KT-394-535

8  7

5 Landscape with farm spring near Volterra
6 Autumn mist at twilight
7 Trees and vineyard
8 Landscape with cypress trees

9 Landscape with clover near Volterra
10 Campanio grapes
11 Chianti barrels
12 Landscape with cypress trees near Volterra
13 Brunello di Montalcino vineyard

10

11

12

14 San Miniato al Monte, Florence

15

15 Palio, Siena
16 Duomo, Sovana
17 Mural, Massa Marittima

16

17

18

18 Castello Aldo, Certaldo
19 Pecorino cheese with herbs
20 Panforte
21 Il Campo, Siena
22 Detail of the Leaning Tower, Pisa

22

19

20

21

23 View over Lucca

24 Duomo, Florence

# About the authors

**Dana Facaros** and **Michael Pauls** are professional travel writers. They spent three years in a tiny Italian village, where they suffered massive overdoses of food, art and wine, and enjoyed every minute of it. They reckon they could whip 98 per cent of the world's non-Italian population at Trivial Pursuit (except for the sports questions). They now live in southwest France. They have written over 40 guides for Cadogan.

# About the updaters

**Nicky Swallow**, a professional musician, has lived in Italy for 18 years. Her enthusiasm for Italian life has led to an intimate knowledge of the country, where she has travelled extensively. She is a regular contributor to travel guides and magazines.

**Helen Holubov** moved to Florence in 1988 for one year. She has lived there ever since and has spent the subsequent time teaching English, working freelance for travel guides and trying to think of a good reason to leave.

# Contents

**Cadogan Guides**
2nd Floor, 233 High Holborn,
London, WC1V 7DN
info@cadoganguides.co.uk
www.cadoganguides.com

**The Globe Pequot Press**
246 Goose Lane, PO Box 480, Guilford,
Connecticut 06437–0480

Copyright © Dana Facaros and Michael Pauls
   1996, 1998, 2000, 2002, 2006

Cover photographs: © Jon Arnold Images/Alamy;
   ©Art Kowalsky/Alamy
Photo essay: © John Ferro Sims
Maps © Cadogan Guides,
   drawn by Map Creation Ltd

Art Director: Sarah Rianhard-Gardner
Managing Editor: Natalie Pomier
Editor: Dominique Shead
Editorial Assistant: Nicola Jessop
Proofreading: Daphne Trotter
Indexing: Isobel McLean

Printed in Italy by Legoprint
A catalogue record for this book is available
   from the British Library
ISBN 10: 1-86011-317-6
ISBN 13: 978-186011-317-8

# Introduction

A Guide to the Guide **2**
Itineraries **4**

A glass of wine before dinner on the garden terrace, the olives glinting in the last flash of the setting sun as the geometric vineyards lose their rigid order in the melting darkness, and only the black daggers of the cypresses stand out against the first stars of the evening – where could you be but Tuscany? It needs no introduction, this famous twilit land, where Titans of art five hundred years ago copied and then outdid nature, and where nature gets her gentle revenge by rivalling art.

Travellers have been coming to central Italy ever since the Middle Ages, to learn, to see and to understand. Most have come with their Baedekers or Ruskins or Berensons in hand, and even today it isn't easy to escape the weight of generations of worthy opinions or to avoid treading on those same old grapes of purple prose. After all, most of what we call Western civilization was either rediscovered or invented here, leaving behind works that have lost none of their power; at times it seems as if the artists of the early 1400s descended from outer space with their secret messages for the imagination. Anyway, to the mass of accumulated opinion we now add ours, for better or worse, but mostly in the hope of provoking some of your own.

But at the end of the day – or, as we are, at the dawn of the 21st century, when times seem to be changing faster than we can or care to – the enduring charm of Tuscany is in that dreamy glass of wine, in those hills that look exactly as they did when Piero painted them, in the bartender who's a dead ringer for Lorenzo de' Medici, in those bewitching Etruscan smiles that seem to have been smiled only yesterday. Things have stayed the same way for centuries not by any accident, or economic reason, or by divine decree of some Tuscan National Trust, but because that's the way people like them. People here make as few concessions to the new millennium as possible, and their Brigadoon may not be for everyone. They're not catching up with the world; the world's catching up with them.

## A Guide to the Guide

After a photo essay to inspire and delight you, the beginning of this guide gives you the background information you need to understand Tuscany. The chapter on **History and Art** provides a detailed background to the development and culture of the region, one of the most artistically rich in the world, and includes a directory of some of the artists you are most likely to encounter. **Topics**, a series of short essays, gives more insights into the people of Tuscany and their customs, while **Food and Drink** provides an overview of regional specialities as well as an Italian menu vocabulary.

The comprehensive **Travel** section covers how to get to and around Tuscany. **Practical A–Z** supplies all the information you are likely to need, on subjects ranging from the climate to official holidays, dealing with the police and even buying a house.

The gazetteer section starts in the treasure-house of **Florence**, and then moves out to the delights of the surrounding countryside with its villages and hill towns, and other major art centres including **Pisa**, **Siena** and **Arezzo**. The gazetteer is divided into sections which focus on a key city or town and the area around it, or on a journey between two featured places. The book concludes with a **Glossary**, a chapter on **Language**, and some suggestions for **Further Reading**.

# Chapter Divisions

EMILIA-ROMAGNA

Pontremoli

**10**
**LUCCA,**
**THE GARFAGNANA**
**& LUNIGIANA**

Abetone

**08**
**CHIANTI & THE**
**MUGELLO**

Pistoia

Prato

**11**
**THE**
**TUSCAN**
**COAST**

Lucca

**07**
**FLORENCE**

Florence

**09**
**THE**
**VALDARNO,**
**PRATO & PISTOIA**

Pisa

THE
MARCHES

Livorno

Gorgona

Casciana Terme

**08**
**CHIANTI & THE**
**MUGELLO**

**15**
**AREZZO &**
**ITS PROVINCE**

Sestino

S. Gimignano

Castellina in Chianti

Volterra

Arezzo

TUSCANY

Siena

**12**
**SIENA**

**13**
**HILL TOWNS**
**WEST OF SIENA**

Montepulciano

Massa
Marittima

Capraia

**14**
**SOUTHERN**
**TUSCANY**

UMBRIA

Piombino

**11**
**THE**
**TUSCAN**
**COAST**

Elba

Pianosa

Orbetello

LAZIO

Montecristo

Giglio

Giannutri

N

20 km

10 miles

*Tyrrhenian Sea*

# Itineraries

## A Week of Roman and Etruscan Sites

1 **Florence** (Archaeology Museum; Etruscan tombs at Sesto Fiorentino) and **Fiesole** (Etruscan walls, Roman theatre, and museum).

2 **Volterra** (museum, Etruscan arch and Roman theatre).

3–4 The Etruscan cities of the coast: **Populonia**, **Vetulonia**, **Roselle** and **Ansedonia**, with stops at the Archaeology Museum in **Grosseto** and 'Frontone' (temple pediment) in **Orbetello**.

5 **Chiusi** (fine museum and only painted Etruscan tombs in Tuscany).

6 **Arezzo** (Roman amphitheatre and museum).

7 **Cortona** (Etruscan walls, gate, tombs and museum).

## Early Medieval Art and Architecture, in 10 Days

The best in Tuscany before 1200:

1 **Florence** (Baptistry, San Miniato).

2 **Pistoia** (Sant'Andrea, San Giovanni Fuorcivitas).

3 The bizarre **Pieve di Castelvecchio**, near **Pescia**, and **Barga** cathedral.

4 **Lucca** (Cathedral and San Michele).

5 **Pisa** (Piazza of Miracles, museums and San Piero a Grado).

6 **Rosia**, **Sovicille** and the other churches just west of **Siena**.

7 **Sant'Antimo**, outside **Montalcino** and **Abbadia San Salvatore** (town and abbey).

8 The well-preserved medieval town of **Sovana**, near **Pitigliano**.

9 **Grópina**, near Loro Ciuffenna in the Valdarno, and **Poppi** (Castle).

10 **Stia** (San Pietro and Castello di Romena).

## 8-Day Tour of High Medieval Art and Architecture

1–2 **Florence**: Orsanmichele, Bargello, Cathedral, Palazzo Vecchio, Palazzo Davanzati.

2 **Empoli** (Collegiata and museum) and **Certaldo** (Boccaccio's well-preserved home town).

3 **San Gimignano**: Collegiata frescoes and the city itself – a genuine, extraordinary, medieval monument.

4 **Volterra**: civic buildings and art in Cathedral, San Francesco.

5 **Massa Marittima** and **San Galgano**.

6–8 **Siena**: Palazzo Pubblico, Cathedral – and nearly everything else!

## 11 Days Shooting a Renaissance Loop outside Florence

Renaissance art somehow seems especially rarefied out in the provinces. Once you've paid your respects to Great Aunt Florence, visit:

1 **Impruneta** (Collegiata), **Certosa di Galluzzo**, **Lastra a Signa** (Alberti's church) and **Poggio a Caiano**, the archetypal Renaissance villa.

2 **Prato** (Santa Maria delle Carceri, Filippo Lippi's fresco cycle in the Cathedral, Donatello and Michelozzo's pulpit).

3 **Lucca**, for the sculpture of Matteo Civitali and Jacopo della Quercia.

4 **San Gimignano**, which has much of the best painting outside Florence, by Gozzoli, Ghirlandaio, Sodoma and more.

5 **Siena**, for the Sienese side of the Renaissance (Cathedral, especially pavements, tombs, and Piccolomini Library, and the Pinacoteca).

6–7 The exquisite monastic complex and frescoes at **Monte Oliveto Maggiore**, on the way to Pius II's planned city of **Pienza**; nearby **Montepulciano** for the best of classic Renaissance temples, Sangallo's San Biagio, as well as other churches and palaces.

8 **Cortona** (Renaissance temples, Signorelli and Fra Angelico) and **Monte San Savino**.

9 **Arezzo** (Piero della Francesco's frescoes and Santa Maria delle Grazie).

10 More Pieros in **Monterchi** and **Sansepolcro**.

11 **La Verna** (Andrea della Robbia) and over the Passo di Consuma to Florence.

## Villas and Gardens, in a Week or So

This would be a 'Two-Centre Holiday' as all the villas and gardens mentioned are located near Florence and Lucca. Do check the opening hours and do the necessary telephoning before setting out. In **Florence** itself there are beautiful walks around the Boboli Gardens, the villas and gardens of **Arcetri**, the **Villa Stibbert and Garden**, and the villas and gardens in and around **Fiesole**. Then:

1 Medici villas and gardens of **La Petraia**, **Castello** and **Careggi**.

2 Into the Mugello: Gardens of **Pratolino**, and Medici Villas at **Cafaggiolo** and **Trebbio**.

3 More Medici villas and gardens: **Poggio a Caiano**, **Villa Artimino** and Cerreto Guidi.

4–5 Villas in Chianti: although only the **Castello di Brolio** and **Badia a Coltibuono** are open to the public; other striking estates include: Villa Tattali, Palazzo al Bosco, Villa Le Corti, Poggio Torselli, Vignamaggio and several around Castellina.

6–7 From **Lucca**, **Castello Garzoni**, with fabulous gardens, near Collodi, and the three villas northeast of Lucca itself: **Villa Mansi**, **Villa Torrigiani** and **Villa Pecci-Blunt**.

## Nature and Scenery

For Tuscany at its least civilized: starting with southern Tuscany's **Monte Amiata**, an isolated patch of lovely mountain forests. **Mediterranean Coastal Scenery**: maquis and pine forests, on **Monte Argentario**, with side trips to **Giglio** and the surrounding marshlands with wildlife reserves and exotic birds, like the **Monti dell'Uccellina**. Further north, there are ancient coastal forests around **Pietrasanta** and **San Rossore**.

**Coastal Mountains**: the **Apuan Alps**, lush, streaked with marble, are located along the coast from Carrara down, while a bit further inland are the dense forests of the **Garfagnana**. Serious **Apennines**: the ridge between Tuscany and Emilia-Romagna, around **Abetone**, **Firenzuola**, **Camaldoli** (with its ancient forest), **Pratomagno** (Monte Secchieta, and its panoramic roads), and the enchanting **Casentino**.

## Two Weeks of Wine

For the best of Tuscan DOC wines, and some of the most ravishing scenery:

1 **Florence** to **Carmignano, Cerreto Guidi** and **Vinci** (wines: Carmignano and Chianti).

2 **Montecatini Alta, Collodi** and **Montecarlo** (wines: Bianco della Valdinievole and Montecarlo).

3 South of the Arno to **San Miniato** and environs, and **Certaldo** (wines: Bianco Pisano di S. Torpè and Chianti).

4 **San Gimignano** and **Colle di Val d'Elsa** (wines: Vernaccia di San Gimignano and Chianti Colli Senesi).

5 **Barberino Val d'Elsa** and **San Casciano** to the Florence–Siena wine route, the Chiantigiana and **Greve in Chianti** (wines: Chianti, Chianti Colli Fiorentini and Chianti Classico).

6 **Panzano** and **Radda in Chianti** (wine: Chianti Classico).

7 **Gaiole in Chianti, Castello di Brolio** and **Siena**, with a stop at the Enoteca Nazionale (wines: Chianti Classico and Chianti Colli Senesi).

8 **Montalcino** (wine: Brunello).

9 **Montepulciano** (wine: Vino Nobile).

10 **Cortona** (wine: Bianco Vergine della Valdichiana).

11 **Sovana, Pitigliano, Saturnia** (wines: Morellino di Scansano and Bianco di Pitigliano).

12 Check in at the spa at **Chianciano Terme** for liver repairs!

## One Week of Curiosities

The unexpected, unique side of Tuscany doesn't jump out at you; you'll have to look for it. In **Florence** you spend

1–3 seeing **Galileo's Forefinger** at the Museum of the History of Science; gruesomely realistic **wax anatomical models** at La Specola museum; a **151kg topaz** at the Museum of Mineralogy; a **16th-century Mexican bishop's mitre** made out of feathers, in the Museo degli Argenti; **Islamic and Japanese armour** in the Villa Stibbert; or an ornate **Mozarabic Synagogue** or onion-domed **Russian Orthodox Church**. From there, head to Tuscany's northernmost town, **Pontrémoli**...

4 to see the mysterious **Neolithic statue-steles**, and then down to **Carrara** for the eerie, almost black whiteness of the **marble quarries**.

5 **Pisa**: the **Leaning Tower** is only one of a score of oddities in the Piazza of Miracles; also take a look at the **Turkish war pennants** in Santo Stefano.

6 **Volterra**, to see the *balze* and the unusual **Etruscan sculpture** in the Guarnacci Museum, on your way to the geothermal carnival of the **Metal Hills – geysers and sulphur lakes** around Larderello and Monterotondo.

7 Detour to Elba for **Napoleon's Death Mask**, or even better, inland to **San Galgano**, with its ruined Gothic abbey and genuine **Sword-in-the-stone**.

8 If it's Saturday or Sunday, try the **Giardino dei Tarocchi** (at Capalbio, east of Orbetello), a bizarre collection of colossal modern sculptures, covered in bright ceramics and mirrors, dedicated to the 22 major arcana of the Tarot deck.

# History and Art

02

# Historical Outline

At times, the history of Tuscany has been a small part of a bigger story – Rome's, or modern Italy's. However, the crucial eras of the Middle Ages and the Renaissance provided a tremendous chronicle of contending city states, each with a complex history of its own. For that reason, we have included detailed histories of the most important towns – Florence, Siena and Pisa – and covered the rest to a lesser extent. Here is a brief historical outline for the region as a whole.

## The Etruscans

Neolithic cultures seem to have occupied this region of Italy since about 4500 BC without distinguishing themselves artistically or politically. The dawn of history in these parts comes with the arrival of the **Etruscans**, though where they came from and precisely when they arrived remains one of the major mysteries of early Mediterranean history. According to their traditions, the Etruscans migrated from western Anatolia, c. 900 BC. Classical authors were divided on this point; some believed the migration theory, while others saw the Etruscans as the indigenous inhabitants of west-central Italy. Their language remains murky to modern scholars, but the discovery of Etruscan inscriptions on the Greek island of Lemnos, along with other clues, tends to support the Etruscan story.

Whatever it was, they were a talented people, and the great wealth they derived from intensive agriculture, manufacturing, and above all mining (Elba and the Metal Hills) allowed these talents to blossom into opulence by the 7th century BC. Though they gave their name to modern Tuscany, the real centre of Etruscan civilization lay to the south; roughly the coast from Orbetello to Cervéteri (Caere) in Lazio and around Lakes Bolsena and Trasimeno. Never a unified nation, the Etruscans preferred the general Mediterranean model of the independent city state; the 12 greatest dominated central Italy in a federation called the **Dodecapolis**. Which cities were members is uncertain, but the 14 possible cities include *Veii, Cervéteri, Tarquinia* and *Vulci* (in Lazio), *Roselle, Vetulonia* and *Populonia* (on or near the Tuscan coast), *Volterra, Fiesole, Arezzo, Chiusi, Orvieto, Cortona* and *Perugia*.

The Etruscans always maintained extremely close trade and cultural ties with classical Greece. They sold Elban iron and bought Greek culture wholesale; the artistic thieving magpies of antiquity, they adapted every style of Greek art, from the Minoan-style frescoes at Tarquinia to the classical bronzes now in the Florence Museum, and created something of their very own. In expressive portrait sculpture, though, they surpassed even the Greeks.

A considerable mythology has grown up around the Etruscans. Some historians and poets celebrate them as a nation of free peoples, devoted to art, good food and easy living. A less sentimental view shows a slave society run for the benefit of a military, aristocratic élite. Whichever, the art they left behind gives them a place as the most enigmatic, vivid and fascinating people of early Italy. It isn't difficult to see echoes of their culture in everything that has happened in this part of Italy for the last 2,000 years.

# Romans

Etruscan kings once ruled in Rome, but after the establishment of the Republic, this precocious city was to prove the end of the Etruscan world. All of southern Etruria was swallowed up by 358 BC, and internal divisions between the Etruscan cities allowed the Romans to push their conquest inevitably northwards. After the conquest of an Etruscan city, Roman policy was often diabolically clever; by establishing veterans' colonies in new towns nearby to draw off trade, Rome was able to ensure the withering of Etruscan culture and the slow extinction of many of Etruria's greatest cities.

Most of the Etruscan cities joined with neighbouring peoples, the Unbrii of Umbria and Piceni of the Marches, in the Social Wars of 92–89 BC, the last doomed attempt of the Italians to fight free of Roman imperialism. Two distinct cultures occupied the northern fringes. The wandering **Celts**, who occupied all northern Italy, often made themselves at home in the Apennines and northern Etruria; their influence on the region's culture is slight. Finally there was the unnamed culture of the rugged **Lunigiana**, around Pontrémoli, a people who carried their Neolithic customs and religion (see the statue-steles in the Pontrémoli museum) well into the modern era.

Under the empire, Etruria was relatively quiet, though the region experienced a north–south economic split to mirror the bigger one beginning across Italy. Southern Etruria, the old Etruscan heartland, shrivelled and died under Roman misrule, never to recover. The north became more prosperous, and important new cities appeared: Lucca, Pisa, Florence and, to a lesser extent, Gubbio and Siena.

# The Dark Ages

Later Italians' willingness to create fanciful stories about the 'barbarian invasions' makes it hard to define what did happen in this troubled time. The first (5th-century) campaigns of the **Goths** in Italy did not seem to cause too much damage, but the curtain finally came down on Roman civilization with the Greek-Gothic wars of 536–563, when Eastern Emperor Justinian and his generals Belisarius and Narsus attempted to recapture Italy for Byzantium. The chronicles of many cities record the devastation of the Gothic King, Totila (the sack of Florence), though the Imperial aggressors were undoubtedly just as bad. In any case, the damage to an already weakened society was fatal, and the wars opened the way for the conquest of much of Italy by the terrible **Lombards** (568), who established the Duchy of Spoleto, with loose control over much of central Italy. Lucca, the late Roman and Gothic capital of Etruria, alone managed to keep the Lombards out. By this time, low-lying cities like Florence had practically disappeared, while the remnants of the other towns survived under the control of local barons, or occasionally under their bishops. Feudal warfare and marauding became endemic. In the 800s even a band of Arabs came looting and pillaging up the Valnerina, almost in the centre of the peninsula.

By the 10th century, things were looking up. Florence had re-established itself, and built its famous baptistry. The old counts of Lucca extended their power to become counts of Tuscany, under the Attoni family, lords of Canossa. As the leading power in the region, they made themselves a force in European affairs. In 1077, the great

Countess Matilda, allied with the Pope, humbled Emperor Henry IV at Canossa – the famous 'penance in the snow' during the struggles over investiture. Perhaps most important of all was the growth of the maritime city of **Pisa** which gave Tuscany a window on the world, building wealth through trade and inviting cultural influences from France, Byzantium and the Muslim world.

## Medieval Tuscany

By 1000, with the new millennium, all of northern Italy was poised to rebuild the civilization that had been lost centuries before. In Tuscany, as elsewhere, increasing trade had created a rebirth of towns, each doing its best to establish its independence from local nobles or bishops, and to increase its influence at the expense of its neigh-bours. Thus a thousand minor squabbles were played out against the background of the major issues of the day; first the conflict over investiture in the 11th century, evolving into the endless factional struggles of **Guelphs** and **Ghibellines** after 1215 (*see* pp.105–7). Throughout, the cities were forced to choose sides between the partisans of the popes and those of the emperors. The Ghibellines' brightest hours came with the reigns of strong Hohenstaufen emperors **Frederick I Barbarossa** (1152–90) and his grandson **Frederick II** (1212–46), both of whom spent much time in Tuscany. An early Guelph wave came with the papacy of **Innocent III** (1198–1216), most powerful of the medieval pontiffs, and the Guelphs would come back to dominate Tuscany after the invasion of Charles of Anjou in 1261. Florence, Arezzo and Lucca were the mainstays of the Guelphs, while Pisa, Pistoia and Siena usually supported the Ghibellines.

In truth, it was every city for itself. By 1200, most towns had become free *comuni*; their imposing public buildings can be seen in almost every corner of Tuscany. All the trouble they caused fighting each other (at first with citizen militias, later increasingly with the use of hired *condottieri*) never troubled the booming economy. Florence and Siena became bankers to all Europe, great building programmes went up, beginning with the Pisa cathedral complex in the 1100s, and the now tamed and urbanized nobles built fantastical skyscraper skylines of tower-fortresses in the towns. Above all, it was a great age for culture, the age of Dante (b. 1265) and Giotto (b. 1266). Another feature of the time was the 13th-century religious revival, dominated by the figure of St Francis of Assisi.

## Background of the Renaissance

Florence, biggest and richest of the Tuscan cities, increased its influence all through the 1300s, gaining Prato and Pistoia, and finally winning a seaport with the capture of declining Pisa in 1406. This set the stage for the relative political equilibrium of Tuscany during the early Renaissance, the height of the region's wealth and artistic achievement. The popes, newly established in Rome, sent Cardinal Albornoz across the territory in the 1360s with the aim of binding the region more closely to the Papal State; he built a score of fortresses across Umbria.

The **Wars of Italy**, beginning in 1494, put an end to Renaissance tranquillity. Florence was once more lost in its internal convolutions, twice expelling the **Medici**, while French and Imperial armies marched over the two regions. When the dust had cleared, the last of the free cities (with the exception of Lucca) had been extinguished, and most of Tuscany came under the rule of the Grand Duke **Cosimo I** (1537–74), the Medici propped on a newly made throne by Emperor Charles V. Tuscany's economic and artistic decline was gentle until 1600. After that, it was precipitate; the old banking and textile businesses collapsed, and serious artistic production practically ceased.

## The Modern Era

Though maintaining a relative independence, Tuscany had little to say in Italian affairs. After the Treaty of Câteau-Cambrésis in 1559, the Spaniards established a military enclave, called the Presidio, around Orbetello, precisely to keep an eye on central Italy. Cosimo I proved a vigorous ruler, though his successors gradually declined in ability. By 1600 it didn't matter. The total exhaustion of the Florentine economy kept pace with that of the Florentine imagination. By 1737, when the Medici dynasty became extinct, Tuscany was one of the torpid backwaters of Europe. It had no chance to decide its own destiny; the European powers agreed to bestow Tuscany on the House of Lorraine, cousins to the Austrian Habsburgs. Surprisingly enough, the Lorraines proved able and popular rulers, especially during the rule of the enlightened, progressive Peter Leopold (1765–90).

The languor of Lorraine and Papal rule was interrupted by Napoleon, who invaded central Italy twice and established a Kingdom of Etruria from 1801 to 1807. Austrian rule returned after 1815, continuing the series of well-meaning, intelligent Grand Dukes. By now, however, the Tuscans and the rest of the Italians wanted something better. In the tumults of the Risorgimento, one of the greatest and kindest of the Lorraines, Leopold II, saw the writing on the wall and allowed himself to be overthrown in 1859. Tuscany was almost immediately annexed to the new Italian kingdom.

Since then, the region has followed the history of modern Italy. The head start Tuscany gained under the Lorraine dukes allowed it to keep up economically with northern Italy. Florence had a brief moment of glory (1865–70) as capital of Italy, awaiting the capture of Rome. More recently, the biggest affair was the Second World War, with a long, tortuous campaign dragging across Tuscany. The Germans based their Gothic Line on the Arno, blowing up all but one of Florence's bridges.

# Art and Architecture

## Etruscans

Although we have no way of knowing what life was like for the average man in Camars or Velathri, their tomb sculptures and paintings convince us that they were a talented, likeable people. Almost all their art derives from the Greek; the Etruscans built classical temples (unfortunately of wood, with terracotta embellishments, so little survives), carved themselves sarcophagi decorated with scenes from Homer, and painted their pottery in red and black after the latest styles from Athens or Corinth.

They excelled at portrait sculpture, and had a remarkable gift for capturing personality, sometimes seriously, though never heroically, often with an entirely intentional humour, and the serene smiles of people who truly enjoyed life.

Etruscan art in museums is often maddening; some of the works are among the finest productions of antiquity, while others – from the same time and city – are awkward and childish. Their talent for portraiture, among much else, was carried on by the Romans, and they bequeathed their love of fresco painting to the artists of the Middle Ages and Renaissance, who of course weren't even aware of the debt. After introducing yourself to the art of the Etruscans, it will be interesting to reconsider all that came later – in Tuscany, and indeed all Italy, you will find subtle reminders of this enigmatic people.

## Romans and Dark Ages

After destroying the Etruscan nation, the Romans also began the extinction of its artistic tradition; by the time of the Empire, there was almost nothing left that could be called distinctively Etruscan. Tuscany contributed little under the Empire. In the chaos that followed, there was little room for art. What painting survived followed styles current in Byzantium.

## The Middle Ages

In both architecture and sculpture, the first influence came from the north. Lombard masons filled Tuscany with simple Romanesque churches; the first (Spoleto, Bevagna, Grópina, Abbadia S. Salvatore and in the Garfagnana, to name a few) follow the northern style, although it wasn't long before two distinctive Tuscan forms emerged: the Pisan style, characterized by blind rows of colonnades, black and white zebra stripes, and lozenge-shaped designs; and the 'Tuscan Romanesque' which developed around Florence, notable for its use of dark and light marble patterns and simple geometric patterns, often with intricate mosaic floors to match (the Baptistry and San Miniato in Florence are the chief examples). In the cities in between – Lucca, Arezzo and Pistoia – there are interesting variations on the two different styles, often carrying an element like stripes or arcades to remarkable extremes. The only real example of French Gothic in Tuscany is San Galgano built by Cistercians in the 1200s, although the style never caught on here or anywhere else in Italy.

From the large pool of talent working on Pisa's great cathedral complex in the 13th century emerged Italy's first great sculptor, **Nicola Pisano**, whose Baptistry pulpit, with its realistic figures, derived from ancient reliefs. His even more remarkable son, **Giovanni Pisano**, prefigures Donatello in the expressiveness of his statues and the vigour of his pulpits; his façade of Siena cathedral, though altered, is a unique work of art. **Arnolfo di Cambio**, a student of Nicola Pisano, became chief sculptor-architect of Florence during its building boom in the 1290s, designing its cathedral and Palazzo Vecchio with a hitherto unheard-of scale and grandeur, before moving on to embellish Orvieto with statues and tombs. Orvieto, however, hired the more imaginative **Lorenzo Maitani** in the early 1300s to create a remarkable cathedral façade as individualistic as Siena's, a unique combination of reliefs and mosaics.

Painting at first lagged behind the new realism and more complex composition of sculpture. The first to depart from Byzantine stylization, at least according to the account in Vasari's *Lives of the Artists* (*see* **Topics**, pp.29–30), was **Cimabue**, in the late 1200s, who forsook Greek forms for a more 'Latin' or 'natural' way of painting. Cimabue found his greatest pupil, **Giotto**, as a young shepherd, chalk-sketching sheep on a piece of slate. Brought to Florence, Giotto soon eclipsed his master's fame (artistic celebrity being a recent Florentine invention) and achieved the greatest advances on the road to the new painting with a plain, rather severe approach that shunned Gothic prettiness while exploring new ideas in composition and expressing psychological depth in his subjects. Even more importantly, Giotto through his intuitive grasp of perspective was able to go further than any previous artist in representing his subjects as actual figures in space. In a sense Giotto actually invented space; it was this, despite his often awkward and graceless draughtsmanship, that so astounded his contemporaries. His followers, **Taddeo and Agnolo Gaddi** (father and son), **Giovanni da Milano** and **Maso di Banco** filled Florence's churches with their own interpretations of the master's style. In the latter half of the 1300s, however, there also appeared the key figure of **Andrea Orcagna**, the most important Florentine sculptor, painter and architect of his day. Inspired by the more elegant style of **Andrea Pisano**'s Baptistry doors, Orcagna broke away from the simple Giottesque forms for a more elaborate, detailed style in his sculpture, while the fragments of his frescoes that survive have a vivid dramatic power, which undoubtedly owes something to the time of the Black Death and social upheavals in which they were painted.

Siena never produced a Vasari to chronicle its accomplishments, though they were considerable; in the 13th and 14th centuries, Siena's Golden Age, the city's artists, like its soldiers, rivalled and often surpassed those of Florence. For whatever reason, it seemed purposefully to seek inspiration in different directions from Florence; at first from central Italian styles around Spoleto, then, with prosperity and the advent of **Guido da Siena** in the early 1200s to the more elegant line and colour of Byzantium. Guido's work paved the way for the pivotal figure of **Duccio di Buoninsegna**, the catalyst who founded the essentials of Sienese art by uniting the beauty of Byzantine line and colour with the sweet finesse of western Gothic art. With Duccio's great followers **Pietro and Ambrogio Lorenzetti** and **Simone Martini**, the Sienese produced an increasingly elegant and rarefied art, almost oriental in its refined stylization. They were less innovative than the Florentines, though they brought the 'International Gothic' style – flowery and ornate, with all the bright tones of May – to its highest form in Italy. Simone Martini introduced the Sienese manner to Florence in the early 1400s, where it influenced most notably the work of **Lorenzo Monaco**, **Masolino** and the young goldsmith and sculptor, **Ghiberti**.

## The Renaissance

Under the assaults of historians and critics over the last two centuries, the term 'Renaissance' has become a vague and controversial word. Nevertheless, however you choose to interpret this rebirth of the arts, and whatever dates you assign to it, Florence inescapably takes the credit for it. This is no small claim. Combining art,

# Masters and Students: the Progress of the Renaissance

*The purpose of this chart is to show who learned from whom: an insight into some 300 years of artistic continuity.*

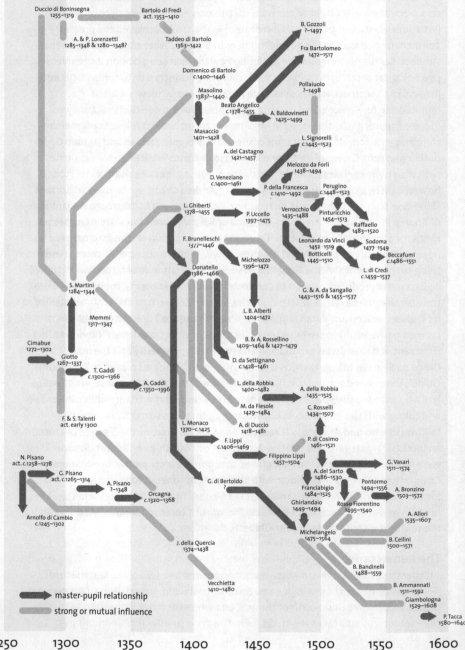

Duccio di Boninsegna 1255–1319

Bartolo di Fredi act. 1353–1410

A. & P. Lorenzetti 1285–1348 & 1280–1348?

Taddeo di Bartolo 1363–1422

B. Gozzoli ?–1497

Fra Bartolomeo 1472–1517

Domenico di Bartolo c.1400–1446

Masolino 1383?–1440

Pollaiuolo ?–1498

Beato Angelico c.1378–1455

A. Baldovinetti 1425–1499

Masaccio 1401–1428

L. Signorelli c.1445–1523

A. del Castagno 1421–1457

Melozzo da Forlì 1438–1494

D. Veneziano c.1400–1461

P. della Francesca c.1410–1492

Perugino c.1448–1523

L. Ghiberti 1378–1455

P. Uccello 1397–1475

Verrocchio 1435–1488

Pinturicchio 1454–1513

Raffaello 1483–1520

F. Brunelleschi 1377–1446

Leonardo da Vinci 1452 1519

Sodoma 1477 1549

Botticelli 1445–1510

Beccafumi c.1486–1551

Michelozzo 1396–1472

Donatello 1386–1466

L. di Credi c.1459–1537

G. & A. da Sangallo 1443–1516 & 1455–1537

S. Martini 1284–1344

L. B. Alberti 1404–1472

Memmi 1317–1347

B. & A. Rossellino 1409–1464 & 1427–1479

Cimabue 1272–1302

D. da Settignano c.1428–1461

Giotto 1267–1337

T. Gaddi c.1300–1366

L. della Robbia 1400–1482

A. della Robbia 1435–1525

A. Gaddi c.1350–1396

M. da Fiesole 1429–1484

C. Rosselli 1434–1507

F. & S. Talenti act. early 1300

L. Monaco 1370–c.1425

A. di Duccio 1418–1481

P. di Cosimo 1461–1521

F. Lippi c.1406–1469

N. Pisano act. c.1258–1278

Filippino Lippi 1457–1504

G. Vasari 1511–1574

G. Pisano act. c.1265–1314

A. Pisano ?–1348

A. del Sarto 1486–1530

Orcagna c.1320–1368

G. di Bertoldo ?

Franciabigio 1484–1525

Pontormo 1494–1556

A. Bronzino 1503–1572

Arnolfo di Cambio c.1245–1302

Ghirlandaio 1449–1494

Rosso Fiorentino 1495–1540

A. Allori 1535–1607

Michelangelo 1475–1564

B. Cellini 1500–1571

J. della Quercia 1374–1438

B. Bandinelli 1488–1559

B. Ammannati 1511–1592

Vecchietta 1410–1480

master-pupil relationship

strong or mutual influence

Giambologna 1529–1608

P. Tacca 1580–1640

1250    1300    1350    1400    1450    1500    1550    1600 science and humanist scholarship into a visual revolution that often seemed pure sorcery to their contemporaries, a handful of Florentine geniuses taught the Western eye a new way of seeing. Perspective seems a simple enough trick to us now, but its discovery determined everything that followed, not only in art, but in science and philosophy as well.

Leading what scholars used self-assuredly to call the 'Early Renaissance' is a triumvirate of geniuses: Brunelleschi, Donatello and Masaccio. **Brunelleschi**, neglecting his considerable talents in sculpture for architecture and science, not only built the majestic dome of Florence cathedral, but threw the Pandora's box of perspective wide open by mathematically codifying the principles of foreshortening. His good friend **Donatello**, the greatest sculptor since the ancient Greeks, inspired a new generation of both sculptors and painters to explore new horizons in portraiture and three-dimensional representation. The first painter to incorporate Brunelleschi's and Donatello's lessons of spatiality, perspective and expressiveness was the young prodigy **Masaccio**, who along with his master Masolino painted the famous Brancacci Chapel in the Carmine, studied by nearly every Florentine artist down to Michelangelo.

The new science of architecture, sculpture and painting introduced by this triumvirate ignited an explosion of talent unequalled before or since – a score of masters, most of them Tuscan, each following the dictates of his own genius to create a remarkable range of themes and styles. To mention only the most prominent: **Lorenzo Ghiberti**, who followed Donatello's advice on his second set of Baptistry doors to cause a Renaissance revolution; **Leon Battista Alberti**, who took Brunelleschi's ideas to their most classical extreme in architecture, creating new forms in the process; **Paolo Uccello**, one of the most provocative of artists, who according to Vasari drove himself bats with the study of perspective and the possibilities of illusionism; **Piero della Francesca** of Sansepolcro, who explored the limits of perspective and geometrical forms to create the most compelling, haunting images of the quattrocento; **Fra** (now **Beato**) **Angelico**, who combined Masaccio's innovations and International Gothic colours and his own deep faith to create the most purely spiritual art of his time; **Andrea del Castagno**, who made use of perspective to create monumental, if often restless, figures.

Some of Donatello's gifted followers were **Agostino di Duccio, Benedetto da Maiano, Desiderio da Settignano, Antonio and Bernardo Rossellino, Mino da Fiesole** and perhaps most famously, **Luca della Robbia**, who invented the coloured terracottas his family spread throughout Tuscany. And still more: **Benozzo Gozzoli**, whose enchanting springtime colours and delight in detail are a throwback to the International Gothic; **Antonio and Piero Pollaiuolo**, sons of a poultryman, whose new, dramatic use of line and form, often violent and writhing, would be echoed in Florentine Mannerism; **Fra Filippo Lippi**, a monk like Fra Angelico but far more earthly, the master of lovely Madonnas, teacher of his talented son **Filippino Lippi; Domenico Ghirlandaio**, whose gift of easy charm and flawless technique made him society's fresco painter; **Andrea del Verrocchio**, who could cast in bronze, paint, or carve with perfect detail; **Luca Signorelli**, who achieved apocalyptic grandeur in Orvieto Cathedral; **Perugino** (Pietro Vannucci) of Umbria, who painted the stillness of his native region into his landscapes and taught the young **Raphael** of Urbino; and finally **Sandro Botticelli**, whose highly intellectual but lovely and melancholy, mythological paintings are in a class of their own.

The 'Early Renaissance' came to a close near the end of the 1400s with the advent of **Leonardo da Vinci**, whose unique talent in painting, only one of his hundred interests, challenged the certainty of naturalism with a subtlety and chiaroscuro that approaches magic. One passion, however, obsessed the other great figure of the 'High Renaissance', **Michelangelo Buonarroti**: his consummate interest was the human body, at first graceful and serene as in most of his Florentine works, later contorted and anguished after he left for Rome.

## Mannerism

Michelangelo left in Florence the seeds for the bold, neurotic avant-garde art that has come to be known as Mannerism. The first conscious 'movement' in Western art can be seen as a last fling amidst the growing intellectual and spiritual exhaustion of 1530s Florence, conquered once and for all by the Medici. The Mannerists' calculated exoticism and exaggerated, tortured poses, together with the brooding self-absorption of Michelangelo, are a prelude to Florentine art's remarkably abrupt turn into decadence, and prophesy its final extinction. Foremost among the Mannerist painters are two surpassingly strange characters, **Jacopo Pontormo** and **Rosso Fiorentino**, who were not in such great demand as the coldly classical **Andrea del Sarto** and **Bronzino**, consummate perfectionists of the brush, both much less intense and demanding. There were also charming reactionaries working at the time, especially **Il Sodoma** and **Pinturicchio**, both of whom left their best works in Siena. In sculpture **Giambologna** and to a lesser extent **Bartolomeo Ammannati** specialized in virtuoso *contrapposto* figures, each one more impossible than the last. With their contemporary, **Giorgio Vasari**, Florentine art lost almost all imaginative and intellectual content, and became a virtuoso style of interior decoration perfectly adaptable to saccharine holy pictures, portraits of newly enthroned dukes, or absurd mythological fountains and ballroom ceilings. In the cinquecento, with plenty of money to spend and a long Medici tradition of patronage to uphold, this tendency soon got out of hand. Under the reign of Cosimo I, indefatigable collector of *pietra dura* tables, silver and gold gimcracks, and exotic stuffed animals, Florence gave birth to the artistic phenomenon modern critics call 'kitsch'.

## The Rest Compressed

In the long, dark night of later Tuscan art a few artists stand out – the often whimsical architect and engineer, **Buontalenti**; **Pietro Tacca**, Giambologna's pupil with a taste for the grotesque; the charming Baroque fresco master **Pietro da Cortona**. Most of Tuscany, and particularly Florence, chose to sit out the Baroque – almost by choice, it seems, and we can race up to the 19th century for the often delightful 'Tuscan

Impressionists' or *Macchiaioli* ('Splatterers'; best collection in Modern Art section of Pitti Palace); and in the 20th century, **Modigliani** of the oval faces (from Livorno); the Futurist **Gino Severini** (from Cortona); and **Alberto Burri**, one of the first to use junk as a medium (from Città di Castello, where there's a museum). There is an exceptionally good collection of contemporary art, the Centro per l'Arte Contemporanea Luigi Pecci, in Prato, with frequent exhibitions; others include a museum dedicated to sculptor **Marino Marini** in Florence, although newest and most entertaining of all is the late French artist Niki de Saint-Phalle's Giardino dei Tarocchi, south of Orbetello.

# Artists' Directory

This includes the principal architects, painters and sculptors of Tuscany and its nearby regions. The works listed are far from exhaustive, bound to exasperate partisans of some artists and do scant justice to the rest, but we have tried to include only the best and most representative works to be found locally.

**Agostino di Duccio** (Florentine, 1418–81). A precocious and talented sculptor, his best work is in the Malatesta Temple at **Rimini** – he was exiled from Florence after being accused of theft (**Florence**, Bargello; **Pontrémoli**, S. Francesco).

**Alberti, Leon Battista** (Florentine, b. Genoa 1404–72). Architect, theorist and writer, also a sculptor and painter. His greatest contribution was recycling the classical orders and the principles of Vitruvius into Renaissance architecture; he was a consultant to the architecture-loving Duke of Urbino. (**Florence**, Palazzo Rucellai, façade of S. Maria Novella, SS. Annunziata; **Lastra a Signa**, S. Martino).

**Allori, Alessandro** (1535–1607). Florentine Mannerist painter, prolific follower of Michelangelo and Bronzino (**Florence**, SS. Annunziata, S. Spirito, Spedale degli Innocenti).

**Ammannati, Bartolomeo** (1511–92). Florentine architect and sculptor. Restrained, elegant architect (**Florence**, S. Trínita bridge, courtyard of Pitti Palace); neurotic, twisted Mannerist sculptor (**Florence**, Fountain of Neptune, Villa di Castello).

**Andrea del Castagno** (c. 1423–57). Precise, dry Florentine painter, one of the first and greatest slaves of perspective. Died of the plague (**Florence**, Uffizi, S. Apollonia, SS. Annunziata).

**Angelico, Fra** (or **Beato**) (Giovanni da Fiesole, c. 1387–1455). Monk first and painter second, but still one of the great visionary artists of the Renaissance (**Florence**, S. Marco – spectacular Annunciation and many more; **Cortona**, Cathedral Museum; **Fiesole**, S. Domenico).

**Arnolfo di Cambio** (born in Colle di Val d'Elsa, c. 1245–1302). Architect and sculptor, pupil of Nicola Pisano and a key figure in his own right. Much of his best sculpture is in Rome, but he changed the face of Florence as main architect to the city's greatest building programme of the 1290s (**Florence**, cathedral and Palazzo Vecchio).

**Baldovinetti, Alesso** (Florentine, 1425–99). A delightful student of Fra Angelico who left few tracks; most famous for fresco work in **Florence** (SS. Annunziata, Uffizi, S. Niccolò sopr'Arno, S. Miniato).

**Bandinelli, Baccio** (1488–1559). Florence's comic relief of the late Renaissance; supremely serious, vain, and so awful it hurts – of course he was court sculptor to Cosimo I (**Florence**, Piazza della Signoria and SS. Annunziata).

**Barna da Siena** (active mid–late 1300s). One of the chief followers of Simone Martini, more dramatic and vigorous than the usual ethereal Sienese (**San Gimignano**, Collegiata).

**Bartolo di Fredi** (Sienese, active *c*. 1353–1410). Student of Ambrogio Lorenzetti, a genuine pre-Raphaelite soul, entirely at home in the Sienese trecento; employs colours never before seen on this planet (**Montepulciano**, Duomo; **San Gimignano**, Collegiata).

**Bartolommeo, Fra** (*c*. 1472–1517). Florentine painter, master of the High Renaissance style (**Florence**, San Marco, Pitti Palace).

**Beccafumi, Domenico** (*c*. 1486–1551). Sienese painter; odd mixture of Sienese conservatism and Florentine Mannerism (**Siena**, Pinacoteca, Palazzo Pubblico, cathedral pavement).

**Benedetto da Maiano** (Florentine, 1442–97). Sculptor, specialist in narrative reliefs (**Florence**, S. Croce, Strozzi Palace, Bargello; he also designed the loggia of S. Maria delle Grazie, **Arezzo**).

**Bigarelli, Guido** (13th century). Talented travelling sculptor from Como, who excelled in elaborate and sometimes bizarre pulpits (**Barga**; **Pistoia**, S. Bartolomeo, and **Pisa**, Baptistry).

**Bonfigli, Benedetto** (Perugia, *c*. 1420–96). Meticulous Umbrian painter, known for his painted banners in many Perugia churches; best works, especially the Cappella dei Priori frescoes, are in that city's National Gallery.

**Botticelli, Sandro** (Florentine, 1445–1510). Though technically excellent in every respect, and a master of both line and colour, there is more to Botticelli than this. Above every other quattrocento artist, his works reveal the imaginative soul of the Florentine Renaissance, particularly the great series of mythological paintings (**Florence**, Uffizi). Later, a little deranged and under the spell of Savonarola, he reverted to intense, though conventional religious paintings. He was almost forgotten in the philistine 1500s and not rediscovered until the 19th century, and thus many of his best works are probably lost (**Florence**, Accademia; **Montelupo**, S. Giovanni Evangelista).

**Bronzino, Agnolo** (1503–72). Virtuoso Florentine Mannerist with a cool, glossy hyper-elegant style, at his best in portraiture; a close friend of Pontormo (**Florence**, Palazzo Vecchio, Uffizi, S. Lorenzo, SS. Annunziata).

**Brunelleschi, Filippo** (1377–1446). Florentine architect, credited in his own time with restoring the ancient Roman manner of building – but really deserves more credit for developing a brilliant new approach of his own (**Florence**, Duomo cupola, Spedale degli Innocenti, S. Spirito, S. Croce's Pazzi Chapel, S. Lorenzo). Also a sculptor (he lost the competition for the Baptistry doors to Ghiberti), and one of the first theorists on perspective.

**Buontalenti, Bernardo** (1536–1608). Late Florentine Mannerist architect and planner of the new city of **Livorno**, better known for his Medici villas (**Artimino**; also the fascinating grotto in **Florence**'s Boboli Gardens, and Belvedere Fort, Uffizi Tribuna).

**Cellini, Benvenuto** (1500–71). Goldsmith and sculptor. Though a native of Florence, Cellini spent much of his time in Rome. In 1545 he came to work for Cosimo I and to torment Bandinelli (*Perseus*, Loggia dei Lanzi; also works in the Bargello). As famed for his catty *Autobiography* as for his sculpture.

**Cimabue** (*c.* 1240–1302). Florentine painter credited by Vasari with initiating the 'rebirth of the arts'; one of the first painters to depart from the stylization of the Byzantine style (**Florence**, mosaics in Baptistry, Crucifix in Santa Croce; **Pisa**, cathedral mosaic).

**Civitali, Matteo** (Lucchese, *c.* 1435–1501). Sweet yet imaginative sculptor, apparently self-taught. He would be much better known if all of his works weren't in Lucca (**Lucca**, cathedral, Guinigi Museum).

**Coppo di Marcovaldo** (Florentine, active *c.* 1261–75). Another very early painter, as good as Cimabue if not as well known (**San Gimignano**; **Pistoia**, cathedral).

**Daddi, Bernardo** (active 1290–*c.* 1349). Florentine master of delicate altarpieces (**Florence**, Orsanmichele, S. Maria Novella's Spanish chapel).

**Desiderio da Settignano** (Florentine, 1428/31–61). Sculptor, follower of Donatello (**Florence**, S. Croce, Bargello, S. Lorenzo).

**Dolci, Carlo** (Florentine, 1616–86). Unsurpassed Baroque master of the 'whites of their eyes' school of religious art (**Florence**, Palazzo Corsini; **Prato**, Museo del Duomo).

**Domenico di Bartolo** (Sienese, *c.* 1400–46). An interesting painter, well out of the Sienese mainstream; the unique naturalism of his art is a Florentine influence. (Spedale di Santa Maria della Scala, Pinacoteca in **Siena**).

**Domenico Veneziano** (Florentine 1404–61). Painter, teacher of Piero della Francesca; master of perspective with few surviving works (**Florence**, Uffizi).

**Donatello** (Florentine, 1386–1466). The greatest Renaissance sculptor appeared as suddenly as a comet at the beginning of Florence's quattrocento. Never equalled in technical ability, expressiveness or imaginative content, his works influenced Renaissance painters as much as sculptors. A prolific worker, the favourite of Old Cosimo de' Medici, and a quiet fellow who lived with his mum, Donatello was the perfect model of the early Renaissance artist – passionate about art, self-effacing, and a little eccentric (**Florence**, Bargello – the greatest works including the original *St George* from Orsanmichele, *David* and *Cupid-Atys*, also the great pulpits, the masterpiece of his old age in San Lorenzo; other works in Palazzo Vecchio, and the Cathedral Museum; **Siena**, cathedral, baptistry).

**Duccio di Buoninsegna** (d. 1319). One of the first and greatest Sienese painters, Duccio was to Sienese art what Giotto was to Florence; ignored by Vasari, though his contributions to the new visual language of the Renaissance are comparable to Giotto's (**Siena**, parts of the great Maestà in the Cathedral Museum, also Pinacoteca; **Florence**, altarpiece in the Uffizi; **Massa Marittima**, Cathedral; **Castelfiorentino**, Pinacoteca).

**Francesco di Giorgio Martini** (Sienese, 1439–1502). Architect – mostly of fortresses – sculptor and painter, his works are scattered all over Italy (**Siena**, Cathedral, Pinacoteca; **Cortona**, S. Maria di Calcinaio).

**Franciabigio** (Florentine, 1482–1525). Most temperamental of Andrea del Sarto's pupils but only mildly Mannerist (**Florence**, Poggio a Caiano and SS. Annunziata).

**Gaddi, Taddeo** (c. 1300–c. 1366). Florentine; most important of the followers of Giotto. He and his son **Agnolo** (d. 1396) contributed some of the finest trecento fresco cycles (notably at S. Croce, and S. Ambrogio, **Florence**).

**Gentile da Fabriano** (c. 1360–1427). Master nonpareil of the International Gothic style, from Fabriano in the Marches. Most of his work is lost (**Florence**, Uffizi).

**Ghiberti, Lorenzo** (1378–1455). Goldsmith and sculptor. The first artist to write an auto-biography was naturally a Florentine. He would probably be better known had he not spent most of his career working on the doors for the Florence Baptistry after winning the famous competition of 1401 (also **Florence**, statues at Orsanmichele; **Siena** Baptistry).

**Ghirlandaio, Domenico** (Florentine, c. 1448–94). The painter of the quattrocento estab-lishment, master of colourful, lively fresco cycles (with the help of a big workshop) in which he painted all the Medici and Florence's banking élite. A great portraitist with a distinctive, dry, restrained style (**Florence**, Ognissanti, S. Maria Novella, S. Trínita, Spedale degli Innocenti; **San Gimignano**, Collegiata).

**Giambologna** (1529–1608). A Fleming, born Jean Boulogne; court sculptor to the Medici after 1567 and one of the masters of Mannerist virtuosity – also a man with a taste for the outlandish (**Florence**, Loggia dei Lanzi, Bargello, Villa della Petraia; **Pratolino**, the *Appennino*).

**Giotto** (c. 1266–1337). Shepherd boy of the Mugello, discovered by Cimabue, who became the first great Florentine painter – and recognized as such in his own time. Invented an essential and direct approach to portraying narrative fresco cycles, but is even more important for his revolutionary treatment of space and of the human figure. (**Florence**, S. Croce, cathedral campanile, Horne Museum, S. Maria Novella).

**Giovanni da Milano** (14th century). An innovative Lombard inspired by Giotto (**Florence**, S. Croce; **Prato**, Cathedral Museum).

**Giovanni di Paolo** (d. 1483). One of the best of the quattrocento Sienese painters; like most of them, a colourful, often eccentric reactionary who continued the traditions of the Sienese trecento (**Siena**, Pinacoteca).

**Giovanni di San Giovanni** (1592–1633). One of Tuscany's more prolific, but likeable Baroque fresco painters (**Florence**, Pitti Palace, Villa della Petraia).

**Gozzoli, Benozzo** (Florentine, d. 1497). Learned his trade from Fra Angelico, but few artists could have less in common. The most light-hearted and colourful of quattro-cento artists, Gozzoli created enchanting frescoes at **Florence**, Medici chapel; **San Gimignano**, S. Agostino; **Pisa**, Camposanto.

**Guido da Siena** (13th century). One of the founders of Sienese painting, still heavily Byzantine in style; little is known about his life (**Siena**, Palazzo Pubblico, Pinacoteca; **Grosseto**, museum).

**Leonardo da Vinci** (1452–1519). We could grieve that Florence's 'universal genius' spent so much time on his scientific interests and building fortifications, and that his meagre artistic output was largely unfinished or lost. All that is left in Tuscany is the *Annunciation* (**Florence**, Uffizi) and also models of all his gadgets at his birthplace, **Vinci**. As the pinnacle of the Renaissance marriage of science and art, Leonardo requires endless volumes of interpretation. As for his personal life, Vasari records him buying up caged birds in the market-place just to set them free.

**Lippi, Filippino** (Florentine, 1457–1504). Son and artistic heir of Fra Filippo. Often seems a neurotic Gozzoli, or at least one of the most thoughtful and serious artists of the quattrocento (**Florence**, S. Maria Novella, S. Maria del Carmine, Badia, Uffizi).

**Lippi, Fra Filippo** (Florentine, 1406–69). Never should have been a monk in the first place. A painter of exquisite, ethereal Madonnas, with one of whom he ran off (the model, at least, a brown-eyed nun named Lucrezia). The pope forgave them both. Lippi was a key figure in the increasingly complex, detailed painting of the middle 1400s (**Florence**, Uffizi; **Prato**, cathedral and Civic Museum).

**Lorenzetti, Ambrogio** (Sienese, d. 1348). He could crank out golden Madonnas as well as any Sienese painter, but was also a great innovator in subject matter and the treatment of landscapes. Created the first and greatest of secular frescoes, the *Allegories of Good and Bad Government* in **Siena**'s Palazzo Pubblico, while his last known work, the 1344 *Annunciation* in Siena's Pinacoteca is one of the 14th century's most revolutionary treatments of perspective (also **Massa Marittima**, museum).

**Lorenzetti, Pietro** (Sienese, d. 1348). Ambrogio's big brother, and also an innovator, standing square between Duccio di BuonInsegna and Giotto; one of the precursors of the Renaissance's new treatment of space (**Siena**, S. Spirito; **Arezzo**, Pieve di S. Maria; **Cortona**, Cathedral Museum). Both Lorenzettis seem to have died in Siena during the Black Death.

**Lorenzo di Credi** (1439–1537). One of the most important followers of Leonardo da Vinci, always technically perfect if occasionally vacuous (**Florence**, Uffizi).

**Lorenzo Monaco** (b. Siena 1370–1425). A monk at S. Maria degli Angeli in Florence and a brilliant colourist, Lorenzo forms an uncommon connection between the Gothic style of Sienese painting and the new developments in early Renaissance Florence (**Florence**, Uffizi, S. Trínita).

**Manetti, Rutilio** (1571–1639). Quirky but somehow likeable Baroque painter, the last artist of any standing produced by Siena (**Massa Marittima**, cathedral).

**Margarito d'Arezzo** (Arezzo, 13th century). Also called Margaritone. A near contemporary of Giotto who stuck firmly to his Byzantine guns (**Arezzo**, museum).

**Martini, Simone** (Sienese, d. 1344). Possibly a pupil of Giotto, Martini took the Sienese version of International Gothic to an almost metaphysical perfection, creating luminous, lyrical and exquisitely drawn altarpieces and frescoes perhaps unsurpassed in the trecento (**Siena**, Palazzo Pubblico; **Pisa**, Museo S. Matteo; **Florence**, Uffizi).

**Masaccio** (Florentine, 1401–c. 1428). Though he died young and left few works behind, this precocious 'shabby Tom' gets credit for inaugurating the Renaissance in painting by translating Donatello and Brunelleschi's perspective on to a flat surface.

Also revolutionary in his use of light and shadow, and in expressing emotion in his subjects' faces (**Florence**, S. Maria del Carmine, S. Maria Novella; **Pisa**, Museo S. Matteo).

**Maso di Banco** (Florentine, active 1340s). One of the more colourful and original followers of Giotto (**Florence**, S. Croce).

**Masolino** (Florentine, d. 1447). Perhaps 'little Tom' also deserves much of the credit, along with Masaccio, for the new advances in art at the Carmine in **Florence**; art historians dispute endlessly how to attribute the frescoes. It's hard to tell, for this brilliant painter left little other work behind to prove his case (**Empoli**, civic museum; also attributed Tau chapel, **Pistoia**).

**Matteo di Giovanni** (Sienese, 1435–95). One Sienese quattrocento painter who could keep up with the Florentines; a contemporary described him as 'Simone Martini come to life again' (**Siena**, Pinacoteca, Cathedral pavement, S. Agostino, S. Maria delle Neve; **Grosseto**, museum).

**Memmi, Lippo** (Sienese, 1317–47). Brother-in-law and assistant of Simone Martini (**Siena**, S. Spirito; **San Gimignano**, museum).

**Michelangelo Buonarroti** (Florentine, 1475–1564). Born in Caprese (now Caprese Michelangelo) into a Florentine family of the minor nobility come down in the world, Michelangelo's early years and artistic training are obscure; he was apprenticed to Ghirlandaio, but showing a preference for sculpture was sent to the court of Lorenzo de' Medici. Nicknamed Il Divino in his lifetime, he was a complex, difficult character, who seldom got along with mere mortals, popes or patrons. What he couldn't express by means of the male nude in paint or marble, he did in his beautiful but difficult sonnets. In many ways he was the first modern artist, unsurpassed in technique but also the first genius to go over the top (**Florence**, Medici tombs and library in San Lorenzo, three works in the Bargello, the *Pietà* in the Museo del Duomo, the *David* in the Accademia, Casa Buonarroti, and his only oil painting, in the Uffizi).

**Michelozzo di Bartolomeo** (Florentine, 1396–1472). Sculptor who worked with Donatello (**Prato**, pulpit of the Holy Girdle, and the tomb in **Florence**'s Baptistry), he is better known as the classicizing architect favoured by the elder Cosimo de' Medici (**Florence**, Medici Palace, Chiostro of SS. Annunziata, library of San Marco; Villas at **Trebbio** and **Cafaggiolo**, **Montepulciano**, S. Agostino; **Impruneta**, Tempietto).

**Mino da Fiesole** (Florentine, 1429–84). Sculptor of portrait busts and tombs; like the della Robbias a representative of the Florentine 'sweet style' (**Fiesole**, cathedral; **Empoli**, museum; **Volterra**, cathedral; **Florence**, Badia, Sant'Ambrogio; **Prato**, cathedral).

**Nanni di Banco** (Florentine, 1384–1421). Florentine sculptor at the dawn of the Renaissance (**Florence**, Orsanmichele, Porta della Mandorla).

**Orcagna, Andrea** (Florence, d. 1368). Sculptor, painter and architect who dominated the middle 1300s in Florence, though greatly disparaged by Vasari, who destroyed much of his work. Some believe he is the 'Master of the Triumph of Death' of Pisa's

Camposanto (**Florence**, Orsanmichele, S. Croce, S. Maria Novella, *Crucifixion* in refectory of S. Spirito, also often given credit for the Loggia dei Lanzi).

**Perugino** (Pietro Vannucci, b. Perugia, *c.* 1450–1523). Perhaps the most distinctive of the Umbrian painters; created some works of genius, along with countless idyllic nativity scenes, each with its impeccably sweet Madonna and characteristic blue-green tinted background. Some of his later works are awful, although he may not always be responsible: in his cynical old age he let his workshop sign his name to anything (**Florence**, Uffizi, S. Maddalena dei Pazzi, Cenacolo di Foligno).

**Piero della Francesca** (*c.* 1415–1492). Painter, born at Sansepolcro, and one of the really unique quattrocento artists. Piero, a leading light in the famous court of Urbino, wrote two of the most important theoretical works on perspective, then illustrated them with a lifetime's work reducing painting to the bare essentials: geometry, light and colour. In his best work his reduction creates nothing dry or academic, but dreamlike, almost eerie scenes similar to those of Uccello. And like Uccello or Botticelli, his subjects are often archetypes of immense psychological depth, not to be fully explained now or ever (**Arezzo**, S. Francesco and the cathedral; **Sansepolcro**, civic museum; **Monterchi**, cemetery church; **Florence**, Uffizi).

**Piero di Cosimo** (Florentine, 1462–1521). Painter better known for his personal eccentricities than his art, which in itself is pretty odd. Lived on hard-boiled eggs which he boiled with his glue (**Florence**, Uffizi; **Fiesole**, S. Francesco).

**Pietro da Cortona** (Cortona, 1596–1699). The most charming of Tuscan Baroque painters; his best is in Rome, but there are some florid ceilings in the Pitti Palace (**Florence**; also works in **Cortona**).

**Pinturicchio** (Perugia, 1454–1513). This painter got his name for his use of gold and rich colours. Never an innovator, but as an absolute virtuoso in colour, style and grace no one could beat him. Another establishment artist, especially favoured by the popes, and, like Perugino, he was slandered most vilely by Vasari (**Siena**, Piccolomini Library).

**Pisano, Andrea** (b. Pontedera, *c.* 1290–1348). Artistic heir of Giovanni and Nicola Pisano and teacher of Orcagna; probably a key figure in introducing new artistic ideas to **Florence** (Baptistry, south doors). Not related to the other Pisani.

**Pisano, Nicola** (active *c.* 1258–78). The first great medieval Tuscan sculptor really came from down south in Apulia, which was then enjoying a flowering of classically orientated art under Emperor Frederick II. He created a little Renaissance all his own, when he adapted the figures and composition of ancient reliefs to make his wonderful pulpit reliefs in **Siena** and **Pisa's** Baptistry. His son **Giovanni Pisano** (active *c.* 1265–1314) carried on the tradition, notably in the façade sculptures at **Siena** cathedral (also **Perugia**, S. Domenico, Fontana Maggiore; great relief pulpits in **Pisa** cathedral, Sant'Andrea, and **Pistoia**).

**Pollaiuolo, Antonio** (Florentine, d. 1498). A sculptor, painter and goldsmith whose fame rests on his brilliant, unmistakable line; he occasionally worked with his less gifted brother **Piero** (**Florence**, Uffizi and Bargello).

**Pontormo, Jacopo** (Florentine, b. Pontormo, 1494–1556). You haven't seen pink and orange until you've seen the work of this determined Mannerist eccentric. After the initial shock, though, you'll meet an artist of real genius, one whose use of the human body as sole means for communicating ideas is equal to Michelangelo's (**Florence**, S. Felicità – his *Deposition* – and Uffizi; **Carmignano**; **Poggio a Caiano**).

**Quercia, Jacopo della** (Sienese, 1374–1438). Sculptor who learned his style from Pisano's cathedral pulpit; one of the unsuccessful contestants for the Florence baptistry doors. Maybe Siena's greatest sculptor, though his most celebrated work, that city's Fonte Gaia, is now ruined (**Lucca**, cathedral *tomb of Ilaria del Carretto*; **San Gimignano**, Collegiata; **Siena**, Baptistry; **Volterra**, cathedral).

**Raphael** (Raffaello Sanzio, 1483–1520). Born in Urbino, Raphael spent time in Città di Castello, Perugia and Florence before establishing himself in Rome. Only a few of the best works of this High Renaissance master remain in the region; those are in the Pitti Palace and Uffizi, **Florence**.

**Robbia, Luca della** (Florentine, 1400–82). Greatest of the famous family of sculptors; he invented the coloured glaze for terracottas that we associate with the della Robbias, but was also a first-rate relief sculptor (the *cantorie* in **Florence**'s cathedral museum; **Impruneta**, Collegiata). His nephew **Andrea della Robbia** (1435–1525; best works in convent of **La Verna** and the Tempietto at **Montevarchi**) and Andrea's son **Giovanni** (1469–1529; best work, **Pistoia**, Ospedale del Ceppo) carried on the blue and white terracotta sweet style in innumerable buildings across Tuscany.

**Rosselli, Cosimo** (Florentine, 1434–1507). Competent middle of the road Renaissance painter who occasionally excelled (**Florence**, S. Ambrogio).

**Rossellino, Bernardo** (1409–64). Florentine architect and sculptor best known as the planner and architect of the new town of **Pienza**. Also a sculptor (**Florence**, S. Croce, S. Miniato; **Empoli**, Pinacoteca). His brother **Antonio Rossellino** (1427–79) was also a talented sculptor (**Florence**, S. Croce).

**Rossi, Vicenzo de'** (1525–87). Florentine Mannerist sculptor of chunky male nudes (**Florence**, Palazzo Vecchio).

**Rosso Fiorentino** (Giovanni Battista di Jacopo, 1494–1540). Florentine Mannerist painter, he makes a fitting complement to Pontormo, both for his tortured soul and for the exaggerations of form and colour he used to create gripping, dramatic effects. Fled Italy after the Sack of Rome and worked for Francis I at Fontainebleau. (**Volterra** Pinacoteca has his masterpiece, the *Deposition*; **Florence**, Uffizi and S. Lorenzo; **Città di Castello**, Duomo).

**Salviati, Francesco** (Florentine, 1510–63). Friend of Vasari and a similar sort of painter – though much more talented. Odd perspectives and decoration, often bizarre imagery (**Florence**, Palazzo Vecchio and Uffizi).

**Sangallo, Antonio da** (brother of Giuliano, 1455–1537). Architect at his best in palaces and churches in the monumental style – notably at the great temple of S. Biagio, **Montepulciano**; the son, **Antonio da Sangallo the Younger**, also an architect, and the family's best, practised mainly in Rome.

**Sangallo, Giuliano da** (Florentine, 1443–1516). Architect of humble origins who became the favourite of Lorenzo de' Medici. Often tripped up by an obsession, inherited from

Alberti, with making architecture conform to philosophical principles (**Poggio a Caiano; Florence**, S. Maddalena dei Pazzi; **Prato**, S. Maria delle Carceri).

Il **Sassetta** (Stefano di Giovanni; active c.1390–1450). One of the great Sienese quattrocento painters, though still working in a style the Florentines would have found hopelessly reactionary; an artist who studied Masaccio but preferred the Gothic elegance of Masolino. His masterpiece, the Borgo Sansepolcro polyptych, is dispersed through half the museums of Europe.

**Signorelli, Luca** (b. Cortona, d. 1523). A rarefied Umbrian painter and an important influence on Michelangelo. Imaginative, forceful compositions, combining geometrical rigour with a touch of unreality, much like his master Piero della Francesca (**Cortona**, civic and cathedral museums; **Monte Oliveto Maggiore**; **Sansepolcro**, museum).

Il **Sodoma** (Giovanni Antonio Bazzi, 1477–1549). Born in Piedmont, but a Sienese by choice, he was probably not the libertine his nickname and Vasari's biography suggest. An endearing, serene artist, who usually eschewed Mannerist distortion, he got rich through his work, then blew it all feeding his exotic menagerie and died in the poorhouse (**Monte Oliveto Maggiore**; **Siena**, Pinacoteca and S. Domenico).

**Spinello Aretino** (b. Arezzo, late 14th century–1410). A link between Giotto and the International Gothic style; imaginative and colourful in his compositions (**Florence**, S. Miniato; **Siena**, Palazzo Pubblico; **Arezzo**, museum). His son **Parri di Spinello** did many fine works, all around **Arezzo** (S. Maria delle Grazie).

**Tacca, Pietro** (1580–1640). Born in Carrara, pupil of Giambologna and one of the best early Baroque sculptors (**Livorno**, *Quattro Mori*; **Florence**, Piazza SS. Annunziata fountains; **Prato**, Piazza del Comune).

**Taddeo di Bartolo** (Volterra, 1363–1422). The greatest Sienese painter of the late 1300s – also the least conventional; never a consummate stylist, he often shows a remarkable imagination in composition and treatment of subject matter (**Siena**, Palazzo Pubblico, S. Spirito; **Perugia**, Pinacoteca; **Colle di Val d'Elsa** museum and Collegiata; **Volterra**, Pinacoteca; **San Gimignano**, Museo Civico).

**Talenti, Francesco** (early 14th century). Chief architect of **Florence** cathedral and campanile after Arnolfo di Cambio and Giotto; his son **Simone** made the beautiful windows in **Orsanmichele** (and perhaps the Loggia dei Lanzi) in **Florence**.

**Torrigiano, Pietro** (1472–1528). Florentine portrait sculptor, famous for his work in Westminster Abbey and for breaking Michelangelo's nose (**Siena**, cathedral).

**Uccello, Paolo** (Florentine, 1397–1475). No artist has ever been more obsessed with the possibilities of artificial perspective. Like Piero della Francesca, he used the new technique to create a magic world of his own; contemplation of it made him increasingly eccentric in his later years. Uccello's provocative, visionary subjects (*Noah* fresco in S. Maria Novella, and *Battle of San Romano* in the Uffizi, and cloister of San Miniato, **Florence**) put him up with Piero della Francesca and Botticelli as the most intellectually stimulating of quattrocento artists (also attributed frescoes, **Prato** cathedral).

**Vasari, Giorgio** (Arezzo, 1511–74). Florentine sycophant, writer and artist. Also a pretty good architect (**Florence**, Uffizi, Corridoio, and Fish Loggia, and the palace in **Città di Castello**).

**Il Vecchietta** (Lorenzo di Pietro, 1412–80). Sienese painter and sculptor, dry and linear, part Sienese Pollaiuolo and part Donatello. One wonders what he did to acquire his nickname, 'Little Old Woman' (**Siena**, Loggia della Mercanzia, Baptistry).

**Verrocchio, Andrea del** (1435–88). Florentine sculptor who worked in bronze; spent his life trying to outdo Donatello. Also a painter, a mystic alchemist in his spare time, and interestingly enough the master of both Botticelli and Leonardo (Uffizi, S. Lorenzo, Orsanmichele, Palazzo Vecchio, and Bargello, **Florence**).

# Topics

# A Country Calendar

If there's a great sense of continuity in the land, it is the same with the rhythms of rural life in central Italy. Old traditions and seasonal changes are still of primary importance – Italians, for the most part, won't buy imported fruit or vegetables (although this is unfortunately changing); even in the cities it's difficult to find a decent tomato in January. Even chocolates disappear off the counter in July. Tuscany, like most of Italy, chooses to follow the calendar as a sort of sentimental journey through the rise and fall of the year.

The traditional Florentine New Year began on Annunciation Day in March, the time when the countryside really did seem to awaken – until the Medici Grand Dukes finally aligned Tuscany to the papal calendar in the 1500s. **January** still hibernates; if the ground is soft farmers may put in peas and garlic; roast chestnuts, polenta, *bruschetta* and game dishes are the highlights of the table. **February** is the month of pruning and planting garden vegetables in frames. Sticky sweet carnival pastries are unavoidable. In **March** new fruit trees are planted and the vines are pruned; potatoes, fennel, spinach, carrots, parsley and lettuce are planted directly in the garden. Blood oranges (from Sicily) and artichokes appear in the shops. The fruit trees burst into blossom, and continue through **April**, the time to plant sunflowers and corn, the other garden vegetables and most flowers. Lambs are slaughtered for Easter; young turkeys and pigs are purchased. The hunt for wild asparagus and salad greens is in full swing.

Strawberries and medlars are the fruits of **May**, central Italy's most glorious month, when the irises and roses bloom in profusion. *Fave* (broad beans) are the big treat, and in the mountains, in most years, you can stop lighting fires to stay warm in the evening. The first garlic, French beans and potatoes are harvested in **June**, which is also the time to plant cabbage and cauliflowers. Cherries, apricots, plums, the first watermelons and fresh tomatoes appear; everyone's eating melon and prosciutto *antipasti* and dishes with courgette flowers (*fiori di zucca*).

**July** brings an avalanche of *zucchini* and peaches. Country folk begin staying up past 10pm, and scorpions come into your house to cool off. In **August** chickens meet their maker, while the end of the month brings masses upon masses of tomatoes, which country families join together to conserve – a messy operation of steaming kettles and grinders that puts up a year's supply of tomato sauce. Apples, pears and fresh figs are harvested in **September**, a golden, placid month when the village stationery shops begin stocking the schoolbooks for the new year.

**October** is the *vendemmia*, or grape harvest, the highlight of the year for everyone outside the Umbrian Apennines; to make *vin santo* it's essential to pick out very mature bunches and hang them up to dry. The hunting season opens, and folks begin to poke around for wild mushrooms. **November** is a busy month, the time to hunt for truffles, harvest olives, pomegranates and chestnuts, and take care of wine business. In **December** the family pig is slaughtered for next year's *prosciutto* and sausages. Orange persimmons hang like ornaments on the trees and plague the table – no one likes them, but everyone has plenty to give away; if they are indeed the apples of the

Hesperides, as some scholars suggest, the afterlife must be a major disappointment. Stick to the tiny tangerines from the south that flood the market. Christmas turkeys realize their time has come; and cakes are everywhere: dense confections of walnuts, raisins, chocolates and pepper (*panforte* of Siena) or tall, airy *panettone* sold in cylindrical boxes.

# The First Professional Philistine

Many who have seen Vasari's work in Florence will be wondering how such a mediocre painter should rate so much attention. Ingratiating companion of the rich and famous, workmanlike over-achiever and tireless self-promoter, Vasari was the perfect man for his time. Born in Arezzo, in 1511, a fortunate introduction to Cardinal Silvio Passerini gave him the chance of an education in Florence with the young Medici heirs Ippolito and Alessandro. In his early years, he became a fast and reliable frescoist gaining a reputation for customer satisfaction – a real innovation in an age when artists were increasingly becoming eccentric prima donnas. In the 1530s, after travelling around Italy on various commissions, he returned to Florence just when Cosimo I was beginning his plans to remake the city in the image of the Medici. It was a marriage made in heaven. Vasari became Cosimo's court painter and architect, with a limitless budget and a large group of assistants, the most prolific fresco machine ever seen in Italy – painting over countless good frescoes of the 1300s.

But more than for his paintings, Vasari lives on through his book, the *Lives of the Painters, Sculptors and Architects*, a series of exhaustive, gossipy biographies of artists. Beginning with Cimabue, Vasari traces the rise of art out of Byzantine and Gothic barbarism, through Giotto and his followers, towards an ever-improving naturalism, finally culminating in the great age of Leonardo, Raphael and the divine Michelangelo, who not only mastered nature but outdid her. Leon Battista Alberti gets the credit for drafting the first principles of artistic criticism, but it was Vasari who first applied such ideas on a grand scale. His book, being the first of its kind, and containing a mine of valuable information on dozens of Renaissance artists, naturally has had a tremendous influence on all subsequent criticism. Art critics have never really been able to break out of the Vasarian straitjacket.

Much of Vasari's world seems quaint to us now: the idea of the artist as a kind of knight of the brush, striving for Virtue and Glory, the slavish worship of anything that survived from ancient Rome, artistic 'progress' and the conviction that art's purpose was to imitate nature. But many of Vasari's opinions have had a long and mischievous career in the world of ideas. His blind disparagement of everything medieval – really the prejudice of his entire generation – lived on until the 1800s. His dismissal of Sienese, Umbrian and northern artists – of anyone who was not a Florentine – has not been entirely corrected even today. Vasari was the sort who founded academies, a cheerful conformist who believed in a nice, tidy art that went by the book. With his interior decorator's concept of Beauty, he created a style of criticism in which virtuosity, not imagination, became the standard by which art was to be judged;

history offers few more instructive examples of the stamina and resilience of dubious ideas.

# Flora and Fauna

No one would come to this part of Italy expecting to find an unspoiled wilderness. Most of Tuscany, in particular, has been cultivated so long and so intensively that wildlife is completely pushed to the fringes. Nevertheless, there is a great variety of birds and beasts to complement the surprisingly wide range of landscapes. Cultivated Tuscany (*see* below, 'Landscapes') is another world, a land of vineyards and olive groves, cypresses, poplars and the occasional umbrella pine. The rest of the territory divides neatly into three parts: the coastal zone, with its beaches and wetlands, the central hills and the mountains.

For nature-lovers, the coast will be by far the most interesting region; the malaria mosquito kept much of the southern Maremma undeveloped for centuries, leaving vast stretches of pine forest, along with cork oak and holm oak, a thriving wildlife (including, even, some wild horses) and marshlands that host a marvellous array of birds, from eagles to woodpeckers. Its protected nesting grounds (*see* the Monti dell'Uccellina, pp.303–4, Orbetello lagoons, p.305, and Lago di Burano, p.310) are Italy's greatest stopover for migrating waterfowl – herons, cormorants, storks, kingfishers, osprey and the only flamingoes left on the mainland. Deforested land beyond the marshes is covered with the characteristic Mediterranean scrub, or maquis (*macchia*, in Italian); either *macchia alta* with shrub versions of pines (they harvest the pine nuts), oaks, beech, cypress and laurel; or the *macchia bassa* in drier regions, thick patches of broom, heather, lentisk and other fragrant plants.

As for the **animals**, there are pretty much the same characters throughout Tuscany starting with those two regional totems, the viper and the boar. The bad old viper, the only really unpleasant thing you may meet out in the woods and fields, proliferates especially where farmlands have been abandoned; he's brownish-grey, about a foot and half long (never more than a yard), and has a vaguely diamond-shaped head. Vipers are a nuisance only because there are so many of them, and because they object to being stepped on. If one bites you, you've got half an hour to find someone with the serum – or you can buy your own in any pharmacy and keep it in the fridge. The boar, a shy, well-mannered creature, flourishes everywhere despite the Italians' best efforts to turn him into salami or *prosciutto*. In summer, you may hear them nosing around the villages at night looking for water.

Beyond these, there are plenty of hares and rabbits, foxes and weasels, also polecats, badgers and porcupine in the wilder areas. Wolves, lynxes and deer were once common, and a few of each survive in the higher reaches of the Apennines; deer have been reintroduced in the Maremma coastal parks. There is a little isolated region in Tuscany, the Val di Farma north of Roccastrada, where you can find all of these, and even wildcats. The only mountain goats are found on the island of Montecristo.

Many writers on this part of Italy comment on the absence of **birdsong**. They're exaggerating. Italian hunters do shoot anything that flies, but there are still quite a few thrushes, starlings, wrens and such, along with the white doves that always make you think of Assisi and St Francis. Cuckoos unfailingly announce the spring, pheasants lie low during the hunting season, and an occasional owl can be heard in the country. Nightingales are rare, but there are supposed to be some around Lago di Massacuccioli and the northern coasts – in the evening you're far more likely to see bats.

The **insect** world is well represented, and if you spend time in the country, you'll meet many of them: lovely butterflies and moths, and delicate white creatures with wings apparently made of feathers; rather forbidding black bullet bees, and wasps that resemble vintage fighter planes. Beetles especially reach disproportionate sizes – if you're lucky you may see a *diavolo*, a large black or red beetle with long, gracefully curving antlers that sings when you trap it; Leonardo drew one in his notebooks. There are enough mosquitoes, midges and little biting flies to be a nuisance in the summer, and, perhaps most alarming at first sight, the shiny black scorpion, who may crawl inside through the window or up drains (you may want to keep the plugs in) or come in with the wood if you have a fire. Once inside they head for dark places like beds or shoes. One thwack with a shoe will do in even the largest scorpion (they're actually quite soft). If you happen to be stung, it may be painful but not deadly; the Italians recommend a trip to the doctor for treatment against an infection or allergic reaction. One of the most stunning insect spectacles is the fireflies in midsummer. In a cornfield it is a truly magical sight – and they are such dull little creatures in daylight.

As for the **forests**, oaks, chestnuts and beech predominate, along with tall, upright poplars ('Lombardy' type), pines, willows (not the weeping variety) and a few maples – with rounded leaves, not pointed as in northern Europe and America. Cypress trees are common. Incidentally the idea that there are erect, needle-like 'male' cypresses and blowsy 'female' ones is a misconception; the tidier ones have been planted, while shaggy cypresses are the wild variety. Parasol or umbrella pines (really the maritime pine), that most characteristic Italian tree, make a grand sight isolated on a hill crest, or in large groves along the Maremma coast. At higher altitudes, there are large beech forests, along with pines and firs – some beautiful groves of silver firs grow around Monte Amiata, while in the Casentino near Camaldoli is a vast stretch of old, protected beech and pine forest; another, primarily chestnut forest, is contained in the Garfagnana's *Parco Naturale dell'Orecchiella*.

Though at first **wild flowers** may seem unfamiliar, many of the most common Italian wild flowers are close cousins to those seen in northern Europe and America. There are a million varieties of buttercup, usually tiny ones like the *ranuncolo* and *bottoncini d'oro*, and of bluebell, often called *campanella* or *campanellina*. Many of the common five-petalled pink blossoms in spring fields are really small wild geraniums (*geranio*), with pointed leaves like the anemone, and you'll see quite a few varieties of violets (*violette*) with round or spade-shaped leaves (a few species are yellow). A daisy, in Italian, is a *margherita*, and they come in all sizes. Tiniest of all are the wild pink and blue forget-me-nots (*non ti scordar di me*); you'll have to look closely to see them in overgrown fields. Large swatches of lavender are one of the charms of the hills of Chianti.

The real star of Italian fields is the poppy, bright red and thriving everywhere. Dandelions and wild mustard are also plentiful, along with white, umbrella-like bunches of florets called *tragosellino* or *podragraria*, similar to what Americans call Queen Anne's Lace. More exotic flowers include wild orchids, some with small florets growing in spiky shoots, rhododendrons (in mountainous areas), five-petalled wild roses and water lilies in the coastal Maremma. The best wildflowers are found up in the Sibillini mountains; the Piano Grande blooming in early summer is an unforgettable sight.

There are other **plants** to look for; a dozen kinds of greens that go into somewhat bitter salads, anise, fennel, mint, rosemary and sage are common. The Italians beat the bushes with fervour every spring looking for wild asparagus and repeat the performance in autumn searching for truffles and *porcini* (boletus) mushrooms.

## A Florentine Puzzle

In a city as visually dry and restrained as Florence, every detail of decoration stands out. In the Middle Ages and Renaissance, Florentine builders combined their passion for geometry with their love of making a little go a long way; they evolved a habit of embellishing buildings with simple geometrical designs. Though nothing special in themselves – most are easily drawn with a compass and straight edge – in their context they stand out like mystic hieroglyphs, symbols upon which to meditate while contemplating old Florence's remarkable journey through the western mind.

The city is full of them, incorporated into façades, mosaics, windows and friezes. Here are eight of them, a little exercise for the eye while tramping the hard pavements of Florence. Your job is to find them. Some are really obvious, others obscure. For No.6 you should be able to find at least three examples (two across the street from each other) and if you're clever you'll find not only No.5, a rather late addition to the cityscape, but also the medieval work that inspired it. Don't worry too much about the last one. But if you're an art historian or a Florentinophile, it's only fair that you seek out this hard one too. For the answers, *see* the last page of the index, p.442.

# Landscapes

Other regions in Italy are lusher, have taller mountains and more fertile valleys, support a far greater variety of flora and enjoy a more temperate climate. Yet, when all is said and done, the landscapes of Tuscany exert the most lasting charm. In the painting of the Renaissance, the background of rolling hills, cypresses, poplars and parasol pines, the vineyards and winding lanes are often more beautiful than the nominally religious subject in the foreground. Very early on, beginning with Giotto, artists took care to relate the figures in their composition to the architecture and the landscape around them, epitomized in the paintings of Leonardo da Vinci, where each tree and rock takes on an almost mystic significance.

Every Italian is born with an obsessive instinct to put in order, or '*sistemare*' things; with a history of wars, earthquakes, foreign rulers, and an age-old tendency to extremes of all descriptions, the race has had a bellyful of disorder and unpredictability. The tidy, ordered geometry and clipped hedges of an Italian garden are a perfect example of the urge to *sistemare* nature, and you'll find good examples of these in the Boboli Gardens and the Medici villas at Castello; the Tuscans, in the vanguard of Italy in so many ways, were the first to *sistemare* their entire territory. The vicious wars of the Middle Ages between cities and the Guelphs and Ghibellines devastated the countryside and much of the forests (as is visible in the harsh, barren brown and grey hills of trecento painting); the Black Death in the 1300s depopulated the cultivated areas, giving the Tuscans the unique opportunity to arrange things just so. Not entirely by coincidence, the late 14th century was the time when the élite, weary of the strife in the city, were discovering the joys of the country and building villas, playing the country squire and gentleman farmer whenever possible – already, in the *Decameron*, the nobles had estates in the environs of Florence. And they planted everything in its place according to elegance and discipline, each tree with its own purpose, a boundary marker, for shade, or to support a vine. Often cypresses and parasol pines stand strikingly along the crest of hills, not for aesthetics or a study in perspective, but for a windbreak. Strongest of all is the feeling that nothing has changed for centuries, that in the quattrocento Gozzoli and Fra Angelico painted the same scene you see today. Few landscapes anywhere are more ancient, or civilized.

# Tuscany on Wheels

Tuscans have always loved a parade, and to the casual reader of Renaissance history, it seems they're forever proceeding somewhere or another, even to their own detriment – during outbreaks of plague, holy companies would parade through an inflicted area, invoking divine mercy, while in effect aiding the spread of the pestilence. They also had a great weakness for allegorical parade floats. During the centuries of endless war each Tuscan city rolled out its war chariot or battle wagon, called the *Carroccio*, invented by a Milanese bishop in the 11th century. A *Carroccio*, drawn by six white oxen, was a kind of holy ship of state in a hay cart; a mast held up a crucifix while a battle standard flew from the yard-arm, there was an altar for priests to say mass during the battle and a large bell to send signals over the din to the armies. The worst possible outcome of a battle was to lose one's Carroccio to the enemy, as Fiesole did to Florence. One is still in operation, in Siena, rumbling out twice a year for the Palio (*see* p.323).

Medieval clerical processions, by the time of Dante, became melded with the idea of the Roman 'triumph' (*trionfo*); in Purgatory, the poet finds Beatrice triumphing with a cast of characters from the Apocalypse. Savonarola wrote of a *Triumph of the Cross*; Petrarch and Boccaccio wrote allegorical triumphs of virtues, love and death. More interesting, however, are the secular Roman-style Triumphs staged by the Medici, especially at Carnival (the name of which, according to Burckhardt, comes from a cart, the pagan *carrus navalis*, the ship of Isis, launched every 5 March to symbolize the reopening of navigation). You can get a hint of their splendour from the frescoes at Poggio a Caiano; the best artists of the day would be commissioned to design the decorations – two particularly famous *trionfi* in Florence celebrated the election of the Medici Pope Leo X. The last relics of these parades are the huge satirical carnival floats at Viareggio.

Two lovely memories of Florence's processions remain. One is Gozzoli's fairy-tale frescoes in the chapel of the Medici palace, of the annual procession staged by the Compagnia de' Re Magi, the most splendid and aristocratic of pageants. The other comes from the Florentine Carnival, famous for its enormous floats, in which scenes from mythology were portrayed to songs and music. One year, for the masque of Bacchus and Ariadne, Lorenzo de' Medici composed the loveliest Italian poem to come out of the Renaissance, with the melancholy refrain:

| | |
|---|---|
| *Quanto è bella giovinezza,* | *How fair is youth,* |
| *Che si fugge tuttavia!* | *How fast it flies away!* |
| *Chi vuol esser lieto, sia:* | *Let him who will, be merry:* |
| *Di doman non c'è certezza.* | *Of tomorrow nothing is certain.* |

# Florentines 2, Giants 1

*Sono vulgari, quei Fiorentini...* You won't spend much time in Italy (or especially in Tuscany) before you hear someone commenting on the vulgarity of the Florentines. Such a remark may be occasioned by a lad standing next to an Alfa with Florence number plates, leaning on the horn and waking up the babies, or by a couple with sunglasses in a dark restaurant who manage to get in three cigarettes after each course. As everyone knows, Florentines are also the most arrogant and conceited people in the universe, surpassing even the Romans and Milanese.

After some initial dismay, you may find it refreshing to encounter a people with so many peculiar facets to their personality. We know about the Florentines of old, their fascination with mathematics and technology, and their matchless talent for art, and we know about the foppish prancing Florentine courtiers of the decadent 1600s. But more up-to-date models are not entirely without interest. Florentines are famous for their dry wit, and their penny-pinching economy, a talent for making a little go a long way. Their tenaciously conservative *dov'era com'era* mentality towards their museum city-home is extreme even by Italian standards. And a redeeming share of their old Renaissance craftsmanship remains, an attention to detail that makes them skilled seamstresses and the best art restorers in the world.

The refinement, as well as the arrogance and conceit, are one side of the coin; on the other we find a surprising streak of down-to-earth hillbilly cussedness. Florentines and the rest of the Tuscans are after all dismissed as *mangiafagioli*, 'bean-eaters', by other Italians. According to one perceptive observer, all the shortcomings of the Florentines are due to a diet of too much beans, tripe and cockscombs – the very mention of these conjures up the uneasy shade of the bloated, horrible Catherine de' Medici up in Paris, gorging herself on cockscombs and puking all over the Louvre.

For all these singular qualities, it is surprising that Florentines hardly ever make it into literature; it's hard to imagine a novel that could not be improved by giving a Florentine a small role. The only interesting one we have been able to find is the star of a fairy-tale heard in Pisa, one of those transcribed by Italo Calvino in his wonderful collection *Italian Folktales*. It seems there was this Florentine who had never in his entire life left Florence. Unable to talk knowledgeably about the comings and goings of the wide world, he felt at a loss in polite conversation, and finally he resolved to go out and do some travelling. He packed his bags and hit the road, in no particular direction, and along the way he met first a priest and then a farmer, both of whom felt the same way about their own lives and decided to join the Florentine as travelling companions. Eventually the three of them came to the house of a giant. The Florentine thought they should go and knock on the door, so that he could tell the folks back home about meeting a giant, and when they did they found the giant a rather courteous fellow who had need of a priest for his village church, and a farmer for his farm. He couldn't think of any particular use for a Florentine, but he took him in too.

Now, in fact this giant's courtesy was but a devious façade concealing a giant-size black-hearted stinker. He took the priest aside, supposedly to show him his duties, but once the door was closed he whacked off his head and kicked the corpse through a trap door. He did the same to the farmer – but the Florentine was watching through the keyhole this time, as Florentines will do, and while he was pretty excited about the story he would have to entertain folks back home, it dawned on him that he would most certainly be next. At this point the storyteller, for lack of something better, gives the tale a turn straight from Homer (remember Odysseus and the Cyclops?). The giant had a squinty eye, and the Florentine had the presence of mind to tell him that he could cure it with a decoction made from a certain herb, which he had noticed growing in those parts. The giant was delighted to let him try, and the Florentine tied him to a marble table and poured the boiling mess into both his eyes. Now comes the chase scene, but the blinded giant couldn't very well catch a Florentine with a marble table tied to his back, and he tried to trick him by offering him his gold ring to finish the cure for his eyes. This was a magic ring, unfortunately, and when the poor guy put it on, his finger became as heavy as stone and weighed him to the ground. The Florentine couldn't get it off again (because it was a magic ring, remember), but he saved himself by chopping off the finger with a penknife. He made it home to Florence, finally, but he never bothered to tell anyone about his wonderful adventures, and whenever anyone asked him about the finger he said he'd had an accident while cutting the grass.

## The First Tuscans

Up in Rome's Capitoline Museum you can see the famous bronze statue of the she-wolf suckling Romulus and Remus, the symbol of Rome since ancient times. Not many people know that this was actually not the work of a Roman artist, but an Etruscan. There are plenty of other things they never taught you in school about the Romans. Specifically, nearly every art or talent we usually give them credit for was bought or more likely stolen from somebody else. Roman painting, sculpture and architecture were seldom more than a grandiose pastiche of the Greek, and plenty of the other Roman trademarks – religion and superstition, gladiators, rectilinear surveying and town planning, portrait sculpture, sewers, togas and even concrete – were simply taken over whole from Rome's nearest neighbours and favourite victims, the Etruscans.

We often forget that, long before Brunelleschi and Donatello, Tuscany was home to another great civilization – Italy's first. But when Rome was still a collection of mud and timber huts among the miasmal swamps of the Tiber, the people of Etruria were collecting Greek urns, reclining on couches at their lavish banquets and dressing up for the races. Etruscan culture blossomed in the 8th century for the usual reasons – most importantly, a nice surplus of ready cash. Just as classical Athens's rise to prominence was financed by the silver mines at nearby Laurion, Etruria exploited the mineral wealth of the Colline Metallifere and Elba; there was plenty of iron, especially, for weapons and for exports. Cities grew opulent as trade boomed, and to protect their trade routes the cities developed powerful navies that dominated the Etruscan *mare nostrum*, the Tyrrhenian (so named because the Greeks called this people *Tyrrhenoi*; to the Romans they were *Tuscii* or *Etruscii*, while in their own language they are properly called the *Rasena*).

The overwhelming impression given by painting and sculpture is of a people who, whatever their flaws, were wonderfully alive. Etruscan art is full of expressive faces that either wear a smile, or are blissfully caught on the verge of breaking into one. Some of the jolly sculptures in the museums of Volterra and Rome must rank among the first conscious caricatures in art. Everything about this art paints a picture, true or not, of a people cheerfully devoted to the joys of this world. Indeed, their contemporaries dropped plenty of gossip about Etruscan hedonism and licentiousness (much of this comes from the devoutly male-chauvinist Greeks and Romans, shocked at a society where women seem to have enjoyed considerable rights and respect).

In any case, it would be difficult to find anyone in antiquity more fashion-conscious. Elaborately carved mirrors and make-up cases constitute a large part of the Etruscan collection in any museum, and the evidence from tomb frescoes suggests the ladies also liked to dye their hair blonde. The jewellery is remarkable – as good as anything between the Minoans and Fabergé. Some of it goes completely over the top, filigree work and granulation so ornate and flashy it could be worn in Las Vegas. Or whatever was the Etrurian equivalent thereof – after considering the Etruscans closely you'll begin to suspect they must have had one somewhere (perhaps Tuscany's thermal spas; the Etruscans, celebrated for their medical skills, were the first to develop these, and passed the habit down to the Romans). Coiffures and clothes could be equally elaborate; in art you will hardly ever find two Etruscan ladies with the same hairdo. Then, as now, Tuscan shoemakers were famous around the known world; the fashions of the 5th century, as shown in frescoes, featured pointed, curling toes.

Another of their talents was music; Etruscans are often pictured dancing or playing the trumpet, the lyre and, most commonly of all, a type of pan-pipes. According to a Hellenistic Greek account, they even used music in their hunting; pipers would play charmed melodies to draw the animals out of their lairs and towards the nets. Such a story is not surprising, considering another essential Etruscan trait, an attachment to magic and fortune-telling unsurpassed in the ancient world. Etruscan augurs, or *haruspices*, scrutinized the livers of sacrificed animals and scanned the skies for birds to fortell the future. Their skill was so great that *haruspices* were still employed around the Roman Empire in the 4th century AD, the last people on earth who understood the Etruscan language.

Nobody knows quite why, but after 500 BC everything started to fall apart for the Etruscans. Manufacture and art declined, slave revolts became common, and the archaeologists report that everything from tombs to pottery were being made less skilfully, more cheaply. The once-formidable Etruscan navy was getting regularly whipped by the Greeks, while the Celts destroyed the colonies in the north that had been built up with so much painstaking effort for so long. Most dire of all were the Romans. Rome's closest Etruscan neighbours, Fidenae and Veii, were captured and wiped out in 425 and 396. Veii suffered an epic siege of ten years, and, typically, during that time none of the other Etruscan cities did much to help. Chronic disunity among the members of the Dodecapolis allowed Rome to gobble up Etruria a bit at a time. The last important city, Volsinii, fell about 350, and from then on Etruria was nothing more than a Roman province – the first of many.

But the cultural heritage of these gifted people was too great to disappear completely. The Romans, as we have seen, swallowed Etruscan culture whole, and they passed quite a bit of it on to us. Hundreds of words in modern languages probably stem from the Etruscan, by way of Latin: *person*, for example, which originally meant an Etruscan theatre or ritual mask, or *temple* (this meant one of the 16 sections into which the Etruscan augurs divided the sky for divination by birdflight).

The Etruscan influence on the art of the Renaissance is a fascinating subject that has never been thoroughly explored. When medieval Tuscans revived the art of fresco painting, they probably had no idea they were simply following in the footsteps of their ancestors. Raymond Bloch, an authority on the Etruscans, noticed an eerily perfect resemblance between Donatello's famous *St George* , the very model of quattrocento *prontezza*, and an Etruscan head found long ago at Veii. In one of Michelangelo's sketchbooks we see an image of the Etruscan god Atia, undoubtedly copied from the frescoes in a tomb. And all those little faces we see staring out at us from Renaissance sculptural friezes, frescoes and book decorations are called 'grotesques', because Raphael found their originals in a painted 'grotto' in Rome. This was really a floor of buried rooms of Emperor Nero's palace, the famous Golden House, decorated in a style inherited from the Etruscans of old.

# Food and Drink

04

In Italy, the three Ms (the *Madonna*, *Mamma* and *Mangiare*) are still a force to be reckoned with, and in a country where millions of otherwise sane people spend much of their waking hours worrying about their digestion, standards both at home and in the restaurants are understandably high. Everybody is a gourmet, or at least thinks he or she is, and food is not only something to eat but a subject approaching the heights of philosophy – two Umbrian businessmen once overheard on a train heatedly discussed mushrooms for over *four* hours. Although ready-made pasta, tinned *minestrone* and frozen pizza in the *supermercato* tempt the virtue of the Italian cook, few give in (although many a working mother wishes she could at times).

For the visitor this national culinary obsession comes as an extra bonus to the senses – along with Italy's remarkable sights, music and the warm sun on your back, you can enjoy some of the best tastes and smells the world can offer, prepared daily in Italy's kitchens and fermented in its countless wine cellars. Eating *all'italiana* is not only delicious and wholesome, but now undeniably trendy. Foreigners flock here to learn the secrets of Italian cuisine and the even more elusive secret of how the Italians can live surrounded by such a plethora of delights and still fit into their sleek Armani trousers.

# Restaurant Generalities

**Breakfast** (*colazione*) in Italy is no lingering affair, but an early morning wake-up shot to the brain: a *cappuccino* (*espresso* with hot foamy milk, often sprinkled with chocolate – incidentally first thing in the morning is the only time of day at which any self-respecting Italian will touch the stuff), a *caffè latte* (white coffee) or a *caffè lungo* (a generous portion of *espresso*), accompanied by a croissant-type roll, called a *cornetto* or *brioche*, or a fancy pastry. This repast can be consumed in any bar and repeated during the morning as often as necessary. Breakfast in most Italian hotels seldom represents great value.

**Lunch** (*pranzo*), generally served around 1pm, is the most important meal of the day for the Italians, with a minimum of a first course (*primo piatto* – any kind of pasta dish, broth or soup, or rice dish or pizza), a second course (*secondo piatto* – a meat dish, accompanied by a *contorno* or side dish – a vegetable, salad or potatoes usually), followed by fruit or dessert and coffee. You can, however, begin with a platter of *antipasti* – the appetizers Italians do so brilliantly, ranging from warm seafood delicacies, to raw ham (*prosciutto crudo*), salami in a hundred varieties, lovely vegetables, savoury toasts, olives, pâté and many many more. There are restaurants that specialize in *antipasti*, and they usually don't take it amiss if you decide to forget the pasta and meat and just nibble on these scrumptious hors-d'œuvres (though in the end it may well cost more than a full meal). Most Italians accompany their meal with wine and mineral water – *acqua minerale*, with or without bubbles (*con* or *senza gas*), which supposedly aids digestion – concluding their meals with a *digestivo* liqueur.

*Cena*, the **evening meal,** is usually eaten around 8pm – earlier in the north and later in the south. This is much the same as *pranzo* although lighter, without the pasta;

a *pizza* and beer, eggs or a fish dish. In restaurants, however, they offer all the courses whatever the time of day, so if you have only a sandwich for lunch you can have a full meal in the evening.

In Italy the various terms for types of **restaurants** – *ristorante*, *trattoria* or *osteria* – have been confused. A *trattoria* or *osteria* can be just as elaborate as a restaurant, though rarely is a *ristorante* as informal as a traditional *trattoria*. Unfortunately the old habit of posting menus and prices in the windows has fallen from fashion, so it's often difficult to judge variety or prices. Invariably the least expensive eating place is the *vino e cucina*, a simple establishment serving simple cuisine at simple everyday prices. It is essential to remember that the fancier the fittings, the fancier the **bill**, though neither of these points has anything at all to do with the quality of the food. If you're uncertain, do as you would at home – look for lots of locals.

People who haven't visited Italy for years and have fond memories of eating full meals for under a pound will be amazed at how much **prices** have risen; though in some respects eating out in Italy is still a bargain, especially when you figure out how much all that wine would have cost you at home. In many places you'll often find restaurants offering a *menu turistico* – full, set meals of usually meagre inspiration for a reasonable set price. More imaginative chefs often offer a *menu degustazione* – a set-price gourmet meal that allows you to taste their daily specialities and seasonal dishes. Both of these are cheaper than if you had ordered the same food *à la carte*.

As the pace of modern urban life militates against traditional lengthy home-cooked repasts with the family, followed by a siesta, alternatives to sit-down meals have mushroomed. Many office workers now behave much as their counterparts else-where in Europe and consume a rapid snack at lunchtime, returning home after a busy day to throw together some pasta and salad in the evenings.

The original Italian fast food alternative is known as the 'hot table' (*tavola calda*), a buffet serving hot and cold foods, where you can choose a simple prepared dish or a whole meal, depending on your appetite. The food in these can occasionally be truly impressive, though nowadays they are becoming harder to find among the growing number of international and made-in-Italy fast food franchises. However, bars often double as *paninotecas* (these make sandwiches to order), and if everywhere else is closed, you can always try the railway station bars – these will at least have sand-wiches and drinks. Some of the station bars also prepare *cestini di viaggio*, full-course meals in a basket to help you survive long train trips.

Common snacks you'll encounter include *panini* of prosciutto, cheese and tomatoes, or other meats; *tramezzini*, little sandwiches on plain, square white bread that are always much better than they look; *pizza*, of course, or the traditional sandwich of Tuscany and Umbria, a hard roll filled with fat slices of warm *porchetta* (roast whole pig stuffed with fennel and garlic, complete with all the fat and gristle). Little shops that sell pizza by the slice (*al taglio*) are common in city centres; some, called *gastronomie*, offer other take-out delicacies as well. At any delicatessen (*pizzicheria*), or grocer's (*alimentari*) or market (*mercato*) you can buy the materials for countryside picnics; some places in smaller towns will make the sandwiches for you.

### Siena's Salami

There are hundreds of different types of salami in Tuscany, each made to an age-old, much treasured recipe, and tasting far better than some of the ingredients might suggest. Siena has several of its own. *Buristo* is a cooked salami made from the blood and fatty leftovers of sausages and heavily spiced; *finocchiona* is peppered sausage meat seasoned with fennel seeds and stuffed into the sausage skin; *soppressata* is a boiled salami made from a mixture of rind and gristle; the alternative version, *soppressata in cuffia*, is made in the same way and then stuffed into a boned pig's head. The *salsiccioli secchi* are perhaps the most appetising salami of all, made from the leanest cuts of pork or wild boar, enhanced with garlic and black or red pepper.

# Regional Specialities

Regional traditions are strong in Italy, not only in dialect but in the kitchen. Tuscany is no exception and firmly maintains its distinctive cuisine. Although Tuscany does not rank as one of the great culinary regions of Italy, it offers good, honest, traditional dishes, often humble, rarely elaborate. The Medici may have put on some legendary feedbags, but the modern Tuscan is known by his fellow Italians as a *mangiafagioli*, or bean-eater. Some observers hold it as part of the austere Tuscan character, others as another sign of their famous alleged miserliness.

The truth is that, although beans and tripe often appear on the menu, most people when dining out want to try something different, from other regions, perhaps, or the recent concoctions of Italian nouvelle cuisine, or *cucina nuova*, or perhaps a recipe from the Middle Ages or Renaissance. Some of the country's finest restaurants are in Tuscany; in practice, the diversity of dishes in the region, from traditional to bizarre, is almost endless.

# Food

The Tuscans will tell you the basic simplicity of their kitchen is calculated to bring out the glories of their wine, which may well be true, as it tends to be the perfect complement to a glass of Chianti or Vino Nobile. Nearly all Tuscan dishes, however, are born more of thrift than anything else, like **bruschetta**, a Tuscan favourite that takes sliced stale bread, roasted over the fire, covered with olive oil and rubbed with garlic. *Acqua cotta*, popular in southern Tuscany, is *bruschetta* with an egg; another version adds mashed tomatoes. Another traditional Tuscan *antipasto* is **crostini**, thin slices of toast with a piquant pâté spread of chicken livers, anchovies, capers and lemons, or other variations.

For **primo**, the traditional Tuscan relies mostly on **soups**. Perhaps most traditional is *ribollita* ('reboiled'), a thick, hearty soup made with chunks of yesterday's bread, beans, black cabbage and other vegetables. Similar is *pappa col pomodoro*, another bread-based soup flavoured with fresh tomatoes, basil and sludgy local olive oil. *Panzanella*, or Tuscan *gazpacho* (a cold soup of tomatoes, cucumbers, onions, basil, olive oil and bread) can be a godsend on a hot summer's day. The prince of Tuscan soups is Livorno's *cacciucco*, a heavenly fish soup that you have to go to Livorno to try. Other first courses you'll find are *fagioli al fiasco* (beans with oil and black pepper simmered in an earthenware pot) or *fagioli all'uccelletto* (beans with garlic and tomatoes); the most Tuscan of pasta dishes is *pappardelle alla lepre* (wide egg-noodles with a sauce of stewed hare); others are the simple but delicious *spaghetti con briciolata* (with olive oil, breadcrumbs and parsley); *nastri alla Borracina* (ribbons of pasta served with a 'moss' of freshly chopped spinach and marjoram, basil, rosemary, mint and sage); and, most splendid of all, *turtui cu la cua* (tortellini with tails), filled with mascarpone, ricotta and spinach, with a butter and basil sauce.

On the whole, Tuscany does not offer exceptional **secondi**: grilled meats, salad, and fried potatoes are the typical *trattoria* standby. Tuscany has its famous steak, *bistecca alla fiorentina* (*see* 'Florence's Most Ephemeral Art', below); otherwise Tuscans are content with grilled chops – lamb, pork or veal. *Fritto misto* is an interesting alternative, where lamb chops, liver, sweetbreads, artichokes and courgettes (*zucchini*) are dipped in batter and deep fried. Otherwise look for *arista di maiale* (pork loin with rosemary and garlic), *francesina* (meat, onion and tomato stew in Vernaccia di San Gimignano wine), *anatra* (duck, often served with truffles in Umbria), *piccione*

## Florence's Most Ephemeral Art

Florence in its loftier moods likes to call itself the 'birthplace of international haute cuisine', a claim that has very much to do with Catherine de' Medici, a renowned trencherwoman, who brought a brigade of Florentine chefs with her to Paris and taught the Frenchies how to eat artichokes, but has little to do with the city's contribution to the Italian kitchen. Florentine food is on the whole extremely simple, with the emphasis on the individual flavours and fresh ingredients. A typical *primo* could be *pappardelle* (*see* above), usually served with a meat sauce, or game such as wild boar, rabbit and duck. Soups are also popular: try the *ribollita*, unique to the region, or *pappa col pomodoro* (*see* opposite).

The most famous main course in Florence is the *bistecca alla fiorentina*, a large steak on the bone, two inches thick, cut from loin of beef and cooked over coals. It is served charred on the outside and pink on the inside and simply seasoned with salt and black pepper. As for the vegetables, you could try *piselli alla fiorentina*, peas cooked with oil, parsley and diced bacon; or *tortino di carciofi*, a delicious omelette with fried artichokes; *fagioli all'uccelletto*, cannellini beans stewed with tomatoes, garlic and sage; and *spinaci saltati* – fresh spinach sautéed with garlic and olive oil. Florentine desserts tend to be sweet and fattening: *bomboloni alla crema* are vanilla-filled doughnuts and *le fritelle di San Giuseppe* are bits of deep-fried batter covered in sugar. If you prefer cheese, try the sturdy *pecorino toscano*. For better or worse, real Florentine soul food rarely turns up on many restaurant menus, and unless you make an effort you'll never learn what a Florentine cook can do with cockscombs, intestines, calves' feet and tripe.

# Italian Menu Vocabulary

## Antipasti

These before-meal treats can include almost anything; these are among the most common.

*antipasto misto*  mixed antipasto
*bruschetta*  garlic toast (sometimes with tomatoes)
*carciofi (sott'olio)*  artichokes (in oil)
*frutti di mare*  seafood
*funghi (trifolati)*  mushrooms (with anchovies, garlic and lemon)
*gamberi ai fagioli*  prawns (shrimps) with white beans
*mozzarella (in carrozza)*  cow/buffalo cheese (fried with bread in batter)
*olive*  olives
*prosciutto (con melone)*  raw ham (with melon)
*salami*  cured pork
*salsicce*  sausages

## Minestre (Soups) and Pasta

*agnolotti*  ravioli with meat
*cacciucco*  spiced fish soup
*cannelloni*  meat/cheese rolled in pasta tubes
*cappelletti*  small ravioli, often in broth
*crespelle*  crêpes
*fettuccine*  long strips of pasta
*frittata*  omelette
*gnocchi*  potato dumplings
*lasagne*  sheets of pasta baked with meat and cheese sauce
*minestra di verdura*  thick vegetable soup
*minestrone*  soup with meat, vegetables and pasta
*orecchiette*  ear-shaped pasta, served with turnip greens
*panzerotti*  ravioli with mozzarella, anchovies and egg
*pappardelle alla lepre*  pasta with hare sauce
*pasta e fagioli*  soup with beans, bacon, and tomatoes
*pastina in brodo*  tiny pasta in broth

*penne all'arrabbiata*  quill-shaped pasta with tomatoes and hot peppers
*polenta*  cake or pudding of corn semolina
*risotto (alla milanese)*  Italian rice (with stock, saffron and wine)
*spaghetti all'amatriciana*  with spicy pork, tomato, onion and chilli sauce
*spaghetti alla bolognese*  with ground meat, ham, mushrooms etc.
*spaghetti alla carbonara*  with bacon, eggs and black pepper
*spaghetti al pomodoro*  with tomato sauce
*spaghetti al sugo/ragù*  with meat sauce
*spaghetti alle vongole*  with clam sauce
*stracciatella*  broth with eggs and cheese
*tagliatelle*  flat egg noodles
*tortellini*  pasta caps filled with
   *al pomodoro*  meat, cheese or vegetables, with tomato sauce
   *con panna*  with cream
   *in brodo*  in broth
*vermicelli*  very thin spaghetti

## Carne (Meat)

*abbacchio*  milk-fed lamb
*agnello*  lamb
*animelle*  sweetbreads
*anatra*  duck
*arista*  pork loin
*arrosto misto*  mixed roast meats
*bistecca alla fiorentina*  Florentine beef steak
*bocconcini*  veal mixed wih ham and cheese and fried
*bollito misto*  stew of boiled meats
*braciola*  chop
*brasato di manzo*  braised beef with veg
*bresaola*  dried raw meat
*capretto*  kid
*capriolo*  roe-buck
*carne di castrato/suino*  mutton/pork
*carpaccio*  thinly sliced raw beef
*cassueola*  pork stew with cabbage
*cervello (al burro nero)*  brains (in black butter sauce)

(stuffed wild pigeon), *cinghiale* (boar), either roasted, in sausages or *stufato* (stewed). Both Tuscans and Umbrians are rather too fond of their *girarrosto*, a great spit of tiny birds and pork livers.

In Tuscany it's fairly easy to find **seafood** as far inland as Florence – one traditional dish is *seppie in zimino*, or cuttlefish simmered with beets. Hardy souls in Florence can try *cibreo* (cockscombs with chicken livers, beans and egg yolks).

*cervo* venison
*cinghiale* boar
*coniglio* rabbit
*cotoletta* veal cutlet
  *alla milanese* fried in breadcrumbs
  *alla bolognese* with ham and cheese
*fagiano* pheasant
*faraona* guinea fowl
  *alla creta* in earthenware pot
*fegato alla veneziana* thinly sliced liver
  sautéed with chopped onion
*lepre (in salmi)* hare (marinated in wine)
*lombo di maiale* pork loin
*maiale (al latte)* pork (cooked in milk)
*manzo* beef
*osso buco* braised veal knuckle
*pancetta* rolled pork
*pernice* partridge
*petto di pollo* boned chicken breast
  *alla fiorentina* fried in butter
  *alla bolognese* with ham and cheese
  *alla sorpresa* stuffed and deep fried
*piccione* pigeon
*pizzaiola* beef steak in tomato and oregano
*pollo* chicken
  *alla cacciatora* with tomatoes and
  mushrooms, cooked in wine
  *alla diavola* grilled
  *alla Marengo* fried with tomatoes, garlic
  and wine
*polpette* meatballs
*quaglie* quails
*rane* frogs
*rognoni* kidneys
*saltimbocca* veal scallop with prosciutto and
  sage, cooked in wine and butter
*scaloppine* thin slices of veal sautéed in butter
*spezzatino* pieces of beef/veal, usually stewed
*spiedino* meat on a skewer/stick
*stufato* beef and vegetables braised in wine
*tacchino* turkey
*trippa* tripe
*uccelletti* small birds on a skewer
*vitello* veal

## Pesce (Fish)

*acciughe* or *alici* anchovies
*anguilla* eel
*aragosta* lobster
*aringa* herring
*baccalà* dried salt cod
*bonito* small tuna
*branzino* sea bass
*calamari* squid
*cappesante* scallops
*cefalo* grey mullet
*coda di rospo* angler fish
*cozze* mussels
*datteri di mare* razor (or date) mussels
*dentice* dentex (perch-like fish)
*dorato* gilt head
*fritto misto* mixed fried delicacies, mainly fish
*gamberetto* shrimp
*gamberi (di fiume)* prawns (crayfish)
*granchio* crab
*insalata di mare* seafood salad
*lampreda* lamprey
*merluzzo* cod
*nasello* hake
*orata* bream
*ostriche* oysters
*pesce spada* swordfish
*polipi/polpi* octopus
*pesce azzurro* various small fish
*pesce di San Pietro* John Dory
*rombo* turbot
*sarde* sardines
*seppie* cuttlefish
*sgombro* mackerel
*sogliola* sole
*squadro* monkfish
*stoccafisso* wind-dried cod
*tonno* tuna
*triglia* red mullet (rouget)
*trota* trout
*trota salmonata* salmon trout
*vongole* small clams
*zuppa di pesce* mixed fish in sauce or stew

Tuscany's tastiest **cheese** is *pecorino*, made from ewe's milk; the best is from around Pienza. When aged it becomes quite sharp and is grated over pasta dishes.

Typical **desserts**, to be washed down with a glass of *vin santo*, include Siena's *panforte* (a rich, spicy dense cake full of nuts and candied fruit), *cenci*, a carnival sweet (deep-fried strips of dough), *castagnaccio* (chestnut cake, with pine nuts, raisins and rosemary), Florentine *zuccotto* (a cake of chocolate, nuts and candied fruits), *biscottini di Prato* (almond biscuits softened in wine), or *crostate* (fruit tarts).

## Contorni (Side Dishes, Vegetables)
*asparagi* asparagus
  *alla fiorentina* with fried eggs
*broccoli* broccoli
*carciofi (alla giudia)* (deep-fried) artichokes
*cardi* cardoons/thistles
*carote* carrots
*cavolfiore* cauliflower
*cavolo* cabbage
*ceci* chickpeas
*cetriolo* cucumber
*cipolla* onion
*fagioli* white beans
*fagiolini* French (green) beans
*fave* broad beans
*finocchio* fennel
*funghi (porcini)* (boletus) mushrooms
*insalata (mista/verde)* (mixed/green) salad
*lattuga* lettuce
*lenticchie* lentils
*melanzane* aubergine/eggplant
*patate (fritte)* (fried) potatoes
*peperoncini* hot chilli peppers
*peperoni* sweet peppers
*peperonata* stewed peppers, onions, etc.
  (similar to ratatouille)
*piselli (al prosciutto)* peas (with ham)
*pomodoro/i* tomato(es)
*porri* leeks
*radicchio* red chicory
*radice* radish
*rapa* turnip
*rucola* rocket
*sedano* celery
*spinaci* spinach
*verdure* greens
*zucca* pumpkin
*zucchini* courgettes

## Formaggio (Cheese)
*bel paese* soft white cow's cheese
*cacio/caciocavallo* pale yellow, sharp cheese
*caprino* goat's cheese
*fontina* rich cow's cheese

*groviera* mild cheese (Gruyère)
*gorgonzola* soft blue cheese
*parmigiano* Parmesan cheese
*pecorino* sharp sheep's cheese
*provolone* sharp, tangy; *dolce* is less strong
*stracchino* soft white cheese

## Frutta (Fruit, Nuts)
*albicocche* apricots
*ananas* pineapple
*arance* oranges
*banane* bananas
*cachi* persimmon
*ciliege* cherries
*cocomero* watermelon
*datteri* dates
*fichi* figs
*fragole (con panna)* strawberries (with cream)
*lamponi* raspberries
*limone* lemon
*macedonia di frutta* fruit salad
*mandarino* tangerine
*mandorle* almonds
*melagrana* pomegranate
*mele* apples
*mirtilli* bilberries
*more* blackberries
*nespola* medlar fruit
*nocciole* hazelnuts
*noci* walnuts
*pera* pear
*pesca* peach
*pesca noce* nectarine
*pinoli* pine nuts
*pompelmo* grapefruit
*prugna/susina* prune/plum
*uva* grapes

## Dolci (Desserts)
*amaretti* macaroons
*cannoli* crisp pastry tubes filled with ricotta, cream, chocolate or fruit
*coppa gelato* assorted ice cream

# Tuscan Wines

Quaffing glass after glass of Chianti inspired Elizabeth Barrett Browning to write her best poetry, and there's no reason why the wines of Tuscany shouldn't bring out the best in you as well. The first person to really celebrate Tuscan wines was a naturalist by the name of Francesco Redi in the 1600s, who, like many of us today,

*crema caramella* caramel-topped custard
*crostata* fruit flan
*gelato (produzione propria)* (home-made) ice cream
*granita* flavoured ice, often lemon or coffee
*monte bianco* chestnut pudding with cream
*panettone* sponge cake with candied fruit and raisins
*panforte* dense cake of chocolate, almonds and preserved fruit
*saint honoré* meringue cake
*semifreddo* refrigerated cake
*sorbetto* sorbet/sherbet
*spumone* a soft ice cream
*tiramisù* layers of sponge, mascarpone, coffee and chocolate
*torrone* nougat
*torta* cake, tart
*torta millefoglie* layered pastry and custard cream
*zabaglione* eggs and Marsala wine, served hot
*zuppa inglese* trifle

## Bevande (Beverages)
*acqua minerale* mineral water
  *con/senza gas* with/without fizz
*aranciata* orange soda
*birra (alla spina)* (draught) beer
*caffè (freddo)* (iced) coffee
*cioccolata* chocolate
*gassosa* lemon-flavoured soda
*latte (intero/scremato)* (whole/skimmed) milk
*limonata* lemon soda
*succo di frutta* fruit juice
*tè* tea
*vino* wine
  *rosso* red
  *bianco* white
  *rosato* rosé

## Cooking Terms (Miscellaneous)
*aceto (balsamico)* (balsamic) vinegar
*affumicato* smoked

*aglio* garlic
*alla brace* on embers
*bicchiere* glass
*burro* butter
*cacciagione* game
*conto* bill
*costoletta/cotoletta* chop
*coltello* knife
*cucchiaio* spoon
*filetto* fillet
*forchetta* fork
*forno* oven
*fritto* fried
*ghiaccio* ice
*griglia* grill
*in bianco* without tomato
*magro* lean meat/pasta without meat
*marmellata* jam
*menta* mint
*miele* honey
*mostarda* candied mustard sauce
*olio* oil
*pane* bread
*pane tostato* toasted bread
*panini* sandwiches (in roll)
*panna* cream
*pepe* pepper
*piatto* plate
*prezzemolo* parsley
*ripieno* stuffed
*rosmarino* rosemary
*sale* salt
*salmì* wine marinade
*salsa* sauce
*salvia* sage
*senape* mustard
*tartufi* truffles
*tavola* table
*tazza* cup
*tovagliolo* napkin
*tramezzini* triangular sandwiches
*umido* cooked in sauce
*uovo* egg
*zucchero* sugar

made a wine tour of the region, then composed a dithyrambic eulogy called 'Bacchus in Tuscany'. Modern Bacchuses in Tuscany will find quite a few treats, some of which are famous and some less so, along with plenty of cellars and *enoteche* (wine bars) where you can do your own survey – one particularly renowned place in Siena boasts a stock including not only every wine produced in Tuscany, but the rest of Italy as well.

Most Italian wines are named after the grape and the district they come from. If the label says DOC (*Denominazione di Origine Controllata*) it means that the wine comes from a specially defined area and was produced according to a certain traditional method; DOCG (the G stands for *Garantita*) means that a high quality is also guaranteed, a badge worn only by the noblest wines. *Classico* means that a wine comes from the oldest part of the zone of production; *Riserva*, or *Superiore*, means a wine has been aged longer. Most Tuscan farmers also make a cask of *vin santo*, a dessert wine that can be sweet or almost dry, and which according to tradition is holy only because priests are so fond of it.

Tuscany produces 19 DOC and DOCG wines, including some of Italy's noblest reds: the dry, ruby **Brunello di Montalcino** and the garnet **Vino Nobile di Montepulciano**, a lovely deep red with the fragrance of violets. The famous Chianti may be drunk either young or as a *Riserva*, especially the higher octane **Chianti Classico**. There are seven other DOC Chianti wines (**Montalbano, Rufina, Colli Fiorentini, Colli Senesi, Colli Aretini, Colline Pisa** and simple **Chianti**). The chief grape in the Chianti region is Sangiovese, shared by all the classified red wines of Tuscany.

Lesser known DOC reds include a dry, bright red named **Rosso delle Colline Lucchesi**, from the hills north of Lucca; the hearty **Pomino Rosso**, from a small area east of Rufina in the Mugello; **Carmignano**, a consistently fine ruby red that can take considerable ageing, produced just west of Florence; and **Morellino di Scansano**, from the hills south of Grosseto, a dry red to be drunk young or old. The three other DOC reds from the coast are **Parrina Rosso**, from Parrina near Orbetello, **Montescudaio Rosso**, and **Elba Rosso**, a happy island wine, little of which makes it to the mainland. All three have good white versions as well.

Of the Tuscan whites, the most notable is **Vernaccia di San Gimignano** (also a *Riserva*), dry and golden in colour, the perfect complement to seafood; delicious but more difficult to find are dry, straw-coloured **Montecarlo** from the hills east of Lucca and **Candia dei Colli Apuani**, a light wine from the mountains of marble near Carrara.

From the coast comes **Bolgheri**, white or rosé, both fairly dry. Cortona and its valley produce **Bianco Vergine Valdichiana**, a fresh and lively wine; from the hills around Montecatini comes the golden, dry **Bianco della Valdinievole**. **Bianco di Pitigliano**, of a yellow straw colour, is a celebrated accompaniment to lobster.

# Travel

# Getting There

## By Air from the UK and Ireland

From London Heathrow **Alitalia** will fly you to Florence, Pisa or Bologna. With **British Airways**, you can reach Bologna from London Gatwick, and Pisa from London Gatwick or Manchester. As for low-cost carriers, **Jet2** will fly you to Pisa from Manchester or Leeds; **Ryanair** goes to Pisa from Liverpool, London Stansted or Glasgow, and also flies to Bologna (Forli) from London Stansted; **Thomsonfly** goes to Pisa from Bournemouth or Doncaster; and **easyJet** flies to Bologna from London Stansted, and to Pisa from Bristol.

From Ireland, **Alitalia** flies from Dublin to Bologna, Pisa and Florence, and **Aer Lingus** flies from Dublin to Bologna. Keep your eyes open for bargains and charters in the papers.

See the airlines' own websites for special offers, or visit UK flight websites, including: *www.cheapflights.co.uk*, *www.flightline.co.uk*, *www.airflights.co.uk*, *www.flights4less.co.uk*, *www.flightsdirect.com*.

**Florence's airport**, Amerigo Vespucci, **t** 055 315874, *www.aeroporto.firenze.it*, lies 4km (3 miles) west of the city centre. The runway has been lengthened, and it now handles as much international traffic as Pisa. A special airport bus (the Volainbus) connects with the city centre every 30mins (every hour after 8pm).

**Pisa International Airport**, Galileo Galilei, **t** 050 500707, *www.pisa-airport.com*, is just outside the city and some 80kms (50 miles) west of Florence. It is connected to Florence by a dual carriageway (the 'Firenze–Pisa–Livorno') which runs into the airport. To get into Pisa city centre, either take the CPT No.1 bus from outside the arrivals building which runs every 20mins into Pisa Centrale train station (tickets from the info desk) or take a taxi. Buses also run to Florence, Livorno and Lucca (*see* website). Trains run from the airport to Florence and stations in between (Pisa Centrale, Pontedera and Empoli). For Siena, change at Empoli, for Livorno, Viareggio and Massa Carrara change at Pisa Centrale. For Arezzo change in Florence. There is also an infrequent service which runs to Lucca. Trains to Florence do not always coincide with flight arrivals and departures; they run roughly every hour from 10am–5pm, but are much more infrequent before and after these times.

**Aeroporto G. Marconi, Bologna, t** 051 647 9615, *www.bologna-airport.it*, handles more flights than either Pisa or Florence and has two terminals. The airport lies 6km north of central Bologna and is connected to the central station by a special bus service. From Bologna Centrale station, trains into Florence can take from 50mins to 1½ hours depending on the type of train. There are direct buses from the airport to Siena; visit *www.sena.it*. If you hire a car, take the horrendous A1 motorway south to Florence; journey time is about 1 hour 20mins.

## By Air from the USA and Canada

From the **United States**, the major carriers fly only to Rome or Milan, though British Airways has a New York–London Gatwick–Pisa service that departs New York around 6pm and has you in Pisa around 1pm the next day. Your travel agent may be able to find a much cheaper fare from your home airport to your Italian airport by way of London, Brussels, Paris, Frankfurt or Amsterdam. From **Canada**, only Alitalia flies direct to Italy (from Toronto/ Montréal to Rome/Milan).

To be eligible for Apex fares, you'll have to have fixed arrival and departure dates and spend at least a week in Italy, but no more than 90 days. Some Apex fares must be purchased at least 14 days (or sometimes 21 days) in advance and there are penalties to pay if you change your flight dates. At the time of writing the lowest midweek Apex between New York and Rome in the off-season is around $750, rising into the $1,000 zone in summer; from Canada, low-season fares start at around $1,000 and move up to about $2,750. To sweeten the deal, some carriers, such as Alitalia, offer promotional packages that might include car rental (Jetdrive) or discounts on Italian hotels, domestic flights or excursions. Ask your travel agent for details. Children under the age of two usually travel for free and both British Airways and Alitalia

# Major Airlines

## From the UK and Ireland

Only Alitalia, BA, Meridiana and Aer Lingus fly direct UK/Ireland–Italy.

**Aer Lingus**, Ireland t 0818 365 000; UK t 0845 084 4444, *www.aerlingus.com.*

**Alitalia**, t 0870 544 8259, *www.alitalia.co.uk.*

**British Airways**, UK t 0870 850 9850; Ireland t 1 890 626747, *www.britishairways.com.*

**KLM Direct**, t 0870 507 4074, *www.klm.com.*

**Lufthansa**, t 0870 837 7747, *www. lufthansa.com.*

**Meridiana**, *www.meridiana.it.*

**SN Brussels Airlines**, t 0870 735 2345, *www.brussels-airlines.com.*

## From the USA and Canada

**Air Canada**, t 1 888 247 2262, *www.aircanada.ca.*

**Alitalia**, (USA) t 800 223 5730, *www. alitaliausa.com.*

**British Airways**, t 800 AIRWAYS, *www.britishairways.com*

**Continental**, t 800 231 0856, t 800 343 9195 (hearing impaired), *www.continental.com.*

**Delta**, t 800 221 1212, *www.delta.com.*

**Northwest Airlines**, t 800 447 4747, *www.nwa.com.*

**United Airlines**, t 800 864 8331, *www.united.com.*

# Low-cost Airlines

**easyJet**, t 0905 821 0905, *www.easyJet.com.*

**Ryanair**, t 0906 270 5656, *www.ryanair.com.*

**Jet2**, t 0871 226 1 737, *www.jet2.com.*

**Thomsonfly**, t 0870 190 0737, *www. thomsonfly.com.*

# Discounts and Youth Fares

## From the UK and Ireland

**Budget Travel**, 134 Lower Baggot Street, Dublin 2, t (01) 631 1075, *www.budgettravel.ie.*

**Italflights**, 125 High Holborn, London WC1V 6QA, t (020) 7404 0470.

**Trailfinders**, 194 Kensington High Street, London W8, t 0845 058 5858, *www. trailfinders.co.uk.* Several branches in London, as well as in other major UK cities. In Ireland: 4–5 Dawson St, Dublin 2, t (01) 677 7888, *www.trailfinders.ie.*

**United Travel**, 2 Old Dublin Road, Stillorgan, County Dublin, t (01) 215 9300, *www.unitedtravel.ie.*

Besides saving 25% on regular flights, people under 26 have the choice of flying on special discount charters.

**STA**, t 0870 160 0599, *www.statravel.co.uk.* Several branches in London, as well as in other major UK towns and cities.

**USIT Now**, 19–21 Aston Quay, Dublin 2, t (01) 602 1904, *www.usitnow.ie.* Ireland's no.1 specialist student travel agent also has other branches in Ireland.

## From the USA and Canada

**Airhitch**, 481 Eighth Ave, Suite 1771, New York, NY, 10001, t 1 877 AIRHITCH, *www. air-hitch.org.*

**STA**, toll free t 800 781 4040, *www.sta travel.com.* Has branches at most universities and also at 10 Downing Street, New York, NY 10014, t (212) 627 3111, and ASUC Building, 1st Floor, University of California, Berkeley, CA 94720, t (510) 642 3000.

**TFI Tours**, 34 West 32nd Street, New York, NY 10001, t (212) 736 1140, outside New York, t (800) 745 8000, *www. lowestairprice.com.*

**The Last Minute Club**, 150 Ferrand Drive, 6th Floor, Toronto, Ontario M3C 3E5, t (416) 449 5400, *www.lastminuteclub.com.*

**Travel Cuts**, 187 College St, Toronto, Ontario M5T 1P7, t 866 246 9762, *www. travelcuts. com.* Canada's largest specialist agent for student travel, with branches in most provinces.

Also see the following websites:

*www.xfares.com* (carry-on luggage only)

*www.smartertravel.com*

*www.hotwire.com*

*www.priceline.com* (bid for tickets)

offer cheaper tickets on some flights for students and the under 26s.

It may be worth catching a cheap flight to London (New York–London fares are always very competitive) and then flying on from there using some of the British low-cost carriers such as easyJet and Ryanair (*see* box, p.51, for website details). Prices are rather more from Canada, so you may prefer to fly from the States.

For discounted flights, try looking through the small ads in newspaper travel pages (e.g. *New York Times*, *Chicago Tribune*, *Toronto Globe & Mail*). Numerous travel clubs and agencies also specialize in discount fares, but may require an annual membership fee. You could also do some initial research on your fare by visiting some of the US cheap flight websites including: *www.priceline.com*, *www.expedia.com*, *www.bestfares.com*, *www.travelocity.com*, *www.cheaptrips.com*. Other websites are listed in the box on the previous page.

# By Train

By Eurostar from London the journey time to Florence is about 17 hours. Services run daily and return fares cost around £225. The journey involves changing trains and stations in Paris, from where a sleeper or couchette is available on the evening train.

**Eurostar**, EPS House, Waterloo Station, London SE1, t 08705 186 186, *www.eurostar.com*.

Travelling by train and ferry takes about 22 hours and costs around £176 for a second-class return (including the couchette). There are also Motorail links from Denderleeuw in Belgium to Bologna (contact Rail Choice, *see* below, for more details).

In an age of low-cost airlines, rail travel is not much of an economy unless you're able to take advantage of student, youth, family and young children or senior citizen discounts. **Interail** (UK) or **Eurail** (USA/Canada) passes offer unlimited travel for all ages throughout Europe for one or two months.

**Rail Choice**, 15 Colman House, Empire Square, High Street, London SE20 7EX, t 0870 165 7300, *sales@railchoice.co.uk*.

**Rail Europe Travel Centre**, (UK) 178 Piccadilly, London W1V 0BA, t 08708 371 371, *www.raileurope.co.uk*.

(USA/Canada) 226 Westchester Ave, White Plains, NY 10064, t 877 257 2887 or Canada t 800 361 RAIL, *www.raileurope.com*.

Various youth fares and inclusive rail passes are also available within Italy, and if you're planning on doing a lot of train travel solely in Italy you can organize these before leaving home at Rail Choice (*see* above). They can even send rail passes and Motorail tickets from the UK to the USA by Fedex.

The **Trenitalia Pass** is available to travellers who are not resident in Italy; it allows first- or second-class travel on all Trenitalia trains for 4–10 days within a two-month period (consecutive or non-consecutive). There are three versions of the pass available: **Trenitalia Pass** for adults over 26 (prices from £132 for 4-day, 2nd class pass up to £265 for 10-day, first class pass); **Trenitalia Pass Youth** for young people under 26 (from £108–178, depending on length of validity; 2nd class travel only); **Trenitalia Pass Saver** for groups of 2–5 people (from £113 for 4-day, second class pass up to £219 for 10-day, first class pass). Supplements are payable for Eurostar Italia upgrades, couchettes and travel on Artesia trains.

Rail Choice have further discounts for those students and under-26s using Eurostar (*see* 'Getting Around', p.55, for details on purchasing the rail passes in Italy).

# By Coach

Usually more expensive than a cheap flight, the coach is the last refuge of aerophobic bargain-hunters. The journey time from London to Florence is around 30 hours; the return full fare is around £115. There are, again, discounts for students, senior citizens and children as well as off-peak travel.

**Eurolines**, 52 Grosvenor Gdns, London W1, t 0870 514 3219, *www.gobycoach.com. Open Mon–Fri 8am–8pm, Sun 10–12*.

# By Car

Driving to Italy from the UK is a rather lengthy and expensive proposition, and if you're only staying for a short time compare your costs against Alitalia's or other airlines' fly-drive scheme. No matter how you cross the Channel, it is a good two-day drive – about 1,600km from Calais to Rome.

**Eurotunnel trains,** t 08705 353 535, *www.eurotunnel.co.uk,* shuttle cars and their passengers through the Channel Tunnel from Folkestone to Calais on a simple drive-on-drive-off system (journey time 35mins). Eurotunnel runs 24 hours a day, year round, with a service at least once an hour through the night. Standard return fares range from £104 to £349, but special offers can bring them as low as £49 one way. **Ferry information** is available from any travel agent or direct from the ferry companies.

You can cut many of the costly motorway tolls by going to Calais, travelling through France to Basle, Switzerland, and from there through the Gotthard Tunnel over the Alps. In the summer you can save the expensive tunnel tolls, and see some marvellous scenery, by taking one of the mountain passes instead.

To bring your car into Italy, you need your car registration (log book), valid driving licence and valid insurance (a Green Card is not necessary, but you'll need one if you go through Switzerland). If your driving licence is of the old-fashioned sort without a photograph the AA strongly recommends that you apply for an international driving permit as well (available from the AA or RAC).

Make sure everything is in excellent working order; it's not uncommon to be stopped, checked and fined by the police, and spare parts for some non-Italian cars are difficult to come by.

Foreign-plated cars are no longer entitled to free breakdown service from the **Italian Auto Club** (ACI), but their prices are fair. Phone ACI on t (06) 44 77 to find out the current rates (*see* also p.60).

Current motorway tunnel tolls are:

**Fréjus Tunnel,** *www.tunneldufrejus.com*, from Modane (France) to Bardonècchia. Prices from €30.50 one way.

**Gran San Bernardo,** *www.grandsaintbernard.ch*, from Bourg St Pierre (Switzerland) to Aosta. Prices from €18.70 one way.

**Mont Blanc Tunnel,** *www.tunnelmb.com*. €30.50 one way.

For more information on driving in Italy, contact a motoring organization:

**AA,** t 0870 600 0371, *www.theaa.com* (UK).
**AAA,** t 800 222 4357, *www.aaa.com* (USA).
**RAC,** t 0800 092 2222, *www.rac.co.uk*.

# Passports and Customs Formalities

To get into Italy you need a valid passport. EU citizens do not need visas. Nationals from the USA, Canada, Australia and New Zealand do not need visas for stays of up to 90 days. If you plan to stay more than 90 days you must get a *permesso di soggiorno*. For this you will need to state your reason for staying, and be able to prove both a source of income and medical insurance. After a couple of exasperating days at some provincial Questura office filling out forms, you should walk out with your permit.

According to Italian law, you must register with the police within eight days of your arrival. If you check into a hotel this is done automatically. Otherwise you should go to the local police station, but in practice few people do this. If you come to grief in the mesh of rules and forms you need to fill in, you can at least get someone to explain it to you in English by calling the Rome Police Office for visitors, t (06) 4686, ext. 2987.

EU nationals over the age of 17 can now import an unlimited quantity of goods for their personal use.

Arrivals from non-EU countries have to pass through Italian Customs, which are usually benign, although how the frontier police manage to recruit such ugly, mean-looking characters to hold the submachine guns and drug-sniffing dogs from such a famously good-looking population is a mystery. However, they'll leave you alone if you don't look suspicious (sadly, not being Caucasian is often 'suspicious' enough) and aren't carrying more than 150 cigarettes or 75 cigars, or not more than a litre of hard liquor or three bottles of wine, a couple of cameras, a movie camera, 10 rolls of film for each, a tape-recorder, radio, record-player, one canoe less than 5.5m, sports equipment for personal use, and one television (though you'll have to pay for a licence for it at Customs). Pets must be accompanied by a bilingual Certificate of

## Specialist Organizations for Disabled Travellers

### In Italy
CO.IN (Consorzio Cooperative Integrate), Via Ostiense 131L, 00154 ROMA, freephone t 800 810810, t 06 712 9011, f 06 2326 7505, *www.coinsociale.it/turismo*. Their tourist information centre (*open Mon–Fri 9–5*) offers advice and information on accessibility.

Centro Studi Consulenza Invalidi, Via Gozzadini 7, 20148 Milan. Publishes an annual guide, *Vacanze per Disabili*, with details of suitable accommodation in Italy.

### In the UK and Ireland
RADAR (Royal Association for Disability & Rehabilitation), 12 City Forum, 250 City Road, London EC1V 8AF, t (020) 7250 3222, *www. radar.org.uk*. For information and books.

Holiday Care Service, 7th Floor, Sunley House, 4 Bedford Park, Croydon CR0 2AP, t 0845 124 9971, *www.holidaycare.org.uk*. Information on accommodation, trans-portation, equip-ment hire, services, tour operators and contacts.

Royal National Institute for the Blind (RNIB), 105 Judd St, London WC1H 9NE, t (020) 7388 1266, *www.rnib.org.uk*. Its mobility unit offers a 'Plane Easy' audio cassette with advice for visually impaired people travelling by plane. Also advises on accommodation.

Tripscope, The Vassall Centre, Gill Ave, Bristol BS16 2QQ, t 0845 758 5641, *www.tripscope*.

*org.uk*. Practical advice and information on every aspect of travel and transport for disabled travellers. Information can be provided by letter or tape.

Irish Wheelchair Association, Blackheath Drive, Clontarf, Dublin 3, t (01) 8186 400, *www.iwa.ie*. Publishes guides with advice for disabled holiday-makers.

### In the USA and Canada
American Foundation for the Blind, 11 Penn Plaza, Suite 300, New York, NY 10001, t (800) 232 5463, *www.afb.org*. The best source of information in the USA for visually impaired travellers.

Federation of the Handicapped, 40 Ctr St, New York, NY 10007, t (212) 233 4593. Organizes summer tours for members; there is a nominal annual fee.

SATH (Society for Accessible Travel and Hospitality), 347 5th Avenue, Suite 610, New York, NY 10016, t (212) 447 7284, f (212) 725 8253, *www.sath.org*. Travel and access infor-mation. Website has good links and a list of relevant on-line publications.

### Internet Sites
Access Ability, *www.access-ability.org/ travel.html*. Information on travel agenices.

Access-Able Travel Source, *www.access-able.com*. Information for older and disabled travellers.

Emerging Horizons, *www.emerginghorizons. com*. International on-line travel newsletter for people with disabilities.

---

Health from your local veterinary inspector. US citizens may return with $400 worth of merchandise – keep your receipts.

There are no limits to the amount of money you may bring into Italy, and no one is likely to check how much you leave with. If you want to ensure that your suitcase full of bank notes is legal, ask the Guardia di Finanza, t 117, 24-hour service.

## Disabled Travellers

Recent access-for-all laws in Italy have improved the once dire situation: the number of ramps and stair lifts has increased probably a hundredfold in the past few years, and nearly every hotel has one or two rooms with facilities for the disabled – although the older ones may not have a lift, or not one large enough for a wheelchair. Although service stations on the *autostrade* have equipped restrooms, you could get very stuck in the middle of a city – Florence, visited by zillions of tourists, is notoriously lacking in accessible loos. Local tourist offices are helpful, and have been known to find someone to give you a hand on the spot, while the National Tourist Office can offer suggestions for hill towns that are particularly difficult to get around. Some of these, especially in Umbria, will tire out the fittest tourist. Italian churches are a problem in themselves. Long flights of steps in front were designed to impress on the would-be worshipper the feeling of going upwards to God – another raw deal for the disabled.

# Getting Around

The republic has an excellent network of airports, railways, highways and byways, and you'll find getting around fairly easy – unless one union or another goes on strike (though to be fair, this rarely happens during the main holiday season). There's plenty of talk about passing a law to regulate strikes, but don't count on it happening soon. Instead, learn how to recognize the word in Italian: *sciopero* (SHO-per-o) and be prepared to do as the Romans do when you hear it – quiver with resignation. There's always a day or two's notice, and usually strikes last only 12 or 24 hours – but this is long enough to throw a spanner in the works if you have to catch a plane, so keep your eyes and ears open for advance warnings.

## By Train

*FS information from anywhere in Italy, t 892 021 88088, open 7am–9pm, www.fs-on-line.com, www.trenitalia.com.*

Italy's national railway, the FS (*Ferrovie dello Stato*) is well run and often a pleasure to ride. There are also several private rail lines around cities and in country districts. We have tried to list them all in the Getting Around sections of the Gazetteer chapters in this book. You may find that some of these private companies won't accept Interail or Eurail passes.

Train **fares** have increased greatly over the last couple of years and only those without extra supplements can still be called cheap. Possible FS unpleasantnesses you may encounter, besides a strike, are delays and crowding (especially on Friday nights, weekends and in the summer). Reserve a seat in advance (*fare una prenotazione*). The fee is small and can save you hours of standing. For the upper echelon trains (Eurostars and some intercities), reservations are mandatory. Do check when you purchase your ticket in

advance that the date is correct; tickets are only valid the day they're purchased unless you specify otherwise.

**Tickets** may be purchased not only at stations, but at many travel agents (and some also on-line) and it's wise to buy them in advance as the queues can be long. Make sure that you ask which **platform** (*binario*) your train leaves from; the big permanent boards posted in the stations are not always correct.

Always remember to **stamp your ticket** (*convalidare*) in the not-very-obvious machine at the head of the platform before boarding the train. Failure to do so may result in a fine. If you get on a train without a ticket you can buy one from the conductor, with an added 20% penalty. You can also pay a conductor in order to move up to first class as long as there are places available.

There is a strict hierarchy of **trains**. A *Regionale* travels short-ish distances, and tends to stop at all the stations. There are only a few *Espressi* trains left in service, but they are in poor condition, and mostly serve the long runs from the south of Italy. No supplement is required. *Intercity* trains link Italian cities, with minimum stops. Some carry an obligatory seat reservation requirement (free in this case), and all have a supplement. The true 'Kings of the Rails' are the super-swish and super-fast *Eurostars* (Florence–Rome in 1½ hours). These make very few stops, offer both first and second class carriages, and carry a supplement that includes an obligatory seat reservation. So, the faster the train, the more you pay. Make sure you check all fares at the time of booking.

The **Trenitalia pass** (*see* 'Getting There: By Train', p.52, for prices) has replaced the Flexicard, which no longer exists. Pass holders can also obtain discounts on various ferry services from Italy to Greece, Spain and north Africa; visit *www.railchoice.co.uk*.

Other **discounts**, available only once you're in Italy, are 15% off same-day return tickets and three-day returns (depending on the distance involved), and discounts for families of at least four travelling together. Senior citizens (60 and over) can also get a *Carta d'Argento* ('silver card') for €30, entitling them to a 30% reduction in fares. A *Carta*

*Verde* bestows a 20% discount on people under 26 and costs €40.

**Refreshments** on routes of any great distance are provided by buffet cars or trolleys; you can usually get sandwiches and coffee from vendors along the tracks at intermediary stops. Station bars often have a good variety of take-away travellers' fare; at least consider investing in a plastic bottle of mineral water, since there's no drinking water on the trains.

Italy's stations also offer other facilities. All have a *deposito*, where you can leave your bags for hours or days for a fee. The larger ones have porters (who charge about €2.50 per piece) and luggage trolleys; major stations have an *albergo diurno* ('day hotel', where you can take a shower, get a shave and haircut, etc.), information offices, currency exchanges open at weekends (not at the most advantageous rates), hotel-finding and reservation services, kiosks with foreign papers, restaurants, etc. You can also arrange a rental car to await you at your destination, through hire firms Avis, Hertz or Maggiore.

## By Coach and Bus

Intercity coach travel is often quicker than train travel, but also a bit more expensive. The Italians aren't dumb; you will find regular coach connections only where there is no train to offer competition. Coaches

## Courses for Foreigners and Specialist Holidays

The **Italian Institute**, 39 Belgrave Square, London SW1X 8NX, t (020) 7235 1461, *www. italculture.org.uk*, or 686 Park Avenue, New York, NY 10021, t (212) 879 4242, is the main source of information on courses for foreigners in Italy, including Italian government scholarships and language courses for business students. Graduate students should also contact their nearest Italian consulate to find out about scholarships – apparently many go unused each year because no one knows about them.

One obvious course to take, especially in this linguistically pure land of Dante, is **Italian language and culture**: there are special summer classes offered by the Scuola Lingua e Cultura per Stranieri of the University of Siena, and special classes in August for teachers of Italian. Similar courses are held in Cortona, Viareggio (run by the University of Pisa), and, not surprisingly, Florence – sometimes there seem to be more American students than Florentines in the city.

The following offer courses year-round:
**British Institute**, Piazza Strozzi 2, t 055 267781, f 055 2677 8223, *www.britishinstitute.it*. Runs courses on Florentine art and history, Dante, opera and language.
**Centro Fiorenza**, Via di Santo Spirito, t 055 239 8274, *www.centrofiorenza.com*. Offers history, literature and art at both basic and advanced levels. Also offers cooking courses.
**Centro Linguistico Italiano Dante Alighieri**, Piazza Repubblica 5, t 055 210808, f 055 287828, *www.clida.it*. Specializes in language courses.
**Scuola Lorenzo de' Medici**, Via Faenza 43, t 055 287360, f 055 239 8920, *www.lorenzo demedici.it*. Has classes in language and art.
**Scuola Machiavelli**, Piazza Santo Spirito 4, t 055 239 6966, *www.centromachiavelli.it*. A smaller school than the others listed here, the Machiavelli is run by a co-operative of teachers and offers a more personal approach. You can learn Italian in classes with a maximum of 12 students or through individual lessons, enroll in courses in commercial Italian, art history, art and artisan practical courses in professional workshops, food and drink apprenticeships, cooking and opera singing.

**Music courses** complement the regions' numerous music festivals: the Centro di Studi sull'Ars Nova del Trecento, Borgo Garibaldi 33, 50052 Certaldo, offers seminars in medieval music. Siena's Accademia Musicale Chigiana, Via di Città, *www.chigiana.it*, offers master classes for instrumentalists and conductors; in July and August Barga holds an International Opera workshop.

**Art-lovers** can take a course on medieval art at Florence's Università Internazionale dell'Arte, in the Villa Tornabuoni, Via Incontri 3, *www.uiafirenze.com*; courses are offered from almost always depart from the vicinity of the train station, and tickets usually need to be purchased before you get on. In many regions they are the only means of public transport and are well used, with frequent departures. The base for all country bus lines will be the provincial capitals: we've done our best to explain the connections even for the most out-of-the-way routes, as well as listing coach companies in the relevant areas, in the listings for each chapter.

**City buses** are the traveller's friend. Most cities label routes well; all charge flat fees for rides within the city limits and immediate suburbs, at the time of writing around €1. Bus tickets must always be purchased before you get on, either from a tobacconist's, a news-

paper kiosk, many bars, or from ticket machines near the main stops. Once you are on, you must 'obliterate' your ticket in the machines at the front or back of the bus; controllers stage random checks to make sure you've punched your ticket. Fines for cheats are about €40, and the odds are about 12 to 1 against a check, so you may decide that you can take your chances. If you're good-hearted, you'll buy a ticket and help some overburdened municipal transit line meet its annual deficit.

## By Taxi

Tariffs from town to town start at about €2.50 but as a rough guideline add €0.80 per

October to April in history of art, restoration and design, while the Istituto per l'Arte e il Restauro, in Palazzo Spinelli, Borgo Santa Croce 10, *www.spinelli.it*, holds workshops in art restoration.

### Specialist Tour Operators in the UK

**Abercrombie & Kent**, St George's House, Ambrose St, Cheltenham, Gloucestershire GL50 3LG, t 0845 0700 610, f 0845 0700 607, *www.abercrombiekent.co.uk*. Luxury tours, villas and walking in Tuscany and Umbria.

**Ace Study Tours**, Babraham, Cambridge CB2 4AP, t (01223) 835055, f (01223) 837394, *www.study-tours.org*. Cultural tours through Tuscany and Umbria: Tuscan Villas and Gardens.

**Alternative Travel**, 69–71 Banbury Road, Oxford OX2 6PE, t (01865) 315678, f (01865) 3156j99, *www.atg-oxford.co.uk*. Offers walking, wild flower, garden and cycling tours; Piero della Francesca, the Palio in Siena, Renaissance Tuscany; also arranges truffle hunts and painting courses.

**Arblaster & Clarke Wine Tours**, Farnham Road, West Liss, Petersfield, Hants GU33 6JQ, t (01730) 893344, f (01730) 892888, *www. arblasterandclarke.com*. Tuscan wine tours, truffle hunts and gourmet cooking tours.

**Artemisia**, PO Box 7504, Glasgow G42 8ZY, t (0141) 424 0985, *www.artemisia-holidays.com*. Stay in a palazzo in Barga while taking courses in art, music, dance, Italian, creative writing and more.

**Creativity Travel**, 39 Kingsdown Park, Whitstable, Kent CT5 2DE, t (01227) 276 390, t (01227) 280 057, *www.creativitytravel.com*. Cooking, art, shopping, and spa holidays in Tuscany and the Marches.

**Inntravel**, Nr Castle Howard, York YO60 7JU, t (01653) 617722, f (01653) 89288, *www. inntravel.co.uk*. Walking and riding tours, and hand-picked inns.

**Inscape Fine Art Tours**, 1 Farley Lane, Stonesfield, Oxfordshire OX29 8HB, t (01993) 891726, f (01993) 891718, *www.inscapetours. co.uk*. Escorted art 'study' tours with guest lecturers in Florence, Siena and southern Tuscany.

**Italiatour**, 9 Whyteleafe Business Village, Whyteleafe Hill, Whyteleafe, Surrey CR3 0AT, t (01883) 623 363, f (01883) 625 255, *www. italiatour.com*. In Ireland, t 01 671 7821. Offers resort holidays, city breaks, self-catering accommodation, and watercolour and cookery courses.

**JMB Travel Consultants**, Suite Four, High Tree House, Cromwell Road, Powick, Worcester WR2 5QJ, t (01905) 830099, f (01905) 830191, *www.jmb-travel.co.uk*. Opera in Florence and Torre del Lago.

**Kirker**, 4 Waterloo Court, 10 Theed St, London SE1 8ST, t 0870 112 3333, f 0870 066 0628, *www.kirkerholidays.com*. For city breaks and tailor-made tours.

**Kudu Travel**, Teffont Manor, Teffont Ewyas, Salisbury SP3 5RJ, t/f (01722) 782 982, *www.kudutravel.com*. All-in specialist km. There is a minimum charge of €4.50. Each piece of baggage will cost extra, and there are surcharges for trips outside the city limits, trips between 10pm and 6am, and trips on Sundays and holidays.

# By Car

The advantages of driving in Tuscany generally outweigh the disadvantages. Before you bring your own car or hire one, consider the kind of holiday you're planning.

If it's a tour of the major art cities, you'd really be best off not driving at all: parking is impossible, traffic impossible, deciphering one-way streets, signals and signs impossible.

In nearly every other case, however, a car gives you the freedom and possibility of making your way through Italy's delightful open countryside and stopping at the smaller towns and villages.

Be prepared to encounter some of the highest fuel costs in Europe, to spend a very long time looking for a place to park in any town bigger than a peanut, and face drivers who look at motoring as if it were a video game. The Italians, whether 21-year-old madcaps or elderly nuns, turn into aggressive starfighters once behind the wheel; their mission is to reach their destination in a certain allotted time (especially around lunch or dinner, if they think the pasta is already on the boil), regardless of minor nuisances such

---

walking holidays for small groups, often combined with music festivals.

**Magic of Italy, t** 0870 546 2442, *www.magic travelgroup.co.uk*. Offers escorted tours, tailor-made, two-centre and villa holidays.

**Martin Randall Travel**, 10 Barley Mow Passage, Chiswick, London W4 4PH, **t** (020) 8742 3355, **f** (020) 8742 7766, *www.martinrandall.com*. Imaginatively put together cultural tours featuring guest lecturers – art, archaeology, history, architecture, music; Medici Villas and Gardens.

**Painting Holidays with Bettina Schroeder**, Cairns House, Holloway Rd, London, N7 9SA, **t** (020) 7609 0843, *www.art-holidays.com*. Painting holidays in Peralta and Cotto, Tuscany.

**Prospect Art Tours**, 36 Manchester Street, London W1V 7LH, **t** (020) 7486 5704, **f** (020) 7486 5868, *www.prospecttours.com*. Art tours in Florence; specialist holidays devoted to famous local cultural figures, such as Dante and Piero della Francesca.

**Ramblers**, Box 43, Welwyn Garden City, Hertfordshire AL8 6PQ, **t** (01707) 331133, **f** (01707) 333276, *www.ramblersholidays. co.uk*. Walking holidays.

**Real Holidays Travel Agency Ltd**, 66–68 Essex Road, London N1 8LR, **t** (020) 7359 3938, **f** (020) 7226 5800, *www.realhols.co.uk*. An eclectic selection of rural and coastal agrituristic properties, hotels, self-catering houses and apartments.

**Ride World Wide**, Staddon Farm, North Tawton, Devon EX20 2BX, **t** (01837) 82522, **f** (01837) 82179, *www.rideworldwide.co.uk*. Riding holidays in Tuscany.

**Sherpa Expeditions**, 131a Heston Road, Hounslow, Middlesex TW5 0RF, **t** (020) 8577 2717, **f** (020) 8572 9788 *www.sherpa-walking-holidays.co.uk*. Walking and cycling holidays.

**Simply Travel**, Kings Place, Wood Street, Kingston-upon-Thames, Surrey KT1 1SG, **t** (0870) 166 4979, *www.simply-travel.co.uk*. Offers a wide range of places to stay, from opulent villas with pools to country house hotels, plus cookery and painting courses.

**Specialtours**, 2 Chester Row, London SW1W 9JH, **t** (020) 7730 2297, **f** (020) 7823 5035, *www.specialtours.co.uk*. Cultural tours.

**Tasting Places**, Unit 108, Buspace Studios, Conlan Street, London W10 5AP, **t** (020) 7460 0077, **f** (020) 7460 0029, *www.tasting places.com*. Cookery courses and breaks.

**Waymark**, 44 Windsor Road, Slough, **t** (01753) 516477, **f** (01753) 517016, *www.waymark holidays.co.uk*. Walking tours of San Gimignano and Tuscany.

## In the USA/Canada

**Abercrombie & Kent**, 1520 Kensington Road, Suite 212, Oak Brook, IL 60523 2141, **t** 800 554 7016, *www.abercrombiekent.com*. Organizes city breaks and walking holidays.

**Bike Riders' Tours**, PO Box 130254, Boston, MA 02113, **t** 800 473 7040 or **t** (617) 723 2354, as other cars, road signs, traffic signals, solid no-passing lines, or blind curves on mountain roads. No matter how fast you trip along on the *autostrade* (Italy's toll motorways, official speed limit **130km/80 miles** per hour), someone will pass you going twice as fast.

If you aren't intimidated, buy a good road map of Italy or a detailed one of the region you're travelling in (the Italian Touring Club produces excellent ones). Most petrol stations close for lunch in the afternoon, and few stay open late at night, though you may find a 'self-service' one where you feed a machine nice, smooth bank notes. *Autostrada* tolls are high – the website *www.autostrada.it* will help you calculate the cost for your journey. The rest stops and petrol stations along the

motorways are open 24 hours. Other roads – from *superstrade* on down through the Italian grading system – are free of charge. The Italians are good about signposting, and roads are almost all excellently maintained. Some highways seem to be built of sheer brávura – suspended on cliffs, crossing valleys on enormous piers – feats of engineering that will remind you, more than almost anything else, that this is the land of the ancient Romans. Beware that you may be fined on the spot for speeding, a burnt-out headlamp, etc; if you're especially unlucky you may be slapped with a *super multa*, or superfine, of €130–260 or more. You may even be fined for not having a portable triangle danger signal (these can be picked up at the border or from

**f** (617) 723 2355, *www.bikeriderstours.com*. Cycling tours with stops at elegant hotels.

**Da Vinci Capers**, 655 Utica Ave, Bouldor, CO 80304, **t** (303) 284 1383, **f** (303) 444 3636, *www.davincicapers.com*. Inspiring and creative weeks in a villa in the hills of Lucca.

**Italian Renaissance Travel**, 3730 Cabrillo St, San Francisco, CA 94121, **t** (415) 752 5367, **f** (415) 386 8781, *www.italyarttrips.com*. Organizes both customized or group tours on themes such as Total Immersion Medici.

**Italiatour**, 666 5th Ave, New York, NY 10103, **t** 800 845 3365 (USA) and **t** 888 515 5245 (Canada), *www.italiatour.com*. Fly-drive and sightseeing tours organized by Alitalia.

**Randonnée**, 100–162 Albert St, Winnipeg, Manitoba R3B 1E9, **t** (204) 475 6939 or (800) 465 6488, **f** (204) 474 1888, *www.randonnee-tours.com*. Self-guided walking and cycling vacations in Tuscany.

**VIP Tours**, 4971 Ringwood Meadow, Sarasota, FL 34235,toll free **t** 877 782 9878, *www. stay andvisit.com*. Run by an Italian family, with a good introductory tour to Tuscany/Umbria.

### In Italy

**A Taste of Florence**, Via Taddea 31, **t** 055 292578, *www.divinacucina.com*. American cook Judy Witts has lived in Florence for years, and her knowledge of the local food and culture is extensive. Courses are run from her home near the central market, and the day starts with a shopping session, progressing to the kitchen. Groups are limited to six.

**Back Road Tuscany Tours**, Corso Mazzini 54, 06049 Spoleto (PG), **t/f** 0573 470 006, mobile 328 897 0761, *www.backroadtuscany tours.com*. Customized and specialized tours, concentrating on out-of-the-way areas.

**Capezzana Wine and Culinary Centre**, Via Capezzana 100, Loc. Seano, 59015, Carmignano, **t** 055 870 6005, *www. capezzana.it*. This wine- and olive oil-producing estate some 30km from Florence hosts courses for food professionals and skilled cooks. There is also accommodation available in a wing of the villa.

**Faith Willinger**, *www.faithwillinger.com*. Author offers a day of hands-on shopping and cooking in Florence.

**FlorenceArt.net**. Website dedicated to promoting traditional crafts in Florence, offering courses on restoration, *trompe l'oeil* painting, and behind-the-scenes tours.

**Tuscany 4 Families**, Villa Aquilea, Via del Castellaccio 46, 55029 Aquilea (LU), **t** 333 522 8985, *www.tuscany4families.com*. Family-oriented stays and activities outside Lucca.

**Tuscan Women Cook**, Podere Poggio Castagni, 53040 Montefollonico (SI), **t** 0577 669 444, **f** 0577 668 707, *www.tuscanwomencook.com*. Near Siena; learn how to make traditional Tuscan dishes from the locals.

**Vinarium Wine Tours**, Via de' Pepi 56r, 50122 Florence, **t** 055 234 6511, **f** 055 234 6511, *www.vinaio.com*. Food and wine and cookery lessons with accommodation in a restored farmhouse in Chianti.

an ACI office). It is now law a) to keep head-lights dipped on the *autostrada* and in any rural area *at all times* and b) to carry a bright orange fluorescent jacket in the car at all times and to put it on if you break down.

The **Automobile Club of Italy** (ACI) (*Via Marsala 8, Rome, t 800 313535 or t 06 49981, f 06 499 82469, www.aci.it*) is a good friend to the foreign motorist. Besides having bushels of useful information and tips, they can be reached from anywhere by calling t 116 – also use this number if you have an accident, need an ambulance, or simply have to find the nearest service station. If you need major repairs, the ACI can make sure the prices charged are according to their guidelines.

**Hiring a car** is fairly simple if not particularly cheap (around €50 a day for a smallish car, €300 for a week). Italian car rental firms are called *autonoleggi*. There are both large inter-national firms through which you can reserve a car in advance, and local agencies, which often have lower prices. Air or rail travellers should check out possible discount packages.

Most companies will require a deposit amounting to the estimated cost of the hire, and there is 19% VAT added to the final cost. Petrol is as expensive as in the UK; diesel is significantly cheaper. Rates become more advantageous if you take the car for a week with unlimited mileage. If you need a car for more than three weeks, leasing is a more economic alternative. The National Tourist Office has a list of firms in Italy that hire caravans (trailers) and campers.

# By Motorbike and Bicycle

The transport of choice for many Italians; motorbikes, mopeds and Vespas can be a delightful way to get between the cities and see the countryside. You should only consider it, however, if you've ridden them before – Italy's hills and aggravating traffic make it no place to learn. Helmets are compulsory. Hire costs for a *motorino* (moped) range from about €30 per day; scooters are somewhat more (from about €50).

Italians are keen cyclists as well, racing drivers up the steepest hills; if you're not training for the Tour de France, consider the hillyness of the region well before planning a bicycling tour – especially in the hot summer months. Bikes can be transported by train in Italy, either with you or within a couple of days; you need to apply at the luggage office (*ufficio bagagli*). Hire prices range from about €10 per day, and to buy one, upwards of €130, either in a bike shop or through the local clas-sified adverts. If you decide to bring your own bike, do check with the airlines first to see what their policies are on transporting them.

# Practical A–Z

06

# Children

Even though a declining birthrate and the legalization of abortion may hint otherwise, children are still the royalty of Italy, and are pampered, often obscenely spoiled, probably more fashionably dressed than you are, and never allowed to get dirty. Yet most of them somehow manage to be well-mannered little charmers. If you're bringing your own *bambini* to Italy, they'll receive a warm welcome everywhere. Many hotels offer advantageous rates for children and have play areas, and most of the larger cities have permanent **Luna Parks**, or fun fairs. Other activities young children enjoy (besides the endless quantities of pizza, spaghetti and ice cream) are the **Pinocchio Park** in Collodi, near Pisa, the **Pistoia Zoo** and the **Nature Park** in Cavriglia in the Valdarno. If a **circus** visits town, you're in for a treat; it will either be a sparkling showcase of daredevil skill or a poignant, family-run, modern version of Fellini's *La Strada*.

# Climate and When to Go

The climate in Tuscany is temperate along the coasts and in the valleys, and considerably cooler up in the mountains; the higher Apennines and Monte Amiata have enough snow to support skis until April. Summers are hot and humid; in August the Florentines, Sienese and Pisans abandon their cities to the tourists and head for the sea or the mountains. Spring, especially May, when it rains less, is pleasantly warm, as fields and gardens brim with flowers. Autumn, too, is a classic time to visit, in October and November; before the winter rains begin and the air is clear, the colours of the countryside are brilliant and rare. The hills of Tuscany are always beautiful, but in October, they're extraordinary.

Winter can be an agreeable time to visit the indoor attractions of the cities and avoid crowds, particularly in Florence, where it seldom snows but may rain for days at a time. The mountains, especially the Apuan Alps along the coast, also get a considerable amount of rain, with 80–120mm in a year.

# Eating Out

When you leave a restaurant you will be given a receipt (*ricevuto fiscale*) which, according to Italian law, you must take with you out of the door and carry for at least 300 metres. If you aren't given one, it means the restaurant is probably fudging its taxes and thus offering you lower prices. There is a slim chance the tax police may have their eye on both you and the restaurant; if you don't have a receipt they could slap you with a heavy fine.

When you eat out, mentally add to the bill (*conto*) the bread and cover charge (*pane e coperto*, between €1 and €3), and a 15% service charge. This is often included in the bill (*servizio compreso*); if not, it will say *servizio non compreso*. Additional tipping is at your own discretion, but never do it in family-owned and -run places.

In this book, prices quoted for meals are for an average complete meal, Italian-style with house wine, for one person. We have divided restaurants into price categories (*see below*).

## Average Temperatures in °C (°F)

|  | January | April | July | October |
|---|---|---|---|---|
| Florence | 6 (42) | 13 (55) | 25 (77) | 16 (60) |
| Livorno | 9 (47) | 15 (59) | 24 (75) | 15 (59) |
| Siena | 5 (40) | 12 (54) | 25 (77) | 15 (59) |

## Average monthly rainfall in millimetres (inches)

|  | January | April | July | October |
|---|---|---|---|---|
| Florence | 61 (3) | 74 (3) | 23 (1) | 96 (4) |
| Livorno | 71 (3) | 62 (3) | 7 (0) | 110 (4) |
| Siena | 70 (3) | 61 (3) | 21 (1) | 112 (4) |

# Festivals

Although festivals in Tuscany are often more show than spirit (though there are several exceptions to the rule), they can add a note of pageantry or culture to your holiday. Some are great costume affairs, with roots dating back to the Middle Ages, and there are quite a few music festivals, antique fairs and, most of all, festivals devoted to food and drink.

Here is a calendar of the major events and festivals throughout the region.

## January
**1** Feast of the Gift, the mayor's donation of gold, frankincense and myrrh at **Castiglione di Garfagnana**

## February
**Carnival** is celebrated in private parties nearly everywhere, and in **Viareggio** there's an enormous public one, with huge satirical floats, music and parades. In **Bibbiena**, the last day of Carnival is celebrated with a grand dance called the *Bello Ballo* and a huge bonfire, the *Bello Pomo*. The **date of Carnival** varies with Easter: the last day, with the most important festivities, is on Shrove Tuesday (Martedì Grasso), and other parties are thrown on preceding Sundays

## March
**19 Greve in Chianti** Pancake festival; also in San Giuseppe, **Siena** (with rice fritters) and **Torrita di Siena**, with a donkey race and tournament

## April
**Good Friday** Way of the Cross candlelight procession, **Grássina**, near Florence
**Easter** Easter morning, *Scoppio del Carro*, expulsion of the cart in **Florence**
Mary's girdle displayed from Donatello's pulpit in **Prato**
**10** Liberty Festival, **Lucca**, honouring the former Republic of Lucca with a special mass, costumes, etc.
**1st Sunday after Easter** National Kite Festival, **San Miniato**
**2nd Sunday after Easter** Donkey Palio, **Querceta**, near Lucca
**April–June** Music festival, **Lucca**

## May
**All month** Iris Festivals, Florence, **San Polo Robbiana** (Chianti)
**Third week** Historical parade and crossbow tournament, **Massa Marittima**
**Ascension Day** Cricket Festival, with floats, and crickets sold in little cages, **Florence**
**May and June** *Maggio Musicale Fiorentino* music festival, **Florence**

## June
**Early June** Procession on sawdust designs in the streets at **Camaiore** (Lucca)
**1st Sunday** Garlic toast (*bruschetta*) festival, **Montecatini Terme**
**Mid-June–August** *Estate Fiesolana* – music, cinema, ballet and theatre, **Fiesole**
**16–17** *Festa di San Ranieri* – lights festival and historic regatta in **Pisa**
**18** *Festa del Barbarossa*, celebrating the meeting of the pope and emperor, with ballet, archery, snails, beans and *pici* at **San Quirico d'Orcia**

For further information about eating in Italy and a menu decoder, *see* **Food and Drink**, p.39.

### Restaurant Price Categories
We have divided restaurants into the following categories (for full meal, per person, but not including wine):
*very expensive* over €60
*expensive* €40–60
*moderate* €25–40
*cheap* up to €25

# Electricity
Your electrical appliances will work if you adapt them to run on 220 AC with two round prongs on the plug. American appliances need transformers as well.

# Embassies and Consulates
If you have a choice, use the consulate in Florence.

**3 weekends** *Calcio in Costume*, Renaissance football game, in **Florence**

**3rd Sunday** *Palio di Rioni*, neighbourhood horse racing, in **Castiglion Fiorentino**

**24** St John the Baptist's Day, with fireworks, in **Florence**

**25** *Giocco del Ponte*, a traditional tug-of-war game, held on a bridge with a cart in the middle, **Pisa**

**Last Sunday** *La Bruscellata*, a week of dancing and singing old love songs around a flowering tree, **San Donato in Poggio** (Florence province)

## July

**1** Versilian Historical Trophy, with a flag-throwing contest, **Querceta** (Lucca)

**1–15** Lyric season, **Camaiore** (Lucca)

**2** *Palio*, the world-famous horse race around Il Campo, **Siena**

**2nd Sunday** 16th-century archery contest in **Fivizzano** (Massa) between court and country archers

**3rd Sunday** Feast of San Paolino, **Lucca**, featuring a torchlight parade and crossbow contest

**25** Joust of the Bear, a tournament dating back to the 1300s, **Pistoia**

**July–August** Concert and theatre festival, **San Gimignano**

**Late July–August** 10-day chamber music festival, *Inconti in Terra di Siena*, in fabulous settings near **Chianciano Terme**

## August

**All month** Outdoor Opera festival, **Torre del Lago Puccini**

**First weekend** Traditional thanksgiving festival in honour of San Sisto, **Pisa**

**2nd Sunday** Regatta, **Porto Santo Stefano**; *Bruscello* stories, food and wine, in **Montepulciano**; crossbow tournament, **Massa Marittima**

**15** Beefsteak Festival, **Cortona**

**16** *Palio*, dating from 1147, in **Siena**

**17** *Palio Marinaro*, neighbourhood boat races, in **Livorno**

**15–30** International choir contest, **Arezzo**

## September

**1st Sunday** Joust of the Saracen, **Arezzo**; *Palio dei Cerri*, competition between neighbourhoods and Renaissance processions, **Cerreto Guidi**; **Florence**, lantern festival

**2nd Sunday** Crossbow contest with Gubbio in **Sansepolcro**; eating and dancing in **Greve in Chianti**

**13** Holy Procession in honour of the *Volto Santo*, by torchlight in **Lucca**

**3rd Sunday Impruneta** wine festival

## October

**All month** Wine festivals

## November

**22** Santa Cecilia, patroness of music, has concerts held in her honour in **Siena**

## December

**8** Fair of the Immaculate Conception, **Bagni di Lucca**

**13** Santa Lucia, celebrated with a pottery fair in **Siena**

**24** Evergreen bonfire, **Camporgiano** (Lucca)

**25–26** Display of the holy girdle and St Stephen's feast, **Prato**

---

**UK**: Via XX Settembre 80a, Rome, t 06 4220 0001.
  Lungarno Corsini 2, Florence, t 055 284133.
**Ireland**: Piazza Campitelli 3, Rome, t 06 697 9121.
**USA**: Via Vittorio Veneto 119a, Rome, t 06 46741.
  Lungarno Amerigo Vespucci 38, Florence, t 055 239 8276.
**Canada**: Via Zara 30, Rome, t 06 44598.
**Australia**: Via Alessandria 215, Rome, t 06 852721.
**New Zealand**: Via Zara 28, Rome, t 06 440 2928.

# Insurance and Health

*Emergencies, t 113*

You can insure yourself against almost any mishap – cancelled flight, lost baggage, medical bills – for a price. National health services in the UK and Australia have reciprocal health care agreements with Italy, but E111 forms for EU nationals have been replaced by the European Health Insurance Card (EHIC). Like the old system, the card is available for UK residents for free at post offices. Unlike the

E111 forms, however, you'll need to apply for a card for every member of the family (you'll need passports and national insurance numbers). The EHIC must be stamped and signed to be valid, and the card must be renewed annually. Note that you will be expected to pay for all medicine and treatment in the first instance – the cost can be claimed back later, provided that you have the correct documentation. Make sure you get a receipt.

Other nationals should check their current policies to see if they cover you abroad, under what circumstances, and judge whether you need a special travel insurance policy. Travel agencies sell policies, as well as insurance companies, but they are not cheap.

Minor illnesses and problems that crop up in Italy can usually be handled free of charge in a public hospital clinic or *ambulatorio*. If you need minor aid, Italian pharmacists are highly trained and can probably diagnose your problem; look for a *farmacia* (they all have a list in the window with details of which ones are open during the night and on holidays). Extreme cases should head for the *Pronto Soccorso* (Accident and Emergency) of the nearest hospital. Italian doctors are not always great linguists; contact your embassy or consulate for a list of English-speaking doctors.

# Internet

Florence is full of Internet points; you will have no difficulty finding one in the centre of town. Cyber cafés haven't caught on in Italy big-time, so you will most likely find a shop offering anything from basic computer and internet services to those offering much more (proofreading and correction, CD-burning, photocopying, international telephone lines, photo services, etc.) plus, at most, a soft drinks machine.

**Internet Train**: Via Zannoni 1r, **t** 055 263 8555. *www.internettrain.it*. Open daily 9am–11pm. Branches at Borgo San Jacopo 30r; Via dell'Oriuolo 25r; Via de' Benci 30r; Borgo la Croce 33r. Opening hours differ from branch to branch.

**Intotheweb**: Via de' Conti 23r, **t** 055 264 5628. Open daily 10am–midnight. Uses Macs.

**Nettyweb**: Via Santo Spirito 42r, **t** 055 2654549. *www.nettyweb.com*. Open 10–10 Mon–Fri; Sat and Sun 2.30–10.30pm. Meeting and business room available for rent.

**The Netgate**: Via Sant'Egidio 14r, **t** 055 2347967. Open 10–9 daily, *www.thenetgate.it*. Branches: Via Nazionale 156r; Via de' Cimatori 17r; Via dei Serragli 76r; Stazione Santa Maria Novella. Opening hours differ from branch to branch.

# Maps and Publications

The maps in this guide are for orientation only and it is worth investing in a good, up-to-date regional map before you arrive from any of the following bookshops:

**Stanford's**, 12–14 Long Acre, London WC2 9LP, **t** (020) 7836 1321.

**The Travel Bookshop**, 13 Blenheim Crescent, London W11 2EE, **t** (020) 7229 5260.

**The Complete Traveller**, 199 Madison Ave, New York, NY 10016, **t** (212) 685 9007.

Excellent maps are produced by **Touring Club Italiano**, **Michelin** and the **Istituto Geografico de Agostini**. These are available at major bookshops in Italy or sometimes on news-stands. Italian tourist offices are helpful and can often supply good area maps and town plans.

Books are more expensive in Italy than in the UK, but some excellent shops stock English-language books. A few useful ones are listed below.

**The Paperback Exchange**, Via Fiesolana 31r, Florence.

**Feltrinelli**, Via Cavour 12–20r, Florence.

# Media

Many of the main news-stands in Tuscan towns and cities sell English **newspapers**; in the summer months they arrive the same evening. They cost a fortune, though; a Sunday paper will cost nearly €4, and most of them don't come with the colour supplements.

The only American paper available is the *Herald Tribune* which has an 'Italy Daily' insert. The same insert also comes with the Italian-language *Corriere della Sera*. Even smaller news-stands stock *Time* and *Newsweek*. Most good '*giornalaii*' keep a good stock of both American and English glossy magazines – again at a price.

For Italian speakers, a look at the local press always provides insight into the country you are visiting. Tuscany's most popular daily is *La Nazione*, a right-wing rag with lots of gossipy items. Each province has its own insert and it is useful for 'what's on' listings and flats-for-rent searches (in the Sunday edition). *La Repubblica* is a more reliable centre-left bet and has some excellent journalism. It is based in Rome, but has a Florence insert. The Milan-based *Corriere della Sera* is another decent paper with an English-language insert (see above). *Panorama* and *L'Espresso* are both good weekly current affairs magazines with some excellent journalism (in Italian).

Italian **television** is pretty dire and even the more 'serious' state-owned RAI channels (1, 2 and 3) are dominated by game and quiz shows and by appalling 'variety' shows featuring an amazing amount of almost bare bums and cleavage. All channels are dominated by ad breaks. Prime Minister Silvio Berlusconi's Mediaset network, Italia 1, Canale 5 and Rete 4 show endless versions of the above, lots of cheap soaps and the odd decent documentary. Films (the best are on Canale 5) are all dubbed as are such familiar sights as *ER*, *Friends* and other well-known US imports.

There are dozens of smaller TV stations; if you can manage to pick up Pistoia-based TVL, they show Sky News and CNN between about midnight and 8am.

There are endless **radio** stations available in Tuscany. The national networks RAI 1, 2 and 3 broadcast a mix of music and current affairs while there is plenty of choice in music stations. Among the best choices are Florence-based Radio Montebeni (108.5MHz), which relays classical music (albeit of a very dated variety); Radio Montecarlo (104.4MHz), which comes from...Montecarlo; Controradio (93.6MHz); Radio Diffuzione (MHz102.7). All are full of publicity spots.

## Money and Banks

The wide acceptance of credit cards and ATM machines (Bancomats) make them by far the most convenient way to bring money to Italy,

although there are a few things to note. Although it's always wise to have some cash on hand, you'll probably come out ahead by using your card to pay when you can rather than taking out loads of cash from the machine and paying the percentage/commission charges. On the other hand, note that many British credit cards lack the microchip required to work automatic machines such as petrol station pumps.

Also note that to prevent fraud, your credit card company may (much to your embarrassment!) refuse payment in an Italian shop because it's an 'unusual' purchase that deviates from your normal buying habits; it may be wise to let your bank know that you are travelling abroad and may be doing some 'unusual' purchasing.

### Banking Hours

Banks are usually open 8.30am–1pm, and 3–4pm. They are closed on Saturdays, Sundays and national holidays.

## Official Holidays

The Italians have cut down somewhat on their official national holidays, but note that every town has one or two local holidays of its own – usually the feast day of its patron saint. Official holidays, shown on transport timetables and museum opening hours, etc., are treated the same as Sundays. Most museums, as well as banks and shops, are closed.

## Opening Hours and Museums

Most of Tuscany closes down at 1pm until 3 or 4pm, to eat and properly digest the main meal of the day, although things are now beginning to change in the cities. Many more shops in the centre of town now stay open during lunch. Afternoon working hours are from 4 to 7, often from 5 to 8 in the hot summer months. In any case, don't be surprised if you find anywhere in Italy unexpectedly closed (or open for that matter), whatever its official stated hours.

**Food shops** shut on Wednesday afternoons in the winter. They close on Saturday after-

## National Holidays

**1 January** New Year's Day (*Capodanno*).

**6 January** Epiphany, better known to Italians as the day of *La Befana* – a kindly witch who brings the bambini the toys Santa Claus (*Babbo Natale*) somehow forgot.

**Easter Monday** Usually pretty dull.

**25 April** Liberation Day – even duller.

**1 May** Labour Day – lots of parades, speeches, picnics, music and drinking.

**2 June** is now a holiday.

**15 August** Assumption, or *Ferragosto* – the biggest of them all – woe to the innocent traveller on the road or train!

**1 November** All Saints, or *Ognissanti* – liveliest at the cemeteries.

**8 December** Immaculate Conception of the Virgin Mary – a dull one.

**25 December** Christmas Day.

**Boxing Day** *Santo Stefano*.

noons only from the end of June to the beginning of September. Sunday opening is becoming more usual, particularly for shops in the centre of town. Bars are often the only places open during the early afternoon and sometimes on a Sunday. (For **bank** opening hours, *see* p.66.)

**Churches** have always been a prime target for art thieves and as a consequence are usually locked when there isn't a sacristan or caretaker to keep an eye on things. All churches, except for the really important cathedrals and basilicas, close in the afternoon at the same hours as the shops, and the little ones tend to stay closed. Always have a pocketful of coins to feed the light machines in churches, or what you came to see is bound to be hidden in ecclesiastical gloom. Don't do your visiting during services, and don't come to see paintings and statues in churches the week preceding Easter – you will probably find them covered with mourning shrouds.

Most major **museums** are now open all day from 9am to 7pm and tend to close on a Monday and often Sunday afternoons as well. Many are magnificent, many are run with shameful neglect, and many have been closed for years for 'restoration', with slim prospects of reopening in the foreseeable future. With an estimated one work of art per inhabitant, Italy has a hard time financing the preserva-

tion of its national heritage; it would be as well to enquire at the tourist office to find out what is open and what is 'temporarily' closed before setting off on a wild-goose chase.

Entrance charges vary wildly; you should expect to pay between €2 and €5 for museum entrance; expensive ones run to €6.50 (Uffizi, Accademia). The good news is that state-run museums and monuments are free if you're under 18 or over 60 (bring ID). For one week of the year – usually late spring – all state museums are free of charge for the 'Settimana dei Beni Culturali'.

Art-lovers should consider visiting Florence during '**Museum Week**' (usually in April), when all the state-run museums are free for the week.

# Packing

You simply cannot overdress in Italy. Now, whether or not you want to try to keep up with the natives is your own affair and your own heavy suitcase – you may do well to compromise and just bring a couple of smart outfits for big nights out. It's not that the Italians are very formal; they simply like to dress up with a gorgeousness that adorns their cities just as much as those old Renaissance churches and palaces. The few places with dress codes are the major churches and basilicas (no shorts or sleeveless shirts), and the smarter restaurants.

After agonizing over fashion, remember to pack small and light: transatlantic airlines limit baggage by size (two pieces are free, up to 1.5m, in height and width; in second class you're allowed one of 1.5m and another up to 110cm). Within Europe limits are by weight: 20kg (44lbs) in second class, 30kg (66lbs) in first. You may well be penalized for anything bigger. If you're travelling mainly by train, you'll especially want to keep bags to a minimum: jamming big suitcases in overhead racks isn't much fun.

Never take more than you can carry, but do bring the following: any prescription medicine you need, an extra pair of glasses or contact lenses, a torch (for dark frescoed churches and hotel corridors), a travel alarm (for those early trains) and a pocket Italian-English dictionary (for flirting and other emergencies).

You may want to invest in earplugs if you're a light sleeper. European electrical appliances will work in Italy; just change your plug to the two-prong variety or buy a travel plug. American appliances need transformers as well.

# Photography

Film and developing are much more expensive than they are in the USA or UK. You are not allowed to take pictures in most museums and in some churches. Most cities now offer one-hour processing if you need your pics in a hurry.

# Police Business

*Police/Emergency, t 113*

There is a fair amount of petty crime in the cities – purse snatchings, pickpocketing, white-collar thievery (always check your change) and car break-ins – but violent crime is rare. Nearly all mishaps can be avoided with adequate precautions. Stay on the inside of the pavement and keep a firm hold on your property; be aware of pickpockets in crowds; don't carry too much cash and don't keep all that you have in one place. Be extra careful around stations, don't leave valuables in hotel rooms, and park your car in garages, guarded car parks, or on well-lit streets, with any temptations out of sight.

Purchasing small quantities of cannabis is legal, although what a small quantity might be exactly is unspecified, so if the police dislike you to begin with, it may be enough to get you into big trouble.

Once the scourge of Italy, political terrorism has declined drastically in recent years, mainly thanks to special squads of the *Carabinieri*, the black-uniformed national police, technically part of the Italian army. Local matters are usually in the hands of the *Polizia Urbana*; the nattily dressed *Vigili Urbani* concern themselves with directing traffic and handing out parking fines. You probably will not have anything to do with the *Guardia di Finanza*, the financial police, who spend their time chasing corrupt politicians and their friends (unless they catch you leaving a bar or restaurant without a receipt).

# Post Offices

*In cities usually open Mon–Sat 8.10–6; elsewhere Mon–Sat 8.10–1.25.*

The postal service in Italy used to have an extremely poor reputation, but has improved in the last couple of years. The new first-class mail, *posta prioritaria* (€0.62), is supposed to guarantee the arrival of a letter in Italy within 24 hours and to EU countries within 36. Or you can use registered delivery, *raccomandata*, for a €2.58 supplement. Stamps (*francobolli*) may also be purchased at tobacconists (*tabacchi*, identified by their blue signs with a white 'T'). Airmail letters to and from North America can quite often take up to two weeks. This can be a nightmare if you're making hotel reservations and are sending a deposit – emailing, faxing or telephoning ahead is far more secure if time is short.

Ask for mail to be sent to you in Italy either care of your hotel or addressed *Fermo Posta* (poste restante: general delivery) to the central post office where you are staying, or if you're a card-holder, to an AmEx office. When you pick up your mail at the *Fermo Posta* window, bring your passport for identification. You will need to pay a nominal charge.

The Italian post has recently made the process of sending parcels a lot easier. You no longer have to wrap things in a certain way; the post offices have boxes if you want to use them. Whether they will be sent as a *lettera* or *pacco* depends on size, weight and contents. *Posta prioritaria* is good for parcels up to 2kg.

# Purchasing a House

Of all the regions in Italy Tuscany has the most foreigners with homes, so many, in fact, that prices have shot into the stratosphere in the most popular areas (especially around Florence and Siena, and in the Chianti). The more obscure areas of Tuscany still have a number of abandoned farmhouses just waiting for someone to renovate them. Rural real estate is one of Italy's great buys, and the recommended way to do it is to buy a run-down property and restore it to your own needs and taste. But beware the pitfalls.

One agent we know is amazed that all English clients invariably express two major concerns about a property: drainage, and the presence of a bidet in the bathroom, as if it were a tool of the devil. What they should be asking are questions about water supply (a major problem in Tuscany), electricity and road access – often big problems for that isolated, romantic farmhouse that has caught your eye. Another thing to remember before purchasing a home or land is that you need permission from the local *comune* to make any changes or improvements, so it's no good buying anything unless you're pretty sure the *comune* will consent (for a sizeable fee, of course) to let you convert that old cellar or stable into a spare bedroom. A further point to remember is that though there are no annual rates (property tax) to pay, there is a 10% IVA tax (VAT) to be paid on the purchase price for a house and 19% on land, as well as hefty Capital Gains Tax on the selling price and profit to be paid by the seller. Italians tend to get around this by selling at one price and writing down another on the contract. But remember, if you sell you'll be in the same bind.

Once you've agreed to buy, you pay a deposit (usually 25–30%) and sign a *compromesso*, a document that states that if you back out, you lose your deposit, and if the seller changes his mind, he forfeits double the deposit to you (be sure your *compromesso* includes this feature, called *caparra confermatoria*). Always transfer payment from home through a bank, taking care to get and save a certificate of the transaction so you can take the sum back out of Italy when you sell. After the *compromesso*, your affairs will be handled by a *notaio*, the public servant in charge of registering documents and taxes who works for both buyer and seller. If you want to make sure your interests are not overlooked, you can hire a *commercialista* (lawyer-accountant) who will handle your affairs with the notaio, including the final transfer deed (*rogito*), which completes the purchase at the local Land Registry. Upon signing, the balance of the purchase price generally becomes payable within a year.

The next stage for most buyers, restoration, can be a nightmare if you aren't careful. Make sure the crew you hire is experienced and that you're pleased with their work elsewhere – don't hesitate to ask as many other people in your area as possible for advice. Keep all receipts, and beware when builders and agents give you receipts for far less than their charges (or no receipts at all) to avoid taxes; you'll pay the difference in sales tax when you sell. Also expect to pay a lofty surcharge on electricity, water and telephone bills unless you become an Italian resident and your Italian house is your primary residence. Two books that offer some clues on the ins and outs of taxes, inheritance law, residency, work permits, etc., are *Buying a Property: Italy* by Monica Larner and John Howell, and *Working and Living: Italy* by Kate Carlisle, both published by Cadogan.

# Shopping

'Made in Italy' has long been a byword for style and quality, especially in fashion and leather, but also in home design, ceramics, kitchenware, jewellery, lace and linens, glassware and crystal, chocolates, hats, straw-work, art books, engravings, handmade stationery, gold and silverware, a hundred kinds of liqueurs, wine, aperitifs, coffee machines, gastronomic specialities and antique reproductions, as well as antiques themselves. If you are looking for the latter and are spending a lot of money, be sure to demand a certificate of authenticity – reproductions can be very, very good.

Florence, which increasingly resembles a glittering medieval shopping mall, has the best variety of goods in the region. There are major monthly antique fairs in Arezzo (first Sunday), Pistoia (second Sunday), Lucca (third Sunday), and Florence (last Sunday). Ceramics are an old tradition in Montelupo, Deruta; porcelain in Sesto Fiorentino; glassware in Empoli. Volterra is famous for its alabaster and alabaster art; Castelfidardo for its accordions; in Elba you can buy semi-precious stones and minerals, in the Mugello and Casentino wrought-iron and copperware, straw goods in the lower Valdarno, and marble in Carrara, though taking it home may pose a bit of a problem. Wine and olive oil, bags of *porcini* mushrooms, jars of truffles and other 'gastronomic' specialities are available everywhere.

Italians don't like department stores, but there are a few chains – *COIN* stores often have good buys on almost the latest fashions. *Standa* and *UPIM* are more like Woolworth's, with a reasonable selection of clothes, houseware, etc., and often supermarkets in their basements. Most stay open throughout the day, but some take the same break as other Italian shops – from 1pm to 3 or 4pm.

Non-EU nationals should save their receipts for Customs on the way home. Shipping goods is a risky business unless you do it through a very reputable shop. Note that the attraction of shopping in Italy is limited to luxury items; for less expensive clothes and household items you'll always, always do better in Britain or America. Prices for clothes, even in street markets, are often ridiculous. Bargains of any kind are rare, and the cheaper goods are often very poor quality.

Italian clothes are lovely, but if you have a large-boned Anglo-American build, you may find it hard to get a good fit, especially on trousers or skirts (Italians are a long-waisted, slim-hipped bunch). Shoes are often narrower than the sizes at home.

## Smoking

Tobacconists ('*Tabacchi*') display a blue and white 'T' sign outside the shop; they and some bars sell cigarettes which are cheaper than in the UK.

Italy is still a great nation of smokers although recent legislation has banned smoking in public offices (post offices, banks etc.), on public transport (although trains have smoking compartments) and in any public places with inadequate air filtering. However these rules are frequently ignored, and you are unlikely to get much sympathy if you ask someone to stop blowing smoke in your face in a restaurant or in a non-smoking train carriage.

Non-smoking rooms in hotels are as rare as non-smoking sections in bars and restaurants.

## Sports and Activities

### Birdwatching

The islands and coastal parks near Argentario are great places to go birdwatching; ecologically hyper-aware Giglio offers **nature appreciation** and **sketching** classes for Italian speakers, t 0564 809034. The bird park at Lago Burano near Capalbio is another place for bird-watching, t 0564 898829.

### Boats and Sailing

The **sailing** is beautiful among the coves of the Tuscan archipelago and around the Argentario; there's a good sailing school in Torre del Lago Puccini, t 0584 351211. You can bring your boat to Italy for six months without any paperwork if you bring it by car; if you arrive by sea you must report to the Port Authority of your first port to show passports and receive your '*Constituto*' which identifies you and allows you to purchase fuel tax-free. Boats with engines require a number plate, and if they're over 3 horsepower you need insurance. To leave your boat in Italy for an extended period, you must have a Navigation Licence; after a year you have to start paying taxes on it. All yachts must pay a daily berthing fee in Italian ports. The National Tourist office has a list of ports that charter yachts in Tuscan ports.

### Clubs

Sports clubs are usually privately owned and are open only to members, who pay on a yearly basis. Do not expect to be able to use a swimming pool, gym or sailing club by paying a daily rate.

### Diving and Swimming

The **diving** is fabulous around the Argentario and its outlying islands, and very popular.

The best (cleanest) **swimming** is to be found on the islands, especially on the beaches that face away from the mainland.
**Elba Diving Centre**, Marciana Marina, t 0336 709259.
**Giglio Diving Club**, Giglio Porto, t 0564 804065.

## Fishing

Fishing in the sea is possible from the shore, boats or under water (but not with an aqualung) without a permit, though it may not be especially fruitful; the Tyrrhenian has been so thoroughly fished commercially that the government has begun to declare two- and three-month moratoria on all fishing, to give the fish a break. Man-made lakes and streams are well stocked, however, and if you're more interested in the eating than the sport, there are trout farms where you can almost pick the fish out of the water with your hands. To fish in fresh water you need to purchase a year's membership card and you must be resident in Italy. The licence costs about €50 for a year and is available from the Federazione Italiana della Pesca Sportiva. At its offices (in every province) they can inform you on local conditions and restrictions. Bait and equipment are readily available.

## Golf

There are golf courses in Florence, Montecatini Terme, Punta Ala, Tirrenia, Orbetello, and Portoferraio on Elba.

## Horse-riding

Horse-riding is increasingly popular, and Agriturist (see 'Where to Stay', below) has a number of villa and riding holidays on offer in Tuscany. The National Association of Equestrian Tourism (ANTE) is probably more active here than anywhere in Italy. For more information, write directly to the local Agriturist office. There are race and trotting courses in Florence and Montecatini Terme.

## Hunting

The most controversial sport in Italy is hunting, pitting avid enthusiasts against a burgeoning number of environmentalists who stage protests. The Apennines are boar territory, and in autumn the woods are full of hunters. Pathetically tiny birds, as well as ducks and pigeons, are the other principal game.

## Medieval Sports

Some ancient sports like the annual horse races, or palios (two in Siena), are still popular, and not entirely as a tourist attraction; the rivalries between neighbourhoods and cities are intense. The Florentines play three games of Renaissance football a year (calcio in costume); Sansepolcro and Gubbio stage two annual crossbow matches a year against each other, while in Lucca the archers compete from different city quarters. Arezzo and Pistoia have annual jousts; in Pisa it's medieval tug-of-war.

## Potholing

Spelunkers can find caves to explore around Montecatini Alta, Monsummano and Sarteano.
Centro Nazionale di Speleologia Monte Cucco, Costacciaro, t 075 917 0400.

## Rowing

When there's enough water, you can try your skills in the Arno (see Florence, p.86). There is also the annual race between the four old maritime republics of Venice, Amalfi, Genoa and Pisa, which alternates between the cities.

## Skiing

Tuscany has major ski resorts at Abetone, north of Pistoia, and at Monte Amiata.

## Tennis

Tennis courts are nearly everywhere; each comune has at least one or two that you can hire by the hour.

## Walking

Hiking and signed trails are best developed in Tuscany; April to October is the best and safest time to go. There are several scenic routes through the mountains: the four-day High Trail of the Apuan Alps, beginning from the Rifugio Carrara, above Carrara (for information call t 0585 841972, or the Italian Alpine Club (CAI) in Carrara, Via Giorgio, t 0585 776782). A second trail, the Grand Apennine Excursion from Lake Scaffaiolo, goes along the mountain ridge that separates Tuscany from Emilia-Romagna, departing from Pracchia, t 0187 625154 for information.

There's a circular trail through the Garfagnana, starting from Castelnuovo di Garfagnana; contact the Comunità Montana Garfagnana, t 0583 644911. In southern Tuscany, trails cover Monte Amiata from

Abbadia San Salvatore (Comunità Montana dell'Amiata, **t** 0564 969611).

Other fine day trails are in the Casentino, from Badia Prataglia or Stia, or in the Nature Parks of Monti dell'Uccellina from Alberese or the Maremma. Maremmagica organizes trekking and walking tours with guides, **t** 0564 202298 for information. In Florence, you can get information from CAI, Via Mezzetta 2, **t** 055 612 0467.

# Telephones

To **call Italy from abroad**, dial **t** 00 39 followed by the area prefix, including the first zero. For **calls inside Italy** you need to dial the complete regional or city code, including the zero, even from inside the region. So when you are in Florence you still need to use **t** 0 55. **International calls from Italy** may be made by dialling the international prefix (for the UK **t** 00 44, Ireland **t** 00 353, USA and Canada **t** 00 1, Australia **t** 00 61, New Zealand **t** 00 64).

Most Italian **public phones** take either coins or phone cards (*schede telefoniche*), available in €2.50 and €5 amounts at tobacconists – snap off the corner to use them. If you bring your **mobile**, beware the huge roaming charges on receiving and making calls abroad. Before leaving, contact your provider to see what international services are on offer or see *www.0044.co.uk*, *www.SIM4travel.com*, *www.textbay.net* and *www.uk2abroad.com*. Some phones can make use of local providers by changing the SIM card, which requires 'unblocking' your phone, do-able in shops (check first to see if it's necessary by trying someone else's card in your phone).

# Time

Italy is an hour ahead of the UK and clocks go forward and back in spring and autumn on the same day as in the UK.

# Tipping

Refreshingly, there is not a lot of pressure in Italy to leave major tips. It is customary to round restaurant bills up by a few euros, and a few coins are sometimes expected in public loos for the caretaker (in motorway services or in stations.) In hotels, the usual kinds of 'rules' apply; 10–15%, but it should reflect your general satisfaction with the service offered.

Most Florentines feel that taxis are so expensive that drivers deserve no tip; they are right! Any tip should be minimal and drivers don't expect more.

# Toilets

Italy's stakes in toilet cleanliness improve steadily; there are fewer holes in the ground, and paper is more common, though as ever they only exist in places like train and bus stations and bars. If you can't find one, try the nearest bar; they are legally obliged to let you use their *bagno*. You often have to ask for the key at the till. In stations, motorway stops and smarter cafés, there are toilet attendants who expect a small tip. Don't get confused by Italian plurals: *signori* (gents), *signore* (ladies).

# Tourist Offices

For more information before you travel, contact the Italian National Tourist Office in your own country:

**UK**, Italian State Tourist Board, 1 Princes Street, London W1R 8AY, **t** (020) 7408 1254, **f** (020) 7493 6695, *www.italiantourism.com*; Italian Embassy, 14 Three Kings Yard, Davies Street, London W1Y 2EH, **t** (020) 7355 1557, **f** (020) 7312 2230, *www.embitaly.org.uk*.

**USA**, 630 Fifth Ave, Suite 1565, New York, NY 10111, **t** (212) 245 4822, **f** (212) 586 9249, *enitny@italiantourism.com*; 12400 Wilshire Blvd, Suite 550, Los Angeles, CA 90025, **t** (310) 820 1898, **f** (310) 820 6357, *enitla@earthlink.net*; 500 N. Michigan Ave, Suite 2240, Chicago, IL 60611, **t** (312) 644 0996, **f** (312) 644 3019, *enitch@italiantourism.com*, *www.italian tourism.com*.

**Australia**, Level 26, 44 Market Street, Sydney NSW 2000 , **t** (02) 92 621666, **f** (02) 92 625745, *lenitour@ihug.com.au*.

**Canada**, 175 Bloor Street East Suite 907 – South Tower, Toronto M4W 3R8 (ON), **t** (416) 925 4882, **f** (416) 925 4799, *enit-canada@ on.aihn.com*, *www.italiantourism.com*.

New Zealand, c/o Italian Embassy, 34 Grant Road, Thorndon, Wellington, t (04) 736 065.

Tourist and travel information may also be available from **Alitalia** (Italy's national airline) or **CIT** (Italy's state-run travel agency) offices in some countries.

You can pick up more detailed information by writing directly to any of the city or provincial tourist offices (addresses are given in the text). These are usually helpful in sending out lists of flats, villas or farmhouses to hire, or at least lists of agents who handle the properties, and *agriturismo* (*see* p.74).

# Where to Stay

## Hotels

Tuscany is well endowed with hotels (*alberghi*) of every description. These are rated by the government's tourism bureaucracy, on a five-star scale: five at the top, one at the bottom. Ratings take into account such things as a restaurant on the premises, plumbing, air-conditioning, etc., but not character, style or charm. Use the stars, included here, as a quick reference only. Hotels may stay at a lower rating than they've earned, so a three-star hotel could turn out to be as comfortable as a four-star.

Breakfast is not always optional. You might well find that half- or full-board is obligatory, particularly during high season at hotels in seaside, lake or mountain resorts, spas or country villas. Otherwise, meal arrangements are optional. In the majority of cases hotel food is bland, just as it is anywhere else.

## Prices

Prices listed here are for double rooms only in high season. For a single, count on paying two-thirds of a double; to add an extra bed in a double will add 35% to the bill. Taxes and service charges are included in the given rate. If rooms are listed without bath, it simply means the shower and lavatory are in the corridor. For rooms without bath, subtract 20–30%. Prices are by law listed on the door of each room and are printed in the hotel lists available from the local tourist office; any discrepancies should be reported to the tourist office. Room rates are seasonal: it could cost up to 50% less if you travel in the low season. In resorts, hotels may close down for several months of the year.

Hotel prices rise by 6–8% each year, and are often more expensive than in northern Europe. Each province or region sets its own price guidelines for accommodation. In Florence, prices are slightly higher, and the price ranges reflect this. In general, the further south you go, the cheaper the rates.

The National Tourist Office has a complete list and booking information for motels and five- and four-star hotels and chains. If you want to stay in a different kind of accommodation, you'll have to book ahead, several months in advance and preferably by fax rather than by post. A booking is valid once a deposit has been paid. If you have to cancel your reservation, the hotel will keep the deposit unless another agreement has been reached. If you come in the summer without reservations, start calling around for a place in the morning or put yourself at the mercy of one of the tourist office hotel-finding services.

Besides classic hotels, there is an increasing number of alternatives, nearly always in historic buildings, in Umbria classified as *residenza d'epoca* or country houses.

## Inexpensive Accommodation

Bargains are few and far between in Italy. Most cheaper places will always be around the railway station, though in large cities it may be worth looking for something in the historic centre. You could find anything in a

### Hotel Price Categories

**In Florence**
*luxury* over €250
*very expensive* €180–250
*expensive* €130–180
*moderate* €75–130
*inexpensive* up to €75

**Elsewhere in the Region**
*luxury* over €230
*very expensive* €150–230
*expensive* €100–150
*moderate* €60–100
*inexpensive* up to €60

one-star Italian hotel; they might be almost perfect, and memorably bad experiences will be few, and largely limited to major cities. In small towns the tourist office may have a list of *affitta camere* (rooms to rent). These vary from basic accommodation in someone's house to more upmarket places. Besides the youth hostels (*see* below), there are several city-run hostels, with dormitory-style rooms open to all. In some cities religious institutions may rent out extra rooms. Monasteries and convents in the country sometimes take guests as well; if you seek that kind of experience, bring a letter of introduction from your local priest or pastor, etc.

## Youth and Student Hostels

You'll find hostels in Florence, Lucca, Tavarnelle Val di Pesa, in Chianti, Abetone, Cortona, San Gimignano and Marina di Massa e Carrara. You can nearly always buy an IYHF card on the spot. There are no age limits, and senior citizens are often given added discounts.

Accommodation – a bunk bed in single-sex room and breakfast – costs around €10 per day. Curfews are common, and you usually can't check in before 5 or 6pm. Book in advance by sending your arrival and departure dates along with the number of guests (by sex) to the hostel, including international postal coupons for the reply. Avoid the spring, when noisy school groups descend on them for field trips.

The *Centro Turistico Studentesco e Giovanile* (CTS), with offices in most Italian cities (and one in London) can also book cheap accommodation for students.

## Self-catering Holidays: Villas, Farmhouses and Flats

Renting a villa, farmhouse, cottage or flat has always been the choice way to visit Tuscany. The Internet has made finding a place easier than ever, with companies providing detailed listings and photos of their offerings online. Another place to look is the Sunday papers; or, if you're set on a particular area, write to its tourist office for a list of local rental agencies. These should provide photos to give you an idea of what to expect, and you should make sure all pertinent details are written down in your rental agreement so

that you avoid any misunderstandings later.

In general minimum lets are for one week; rental prices (generally per week) usually include insurance, water and electricity, and sometimes linen and maid service. Don't be surprised if when you arrive the owner 'denounces' (*denunciare*) you to the police; according to Italian law, all visitors must be registered upon arrival. Common problems are water shortages, unruly insects (*see* **Topics**, p.31) and low kilowatts. Most companies offer all-inclusive packages, with flights and car-hire. Book as far in advance as possible for the summer season.

## Rural Self-catering or *Agriturismo*

For a breath of rural seclusion, the gregarious Italians head for a spell on a **working farm**, in accommodation (sometimes self-catering) that often approximates to the French *gîte*. The real pull of the place may in fact be cooking by the hosts – a chance to sample home-grown produce. In Tuscany there are now hundreds of *agriturismo* farms offering rooms. They vary enormously in standard and price, from quite modest to very up-market. This branch of the Italian tourist industry is run by **Agriturist**. It has burgeoned in recent years, with several offices in each region. Prices, compared with the over-hyped 'Tuscan villa', are still reasonable. Local tourist offices will have information on this type of accommodation in their areas.

**Associazione Regionale Agriturist**, Via degli Alfani 67, 50120 Firenze, **t** 055 287838, **f** 055 230 2285.

**Solemar**, Via G Modena 19, 50121 Firenze, **t** 055 552131.

**Turismo Verde Toscana**, Via Jacopo Nardi 41, 50132 Firenze, **t** 055 233 8911, *www.turismoverde.it*.

Or write directly to the individual provincial **Agriturist** offices (UPA):

Via Fabio Fuzi 27, 52100 **Arezzo**, **t** 0575 905355, **f** 0575 902610.

Viale Amendola 46, 50121 **Firenze**, **t** 055 200 41225, **f** 055 239 6423.

Via Manin 20, 58100 **Grosseto**, **t** 0564 417418, **f** 0564 421828.

Via G Marradi 14, 57126 **Livorno**, **t** 0586 812744, **f** 0586 811792.

Viale Barsanti e Matteucci 208, 55100 **Lucca**, **t** 0583 342044, **f** 0583 341920.

Via Resistenza 52/M, **Aulla-Massa** 54011,
t/f 0187 421028.
Via Lavagna 26, 56100 **Pisa**, t 050 26221,
f 050 48533.
Via F Pacini 45, 51100 **Pistoia**, t 0573 21 231,
f 0573 367439.
Via Marco Ronconi 214, 59100 **Prato**,
t 0574 33939, f 0574 34437.

Via Massetana Romana 52, 53100 **Siena**,
t/f 0577 47669.

## Alpine Refuges

The Club Alpino Italiano operates many of
the *Rifugi Alpini*, mountain huts in the
Apennines. Facilities range from basic to
grand; some are exclusively for hikers and

---

# Self-catering Operators

## In the UK and Ireland

**The Apartment Service**, 5–6 Francis Grove,
London SW19 4DT, t (020) 8947 3003, *www.
apartmentservice.com*. Apartments in
Florence.
**CV Travel**, 43 Cadogan Street, London SW3 2PR,
t (020) 7384 5850, *www.cvtravel.net*.
**Home in Italy**, 343 City Rd, London EC1V 1LR,
t (020) 7404 4911, *homeinitaly.com*.
**Individual Travellers Company**, Manor
Courtyard, Bignor, Pulborough, West
Sussex RH20 1QD, t 08700 780 193,
*www.indiv-travellers.com*.
**Interhome**, 383 Richmond Road, Twickenham,
Middx TW1 2EF, t (020) 8891 1294, f (020)
8891 5331, *www.interhome.co.uk*.
**Italian Chapters**, t 0845 0700 618, *www.
villarentals.com*.
**Magic of Italy**, t 0870 888 0222, *www.
magictravelgroup.co.uk*.
**Meon Villas**, t 0870 909 7550, *www.
meonvillas.co.uk*.
**The Owners' Syndicate**, 3 Calico Row,
Plantation Wharf, London SW11 YH, t (020)
7801 9807, *www.ownerssyndicate.com*.
**Simply Travel**, Kings House, Wood St, Kingston-
upon-Thames KT1 18G, t 0870 166 979,
*www.simply-travel.co.uk*.
**Topflight**, Third Floor, Jervis House, Jervis
Street, Dublin 1, t (01) 240 1700, f (01) 240
1707, *www.topflight.ie*.
**Traditional Tuscany**, Park Farm, 38 Mill Rd,
Magdalen, Kings Lynn, Norfolk PE34 3BZ,
t (01533) 810 003, *www.traditionaltuscany.
co.uk*
**Travel à la Carte**, First Floor, 30 High Street
Thatcham, Berks RG19 3JD, t (01635) 863030,
f (01635) 867272, *www.anotheritaly.co.uk*.
**Tuscany Now**, t (020) 7684 8884, *www.
tuscanynow.com*

## In the USA

**Exclusive Resorts**, 1530 16th St, Suite 500,
Denver, CO 80202, t 800 447 8988,
*www.exclusiveresorts.com*.
**Hideaways International**, 767 Islington St,
Portsmouth, NH 03801, t 800 843 4433,
*www.hideaways.com*.
**Homebase Abroad**, 29 Mary's Lane, Scituate,
MA 02006, t (781) 545 5112, *www.homebase-
abroad.com*.
**Italianvillas.com**, t 800 700 9549, *www.
italianvillas.com*.
**Rentals in Italy (and Elsewhere!)**, 700 E. Main
St, Ventura, CA 93001, t 800 726 6702,
f (805) 641 1630, *www.rentvillas.com*.
**Via Travel Design**, 7458 Devon St, Philadelphia,
PA 19119, t 888 477 2740, *www.viatravel
design.com*.

## In Italy

**The Best in Italy**, Via Ugo Foscolo 72, 50124
Firenze, t 055 223064, *www.
thebestinitaly.com*.
**Cuendet**, Strada di Strove 17, 53035
Monteriggioni, t 0577 576330, f 0577 301193,
*www.cuendet.com*.
**Euro Casa**, Piazza Silvio Pellico 1, Marchiano
della Chiana (AR), t 0575 845 348, *www.
eurocasa.com*.
**Florence Dreams**, Via S. Lucia 16r, 50123 Florence,
t 055 264 5162, *www.florencedreams.com*.
**Houses of Charme**, Piazza Baronale 4, 05020
Montoro, t 0744 793051, f 0744 793233,
*www.vacation-rentals-italy.net*.
**MB Rent Tuscany**, Via L. da Vinci 9, 53044
Chiusi (SI), t 0578 21192, *www.
immobiliaremb.com*.
**Toscanamare**, Via W della Gherardesca 5,
Marina di Castagneto Carducci (LI), t 0565
744012, *www.toscanamare.it*. Villas on the
Etruscan coast.
**Tuscany All**, t 055 713655, f 055 7193507,
*www.tuscanyall.com*.

climbers, while others are reached by *funivie*, used by skiers in winter and holiday-makers in summer. Rates range from about €10–28 a night, depending on whether you are a CAI member, but rise by 20% December to April. Write to the club at Via E Petrella 19, 20124 Milano, **t** 02 205 7231, *www.cai.it*, for a list of huts, dates available, and booking information.

## Camping

Most official campsites are near the sea, the mountains or the lakes; and there is usually one within commuting distance of major tourist centres. Details are published in the Italian Touring Club's *Campeggi e Villaggi Turistici*, available in Italian bookshops for €18; ask for an abbreviated list free from:

**Centro Internazionale Prenotazioni Federcampeggio**, Casella Postale 23, 50041 Calenzano (FI), **t** 055 882391, *www. federcampeggio.it*.

Camping prices vary enormously, so check with the individual sites, and request a booking form to reserve a space – in summer the tents and caravans are packed cheek by jowl. You may camp outside an official site if you ask the landowner's permission. Hiring a caravan is expensive: ask the tourist office for a list of firms.

# Florence

# Getting There

Florence is the central transport node for Tuscany and harder to avoid than to reach.

## By Air

Florence's **Vespucci airport** was lengthened in 1996, and now bustles with at least as much international traffic as Pisa. It is 4km out at Peretola, t 055 315874, flight information t 055 306 1300 (recorded message in Italian and English). There is a regular bus to Florence, terminating at Santa Maria Novella station (15mins). A taxi to the centre will cost €15–20.

**Alitalia**: Lungarno Acciaioli 10/12r, t 055 27881 (reservations, t 848 865642), *www.alitalia.it*.

**British Airways**: t 199 712266 or contact Pisa office, t 050 40866, *www.britishairways.com*.

**Meridiana** (for London Gatwick): Peretola Airport 28r, t 199 111333.

## By Train

The central station is **Santa Maria Novella**, call t 892021 for information, *www.trenitalia. com*. Many long-distance trains arriving at night use **Campo di Marte** station, bus nos.12 or 91.

## By Bus

It's possible to reach nearly every city, town and village in Tuscany from Florence – once you know which of several bus companies to patronize. The tourist office has a complete list, but here are some of the most popular:

**SITA** (near station, Via S. Caterina da Siena 15, t 055 294955, t 800 373760, *www.sita-on-line.it*): towns in the Val d'Elsa, Chianti, Val di Pesa, Mugello and Casentino; Anghiari, Arezzo, Bibbiena, Castelfiorentino, Certaldo, Città di Castello, Consuma, Figline Valdarno, Firenzuola, Marina di Grosseto, Montevarchi, Poggibonsi (for San Gimignano and Volterra), Pontassieve, Poppi, Pratovecchio, Sansepolcro, Scarperia, Siena, Stia and Vallombrosa.

**LAZZI** (Piazza Stazione 47r, t 055 351061 Mon–Fri, t 166 845010 24-hour recorded message, *www.lazzi.it*): along the Arno to the coast, including Calenzano, Cerreto Guidi, Empoli, Forte dei Marmi, Livorno, Lucca, Marina di Carrara, Marina di Massa, Montecatini Terme, Montelupo, Montevarchi, Pescia, Pisa, Pistoia, Pontedera, Prato, Signa, Tirrenia, Torre del Lago, Viareggio.

**CAP** (Via Nazionale 13, t 055 214637): Borgo S. Lorenzo, Impruneta, Pistoia, Prato.

**COPIT** (Piazza S. Maria Novella, t 055 214637): Abetone, Cerreto Guidi, Pistoia, Poggio a Caiano, Vinci.

**RAMA** (Lazzi station, t 055 239 8840): Grosseto.

# Getting Around

Florence is a relatively easy city to get around, because nearly everything you'll want to see is within easy walking distance and large areas in the centre are pedestrian zones. In addition, there are no hills to climb, and it's hard to lose your way for very long.

Just to make life difficult, Florence has two sets of **address numbers** on every street – red ones for business, blue or black for residences; your hotel could be either. However, there has been some improvement in recent years: every major piazza, landmark or monument now has a plaque offering relevant background information, and helpful maps have been posted in strategic positions throughout the city.

## By Bus

**City buses** (ATAF; *www.ataf.net*) can whizz or inch you across Florence, and are an excellent means of reaching sights on the periphery. Most useful lines begin at Santa Maria Novella station, and pass by Piazza del Duomo or Piazza San Marco. ATAF supply a comprehensive booklet, including a clear map, with details of all bus routes, available at the information/ ticket booth at the station, tourist offices, some bars, and at ATAF's central office in Piazza della Stazione, t 800 424 500. Ticket prices: €1 for 60mins, €1.80 for 3hrs, €4.50 for 24hrs. The most useful buses for visitors are listed below.

| | |
|---|---|
| 6 | Via Rondinella–Piazza San Marco–Duomo–Station–Soffiano |
| 7 | Station–Duomo–San Domenico–Fiesole |
| 10 | Station–Duomo–S. Marco–Ponte a Mensola–Settignano |
| 11 | Viale Calatafimi–S. Marco–Piazza Indipendenza–Station–Porta Romana–Poggio Imperiale |
| 11a | Viale Calatafimi–Duomo–Porta Romana–Poggio Imperiale |
| 13 | Station–Ponte Rosso–Parterre (car park)–Piazza Libertà–Viale Mazzini–Campo di |

Marte–Piazzale Michelangelo–Porta Romana

14c Rovezzano–Duomo–Station–Careggi (hospital)

17 Cascine–Station–Duomo–Via Lamarmora–Salviatino (for the youth hostel)

25 Station–S. Marco–Piazza Libertà–Via Bolognese–Pratolino

28 Station–Via R Giuliani–Castello–Sesto Fiorentino

37 Station–Ponte alla Carraia–Porta Romana–Certosa del Galluzzo

38 Porta Romana–Pian del Giullari (you need to book this one from the telephone near the bus stop at Porta Romana, t 0167 019794)

As part of the continuing campaign against city smog, a fleet of Lilliputian electric buses, routes A, B and D, have recently been introduced in the city. These mainly serve the centre, often taking circuitous routes 'round the houses', and are a good way of seeing some of the sights if you've had enough walking. Details of routes can be found on the ATAF maps.

## By Taxi

Taxis in Florence don't cruise; you'll find them in ranks at the station and in the major *piazze*, or else ring for a radio taxi: t 055 4798 or 4390. Taxi meters start at €2.54 plus extras, adding €0.82 per km. There is a minimum charge of €4.55.

## By Car

Until the late 1980s, Florence had the most carcinogenic traffic problems in Italy. But in 1988, with great fanfares and accompanied by howls of protest, the city tried to do something about the cars that were choking it to death, by enlarging the limited access zone, the *zona di traffico limitato* (ZTL).

Within the ZTL only buses, taxis and cars belonging to residents are permitted; otherwise, you are permitted to pay to park in one of the city's **car parks** (there's the underground car park at the station, or the cheaper, big park at the Parterre, near Piazza Libertà) or take your chances on a side street or on metered parking areas as shown on the maps at the beginning of this chapter.

This new regulation was then followed by whole areas, especially around Piazza della Signoria and the Duomo, becoming totally traffic-free zones. The only danger is the odd ambulance or police car, the speeding mopeds (all of which you can easily hear) and the deadly silent bicycle.

## Bicycle, Scooter, Golf Cart and Car Hire

Hiring a bike can save you tramping time and angst but it's not risk free. Watch out for cars and pedestrians. Electric golf cars holding up to four people have access to pedestrian zones.

**Biancaneve**, t 055 7139270.

You can hire a motorbike at:

**Alinari**, Via Guelfa 85r, t 055 280500.

**Motorent**, Via S. Zanobi 9r, t 055 490113.

**Florence by Bike**, Via S. Zanobi 120/122r, t 055 488992, *www.florencebybike.it*.

Between 8am and 7.30pm, visitors can now take advantage of one of the (almost) free bicycles supplied by the *comune* of Florence. There are various pick-up points around town, the most central being the Fortezza, the Parterre (for the car parks), Piazza Strozzi, Piazza Stazione, Piazza San Marco, the central market and Porta Romana. They cost about €1 for the day.

When you can't take any more art, hire a car and escape into the ravishing countryside. Most rental firms are within easy walking distance of the station.

**Avis**, Borgo Ognissanti 128r, t 055 213629.

**Europcar**, Borgo Ognissanti 53r, t 800 014410.

**Hertz**, Via M Finiguerra 33, t 199 112211, t 055 239 8205.

**Italy by Car**, Borgo Ognissanti 134r, t 055 287161.

**Maggiore-Budget**, Via M Finiguerra 31r, t 055 210238.

**Program**, Borgo Ognissanti 135, t 055 282916.

# Tourist Information

APT tourist service: *www.firenzeturismo.it*.

Florence becomes more tourist-friendly all the time and there is now a genuine effort on the part of the city administration to provide helpful tourist information. The *comune* publishes a leaflet listing bars and cafés that 'offer their clients a welcoming reception, politeness and, should they need it, bathroom facilities...'; believe it or not, finding a loo you could use in a bar or café used to be difficult.

In addition, there are two **guides for the disabled**, both available at the tourist office. The more comprehensive is in Italian, but it has a good map and covers access to sites and restaurants, etc. in great detail. (For further information on travel and specialist organizations, see p.54.)

### Florence

The main tourist office is a bit out of the way, near Piazza Beccaria on **Via Manzoni 16**, t 055 23320 (open Mon–Fri 8–6, Sat 8–2).

There is a branch at Via Camillo Cavour 1r, t 055 290832, infoturismo@provincia.fi.it (open Mon–Sat 8.30–6.30, Sun 8.30–1.30).

There is also an office at Borgo Santa Croce 29r, t 055 234 0444, f 055 226 4524 (open Mon–Sat 9–7, Sun & hols 9–2).

A new office has opened on the south side of the station in Piazza della Stazione, t 055 212245, f 055 238 1226, www.comune.firenze.it (open Mon–Sat 8.30–7, Sun 8.30–2).

In the summer, look out for the temporary mobile 'Tourist Help Points' run by the Vigili Urbani (the traffic police), in the centre of town.

### Fiesole

**Via Portigiani 3**, t 055 598720/055 597 8373, f 055 598822, www.comune.fiesole.fi.it (Mon–Sat 9–6, Sun 10–1 and 2–6, closes an hour earlier in winter).

## Practical A–Z

**American Express**: Via Dante Alighieri 22r, t 055 50981, just off Piazza della Repubblica.
**Central Post Office**: Via Pellicceria, near Piazza della Repubblica, t 055 27631 (open Mon–Fri 8.15–7, Sat 8.15–12.30; telegram office open Mon–Sat 8.15–7; call t 160 for information).
**Consulates**: UK, Lungarno Corsini 2, t 055 284133; USA, Lung. Vespucci 38, t 055 239 8276.
**E-mail services**: you can send e-mail, use the Internet or fax from all over the city nowadays; one such service is **Internet Train**, Via Zannoni 1r, t 055 263 8555, www.internettrain.it, or Via Guelfa 24a, t/f 055 214794 (opening

hours differ from branch to branch); they are also agents for the Swiss Post International if you want to avoid the bureaucratic slowpokes in the Posta Italiana. Mac users might try **Intotheweb**, Via de' Conti 23r, t 055 264 5628 (open daily 10am–midnight).
**Libraries**: British Institute Library, Lungarno Guicciardini 9, t 055 2677 8270 (open 9.45–1 and 3.15–6.30, closed Sat and Sun). American Library, Via S. Gallo 10 (open 9–12.30, closed Sat and Sun). There are so many other libraries in Florence that one, the Biblioteca del Servizio Beni Librari, Via G. Modena 13, t 055 438 2655, does nothing but dispense information on all the others.
**Lost property** in Italian is Oggetti smarriti or Oggetti ritrovati. The office is in Via Circondaria 17b, t 055 328 3942.
**Medical**: for an ambulance or first aid, Misericordia, Piazza del Duomo 20, t 055 212222. Doctor's night service, t 055 287788. For general medical **emergencies** call t 118. The general **hospital** Santa Maria Nuova, in Piazza S. M. Nuova, t 055 27581, is the most convenient. **Tourist Medical Service** (24hrs a day) is staffed by English- and French-speaking physicians at Via Lorenzo il Magnifico 59; ring first on t 055 475411. If you find yourself hospitalized while in Florence, the **AVO** (Association of Hospital Volunteers) provides volunteer interpreters to deal with language problems, t 055 425 0126/055 234 4567.
**Pharmacies**: open 24hrs every day in **S. Maria Novella** station, also **Molteni**, Via Calzaiuoli 7r and **Taverna**, Piazza S. Giovanni 20r, by the baptistry.
**Police**: emergency t 113. The Ufficio Stranieri, in the questura, Via Zara 2, t 055 49771 (open Mon–Fri 8.30–12.30), handles most foreigners' problems, and usually has someone around who speaks English. Go there for residents' permits, etc.
**Tourist Aid Police**: Via Pietrapiana 50, t 055 203911 (open Mon–Fri 8.30–7.30, Sat 8.30–1.30). Interpreters available to help you report thefts or resolve other problems.
**Towed-away cars**: there is one car pound if your car gets towed away, in the Ponte a Greve car park, near the Ponte al Indiano in the west of the city, t 055 783882 (open 24hrs; bus 44).

# Festivals and Events

Traditional festivals in Florence date back for centuries. The following are listed roughly in the order they take place in the year:

*Scoppio del Carro* (Explosion of the Cart), *Easter Sunday*. Commemorates Florentine participation in the First Crusade, which took place in 1096. The Florentines were led by Pazzino de' Pazzi, who was the first over the walls of Jerusalem and who, upon returning home, received the special custody of the flame of Holy Saturday, with which the Florentines traditionally relit their family hearths. To make the event more colourful, the Pazzi constructed a decorated wooden ox cart to carry the flame. They lost the job after the Pazzi conspiracy in 1478, and since then the city has taken over the responsibility. In the morning, a firework-filled wooden float is pulled by white oxen from Il Prato to the cathedral, where, at 11am, during the singing of the Gloria, it is ignited by an iron 'dove' that descends on a wire from the high altar.

*Maggio Musicale Fiorentino*, Teatro del Maggio Musicale Fiorentino, Corso Italia 12 (off Lungarno Vespucci), **t** 055 211158, *www.maggiofiorentino.com* for ticket information, *late April–early July*. The city's big music festival, brings in big-name concert and opera stars. Some performances may also be held at Teatro della Pergola, or other venues.

**Flower and Plant Show**, Giardino di Orticoltura, Via Vittorio Emanuele 4, *late April*. A huge show, a must for horticulture fans. Centred around a 19th-century glasshouse.

**International Iris festival**, Piazzale Michelangelo, *May*.

*Festa del Grillo* (cricket festival), Cascine, Ascension Day, *May*. Michelangelo was thinking of the festival's little wooden cricket cages when he mocked Ammannati's gallery on the cathedral dome.

*Calcio Storico in Costume*, Piazza Santa Croce, *June*. Each June, four matches of historical football are played in 16th-century costume by 27-man teams from Florence's four quarters, in memory of a defiant football match played there in 1530, during the siege by Charles V. It's great fun with flag-throwing and a parade in historical costume as part of the pre-game ceremonies. The only fixed date is 24 June; the dates for the other matches are pulled out of a hat on Easter Sunday.

*Festa di San Giovanni*, *24 June*. The festival of Florence's patron saint, marked by a big firework display near Piazzale Michelangelo at 10pm.

*Estate Fiesolana*, *late June–Aug*. This is one of the annual cultural events generally adored by Florentines, when the old Roman theatre is made the venue for concerts, dance, theatre and films, for reasonable prices.

**Summer concerts**, Piazza Signoria, *summer months*. The piazza occasionally plays host to concerts and other events during the summer. Countless smaller scale concerts are given, often outdoors or in cloisters, churches and villas. Look out for posters or ask at the tourist office.

*Maggio Musicale* **festival closing concert**, *late June–early July*. A free-for-all heralding the end of the annual music festival.

*MaggioDanza* **ballet company**, *late June–early July*. An evening of dance, held annually, also a free-for-all.

**Florence Dance Festival**, **t** 055 289276 for information, *July*. Presents an interesting combination of classical and contemporary dance performances. Usually held in Fiesole's Roman Theatre.

*Festa della Rificolona*, *7 Sept*. A children's festival: Florentine kids gather in the evening in Piazza SS. Annunziata and along the river armed with paper lanterns, and then, after dark, they parade singing around the streets.

# Shopping

## Fashion

Although central Florence sometimes seems like one solid boutique, the city is no longer the queen of Italian fashion – the long lack of a central airport, more than anything else, sent most of the big designers to Milan. Even so, the big fashion names of the 1960s and 70s, and the international chain stores, are well represented in smart Via Tornabuoni, Via Calzaiuoli and around the Duomo, and the new overhaul of Gucci and the arrival of Prada has updated the city's slightly fusty image.

## Leather

**Via della Vigna Nuova.** Leather is something Florence is still known for, and you'll see plenty of it in this central street.

**The Leather School,** entrance at Piazza Santa Croce 16 or Via S. Giuseppe 5r. An unusual institution, occupying part of Santa Croce's cloister, with less expensive goods.

**Piazza Santa Croce** and surrounding streets.

## Jewellery

**Ponte Vecchio.** Florence is famous for jewellery. The shops on, and around, the bridge are forced, by the nature of their location, into wide-open competition. Good prices for Florentine brushed gold (although much of it is made in Arezzo these days) and antique jewellery are more common than you may think. Elsewhere, there are two other stores worth seeking out.

**Il Gatto Bianco,** Borgo SS. Apostoli 12r. Modern designs (earrings, rings, necklaces, etc.) are crafted on the premises in silver, gold and other metals with pearls and precious stones.

**Pepita Studio,** Borgo degli Albizi 23r. Fun, chunky, young designs in plexiglass, wood and glass. Prices are very reasonable.

## Marbled Paper

Florence is one of the few places in the world that makes marbled paper, an art brought from the Orient in the 12th century. Each sheet is hand-dipped to create a delicate, lightly coloured clouded design; no two sheets are alike. Stationery items or just sheets of marbled paper are available at:

**Giulio Giannini e Figlio,** Piazza Pitti 36r. The oldest manufacturer in Florence.

**Il Papiro,** with three shops at: Via Cavour 55r; Piazza del Duomo 24r; Lung. Acciaiuoli 42r.

**La Bottega Artigiana del Libro,** Lungarno Corsini 40r.

**Il Torchio,** Via dei Bardi 17, t 055 234 2862. Here the workbench is in the shop so you can see the artisans in action. These shops (and many others) also carry Florentine paper with its colourful Gothic patterns.

## Books

Bookworms do better in Florence than most Italian cities, and prices of books in English seem to have come down in recent years, so there are a fair number of places to browse.

**The Paperback Exchange,** Via Fiesolana 31r. A wide selection in English, with many books about Florence.

**Seeber,** Via Tornabuoni 70r. An alternative to the Exchange, also has a good selection.

**Feltrinelli,** Via Cavour 12–20r. Books in English and an excellent range of art books.

**BM Bookshop,** Borgo Ognissanti 4r. Ditto here.

**Franco Maria Ricci,** Via delle Belle Donne 41r. A fabulous collection of art books.

**Edition,** Piazza della Repubblica 27r. Florence's biggest bookshop with plenty of titles in English, travel guides and maps (also in English), Internet points, video services and a café.

## Antiques and Art Galleries

Borgo Ognissanti and the various Lungarni are the places to look. Also check out: Piazza dei Ciompi's flea market and monthly flea market (2nd Sunday of month) held in Piazza Santo Spirito.

**P. Bazzanti e Figli,** Lungarno Corsini 44. Here you can pick up an exact replica of the bronze boar in the Mercato Nuovo.

**Atelier Alice,** Via Faenza 72r. Much easier to carry is an Italian carnival mask, available here, and for those who are keen to learn more about the art of the mask, the shop runs five-lesson courses. Ring Prof A Dessi on t 055 215961 for details.

**Via Maggio.** This street is full of upmarket antique shops.

Serious collectors may want to check Florence's busy auction houses:

**Casa d'Aste Pandolfini,** Borgo degli Albizi 26, t 055 234 0888.

**Casa d'Aste Pitti,** Via Maggio 15, t 055 239 6382.

**Sotheby's Italia,** Via G Capponi 26, t 055 247 9021 (*call for appointment*).

## Cloth

**Casa dei Tessuti,** Via de' Pecori 20–24r, t 055 215961. Keeps Florence's ancient cloth trade alive with lovely linens, silks and woollens. During the lunch break, you might catch a lecture on the history of Florence with special reference to the textile industry.

## Silver, Crystal and Porcelain

**A Poggi**, Via Calzaiuoli 105r and 116r. One of the city's widest selections (including Florence's own Richard-Ginori).

## Children's Toys and Clothes

**Città del Sole**, Via Cimatori 21r. The best toy shop in Florence.

**Cirri**, Via Por S. Maria 38–40r. If you happen to have or know the kinds of little girls who like to wear white, this has a fairy-tale selection of dresses.

**Anichini**, Via di Parione 59r. Oldest kids' clothes shop in Florence; exquisitely produced dresses (made in store), silk party dresses, romper suits, Christening robes and playwear.

## Wine and Food

**Millesimi**, Borgo Tegolaio 33r. One of the best wine shops in town. Tastings by appointment.

**Mercato Centrale**. Good for a number of speciality food shops.

**Allrientar Gastronomia**, Borgo SS. Apostoli. Pick up items such as truffle cream here.

**La Porta del Tartufo**, Borgo Ognissanti 133r. Virtually confines itself to different types of truffles or 'truffled' foods ranging from *grappa* to salmon paste.

**Il Procacci**, Via Tornabuoni 64r. A high-quality *alimentari* (food shop) selling regional specialities as well as foreign foods. It's most famous as the venue for a lunch time *Prosecco* and *panino tartufato*, a glass of sparkling white wine and a truffle-filled sandwich. Also a bar.

**Pitti Gola e Cantina**, Piazza Pitti 16. Offers a good selection of wines, oils and vinegars, and cookery books (in both English and Italian) to go with them.

**La Bottega del Brunello**, Via Ricasoli 81r. Divided in two parts, one for display and one for tasting the wine and specialities on sale.

**Casa del Vino**, Via dell'Ariento 16r. With wine tastings plus snacks in the San Lorenzo street market.

**Enoteca dei Giraldi**, Via Giraldi. Exclusively in Tuscan wines from lesser known producers, with over 140 labels (you can also eat there).

**Le Volpi e L'Uva**, Piazza de' Rossi 1. Situated behind the Ponte Vecchio on the square, this also stocks lesser known labels.

**Enoteca Murgia**, Via dei Banchi 57, off Piazza S. Maria Novella. Good for wines and spirits in general.

**Marchesi de' Frescobaldi**, Via di S. Spirito 11. One of the largest wine suppliers in Italy; visit their ancient cellars.

## Markets

Florence's lively street markets offer good bargains, fake designer glad rags and even some authentic labels.

**San Lorenzo**. Easily the largest and most boisterous: food (*open Mon–Sat 8–2*) and clothes and party gifts (*open Tues–Sat*).

**Sant'Ambrogio**. A bustling food market.

**Mercato Nuovo** (Straw Market). The most touristic, but not flagrantly so.

**Piazza Santo Spirito**. Home to different markets on different days: Food, clothes and shoes (small). *Open daily exc Sun.* Craft and flea market (big). *Open every 2nd Sun of month.* Organic food market. *Open every 3rd Sun.*

**Cascine**, along the river. A weekly market where many Florentines buy their clothes. Here you may easily find designer clothes off the back of a lorry, shoes and lots more besides. *Open Tues am.*

**Mercato delle Pulci** (Flea Market), Piazza dei Ciompi. Perhaps the most fun market, offering all kinds of desirable junk. *Open Sun.*

# Sports and Activities

## On the Water

The one activity most summertime visitors begin to crave after tramping through the sights is a dip in a pool.

**Piscina le Pavoniere**, Cascine. The prettiest in Florence. *Open June–Sept 10–6.30.*

**Bellariva**, up the Arno at Lungarno Colombo 2. *Open June–Sept 11–5.*

**Amici del Nuoto**, Via del Romito 38, t 055 483951. *Open all year.*

**Costoli**, Via Paoli, near Campo di Marte, t 055 623 6027. *Open all year.*

If there's enough water in the Arno, you can try rowing or canoeing:

**Società Canottieri Comunali**, Lungarno Ferrucci 6, **t** 055 681 2151.

**Società Canottieri Firenze**, Lungarno dei Medici 8, **t** 055 238 1010 (membership only).

## Horse-racing and Riding

**Ippodromo Il Visarno**, Cascine, **t** 055 422 6076. Florence's flat race course.

**Ippodromo della Mulina**, Cascine, **t** 055 422 6076.

**Maneggio Mirinelle**, Via di Macia 21, **t/f** 055 887 8066. The nearest place to go riding in the Tuscan hills.

**Centro Ippico Ugolino**, Via Oliveta 12, **t** 055 230 1289. You can also ride here, near the golf course.

## Golf

**Golf Club Ugolino**, on the Chiantigiana, **t** 055 230 1009, *www.golfugolino.it*. The nearest 18-hole golf course to Florence is in Gràssina, 7km southeast of the city; a lovely course.

## Squash and Tennis

**Centro Squash**, Via Empoli 16, **t** 055 732 3055.

**Circolo Tennis Firenze**, Viale Visarno, **t** 055 354326.

# Where to Stay

## Florence ✉ 50100

Florence has some lovely hotels, and not all of them at Grand Ducal prices, although base rates are the highest in Tuscany. As in any city, the higher cost of living means you won't find much *inexpensive* accommodation. Florence, Venice and Rome are the most expensive places to stay in Italy, and you should count on having to pay around 25% more for a room here than you would anywhere else (*see* p.73).

Historic old palace-hotels are the rule rather than the exception; those listed below are some of the more atmospheric and charming, but to be honest, few are secrets, so reserve as far in advance as possible. Note that many hotels will try to lay down a heavy breakfast charge that is supposed to be optional.

There are almost 400 hotels in Florence but not enough for anyone who arrives in June and September without a reservation (Easter is even more busy). But don't despair; there are several hotel consortia that can help you find a room in nearly any price range for a small commission. If you're arriving by car or train, the most useful will be ITA.

**ITA**: in Santa Maria Novella station, **t** 055 282893, *open 8.30–7*. Bookings can be made by phone and a booking fee of between €3 and €8 is charged, according to the category of hotel.

**Florence Promhotels**: Viale A. Volta 72, **t** 055 570481, **f** 055 587189. Free booking service.

For *agriturismo* or farmhouse accommodation in the surrounding countryside (self-catering or otherwise), contact: Agriturist Toscana, Piazza S. Firenze 3, **t/f** 055 287838, *www.agriturist.it*; or Turismo Verde Toscana, Via Jacopo Nardi 41, **t** 055 233 8911.

### Luxury

*****Excelsior**, Piazza Ognissanti 3, **t** 055 2715, **f** 055 210278, *www.westin.com/excelsiorflorence*. In the city the luxury leader is the former Florentine address of Napoleon's sister, Caroline. Lots of marble, neoclassically plush, lush and green with plants, immaculately staffed, with decadently luxurious bedrooms, many of which have river views (for a price).

*****Helvetia & Bristol**, Via dei Pescioni 2, **t** 055 287814, **f** 055 288353, *www.charminghotels.it*. If you prefer luxury on a smaller scale, this has 52 exquisitely furnished bedrooms, each one different, all with rich fabrics adorning windows, walls and beds; Stravinsky, Bertrand Russell and Pirandello stayed here; added pluses are the restaurant and the winter garden.

*****The Savoy**, Piazza della Repubblica 7, **t** 055 283313, **f** 055 284840, *www.roccofortehotels.com*. The old, crumbling Savoy reopened in spring 2000 under the Forte Group, now striking a minimalist tone with décor in shades of cream, beige and grey; it has a bar and restaurant where you can sit out on the piazza.

*****Villa La Vedetta**, Viale Michelangiolo 78, **t** 055 658 0237, **f** 055 658 2544, *www.villalavedettahotel.com*. This recently opened luxury hotel occupies an elegant villa in a superb position near Piazzale Michelangelo with panoramic views over the city from its terraces and some of the rooms. Downstairs, cool grey and white marble prevail while the bedrooms are sumptuously-but not ostentatiously-done out in silks. The restaurant (which has just been awarded a Michelin star), serving creative gourmet fare, is superb; in summer you can eat on the terrace overlooking the city lights.

★★★★**Astoria**, Via del Giglio 9, **t** 055 239 8095, **f** 055 214632, *www.boscolohotels.com*. Recently refurbished, in a grand 16th-century palazzo near San Lorenzo market, this has more character than many of those located near the station. Public rooms are suitably impressive and some of the bedrooms likewise; avoid those on the lower floors by the street.

★★★★**Gallery Hotel Art**, Vicolo dell'Oro 2, **t** 055 27263, **f** 055 268557, *galleryhotel@ lungarnohotels.it*. Florence's most exciting hotel is a shrine to contemporary interior design. It is by no means stark, however, and the position (a mere two minutes from the Ponte Vecchio) is superb. It has a comfortable library, a smart bar and a restaurant serving trendy fusion food.

★★★★**J.K. Place**, Piazza Santa Maria Novella 7, **t** 055 2645181, **f** 055 2658387, *www.jkplace. com*. This tall, elegant townhouse stands on smartened-up Piazza Santa Maria Novella with rooms that overlook Alberti's glorious church façade. The interior is luxuriously designer-chic (and attracts the fashion crowd), but manages to be warm and welcoming at the same time. Some of the bedrooms are on the small side, but are equipped with every mod con; there is a wonderful rooftop terrace and bar. Breakfast is served at a large communal table in a glassed-in courtyard and there is a selection of complimentary soft drinks and snacks available to guests.

★★★★**Kraft**, Via Solferino 2, **t** 055 284273, **f** 055 239 8267, *www.krafthotel.it*. Frequently used by upmarket tour groups, this is handy for the opera season (it is two minutes' walk from the Teatro del Maggio Musicale Fiorentino), and has the added advantage of a small rooftop pool. Bedrooms are light and sunny, and comfortably furnished with

cheerful fabrics. The suites on the top floor have great views. There is a restaurant.

★★★★**Lungarno**, Borgo San Jacopo 14, **t** 055 27261, **f** 055 268437, *www.lungarnohotels. com*. A discreet hotel enjoying a marvellous location on the river, only two minutes' walk from the Ponte Vecchio. The ground-floor sitting/breakfast room and bar, and the new restaurant, which specializes in fish, look out on to the water. The building is modern, but incorporates a medieval tower, and has recently been refurbished; the smallish bedrooms are decorated in smart blue and cream. The best have balconies with 'The View'. Book ahead for these.

★★★★**Monna Lisa**, Borgo Pinti 27, **t** 055 247 9751, **f** 055 247 9755, *www.monnalisa.it*. This Renaissance palace, now owned by the descendants of sculptor Giovanni Dupre, may have a stern façade and, it is said, staff to match, but it is also one of the loveliest small hotels in Florence – well preserved and filled with family heirlooms and works of art. Rooms vary wildly; try to reserve one that overlooks the garden; breakfast is available, as is private parking.

## Very Expensive

★★★★**Villa Carlotta**, Via Michele di Lando 3, **t** 055 233 6134, **f** 055 233 6147, *www. panoramichotelsitaly.it*. Located in a quiet residential district in the upper Oltrarno, close to the Porta Romana, this Tuscan–Edwardian building has 26 sophisticated rooms which have been tastefully refurnished and have every mod con. There's a garden and glassed-in veranda, where the large breakfasts are served; a private garage offers safe parking.

★★★**Aprile**, Via della Scala 6, **t** 055 216237, **f** 055 280947, *www.hotelaprile.it*. Convenient for the station and recently given a facelift, this was once a Medici palace and appropriately has a bust of Cosimo I above the door. Vaulted ceilings and frescoes remain intact, and the bedrooms all have period furniture although some are on the gloomy side; there's a shady courtyard.

★★★**Calzaiuoli**, Via Calzaiuoli 6, **t** 055 212456, **f** 055 268310, *www.calzaiuoli.it*. Just a few steps from Piazza Signoria and on a traffic-free street is a comfortable hotel with modern, nicely decorated rooms and wonderful views from the top floor.

***Beacci Tornabuoni**, Via Tornabuoni 3, t 055 212645, f 055 283594, *www.tornabuoni hotels.com*. Another excellent small hotel that puts you in the centre of fashionable Florence, on the top three floors of an elegant Renaissance palace. The rooms are comfortable, air-conditioned and equipped with minibars, though it's more fun to sit over your drink on the panoramic roof terrace.

***Hermitage**, Vicolo Marzio 1, t 055 287216, f 055 212208, *www.hermitagehotel.com*. Tucked away behind the Ponte Vecchio on the north side of the river, this little hotel is built upside down; the lift takes you to the fifth floor with its ravishing roof garden, reception and elegant blue and yellow sitting room. The bedrooms below are on the small side, but charmingly furnished with antiques and tasteful fabrics. Some have river views.

***Loggiato dei Serviti**, Piazza SS. Annunziata 3, t 055 289592, f 055 289595, *www.loggiato deiservitihotel.it*. Located on Florence's most beautiful square (now traffic-free), the front rooms of this delightful hotel overlook Brunelleschi's famous portico. The 16th-century building was originally a convent, and many of the architectural features remain. Rooms are furnished with antiques and tasteful fabrics; each is very different from the next. Recommended.

***Torre Guelfa**, Borgo SS. Apostoli 8, t 055 239 6338, f 055 239 8577, *www. torreguelfa.com*. Boasting the tallest privately owned tower in Florence, bang in the middle of the *centro storico*. There's a grand double salon, a sunny breakfast room, and stylish bedrooms in pastel shades with wrought iron and hand-painted furniture, as well as the chance to sip an *aperitivo* while contemplating a 360° view.

**Casa Howard**, Via della Scala 18, t 06 (yes...reservations are made through Rome) 6992 4555, *www.casahoward.com*. Following in the footsteps of the two very popular Casa Howards in Rome and only a stone's throw from the train station, this elegant guest house offers 11 individually decorated rooms (there is one for kids, one with a library in it, one for dogs) at remarkably reasonable prices in a home-from-home

atmosphere. All rooms have tea- and coffee-making facilities and some have a private terrace; there's even a Turkish hammam.

## Expensive

****Villa Belvedere**, Via Benedetto Castelli 3, t 055 222501, f 055 223163, *www.villa-belvedere.com*. Not the more interesting building in this part of peripheral Florence (1km above Porta Romana), but a pleasant alternative to central accommodation, nonetheless, with a beautiful garden, tennis court, a nice little pool and good views. Rooms are modern and comfortable with lots of wood and plenty of space. For trips into town, you can leave your car and catch a nearby bus. Light meals are served in the restaurant. Excellent value for a 4-star hotel.

***Hotel delle Arti**, Via dei Servi 38/A, t 055 267 8553, f 055 290140, *www.hoteldellearti.it*. Under the same ownership as the Loggiato dei Serviti (*see* above), this nine-bedroom hotel has a simpler, more country look than its big sister up the road. The stylish bedrooms are decorated in restful shades of green and cream and have wood floors; a couple have pine four-posters. The three corner rooms are particularly spacious and light and there is a pretty breakfast room on the top floor with a wraparound terrace.

***Morandi alla Crocetta**, Via Laura 50, t 055 234 4747, f 055 248 0954, *www.hotel morandi.it*. Small but popular, with 10 rooms in the university area northeast of Piazza San Marco. The building was a convent in the 16th century, and some of the comfortable and pleasant rooms still have the odd fresco. Two rooms have private terraces.

***Silla**, Via dei Renai 5, t 055 234 2888, f 055 234 1437, *www.hotelsilla.it*. Ten minutes' walk east of the Ponte Vecchio on the south bank of the river, this manages to be central, yet in a quiet and relatively green neighbourhood. This old-fashioned *pensione* is on the first floor of a 16th-century palazzo and the spacious breakfast terrace has great views over the Arno and beyond.

****Alessandra**, Borgo SS. Apostoli 17, t 055 283438, f 055 210619, *www.hotelalessandra. com*. A modest hotel in a palazzo designed by Michelangelo's pupil, Baccio d'Agnolo, on a central but quiet back street; there are 25 rooms of varying standards. Not all have private baths; the best have waxed parquet floors and antiques.

**\*\*Casci**, Via Cavour 13, **t** 055 211686, **f** 055 239 6461, *www.hotelcasci.com*. The Lombardis, owners of this 15th-century palazzo (once home to Rossini), run a relaxed and cheerful ship. The reception area is full of helpful information, the breakfast room has a frescoed ceiling while the recently refurbished bedrooms are bright and modern. The choice few look on to a garden at the back.

**Relais Uffizi**, Chiasso de' Baroncelli/Chiasso del Buco 16, **t** 055 267 6239, **f** 055 265 7909, *www.relaisuffizi.it*. The only hotel which overlooks Piazza della Signoria, the Relais Uffizi is hidden down a series of narrow lanes. The 13 rooms of varying shapes and sizes are decorated and furnished with style, while the atmosphere is informal. You can relax in the sitting room and watch the ever-changing piazza below.

## Moderate

**\*\*\*Locanda degli Artisti**, Via Faenza 56, **t/f** 055 213806, *www.hotelazzi.it*. This hotel, a stone's throw from the San Lorenzo market and the train station, offers pleasant rooms and has an arty, alternative feel to it. On the ground floor, bedrooms are a little more sophisticated (there are even a couple of suites) while upstairs, rooms are clean but quite Spartan and none have private baths. There's a sauna, a sunny terrace and a breakfast room where organic produce is served.

**\*\*\*Classic Hotel**, Viale Machiavelli 25, **t** 055 229351, **f** 055 229353, *www.classichotel.it*. A good alternative in a very pleasant location just above Porta Romana on the way to Piazzale Michelangelo, a five-minute walk to a bus stop for downtown. The pink-washed villa stands in a shady garden (a welcome respite from the heat of the city), and breakfast is served in the conservatory in summer.

**\*\*Belletini**, Via de' Conti 7, **t** 055 213561, **f** 055 28355, *www.firenze.net/hotelbelletini*. A friendly place near the Medici chapels, decorated in traditional Florentine style; a couple of rooms have stunning views of the nearby domes. There's a good, generous

breakfast. An annexe around the corner houses an additional six stylishly furnished rooms, which are slightly more expensive. TV, air-conditioning, cots, and parking nearby.

**\*\*Boboli**, Via Romana 63, **t** 055 229 8645, **f** 055 233 7169, *www.hotelboboli.com*. As the name suggests, this modest hotel is located near the back entrance of the Boboli gardens. The brightest rooms are right at the top of the four-storey building. A lift has recently been installed. Or if you want quiet (Via Romana is quite noisy), go for a room on the inner courtyard. Breakfast is served on a little terrace in summer.

**\*\*Residenza Johanna Cinque Giornate**, Via Cinque Giornate 12, **t/f** 055 473377, *www.johanna.it*. Good value for money in a city where bargains are few and far between, located some way from the centre (near the Fortezza da Basso). The villa stands in its own garden and there are six comfortable rooms, each equipped with a breakfast tray and kettle, as well as a sitting room with plenty of reading material. Guests are left to themselves, but other facilities are of a three-star standard; parking available.

**\*\*La Scaletta**, Via Guicciardini 13, **t** 055 283028, **f** 055 289562, *www.lascaletta.com*. Between the Ponte Vecchio and the Pitti Palace is a friendly *pensione* with a roof garden and great views into Boboli. The 12 bedrooms (not all with bathrooms and some of which sleep up to four) are decently furnished, the nicest with some antique pieces. Very moderately priced dinner available.

**\*Bavaria**, Borgo degli Albizi 26, **t/f** 055 234 0313, *www.welcomehotels.com*. Housed in a grand, 16th-century palazzo whose façade is said to be frescoed by Vasari, this once-crummy hotel has had a facelift. While it is still on one floor and only a handful of rooms have private baths, the rooms are stylish, and some have splendid views of the city.

**\*Maxim**, Via dei Medici 4, **t** 055 217474, **f** 055 283729, *www.firenzealbergo.it/home/hotelmaxim*. This centrally located budget hotel has had a recent facelift. The reception area is bright and elegant, and the bedrooms (which sleep two or three) are well furnished and modern. All are en suite and one even has a jacuzzi. Air-conditioning, and parking nearby.

\***Sorelle Bandini**, Piazza Santo Spirito 9, t 055 215308, f 055 282761. Remains popular, despite its state of disrepair and relatively high prices. This is partly due to the romantic loggia along one side of the fourth-storey hotel, but also to its location on Piazza Santo Spirito, bustling by day and lively (and noisy) at night. Expect uncomfortable beds, cavernous rooms, heavy Florentine furniture and a certain shabby charm.

**Antica Dimora**, Via San Gallo 72n, t 055 462 7296, f 055 463 4450, *www.anticadimorafirenze.it*. This delightful new guest house, situated ten minutes' walk north of the Duomo, has six beautifully furnished rooms and the warm atmosphere of an elegant private apartment. Four-posters are hung with fine linens and silks and all rooms have DVDs and modem connections. Prices are remarkably low for what is on offer.

**Residenza Johlea**, Via San Gallo 80, t 055 463 3292, f 055 463 4552, *www.johanna.it*. Really two small hotels a few doors from each other. A remarkable bargain in terms of what it offers for the price, the Johlea is under the same ownership as the Johannas (*see* below). Situated 10mins' walk north of the central market, the rooms are comfortable and well furnished with taste and style and all have excellent bathrooms. Breakfast is supplied on trays in the rooms. On the top floor is a small sitting room and a roof terrace affording 360° views of the city. If all the rooms are full, there is a sister 'residenza' (the Johlea Due) a few doors down.

## Inexpensive

\***Dali**, Via dell'Oriuolo 17, t/f 055 234 0706, *www.hoteldali.com*. Just a few minutes' walk from the Duomo, this little hotel is run by a genuinely friendly young couple who have decorated the rooms with care and attention to detail in spite of the low prices. Only three of the ten rooms have en suite bathrooms, but all are bright and homely. There's free parking in the internal courtyard. No breakfast.

\***Orchidea**, Borgo degli Albizi 11, t/f 055 248 0346, *hotelorchidea@yahoo.it*. Run by an Anglo-Italian family in a 12th-century building where Dante's in-laws once lived.

One of the seven cheerful rooms has a private shower; the best of the rest look on to a garden at the back.

\***Scoti**, Via de' Tornabuoni 7, t 055 292128, *www.hotelscoti.com*. A simple and cheap *pensione* with a surprisingly upmarket address, which could be ideal if you would rather splurge on the wonderful clothes in the surrounding shops. A recent facelift means that all the simple rooms are now en suite; luckily the atmosphere has not been spoilt, and there are still wonderful faded floor-to-ceiling frescoes in the sitting room. The owners are friendly.

**Istituto Gould**, Via dei Serragli 49, t 055 212576, f 055 280274, *gould.reception@ dada.it*. An excellent budget choice near Santo Spirito, the Istituto Gould is run by the Valdese church. Rooms vary in size from singles (a couple) to quads and not all have their own bathrooms; book early to secure singles or doubles. The best rooms have access to a terrace and the noisiest are on Via dei Serragli. No smoking is allowed in the building and you have to check in during office hours.

**Residenza Johanna**, Via Bonifacio Lupi 14, t 055 481896, f 055 482721, *www.johanna.it*. Only a tiny brass plaque over the bell identifies this building, just north of Piazza San Marco. There are no TVs or phones in the rooms, no doorman, and not all rooms have private baths, but the furnishings are comfortable, the bedrooms are prettily decorated and there's lots of reading material to hand. Breakfast is on a do-it-yourself tray in each room, and there are kettles out in the corridor.

## Rooms to Let

Besides hotels, a number of institutions and private homes let rooms – there's a complete list in the back of the annual provincial hotel book. Many take women only, and fill up with students in the spring.

## Youth Hostels

**Archi Rossi**, Via Faenza 94r, t 055 290804, *www.hostelarchirossi.com*. Purpose-built and fully wheelchair-accessible, this is the nearest hostel to the station, and is well equipped. You can book a place after 6am and occupy your room after 2.30pm. Phone bookings are accepted and there is a 12.30am curfew.

**Ostello Europa Villa Camerata**, Viale A Righe 2/4 (bus from the station), **t** 055 601451, *www.iyhf.org*. Has 500 beds for people with IYHF cards. Located in an old palazzo with gardens, it is a popular place, and you'd be wise to show up at 2pm to get a spot in the summer; maximum stay three days.

**Ostello Santa Monaca**, Via Santa Monaca 6, **t** 055 268338, *www.ostello.it*. Has 111 beds near the Carmine church; sign up for a place in the morning.

## Camping

There are a few campsites within easy striking distance of Florence:

**Camping Internazionale**, Via S. Cristofano 2, **t** 055 237 4704, *www.florencecamping.com*. South of the city in Bottai Tavarnuzze, near the A1 exit Autostrada Firenze–Certosa. *Open end Mar–1st Nov.*

**Camping Michelangelo**, Viale Michelangelo 80, **t** 055 681 1977, **f** 055 689348, *www.ecvacanze.it*. Fine views over the city and free hot showers; arrive early to get a spot. On the other hand, there's no shade and the disco goes on until 1am. Bus 13 will take you there from the station. *Open all year.*

**Camping Panoramico Fiesole**, Via Peramonda 1, **t** 055 599069, *www.florencecamping.com*. A beautifully situated campsite, just above Fiesole on a hill with fabulous views over Florence, but packed and expensive in the summer. *Open all year.*

**Mugello Verde International Camping**, Via Masso Rondinaio 2, in San Piero a Sieve, **t** 055 848511, **f** 055 848 6910, *www.florencecamping.com*. 25km north of Florence on the road to Bologna, with a very pleasant setting among hills and forests, and frequent buses down to Florence. *Closed Nov–mid-Mar.*

## Fiesole ✉ 50014

Many frequent visitors to Florence wouldn't stay anywhere else: it's cooler, quieter, and at night the city far below twinkles as if made of fairy lights.

★★★★★**Villa San Michele**, Via Doccia 4, **t** 055 567 8200, **f** 055 567 8250, *www.orient/expresshotels.com* (*luxury*). Built as a monastery in the 14th century, this hotel is the superb choice if money happens to be no object, set in a breathtaking location just below Fiesole with a façade and loggia reputedly designed by Michelangelo himself. After suffering bomb damage during the Second World War, it was carefully reconstructed to create one of the most beautiful hotels in Italy, set in a lovely Tuscan garden, complete with a pool. Each of its 29 rooms is richly and elegantly furnished and air-conditioned; the more plush suites have jacuzzis. The food is delicious, and the reasons to go down to Florence begin to seem insignificant; a stay here is complete in itself. Paradise, however, comes at a price.

★★★★**Villa Aurora**, Piazza Mino 38, **t** 055 59363, **f** 055 59587, *www.aurorafiesole.com* (*very expensive*). An agreeable 19th-century villa, located right on Fiesole's famous piazza from where the no.7 bus will whisk you down to central Florence in 20mins. The 25 bedrooms have rustic antiques and splendid views over the city. Some of the bathrooms are poky. There is a restaurant – on a terrace overlooking Florence in the summer – and the bar next door (which can be noisy at times) is under the same ownership.

★★★**Pensione Bencistà**, Via Benedetto di Maiano 4, **t/f** 055 59163, *pensione bencista@iol.it* (*moderate – half-board*). Another former monastery with views from its flower-decked terrace which are every bit as good as those at Villa San Michele, and the welcome will be more friendly. Bedrooms, each one different from the next, are all comfortably furnished with solid antique pieces. The three little sitting rooms are particularly inviting in cooler weather when fires are lit. Half-board – breakfast and either lunch or dinner – is obligatory here, but prices are reasonable. NB: *No credit cards*.

★★★**Villa Fiesole**, Via Beato Angelico 35, **t** 055 597252, **f** 055 599133, *www.villafiesole.it* (*luxury*). This new hotel was once part of the San Michele convent, and shares part of its driveway with the hotel of the same name. The smart, neoclassical-style interiors are variations on a fresh blue and yellow colour scheme. Light meals are served in a sunny dining room or on the adjacent terrace, and there is a pool. The facilities (and prices) here are decidedly four-star. Wheelchair-accessible.

★**Villa Baccano**, Via Bosconi 4, t/f 055 59341, *www.villabaccano.it* (*inexpensive*). In the hills 2km out of the centre of Fiesole, in a lovely garden setting.

★**Villa Sorriso**, Via Gramsci 21, t 055 59027, f 055 597 8075, *www.paginegialle.it/ albergosorriso.01* (*inexpensive*). An unpretentious, comfortable hotel in the centre of Fiesole, with a terrace overlooking Florence.

**Le Cannelle**, Via Gramsci 52–6, t 055 597 8336, f 055 597 8292, *www.lecannelle.com* (*expensive–moderate*). A new, friendly B&B run by two sisters on the main street. Rooms are comfortably rustic and there is a pretty breakfast room.

## Villa Hotels in the Florentine Hills

If you're driving, you may consider lodging outside the city where parking is hassle-free and the summer heat is less intense.

### Luxury

★★★★★**Villa La Massa**, Via La Massa 6, t 055 62611, f 055 633102, *www. villalamassa.com*. A lovely choice, located up the Arno some 6km from Florence at Candeli. This is the former 15th-century villa of Count Giraldi, and retains the old dungeon (now one of two restaurants), the family chapel (now a bar), and other early Renaissance amenities, combined with 20th-century features like tennis courts, a pool and air-conditioning. The recently refurbished interiors are fit for a Renaissance princeling, there's dining and dancing by the Arno in the summer, a shady garden, and a hotel bus to whizz you into the city. Excellent restaurant.

★★★★★**Grand Hotel Villa Cora**, Viale Machiavelli 18–20, t 055 229 8451, f 055 229086, *www.villacora.com*. Near Piazzale Michelangelo is another luxury choice, an opulent 19th-century mansion set in a beautiful formal garden overlooking the Oltrarno. Built by Baron Oppenheim, it later served as the residence of the wife of Napoleon III, Empress Eugénie. Its conversion to a hotel has dimmed little of its splendour; some of the bedrooms have frescoed ceilings and lavish 19th-century furnishings – all are air-conditioned and have frigo-bars, and there's a pretty pool. In the summer meals are served in the garden, and there's a fine view of Florence from the roof terrace.

★★★★**Torre di Bellosguardo**, Via Roti Michelozzi 2, t 055 229 8145, f 055 229008, *www.torrebellosguardo.com*. In the 12th century a tower was built at Bellosguardo, enjoying one of the most breathtaking views over the city. It was later purchased by the Cavalcanti, friends of Dante, and a villa was added below the tower; after that, Cosimo I confiscated it, the Michelozzi purchased it from the Medici, Elizabeth Barrett Browning wrote about it, and finally, in 1988, it opened its doors as a small hotel. There are frescoes by Baroque master Poccetti in the entrance hall, and fine antiques adorn the rooms, each of which is unique and fitted out with modern bath. The large, beautiful terraced garden has a pool. For a splurge, reserve the two-level tower suite, with fabulous views in four directions. Superb formal gardens look down to the city below, and lunch is served around the pool.

### Very Expensive

★★★★**Paggeria Medicea**, Viale Papa Giovanni XXIII 3, Artimino, near Carmignano, t 055 871 8081, f 055 875 1470, *www.artimino.com*. You can play the Medici in the refurbished outbuildings of Grand Duke Ferdinand's villa, which has some unusual amenities – a hunting reserve and a lake stocked with fish, also a pool and tennis court, and pleasant modern rooms, many with balconies, all air-conditioned. A short walk across the gardens brings you to the restaurant Biagio Pignatta, which specializes in Medici dishes, in the former butcher's quarters.

★★★**Villa le Rondini**, Via Vecchia Bolognese 224, t 055 400081, f 055 268212, *www.villa lerondini.it*. Occupying several buildings in a pleasant setting 7km north of Florence, surrounded by olive and cypress trees. The most interesting rooms are in the 16th-century villa. There is a very pleasant pool.

★★★**Villa Villoresi**, Via Campi 2, Colonnata di Sesto Fiorentino, **t/f** 055 443212, *www.ila-chateau.com/villoresi*. Contessa Cristina Villoresi's family home is a lovely oasis (in the middle of one of Florence's more un-lovely suburbs), which hasn't been too pristinely restored, retaining much of its slightly faded appeal as well as its frescoed ceilings, antiques and chandeliers. The villa boasts the longest loggia in Tuscany, to which five of the best, and grandest, bedrooms have direct access. Other rooms are a good deal plainer and somewhat cheaper.

**Villa Poggio San Felice**, Via S. Matteo Arcetri 24, **t** 055 220016, **f** 055 233 5388, *www.villapoggiosanfelice.com*. A delightful alternative to city hotels, this is a 15th-century villa on a hill just south of Porta Romana, near the observatory. It was once owned by a Swiss hotel magnate, whose descendants have restored the house and gardens (designed by Porcinaie) and opened them up to guests. There are five double bedrooms, all furnished with family antiques, and all with stunning views. There is also a small pool. *Bed and breakfast only, closed Dec–Feb.*

## Moderate

★★★**Hermitage**, Via Gineparia 112, Bonistallo, **t** 055 877040, **f** 055 879 7057, *www.hotel hermitageprato.it*. Several miles from Florence, near Poggio a Caiano, this is a fine, affordable choice for families; there's a pool in the grounds and air-con rooms, not to mention gallons of fresh air and quiet.

# Eating Out

Like any sophisticated city with many visitors, Florence has plenty of fine restaurants; even in the cheaper places standards are high, and if you don't care for anything fancier, there will be lots of good red Chianti to wash down your meal. By popular demand, the city centre is full of *tavole calde*, pizzerias and snack bars, where you can grab a sandwich or a salad instead of a full sit-down meal (one of the best pizza-by-the-slice places is just across from the Medici Chapels).

Please note that many of the best places are likely to close for all or part of August; you would also be wise to call ahead and reserve, even a day or two in advance.

## Very Expensive

**Alle Murate**, Via Ghibellina 52r, **t** 055 240618, *www.caffeitaliano.it*. By the Bargello, this 'creative traditional' restaurant is elegant but relaxed, serving two set menus, one Tuscan and one different – spaghetti with sea bass, or pigeon stuffed with peppers and potatoes, or ducks' livers with ceps and rosemary. *Dinner only, closed Mon.*

**Cibreo**, Via dei Macci 118r, **t** 055 234 1100. One of the most Florentine of Florentine restaurants is close to the market of Sant' Ambrogio. The décor is simple – yet elegant – food is the main concern, and all of it is market-fresh. You can go native and order tripe, cockscombs and kidneys, or play it safe with prosciutto from the Casentino, a fragrant soup (no pasta here) of tomatoes, mussels and bell peppers, leg of lamb stuffed with artichokes, topped off with a delicious lemon *crostata*, cheesecake or a chocolate cake to answer every chocaholic's dream. Booking is essential. *Open Tues–Sat 12.50–2.30 and 7.30–11.15, closed Aug.*

**Don Chisciotte**, Via C Ridolfi 4r, **t** 055 475430. A small place between the Fortezza Basso and Piazza dell'Indipendenza, serving inventive Italian food with a particular emphasis on fish and vegetables. Let yourself be tempted by tagliatelle with scampi and asparagus, fresh tuna steak with an onion cream, warm fish salad. *Closed Aug.*

**Enoteca Pinchiorri**, Via Ghibellina 87, near the Casa Buonarroti, **t** 055 242777. One of the finest gourmet restaurants in Italy, boasting two Michelin stars. The owners inherited the wine shop and converted it into a beautifully appointed restaurant, with meals served in a garden court in the summer; the cellars contain some 80,000 bottles of the best Italy and France have to offer. The cooking, a mixture of *nouvelle cuisine* and traditional Tuscan recipes, wins prizes every year. Italians tend to complain about the minute portions. Prices are reckoned to be over €200 excluding wine, but the sky's the limit if you go for a more interesting bottle.

*Open Mon and Wed 7.30–10, Tues, Thurs–Sat 12.30–2 and 7.30–10, closed Aug.*

## Expensive

**Beccofino**, Piazza degli Scarlatti, t 055 290076, *www.beccofino.com*. On the river under the British Institute, you could almost be in London or New York once inside this trendy restaurant, but the food is decidedly Italian. Dishes are enhanced by a creative touch and are elegantly presented. Both fish and meat dishes are excellent and change with the seasons: octopus salad, pasta flavoured with courgettes and saffron, sea bass on a bed of truffle-flavoured mash, steak fillet with caramelized shallots, and a fabulous *bistecca alla fiorentina*. You can also eat a light meal in the wine bar where prices are considerably lower. *Closed Mon.*

**Buca Lapi**, Via del Trebbio 1r, t 055 213768. Located since 1800 in the old wine cellar of the lovely Palazzo Antinori, serving traditional favourites, from *pappardelle al cinghiale* (wide pasta with boar) and a *bistecca fiorentina con fagioli* that is hard to beat, downed with many different Tuscan wines. *Closed Sun and Mon lunch.*

**Coco Lezzone**, Via del Parioncino 26r (off Lungarno Corsini), t 055 287178. In old Florentine dialect, this means big, smelly cook, but don't let this unpromising name put you off. The atmosphere is informal and the food is classic Tuscan using the highest quality fresh ingredients. *Open Mon–Sat 12.30–2 and 8–10.30.*

**Oliviero**, Via delle Terme 51r, t 055 212421. Five minutes from the Piazza della Signoria, this has somewhat passé décor and a slightly bizarre clientele, but it also has excellent food, serving curiosities such as *gnudi di fiori di zucchini e ricotta* (ravioli stripped of its pasta coating with ricotta cheese and courgette flowers) and boned pigeon stuffed with chestnuts. *Eves only, closed Sun.*

**Pane e Vino**, Via San Niccolò 70r (in the Oltrarno, just in from Ponte alla Grazie), t 055 247 6956. This pleasant and informal place has a superb wine list, and very knowledgeable staff to go with it. The *menu degustazione* changes daily, and offers seven small courses; with any luck,

the superb porcini mushroom flan will be available. *Mon–Sat 7.30–midnight.*

**Ristorante Ricchi**, Piazza S. Spirito 8r, t 055 215864, *www.caffericchi.it*. This small fish restaurant has tables on magical Piazza Santo Spirito. Inside, the décor is contemporary and elegant, with tables lined up against the walls. The generous plate of *antipasto* is good and main courses include the catch of the day roasted on a bed of potatoes and tomatoes. There are a few meat dishes too. *Open Mon–Sat 8–10.30.*

**Targa**, Lungarno C Colombo 7, t 055 677377. From the rather dated ashes of Caffè Concerto has risen Targa with a re-vamped, more casual menu and a fresh approach to eating out. The space (a delightfully warm wood-and-glass room on the Arno) has not changed, but the food on offer is simpler (and a bit cheaper) while still providing a creative take on regional dishes such as crepes with talaggio cheese and artichokes, seared tuna fillet with braised leeks, rack of lamb with baby broad beans and asparagus. Save room for the sinful hot chocolate soufflé and choose a wine from a formidable list which includes labels from all of Italy and beyond. *Closed Sun and first 3 weeks in Aug.*

**Taverna del Bronzino**, Via delle Ruote 25–27r, t 055 495220. An elegant, traditional restaurant north of the Duomo, featuring plenty of Tuscan dishes – the *bistecca alla fiorentina* is succulent and tender – and delights like truffle-flavoured tortellini; there are several seafood choices for each course. *Open Mon–Sat 12.30–2.30 and 7.30–10.30, closed 3 weeks in Aug.*

## Moderate

**Angiolino**, Via Santo Spirito 57r, t 055 239 8976. It has lost some of its genuinely 'characteristic' qualities after renovation, but it's still a reliable place to eat Tuscan standards. The vegetable *antipasti* are especially good, and the simple *pollastrina sulla griglia* (grilled spring chicken) is succulent and tasty. *Closed Mon.*

**Antico Fattore**, Via Lambertesca 1/3r, t 055 288975, *www.anticofattore.it*. This traditional Florentine *trattoria*, popular with locals and tourists alike, suffered serious damage in the 1993 Uffizi bomb, but it is back in business now and serving excellent and reasonably priced local dishes. Try pasta with wild boar or deer sauce, *Il Fritto* (deep-fried rabbit, chicken and brains) and *involtini* with artichoke hearts. *Open Mon–Sat 12.15–2.45 and 7.15–10.30, closed 2 weeks in Aug.*

**Antico Ristoro di Cambi**, Via Sant'Onofrio 1r, **t** 055 217134. In the Oltrarno, some way to the west of the centre, is a place very popular with the Florentine *intellighenzia*. The food is genuinely Florentine, the classic soups – *ribollita* and *pappa al pomodoro* – are tasty and warming, and the *bistecca alla fiorentina* impressive. *Open Mon–Sat noon–2.30 and 7.30–10.30.*

**Baldovino**, Via Giuseppe 22r (Piazza S. Croce), **t** 055 241773. An excellent *trattoria*/pizzeria where you can eat anything from a big salad, filled focaccia or pizza (from a wood-burning oven) to a full menu of pasta, fish and steaks from the Val di Chiana. *Open Tues–Sun 11.30–2.30 and 7–11.30.*

**Buca Mario**, Piazza degli Ottaviani 16r, **t** 055 214179. Steep stairs take you down into one of Florence's traditional 'cellar restaurants'; a place full of Florentine atmosphere with a menu to match. The soups here are superb – *pappa al pomodoro* and *ribollita*, or you could try the tagliatelle with porcini. *Osso buco* is also excellent (cooked in tomato sauce, Florentine-style), and the *bistecca* is of the best quality. *Open Thurs–Tues 12.30–2.30 and 7.30–10.30.*

**Cavolo Nero**, Via dell'Ardiglione 22, **t** 055 294744. This little restaurant, tucked away in a side street near Piazza del Carmine, has quite a following among Florentine trendies. The interior is white on yellow with as many tables as possible crowded into the attractive room and there is a pretty garden at the back. The food is mainly Mediterranean with a twist (curried monkfish, rabbit with wild fennel), but there are also plenty of local standards such as spaghetti with clams. *Open Mon–Sat noon–2.30 and 8–11, closed 2 weeks mid-Aug.*

**Coquinarius**, Via delle Oche 15r, **t** 055 230 2153. You can eat or drink just about anything at this café/wine bar/restaurant. It is a useful stop off for a light meal or snack in the centre of tourist land. Snacks include a series of hot *crostoni* (toasted Tuscan bread with

various toppings) and various salads, but you can also order a pasta dish or a *carpaccio*. Wines by the bottle or the glass. *Open Sept–April daily 9am–11pm; May–Aug Mon–Sat 9am–11pm.*

**Finisterrae**, Via de' Pepi 3-5r, **t** 055 2638675. A great place to go if you are tired of *ribollita* and the typical *trattoria* look, Finisterrae serves food from Mediterranean countries from southern Italy and France to Greece, Turkey, Tunisia and Spain. The standard of the food is not always up to scratch, but the atmosphere is wonderful with a series of rooms decorated in the style of the various countries concerned. While you wait for a table, you can sip an *aperitivo* in the Moroccan-style bar and feast on excellent nibbles provided.

**Il Latini**, Via dei Palchetti 6r (by Palazzo Rucellai), **t** 055 210916, *www.illatini.com*. Something of an institution in Florence, crowded (prepare to queue; they don't accept bookings) and noisy but fun, where you eat huge portions of Florentine classics at long tables. Try one of the hearty soups followed by the *bistecca* or, more unusual, the *gran pezzo* – a vast rib-roast of beef. The house wine is good; try a *riserva*. *Closed Mon and all of Aug.*

**La Vecchia Bettola**, Viale Ariosto 32–34r, **t** 055 224158. A noisy *trattoria*, west of the Carmine, with great food; the menu changes daily, but you can nearly always find their classic *tagliolini con funghi porcini*. The grilled meats are tasty and succulent, and the ice cream comes from Vivoli. *Closed Sun and Mon.*

**Osteria Santo Spirito**, Piazza Santo Spirito 16r, **t** 055 238 2383. If there is no room at Borgo Antico, this is just a walk across the piazza. Sit outside and enjoy a choice of cold dishes, pastas (try the gnocchi with melted cheese infused with truffle oil), vegetarian dishes and more. The décor inside is unusual for Florence – warm red paintwork with contemporary lighting. *Open daily 12.30–2.30 and 7.30–11.30.*

**Sostanza**, Via della Porcellana 25r, **t** 055 212691. Just west of Santa Maria Novella is one of the last authentic Florentine *trattorias*, a good place to eat *bistecca*. One of their most famous dishes is the simple, but delectable, *petto di pollo al burro*, chicken breast sautéed in butter. *Open Mon–Fri 12.30–2 and 7.30–9.30*.

**Zibibbo**, Via di Terzollina 3r, **t** 055 433383. A wonderful restaurant serving traditional Tuscan fare but in a stylish, un-Tuscan setting (pink-varnished floorboards, contemporary furniture). Plenty of choice between meat and fish dishes; *pasta e fagioli*, delicious *spaghetti alle vongole*, *in zimino* (squid stew with Swiss chard), tripe *alla fiorentina*, *fricassée* of rabbit and pigeon wrapped in 'lardo' and cooked with prunes. Worth the trip up to the northernmost extremes of town. *Open Mon–Sat 1–3 and 8–11*.

## Cheap

**Aquacotta**, Via dei Pilastri 51r, **t** 055 242907. This restaurant, north of Piazza S. Ambrogio, is named for the simple but delicious bread soup, one of its specialities; you could follow that by deep-fried rabbit accompanied by crisply fried courgette flowers. *Open Mon–Sat 7.30–10*.

**Borgo Antico**, Piazza Santo Spirito 6, **t** 055 210437. Popular with a young trendy crowd, so you may have to wait for a table, especially in summer. Inside, the music can be unbearably loud, but the pizza is decent, and there are plenty of other choices – interesting pastas, big salads and more substantial meat and fish dishes. *Open daily 12.30–2.30 and 7.30–11.30*.

**La Casalinga**, Via Michelozzi 9r, **t** 055 218624. A family-run *trattoria*, also near Piazza Santo Spirito, and always busy, which is not surprising given the quality of the simple home cooking and the low prices. The *ribollita* is excellent. *Open Mon–Sat noon–2.30 and 7–9.45*.

**Trattoria Cibreo**, Via dei Macci 114, **t** 055 234 1100. A little annexe to smart Cibreo (*see* p.93), this is one of the best deals in town; the food is the same (excluding the odd more extravagant dish), but served in a rustic setting on cheaper porcelain – and your bill will be a third of that of those dining next door. *Open Tues–Sat 12.50–2.30 and 7.30–11.15*.

**Trattoria del Carmine**, Piazza del Carmine 18r, **t** 055 218601. A traditional, bustling *trattoria* in the San Frediano district, often

full. The long menu includes such staples as *ribollita*, *pasta e fagioli* and roast pork, but also features seasonal dishes such as risotto with asparagus or mushrooms, pasta with wild boar sauce and *osso buco*. *Closed Sun and 3 weeks in Aug*.

**Da Mario**, Via della Rosina 2r, **t** 055 218550. Mario's *trattoria*, located at the back of the central market, is always buzzing, and there is usually a queue for the few rather cramped tables; don't expect a table to yourself. The food is pure Tuscan, excellent and cheap; *ribollita*, *spezzatino con patate* (beef stew with potatoes) and mixed boiled meats with a deliciously pungent *salsa verde*. *Open Mon–Sat noon–2pm; cash only*.

**Il Pizzaiuolo**, near the Sant'Ambrogio market at Via dei Macci 113r, **t** 055 241171. One of the best, boasting a real Neapolitan pizza-maker, whose creations are puffy and light. There's lots more to choose from, but long queues. *Open Mon–Sat 12.30–3.30 and 7.30–1am, closed Aug*.

**Da Ruggero**, Via Senese 89r, **t** 055 220542. A tiny, family-run *trattoria* a little way from the centre of town; it's always full, so book. The traditional food is home cooked; try the excellent *pappardelle alla lepre* (with hare sauce) and good puddings. *Closed Tues and Wed, and 3 weeks July–Aug*.

**Sabatino**, Via Pisana 2r, **t** 055 225955. Just outside the old city gate of San Frediano, this simple, family-run *trattoria* feels as if it has always been this way. Cooking methods, too, are old-fashioned and suitably rustic, and prices are similarly retro. *Open Mon–Fri noon–2.30 and 7.30–10.30, closed Aug*.

**Santa Lucia**, Via Ponte alle Mosse 102r, **t** 055 353255. North of the Cascine there is a genuine Neapolitan pizzeria. It's a noisy, steamy and unromantic place but it makes up for its lack of glamour by serving what is possibly the best pizza in Florence, topped with the sweetest tomatoes and the creamiest *mozzarella di buffala*. *Open 7.30–1am, closed Wed and Aug; cash only*.

**Al Tranvai**, near the Carmine in Piazza Torquato Tasso 14r, **t** 055 225197. The two rows of tables in this cheerful little place are always full, and you may not get much elbow room. The menu changes daily, but the *crostini misti* are always on offer, and there's lots of offal: tripe, *lampredotto* (intestines), chicken gizzards etc. *Open Mon–Fri 7.30–10.30.*

There aren't many **vegetarian** restaurants as such in Florence, though non-meat eaters will find plenty of choice (pastas, risotto, etc.) to tempt them. Specifically **vegetarian** restaurants include:

**Ruth's**, Via Farini 2/A, **t** 055 248 0888. A new, bright and modern kosher vegetarian restaurant next to the synagogue, serving fish and Middle Eastern dishes. Try a *brick*, a savoury pastry, filled with fish, potatoes or cheese that tastes better than it sounds. *Open 12.30–2.30 and 8–10.30, closed Fri dinner and Sat lunch.*

**Il Vegetariano**, Via delle Ruote 30r, **t** 055 47030. Located to the west of San Marco; self-service with excellent fresh food including a wide choice of soups, salads and more substantial dishes. *Closed Sun lunch and Mon.*

## Restaurants Around Florence

**Biagio Pignatta**, Artimino, **t** 055 875 1406 (*expensive*). Near the Medici villa in Artimino and named after a celebrated Medici chef, this serves Tuscan dishes with a Renaissance flavour – such as pork fillet with prunes and *vin santo* – on a terrace overlooking vines and olives. *Closed Wed, and Thurs lunch in winter.*

**Bibé**, Via delle Bagnese 1r, **t** 055 204 9085 (*moderate*). A couple of kilometres south of Porta Romana, occupying an old farmhouse with a lovely garden (somewhat marred by its proximity to the road and mosquitoes). Try the *crespelle alla fiorentina* – crêpes filled with ricotta and spinach – and the roast meats, fried chicken and rabbit. Desserts here are creative and divine. *Open 12.30–2 and 7.30–9.45, closed Wed and Thurs lunchtime.*

**Centanni**, Via di Centanni, Bagno a Ripoli, **t** 055 630122 (*expensive*). An elegant restaurant to the east of Florence, set in an olive grove with a lovely terrace for warm weather. Dishes are along traditional lines – home-made pasta with pigeon or wild boar sauce, *bistecca*, deep-fried chicken or brains

– and there is an excellent wine list. *Closed Sat lunch and Sun.*

**Da Delfina**, Via della Chiesa, Artimino, near Carmignano, **t** 055 871 8074 (*expensive*). In the same village, this is worth the drive out for its enchanting surroundings, lovely views, the charming atmosphere and sublime cooking – home-made tagliatelle with a sauce made from greens, risotto with garden vegetables, asparagus, succulent kid and lamb dishes. Outdoor seating too. *Open Tues–Sat 12.30–2.30 and 8–10.30, Sun 12.30–2.30.* NB: *No credit cards.*

**Omero**, Via Pian de' Giuliari 11r, **t** 055 220053. The main reason for a trip to Omero's rustic restaurant a ten-minute taxi ride from the centre of town is the wonderful view from the picture windows over hills dotted with elegant villas, olive groves and cypresses; make sure you get a table in the top room. The typically Tuscan food is reliable without being exceptional while the atmosphere is old-fashioned and charming. *Closed Tues.*

## Cafés and *Gelaterie*

**Caffè Italiano**, Via Condotta 56r, **t** 055 291082. Right in the centre of town, a popular lunch time stop for locals who crowd in for the excellent hot and cold dishes. On two levels: downstairs for standing at the bar, upstairs for a longer sit. The atmosphere is old-fashioned, particularly in the tearoom upstairs. Newspapers are on offer for browsing.

**Caffè Ricchi**, Piazza Santo Spirito. A local institution. It continues to serve excellent light lunches and wonderful ice cream. The outside tables enjoy the benefit of one of the most beautiful piazzas in Florence, at a price. At *aperitivo* time (6pm–8pm) there's a great spread of 'free' nibbles to go with your Campari.

**Capocaccia**, Lungarno Corsini 12r, **t** 055 210751. Popular as a night spot as well as a day-time bar and café, Capocaccia enjoys a great location on the river beside the British Consulate. It opens at lunchtimes (except at weekends when it does a brisk brunch trade) for light meals and is great for an *aperitivo* with free nibbles in the evening or as an evening venue for music and drinks. *Closed Mon.*

**Dolci e Dolcezze**, Piazza Cesare Beccaria 8r, **t** 055 234 5438. East of Sant'Ambrogio market, this has the most delicious cakes, pastries and marmalades in the city – the *crostate*, *torte* and *bavarese* are expensive but worth every euro. It now has another shop at Via del Corso 41r. *Closed Mon*.

**Dolce Vita**, **t** 055 284595. Piazza del Carmine. This is the place where fashionable young Florentines strut their latest togs – a favourite pastime since the 14th century. *Closed Mon and 2 weeks in Aug*.

**Festa del Gelato**, Via del Corso 75r. Boasts over 100 variations of ice cream.

**Gelateria de' Ciompi**, Via dell'Agnolo 121r. This traditional Florentine ice cream parlour, tucked around the corner from Santa Croce, prides itself on its authentic home-made recipes, some of which are over 50 years old.

**Gilli**, Piazza della Repubblica 36–39r. Many of Florence's grand old cafés were born in the last century, though this one, the oldest, dates back to 1733, when the Mercato Vecchio still occupied this area; its two panelled back rooms are especially pleasant in the winter. *Open Wed–Mon*.

**Giubbe Rosse**, Piazza della Repubblica 13–14r. Famous as the rendezvous of Florence's literati at the turn of the last century; the chandelier-lit interior has changed little since.

**Il Granduca**, Via dei Calzaiuoli 57r. Yet another *gelato* option, with creamy concoctions that challenge those of nearby rival Perché No (Why Not). *Closed Wed*.

**Hemingway**, Piazza Piattellina 9r, **t** 055 284781 (*booking advised*). A beautifully appointed bar done out in pale blues with rattan furniture. You can enjoy teas and coffees, as well as cocktails, interesting light meals and an excellent brunch on Sundays. The owner is a chocaholic, so the hand-made chocolates and puddings are a dream. Try the *sette veli* chocolate cake. *Open weekdays 4.30–late, Sun 11–8*.

**L'Oasi**, Via dell'Oriuolo 5, near the Duomo. Sophisticated ice cream flavours, and a good choice of cakes.

**Il Triangulo delle Bermude**, Via Nazionale 61r. Has a superb choice of ice cream.

**La Via del' Té**, Piazza Ghiberti 22r. Looking on to the Sant'Ambrogio food market, this offers a huge range of teas to choose from plus sweet and savoury snacks.

**Perché No**, Via Tavolini 194. Arctic heaven near Via Calzaiuoli, with wonderful ice cream in 1940s surroundings.

**Rivoire**, Piazza della Signoria 5r. Florence's most elegant and classy watering hole, with a marble-detailed interior as lovely as the Piazza della Signoria itself. Terrace on the square.

**Vivoli**, Via Isola delle Stinche 7r, between the Bargello and S. Croce. Florence lays some claim to being the ice cream capital of the world, a reputation that owes much to the decadently delicious confections and rich *semifreddi* served here. *Closed Mon*.

## Wine Bars

Florence is full of wine bars, from new-generation places to simple 'holes in the wall'.

**Cantinetta dei Verrazzano**, Via dei Tavolini 18–20r. Part bakery (selling delicious bread and cakes), part wine bar, this centrally located place belongs to the Verrazzano wine estate and serves its own very good wine exclusively; sip it with a plate of mixed *crostini* at hand.

**Enoteca Baldovino**, Via San Giuseppe 18r, **t** 055 234 7220. A bright and cheerful wine bar down the northern side of Santa Croce with snacks and pasta dishes. There is a comprehensive wine list and plenty of wines by the glass. *Open daily but closed Mon in winter*.

**Enoteca dei Giraldi**, Via dei Giraldi. Near the Bargello, this hosts art exhibitions and runs wine-tasting courses as well as supplying excellent food and drink.

**Frescobaldi Wine Bar**, Vicolo dei Gondi (off Via della Condotta), **t** 055 284724. One of Tuscany's best-known wine-growing families recently opened this pleasant little wine bar, annexe to a full-blown (and very elegant) restaurant. The wines on offer are, naturally, all Frescobaldi produced on their estates in Tuscany and the rest of Italy; some are the result of joint ventures in California and Chile. Delicious snacks include cheeses and cold meats, or you can pop next door for dinner. *Closed Sun*.

**Fuori Porta**, Via Monte alle Croci 10r, **t** 055 234 2483, *www.fuoriporta.it*. Possibly the most famous of all, where there are some 600 labels on the wine list and dozens of whiskeys and grappas. Among the snacks and hot dishes on offer, try one of the *crostoni*, huge slabs of local bread topped with something delicious and heated under the grill. *Closed Sun*.

**Pitti Gola e Cantina**, Piazza Pitti 16, t 055 212704. A delightful little place situated bang opposite the Pitti palace, with a good choice of wines from Tuscany and beyond, snacks and other more substantial dishes, as well as a few outside tables. *Closed Mon*.

**Vini**, Via dei Cimatori 38r. A hole in the wall and one of the last of its kind in Florence, where you can join the locals standing on the street, glass and *crostino* in hand. *Closed Sun*.

**Le Volpi e l'Uva**, Piazza dei Rossi, t 055 239 8132. The knowledgeable and helpful owners specialize in relatively unknown labels, and snacks include a marvellous selection of French and Italian cheeses.

# Entertainment and Nightlife

Nightlife with Great Aunt Florence is still awaiting its Renaissance; according to the Florentines she's conservative, somewhat deaf and retires early – 1am is late in this city. However, there are plenty of people who wish it weren't so, and slowly, slowly Florence by night is beginning to mean more than the old *passeggiata* over the Ponte Vecchio and an ice cream, and perhaps a late trip up to Fiesole to contemplate the lights.

Look for listings of concerts and events in Florence's daily, *La Nazione*. The tourist office's free *Florence Today* contains bilingual monthly information and a calendar, as does a booklet called *Florence Concierge Information*, available in hotels and tourist offices. The monthly *Firenze Spettacolo*, sold at newsstands, contains a brief section on events in English, but the comprehensive listings (including anything from ecology and trekking events, film societies, clubs, live music, opera and concerts) are easy to understand even in Italian. The annual *Guida locali di Firenze* also gives listings. For all current films being shown in Florence, look in the local paper.

## Performance Arts

The opera and ballet season runs from September to Christmas and concerts from January to April at the **Teatro del Maggio Musicale Fiorentino**, and in the **Maggio Musicale** festival, which features all three, from mid-April until the end of June. There is usually more opera in July.

## Classical Concerts

Concerts are held mainly in the following venues:

**Teatro del Maggio Musicale Fiorentino**, Via del Corso 16, t 055 211158, *www.maggio fiorentino.com*. Symphony concerts, recitals, opera and ballet are all held at Florence's municipal opera house.

**Teatro della Pergola**, Via della Pergola 12–32, t 055 226 4316, *www.amicimusica.fi.it*. The excellent chamber music series held here, in the stunning 18th-century Teatro della Pergola, is promoted by the Amici della Musica.

**Teatro Verdi**, Via Ghibellina 99, t 055 212320, *www.teatroverdifirenze.it*. The red and gold Teatro Verdi is home to Tuscany's regional orchestra who perform there regularly from late Nov–May.

**Scuola di Musica di Fiesole**, Villa la Torraccia, San Domenico, Fiesole, t 055 597851, *www.scuolamusica.fiesole.fi.it*. One of Italy's best-known music schools promotes a series of chamber music concerts.

Many smaller events take place year-round in churches, cloisters and villas, with plenty of outdoor concerts in summer. Look out for posters: they are not always well publicized.

## Rock and Jazz Concert Venues

**Auditorium Flog**, Via M Mercati 24b, t 055 487145, *www.flog.it*. One of the best places in Florence to hear live music year-round, often hosting ethnic music events. Look out for the Musica dei Popoli festival in November.

**Teatro Verdi**, Via Ghibellina 99, t 055 212320.

**Tenax**, Via Pratese 46, t 055 308160, *www.tenax.org*. A spacious venue on the outskirts of town, which is very popular and so usually crowded. Stages lots of live rock concerts, with bands ranging from international names to local groups. DJs take over after the live music stops.

**Palasport**, Viale Paoli, **t** 055 678841, *www. boxoffice.it*. Big-name rock and jazz bands nearly always play at this venue in Campo di Marte, which seats 7,000.

**Saschall**, Lungarno Aldo Moro 3, **t** 055 650 4112, *www.saschall.it*. Risen from the ashes (not literally) of the old Teatro Tenda, this 3,000-seat venue plays host to all kinds of music (including musicals). See local press for details.

In the summer, there are lots of live music venues all over the city, many of them free, for when the Florentines move outdoors to cool off.

**Musicus Concentus**, Piazza del Carmine 14, **t** 055 287347, *www.musicusconcentus.com*. This venue brings big-name jazz performers in to Florence.

**Box office**, Via Alamanni 39, **t** 055 210804, *www.boxoffice.it*. A central ticket agency for all the major events in Tuscany and beyond, including classical, rock, jazz, etc.

## Cinemas

Summer is a great time to catch the latest **films**. English-language films are shown throughout the summer three evenings a week at the Odeon in Piazza Strozzi and open-air screens are erected in several venues in Florence with two different films in Italian each evening from mid-June until mid-Sept. Details appear in the local newspapers.

The following show original language (usually English) films:

**Odeon Cinehall**, Piazza Strozzi, **t** 055 214068, *www.cinehall.it*. Shows latest releases on Mon, Tues and Thurs.

**Spazio Uno**, Via del Sole 10, **t** 055 215634. Occasionally has original language films.

## Clubs

Many clubs have themed evenings; keep an eye out for posters or handouts or buy the listings magazine *Firenze Spettacolo*. Places are somewhat seasonal as well.

**Caffedecò**, Piazza della Libertà 45–46r. There's often live jazz here, in elegant Art Deco surroundings, where Florence's swells put on the dog. *Closed Mon.*

**Caffè La Torre**, Lungarno Cellini 65r, **t** 055 680643. A small club which hosts regular jazz and Latin events.

**Central Park**, Parco delle Cascine. In summer, possibly the trendiest place in Florence, full of serious clubbers dancing to live music on three dance floors. *Open Tues–Sat 11pm–4am.*

**"Ex-Mud"**, Corso dei Tintori 4. The old Mood club has been re-vamped and given an appropriate new name. Still a cool venue, it is located below ground in a cavernous basement with bar and decent dance space. *Open Wed–Sun 10pm–4am.*

**Full-Up**, Via della Vigna Vecchia 25r. Another possibility, with mirrored walls, disco lighting and dated music. *Open Tues–Sat 11pm–4am.*

**Girasol**, Via del Romito 1, **t** 055 474948. If it's Latin sounds you are into, head north of the city to Girasol for live bands and DJs who supply a good mix of Cuban, Flamenco, Brazilian, Caribbean and salsa rhythms. The space is small, so be sure to arrive early. *Open Tues–Sun 8pm–2.30am.*

**Jazz Club**, Via Nuova de' Caccini 3, **t** 055 247 9700. A small club, with regular live jazz.

**Lido**, Lungarno Pecori Giraldi 1. A small place in a pretty setting on the Arno, playing a wide variety of music to a mixed crowd. *Closed Mon.*

**Mago Merlino**, Via dei Pilastri 31r. A relaxed tearoom/bar with live music, theatre, shows and games.

**Maracanà**, Via Faenza 4. Try this for live music with a Latin feel – samba, mambo and bossanova. *Closed June–Aug.*

**Maramao**, Via dei Macci 79r. Slick and cool; the music ranges from acid jazz to hip-hop and house. *Closed Mon.*

**Rex Caffé**, Via Fiesolana 25r, **t** 055 248 0331. The number one winter hotspot until Universale opened its doors, featuring an unusual décor, tapas, music and dancing. *Closed June–Aug.*

**Rio Grande**, Viale degli Olmi 1, **t** 055 331371. A huge and hugely popular venue with an outside dancefloor in summer where the music is mostly Latin. *Open Tues–Sat (winter also Mon).*

**Soulciety**, Via San Zanobi 114b, **t** 055 830 3513. Popular with Florence's Senegalese community but otherwise a relatively little-known dance venue. It's a good alternative to the city's run-of-the-mill clubs and, with its Rococo décor, has an exotic feel to it. *Open Tues–Sun 11.30pm–4am, closed June–Sept.*

**Universale**, Via Pisana 77r, *www.universale firenze.it* A vast ex-cinema, with designer décor, a restaurant, several bars and a pizzeria, all accompanied by live music and a giant cinema screen. Fast becoming the hottest hang-out in town, these are chic, sleek surroundings for a chic, sleek crowd. *Open 7pm–3am, closed Mon and June–Sept.*

**Yab**, Via Sassetti 5r, **t** 055 215168, *www.yab.it.* Yab has been around for a long time, and so have some of the punters who hang out there – it is favoured by a decidedly older crowd. It has recently been completely redesigned and has a vast dance space and a great sound system. *Closed May–Sept.*

## Pubs

Irish pubs are big in Florence, and you will also find the odd English and Scottish version.

**The Fiddler's Elbow**, Piazza Santa Maria Novella 7r, **t** 055 215056. One of the original pubs in Florence, with some live music and an ex-pat atmosphere. A handy place to wait for a train, but otherwise a bit grim. Terrace on the piazza.

**James Joyce**, Lungarno B. Cellini 1r, **t** 055 658 0856. An Irish pub with literary pretensions, the James Joyce enjoys a pleasant location with a big garden near the river. Books and magazines are on hand for browsing.

**JJ Cathedral Pub**, Piazza San Giovanni 44r, **t** 055 280260. An almost authentic atmosphere prevails in this pub sitting in the shadow of the Duomo; try and get the sole table on the tiny terrace overlooking the cathedral itself.

**The Lion's Fountain**, Borgo degli Albizi 34r, **t** 055 234 4412. A nice place which also serves food until late.

**Il Rifrullo**, Via S. Niccolò 55r, **t** 055 234 2621. Year-round, an older pub/wine bar; probably the most popular of all and one of the first to attract people to the Oltrarno. There's no word for 'cosy' in Italian, but the Rifrullo does the best it can.

## Gay Clubs

There are a few gay clubs in Florence.

**Crisco**, Via Sant'Egidio 43r, **t** 055 248 0580. *Closed Tues.*

**Il Piccolo Café**, Borgo Santa Croce 23, **t** 055 200 1057. A tiny, friendly, arty bar. *Open daily from 5pm.*

**Silver Stud**, Via della Fornace 9, **t** 055 688466, *www.silverstud.it*. A new bar in the Oltrano. *Closed Sun.*

**Tabasco**, Piazza Santa Cecilia 3r, **t** 055 213000, *www.tabascogay.it*. Italy's first gay bar, opened in the 1970s.

## Summer venues

In the summer, nightlife in Florence moves out of doors and a series of venues open up between late May and mid-September in some of the city's squares and open spaces. A torrid Florentine summer evening is no time to sit indoors (unless there's air conditioning of course), and these venues usually incorporate food and drink and some kind of live entertainment. Admission is usually free.

**Le Murate**, Via dell'Agnolo, **t** 338 506 0253. Housed in the courtyard of a former prison, the Murate provides music and dancing, food, drink, film and live music.

**Parterre**, Piazza della Libertà. Club and live music venue.

**Piazza Santissima Annunziata**. Live music and dance, plus a bar and pizzeria, with the incomparable backdrop of Brunelleschi's loggia.

**Le Rime Rampanti**. A great spot overlooking the river above Piazza Poggi with a bar, snacks and live music and dancing.

## Discos

**Auditorium Flog**, Via M Mercanti 24b, **t** 055 490437. A favourite and usually packed student venue.

**Jackie O**, Via dell'Erta Canina 24. An old favourite for the 30ish crowd which includes a piano bar. *Closed Mon, Tues, Wed.*

**Space Electronic**, Via Palazzuolo 37, **t** 055 293082. A high-tech noise box. *Open daily.*

**Tenax**, Via Pratese 46, **t** 055 308160, *www. tenax.org*. Lots of live music – the current place to go in Florence, out near the airport. *Closed Sun–Wed and mid-May–Sept.*

*Fine balm let Arno be;*
*The walls of Florence all of silver rear'd,*
*And crystal pavements in the public way...*
14th-century madrigal by Lapo Gianni

*Magari!* – if only! – the modern Florentine would add to this vision, to this city of art and birthplace of the Renaissance, built by bankers and merchants whose sole preoccupation was making more florins. The precocious capital of Tuscany began to slip into legend back in the 14th century, during the lifetime of Dante; it was noted as *different* even before the Renaissance, before Boccaccio, Masaccio, Brunelleschi, Donatello, Leonardo da Vinci, Botticelli, Michelangelo, Machiavelli, the Medici...

*This city of Florence is well populated, its good air a healthy tonic; its citizens are well dressed, and its women lovely and fashionable, its buildings are very beautiful, and every sort of useful craft is carried on in them, more so than any other Italian city. For this many come from distant lands to see her, not out of necessity, but for the quality of its manufactures and arts, and for the beauty and ornament of the city.*
Dino Compagni in his *Chronicle* of 1312

According to the tourist office, in 1997, 685 years after Dino, a grand total of over seven million tourists (Americans, Germans, French and Britons are still the top four groups) spent at least one night in a Florentine hotel. Some, perhaps, had orthodontist appointments. A large percentage of the others came to inhale the rarefied air of the cradle of Western civilization, to gaze at some of the loveliest things made by mortal hands and minds, to walk the streets of new Athens, the great humanist 'city built to the measure of man'. Calling Florence's visitors 'tourists', however, doesn't seem quite right; 'tourism' implies pleasure, a principle alien to this dour, intellectual, measured town. 'Pilgrims' is perhaps the better word, cultural pilgrims who throng the Uffizi, the Accademia, the Bargello to gaze upon the holy mysteries of our secular society, to buy postcards and replicas, the holy cards of our day.

Someone wrote a warning on a wall near Brunelleschi's Santo Spirito, in the Oltrarno: *'Turista con mappa/alla caccia del tesoro/per finire davanti ad un piatto/di spaghetti al pomodoro'* ('Tourist with a map, on a treasure hunt, only to end up in front of a plate of spaghetti with tomato sauce'). Unless you come with the right attitude, Florence can be as disenchanting as cold spaghetti. It only blossoms if you apply your mind as well as your vision, if you go slowly and do not let the art bedazzle until your eyes glaze over in dizzy excess (a common complaint, known in medical circles as the Stendhal syndrome). Realize that loving and hating Florence at the same time may be the only rational response. It is the capital of contradiction; you begin to like it because it goes out of its way to annoy.

## History

The identity of Florence's first inhabitants is a matter of dispute. There seems to have been some kind of settlement along the Arno long before the Roman era, perhaps as early as 1000 BC; the original founders may have been either native Italics

# Florentine Duality

Dante's *Vita Nuova*, the autobiography of his young soul, was only the beginning of Florentine analysis; Petrarch, the introspective 'first modern man', was a Florentine born in exile; Ghiberti was the first artist to write an autobiography, Cellini wrote one of the most readable; Alberti invented art criticism; Vasari invented art history; Michelangelo's personality, in his letters and sonnets, looms as large as his art. In many ways Florence broke away from the medieval idea of community and invented the modern concept of the individual, most famously expressed by Lorenzo de' Medici's friend, Pico della Mirandola, whose *Oration on the Dignity of Man* tells us what the God on the Sistine Chapel ceiling was saying when he created Adam: '…And I have created you neither celestial nor terrestrial, neither mortal nor immortal, so that, like a free and able sculptor and painter of yourself, you may mould yourself entirely in the form of your choice.'

To attempt to understand Florence, remember one historical constant: no matter what the issue, the city always takes both sides, vehemently and often violently, especially in the Punch and Judy days of Guelphs and Ghibellines. In the 1300s this was explained by the fact that the city was founded under the sign of Mars, the war god; but in medieval astronomy Mars is also connected with Aries, another Florentine symbol and the sign of the time of spring blossoms. (The Annunciation, at the beginning of spring, was Florence's most important festival.) One of the city's oldest symbols is the lily (or iris), flying on its oldest gonfalons. Perhaps even older is its *marzocco*, originally an equestrian statue of Mars on the Ponte Vecchio, later replaced by Donatello's grim lion.

Whatever dispute rocked the streets, Great Aunt Florence often expressed her schizophrenia in art, floral Florence versus stone Florence, epitomized by the irreconcilable differences between the two most famous works of art: Botticelli's graceful *Primavera* and Michelangelo's cold, perfect *David*. The 'city of flowers' seems a joke; it has nary a real flower, nor even a tree, in its stone streets; indeed, all effort has gone into keeping nature at bay, surpassing it with geometry and art. And yet the Florentines were perhaps the first since the Romans to discover the joys of the countryside. The rusticated stone palaces, like fortresses or prisons, hide charms as delightful as Gozzoli's frescoes in the Palazzo Medici-Riccordi. Luca della Robbia's dancing children and floral wreaths are contemporary with the naked, violent warriors of the Pollaiuolo brothers; the writhing, quarrelsome statuary in the Piazza della Signoria is sheltered by one of the most delicate *loggie* imaginable.

After 1500, all the good, bad and ugly symptoms of the Renaissance peaked in the mass fever of Mannerism. Then, drifting into a debilitating twilight, Florence gave birth to the artistic phenomenon known as kitsch – the Medici Princes' chapel is an early kitsch classic. Since then, worn out perhaps, or embarrassed, this city built by merchants has kept its own counsel, expressing its argumentative soul in overblown controversies about traffic, art restoration and the undesirability of fast-food counters and cheap *pensioni*. We who find her fascinating hope she some day comes to remember her proper role, bearing the torch of culture instead of merely collecting tickets for the culture torture.

or Etruscans. Throughout the period of Etruscan dominance, the village on the river lived in the shadow of *Faesulae* – Florence's present-day suburb of Fiesole was then an important city, the northernmost member of the Etruscan Dodecapolis. The Arno river cuts across central Italy like a wall. This narrow stretch of it, close to the mountain pass over to Emilia, was always the most logical place for a bridge.

Roman Florence can claim no less a figure than **Julius Caesar** for its founder. Like so many other Italian cities, it began as a planned urban enterprise in an under-developed province – a colony for army veterans in 59 BC. The origin of the name – so suggestive of springtime and flowers – is another mystery. First it was *Florentia*, then *Fiorenza* in the Middle Ages, and finally *Firenze*. One guess is that its foundation took place in April, when the Romans were celebrating the games of the Floralia.

The original street plan of *Florentia* can be seen today in the neat rectangle of blocks between Via Tornabuoni and Via del Proconsolo, between the Duomo and Piazza della Signoria. Its forum occupied roughly the site of the modern Piazza della Repubblica, and the outline of its amphitheatre can be traced in the oval of streets just west of Piazza Santa Croce. Roman *Florentia* never really imposed itself on the historian. One writer mentions it as a major town and river crossing along the Via Cassia, connected to Rome and the thriving new cities of northern Italy, such as Bononia and Mediolanum (Bologna and Milan). At the height of the empire, the municipal bound-aries had expanded out to Via de' Fossi, Via S. Egidio, and Via de' Benci. Nevertheless, Florentia did not play a significant role either in the Empire's heyday or in its decline.

After the fall of Rome, Florence weathered its troubles comparatively well. We hear of it withstanding sieges by the Goths around the year 400, when it was defended by the famous imperial general Stilicho, and again in 541, during the campaigns of Totila and Belisarius; all through the Greek–Gothic wars Florence seems to have taken the side of Constantinople. The Lombards arrived around 570; under their rule Florence was the seat of a duchy subject to the then Tuscan capital of Lucca. The next mention in the chronicles refers to Charlemagne spending Christmas with the Florentines in the year 786. Like the rest of Italy, Florence had undoubtedly declined; a new set of walls went up under Carolingian rule, about 800, enclosing an area scarcely larger than the original Roman settlement of 59 BC. Most likely throughout the Dark Ages the city was gradually increasing its relative importance and strength at the expense of its neighbours. The famous baptistry, erected some time between the 6th and 9th centuries, is the only important building from that troubled age in all Tuscany.

By the 1100s, Florence was the leading city of the County of Tuscany. **Countess Matilda**, ally of Pope Gregory VII against the emperors, oversaw the construction of a new set of walls in 1078, coinciding with the widest Roman-era boundaries. The city had recovered all the ground lost during the Dark Ages, and the momentum of growth did not abate. New walls again in the 1170s enclosed what was becoming one of the largest cities in Europe. In this period, Florence owed its growth and prosperity largely to the textile industry – weaving and 'finishing' cloth not only from Tuscany but wool shipped from as far afield as Spain and England. The capital gain from this trade, managed by the *Calimala* and the *Arte della Lana*, Florence's richest guilds, led naturally to an even more profitable business – banking and finance.

## The Florentine Republic Battles with the Barons

In 1125, Florence once and for all conquered its ancient rival Fiesole. Wealth and influence brought with them increasing political responsibilities; the city often found itself at war with its neighbours. Since Countess Matilda's death in 1115, Florence had become a self-governing *comune*, largely independent of the emperor and local barons. The new city republic's hardest problems, however, were closer to home. The nobles of the county, encouraged in their anachronistic feudal behaviour by representatives of the imperial government, proved irreconcilable enemies to the new merchant republic, and Florence spent most of the 12th century trying to keep them in line. Often the city actually declared war on a noble clan, as with the Alberti, or the Counts of Guidi, and razed their castles whenever they captured one. To complicate the situation, nobles attracted by the stimulation of urban life – along with the opportunities for making money – often moved their families into Florence itself.

They brought their country habits with them: a boyish eagerness to brawl with their neighbours on the slightest pretext, and a complete disregard for the laws of the *comune*. Naturally, they couldn't feel secure without a little urban castle of their own, and before long Florence's skyline, like that of any prosperous Italian city of the Middle Ages, featured hundreds of tower-fortresses, built as much for status as for defence. Many were over 200ft in height. It wasn't uncommon for the honest citizen to come home from work hoping for a little peace and quiet, only to find siege engines in front of the house and a company of bowmen in the children's bedroom.

But just as Florence was able to break the power of the rural nobles, those in the town also eventually had to succumb. The last tower-fortresses were chopped down to size in the early 1300s. But even without the nobles raising all manner of hell, the Florentines managed to find brand new ways to keep the pot boiling. The rich merchants who dominated the government, familiarly known as the *popolari grossi*, resorted to every sort of murder and mayhem to beat down the demands of the lesser guilds, the *popolari minuti*, for a fair share of the wealth; the two only managed to settle their differences when confronted by murmurs of discontent from what was then one of Europe's largest urban proletariats. But even beyond simple class issues, the city born under the fiery sign of Mars always found a way to make trouble. Not only did Florentines pursue the Guelph–Ghibelline conflict with greater zest than almost any Tuscan city; according to the chronicles of the time, they actually started it. In 1215, men of the Amidei family murdered a prominent citizen named Buondelmonte dei Buondelmonti over a broken wedding engagement, the spark that ignited the factionalist struggles first in Florence, then quickly throughout Italy.

## Guelphs and Ghibellines

In the 13th century, there was never a dull moment in Florence. Guelphs and Ghibellines, often more involved with some feud between powerful families than with real political issues, cast each other into exile and confiscated each other's property with every change of the wind. Religious strife occasionally pushed politics off the front page. In the 1240s, a curious foreshadowing of the Reformation saw Florence wrapped up in the **Patarene heresy**. This sect, closely related to the

Albigensians of southern France, was as obsessed with the presence of Evil in the world as John Calvin – or Florence's own future fire-and-brimstone preacher, Savonarola. Exploiting a streak of religious eccentricity that has always seemed to be present in the Florentine psyche, the Patarenes thrived in the city, even electing their own bishop. The established Church was up to the challenge; St Peter Martyr, a blood-thirsty Dominican, led his armies of axe-wielding monks to the assault in 1244, exterminating almost the entire Patarene community.

In 1248, with help from Emperor Frederick II, Florence's Ghibellines booted out the Guelphs – once and for all, they thought – but two years later the Guelphs were back, and it was the Ghibellines' turn to leave. The new Guelph regime, called the *primo popolo*, was for the first time completely in the control of the bankers and merchants. It passed the first measures to control the privileges of the turbulent, largely Ghibelline nobles, and forced them all to chop the tops off their tower-fortresses. The next decades witnessed a series of wars with the Ghibelline cities of Tuscany – Siena, Pisa and Pistoia, not just by coincidence Florence's habitual enemies. Usually the Florentines were the aggressors, and more often than not fortune favoured them. In 1260, however, the Sienese, reinforced by Ghibelline exiles from Florence and a few imperial cavalry, destroyed an invading Florentine army at the **Battle of Monteaperti**. Florence was at the Ghibellines' mercy. Only the refusal of Farinata degli Uberti, the leader of the exiles, to allow the city's destruction kept the Sienese from torching it – a famous episode recounted by Dante in the *Inferno*. (In a typical Florentine gesture of gratitude, Dante found a home for Uberti in one of the lower circles of hell.)

In Florence, a Ghibelline regime under Count Guido Novello made life rough for the wealthy Guelph bourgeoisie. As luck would have it, though, only a few years later the Guelphs were back in power, and Florence was winning on the battlefield again. The new Guelph government, the *secondo popolo*, earned a brief respite from factional strife. In 1289, Florence won a great victory over another old rival, Arezzo. This was the **Battle of Campaldino**, where the Florentine citizen army included young Dante Alighieri. In 1282, and again in 1293, Florence tried to clean up an increasingly corrupt government with a series of reforms. The 1293 Ordinamenti della Giustizia once and for all excluded the nobles from the important political offices. By now, however, the real threat to the Guelph merchants' rule did not come so much from the nobility, which had been steadily falling behind in wealth and power for two centuries, but from the lesser guilds, which had been excluded from a share of the power, and also from the growing working class employed in the textile mills and the foundries.

Despite all the troubles, the city's wealth and population grew tremendously throughout the 1200s. Its trade contacts spread across Europe, and crowned heads from London to Constantinople found Florentine bankers ready to float them a loan. About 1235 Florence minted modern Europe's first gold coin, the *florin*, which soon became a standard currency across the continent. By 1300 Florence counted over 100,000 souls – a little cramped, even inside the vast new circuit of walls built by the *comune* in the 1280s. It was not only one of the largest cities in Europe, but certainly one of the richest. Besides banking, the wool trade was also booming: by 1300 the wool guild, the Arte della Lana, had over 200 large workshops in the city alone.

Naturally, this new opulence created new possibilities for culture and art. Florence's golden age began perhaps in the 1290s, when the *comune* started its tremendous programme of public buildings – including the Palazzo della Signoria and the cathedral; important religious structures, such as Santa Croce, were under way at the same time. Cimabue was the artist of the day; Giotto was just beginning, and his friend Dante was hard at work on the *Commedia*.

As in so many other Italian cities, Florence developed its republican institutions slowly and painfully. At the beginning of the *comune* in 1115, the leaders were a class called the *boni homines*, which was made up mostly of nobles. Only a few decades later, these were calling themselves *consules*, evoking a memory of the ancient Roman republic. When the Ghibellines took over, the leading official was a *podestà* appointed by the emperor. Later, under the Guelphs, the *podestà* and a new officer called the *capitano del popolo* were both elected by the citizens. With the reforms of the 1290s Florence's republican constitution was perfected – though it satisfied only a few citizens and guaranteed future trouble. Power was invested in the council of the richer guilds, the *Signoria*; the new Palazzo della Signoria was designed expressly as a symbol of their authority, replacing the old Bargello, which had been the seat of the *podestà*. The most novel feature of the government, designed to avoid the violent factionalism of the past, was the selection of officials by lot from among the guild members. In effect, politics was to be abolished.

## Business as Usual: Riot, War, Plagues and Revolution

Despite the reforms of the Ordinamenti, Florence found little peace in the new century. As if following some strange and immutable law of city-state behaviour, no sooner had the Guelphs established total control than they themselves split into new factions. The radically anti-imperial **Blacks** and the more conciliatory **Whites** fought each other through the early 1300s with the same fervour that both had once exercised against the Ghibellines. The Whites, who included Dante among their partisans, came out losers when the Blacks conspired with the pope to bring Charles of Valois' French army into Florence; almost all the losing faction were forced into exile in 1302. Some of them must have sneaked back, for the chronicles of 1304 record the Blacks trying to burn them out of their houses with incendiary bombs, resulting in a fire that consumed a quarter of the city.

Beginning in 1313, Florence was involved in a constant series of inconclusive wars with Pisa, Lucca and Arezzo, among others. In 1325, the city was defeated and nearly destroyed by the great Lucchese general **Castruccio Castracani** (*see* p.225). Castruccio died of a common cold while the siege was already under way, another instance of Florence's famous good luck, but unfortunately one of the last. The factions may have been suppressed, but fate had found some more novel disasters for the city. One far-off monarch did more damage to Florence than its Italian enemies had ever managed – King Edward III of England, who in 1339 found it expedient to repudiate his foreign debts. Florence's two biggest banks, the Bardi and the Peruzzi, immediately went bust, and the city's standing as the centre of international finance was gravely damaged.

One constant throughout the history of the republic was the oppression of the poor. The ruling bankers and merchants exploited the labour of the masses and gave them only the bare minimum in return. In the 14th century, overcrowding, undernourishment and plenty of rats made Florence's poorer neighbourhoods a perfect breeding ground for epidemics. Famine, plagues and riots became common in the 1340s, causing a severe political crisis. At one point, in 1342, the Florentines gave over their government to a foreign dictator, Walter de Brienne, the French–Greek 'Duke of Athens'. He lasted only for a year before a popular revolt ended the experiment. The **Black Death** of 1348, which was the background for Boccaccio's *Decameron*, carried off perhaps one-half of the population. Coming on the heels of a serious depression, it was a blow from which Florence would never really recover.

In the next two centuries, when the city was to stake its position as the great innovator in Western culture, it was already in relative decline, a politically decadent republic with a stagnant economy, barely holding its own among the changes in trade and diplomacy. For the time being, however, things didn't look too bad. Florence bought control of Prato, in 1350, and was successful in a defensive war against expansionist Milan in 1351. War was almost continuous for the last half of the century, a strain on the exchequer but not usually a threat to the city's survival; this was the heyday of the mercenary companies, led by *condottieri* like **Sir John Hawkwood** (Giovanni Acuto), immortalized in Florence's cathedral. Before the Florentines made him a better offer, Hawkwood was often in the employ of their enemies.

Throughout the century, the Guelph party had been steadily tightening its grip over the republic's affairs. Despite the selection of officials by lot, by the 1370s the party organization bore an uncanny resemblance to some of the big-city political machines common not so long ago in America. The merchants and the bankers who ran the party used it to turn the Florentine republic into a profit-making business. With the increasingly limited opportunities for making money in trade and finance, the Guelph ruling class tried to make up the difference by soaking the poor. Wars and taxes stretched Florentine tolerance to breaking point, and finally, in 1378, came revolution. The **Ciompi Revolt** (*ciompi* – wage labourers in the textile industries) began in July, when a mob of workers seized the Bargello. Under the leadership of a wool-carder named Michele di Lando, they executed a few of the Guelph bosses and announced a new, reformed constitution. They were also foolish enough to believe the Guelph magnates when they promised to abide by the new arrangement if only the *ciompi* would go home. Before long di Lando was in exile, and the ruling class firmly back in the seat of power, more than ever determined to eliminate the last vestiges of democracy from the republic.

## The Rise of the Medici

In 1393, Florentines celebrated the 100th anniversary of the great reform of the Ordinamenti, while watching their republic descend into oligarchy. In that year **Maso degli Albizzi** became *gonfaloniere* (the head of the Signoria) and served as virtual dictator for many years afterwards. The ruling class of merchants, more than a bit paranoid after the Ciompi Revolt, were relieved to see power concentrated in strong hands. In an atmosphere of repression and conspiracy, the Signoria's secret police hunted down malcontents while Florentine exiles plotted against the republic in foreign courts. Florence was almost constantly at war. In 1398 she defeated an attempt at conquest by Giangaleazzo Visconti of Milan. The imperialist policy of the Albizzi and their allies resulted in important territorial gains, including the conquest of Pisa in 1406, and the purchase of Livorno from the Genoese in 1421, but unsuccessful wars against Lucca finally disenchanted the Florentines with Albizzi rule. An emergency *parlamento* (the infrequent popular assembly usually called when a coming change of rulers was obvious) in 1434 decreed the recall from exile of the head of the popular opposition, **Cosimo de' Medici**.

Perhaps it was something that could only have happened in Florence – the darling of the plebeians, the great hope for reform, was also the head of Florence's biggest bank. The Medici family had their roots in the Mugello region north of Florence. Their name seems to suggest that they once were pharmacists (later enemies would jibe at the balls on the family arms as 'the pills'). For two centuries they had been active in Florentine politics; many had acquired reputations as troublemakers; their names turned up often in the lists of exiles and records of lawsuits. None of the Medici had ever been particularly rich until **Giovanni di Bicci de' Medici** (1360–1429) parlayed his wife's dowry into the founding of a bank. Good fortune – and a temporary monopoly on the handling of the pope's finances – made the Medici Bank Florence's biggest.

Giovanni had been content to stay on the fringe of politics; his son, **Cosimo** (known in Florentine history as **'il Vecchio'**, the 'old man'), took good care of the bank's affairs but aimed his sights much higher. His strategy was as old as Julius Caesar – the patrician reformer, cultivating the best men, winning the favour of the poor with largesse and gradually, carefully forming a party under a system specifically designed to prevent such things. In 1433 Rinaldo degli Albizzi had him exiled, but it was too late; continuing discontent forced his return only a year later, and for the next 35 years Cosimo would be the unchallenged ruler of Florence. Throughout this period, Cosimo occasionally held public office – this was done by lottery, with the electoral lists manipulated to ensure a majority of Medici supporters at all times. Nevertheless, he received ambassadors at the new family palace (built in 1444), entertained visiting popes and emperors, and made all the important decisions. A canny political godfather and usually a gentleman, Cosimo was also a useful patron to the great figures of the early Renaissance – including Donatello and Brunelleschi. His father had been one of the judges in the famous competition for the baptistry doors, and Cosimo was a member of the commission that picked Brunelleschi to design the cathedral dome.

Under Cosimo's leadership Florence began Europe's first progressive income tax, and invented the concept of the national debt – endlessly rolling over bonds to keep the republic afloat and the creditors happy. The poor, with fewer taxes to pay, were also happy, and the ruling classes were positively delighted; never in Florence's history had any government so successfully muted class conflict and the desire for a genuine democracy. Wars were few, and the internal friction negligible. Cosimo died in August 1464; his tomb in San Lorenzo bears the inscription *Pater patriae,* and no dissent was registered when his 40-year-old son **Piero** took up the boss's role.

## Lorenzo il Magnifico

Piero didn't quite have the touch of his masterful father, but he survived a stiff political crisis in 1466, when he outmanoeuvred a new faction led by wealthy banker Luca Pitti. In 1469 he succumbed to the Medici family disease, gout, and his 20-year-old son **Lorenzo** succeeded him in an equally smooth transition. He was to last for 23 years. Not necessarily more 'magnificent' than other contemporary princes, or other Medici, Lorenzo's honorific reveals something of the myth that was to grow up around him in later centuries. His long reign corresponded with the height of the Florentine Renaissance. It was a relatively peaceful time, and in the light of the disasters that were to follow, Florentines could not help looking back on it as a golden age.

As a ruler, Lorenzo showed many virtues. Still keeping up the pretence of being a private citizen, he lived relatively simply, always accessible to the concerns of his fellow citizens, who would often see him walking the city streets. In the field of foreign policy he was indispensable to Florence and indeed all Italy; he did more than anyone to keep the precarious peninsular balance of power from disintegrating. The most dramatic affair of his reign was the **Pazzi conspiracy**, an attempt to assassinate Lorenzo plotted by Pope Sixtus IV and the wealthy Pazzi family, the pope's bankers and ancient rivals of the Medici. In 1478, two of the Pazzi attacked Lorenzo and his brother Giuliano during mass at the cathedral. Giuliano was killed, but Lorenzo managed to escape into the sacristy. The botched murder aborted the planned revolt; Florentines showed little interest in the Pazzis' call to arms, and before nightfall most of the conspirators were dangling from the cornice of the Palazzo Vecchio.

Apparently, Lorenzo had angered the pope by starting a syndicate to mine for alum in Volterra, threatening the papal monopoly. Since Sixtus failed to murder Lorenzo, he had to settle for excommunicating him, and declaring war in alliance with King Ferrante of Naples. The war went badly for Florence and, in the most memorable act of his career, Lorenzo walked into the lion's cage, travelling to negotiate with the terrible Neapolitan, who had already murdered more than one important guest. As it turned out, Ferrante was only too happy to dump his papal entanglements; Florence found itself at peace once more, and Lorenzo returned home to a hero's welcome.

In other affairs, both foreign and domestic, Lorenzo was more a lucky ruler than a skilled one. Florence's economy was entering a long, slow decline, but for the moment the banks and mills were churning out just enough profit to keep up the accustomed level of opulence. The Medici Bank was on the ropes. Partly because of Lorenzo's neglect, it came close to collapsing on several occasions – and it seems that Lorenzo blithely made up the losses with public funds. Culturally, he was fortunate to be the nabob of Florence at its most artistically creative period; later historians and Medici propagandists gave him a reputation as an art patron that is entirely undeserved. His own tastes tended towards bric-a-brac, jewellery, antique statues and vases; there is little evidence that he appreciated the extraordinary talents of the great artists around him. Perhaps because he was too nearsighted to see anything clearly, he did not commission a single important canvas or fresco in Florence (except for Luca Signorelli's mysterious *Pan*, lost in Berlin during the last war). His favourite architect was the hack Giuliano da Sangallo.

Lorenzo was brought up with some of the leading humanist scholars of Tuscany for tutors and his real interests were literary. His well-formed lyrics and winsome pastorals have earned him a place among Italy's greatest 15th-century poets; they neatly reflect the private side of Lorenzo, the retiring, scholarly family man who enjoyed life better in one of the many rural Medici villas than in the busy city. In this, he was perfectly in tune with his class and his age. Plenty of Florentine bankers were learning the joys of country life, reading Horace or Catullus in their geometrical gardens and pestering their tenant farmers with well-meant advice.

Back in town, they had thick, new walls of rusticated sandstone between them and the bustle of the streets. The late 15th century was the great age of palace-building in Florence. Following the example of Cosimo de' Medici, the bankers and merchants erected dozens of palaces (some of the best can be seen around Via Tornabuoni), each with blank walls and iron-barred windows to the street. Historians always note a turning inward, a 'privatization' of Florentine life in this period. In a city that had become a republic only in name, civic interest and public life ceased to matter so much. The rich began to assume the airs of an aristocracy, and did everything they could to distance themselves from their fellow citizens. Ironically, just at the time when Florence's artists were creating their greatest achievements, the republican ethos, the civic soul that had made Florence great, began to disintegrate.

## Savonarola

Lorenzo's death, in 1492, was followed by another apparently smooth transition of power to his son **Piero**. But after 58 years of Medicean quiet and stability, the city was ready for a change. The opportunity came soon enough, when the timid and inept Piero allowed the invading King of France, **Charles VIII**, to occupy Pisa and the Tuscan coast. A spontaneous revolt chased Piero and the rest of the Medici into exile, while a mob sacked the family's palace. A new regime, under **Piero Capponi**, dealt sternly with the French and tried to pump new life into the long-dormant republican constitution.

The Florence that threw out the Medici was a city in the mood for some radical reform. Already, the dominating figure on the political stage was an intense Dominican friar from Ferrara named **Girolamo Savonarola**. Perhaps not surprisingly, this oversophisticated and overstimulated city was also in the mood to be told how wicked and decadent it was, and Savonarola was happy to oblige. A spellbinding revival preacher with a touch of erudition, Savonarola packed as many as 10,000 into the Duomo to hear his weekly sermons, which were laced with political sarcasm and social criticism. Though an insufferable prig, he was also a sincere democrat. There is a story that the dying Lorenzo called Savonarola to his bedside for the last rites, and that the friar refused him absolution unless he 'restored the liberty of the Florentines', a proposal that only made the dying despot sneer with contempt.

Savonarola also talked Charles VIII into leaving Florence in peace. Pisa, however, took advantage of the confusion to revolt, and the restored republic's attempts to recapture it were in vain. Things were going badly. Piero Capponi's death in 1496 left Florence without an able leader, and Savonarolan extremists became ever more influential. The French invasion and the incessant wars that followed cost the city dearly in trade, while the Medici, now in Rome, intrigued to destroy the republic. Worst of all, Savonarola's attacks on clerical corruption made him another bitter enemy in Rome – **Pope Alexander VI**, the most corrupt cleric who ever lived – who scraped together a league of allies to make war on Florence in 1497.

This war proceeded without serious reverses for either side, but Savonarola was able to exploit it brilliantly, convincing the Florentines that they were on a moral crusade against the hated and dissolute Borgias, Medici, French, Venetians and Milanese. The year 1497 was undoubtedly the high point of Savonarola's career. The good friar's spies – mostly children – kept a close eye on any Florentines who were suspected of enjoying themselves, and collected books, fancy clothes and works of art for the famous **Bonfire of Vanities**. It was a climactic moment in the history of Florence's delicate psyche. Somehow the spell had been broken; like the deranged old Michelangelo, taking a hammer to his own work, the Florentines gathered the objects that had once been their greatest pride and put them to the torch. The bonfire was held in the centre of the Piazza della Signoria; a visiting Venetian offered to buy the whole lot, but the Florentines had someone sketch his portrait and threw that on the flames, too.

One vanity the Florentines could not quite bring themselves to part with was their violent factionalism. On one side were the Piagnoni ('weepers') of Savonarola's party, on the other the party of the Arrabbiati ('the angry'), including the gangs of young delinquents who would demonstrate their opposition to piety and holiness by sneaking into the cathedral and filling Savonarola's pulpit with cow dung. A Medicean party was also gathering strength, a sort of fifth column sowing discontent within the city and undermining the war effort. Three times, unsuccessfully, the exiled Medici attempted to seize the city with bands of mercenaries. The Pisan revolt continued, and Pope Alexander had excommunicated Savonarola and was threatening to place all Florence under an interdict. In the long hangover after the Bonfire of Vanities, the Florentines were growing weary of their preacher. When the Arrabbiati won the elections of 1498, his doom was sealed. A kangaroo court found the new scapegoat guilty of heresy and treason. After some gratuitous torture and public mockery, the very spot where the Bonfire of Vanities had been held now witnessed a bonfire of Savonarola.

Pope Alexander still wasn't happy. He sent an army under his son, Cesare Borgia, to menace the city. Florence weathered this threat, and the relatively democratic 'Savonarolan' constitution of 1494 seemed to be working out well. Under a new and innovative idea, borrowed from Venice and designed to circumvent party strife, a public-spirited gentleman named **Piero Soderini** was elected *gonfaloniere* for life in 1502. With the help of his friend and adviser, **Niccolò Machiavelli**, Soderini managed to keep the ship of state on an even keel. Pisa finally surrendered in 1509. Serious trouble returned in 1512, and once more the popes were behind it. As France's only ally in Italy, Florence ran foul of Julius II. Papal and Spanish armies invaded Florentine territory and, after their gruesome sack of Prato, designed specifically to overawe Florence, the frightened and politically apathetic city was ready to submit to the pope's conditions – the expulsion of Soderini, a change of alliance and the return of the Medici.

## The End of the Republic

At first, the understanding was that the Medici would live in Florence as private citizens. But **Giuliano de' Medici**, son of Lorenzo and current leader, soon united the upper classes for a rolling back of Savonarolan democracy. With hired soldiers to intimidate the populace, a rigged *parlamento* in September 1512 restored Medici control. The democratic Grand Council was abolished; its new meeting hall in the Palazzo Vecchio (where Leonardo and Michelangelo were to have their 'Battle of the Frescoes') became apartments for soldiers. Soldiers were everywhere, and the Medicean restoration took on the aspect of a police state. Hundreds of political prisoners were tortured in the Palazzo Vecchio's dungeons, among them Machiavelli.

Giuliano died in 1516, succeeded by his nephew **Lorenzo, Duke of Urbino**, a snotty young sport with a tyrant's bad manners. Nobody mourned much when syphilis carried him off in 1519, but the family paid Michelangelo to give both Lorenzo and Giuliano fancy tombs. Ever since Giuliano's death, however, the real Medici boss had been not Lorenzo, but his uncle Giovanni, who in that year became **Pope Leo X**. The Medici, original masters of nepotism, had been planning this for years. Back in the 1470s, Lorenzo il Magnifico realized that the surest way of maintaining the family fortunes would be to get a Medici on the papal throne. He had little Giovanni ordained at the age of eight, purchased him a cardinal's hat at 13, and used bribery and diplomacy to help him accumulate dozens of benefices all over France and Italy. For his easy-going civility (as exemplified in his famous quote: 'God has given us the papacy so let us enjoy it'), and his patronage of scholars and artists, Leo became one of the best-remembered Renaissance popes. On the other side of the coin was his criminal mismanagement of the Church. Upper-class Florentines descended on Rome like a plague of locusts, occupying all the important sinecures and rapidly emptying the papal treasury. Their rapacity, plus the tremendous expenses involved in building the new St Peter's, caused Leo to step up the sale of indulgences all over Europe – disgusting reformers like Luther and greatly hastening the onset of the Reformation.

Back in Florence, Lorenzo Duke of Urbino's successor Giulio, bastard son of Lorenzo il Magnifico's murdered brother Giuliano, was little more than a puppet; Leo found enough time between banquets to manage the city's affairs. Giulio himself became pope in 1523, as **Clement VII**, thanks to the new financial interdependence between Florence and Rome, and now the Medici presence in Florence was reduced to two more unattractive young bastards, Ippolito and Alessandro, under the guardianship of Cardinal Silvio Passerini. Clement attempted to run the city from Rome as Leo had done, but high taxes and the lack of a strong hand made the new Medici regime increasingly precarious; its end followed after the sack of Rome in 1527. With Clement a prisoner in the Vatican and unable to intervene, a delegation of Florentine notables informed Cardinal Passerini and the Medicis that it was time to go. For the third time in less than a century, Florence had succeeded in getting rid of the Medici.

The new republic, though initiated by the disillusioned wealthy classes, soon found radical Savonarolan democrats gaining the upper hand. The Grand Council met and extended the franchise to include most of the citizens. Vanities were cursed again, books were banned and carnival parades forbidden; the council officially pronounced

Jesus Christ 'King of the Florentines', just as it had done in the heyday of the Savonarolan camp meetings. In an intense atmosphere of republican virtue and pious crusade, Florence rushed headlong into the apocalyptic climax of its history. This time it did not take the Medici long to recover. In order to get Florence back, the witless Clement became allied to his former enemy, **Emperor Charles V**, a sordid deal that would eventually betray all Italy to Spanish control. Imperial troops were to help subdue Florence, and Clement's illegitimate son Alessandro was to wed Charles' illegitimate daughter. Charles' troops put Florence under siege in December 1529. The city had few resources for the struggle, and no friends, but a heroic resistance kept the imperialists at bay all through the winter and spring. Citizens gave up their gold and silver to be minted into the republic's last coins. The councillors debated seizing little Catherine de' Medici, future Queen of France, but then a prisoner of the republic, and dangling her from the walls to give the enemy a good target. Few artists were left in Florence, but Michelangelo stayed to help with his city's fortifications (by night he was working on the Medici tombs in San Lorenzo; both sides gave him safe passage when he wanted to leave Florence).

In August of 1530, the Florentines' skilful commander, Francesco Ferruccio, was killed in a skirmish near Pistoia; at about the same time the republic realized that its mercenary captain within the walls, Malatesta Baglioni, had sold them out to the pope and emperor. When they tried to arrest him, Baglioni only laughed, and directed his men to turn their artillery on the city. The inevitable capitulation came on 12 August; after almost 400 years, the Florentine republic had breathed its last.

At first, this third Medici return seemed to be just another dreary round of history repeating itself. Again, a packed *parlamento* gutted the constitution and legitimized the Medici takeover. Again the family and its minions combed the city, taking back every penny's worth of property that had been confiscated from them. This time, however, was to be different. Florence had gone from being a large fish in a small Italian pond to a minuscule but hindersome nuisance in the pan-European world of papal and imperial politics. Charles V didn't much like republics, or disorderly politicking, or indeed anyone who might conceivably say no to him. The orders came down from the emperor in Brussels; it was to be Medici for ever.

## Cosimo I: the Medici as Grand Dukes

At first little was changed; the shell of the republican constitution was maintained, but with the 20-year-old illegitimate **Alessandro** as 'Duke of the Florentine Republic'; the harsh reality was under construction above the city's west end – the Fortezza da Basso, with its Spanish garrison, demanded by Charles V as insurance that Florence would never again be able to assert its independence. If any further symbolism was necessary, Alessandro ordered the great bell to be removed from the tower of the Palazzo Vecchio – the bell that had always summoned the citizens to political assemblies and the mustering of the army. In 1537, Alessandro was treacherously murdered by his jealous cousin Lorenzaccio de' Medici. With no legitimate heirs in the direct line Florence was in danger of falling under direct imperial rule, as had happened to Milan two years earlier, upon the extinction of the Sforza dukes. The assassination was kept secret while the Medici and the diplomats angled for a solution. The only reasonable choice turned out to be 18-year-old **Cosimo de' Medici**, heir of the family's cadet branch. This son of a famous mercenary commander, Giovanni of the Black Bands, had grown up on a farm; both the elder statesmen of the family and the imperial representatives thought they would easily be able to manipulate him.

It soon became clear that they had picked the wrong boy. Right from the start, young Cosimo had a surprisingly complete idea of how he meant to rule Florence, and also the will and strength of personality to see his commands carried out. No one ever admitted liking him; his puritanical court dismayed even the old partisans of Savonarola, and Florentines enjoyed grumbling over his high taxes, going to support 'colonels, spies, Spaniards, and women to serve Madame' (his Spanish consort Eleanor of Toledo). More surprising, when bowing and scraping Italians were everywhere else losing their liberty, Cosimo held his own against both pope and Spaniard. To back up his growing independence, Cosimo put his domains on an almost permanent war footing. New fortresses were built, a big fleet begun, and a paid standing army took the place of mercenaries and citizen levies. The skeleton of the old republic was revamped into a modern, bureaucratic state, governed scientifically and rationally as any in Europe. Early in his reign Cosimo defeated the last-ditch effort of the republican exiles, unreconstructed oligarchs led by the banker Filippo Strozzi, at the **Battle of Montemurlo**, the last threat ever to Medici rule. Cosimo's masterstroke came in 1557, when with the help of an imperial army he took the entire Republic of Siena. Now the Medicis controlled roughly the boundaries of modern Tuscany; Cosimo was able to cap off his reign in 1569 by purchasing the title of Grand Duke of Tuscany.

## Knick-knacks and Tedium: the Later Medici

For all Cosimo's efforts, Florence was entering a very evident decline. Banking and trade did well throughout the late 16th century, a prosperous time for almost all of Italy, but there were few opportunities for growth. More than ever, wealth was going into land, palaces and government bonds; the tradition of mercantile venture was becoming a thing of the past. For culture and art, Cosimo's reign turned out to be a disaster. It wasn't what he intended; indeed the Duke brought to the field his accustomed energy and compulsion to improve and organize. Academies were founded, and research underwritten. Cosimo's emphasis on art as political propaganda helped change the Florentine artist from a guild artisan to a flouncing courtier, ready to roll over at his master's command. The city had as great an influence in its age of decay as in its age of greatness. The cute, well-educated Florentine pranced across Europe, praised as the paragon of culture and refinement. Even in England – though that honest nation soon found him out:

*A little Apish hatte, couched fast to the Pate, like an Oyster,*
*French Camarick Ruffes, deepe with a witnesse, starched to the purpose,*
*Delicate in speach, queynte in arraye: conceited in all poyntes:*
*In Courtyly guyles, a passing singular odde man...*
                    *Mirror of Tuscanism*, Gabriel Harvey, 1580

Michelangelo, despite frequent entreaties, always refused to work for Cosimo. Most of the other talented Florentines eventually left for Rome or further afield, leaving lapdogs like **Giorgio Vasari** to carry on the grand traditions of Florentine art. Vasari, with help from such artists as Ammannati and Bandinelli, transformed much of the city – especially the interiors of its churches and public buildings. Florence began to fill up with equestrian statues of Medici, pageants and plaster triumphal arches displaying the triumphs of the Medici, sculptural allegories (like Cellini's *Perseus*) reminding us of the inevitability of the Medici and, best of all, portraits of semi-divine Medici floating in the clouds with little Cupids and Virtues. It was all the same to Cosimo and his successors, whose personal tastes tended more to engraved jewels, exotic taxidermy and sculptures made of seashells. But it helped to hasten the extinction of Florentine culture. Cosimo grew ill, abdicating most responsibility to his son **Francesco** from 1564 to his death 10 years later. Francesco, the genuine oddball among the Medici, was a moody, melancholic sort who cared little for government, preferring to lock himself up in the family palaces to pursue his passion for alchemy, as well as occasional researches into such subjects as perpetual motion and poisons – he received consignments of crates of scorpions every now and then. Despite his lack of interest, Francesco was a capable ruler, best known for his founding of Livorno.

Later Medici followed the general course established by other great families, such as the Habsburgs and Bourbons – each one was worse than the last. Francesco's death in 1587 gave the throne to his brother, **Ferdinando I**, founder of the Medici Chapels at San Lorenzo and another indefatigable collector of bric-a-brac. Next came **Cosimo II** (1609–21), a sickly nonentity who eventually succumbed to tuberculosis, and **Ferdinando II** (1621–70), whose long and uneventful reign oversaw the impoverishment of Florence and most of Tuscany. For this the Medici do not deserve much blame. A long string of bad harvests, beginning in the 1590s, plagues that recurred with terrible frequency as late as the 1630s, and general trade patterns that redistributed wealth and power from the Mediterranean to northern Europe, all set the stage for the collapse of the Florentine economy. The fatal blow came in the 1630s, when the long-deteriorating wool trade collapsed with sudden finality. Banking was going too, partly a victim of the age's continuing inflation, partly of high taxes and lack of worthwhile investments. Florence, by the mid-century, found itself with no prospects at all, a pensioner city drawing a barely respectable income from its glorious past.

With **Cosimo III** (1670–1723), the line of the Medici crossed over into the ridiculous. A religious crank and anti-Semite, this Cosimo temporarily wiped out free thought in the universities, allowed Tuscany to fill up with nuns and Jesuits, and decreed fantastical laws like the one that forbade any man to enter a house where an unmarried woman lived. To support his lavish court and pay the big tributes demanded by Spain and Austria (something earlier Medici would have scorned) Cosimo taxed what was left of the Florentine economy into an early grave. His heir, **Gian Gastone** (1723–37), was an obese drunkard, senile and slobbering at the age of 50. He had to be carried up and down stairs on the rare occasions that he got out of bed (mainly to disprove rumours that he was dead); on the one occasion he appeared in public, the chronicles report him vomiting repeatedly out of the carriage window.

As a footnote on the Medici there is Gian Gastone's perfectly sensible sister, **Anna Maria Ludovica**. As the very last surviving Medici, it fell to her to dispose of the family's vast wealth and hoards of art. When she died, in 1743, her will revealed that the whole bundle was to become the property of the future rulers of Tuscany – whoever they should be – with the provision that not one bit of it should ever, ever, be moved outside Florence. Without her, the great collections of the Uffizi and the Bargello might long ago have been packed away to Vienna or to Paris.

## Post-Medici Florence

When Gian Gastone died in 1737, Tuscany's fate had already been decided by the powers of Europe. The Grand Duchy would fall to **Francis Stephen**, Duke of Lorraine and husband-to-be of the Austrian Empress Maria Theresa; his troops had been installed in the Fortezza da Basso a year before. For most of the next century, Florence slumbered under benign Austrian rule. Already the first Grand Tourists were arriving on their way to Rome and Naples, sons of the Enlightenment like Goethe, who didn't stop because 'nothing in Florence could interest him', or relics like the Pretender Charles Edward Stuart, 'Bonnie Prince Charlie', who stayed two years. Napoleon's men occupied the city for most of two decades without making much impression.

After the Napoleonic Wars, the Habsburg restoration brought back the Lorraine dynasty. From 1824 to 1859, Florence and Tuscany were ruled by **Leopold II**, that most likeable of all Grand Dukes. This was when Florence first became popular among the northern Europeans and the time when the Brownings, Dostoevsky, Leigh Hunt and dozens of other artists and writers took up residence, rediscovering the glories of the city and of the early Renaissance. Grand Duke Leopold was decent enough to let himself be overthrown in 1859, during the tumults of the Risorgimento. In 1865, when only the Papal State remained to be incorporated into the Kingdom of Italy, Florence briefly became the new nation's capital. King Vittorio Emanuele moved into the Pitti Palace, and the Italian Parliament met in the great hall of the Palazzo Vecchio.

It was not meant to last. When the Italian troops entered Rome in 1870, Florence's brief hour as a major capital was at an end, but it had given the staid old city a jolt towards the modern world. In an unusual flurry of exertion, Florence finally threw up a façade for its cathedral, and levelled the picturesque though squalid market area and Jewish ghetto to build the dolorous Piazza della Repubblica. Fortunately, the city regained its senses before too much damage was done. Throughout the 20th century, Florence's role as a museum city was confirmed with each passing year. The Second World War allowed the city to resume briefly its ancient delight in black-and-white political epic. In 1944–5, Florence offered some of the most outrageous spectacles of Fascist fanaticism, and also some of the most courageous stories of the Resistance – including that of the German consul Gerhard Wolf, who used his position to protect Florentines from the Nazi terror, often at great personal risk.

In August 1944, the Allied armies were poised to advance through northern Tuscany. For the Germans, the Arno made a convenient defensive line, requiring that all the bridges of Florence be demolished. They all were, except for the Ponte Vecchio, saved in a last-minute deal, though the buildings on either side of it were destroyed to provide piles of rubble around the bridge approaches. After the war, all were repaired; the city had the Ponte della Trínita rebuilt stone by stone exactly as it was. No sooner was the war damage redeemed, however, than a greater disaster attacked Florence's heritage. The flood of 1966, when water reached 21ft, did more damage than Nazis or Napoleons; an international effort was raised to preserve and restore the city's art and monuments. Since then the Arno has been deepened under the Ponte Vecchio and 18ft earthen walls have been erected around Ponte Amerigo Vespucci; video screens and computers monitor every fluctuation in the water level. Should another flood occur, Florence will have time to protect herself. Far more insoluble is terrorism, which touched the city in May 1993, when a bomb destroyed the Gregoriophilus library opposite the Uffizi, damaged the Vasari Corridor and killed a family. Florence, shocked by this intrusion from the outside world into its holy of holies, repaired most of the damage in record time with funds raised by a national subscription.

Careful planning has saved the best of Florence's immediate countryside from post-war suburbanization – but much of the other territory around the city has been coated by a suburban sprawl that is not exactly attractive. A new airport extension is being built, which the Florentines hope will help make up some of the economic ground they've lost to Milan, and a whole new satellite city is planned – a new Florence ('Firenze Nuova'), nothing less than 'the greatest urban planning operation of the century', they say, with some of the old audacity of Brunelleschi. The buildings on the marshland (northwest of the city) have been demolished, the land flattened and the project for a new city to include housing, shops, leisure facilities, a new law court and a new Fiat factory (Fiat along with the insurance group, La Fondiaria, are the sponsors) is already under way, with some apartment blocks nearing completion. The law court building was actually started in 1999. Work is progressing and the main structure is up, but it will be a while before it's finished.

Meanwhile Florence works hard to preserve what it already has. Although new measures to control the city's bugbear – the traffic problems of a city of 500,000 that receives seven million visitors a year – have been enacted to protect the historic centre, pollution from nearby industry continues to eat away at monuments; Donatello's statue of St Mark at Orsanmichele, perfectly intact 50 years ago, is now a mutilated leper. Private companies, banks and even individuals finance 90 per cent of the art restoration in Florence, with techniques invented by the city's innovative Institute of Restoration. Increasingly, copies are made to replace original works. Naturally, half the city is for them, and the other half against.

# Piazza del Duomo

Tour groups circle the three great spiritual monuments of medieval Florence like sharks around their prey. Postcard vendors prey, and sax players play to a human carnival from a hundred nations that mills about the cathedral good-naturedly while ambulances of a medieval brotherhood dedicated to first aid stand at the ready in case anyone swoons from ecstasy or art-glut.

## The Baptistry

*Open Mon–Sat 12–7, Sun 8.30–2; adm.*

To begin to understand what magic made the Renaissance first bloom by the Arno, look here; this ancient, mysterious building is the egg from which Florence's golden age was hatched. By the quattrocento, Florentines firmly believed their baptistry was originally a Roman temple to Mars, a touchstone linking them to a legendary past. Scholarship sets its date of construction between the 6th and 9th centuries, in the darkest Dark Ages, which makes it even more remarkable; it may as well have dropped from heaven. Its distinctive dark green and white marble facing, the tidily classical pattern of arches and rectangles that deceived Brunelleschi and Alberti, was probably added around the 11th century. The masters who built it remain unknown, but their strikingly original exercise in geometry provided the model for all Florence's great church façades. When it was new, there was nothing remotely like it in Europe; to visitors from outside the city it must have seemed almost miraculous.

Every 21 March, New Year's Day on the old Florentine calendar, all the children that had been born over the last 12 months would be brought here for a great communal baptism, a habit that helped make the baptistry not merely a religious monument but a civic symbol, in fact the oldest and fondest symbol of the republic. As such the Florentines never tired of embellishing it. Under the octagonal cupola, the glittering 13th- and 14th-century gold-ground mosaics show a strong Byzantine influence, perhaps laid by mosaicists from Venice. The decoration is divided into concentric strips: over the apse, dominated by a 28ft figure of Christ, is a *Last Judgement*, while the other bands, from the inside out, portray the *Hierarchy of Heaven*, *Story of Genesis*, *Life of Joseph*, *Life of Christ* and the *Life of St John the Baptist*, the last band believed to be the work of Cimabue. The equally beautiful mosaics over the altar and in the vault are the earliest, signed by a monk named Iacopo in the early 1200s. New lighting installed in 1999 has vastly improved visitors' view of the ceiling.

To match the mosaics, there is an intricate tessellated marble floor, decorated with signs of the Zodiac; the octagonal space in the centre was formerly occupied by the huge font. The green and white patterned walls of the interior are remarkable, combining influences from the ancient world and modern inspiration for something new, the perfect source that architects of the Middle Ages and Renaissance would strive to match. Much of the best design work is in the **galleries**, partially visible from the floor. The baptistry is hardly cluttered; besides a 13th-century Pisan-style baptismal font, only the **Tomb of Anti-Pope John XXIII** by Donatello and Michelozzo stands out. This funerary monument, with marble draperies softening its classical lines, is one of the prototypes of the Early Renaissance. But how did Anti-Pope John, deposed by the Council of Constance in 1415, earn the privilege of a tomb here? Why, it was thanks to him that Giovanni di Bicci de' Medici made a fortune as head banker to the Curia.

## The Gates of Paradise

Historians used to pinpoint the beginning of the 'Renaissance' as the year 1401, when the merchants' guild, the Arte di Calimala, sponsored a competition for the

## Highlights of Florence

Florence's museums, palaces and churches contain more good art than perhaps any city in Europe, and to see it all without hardship to your eyes, feet and sensibilities would take at least three weeks. If you have only a few days to spend, the highlights will easily take up all of your time – the **Cathedral** and **Baptistry**, the paintings in the **Uffizi** (preferably not all in the same day) and the sculptures in the **Bargello**, which is more worthy of your brief time than the **Accademia**, where the rubbernecks pile in to see Michelangelo's *David*. Stop in for a look at the eccentric **Orsanmichele**, and see the Arno from the **Ponte Vecchio**, taking in some of the oldest streets in the city.

If your heart leans towards the graceful lyricism of the 1400s, don't miss the **Cathedral Museum** and the Fra Angelicos in **San Marco**; if the lush virtuosity of the 1500s is your cup of tea, visit the Pitti Palace's Galleria Palatina. Two churches on the edges of the centre, **Santa Maria Novella** and **Santa Croce**, are galleries in themselves; **Santa Maria del Carmine** has the restored frescoes of Masaccio. Devotees of the Michelangelo cult won't want to miss the Medici Chapels and library at **San Lorenzo**. Or head for the oasis of the **Boboli Gardens**. Finally, climb up to **San Miniato**, for the beautiful medieval church and enchanting view over the city.

Florence's 'secondary' sights are just as interesting. You could spend a day walking around old **Fiesole**, or 15 minutes looking at Gozzoli's charming fresco in the **Palazzo Medici-Riccardi**. The **Palazzo Vecchio** has more, but less charming, Medici frescoes. You can see how a wealthy medieval Tuscan merchant lived at the **Palazzo Davanzati**, while the **Museum of the History of Science** will tell you about the scientific side of the Florentine Renaissance; **Santa Trinita**, **Santo Spirito**, **Ognissanti** and the **Annunziata** all contain famous works from the Renaissance. The **Casa Buonarroti** has some early sculptures of Michelangelo; the **Archaeology Museum** has even earlier ones by the Etruscans, Greeks and Egyptians; the Pitti Palace's **Museo degli Argenti** overflows with Medicean jewellery and trinkets. Take a bus or car out to Lorenzo il Magnifico's villa at **Poggio a Caiano**, or to the other Medici garden villas: **La Petraia** and **Castello**, or Villa Demidoff at **Pratolino**.

There are two museums with 19th- and 20th-century collections to bring you back to the present: the recently expanded **Galleria d'Arte Moderna** in the Pitti Palace, and the **Collezione della Ragione**. There are two museums founded by Englishmen: the **Horne Museum** with Renaissance art, and the eccentric **Stibbert Museum** with everything but the kitchen sink. Strangest of all are the museums in **La Specola**, featuring stuffed animals and wax figures.

Most of the important museums, excluding the Palazzo Vecchio, are state-run and can be pre-booked. Call **t** 055 294883.

baptistry's north doors. The **South Doors** (the main entrance) had already been completed by Andrea Pisano in 1330 in the style of the day. Their 28 panels in quatrefoil frames depict scenes from the life of St John the Baptist and the seven Cardinal and Theological Virtues – formal and elegant works in the best Gothic manner.

The celebrated competition of 1401 – perhaps the first ever held in the annals of art – pitted the seven greatest sculptors of the day against one another. Judgement was based on trial panels of the Sacrifice of Isaac, and in a dead heat at the end of the day were the two by Brunelleschi and Lorenzo Ghiberti, now displayed in the Bargello. Ghiberti's more classical-style figures were eventually judged the better, and it was a serendipitous choice; he devoted nearly the rest of his life to creating the most beautiful bronze doors in the world while Brunelleschi, disgusted by his defeat, went on to build the most perfect dome. Ghiberti's first efforts, the **North Doors** (1403–24), are contained, like Pisano's, in 28 quatrefoil frames. In their scenes on the Life of Christ, the Evangelists, and the Doctors of the Church, you can trace Ghiberti's progress over the 20 years he worked in the increased depth of his compositions, not only visually but dramatically; classical backgrounds begin to fill the frames, ready to break out of their Gothic confines. Ghiberti also designed the floral frame of the doors; the three statues, of John the Baptist, the Levite and the Pharisee, by Francesco Rustici, were based on a design by Leonardo da Vinci and added in 1511.

Ghiberti's work pleased the Arte di Calimala, and they set him loose on another pair of portals, the **East Doors** (1425–52), his masterpiece and one of the most awesome achievements of the age. Here Ghiberti (perhaps under the guidance of Donatello) dispensed with the small Gothic frames and instead cast 10 large panels that depict the Old Testament in Renaissance high gear, reinterpreting the forms of antiquity with a depth and drama that have never been surpassed. Michelangelo declared them 'worthy to be the Gates of Paradise'. The doors (they're actually copies – eight of the original panels, restored after flood damage, are on display in the Museo dell' Opera del Duomo) have been cleaned and stand in gleaming contrast to the others. In 1996 copies of Andrea Sansovino's marble statues of Christ and John the Baptist (1502) and an 18th-century angel were installed over the doors. The originals had begun to fall to bits in 1974; they too are now in the Museo dell'Opera.

Ghiberti wasn't exactly slow to toot his own horn; according to himself, he planned and designed the Renaissance on his own. His unabashedly conceited *Commentarii* were the first attempt at art history and autobiography by an artist, and a work as revolutionary as his doors in its presentation of the creative God-like powers of the artist. In a typical exhibition of Florentine pride he also put busts of his friends among the prophets and sibyls that adorn the frames of the East Doors. Near the centre, the balding figure with arched eyebrows and a little smile is Ghiberti himself.

## The Duomo

*www.duomofirenze.it; open Mon–Wed and Fri 10–5, Thurs 10–3.30, Sat 10–4.45, Sun 1.30–4.45.*

For all its importance and prosperity, Florence was one of the last cities to plan a great cathedral. Work began in the 1290s, with the sculptor Arnolfo di Cambio in charge, and from the beginning the Florentines attempted to make up for their delay with sheer audacity. 'It will be so magnificent in size and beauty,' said a decree of 1296, 'as to surpass anything built by the Greeks and Romans.' In response, Arnolfo planned what in its day was the largest church in Catholicism; he confidently laid the foundations for an enormous octagonal crossing 146ft in diameter, then died before working out a way to cover it, leaving behind the job of designing the biggest dome in the world.

Beyond its presumptuous size, the cathedral of Santa Maria del Fiore shows little interest in contemporary innovations and styles; a visitor from France or England in the 1400s would certainly have found it somewhat drab and architecturally primitive. Visitors today often circle confusedly around its grimy, ponderous bulk. Instead of the striped bravura of Siena or the elegant colonnades of Pisa, they behold an astonishingly eccentric green, white and red pattern of marble rectangles and flowers – like Victorian wallpaper, or as one critic expressed it, 'a cathedral wearing pyjamas'. In the sun, the cathedral under its sublime dome sports festively above the dullish dun and ochre sea of Florence; in dismal weather it sprawls morosely across its piazza like a beached whale tarted up with a lace doily front.

The fondly foolish **façade** cannot be blamed on Arnolfo. His original design, only one-quarter completed, was taken down in a late 16th-century Medici rebuilding programme that never got off the ground. The Duomo turned a blank face to the world until the present neo-Gothic extravaganza was added in 1888. Walk around to the north side to see what many consider a more fitting door, the **Porta della Mandorla** crowned with an Assumption of the Virgin in an almond-shaped frame (hence 'Mandorla'), made by Nanni di Banco in 1420.

## Brunelleschi's Dome

*Open Mon–Fri 8.30–7, Sat 8.30–5.40; adm.*

Brunelleschi's dome, more than any landmark, makes Florence Florence. Many have noted how the dome repeats the rhythm of the surrounding hills, echoing them with its height and beauty; from those city streets fortunate enough to have a clear view, it rises among the clouds with all the confident mastery, proportions and perfect form that characterize the highest aspirations of the Renaissance. But if it seems miraculous, it certainly isn't divine; unlike the dome of the Hagia Sophia, suspended from heaven by a golden chain, Florence's was made by man.

Losing the competition for the baptistry doors was a bitter disappointment to Filippo Brunelleschi. His reaction was typically Florentine: not content with being the second-best sculptor, he turned his talents to a field where he thought no one could beat him, launching himself into a study of architecture and engineering, visiting Rome and probably Ravenna to snatch secrets from the ancients. When proposals were solicited for the cathedral's dome in 1418, he was ready with a brilliant *tour de force*. Not only would he build the biggest, most beautiful dome of the time, but he would do it without any expensive supports while work was in progress, making use of a cantilevered system of bricks that could support itself while it ascended.

Brunelleschi studied, then surpassed the technique of the ancients. To the Florentines, who could have invented the slogan 'form follows function' for their own tastes in building, it must have come as a revelation: the most logical way of covering the space was a work of perfect beauty. Brunelleschi's dome put a crown on the achievements of Florence. After 500 years it is still the city's pride and symbol.

The best way to appreciate Brunelleschi's genius is by touring inside the two concentric shells of the dome (*see* over), but before entering, note the eight marble ribs that define its octagonal shape; hidden inside are the three huge stone chains that bind them together. Work on the balcony around the base of the dome, designed by Giuliano da Sangallo, was halted in 1515 after Michelangelo commented that it resembled a cricket's cage. As for the lantern, the Florentines were famous for their fondness and admiration for Doubting Thomas, and here they showed why. Even though they marvelled at the dome, they still doubted that Brunelleschi could construct a proper lantern, and forced him to submit to yet another competition. He died before it was begun, and it was completed to his design by Michelozzo.

## The Interior

After the façade, the austerity of the Duomo interior is startling. There is plenty of room – contemporary writers mention 10,000 souls packed inside to hear Savonarola's sermons. But, the Duomo hardly seems a religious building – more a *Florentine* building, with simple arches and counterpoint of grey stone and white plaster, full of old familiar Florentine things. Near the entrance, on the right-hand side, are busts of Brunelleschi and Giotto. On the left wall, posed inconspicuously, are the two most conspicuous monuments to private individuals ever erected by the Florentine Republic. The one on the right, is to **Sir John Hawkwood**, the English *condottiere* whose name the Italians mangled to Giovanni Acuto, a commander who served Florence for many years and is perhaps best known to English speakers as the hero of *The White Company* by Sir Arthur Conan Doyle. Hawkwood had the Florentines' promise to build him an equestrian statue after his death; it was a typical Florentine trick to pinch pennies and cheat a dead man, but they hired the greatest master of perspective, Paolo Uccello, to make a fresco that looked like a statue (1436). Twenty years later, they pulled the same trick again, commissioning Andrea del Castagno to paint the non-existent equestrian statue of another *condottiere*, Niccolò da Tolentino. A little further down, Florence commemorates its own secular scripture with Michelino's well-known fresco of Dante, a vision of the poet and his *Paradiso* outside the walls of Florence. Two singular icons of Florence's fascination with science stand at opposite ends of the building: behind the west front, a bizarre clock painted by Uccello, and in the pavement of the left apse, a gnomon fixed by the astronomer Toscanelli in 1475. A beam of sunlight strikes it every year at the summer solstice.

For building the great dome, Brunelleschi was accorded a special honour – he is one of the few Florentines to be buried in the cathedral. His tomb may be seen in the **Excavations of Santa Reparata** (*the stairway descending on the right of the nave; open Mon–Sat 10–5; adm*). Arnolfo di Cambio's cathedral was constructed on the ruins of the ancient church of Santa Reparata, which lay forgotten until 1965. Excavations have revealed not only the palaeo-Christian church and its several reconstructions, but also the remains of its Roman predecessor – a rather confusing muddle of walls that have been tidied up in an ambience that resembles an archaeological shopping centre. A coloured model helps explain what is what, and glass cases display items found in the dig, including the spurs of Giovanni de' Medici, who was buried here in 1351. In the ancient crypt of Santa Reparata are 13th-century tomb slabs, and in another section there's a fine pre-Romanesque mosaic pavement.

There is surprisingly little religious art – the Florentines for reasons of their own have carted most of it off into the Cathedral Museum (*see* opposite). Under the dome are the entrances to the two sacristies, with terracotta lunettes, over the doors, by Luca della Robbia; the scene of the Resurrection over the north sacristy is one of his earliest and best works. He also did the bronze doors beneath it, with tiny portraits on the handles of Lorenzo il Magnifico and his brother Giuliano de' Medici, targets of the Pazzi conspiracy in 1478. In the middle apse, there is a beautiful bronze urn by Ghiberti containing relics of the Florentine St Zenobius. The only conventional religious decorations are the frescoes some 200ft up in the dome, mostly by Vasari. As you stand squinting at them, try not to think that the cupola weighs around 25,000 tons.

A door on the left aisle near the Dante fresco leads up into the **dome** (*open Mon–Fri 8.30–7 and Sat 8.30–5.40; adm*). The complicated network of stairs and walks between the inner and outer domes (not too difficult, if occasionally claustrophobic and vertiginous) was designed by Brunelleschi, and offers an insight on how thoroughly the architect thought out the problems of the dome's construction, even inserting hooks to hold up scaffolding for future cleaning or repairs; Brunelleschi installed restaurants to save workers the trouble of descending for meals. There is also no better place to get an idea of the dome's scale; the walls of the inner dome are 13ft thick, and those of the outer dome 6ft. These give the dome enough strength and support to preclude the need for further buttressing.

From the gallery of the dome you can get a good look at the lovely **stained glass** by Uccello, Donatello, Ghiberti and Castagno, in the seven circular windows, or *occhi*, made during the construction of the dome, which are being restored one by one. Further up, the views through the small windows offer tantalizing hints of the breathtaking panorama from the marble lantern at the top. The bronze ball at the very top was added by Verrocchio, and can hold almost a dozen people when open.

## Giotto's Campanile

The dome steals the show, putting one of Italy's most beautiful bell towers in the shade both figuratively and literally. The dome's great size – 366ft to the bronze ball – makes the campanile look small, though 280ft is not exactly tiny. Giotto was made director of the cathedral works in 1334, and his basic design was completed after his death (1337) by Andrea Pisano and Francesco Talenti. It is difficult to say whether they were entirely faithful to the plan. Giotto was an artist, not an engineer. After he died, his successors realized the thing, then only 40ft high, was about to tumble over, a problem they overcame by doubling the thickness of the walls.

Besides its lovely form, the green, pink and white campanile's major fame rests with Pisano and Talenti's **sculptural reliefs** – a veritable encyclopaedia of the medieval world view with prophets, saints and sibyls, allegories of the planets, virtues and sacraments, the liberal arts and industries (the artist's craft is fittingly symbolized by a winged figure of Daedalus). All of these are copies of the originals now in the Cathedral Museum. If you can take another 400 steps or so, the **terrace** on top (*open daily 8.30–7.30; adm*) offers a slightly different view of Florence and of the cathedral itself.

## Loggia del Bigallo

The most striking secular building on the Piazza del Duomo is the Loggia del Bigallo, south of the baptistry near the beginning of Via de' Calzaiuoli. This 14th-century porch was built for one of Florence's great charitable confraternities, the Misericordia which still has its headquarters across the street and operates the ambulances parked in front; in the 13th and 14th centuries members courageously nursed and buried victims of the plague. The Loggia itself originally served as a lost and found office for children; if unclaimed after three days they were sent to foster homes.

East of the Loggia del Bigallo is a stone bench labelled the 'Sasso di Dante' – **Dante's Stone** – where the poet would sit and take the air, observing his fellow citizens and watching the construction of the cathedral.

## Museo dell'Opera del Duomo

*www.duomofirenze.it; open Mon–Sat 9–7.30, Sun 9–1.40; adm.*

The Cathedral Museum (Piazza del Duomo 9, near the central apse) is one of Florence's finest, and houses both relics from the construction of the cathedral and the masterpieces that once adorned it. It reopened in early 2000 after major restructuring to improve the layout and make it more visitor-friendly: there is now full disabled access, better information, a more logical layout, in a more or less chronological order, and greatly increased floor space. The courtyard has been covered by a glass roof and turned into an exhibition room; and there are long-term plans to incorporate a neighbouring 18th-century theatre into the museum, which has been closed for several centuries and was most recently used as a garage. Restoration work should be finished by 2007 when the museum will have doubled in size.

The entrance leads into the new ticket hall – pristine in marble and stone, the same materials used in the Duomo's construction – and past the bookshop. Just after the entrance are several fragments of Roman reliefs, then two anterooms which contain restored statues or bits of statues that once adorned the façade of the Duomo.

The first hall is devoted to the cathedral's sculptor-architect Arnolfo di Cambio and contains the statues he made to adorn it: the unusual Madonna with the glass eyes, Florence's old patron saints, Reparata and Zenobius, and nasty old Boniface VIII, who sits stiffly on his throne like an Egyptian god. There are the four Evangelists, including a St John by Donatello, and a small collection of ancient works – Roman sarcophagi and an Etruscan cippus carved with dancers. Note the 16th-century 'Libretto', a fold-out display case of saintly odds and ends. The Florentines were never enthusiastic about the worship of relics, and long ago they shipped San Girolamo's jawbone, John the Baptist's index finger and St Philip's arm across the street to this museum.

A nearby room contains a collection of altarpieces, triptychs and paintings of saints including Giovanni del Biondo's *Saint Sebastian*. Also here are a series of marble relief panels by Baccio Bandinelli from the altarpiece of the cathedral. A small room next to this contains a section (several fragments pieced together) of the door known as the 'Porta della Mandorla' on the north side of the Duomo. This is an intricately carved marble relief, including a small figure of Hercules with his stick, significant in that it was the first representation of the adult male nude and a taste of things to come, more of a statue than a relief. Also in this room are two statues known as *The Profetini*, which once stood over the door and are attributed to the young Donatello.

On the landing of the stairs stands the *Pietà* that Michelangelo intended for his own tomb. The artist, increasingly cantankerous in his old age, became exasperated with this complex work and took a hammer to Christ's arm – the first known instance of an artist vandalizing his own creation. His assistant repaired the damage and finished part of the figures of Christ and Mary Magdalene. According to Vasari, the hooded figure of Nicodemus is a self-portrait.

Upstairs, the first room is dominated by the two **Cantorie**, two marble choir balconies with exquisite bas-reliefs, made in the 1430s by Luca della Robbia and Donatello. Both rank among the Renaissance's greatest works. Della Robbia's delightful horde of children dancing, singing and playing instruments is a truly angelic choir, Apollonian in its calm and beauty. It is perhaps the most charming work ever to have been inspired by the forms of antiquity. Donatello's *putti*, by contrast, dance, or rather race, through their quattrocento decorative motifs with fiendish Dionysian frenzy. Grey and weathered prophets by Donatello and others stand along the white walls. These originally adorned the façade of the campanile. According to Vasari, while carving the most famous of these, *Habbakuk* (better known as *lo Zuccone*, or 'baldy'), Donatello would mutter under his breath 'Speak, damn you. Speak!' The next room contains the original panels on the Spiritual Progress of Man from Giotto's campanile, made by Andrea Pisano.

The first thing you see as you enter the last room is Donatello's statue *Mary Magdalene*, surely one of the most jarring figures ever sculpted, ravaged by her own piety and penance, her sunken eyes fixed on a point beyond this vale of tears. This room is dedicated to works removed from the baptistry, especially the lavish silver altar (14th–15th-century), made by Florentine goldsmiths, portraying scenes from the life of the Baptist. Antonio Pollaiuolo used the same subject to design the 27 needle-work panels that once were part of the priest's vestments. There are two 12th-century Byzantine mosaic miniature masterpieces, and a St Sebastian triptych by Giovanni del Biondo that may well be the record for arrows; the poor saint looks like a hedgehog.

A ramp leads into the new part of the museum from the room containing the panels from the campanile. Cases either side display the collection of pulleys and instruments used in the construction of the cathedral. At the bottom of the ramp on the left is Brunelleschi's death mask, facing a model of the lantern, which he was never to see. A window behind this model cleverly gives a close-up view of the cupola itself, which is topped by that self-same lantern.

A series of rooms off a long corridor contain bits and pieces brought out of storage, including the four carved façades, artists' models for the design of the cricket's-cage pattern round the base of the cupola. The corridor leads into a room whose walls are filled with drawings of the Duomo from the 1875 competition to design the façade.

From here, a staircase leads down into the courtyard where eight of Ghiberti's panels from the *Gates of Paradise* are on display. The plan is still to reconstruct the doors and their cornice once the latter and the last two panels are restored. It will be placed in the new space next door to the museum by 2007.

# Via de' Calzaiuoli and Piazza della Repubblica

Of all the streets that radiate from the Piazza del Duomo, most people almost intuitively turn down the straight, pedestrian-only Via de' Calzaiuoli, the Roman street that became the main thoroughfare of medieval Florence, linking the city's religious centre with the Piazza della Signoria. Widening of this 'Street of the Shoemakers' in the 1840s has destroyed much of its medieval character, and the only shoe shops to be seen are designer-label. Its fate seems benign, though, compared with what happened to the Mercato Vecchio, in the fit of post-Risorgimento 'progress' that converted it into the **Piazza della Repubblica**, a block to the right along Via Speziali.

On the map, it's easy to pick out the small rectangle of narrow, straight streets around Piazza della Repubblica; these remain unchanged from the little *castrum* of Roman days. At its centre, the old forum deteriorated through the Dark Ages into a shabby market square and the Jewish ghetto, a densely populated quarter known as the Mercato Vecchio, the epitome of the picturesque for 19th-century tourists but an eyesore for the movers and shakers of the new Italy, who tore it down. They erected a triumphal arch to themselves and proudly blazoned it with the inscription 'THE ANCIENT CITY CENTRE RESTORED TO NEW LIFE FROM THE SQUALOR OF CENTURIES'. The sad result, the Piazza della Repubblica, is one of the most ghastly squares in Italy, a brash intrusion of ponderous 19th-century buildings. Just the same, it is popular with locals and tourists alike, closed to traffic and full of outdoor cafés, something of an oasis among the narrow, stern streets of medieval Florence.

From Piazza della Repubblica the natural flow of street life will sweep you down to the **Mercato Nuovo**, the old Straw Market, bustling under a beautiful loggia built by Grand Duke Cosimo in the 1500s. Nowadays vendors hawk purses, stationery, toys, clothes, umbrellas and knick-knacks. In medieval times this was the merchants' exchange, where any merchant who committed the crime of bankruptcy was publicly spanked before being carted off to prison; in times of peace it sheltered Florence's battle-stained *carroccio*. Florentines often call the market the 'Porcellino' (piglet) after the large bronze boar erected in 1612. The current boar was put in place in 1999, a copy of a copy of the ancient statue in the Uffizi. The drool spilling from the side of its mouth reminds us that Florence is no splashy city of springs and fountains. Rub the piglet's snout, and supposedly destiny will one day bring you back to Florence. The pungent aroma of the tripe sandwiches sold nearby may give you second thoughts.

## Orsanmichele

*Open Mon–Fri 9–12 and 4–6, Sat and Sun 9–1 and 4–6. (However, closed most of the time due to lack of staff!) Open for concerts in the summer.*

There is a wonderfully eccentric church on Via de' Calzaiuoli that looks like no other in the world: Orsanmichele rises up in a tall, neat three-storey rectangle. It was built on the site of ancient San Michele ad Hortum (popularly reduced to 'Orsan-michele'), a 9th-century church located near a vegetable garden, which the *comune* destroyed in 1240 to erect a grain market; after a fire in 1337 the current market building (by Francesco Talenti and others) was erected, with a loggia on the ground floor and emergency storehouses on top where grain was kept against a siege.

The original market had a pilaster with a painting of the Virgin that became increasingly celebrated for performing miracles. The area around the Virgin became known as the Oratory, and when Talenti reconstructed the market, his intention was to combine both its secular and religious functions; each pilaster of the loggia was assigned to a guild to adorn with an image of its patron saint. In 1380, when the market was relocated, the entire ground floor was given over to the functions of the church, and Francesco Talenti's son Simone was given the task of closing in the arcades with lovely Gothic windows, later bricked in.

The church is most famous as a showcase of 15th-century Florentine sculpture; displaying the stylistic innovations through the decades. Each guild sought to outdo the others by commissioning the finest artists of the day to carve their patron saints and create elaborate canopied niches to hold them. The first statue to the left of the door is one of the oldest; Ghiberti's bronze *St John the Baptist*, erected in 1416 for the Arte di Calimala, was the first life-sized Renaissance statue cast in bronze. Continuing to the left on Via de' Lamberti you can compare it with Donatello's *St Mark*, patron of the linen dealers and used-cloth merchants. Finished in 1411, it is considered the first free-standing marble statue of the Renaissance.

The niches continue around Via dell'Arte della Lana, named after the Wool Merchants' Guild, the richest after that of the Bankers. Their headquarters, the **Palazzo dell' Arte della Lana**, is linked by an overhead arch with Orsanmichele; built in 1308, it was restored in 1905 in a William Morris style of medieval picturesque. The first statue on this façade of Orsanmichele is *St Eligio*, patron of smiths, by Nanni di Banco (1415), with a niche embellished with the guild's emblem (black pincers) and a bas-relief below showing one of this rather obscure saint's miracles – apparently he shod a horse by cutting off its hoof, shoeing it, then sticking it back on the leg. The other two statues on this street are bronzes by Ghiberti, the Wool Guild's *St Stephen* (1426) and the Exchange Guild's *St Matthew* (1422), the latter an especially fine work.

On the Via Orsanmichele façade stands a copy of Donatello's famous *St George* (the original now in the Bargello) done in 1417 for the Armourers' Guild, with a dramatic predella of the saint slaying the dragon, also by Donatello, that is one of the first known works making use of perspective; next are the Stonecutters' and Carpenters' Guild's *Four Crowned Saints* (1415, by Nanni di Banco), inspired by Roman statues. Nanni also contributed the Shoemakers' *St Philip* (1415), while the next figure, *St Peter*, is commonly attributed to Donatello (1413). Around the corner on Via Calzaiuoli stands the bronze *St Luke*, patron of the Judges and Notaries, by Giambologna, a work of 1602 in a 15th-century niche, and the *Doubting of St Thomas* by Andrea del Verrocchio (1484), made not for a guild but the Tribunal of Merchandise, who like St Thomas wanted to be certain before making a judgement. In the rondels above some of the niches are terracottas of the guilds' symbols by Luca della Robbia.

Orsanmichele's dark **interior** (*closed for restoration*) is ornate and cosy, with more of the air of a guildhall than a church. It makes a picturebook medieval setting for one of the masterpieces of the trecento: Andrea Orcagna's beautiful Gothic **Tabernacle**, a large, exquisite work in marble, bronze and coloured glass framing a contemporary painting of the Madonna (either by Bernardo Daddi or Orcagna himself), replacing the miraculous one, lost in a fire. The Tabernacle was commissioned by survivors of the 1348 Black Death. On the walls and pilasters are faded 14th-century frescoes of saints, placed as if members of the congregation; if you look at the pilasters on the left as you enter and along the right wall you can see the old chutes used to transfer grain.

# Piazza della Signoria

Now that this big medieval piazza is car-free, it serves as a great corral for tourists, endlessly snapping pictures of the Palazzo Vecchio or strutting in circles like pigeons. In the old days it would be full of Florentines, the stage set for the tempestuous life of their republic. The public assemblies met here, and at times of danger the bells would ring and the piazza fill with citizen militias, assembling under the banners of the quarters and guilds. Savonarola held his Bonfire of Vanities here, and only a few years later the disenchanted Florentines ignited their Bonfire of Savonarola on the same spot. (You can see a painting of the event at San Marco.) Today the piazza is still the favoured spot for political rallies.

The three graceful arches of the **Loggia dei Lanzi**, next to the Palazzo Vecchio, were the reviewing stand for city officials during assemblies and celebrations. Florentines often call it the Loggia dell'Orcagna, after the architect who designed it in the 1370s. In its simple classicism the Loggia anticipates the architecture of Brunelleschi and all those who came after him. The city has made it an outdoor sculpture gallery, with some of the best-known works in Florence: Cellini's triumphant *Perseus*, radiant after recent restoration, and Giambologna's *Rape of the Sabines*, other works by Giambologna, and a chorus of Roman-era Vestal Virgins along the back wall. Cosimo himself stands imperiously at the centre of the piazza, a bronze equestrian statue also by Giambologna.

All the statues in the piazza are dear to the Florentines for one reason or another. Some are fine works of art; others have only historical associations. Michelangelo's *David*, a copy of which stands in front of the palazzo near the spot the artist intended for it, was meant as a symbol of republican virtue and Florentine excellence. At the opposite extreme, Florentines are taught almost from birth to ridicule the **Neptune Fountain**, a pompous monstrosity with a giant marble figure of the god. The sculptor, Ammannati, thought he would upstage Michelangelo, though the result is derisively known to all Florence as Il Biancone ('Big Whitey'). Bandinelli's statue of *Hercules and Cacus* is almost as big and just as awful; according to Cellini, it looks like a 'sack of melons'.

## Palazzo Vecchio

*Open Mon–Wed and Fri–Sun 9–7, Thurs 9–2; adm.*

When Goethe made his blitz-tour of Florence, the Palazzo Vecchio (also called the Palazzo della Signoria) helped pull the wool over his eyes. 'Obviously,' thought the great poet, 'the people...enjoyed a lucky succession of good governments' – a remark which, as Mary McCarthy wrote, could make the angels in heaven weep. But none of Florence's chronic factionalism mars Arnolfo di Cambio's temple of civic aspirations, part council hall and part fortress. In many ways, the Palazzo Vecchio is the ideal of stone Florence: rugged and imposing, with a rusticated façade that was to inspire so many of the city's private palaces, yet designed according to the proportions of the Golden Section of the ancient Greeks. Its dominant feature, the 308ft tower, is a typical piece of Florentine bravado, for long the highest point in the city.

The Palazzo Vecchio occupies the site of the old Roman theatre and the medieval Palazzo dei Priori. In the 13th century this earlier palace was flattened along with the Ghibelline quarter interred under the piazza, and in 1299 the now ascendant Guelphs called upon Arnolfo di Cambio, master builder of the cathedral, to design the most impressive 'Palazzo del Popolo' (as the building was originally called) possible. The palace's unusual trapezoidal shape is often, but rather dubiously, explained as Guelph care not to have any of the building touch land once owned by Ghibellines. One doubts that even in the 13th century property realities allowed such delicacy of sentiments; nor does the theory explain why the tower has swallowtail Ghibelline crenellations, as opposed to the square Guelph ones on the palace itself. Later additions to the rear of the palace have obscured its shape even more, although the façade is essentially as Arnolfo built it, except for the bet-hedging monogram over the door hailing Christ the King of Florence, put up in the nervous days of 1529, when the Imperial army of Charles V was on its way to destroy the last Florentine republic; the inscription replaces an earlier one left by Savonarola. The room at the top of the tower was used as a prison for famous people and dubbed the *alberghetto*; inmates in 'the little hotel' included Cosimo il Vecchio before his brief exile, and Savonarola, who spent his last months, between torture sessions, enjoying a superb view of the city before his execution in the piazza below.

### Inside the Palazzo Vecchio

Today the Palazzo Vecchio serves as Florence's city hall, but nearly all its historical rooms are open to the public. With few exceptions, the interior decorations date from the time of Cosimo I, when he moved his Grand Ducal self from the Medici palace in 1540. To politically 'correct' its acres of walls and ceilings in the shortest amount of time, he turned to his court artist Giorgio Vasari, famed more for the speed at which he could execute a commission than for its quality. On the ground floor of the palazzo, before you buy your ticket, you can take a look at some of Vasari's more elaborate handiwork in the **Courtyard**, redone for the occasion of Francesco I's unhappy marriage to the plain and stupid Habsburg Joanna of Austria in 1565.

Vasari's suitably grand staircase ascends to the vast **Salone dei Cinquecento**, added by Savonarola for meetings of the 500-strong Consiglio Maggiore, the reformed republic's democratic assembly. Leonardo da Vinci and Michelangelo were commissioned in 1503 to paint the two long walls of the *salone* in a kind of Battle of the Brushes. Unfortunately, neither came near to completing the project; Leonardo managed to fresco a section of the wall, using the experimental techniques that were to prove the undoing of his *Last Supper* in Milan, while Michelangelo only completed the cartoons before being summoned to Rome by Julius II, who required the sculptor of the *David* to pander to his own personal megalomania.

In the 1560s Vasari removed what was left of Leonardo's efforts and refrescoed the room as a celebration of Cosimo's military triumphs over Pisa and Siena, complete with an apotheosis of the Grand Duke on the ceiling. These wall scenes are inane; big, busy, crowded with men and horses who appear to have all the substance of overcooked pasta. The sculptural groups lining the walls of this large room (the Italian parliament sat here from 1865 to 1870 when Florence was the capital) are only slightly more stimulating; even Michelangelo's *Victory*, on the wall opposite the entrance, is more virtuosity than vision: a vacuous young idiot posing with one knee atop a defeated old man still half-submerged in stone, said to be a self-portrait of the sculptor. Its neighbour, a muscle-bound *Hercules and Diomedes* by Vicenzo de' Rossi, probably was inevitable in this city obsessed by the possibilities of the male nude.

Beyond the *salone*, behind a modern glass door, is a much more intriguing room the size of a closet. This is the **Studiolo of Francesco I**, designed by Vasari in 1572 for Cosimo's melancholic and reclusive son, where he would escape to brood over his real interests in natural curiosities and alchemy. The little study, windowless and more than a little claustrophobic, has been restored to its original appearance, lined with allegorical paintings by Vasari, Bronzino and Allori, and bronze statuettes by Giambologna and Ammannati, their refined, polished and erotic mythological subjects part of a carefully thought-out 16th-century programme on Man and Nature. The lower row of paintings conceals Francesco's secret cupboards where he kept his most precious belongings, his pearls and crystals and gold.

After the *salone* a certain fuzziness begins to set in. Cosimo I's propaganda machine in league with Vasari's fresco factory produced room after room of self-glorifying Medicean puffery. The first series of rooms, known as the **Quartiere di Leone X**, carry ancestor-worship to extremes, each chamber dedicated to a different Medici: in the first Cosimo il Vecchio returns from exile amid tumultuous acclaim; in the second Lorenzo il Magnifico receives the ambassadors in the company of a dignified giraffe; the third and fourth are dedicated to the Medici popes, while the fifth, naturally, is for Cosimo I, who gets the most elaborate treatment of all.

Upstairs the next series of rooms is known as the **Quartiere degli Elementi**, with more works of Vasari and his studio, depicting allegories of the elements. In a small room, called **Terrazzo di Giunone**, is the original of Verrocchio's boy with the dolphin, from the courtyard fountain. A balcony across the Salone dei Cinquecento leads to the **Quartiere di Eleonora di Toledo**, Mrs Cosimo I's private apartments. Her chapel is one of the masterpieces of Bronzino, who seemed to relish the opportunity to paint something besides Medici portraits. The **Sala dell'Udienza**, beyond the second chapel, has a magnificent quattrocento coffered ceiling by Benedetto and Giuliano da Maiano, and walls painted by Mannerist Francesco Salviati (1550–60).

The last room, the **Sala dei Gigli** ('of the lilies') boasts another fine ceiling by the da Maiano brothers; it contains Donatello's restored bronze *Judith and Holofernes*, a late and rather gruesome work of 1455; the warning to tyrants inscribed on its base was added when the statue was abducted from the Medici palace and placed in the Piazza della Signoria. Off the Sala dei Gigli are two small rooms of interest: the **Guardaroba**, or unique 'wardrobe' adorned with 57 maps painted by Fra Egnazio Danti in 1563, depicting all the world known at the time. The **Cancelleria** was Machiavelli's office from 1498 to 1512, when he served the republic as a secretary and diplomat. He is commemorated with a bust and a portrait. Poor Machiavelli would probably be amazed to learn that his very name had become synonymous with cunning, amoral intrigue. After losing his job upon the return of the Medici, and at one point being tortured and imprisoned on false suspicion of conspiracy, Machiavelli was forced to live in idleness in the country, where he wrote his political works and two fine plays, feverishly trying to return to favour. His concern throughout had been to advise realistically, without mincing words, the fractious and increasingly weak Italians on how to create a strong state. His evil reputation came from openly stating what rulers do, rather than what they would like other people to think they do.

The **Collezione Loeser**, a fine assortment of Renaissance art left to the city in 1928 by Charles Loeser, the Macy's department-store heir, is also housed in the Palazzo Vecchio, in the mezzanine before you exit the museum.

## Raccolta Alberto della Ragione

After the pomposity of the Palazzo Vecchio and a Campari cure at the Piazza della Signoria's Café Rivoire, you may be in the mood to reconsider the 20th century in Florence's only museum of modern art, recently moved to Piazza della Signoria 5 (*open summer Mon, Thurs and Sat 10–7, Wed and Fri 10–10; winter 10–7; closed Tues; adm*). There are typical still lifes by De Pisis; equally still landscapes by Carlo Carrà; mysterious baths by De Chirico; Tuscan landscapes by Mario Mafai, Antonio Donghi and Ottone Rosai; a speedy Futurist horse by Fortunato Depero and a window with doves by Gino Severini; a number of richly coloured canvases by Renato Guttuso, paintings after Tintoretto by Emilio Vedova, and many others.

# The Uffizi

*www.uffizi.firenze.it. Long queues in the summer are very common; try to arrive early. Open Tues–Sun 8.15–6.50; adm exp. Pre-book by phone, t 055 294883: pay at the door when you pick up your ticket.*

Florence has the most fabulous art museum in Italy, and as usual we have the Medici to thank; for the building that holds these treasures, however, credit goes to Grand Duke Cosimo's much maligned court painter. Poor Giorgio Vasari! His roosterish boastfulness and the conviction that his was the best of all possible artistic worlds, set next to his very modest talents, have made him a comic figure in most art criticism. On one of the rare occasions when he tried his hand as an architect, though, he gave Florence something to be proud of. The Uffizi ('offices') were built as Cosimo's secretariat, incorporating the old mint (producer of the first gold florins in 1252), the archives and the large church of San Pier Scheraggio, with plenty of room for the bureaucrats needed to run Cosimo's efficient, modern state. The matched pair of arcaded buildings have coldly elegant façades that conceal Vasari's surprising innovation: iron reinforcements that make the huge amount of window area possible and keep the building stable on the soft sandy ground. It was a trick that would be almost forgotten until the Crystal Palace and the first American skyscrapers. Almost from the start the Medici began to store some of their huge collection in parts of the building. There are galleries in the world with more works of art – the Uffizi counts some 1,800 – but the Uffizi overwhelms by the fact that everything in it is worth looking at.

The Uffizi has undergone major reorganization in the last couple of years. Some of this involved the restoration of remaining damage after the bomb of 1993 (all but a very few paintings are now back on display), but improvements have also been made on a practical level. Major restoration of the vaulted rooms on the ground floor has resulted in a vastly improved space; there are now three entrances (for individuals, for groups and for pre-paid tickets), bookshops, cloakrooms, video and computer facilities and information desks.

If you are particularly keen on seeing a certain painting, note that rooms may be temporarily closed when you visit; this often seems to depend on staff availability. There is a list of these closures at the ticket counters. Some works are still hung out of chronological order, and the rooms containing work by Caravaggio and Rubens are closed until further notice (although two of the Caravaggios are at present hung in Room 16 – see p.136).

From the ticket counter you can take the lift or sweeping grand staircase up to the second floor, where the Medici once had a huge theatre, now home to the **Cabinet of Drawings and Prints**. Although the bulk of this extensive and renowned collection is only open to scholars with special permission, a roomful of tempting samples gives a hint at what they have a chance to see.

Nowadays one thinks of the Uffizi as primarily a gallery of paintings, but when it first opened visitors came for the fine collection of Hellenistic and Roman marbles. Most of these were collected in Rome by Medici cardinals, and not a few were sources of Renaissance inspiration. The **Vestibule** at the top of the stairs contains some of the best, together with Flemish and Tuscan tapestries made for Cosimo I and his successors. **Room 1**, usually shut, contains excellent early Roman sculpture.

## Rooms 2–6: 13th and 14th Centuries

The Uffizi's paintings are arranged in chronological order, the better to educate its visitors on trends in Italian art. The roots of the Early Renaissance are most strikingly revealed in **Room 2**, dedicated to the three great **Maestà** altarpieces by the masters of the 13th century. All portray the same subject of the Madonna and Child enthroned with angels. The one on the right, by Cimabue, was painted around the year 1285 and represents a breaking away from the flat, stylized Byzantine tradition. To the left is the so-called *Rucellai Madonna*, painted around the same period by the Sienese Duccio di Buoninsegna for Santa Maria Novella. It resembles Cimabue's in many ways, but with a more advanced technique for creating depth, and the bright colouring that characterizes the Sienese school. Giotto's altarpiece, painted some 25 years later, takes a great leap forward, not only in his use of perspective, but in the arrangement of the angels, standing naturally, and in the portrayal of the Virgin, gently smiling, with real fingers and breasts.

To the left, **Room 3** contains representative Sienese works of the 14th century, with a beautiful Gothic *Annunciation* (1333) by Simone Martini and the brothers Pietro and Ambrogio Lorenzetti. **Room 4** is dedicated to 14th-century Florentines: Bernardo Daddi, Nardo di Cione, and the delicately coloured *San Remigio Pietà* by Giottino. **Rooms 5 and 6** portray Italian contributions to the International Gothic school, most dazzlingly Gentile da Fabriano's *Adoration of the Magi* (1423), two good works by Lorenzo Monaco, and the *Thebaid* of Gherardo Starnina, depicting the rather unusual activities of the 4th-century monks of St Pancratius of Thebes, in Egypt.

## Rooms 7–9: Early Renaissance

In the Uffizi, at least, it's but a few short steps from the superbly decorative International Gothic to the masters of the Early Renaissance. **Room 7** contains minor works by Fra Angelico, Masaccio and Masolino, and three masterpieces. Domenico Veneziano's pastel *Madonna and Child with Saints* (1448) is one of the rare pictures by this Venetian master who died a pauper in Florence. It is a new departure not only for its soft colours but for the subject matter, unifying the enthroned Virgin and saints in one panel, in what is known as a *Sacra Conversazione*. Piero della Francesca's famous *Double Portrait of the Duke Federigo da Montefeltro and his Duchess Battista Sforza of Urbino* (1465) depicts one of Italy's noblest Renaissance princes – and surely the one with the most distinctive nose. Piero's ability to create perfectly still, timeless worlds is even more evident in the allegorical 'Triumphs' of the Duke and Duchess painted on the back of their portraits. A similar stillness and fascination floats over into the surreal in Uccello's *Rout of San Romano* (1456), or at least the third of it still present (the other two panels are in the Louvre and London's National Gallery; all three once decorated the bedroom of Lorenzo il Magnifico in the Medici palace). Both Piero and Uccello were deep students of perspective, but Uccello went half-crazy; applying his principles to a violent battle scene has left us one of the most provocative works of all time – a vision of warfare in suspended animation, with pink, white and blue toy horses, robot-like knights, and rabbits bouncing in the background.

**Room 8** is devoted to the works of the rascally romantic Fra Filippo Lippi, whose ethereally lovely Madonnas were modelled after his brown-eyed nun. In his *Coronation of the Virgin* (1447) she kneels in the foreground with two children, while the artist, dressed in a brown habit, looks dreamily towards her; in his celebrated *Madonna and Child with Two Angels* (1445) she plays the lead before the kind of mysterious landscape Leonardo would later perfect. Lippi taught the art of enchanting Madonnas to his student Botticelli, who has some lovely works in this room and the next; Alesso Baldovinetti, a pupil of the far more holy Fra Angelico, painted the room's beautiful *Annunciation* (1447).

**Room 9** has two small scenes from the *Labours of Hercules* (1470) by Antonio Pollaiuolo, whose interest in anatomy, muscular expressiveness and violence presages a strain in Florentine art that culminated in the great Mannerists. He worked with his younger brother Piero on the refined, elegant *SS. Vincent, James and Eustace*, transferred here from San Miniato. This room also contains the Uffizi's best-known forgery: *The Young Man in a Red Hat* or self-portrait of Filippino Lippi, believed to have been the work of an 18th-century English art dealer who palmed it off on the Grand Dukes.

## Botticelli: Rooms 10–14

To accommodate the bewitching art of 'Little Barrels' and his 20th-century admirers, the Uffizi converted four small rooms into one great Botticellian shrine. Although his masterpieces displayed here have become almost synonymous with the Florentine Renaissance at its most spring-like and charming, they were not publicly displayed until the beginning of the 19th century, nor given much consideration outside Florence until the early 20th century. Botticelli's best works date from his days as a darling of the Medici – family members crop up most noticeably in the *Adoration of the Magi* (1476), where you can pick out Cosimo il Vecchio, Lorenzo il Magnifico and Botticelli himself (in the right foreground, in a yellow robe, gazing at the spectator). His *Annunciation* is a graceful, cosmic dance between the Virgin and the Angel Gabriel. In the *Tondo of the Virgin of the Pomegranate* the lovely melancholy goddess who was to become his Venus makes her first appearance.

Botticelli is best known for his sublime mythological allegories, nearly all painted for the Medici and inspired by the Neoplatonic, humanistic and hermetic currents that pervaded the intelligentsia of the late 15th century. Perhaps no painting has been debated so fervently as *La Primavera* (1478). This hung for years in the Medici Villa at Castello, and it is believed that the subject of the Allegory of Spring was suggested by Marsilio Ficino, one of the great natural magicians of the Renaissance, and that the figures represent the 'beneficial' planets able to dispel sadness. *Pallas and the Centaur* has been called another subtle allegory of Medici triumph – the rings of Athena's gown are supposedly a family symbol. Other interpretations see the taming of the sorrowful centaur as a melancholy comment on reason and civilization.

Botticelli's last great mythological painting, *The Birth of Venus*, was commissioned by Lorenzo di Pierfrancesco and inspired by a poem by Poliziano, Lorenzo il Magnifico's Latin and Greek scholar, who described how Zephyr and Chloris blew the newborn goddess to shore on a scallop shell, while Hora hastened to robe her, a scene Botticelli portrays once again with dance-like rhythm and delicacy of line. Yet the goddess of love floats towards the spectator with an expression of wistfulness – perhaps reflecting the artist's own feelings of regret. For artistically, the poetic, decorative style he perfected in this painting would be disdained and forgotten in his own lifetime. Spiritually, Botticelli also turned a corner after creating this haunting, uncanny beauty – his and Florence's farewell to a road not taken. Although Vasari's biography of Botticelli portrays a prankster rather than a sensitive soul, the painter absorbed more than any other artist the *fin-de-siècle* neuroticism that beset the city with the rise of Savonarola. So thoroughly did he reject his Neoplatonism that he would only accept commissions of sacred subjects or supposedly edifying allegories like his *Calumny*, a small but rather disturbing work, and a fitting introduction to the dark side of the quattrocento psyche.

This large room also contains works by Botticelli's contemporaries. There are two paintings of the *Adoration of the Magi*, one by Ghirlandaio and one by Filippino Lippi, which show the influence of Leonardo's unfinished but radical work in pyramidal composition (in the next room); Leonardo himself got the idea from the large *Portinari Altarpiece* (1471), at the end of the room, a work by Hugo Van der Goes, brought back from Bruges by Medici agent Tommaso Portinari.

## Rooms 15–24: More Renaissance

**Room 15** is dedicated to the Florentine works of Leonardo da Vinci's early career. Here are works by his master Andrea Verrocchio, including the *Baptism of Christ*, in which Leonardo painted the angel on the left. Art critics believe the *Annunciation* (1475) is almost entirely by Leonardo – the soft faces, botanical details, and misty, watery background would become his trademarks. Most influential was his unfinished *Adoration of the Magi* (1481), an unconventional composition that Leonardo abandoned when he left Florence for Milan. Although at first glance it's hard to make out much more than a mass of reddish chiaroscuro, the longer you stare, the better you'll see the serene Madonna and Child surrounded by anxious, troubled humanity, with an exotic background of ruins, trees and horsemen.

Other artists in Room 15 include Leonardo's peers: Lorenzo di Credi, whose religious works have eerie garden-like backgrounds, and the nutty Piero di Cosimo, whose dreamy *Perseus Liberating Andromeda* includes an endearing mongrel of a dragon that gives even the most reserved Japanese tourist fits of giggles. Tuscan maps adorn **Room 16**, as well as scenes by Hans Memling. Temporarily housed here, away from their normal home in Room 43, are Caravaggio's *Bacchus* and *The Head of Medusa*, believed to be self-portraits. In its day the fleshy, heavy-eyed *Bacchus*, half portrait and half still life, was considered highly iconoclastic.

The octagonal **Tribuna (Room 18)** with its mother-of-pearl dome and *pietra dura* floor and table was built by Buontalenti in 1584 for Francesco I and, like the Studiolo in the Palazzo Vecchio, was designed to hold Medici treasures. For centuries the best-known of these was the *Venus de' Medici*, a 2nd-century BC Greek sculpture, farcically claimed as a copy of Praxiteles' celebrated *Aphrodite of Cnidos*, the most erotic statue in antiquity. In the 18th century, amazingly, this rather ordinary girl was considered the greatest sculpture in Florence; today most visitors walk right by without a second glance. Other antique works include the *Wrestlers* and the *Knife Grinder*, both copies of Pergamese originals, the *Dancing Faun*, the *Young Apollo*, and the *Sleeping Hermaphrodite* in the adjacent room, which is usually curtained off.

The real stars of the Tribuna are the Medici court portraits, many of them by Bronzino, who was not only able to catch the likeness of Cosimo I, Eleanor of Toledo and their children, but could also aptly portray the spirit of the day – these are people who took themselves very seriously indeed. They have for company Vasari's posthumous portrait of *Lorenzo il Magnifico* and Pontormo's *Cosimo il Vecchio*, Andrea del Sarto's *Girl with a Book by Petrarch*, and Rosso Fiorentino's *Angel Musician*, an enchanting work entirely out of place in this stodgy temple.

Two followers of Piero della Francesca, Perugino and Luca Signorelli, hold pride of place in **Room 19**; Perugino's *Portrait of a Young Man* is believed to be modelled on his pupil Raphael. Signorelli's *Tondo of the Holy Family* was to become the inspiration for Michelangelo's (*see* below). The room also contains Lorenzo di Credi's *Venus*, inspired by Botticelli. The Germans appear in **Room 20**: Dürer's earliest known work, the *Portrait of his Father* (1490), done at age 19, and *The Adoration of the Magi* (1504). Also here are Lucas Cranach's Teutonic *Adam and Eve* and his *Portrait of Martin Luther* (1543), not someone you'd necessarily expect to see in Florence. **Room 21** is dedicated to the great Venetians, most famously Bellini and his uncanny *Sacred Allegory* (1490s), the meaning of which has never been satisfactorily explained. There are two minor works by the elusive Giorgione, and a typically weird *St Dominic* by Cosmè Tura.

Later Flemish and German artists appear in **Room 22**, works by Gerard David and proto-Romantic Albrecht Altdorfer, and a portrait attributed to Hans Holbein of *Sir Thomas More*. **Room 23** is dedicated to non-Tuscans Correggio of Parma and Mantegna of the Veneto, as well as Boltraffio's strange *Narcissus*.

## Rooms 25–27: Mannerism

The window-filled South Corridor, with its views over the city and its fine display of antique sculpture, marks only the halfway point in the Uffizi but nearly the end of Florence's contribution. In the first three rooms, however, local talent rallies to produce a brilliantly coloured twilight in Florentine Mannerism. By most accounts, Michelangelo's only completed oil painting, the *Tondo Doni* (1506), was the spark that ignited Mannerism's flaming orange and turquoise hues. Michelangelo was 30 when he painted this unconventional work, in a medium he disliked (sculpture and fresco being the only fit occupations for a man, he believed). It's a typical Michelangelo story that when the purchaser complained the artist was asking too much for it, Michelangelo promptly doubled the price. As shocking as the colours are the spiralling poses of the Holy Family, sharply delineated against a background of five nude, slightly out-of-focus young men of uncertain purpose (are they pagans? angels? boyfriends? or just fillers?) – an ambiguity that was to become a hallmark of Mannerism; as the *Ignudi* they later appear on the Sistine Chapel ceiling. In itself, the *Tondo Doni* is more provocative than immediately appealing; the violent canvas in Room 27, Rosso Fiorentino's *Moses Defending the Children of Jethro*, was painted some 20 years later and at least in its intention to shock the viewer puts a cap on what Michelangelo began.

**Room 26** is dedicated mainly to Raphael, who was in and out of Florence in 1504–8. Raphael was the sweetheart of the High Renaissance. His Madonnas, like *The Madonna of the Goldfinch*, have a tenderness that was soon to be over-popularized by others and turned into holy cards, a cloying sentimentality added over the centuries.

It's easier, perhaps, to see Raphael's genius in non-sacred subjects, like *Leo X with Two Cardinals*, a perceptive portrait study of the first Medici pope with his nephew Giulio de' Medici, later Clement VII.

The same room contains Andrea del Sarto's most original work, the fluorescent *Madonna of the Harpies* (1517), named after the figures on the Virgin's pedestal. Of the works by Pontormo, the best is in **Room 27**, *Supper at Emmaus* (1525), a strange canvas with the Masonic symbol of the Eye of God hovering over Christ's head.

## Rooms 28–45

The Uffizi fairly bristles with masterpieces from other parts of Italy and abroad. Titian's delicious nudes, especially the voluptuous *Venus of Urbino*, raise the temperature in **Room 28**; Parmigianino's hyper-elegant *Madonna with the Long Neck* (1536) in **Room 29** is a fascinating Mannerist evolutionary dead-end. **Room 31** holds Paolo Veronese's *Holy Family with St Barbara*, bathed in a golden Venetian light, with a gorgeously opulent Barbara. Sebastiano del Piombo's *Death of Adonis*, in **Room 32**, is notable for its melancholy, autumn atmosphere, and Venus's annoyed look. Tintoretto's shadowy *Leda* languidly pretends to restrain the lusty swan.

**Room 41** is Flemish domain, with brand-name art by Rubens and Van Dyck; the former's *Baccanale* may be the most grotesque canvas in Florence. **Room 42**, the *Sala della Niobe*, was reopened in December 1998 after the bomb damage was repaired. A series of statues, *Niobe and her Sons* (18th-century copies of Hellenic works), are housed in the high, arched-ceilinged room, which is covered in pristine plaster and gold leaf. **Room 43** houses some striking Caravaggios.

Struggle on gamely to **Room 44**, where there are three portraits by Rembrandt including two self-portraits, and landscapes by Ruysdael. **Room 45** has some fine 18th-century works, including portraits by Chardin, Goya and Longhi, and Venetian landscapes by Guardi and Canaletto. Even more welcome by this time is the **bar**, with a summer terrace and in a superb position overlooking Piazza Signoria.

The **Contini Bonacossi** collection, once housed in the Meridiana Pavilion at Palazzo Pitti, was moved to the Uffizi in 1999. Visits are by appointment only (*t* 055 265 4321), and there is a separate entrance in Via Lambertesca. The Uffizi ticket is also valid for this. This recent bequest includes works of Cimabue, Duccio and Giovanni Bellini, some sculpture and china, and also paintings by El Greco, Goya and Velazquez – the last represented by an exceptional work, *The Water Carrier of Seville*.

## Corridoio Vasariano

*Open for very limited periods during the year. It is now open to individuals, not just groups. Hours are also very limited. Call t 055 265 4321 for info and bookings (obligatory); adm exp.*

In 1565, when Francesco I married Joanna of Austria, the Medici commissioned Vasari to link their new digs in the Pitti Palace with the Uffizi and the Palazzo Vecchio in such a manner that the Archdukes could make their rounds without rubbing elbows with their subjects. With a patina of 400 years, it seems that Florence wouldn't look quite right without this covered catwalk, leapfrogging on rounded arches from the back of the Uffizi, over the Ponte Vecchio, daintily skirting a medieval tower, and darting past the façade of Santa Felicità to the Pitti Palace.

The Corridoio does not only offer interesting views of Florence: it has been hung with a celebrated collection of artists' self-portraits, beginning, reasonably, with Vasari himself before continuing in chronological order, past the Gaddis and Raphael to Rembrandt, Van Dyck, Velazquez, Hogarth, Reynolds, Delacroix and Corot.

## The Museum of the History of Science (Museo di Storia della Scienza)

*Open summer 9.30–5, Tues and Sat 9.30–1, closed Sun; winter 9.30–5, Tues 9.30–1, 2nd Sun of month 10–1; adm.*

For all that Florence and Tuscany contributed to the birth of science, it is only fitting to have this museum in the centre of the city, behind the Uffizi in Piazza Giudici. Much of the first floor is devoted to instruments measuring time and distance: Arabian astrolabes and pocket sundials, Tuscan sundials in the shape of Platonic solids, enormous elaborate armillary spheres and a small reliquary holding the bone of Galileo's finger, erect, like a final gesture to the city that until 1737 denied him a Christian burial. Here, too, are two of his original telescopes and the lens with which he discovered the four moons of Jupiter. Other scientific instruments come from the Accademia del Cimento (of 'trial' or 'experiment'), founded in 1657 by Cardinal Leopoldo de' Medici, the world's first scientific organization, dedicated to Galileo's principle of inquiry and proof by experimentation. 'Try and try again' was its motto.

Upstairs, there's a large room filled with machines used to demonstrate principles of physics, which the women who run the museum will operate if you ask. Two unusual ones are the 18th-century automatic writer and the instrument of perpetual motion. The rooms devoted to medicine contain a collection of 18th-century wax anatomical models, designed to teach budding obstetricians about unfortunate foetal positions, as well as a fine display of surgical instruments from the period.

# The Ponte Vecchio and Ponte Santa Trínita

*Bent bridges seeming to strain like bows*
*And tremble with arrowy undertide...*
Elizabeth Barrett Browning, 'Casa Guidi Windows'

Often at sunset the Arno becomes a stream of molten gold, that is, during those months when it has a respectable flow of water. But even in the torrid days of August, when the Arno shrivels into muck and spittle, its two famous bridges retain their distinctive beauty. The most famous of these, the **Ponte Vecchio** or 'Old Bridge', crosses the Arno at its narrowest point; the present bridge, with its three stone arches, was built in 1345, and replaces a wooden construction from the 970s, which in turn was the successor to a span that may well have dated back to the Romans. On this wooden bridge, at the foot of the *Marzocco*, or statue of Mars, Buondelmonte dei

Buondelmonti was murdered in 1215, setting off the wars of the Guelphs and Ghibellines. The original *Marzocco* was washed away in a 14th-century flood, and Donatello's later version has been carted off to the Bargello.

Like old London Bridge, the Ponte Vecchio is covered with shops and houses. By the 1500s it had become the street of hog butchers, though after Vasari built Cosimo's secret passage on top, the Grand Duke evicted the butchers and replaced them with goldsmiths. They have been there ever since, and shoppers from around the world descend on it each year to scrutinize the traditional Florentine talent for jewellery – not a few of the city's great artists began their careers as goldsmiths, beginning with Ghiberti and Donatello, and ending with Cellini, whose bust adorns the middle of the bridge. In the 1966 flood the shops did not prove as resilient as the Ponte Vecchio itself, and a fortune of gold was washed down the Arno.

In the summer of 1944, the river briefly became a German defensive line during the slow painful retreat across Italy. Before leaving Florence, the Nazis blew up every one of the city's bridges, saving only, on Hitler's special orders, the Ponte Vecchio, though they blasted a large number of ancient buildings on each side of the span to create piles of rubble to block the approaches. Florence's most beautiful span, the **Ponte Santa Trínita**, was the most tragic victim. Immediately after the war the Florentines set about replacing the bridges exactly as they were: for Santa Trínita, old quarries had to be reopened to duplicate the stone, and old methods revived to cut it (modern power saws would have done it too cleanly). The graceful curve of the three arches was a problem; they could not be constructed geometrically, and considerable speculation went on over how the architect (Ammannati, in 1567) did it. Finally, recalling that Michelangelo had advised Ammannati on the project, someone noticed that the same form of arch could be seen on the decoration of the tombs in Michelangelo's Medici Chapel, constructed most likely by pure artistic imagination. Fortune lent a hand in the reconstruction; of the original statues of the 'Four Seasons', almost all the pieces were fished out of the Arno and rebuilt. Spring's head was eventually found by divers completely by accident in 1961.

# Dante's Florence

Dante would contemplate his Beatrice, the story goes, at Mass in the **Badia Fiorentina** (*entrance on Via Dante Alighieri; cloister open Mon 3–6; church open Mon 3–6, Tues–Sat 6.30–6*), a Benedictine church on Via del Proconsolo across from the Bargello, with a lovely Gothic spire to grace this corner of the Florentine skyline. The church has undergone many rebuildings since Willa, widow of a Margrave of Tuscany, began it in around 990, but there is still a monument to Ugo, the 'Good Margrave' mentioned in Dante, and a painting of the Madonna appearing to St Bernard by Filippo Lippi.

Between the Badia and Via de' Calzaiuoli, a little corner of medieval Florence has survived the changes of centuries. In these quiet, narrow streets you can visit the **Casa di Dante** (*closed for restoration work; unknown when it will re-open*), which was actually built in 1911 over the ruins of an amputated tower house, although scholars all agree that the Alighieri lived somewhere in the vicinity. Since 1960 this museum dedicated to Dante has made a game attempt to evoke Dante's life and times, in spite of neglect. Near the entrance is an edition of *The Divine Comedy*, all printed in tiny letters on a poster by a mad Milanese. Upstairs there are copies of Botticelli's beautiful line illustrations for the *Commedia*.

Nearby, the stoutly medieval **Torre del Castagna** is all that remains of the original Palazzo del Popolo, the residence of the *priori*, the governors of the city, before the construction of the Palazzo Vecchio. Dante himself was a *priore* once, and he would have spent his two-month term of office living here, as the law required.

After giving up on Beatrice, Dante married Gemma Donati, in the **Santa Margherita** church on the same block. Another church nearby, **San Martino del Vescovo** (*open Mon–Sat 10–12 and 3–5, closed Sun*), has a fine set of frescoes from the workshop of Ghirlandaio.

## Museo Nazionale del Bargello

*Open daily 8.15–1.50; closed 1st and 3rd Sun, and 2nd and 4th Mon of month; adm.*

Across from the Badia Fiorentina looms the Bargello, a battlemented urban fortress, well proportioned yet of forbidding grace; for centuries it saw duty as Florence's prison. Today its only inmates are men of marble, gathered together to form Italy's finest collection of sculpture, a fitting complement to the paintings in the Uffizi. The Bargello is 'stone Florence' squared to the sixth degree, rugged and austere *pietra forte*, the model for the even grander Palazzo Vecchio. Even the treasures it houses are hard, definite, certain – and almost unremittingly masculine. The Bargello offers the best insight available into Florence's golden age, and it was a man's world indeed.

Completed in 1255, the Bargello was intended as Florence's Palazzo del Popolo, though by 1271 it served instead as the residence of the foreign *podestà*, or chief magistrate, installed by Guelph leader Charles of Anjou. The Medici made it the headquarters of the captain of police (the *Bargello*), the city jail and torture chamber, a function it served until 1859. In the Renaissance it was the peculiar custom to paint portraits of the condemned on the exterior walls of the fortress; Andrea del Castagno was so good at it that he was nicknamed Andrea of the Hanged Men. All of these ghoulish souvenirs have long since disappeared, as have the torture instruments – burned in 1786, when Grand Duke Peter Leopold abolished torture and the death sentence in Tuscany, only a few months after the Venetians led the way. Today the **Gothic courtyard**, former site of the gallows and chopping block, is a delightful place, owing much to an imaginative restoration in the 1860s. The encrustation of centuries of *podestà* armorial devices and plaques in a wild vocabulary of symbols, the shadowy arcades and stately stairs combine to create one of Florence's most romantic corners.

The main ground-floor gallery is dedicated to Michelangelo and his century, although it must be said that the Michelangelo of the Bargello somewhat lacks the accustomed angst and ecstasy. The real star of the room is **Benvenuto Cellini**, who was, besides many other things, an exquisite craftsman and daring innovator.

The stairway from the courtyard leads up to the shady **Loggia**, now converted into an aviary for Giambologna's charming bronze birds, made for the animal grotto at the Medici's Villa di Castello.

The **Salone del Consiglio Generale**, formerly the courtroom of the *podestà*, contains the greatest masterpieces of Early Renaissance sculpture. And when Michelangelo's maudlin self-absorption and the Mannerists' empty virtuosity begin to seem tiresome, a visit to this room will prove a welcome antidote. Donatello's originality and vision are strikingly modern – and mysterious. On the wall hang the two famous trial reliefs for the second set of baptistry doors, by Ghiberti and Brunelleschi, both depicting the Sacrifice of Isaac. The remainder of the first floor houses fascinating collections of decorative arts donated to the Bargello in the last century.

Some of the most interesting items are in the next rooms, especially the works in the **ivory collection** – Carolingian and Byzantine diptychs, an 8th-century whalebone coffer from Northumbria adorned with runes, medieval French miniatures chronicling 'The Assault on the Castle of Love', 11th-century chess pieces, and more.

A stairway from the ivory collection leads up to the **Second Floor**. It houses some of the finest enamelled terracottas of the della Robbia family workshop, a room of portrait busts, works by Antonio Pollaiuolo and Verrocchio, including his *David* and lovely *Young Lady with a Nosegay*. There is also a collection of armour, and the most important collection of small Renaissance bronzes in Italy.

## Piazza San Firenze to the Duomo

The strangely shaped square that both the Badia and the Bargello call home is named after the large church of **San Firenze**, now partially used as Florence's law courts. At the corner of the square and Via Gondi, the **Palazzo Gondi** is a fine Renaissance palace built for a merchant by Giuliano da Sangallo in 1489 but completed only in 1884; it's not easy to pick out the discreet 19th-century additions. A block from the square on Via Ghibellina, the **Palazzo Borghese** (No.110) is one of the finest neoclassical buildings in the city, erected in 1822 for a party in honour of Habsburg Grand Duke Ferdinand III. The host was one of the wealthiest men of his day, the Roman prince Camillo Borghese, husband of Pauline Bonaparte and the man responsible for shipping many of Italy's art treasures off to the Louvre.

From Piazza San Firenze, Via del Proconsolo leads straight to the Piazza del Duomo, passing by way of the **Palazzo Pazzi-Quaratesi** (No.10), the 15th-century headquarters of the banking family that organized the conspiracy against Lorenzo and Giuliano de' Medici. No.12, the Palazzo Nonfinito – begun in 1593 but, as its name suggests, never completed – is now the home of the **Museo Nazionale di Antropologia ed Etnologia** (*open Mon–Wed, Fri and Sat 9–1, Tues 9–1 and 3–5; adm*), founded in 1869, the first ethnological museum in Italy, with an interesting collection of Peruvian mummies, musical instruments collected by Galileo Chini (who decorated the Liberty-style extravaganzas at Viareggio), some lovely and unusual items of Japan's Ainu and Pakistan's Kafiri, and a large number of skulls from all over the world.

# Florence As It Was

Borgo degli Albizi, the fine old street passing in front of the Palazzo Nonfinito, was in ancient times the Via Cassia, linking Rome with Bologna, and it deserves a leisurely stroll for its palaces (especially No.18, the cinquecento Palazzo Valori, nicknamed 'Funny Face Palace' for its surreal, semi-relief herm-busts of Florentine immortals on three floors of the façade). If Borgo degli Albizi, too, fails to answer to the Florence you've been seeking, take Via dell'Oriuolo (just to the left at Piazza G Salvemini) for the **Museo di Firenze Com'Era** (Museum of Florence As It Was), located at the big garden at No.24 (*open Fri–Wed 9–2; adm*). The jewel of this museum is right out in front, the nearly room-sized *Pianta della Catena*, most beautiful of the early views of Florence. It is a copy; the original, made in 1490 by an unknown artist – that handsome fellow pictured in the lower right-hand corner – was lost during the last war in a Berlin museum. This fascinating painting captures Florence at the height of the Renaissance, a city of buildings in bright white, pink and tan; the great churches are without their façades, the Uffizi and Medici chapels have not yet appeared, and the Medici and Pitti palaces are without their later extensions.

The museum is not large. At present it contains only a number of plans and maps, as well as a collection of amateurish watercolours of Florence's sights from the last century, and paintings of Florence's surroundings by Ottone Rosai, a local favourite who died in 1957. Today's Florentines seem much less interested in the Renaissance than in the city of their grandparents. For some further evidence, look around the corner of Via S. Egidio, where some recent remodelling has uncovered posters over the street from 1925, announcing plans for paying the war debt and a coming visit of the *Folies Bergère*. The Florentines have restored them and put them under glass.

From Via dell'Oriuolo, Via Folco Portinari takes you to Florence's main hospital, **Santa Maria Nuova**, founded in 1286 by the father of Dante's Beatrice, Folco Portinari. A tomb in the hospital's church, Sant'Egidio, is all that remains of the family. Readers of Iris Origo's *The Merchant of Prato* will recognize it as the workplace of the good notary, Ser Lapo Mazzei. The portico, by Buontalenti, was finished in 1612.

## Medieval Streets North of the Arno

Just west of Via Por S. Maria, the main street leading down to the Ponte Vecchio, you'll find some of the oldest and best-preserved lanes in Florence. Near the Mercato Nuovo at the top of the street (*see* p.127) stands the **Palazzo di Parte Guelfa**, the 13th-century headquarters of the Guelph party, and often the real seat of power in the city, paid for by property confiscated from the Ghibellines; in the 15th century Brunelleschi added a hall on the top floor and an extension. Next door is the guildhall of the silk-makers, the 14th-century **Palazzo dell' Arte della Seta**, still bearing its bas-relief emblem, or *stemma*, of a closed door, the age-old guild symbol. It's worth continuing around the Guelph Palace to Via Pellicceria to see the fine ensemble of medieval buildings on the tiny square near Via delle Terme, named after the old Roman baths.

## Palazzo Davanzati

*Open 8.30–1.50; closed alternate Sun and Mon.*

To get an idea of what life was like inside these sombre palaces some 600 years ago, stroll over to nearby Via Porta Rossa, site of the elegant Palazzo Davanzati, now arranged as the **Museo della Casa Fiorentina Antica** (re-opened in 2005 after a 10-year restoration programme). One of the city's most delightful museums, it offers a chance to step back into domestic life of yore.

Originally built in the mid-14th century for the Davizzi family, the house was purchased by merchant Bernardo Davanzati in 1578 and stayed in the family until the 1900s. Restored by an antique collector in 1904, it is the best-preserved medieval-Renaissance house in Florence.

## Piazza Santa Trínita

Three old Roman roads – Via Porta Rossa, Via delle Terme and Borgo SS. Apostoli – lead into the irregularly shaped Piazza Santa Trínita. Borgo SS. Apostoli is named after one of Florence's oldest churches, the little Romanesque **Santi Apostoli** (11th century), which is located in the sunken Piazzetta del Limbo, former cemetery of unbaptized babies.

Piazza Santa Trínita itself boasts an exceptionally fine architectural ensemble, grouped around the 'Column of Justice' from the Roman Baths of Caracalla, given by Pius IV to Cosimo I, and later topped with a red statue of Justice by Francesco del Tadda. Its pale granite is set off by the palaces of the piazza: the High Renaissance-Roman **Palazzo Bartolini-Salimbeni** by Baccio d'Agnolo (1520) on the corner of Via Porta Rossa, formerly the fashionable Hôtel du Nord where Herman Melville stayed; the medieval **Palazzo Buondelmonti**, with a 1530 façade by Baccio d'Agnolo, once home to the reading room and favourite haunt of such literati in the 19th century as Dumas, Browning, Manzoni and Stendhal; and the magnificent curving **Palazzo Spini-Ferroni**, the largest medieval palace in Florence, built in 1289 and still retaining its original battlements. This is now home to the heirs of the Florentine designer Ferragamo and houses a retail outlet and a fascinating small **museum** of Ferragamo's life and work, including some of the most beautiful shoes in the world (*open Mon–Fri 9–1 and 2–6 by appt only, t 055 336 0456; free*).

### Santa Trínita

*Open Mon–Sat 8–12 and 4–6, Sun 4–6 only.*

The church of Santa Trínita has stood here, in one form or another, since the 12th century; its unusual accent on the first syllable (from the Latin *Trínitas*) is considered proof of its ancient foundation. Although the pedestrian façade added by Buontalenti in 1593 isn't especially welcoming, step into its shadowy 14th-century interior for several artistic treats, beginning with the **Bartolini-Salimbeni Chapel** (fourth on the right), frescoed in 1422 by the Sienese Lorenzo Monaco; his marriage of the Virgin takes place in a Tuscan fantasy backdrop of pink towers. He also painted the chapel's graceful, ethereally coloured altarpiece, the *Annunciation*.

In the choir, the **Sassetti Chapel** is one of the masterpieces of Domenico Ghirlandaio, completed in 1495 for wealthy merchant Francesco Sassetti and dedicated to the Life of St Francis, but also to the life of Francesco Sassetti, the city and his Medici circle: the scene above the altar, of Francis receiving the Rule of the Order, is transferred to the Piazza della Signoria, watched by Sassetti (to the right, with the fat purse) and Lorenzo il Magnifico; on the steps stands the great Latinist Poliziano with Lorenzo's three sons. The *Death of St Francis* pays homage to Giotto's similar composition in Santa Croce. The altarpiece, the *Adoration of the Shepherds* (1485), is one of Ghirlandaio's best-known works, often described as the archetypal Renaissance painting, a contrived but charming classical treatment; the Magi arrive through a triumphal arch, a Roman sarcophagus is used as manger and a ruined temple for a stable – all matched by the sibyls on the vault; the sibyl on the outer arch is the one who supposedly announced the birth of Christ to Augustus.

Santa Trínita is a Vallombrosan church and the first chapel to the right of the altar holds the Order's holy of holies, a painted crucifix formerly in San Miniato. The story goes that on a Good Friday, a young noble named Giovanni Gualberto was on his way to Mass when he met the man who had recently murdered his brother. Rather than take his revenge, Gualberto pardoned the assassin in honour of the holy day. When he arrived at church to pray, this crucifix nodded in approval of his mercy. Giovanni was so impressed that he went on to found the Vallombrosan order in the Casentino.

The **Sanctuary** was frescoed by Alesso Baldovinetti, though only four Old Testament figures survive. In the second chapel to the left the marble *Tomb of Bishop Benozzo Federighi* (1454) is by Luca della Robbia. In the fourth chapel, a detached fresco by Neri di Bicci portrays San Giovanni Gualberto and his fellow Vallombrosan saints.

# West of Piazza della Repubblica

The streets west of Piazza della Repubblica have always been the choicest district of Florence, and **Via de' Tornabuoni** the city's smartest shopping street. These days you won't find many innovations: Milan's current status as headquarters of Italy's fashion industry is a sore point with Florence.

In the bright and ambitious 1400s, however, when Florence was the centre of European high finance, Via de' Tornabuoni and its environs was the area the new merchant élite chose for their palaces. Today's bankers build great skyscrapers for the firm and settle for modest mansions for themselves; in Florence's heyday, things were reversed. Bankers and wool tycoons really owned their businesses. While their places of work were quite simple, their homes were imposing city palaces, all built in the same conservative style and competing with each other in size like some Millionaires' Row in 19th-century America.

The champion was the **Palazzo Strozzi**, a long block up Via de' Tornabuoni from Piazza Trínita. This rusticated stone cube of fearful dimensions squats in its piazza, radiating almost visible waves of megalomania. There are few architectural innovations in the Palazzo Strozzi, but here the typical Florentine palace is blown up to the level of the absurd: although three storeys like other palaces, each floor is as tall as three or four normal ones, and the rings to tie up horses could hold elephants. Like Michelangelo's *David*, Florence's other beautiful monster, it emits the unpleasant sensation of what Mary McCarthy called the 'giganticism of the human ego', the will to surpass not only antiquity but nature herself. Nowadays, at least, the Strozzi palace is moderately useful as a space to hold temporary exhibitions.

## Palazzo Rucellai

There are two other exceptional palaces in the quarter. At the north end of Via de' Tornabuoni stands the beautiful golden **Palazzo Antinori** (1465, architect unknown), which has Florence's grandest Baroque façade, **San Gaetano** (1648, by Gherardo Silvani), as its equally golden companion, despite being decorated with statues that would look right at home in Rome but look like bad actors in Florence.

The second important palace, Florence's most celebrated example of domestic architecture, is the **Palazzo Rucellai**, in Via della Vigna Nuova. Its original owner, Giovanni Rucellai, was a quattrocento tycoon like Filippo Strozzi, but an intellectual as well, whose *Zibaldone*, or 'commonplace book', is one of the best sources available on the life and tastes of the educated Renaissance merchant. In 1446 Rucellai chose Leon Battista Alberti to design his palace. Actually built by Bernardo Rossellino, it follows Alberti's precepts and theories in its use of the three classical orders; instead of the usual rusticated stone, the façade has a far more delicate decoration of incised irregular blocks and a frieze, elements influential in subsequent Italian architecture – though far more noticeably in Rome than Florence itself. Originally the palace was only five bays wide, and when another two bays were added later the edge was left ragged, unfinished, a nice touch, as if the builders could return at any moment and pick up where they left off. The frieze, like that on Santa Maria Novella, portrays the devices of the Medici and the Rucellai families (Giovanni's son married a daughter of Piero de' Medici), a wedding fêted in the **Loggia dei Rucellai** across the street, also designed by Alberti.

## Piazza Goldoni and Ognissanti

Before taking leave of old Florence's west end, head back to the Arno and **Piazza Goldoni**, named after the great comic playwright from Venice. The bridge here, the **Ponte alla Carraia**, is new and nondescript, but its 1304 version played a leading role in that year's most memorable disaster: a company staging a water pageant of the *Inferno*, complete with monsters, devils and tortured souls, attracted such a large crowd that the bridge collapsed under the weight, and all were drowned.

The most important building on the piazza, the **Palazzo Ricasoli**, was built in the 15th century but bears the name of one of unified Italy's first Prime Ministers, Bettino 'Iron Baron' Ricasoli. Just to the east on Lungarno Corsini looms the enormous

**Palazzo Corsini**, the city's most prominent piece of Roman Baroque extravagance, begun in 1650 and crowned with a bevy of statues. The Corsini, the most prominent family of 17th- and 18th-century Florence, were reputedly so wealthy that they could ride from Florence to Rome entirely on their own property. The **Galleria Corsini** (*adm by appt only, t 055 218994; Mon 9–4, Tues–Fri 9–1, enter from Via Parione*), houses paintings by Giovanni Bellini, Signorelli, Filippino Lippi and Pontormo, and *Muses* from the ducal palace of Urbino, painted by Raphael's first master, Timoteo Viti. It also has the rarest of Florentine amenities: a garden, a 17th-century oasis of box hedges, Roman statues, lemon trees and tortoises. Further east on Lungarno Corsini stood the Libreria Orioli, which caused a scandal when it published the first edition of *Lady Chatterley's Lover* in 1927.

To the west of Piazza Goldoni lies the old neighbourhood of the only Florentine to have a continent named after him. Amerigo Vespucci (1451–1512) was a Medici agent in Seville, and made two voyages from there to America on the heels of Columbus. His parish church, **Ognissanti** (All Saints) (*open 8–12.30 and 5–7.30*), is set back from the river behind a Baroque façade, on property donated in 1256 by the Umiliati, a religious order that specialized in wool-working. The Vespucci family tomb is below the second altar to the right, and Amerigo himself is said to be pictured next to the Madonna in the fresco of the Madonna della Misericordia. Also buried in Ognissanti was the Filepepi family, one of whom was Botticelli.

The best art is to be found in the **Convent**, just to the left of the church at No.42 (*open Sat, Mon and Tues 9–12; you may have to ring*). Frescoed in the refectory is the great *Last Supper*, or *Cenacolo*, painted by Domenico Ghirlandaio in 1480. It's hard to think of a more serene and elegant Last Supper, alike to a garden party with its background of fruit trees and exotic birds; a peacock sits in the window, cherries and peaches litter the lovely tablecloth. On either side of the fresco are two scholarly saints moved from the church itself; Ghirlandaio's *St Jerome* and, on the right, young Botticelli's *St Augustine*.

# Santa Maria Novella

*Open Mon–Thurs and Sat 9.30–5; Fri, Sun and hols 1–5; adm.*

As in so many other Italian cities, the two churches of the preaching orders – the Dominicans' Santa Maria Novella and the Franciscans' Santa Croce – became the largest and most prestigious in the city, where wealthy families vied to create the most beautiful chapels and tombs. In Florence, by some twitch of city planning, both of these sacred art galleries dominate broad, stale squares that do not invite you to linger; in the irregular **Piazza Santa Maria Novella** you may find yourself looking over your shoulder for the ghosts of the carriages that once raced madly around the two stout obelisks set on turtles, just as in a Roman circus, in the fashionable carriage races of the 1700s. The arcade on the south side, the **Loggia di San Paolo**, is very much like Brunelleschi's *Spedale degli Innocenti*, although it suffers somewhat from its use as a busy bus shelter; the lunette over the door, by Andrea della Robbia, is the *Meeting* *of SS. Francis and Dominic.* Santa Maria Novella redeems the anomie of its square with its stupendous black and white marble **façade**, the finest in Florence. The lower part, with its looping arcades, is Romanesque work in the typical Tuscan mode, finished before 1360. In 1456 Giovanni Rucellai commissioned Alberti to complete it, a remarkably fortunate choice. Alberti's half not only perfectly harmonizes with the original, but perfects it with geometrical harmonies to create what appears to be a kind of Renaissance Sun Temple. The original builders started it off by orienting the church to the south instead of west, so that at noon the sun streams through the 14th-century rose window. The only symbol Alberti put on the façade is a blazing sun; the unusual sundials, over the arches on the extreme right and left, were added by Cosimo I's court astronomer Egnazio Danti. The base of the façade is also the base of an equilateral triangle, with Alberti's sun at the apex. The beautiful frieze depicts the Rucellai emblem (a billowing sail), as on the Palazzo Rucellai. The wall of Gothic recesses to the right, enclosing the old cemetery, are *avelli*, or family tombs.

The **interior** is vast, lofty and more 'Gothic' in feel than any other church in Florence – no thanks to Vasari, who was set loose to remodel the church to 16th-century taste, painting over the original frescoes, removing the rood screen and Dominicans' choir from the nave, and remodelling the altars; in the 1800s restorers did their best to de-Vasari Santa Maria with neo-Gothic details. Neither party, however, could touch two of the interior's most distinctive features – the striking stone vaulting of the nave and the perspective created by the columns marching down the aisles, each pair placed a little closer together as they approach the altar.

Over the portal at the entrance is a fresco lunette by Botticelli that has recently been restored. One of Santa Maria Novella's best-known pictures has also recently been restored and is at the second altar on the left: Masaccio's *Trinità*, painted around 1425, one of the revolutionary works of the Renaissance. Masaccio's use of architectural elements and perspective gives his composition both physical and intellectual depth. The flat wall becomes a deeply recessed Brunelleschian chapel, calm and classical, enclosed in a coffered barrel vault; at the foot of the fresco a bleak skeleton decays in its tomb, bearing a favourite Tuscan reminder: 'I was that which you are, you will be that which I am.'

Above this morbid suggestion of physical death kneel the two donors; within the celestially rational inner sanctum the Virgin and St John stand at the foot of the Cross, humanity's link with the mystery of the Trinity. In the nearby pulpit, designed by Brunelleschi, Galileo was first denounced by the Inquisition for presuming to believe that the earth went around the sun.

There is little else to detain you in the aisles, but the first chapel in the left transept, the raised **Cappella Strozzi**, is one of the most evocative corners of 14th-century Florence, frescoed entirely by Nardo di Cione and his brother, Andrea Orcagna; on the vault pictures of St Thomas Aquinas and the Virtues are echoed in Andrea's lovely altarpiece *The Redeemer Donating the Keys to St Peter and the Book of Wisdom to St Thomas Aquinas*; on the left wall there's a crowded scene of Paradise, with the righteous lined up in a medieval school class photograph. On the right, Nardo painted a striking view of Dante's *Inferno*, with all of a Tuscan's special attention to precise

# Santa Maria Novella

1 Masaccio's *Trinità*
2 Brunelleschi's Pulpit
3 Cappella Strozzi
4 Sacristy
5 Cappella Gondi
6 Sanctuary
7 Fillippo Strozzi Chapel
8 Rucellai Chapel
9 Gothic Tombs
10 *Universal Deluge*
11 Spanish Chapel
12 Chiostrino dei Morti
13 Refectory

map-like detail. Dramatically in the centre of the **Nave** hangs Giotto's *Crucifix* (*c.*1300), one of the artist's first works. In the **Gondi Chapel** hangs another famous *Crucifix*, carved in wood by Brunelleschi, which, according to Vasari, so astonished his friend Donatello that he dropped the eggs he was carrying in his apron for their lunch when he first saw it.

The charming fresco cycle in the **Sanctuary** (1485–90), painted by Domenico Ghirlandaio, is the *Lives of the Virgin, St John the Baptist and the Dominican Saints* portrayed in magnificent architectural settings; little Michelangelo was among the students who helped him complete it. Nearly all of the bystanders are portraits of Florentine quattrocento VIPs, including the artist himself (in the red hat, in the *Expulsion of St Joachim from the Temple*), but most prominent are the ladies and gentlemen of the Tornabuoni house. More excellent frescoes adorn the **Filippo Strozzi Chapel**, the finest work ever to come from the brush of Filippino Lippi, painted in 1502 near the end of his life; the exaggerated, dark and violent scenes portray the lives of St Philip (his crucifixion and his subduing of the dragon before the Temple of Mars, which creates such a stench that it kills the heathen prince) and of St John the Evangelist (raising Drusiana from the dead and being martyred in boiling oil). The chapel's beautifully carved tomb of Filippo Strozzi is by Benedetto da Maiano. The **Rucellai Chapel** contains a marble statue of the Madonna and Bambino by Nino Pisano and a fine bronze tomb by Ghiberti, which makes an interesting comparison with the three Gothic tombs nearby in the right transept. One of these contains the remains of the Patriarch of Constantinople, who died in here after the failure of the Council of Florence in 1439 to reunite the Western and Eastern Churches.

## The Green Cloister and Spanish Chapel

More great frescoes, restored after the flood, await the visitor in Santa Maria Novella's Cloisters, open as a city museum (*entrance just to the left of the church; open Sat–Thurs 9–2; adm*). The first cloister, the so-called **Green Cloister**, one of the masterpieces of Paolo Uccello and his assistants, is named for the *terraverde* or green earth pigment used by the artist, which lends the scenes from Genesis their eerie, ghostly quality. Much damaged by time and neglect, they are nevertheless striking for their two Uccellian obsessions – perspective and animals. Best known, and in better condition than the others, is Uccello's surreal *Universal Deluge*, a composition framed by the steep walls of two arks, before and after views, which have the uncanny effect of making the scene appear to come racing out of its own vanishing point, a vanishing point touched by divine wrath in a searing bolt of lightning. In between the claustrophobic walls the flood rises, tossing up a desperate ensemble of humanity, waterlogged bodies, naked men bearing clubs, crowded in a jam of flotsam and jetsam in the dark waters. In the right foreground, amidst all the panic, stands a tall robed man, seemingly a visionary, perhaps even Noah himself, looking heavenward while a flood victim seizes him by the ankles.

The **Spanish Chapel** at the far end of the cloisters, takes its name from the Spanish court followers of Eleonora di Toledo who worshipped here; the Inquisition had earlier made the chapel its headquarters in Florence. The chapel is, again, famous for its frescoes, the masterpiece of a little-known 14th-century artist named Andrea di Buonaiuto, whose subject was the Dominican cosmology, beautifully portrayed so that even the 'Hounds of the Lord' (a pun on the Order's name, the 'Domini canes') on the right wall seem more like pets than militant bloodhounds sniffing out unorthodox beliefs. The church behind the scene with the hounds is a fairy-pink confection of what Buonaiuto imagined the Duomo would look like when finished; it may well be Arnolfo di Cambio's original conception. Famous Florentines, including Giotto, Dante, Boccaccio and Petrarch, stand to the right of the dais supporting the pope, emperor and various sour-faced hierophants. Off to the right the artist has portrayed four rather urbane Vices with dancing girls, while the Dominicans lead stray sheep back to the fold. On the left wall, St Thomas Aquinas dominates the portrayal of the Contemplative Life, surrounded by Virtues and Doctors of the Church.

The oldest part of the monastery, the **Chiostrino dei Morti** (1270s), contains some 14th-century frescoes, while the **Great Cloister** beyond is now off limits, the property of the Carabinieri, the new men in black charged with keeping the Italians orthodox. Off the Green Cloister, the **Refectory** is a striking hall with cross vaulting and frescoes by Alessandro Allori, now serving as a museum.

## Around Santa Maria Novella

Just behind, but a world apart from Santa Maria Novella, another large, amorphous square detracts from one of Italy's finest modern buildings – the **Stazione Centrale**, designed by the architect Michelucci in 1935. Adorned by only a glass block canopy at the entrance (and an early model of that great Italian invention, the digital clock), the station is nevertheless remarkable for its clean lines and impeccable practicality.

Leading south from Piazza Santa Maria Novella, Via delle Belle Donne was once known for its excellent brothels. Today it is worth a short stroll to see one of the very few crossroads in Italy marked by a cross, a Celtic custom that never really caught on here. According to legend, **Croce del Trebbio** (from a corruption of 'trivium') marks the spot of a massacre of Patarene heretics in the 1240s, after the masses had been excited by a sermon given by the fire-eating Inquisitor St Peter Martyr from the pulpit of Santa Maria Novella.

# San Lorenzo and the Medici Chapels

The lively quarter just east of Santa Maria Novella has been associated with the Medici ever since Giovanni di Bicci de' Medici commissioned Brunelleschi to rebuild the ancient church of San Lorenzo in 1420; subsequent members of the dynasty lavished bushels of florins on its decoration and Medici pantheon, and on several projects commissioned from Michelangelo. The mixed result of all their efforts could be held up as an archetype of the Renaissance, described by Walter Pater as 'great rather by what it designed or aspired to do, than by what it actually achieved'. San Lorenzo's façade of corrugated brick, was the most *nonfinito* of all of Michelangelo's unfinished projects; commissioned by Medici Pope Leo X in 1516, the project never got further than Michelangelo's scale model, which may be seen in the Casa Buonarroti. To complete the church's dingy aspect, the piazza in front contains a universally detested 19th-century statue of Cosimo I's dashing father, Giovanni delle Bande Nere, who died at the age of 28 of wounds received fighting against Emperor Charles V.

The **interior** was completed after Brunelleschi's death to his design, classically calm in good grey *pietra serena*. Of the artistic treasures it contains, most riveting are **Donatello's pulpits**, the sculptor's last works, completed by his pupils after his death in 1466. Cast in bronze, the pulpits were commissioned by Donatello's friend and patron Cosimo il Vecchio. Little in Donatello's previous work prepares the viewer for these scenes of Christ's passion and Resurrection with their rough and impressionistic details, their unbalanced, emotional and overcrowded compositions, more reminiscent of Rodin than anything Florentine. Off the left transept the **Old Sacristy** is a beautiful vaulted chamber with calmer sculptural decoration by Donatello.

Just beyond the Bronzino a door leads into the 15th-century **Cloister**, and from there a stair leads up to Michelangelo's **Biblioteca Laurenziana** (*open Mon–Sat 8.30–1.30*).

## The Medici Chapels

*Open daily 8.15–5; closed 2nd and 4th Sun and 1st, 3rd and 5th Mon of month.*

San Lorenzo is most famous, however, for the Medici Chapels, which lie outside and behind the church. The entrance leads through the crypt, a dark and austere place where many of the Medici are actually buried.

Their main monument, the family obsession, is just up the steps, and has long been known as the **Chapel of the Princes**, a stupefying, costly octagon of death that, as much as the Grand Dukes fussed over it, lends their memory an unpleasant aftertaste of bric-a-brac that grew and grew. Perhaps only a genuine Medici could love its trashy opulence; all of Grand Duke Cosimo's descendants worked like beavers to finish it according to the plans left by Cosimo's illegitimate son, Giovanni de' Medici. Yet even today it is only partially completed, the *pietre dure* extending only part of the way up the walls. The 19th-century frescoes in the cupola are a poor substitute for the originally planned 'Apotheosis of the Medici' in lapis lazuli, and the two statues in gilded bronze in the niches over the sarcophagi are nothing like the intended figures to be carved in semi-precious stone. The most interesting feature is the inlaid *pietra dura* arms of Tuscan towns and the large Medici arms above, with their familiar six red boluses. (The balls probably derive from the family's origins as pharmacists (*medici*), and opponents called them 'the pills'. Medici supporters, however, made them their battle cry in street fights: 'Balls! Balls!')

A passageway leads to Michelangelo's **New Sacristy**, commissioned by Leo X to occupy an unfinished room originally built to balance Brunelleschi's Old Sacristy. Michelangelo's first idea was to turn it into a new version of his unfinished, overly ambitious Pope Julius Tomb, an idea quickly quashed by his Medici patrons, who requested instead four wall tombs. Michelangelo only worked on two of the monuments, but managed to finish the New Sacristy itself, creating a silent and gloomy mausoleum, closed in and grey, a chilly introspective cocoon calculated to depress even the most chatty tour groups.

Nor are the famous tombs guaranteed to cheer. Both honour nonentities: that of *Night and Day* belongs to Lorenzo il Magnifico's son, the Duke of Nemours, and symbolizes the Active Life, while the *Dawn and Dusk* is of Guiliano's nephew, Lorenzo, Duke of Urbino (and dedicatee of *The Prince*), who symbolizes the Contemplative Life (true to life in one respect – Lorenzo was a disappointment to Machiavelli and everyone else, passively obeying the dictates of his uncle Pope Leo X). Idealized statues of the two men, in Roman patrician gear, represent these states of mind, while draped on their sarcophagi are Michelangelo's four allegorical figures of the Times of Day, so heavy with weariness and grief they seem ready to slide off on to the floor. The most finished figure, *Night*, has always impressed the critics; she is almost a personification of despair, the mouthpiece of Michelangelo's most bitter verse:

> Sweet to me is sleep, and even more to be like stone
> While wrong and shame endure;
> Not to see, nor to feel, is my good fortune.
> Therefore, do not wake me; speak softly here.

Both statues of the dukes look towards the back wall, where a large double tomb for Lorenzo il Magnifico and his brother Giuliano was originally planned, to be decorated with river gods. The only part of this tomb ever completed is the statue of the *Madonna and Child* now in place, accompanied by the Medici patron saints, the doctors Cosmas and Damian.

In 1975, charcoal drawings were discovered on the walls of the little room off the altar (*ask at the cash desk for a permit, as only 12 people can enter at one time*). They were attributed to Michelangelo, who may have hidden here in 1530, when the Medici had regained Florence and apparently would only forgive the artist for aiding the republican defence if he would finish their tombs. But Michelangelo had had enough of their ducal pretences and went off to Rome, never to return to Florence.

## Mercato Centrale and Perugino

What makes the neighbourhood around San Lorenzo so lively is its street market, which the Florentines run with an almost Neapolitan flamboyance (*open Tues–Sat, also open Mon in summer*). Stalls selling clothes and leather extend from the square up Via dell'Ariento and vicinity (nicknamed 'Shanghai') towards the **Mercato Centrale**, Florence's main food market (*open Mon–Fri 7–2; some stalls also open Sat afternoon*), a cast-iron and glass confection of the 1870s, brimful of fresh fruit and vegetables, leering boars' heads and mounds of tripe.

Beyond the market, at Via Faenza 42, is the entrance to Perugino's **Cenacolo di Foligno** fresco, housed in the ex-convent of the Tertiary Franciscans of Foligno (*open daily 9–12; ring the bell*). This 1490s Umbrian version of the Last Supper was discovered in the 1850s and has recently been restored.

## Palazzo Medici-Riccardi

A block from San Lorenzo and the Piazza del Duomo stands the palace that once held Florence's unofficial court, where ambassadors would call, kings would lodge, and important decisions would be made. Built in 1444 by Michelozzo for Cosimo il Vecchio, it was the principal address of the Medici for a hundred years, until Cosimo I abandoned it for larger quarters in the Palazzo Vecchio and the Pitti Palace. In 1659 the Riccardi purchased the palace, added to it and did everything to keep it glittering until Napoleon and his debts drove them to bankruptcy in 1809. The palace is now used as the city's prefecture.

In its day, though, it was the largest private address in the city, where the family lived with the likes of Donatello's *David* and *Judith and Holofernes*, Uccello's *Battle of San Romano* and other masterpieces now in the Uffizi and Bargello. Frescoes are much harder to move, however, and the Palazzo Medici is worth visiting to see the most charming one in Italy, Benozzo Gozzoli's 1459 *Procession of the Magi*, located in the **Cappella dei Magi** upstairs (*open Thurs–Tues 9–7; adm. Only a few people allowed in at a time; in summer you can reserve, t 055 276 0340*).

Painting in a delightful, decorative manner more reminiscent of International Gothic than the awakening Renaissance style of his contemporaries, Gozzoli took a religious subject and turned it into a merry, brilliantly coloured pageant of beautifully dressed kings, knights and pages, accompanied by greyhounds and a giraffe, who travel through a springtime landscape of jewel-like trees and castles. This is a largely secular painting, representing less the original Three Kings than the annual pageant of the *Compagnia dei Magi*, Florence's richest confraternity. The scene is wrapped around three walls of the small chapel – you feel as if you had walked straight into a glowing fairytale world. Most of the faces are those of the Medici and other local celebrities; Gozzoli certainly had no qualms about putting himself among the crowd of figures on the right wall, with his name written on his red cap. In the foreground, note the black man carrying a bow. Blacks, as well as Turks, Circassians, Tartars and others, were common enough in Renaissance Florence, originally brought as slaves. By the 1400s, however, contemporary writers mention them as artisans, fencing masters, soldiers and one famous archery instructor, who may be the man pictured here. For an extraordinary contrast pop into the **gallery** (up the second set of stairs) with its 17th-century ceiling by Neapolitan Luca Giordano, showing the last, unspeakable Medici floating around in marshmallow clouds. In a small adjoining room is a lovely Madonna and Child by Filippo Lippi, placed here a couple of years ago after restoration.

## San Marco

*Convent open daily 8.15–1.50, Sat 8.15–6.50; closed 1st and 3rd Sun of month and 2nd and 4th Mon of month; adm. Church open 7–12 and 4–7 daily.*

Despite all the others who contributed to this Dominican monastery and church, it has always been best known for the work of its most famous resident. Fra Angelico lived here from 1436 until his death in 1455, spending the time turning Michelozzo's simple **cloister** into a complete exposition of his own deep faith, expressed in bright colours and angelic pastels. Fra Angelico painted the frescoes in the corners of the cloister, and on the first floor there is a small museum of his work, collected from Florentine churches, as well as several early 15th-century portraits by Fra Bartolommeo, capturing some of the most sincere spirituality of the age. The *Last Supper* in the refectory is by Ghirlandaio. Other works by Fra Angelico include the *Life of Christ* series, in which the Saved are well-dressed Italians holding hands. The Bad (mostly princes and prelates) are stripped to receive their interesting tortures.

Right at the top of the stairs to the monks' dormitory, your eyes meet the Angelic Friar's masterpiece, a miraculous *Annunciation* that offers an intriguing comparison with Leonardo's *Annunciation* in the Uffizi. The subject was a favourite with Florentine artists, not only because it was a severe test – expressing a divine revelation with a composition of strict economy – but because the Annunciation, falling near the spring equinox, was New Year's Day for Florence until the Medici adopted the Pope's calendar in the 17th century. In each of the monks' cells, Fra Angelico and students painted the *Crucifixion*, all the same but for some slight differences in pose; glancing in the cells down the corridor in turn gives the impression of a cartoon. One of the cells belonged to Savonarola, who was the prior here during his period of dominance in Florence; it has the simple furniture of the period and a portrait of Savonarola by Fra Bartolommeo. In a nearby corridor, you can see an anonymous painting of the monk and two of his followers being led to the stake on Piazza della Signoria. Michelozzo's Library, off the main corridor, is as light and airy as the cloisters below; in it is displayed a collection of choir books, one illuminated by Fra Angelico.

Near San Marco, at Via G La Pira 4, the **University of Florence** runs several small museums; nearly all the collections were begun by the indefatigable Medici. The **Geology and Palaeontology Museum** (*open winter Tues 9–1 and 2–6, Wed–Sat 9–1; summer Wed and Fri 9–1; adm*) has one of Italy's best collections of fossils, many of which were uncovered in Tuscany. The **Mineralogy and Lithology Museum** (*open Mon–Fri 9–1 and 2nd Sun of month 8–2; adm*) houses a collection of strange and beautiful rocks, especially from Elba. The **Botanical Museum** (*open on request only, t 055 275 7462 for details*) is of less interest to the casual visitor, though it houses one of the most extensive herbariums in the world; most impressive here are the exquisite wax models of plants made in the early 1800s.

Also on Via La Pira is the entrance to the University's **Giardino dei Semplici**, the botanical garden created for Cosimo I. The garden maintains its original layout, with medicinal herbs, Tuscan plants, flowers and tropical plants in its greenhouses (*open summer Wed–Fri 9–1, Tues 9–1 and 3–6; winter Mon–Fri 9–1; adm*).

## Sant'Apollonia and the Scalzo

*Cenacoli*, or frescoes of the Last Supper, became almost *de rigueur* in monastic refectories; in several of these the Last Supper is all that remains of a convent. Until 1860, the Renaissance convent of **Sant'Apollonia**, off Piazza S. Marco at Via XXVII Aprile 1 (*open daily 8.15–1.50; closed 2nd and 4th Mon and 1st, 3rd and 5th Sun of month*) was the abode of cloistered nuns, and the *cenacolo* in their refectory was a secret. When the convent was suppressed, and the painting discovered under the whitewash, the critics believed it to be the work of Paolo Uccello, but lately have unanimously attributed it to Andrea del Castagno, painted 1445–50. The other walls have sinopie of the Crucifixion, Entombment and Resurrection by Castagno; in the vestibule there are good works by Neri di Bicci and Paolo Schiavo.

Not far away you can enter a radically different artistic world in the **Chiostro dello Scalzo**, again off Piazza S. Marco at Via Cavour 69 (*open Mon, Thurs and Sat 8.15–1.50; ring the bell*). Formerly part of the Confraternity of San Giovanni Battista, all that has survived is this cloister, frescoed (1514–24) with scenes of the life of St John the Baptist by Andrea del Sarto and his pupil Franciabigio. Del Sarto, Browning's 'perfect painter', painted these in monochrome grisaille, and while the scene of the *Baptism of Christ* is a beautiful work, some of the other panels are the most unintentionally funny things in Florence – the scene of Herod's banquet is reduced to a meagre breakfast where the king and queen look up indignantly at the man bringing in the platter of the Baptist's head as if he were a waiter who has made a mistake with their order.

# The Galleria dell'Accademia

*Open Tues–Sun 8.15–6.50; adm.*

From Piazza San Marco, Via Ricasoli makes a beeline for the Duomo, but on most days the view is obstructed by the crowds milling around No.60; in the summer the queues are as long as those at the Uffizi, everyone anxious to get a look at

Michelangelo's *David*. Just over a hundred years ago Florence decided to take this precocious symbol of republican liberty out of the rain and install it, with much pomp, in a specially built classical exedra in this gallery.

Michelangelo completed the *David* for the city in 1504, when he was 29, and it was the work that established the overwhelming reputation he had in his own time. The monstrous block of marble – 16ft high but unusually shallow – had been quarried 40 years earlier by the Cathedral Works and spoiled by other hands. The block was offered around to several other artists, including Leonardo da Vinci, before young Michelangelo decided to take up the challenge of carving the largest statue created since Roman times. And it is the dimensions of the *David* that remain the biggest surprise in these days of endless reproductions. Certainly as a political symbol of the Republic, he is excessive – the irony of a David the size of a Goliath is disconcerting – but as a symbol of the artistic and intellectual aspirations of the Renaissance period he is unsurpassed.

And it's hard to deny, after gazing at this enormous nude, that these same Renaissance aspirations by the 1500s began snuggling uncomfortably close to the frontiers of kitsch. Disproportionate size is one symptom; the calculated intention to excite a strong emotional response is another. In the *David*, virtuosity eclipses vision, and commits the even deadlier kitsch sin of seeking the sterile empyrean of perfect beauty – most would argue that Michelangelo here achieves it, perhaps capturing his own feelings about the work in the *David*'s chillingly vain, self-satisfied expression. This is also one of the few statues to have actually injured someone. During a political disturbance in the Piazza della Signoria, its arm broke off and fell on a farmer's toe. In 1991 it was David's toe that fell victim when a madman chopped it off. Since then, the rest of his anatomy has been shielded by glass.

In the Galleria next to the *David* are Michelangelo's famous *nonfiniti*, the four *Prisoners* or *Slaves*, worked on between 1519 and 1536, sculpted for Pope Julius' tomb and left in various stages of completion, although it is endlessly argued whether this is by design or through lack of time. Whatever the case, they illustrate Michelangelo's view of sculpture as a prisoner in stone just as the soul is a prisoner of the body. When Michelangelo left them, the Medici snapped them up to decorate Buontalenti's Grotta fountain in the Boboli gardens.

The Gallery was founded by Grand Duke Pietro Leopold in 1784 to provide Academy students with examples of art from every period. The big busy Mannerist paintings around the *David* are by Michelangelo's contemporaries, among them Pontormo's *Venus and Cupid*, with a Michelangelesque Venus among theatre masks. Other rooms contain a good selection of quattrocento painting, including the *Madonna del Mare* by Botticelli, a damaged Baldovinetti, the *Thebaid* by a follower of Uccello, and Perugino's *Deposition*. The painted frontal of the **Adimari chest** shows a delightful wedding scene of the 1450s with the baptistry in the background that has been reproduced in half the books that have ever been written about the Renaissance.

The hall off to the left of the *David* was formerly the women's ward of a hospital, depicted in a greenish painting by Pontormo. Now it is used as a gallery of plaster models by 19th-century members of the Accademia.

The excellent **Collection of Old Musical Instruments** once housed in the Palazzo Vecchio has moved to the Accademia. The collection of some 150 exhibits, including several violins and cellos by Cremona greats like Stradivarius and Guarneri, are on display in a room on the ground floor, properly organized and labelled.

# Piazza Santissima Annunziata

This lovely square, really the only Renaissance attempt at a unified ensemble in Florence, is surrounded on three sides by arcades. In its centre, gazing down the splendid vista of Via dei Servi towards the Duomo, stands the equestrian statue of Ferdinand I (1607) by Giambologna and his pupil, Pietro Tacca, made of bronze from Turkish cannons captured during the Battle of Lepanto. More fascinating than Ferdinand are the pair of bizarre Baroque fountains, also by Tacca, that share the square. Though of a nominally marine theme, they resemble tureens of bouillabaisse that any ogre would be proud to serve, topped by grinning winged monkeys.

In the 1420s Filippo Brunelleschi struck the first blow for classical calm in this piazza when he built the celebrated **Spedale degli Innocenti** (*open Thurs–Tues 8.30–2; adm*) and its famous portico – an architectural landmark, but also a monument to Renaissance Italy's long, hard and ultimately unsuccessful struggle towards some kind of social consciousness. Even in the best of times, Florence's poor were treated like dirt; if any enlightened soul had been so bold as to propose even a modern conservative 'trickle down' theory to the Medici and the banking élite, their first thought would have been how to stop the leaks. Babies, at least, were treated a little better. The Spedale degli Innocenti was the first hospital for foundlings in Italy and the world (at the left end of the loggia you can still see the original window-wheel where babies were anonymously abandoned until 1875). Today it is a nursery school. The Spedale was Brunelleschi's first completed work and demonstrates his use of geometrical proportions adapted to traditional Tuscan Romanesque architecture. His lovely portico is adorned with the famous blue and white tondi of infants in swaddling clothes by Andrea della Robbia, added as an appeal to charity in the 1480s after several children died of malnutrition. Brunelleschi also designed the two beautiful cloisters of the convent; the **Chiostro delle Donne**, reserved for the hospital's nurses (located up the ramp on the right at No.13), is especially fine. Upstairs, the **Museo dello Spedale** (*open Thurs–Tues 8.30–2; adm*) contains a number of detached frescoes from Ognissanti and other churches, among them an unusual series of red and orange prophets by Alessandro Allori; other works include a *Madonna and Saints* by Piero di Cosimo, a *Madonna and Child* by Luca della Robbia, and the brilliant *Adoration of the Magi* (1488) painted by Domenico Ghirlandaio for the hospital's church, a crowded, colourful composition featuring portraits of members of the Arte della Lana, who funded the Spedale.

## Santissima Annunziata

To complement Brunelleschi's arches, the old church of Santissima Annunziata was rebuilt and given a broad arcaded portico by Michelozzo facing the street. Behind the portico the architect added the **Chiostrino dei Voti**, a porch decorated with a collection of early 16th-century frescoes, including two by Andrea del Sarto. The best of these, faded as it is, is a finely detailed *Nativity* by Alessio Baldovinetti, one of the quattrocento's underappreciated masters.

The church itself is the gaudiest in Florence; its freshly gilded elliptical dome, its unusual polygonal tribune around the sanctuary and megatons of *pietra dura* have helped it become the city's high-society parish, where even funerals are major social events. The huge candlelit chapel in the rear is the Tempietta, also by Michelozzo, sheltering a miraculous painting of *The Annunciation*.

## Archaeology Museum

*www.firenzemusei.it/archeologico; open Mon 2–7, Tues and Thurs 8.30–7, Wed and Fri–Sun 8.30–2; adm.*

From Piazza SS. Annunziata, Via della Colonna leads to Florence's **Museo Archeologico**, housed in the 17th-century Palazzo della Crocetta, originally built for Grand Duchess Maria Maddalena of Austria. Like nearly every other museum in Florence, this impressive collection was begun by the Medici, beginning with Cosimo il Vecchio and accelerating with the insatiable Cosimo I and his heirs. The Medici were especially fond of Etruscan things, while the impressive Egyptian collection was begun by Leopold II in the 1830s.

The **Etruscan collection** is on the first floor, including the famous bronze *Chimera*, a remarkable beast with the three heads of a lion, goat and snake. This 5th-century BC work, dug up near Arezzo in 1555 and immediately snatched by Cosimo I, had a great influence on Mannerist artists. There is no Mannerist fancy about its origins, though; like all such composite monsters, it is a religious icon, a calendar beast symbolizing the three seasons of the ancient Mediterranean agricultural year. In the same corridor stands the *Arringatore*, or Orator, a monumental bronze of the Hellenistic period, a civic-minded and civilized-looking gentleman, dedicated to Aulus Metellus, and the statue of *Minerva*. Also to be found in this section are other Etruscan bronzes, big and small. The cases here are full of wonderful objects, anything from tiny animals to jewellery, carved mirrors and household objects such as plates – there's even a strainer. All these show just how skilled the Etruscans were in casting bronze.

The beautifully lit **Egyptian collection**, also on the first floor, has been expanded and modernized. It includes some interesting small statuettes, mummies, canopic vases, and a unique wood-and-bone chariot, nearly completely preserved, found in a 14th-century BC tomb in Thebes.

On the second floor there is plenty of Greek art; Etruscan noble families were wont to buy up all they could afford. The beautiful Hellenistic horse's head once adorned the Palazzo Medici-Riccardi. The *Idolino*, a bronze of a young athlete, is believed to be a Roman copy of a 5th-century BC Greek original. There is an excellent *Kouros*, a young man in the archaic style from 6th-century BC Sicily. An unusual, recent find, the silver *Baratti Amphora*, was made in the 4th century BC in Antioch and covered with scores of small medallions showing mythological figures. Scholars believe that the images and their arrangement may encode an entire system of belief, the secret teaching of one of the mystic-philosophical cults common in Hellenistic times, and they hope some day to decipher it. There's a vast collection of Greek pottery (including the massive *François vase* in Room 2), and large Greek, Roman and Renaissance bronzes, recently brought out of storage. There are also several fabulous Greek marble sculptures dating from *c.* 500 BC.

There is virtually nothing displayed on the ground floor now although temporary exhibitions are held there. In the garden are several reconstructed Etruscan tombs (*open to visitors on Sat 8.30–2*). The fabulous collection of precious stones, coins and, most notably, cameos (amassed by the Medici) is now permanently on display in the corridor which runs between the museum and the church of Santissima Annunziata.

## Santa Maria Maddalena dei Pazzi and the Synagogue

East of the Archaeological Museum, Via della Colonna becomes one of Florence's typical straight, boring Renaissance streets. It's well worth taking a detour down Borgo Pinti, to No.58, to visit one of the city's least known but most intriguing churches, **Santa Maria Maddalena dei Pazzi** (*open Mon–Sat 9.30–12 and 5–7; Sun 9.30–11 and 5–7*), a fine example of architectural syncretism. The church itself was founded in the 13th century, rebuilt in classically Renaissance style by Giuliano da Sangallo, then given a full dose of Baroque when the church was rededicated to the Counter-Reformation saint of the Pazzi family. Inside it's all high theatre, with a gaudy trompe l'œil ceiling, paintings by Luca Giordano, florid chapels, and a wild marble chancel. From the Sacristy a door leads down into a crypt to the chapterhouse, which contains a frescoed *Crucifixion* (1496), one of Perugino's masterpieces. Despite the symmetry and quiet, contemplative grief of the five figures at the foot of the Cross and the stillness of the luminous Tuscan-Umbrian landscape, the fresco has a powerful impact, giving the viewer the uncanny sensation of being able to walk right into the scene. The fresco has never been restored; in the 1966 flood, the water came within four inches of it, and stopped.

Florence's Jewish community, although today a mere 1,200 strong, has long been one of the most important in Italy, invited to Florence by the republic in 1430, but repeatedly exiled and readmitted until Cosimo I founded Florence's Ghetto in 1551. When the Ghetto was opened up in 1848 and demolished soon after, a new **Synagogue** (1874–82) was built in Via L C Farini: a tall, charming, Mozarabic Pre-Raphaelite hybrid inspired by the Hagia Sophia and the Transito Synagogue of Toledo (*www.fol.it/sinagoga; open April, May, Sept and Oct Sun–Thurs 10–5 and Fri 10–2; June–Aug Sun–Thurs 10–6 and Fri 10–3; Nov–Feb Sun–Thurs 10–2; adm*). Although seriously damaged by the Nazis in August 1944, as well as by the Arno in 1966, it has since been lovingly restored. There's a small **Jewish Museum** upstairs (*opening hours as for Synagogue; call t 055 245252/3 for info*), which has a documentary history of Florentine Jews.

## Sant'Ambrogio and the Flea Market

The streets of Sant'Ambrogio are among the most dusty and piquant in the city centre, a neighbourhood where tourists seldom tread. Life revolves around the church in **Sant'Ambrogio** and its neighbouring food market made of cast iron in 1873; the church (rebuilt in the 13th century, 19th-century façade) is of interest for its artwork: the second chapel on the right has a lovely fresco of the *Madonna Enthroned with Saints* by Orcagna (or his school) and the **Cappella del Miracolo**, just left of the high altar, contains Mino da Fiesole's celebrated marble *Tabernacle* (1481) and his own tomb. The chapel has a fresco of a procession by Cosimo Rosselli, especially interesting for its depiction of 15th-century celebrities, including Pico della Mirandola and Rosselli himself (in a black hat, in the group on the left). Andrea Verrocchio is buried in the fourth chapel on the left; on the wall by the second altar, there's a *Nativity* by Baldovinetti. The fresco of an atypical *St Sebastian* in the first chapel of the left is by Agnolo Gaddi.

From Sant'Ambrogio take Via Pietrapiana to the bustling **Piazza dei Ciompi**, named after the wool-workers' revolt of 1378. In the morning, Florence's flea market or **Mercatino** takes place here, the best place in town to buy that 1940s radio or outdated ball gown you've always wanted. One side of the square is graced with the **Loggia del Pesce**, built by Vasari in 1568 for the fishmongers of the Mercato Vecchio; when that was demolished the loggia was salvaged and re-erected here.

## Casa Buonarroti

*www.casabuonarroti.it; open Wed–Mon 9.30–2; adm; look out for their temporary exhibitions.*

Michelangelo never lived in this house at Via Ghibellina 70, although he purchased it in 1508. That wasn't the point, especially to an artist who had no thought for his own personal comfort, or anyone else's – he never washed, and never took off his boots, even in bed. Real estate was an obsession of his, as he struggled to restore the status of the semi-noble but impoverished Buonarroti family. His nephew Leonardo inherited the house and several works of art in 1564; later he bought the two houses next door to create a memorial to his uncle, hiring artists to paint scenes from Michelangelo's life. In the mid-19th century, the house was opened to the public as a Michelangelo museum.

The ground floor is dedicated to mostly imaginary portraits of the artist, and works of art collected by his nephew's descendants, including an eclectic Etruscan and Roman collection. The main attractions, however, are upstairs, beginning with Michelangelo's earliest known work, the beautiful bas-relief *The Madonna of the Steps* (1490–1), the precocious work of a 16-year-old influenced by Donatello and studying in the household of Lorenzo il Magnifico; the relief of a battle scene, inspired by classical models, dates from the same period. Small models and drawings of potential projects line the walls; there's the wooden model for the façade of San Lorenzo, with designs for some of the statuary Michelangelo intended to fill in its austere blank spaces – as was often the case, his ideas were far too grand for his patron's purse and patience.

The next four rooms were painted in the 17th century to illustrate Michelangelo's life, virtues and apotheosis, depicting a polite, deferential and pleasant Michelangelo hobnobbing with popes. Those who know the artist best from *The Agony and the Ecstasy* may think they painted the wrong man by mistake. One of the best sections is a frieze of famous Florentines in the library. Other exhibits include a painted wooden *Crucifix* discovered in Santo Spirito in 1963 and believed by most scholars to be a documented one by Michelangelo, long thought to be lost; the contrapposto position of the slender body, and the fact that only Michelangelo would carve a nude Christ, weigh in favour of the attribution.

# Santa Croce

*Open Mon–Sat 9.30–5.30, Sun 1–5.30; adm (includes museum).*

No place in Florence so feeds the urge to dispute as the church of Santa Croce, Tuscany's 'Westminster Abbey', the largest Franciscan basilica in Italy, a must-see for every tour group. It was here that Stendhal gushed: 'I had attained to that supreme degree of sensibility where the divine intimations of art merge with the impassioned sensuality of emotion. As I emerged from the port of Santa Croce, I was seized with a fierce palpitation of the heart; I walked in constant fear of falling to the ground.' But don't be put off; most people manage to emerge without tripping over themselves.

The contradictions begin in the **Piazza Santa Croce**, which has its interesting points – the row of medieval houses with projecting upper storeys, supported by stone brackets, the faded bloom of dancing nymphs on the **Palazzo dell' Antella**; the curious 14th-century **Palazzo Serristori-Cocchi**, opposite the church; a grim 19th-century statue of Dante (if Dante really looked like that, it's no wonder Beatrice married someone else). Because this piazza is the lowest-lying in the city, it suffered the worst in the 1966 flood, when 20ft of oily water poured in; note the plaque marking the water line on the corner of Via Verdi.

Dominant over all is Santa Croce's neo-Gothic façade, built in 1857–63 and financed by Sir Francis Sloane, whose Sloane Square in London has more admirers than this black and white design, derived from Orcagna's Tabernacle in Orsanmichele. Yet of all the modern façades built on Italy's churches to atone for the chronic Renaissance inability to finish anything, this is one of the least offensive.

## The Interior

Santa Croce was founded by St Francis himself; during repairs after the flood, vestiges of a small, early 13th-century church were discovered under the present structure. It went by the board in Florence's colossal building programme of the 1290s. The great size of the new church speaks for the immense popularity of Franciscan preaching. Arnolfo di Cambio planned it, and it was largely completed by the 1450s but, as in Santa Maria Novella, Giorgio Vasari and the blinding forces of High Renaissance mediocrity were unleashed upon the interior. Vasari never had

# Santa Croce

1  Madonna del Latte
2  Tomb of Michelangelo
3  Monument to Dante
4  Benedetto da Maiano's Pulpit
5  Vittorio Alfieri's Tomb
6  Tomb of Machiavelli
7  Donatello's *Annunciation*
8  Tomb of Leonardo Bruni
9  Tomb of Carlo Marsuppini
10 Tomb of Rossini
11 Castellani Chapel
12 Baroncelli Chapel
13 Medici Chapel
14 Sacristy
15 Rinuccini Chapel
16 Peruzzi Chapel
17 Bardi Chapel
18 Sanctuary
19 Bardi di Libertà Chapel
20 Bardi di Vernio Chapel
21 Niccolini Chapel
22 Bardi Chapel
23 Salviati Chapel
24 Monument to Alberti
25 Tomb of Lorenzo Ghiberti
26 Galileo's Tomb
27 Museo dell'Opera di Santa Croce

much use for the art of Andrea Orcagna – he not only left him out of his influential *Lives of the Artists* but in Santa Croce he destroyed Orcagna's great fresco cycle that once covered the nave, replacing it with uninspired side altars.

For centuries it was the custom to install monuments to illustrious men in Santa Croce and, as you enter, you can see them lining the long aisles. Like many Franciscan churches, Santa Croce's large size, its architectural austerity and open timber roof resemble a barn, but at the end there's a lovely polygonal sanctuary, which shimmers with light and colour streaming through 14th-century stained glass. The whole interior has been treated to an overhaul, completed in 2000, including restoration of the ceiling.

Perversely, the greater the person buried in Santa Croce, the uglier their memorial. A member of the Pazzi conspiracy, Francesco Nori, is buried by the first pillar in the right aisle, and graced by one of the loveliest works of art, the *Madonna del Latte* (1478), a bas-relief by Antonio Rossellino, while the **Tomb of Michelangelo** (1570, the first in the right aisle) by Vasari is one of the least attractive. Michelangelo died in Rome in 1564, refusing for 35 years to return to Florence while alive, but agreeing to give the city his corpse. Dante has fared even worse, with an 1829 neoclassical monument that's as disappointing as the fact (to the Florentines, anyway) that Dante is buried in Ravenna, where he died in exile in 1321.

Facing the nave, Benedetto da Maiano's **marble pulpit** (1476) is one of the most beautiful the Renaissance ever produced. Behind it, the **Vittorio Alfieri Monument** (1809) was sculpted by neoclassical master Antonio Canova and paid for by his lover, the Countess of Albany. Next is the nondescript 18th-century **Monument of Niccolò Machiavelli**, and then Donatello's *Annunciation* (1430s), a tabernacle in gilded limestone, the angel wearing a remarkably sweet expression as he gently breaks the news to a grave, thoughtful Madonna. Bernardo Rossellino's **Tomb of Leonardo Bruni** (1447), another masterpiece of the Renaissance, is perhaps the one monument that best fits the man it honours. Bruni was a Greek scholar, a humanist, and the author of the first major historical work of the period, *The History of Florence*, a copy of which his tranquil effigy holds. The tomb, with its Brunelleschian architectural setting, proved a great inspiration to other artists, most obviously Desiderio da Settignano and his equally beautiful **Tomb of Carlo Marsuppini** (1453) directly across the nave, and the less inspired, more imitative **Monument to Rossini** crowded in to the left. The last tomb in the aisle belongs to poet and patriot Ugo Foscolo.

Santa Croce is especially rich in trecento frescoes, providing a unique opportunity to compare the work of Giotto with his followers. The south transept's **Castellani Chapel** has some of the later, more decorative compositions by Agnolo Gaddi (*Scenes from the Lives of Saints*, 1380s). The beautiful **Baroncelli Chapel** was painted with scenes from the Life of the Virgin by Agnolo's father Taddeo, Giotto's assistant in the 1330s and includes a bright, gilded altarpiece, the *Coronation of the Virgin* by Giotto and his workshop. The *Annunciation to the Shepherds* by Taddeo, seen to the left of the window, is important as it is thought to be the first nocturnal scene in the history of Western art.

The next portal gives on to a **Corridor** and the **Medici Chapel** (*open for Mass at 6pm*), both designed by Michelozzo, containing one of Andrea della Robbia's finest altarpieces and a 19th-century fake Donatello, a relief of the *Madonna and Child* that fooled the experts for decades. From the corridor a door leads to the **Sacristy**, its walls frescoed by Taddeo Gaddi (*The Crucifixion*), Spinello Aretino and Niccolò di Pietro Gerini. Behind the 14th-century grille, the **Rinuccini Chapel** was frescoed by one of Giotto's most talented followers, the Lombard Giovanni da Milano, in the 1360s.

## Giotto's Chapels

The frescoes in the two chapels to the right of the sanctuary, the **Peruzzi Chapel** and the **Bardi Chapel**, were painted by the legendary Giotto in the 1330s, towards the end of his life when the artist returned from Padua and his work in the Arena chapel. The frescoes have not fared well during the subsequent 660 years. Firstly Giotto painted large parts of the walls *a secco* (on dry plaster) instead of *affresco* (on wet plaster), presenting the same kind of preservation problems that bedevil Leonardo's *Last Supper*; secondly, the 18th century thought so little of the frescoes that they were whitewashed over as eyesores. Rediscovered some 150 years later and finally restored in 1959, the frescoes now, even though fragmentary, may be seen more or less as Giotto painted them. The Peruzzi Chapel contains scenes from the Lives of St John the Evangelist and the Baptist. In the Bardi Chapel is the *Life of St Francis*, which makes an interesting comparison with the frescoes in Assisi. The contrast between Giotto's frescoes and the chapel's 13th-century altarpiece, also showing the *Life of St Francis*, is a fair yardstick for measuring the breadth of the Giottesque revolution.

Agnolo Gaddi designed the stained glass around the **Sanctuary**, as well as the fascinating series of frescoes on the *Legend of the True Cross*.

Further to the left are two more chapels frescoed by followers of Giotto: the fourth, the **Bardi di Libertà Chapel**, by Bernardo Daddi, and the last, the **Bardi di Vernio Chapel**, by Maso di Banco, one of the most innovative and mysterious artists of the trecento. The frescoes illustrate the little-known *Life of St Sylvester* – his baptism of Emperor Constantine, the resurrection of the bull, the closing of the dragon's mouth and resurrection of two sorcerers; on the other wall of the chapel are a *Dream of Constantine* and *Vision of SS. Peter and Paul*. In the corner of the transept, the richly marbled **Niccolini Chapel** offers a Mannerist-Baroque change of pace, built by Antonio Dossi in 1584 and decorated with paintings by Allori (*under restoration*). Next, the second **Bardi Chapel** houses the famous crucifix by Donatello that Brunelleschi disdainfully called 'a peasant on the Cross'. The last funeral monuments, near the door, are those of Lorenzo Ghiberti and Galileo, the latter an 18th-century work. For running foul of the Inquisition, Galileo was not permitted a Christian burial until 1737.

## The Pazzi Chapel

*Open Mon–Sat 9.30–5.30, Sun 1–5.30; entrance through Santa Croce; adm.*

This chapel is well worth a visit. Brunelleschi, who could excel on the monumental scale of the cathedral dome, saved some of his best work for small places. Without

## The Legend of the True Cross

This popular medieval story begins with Noah's son, Seth, as an old man, asking for the essence of mercy. The Angel Gabriel replies by giving Seth a branch, saying that 5,000 years must pass before mankind may know true redemption. Seth plants the branch over Adam's grave on Mount Sinai, and it grows into a magnificent tree. King Solomon orders the tree cut, but as it is too large to move, the trunk stays where it is and is used as the main beam of a bridge. The Queen of Sheba is about to cross the bridge when she has a vision that the saviour of the world will be suspended from its wood, and that his death will mark the end of the Kingdom of the Jews. She refuses to cross the bridge, and writes of her dream to Solomon, who has the beam buried deep underground. Nevertheless, it is dug up and used to make the cross of Christ.

The cross next appears in the dream of Emperor Constantine before the Battle of Milvan Bridge, when he hears a voice saying that under this sign he will conquer. When it proves true, he sends his mother Helen to find the cross in Jerusalem. There she meets Judas Cyriacus, a pious Jew who knows where Golgotha is, but won't tell until Helen has him thrown in a well and nearly starved to death. When at last he agrees to dig, a sweet scent fills the air, and Judas Cyriacus is immediately converted. To discover which of the three crosses they find is Christ's, each is held over the coffin of a youth; the True Cross brings him back to life. After all this trouble in finding it, Helen leaves the cross in Jerusalem, where it is stolen by the Persians. Their King Chosroes thinks its power will bring him a great victory, but instead he loses the battle, and Persia, to Emperor Heraclius, who decides to return the holy relic to Jerusalem. But the gate is blocked by the Angel Gabriel, who reminds the proud Heraclius that Jesus entered the city humbly, on the back of an ass. And so, in a similar manner, the emperor returns the cross to Jerusalem.

knowing the architect, and something about the austere religious tendencies of the Florentines, the Pazzi Chapel is inexplicable, a Protestant reformation in architecture unlike anything ever built before. The 'vocabulary' is essential Brunelleschi, the geometric forms emphasized by the simplicity of the decoration: *pietra serena* pilasters and rosettes on white walls, arches, 12 terracotta *tondi* of the Apostles by Luca della Robbia, coloured rondels of the Evangelists in the pendentives by Donatello, and a small, stained-glass window by Baldovinetti. Even so, that is enough. The contemplative repetition of elements makes for an aesthetic that posed a direct challenge to the International Gothic of the time.

Leaving the Pazzi Chapel (notice Luca della Robbia's terracotta decorations on the portico), a doorway on the left of the cloister leads to Brunelleschi's **Second Cloister**, designed with the same subtlety and one of the quietest spots in Florence.

The old monastic buildings off the first cloister now house the **Museo dell'Opera di Santa Croce** (*open Mon–Sat 9.30–5.30, Sun 1–5.30; adm*), where you can see Cimabue's celebrated *Crucifix*, devastated by the flood, and partly restored after one of Florence's perennial restoration controversies. The refectory wall has another fine fresco by Taddeo Gaddi, of the *Tree of the Cross and the Last Supper*; fragments of Orcagna's frescoes salvaged from Vasari's obliteration offer powerful, nightmarish vignettes of *The Triumph of Death and Hell*. Donatello's huge, gilded bronze statue *St Louis of Toulouse* (1423) – a flawed work representing a flawed character, according to Donatello – was made for the façade of Orsanmichele. The museum also contains works by Andrea della Robbia, and a painting of Mayor Bargellini with a melancholy Santa Croce submerged in the 1966 flood for a backdrop; under the colonnade there's a statue of Florence Nightingale, born in and named after the city in 1820.

## Around Santa Croce: the Horne Museum

The east end of Florence, a rambling district packed with artisans and small manufacturers, traditionally served as the artists' quarter in Renaissance times. It's still one of the livelier neighbourhoods today, with a few lingering artists lodged in the upper storeys, hoping to breathe inspiration from the very stones where Michelangelo walked. It is a good place to observe the workaday Florence behind the glossy façade.

From Santa Croce, the pretty Borgo Santa Croce leads towards the Arno and the delightful **Horne Museum**, housed in a Renaissance palace, at Via de' Benci 6 (*open Mon–Sat 9–1; closed Sun and hols; adm*). Herbert Percy Horne (1844–1916) was an English art historian, biographer of Botticelli, and Florentinophile, who bequeathed his collection to the nation.

# North Bank Peripheral Attractions

## The Cascine

The newer sections of the city are, by and large, irredeemably dull. Much of Florence's traffic problem is channelled through its ring of avenues, or *viali*, laid out in the 1860s by Giuseppe Poggi to replace the demolished walls. On and along them are scattered points of interest, including some of the old city gates; the distances involved and danger of carbon monoxide poisoning on the *viali* make the idea of walking insane.

Bus 17C from the station or Duomo will take you through the congestion to the **Cascine**, the long (3.5km), narrow public park lining this bank of the Arno, originally used as the Medici's dairy farm, or *cascina*, and later as a Grand Ducal hunting park and theatre for public spectacles. A windy autumn day here in 1819 inspired Shelley to compose the 'Ode to the West Wind'. Three years later Shelley's drowned body was burnt on a pyre in Viareggio, by his friend Trelawny; curiously, a similar incineration took place in the Cascine in 1870 when the Maharaja of Kohlapur died in Florence. According to ritual his body had to be burned near the confluence of two rivers, in this case, the Arno and Mugnone at the far end of the park, on a spot now marked by the Maharaja's equestrian statue. Florentines come to the Cascine by day to play; it contains a riding school, race tracks, a small amusement park and zoo for the children, tennis courts, and a swimming pool. At night they come to ogle the transvestites strutting their stuff on the *viale*.

Beyond the train station, cars and buses hurtle around and around the **Fortezza da Basso**, an enormous bulk built by Antonio da Sangallo on orders from Alessandro de' Medici in 1534. It immediately became the most hated symbol of Medici tyranny. Ironically, the duke who built the Fortezza da Basso was one of very few to meet his end within its ramparts – stabbed by his relative and bosom companion 'Lorenzaccio' de' Medici. As a fortress, the place never saw any action as thrilling or vicious as the Pitti fashion shows that take place behind the walls in its 1978 aluminium exhibition hall.

Just east of the Fortezza, at the corner of Via Leone X and Viale Milton, there's an unexpected sight rising above the sleepy residential neighbourhood – the five graceful onion domes of the **Russian Church**, made even more exotic by the palm tree tickling its side. In the 19th century, Florence was a popular winter retreat for Russians who could afford it, among them Dostoevsky and Maxim Gorky. Completed by Russian architects in 1904, it is a pretty jewel box of brick and majolica decoration, open on the third Sunday of the month, when the priest comes from Nice to hold a morning service in Russian.

## The Stibbert Museum

*www.museostibbert.it; open in summer Mon–Wed 10–2, Fri–Sun 10–6; adm.*

From Piazza della Libertà, the dull Via Vittorio Emanuele heads 1km north to Via Stibbert and the Stibbert Museum (alternatively, take bus 31 or 32 from the station). Those who make the journey to see the lifetime's accumulations of Frederick Stibbert (1838–1906), who fought with Garibaldi and hobnobbed with Queen Victoria, can savour Florence's most bizarre museum, and one of the city's most pleasant small parks, laid out by Stibbert with a mouldering Egyptian temple sinking in a pond; and just try to obey the sign on the door: 'Comply with the Forbidden Admittances!'

Stibbert's Italian mother left him a 14th-century house, which he joined to another house to create a Victorian's sumptuous version of what a medieval Florentine house should have looked like – 64 rooms to contain a pack-rat's treasure hoard of all things brilliant and useless, from an attributed Botticelli, to snuff boxes, to what a local guide intriguingly describes as 'brass and silver basins, used daily by Stibbert'.

Stibbert's serious passion, however, was armour, and he amassed a magnificent collection from all times and places. The best pieces are not arranged in dusty cases, but with a touch of Hollywood, on grim knightly mannequins ranked ready for battle.

# The Oltrarno

Once over the Ponte Vecchio, a different Florence reveals itself: greener, quieter, and less burdened with traffic. The Oltrarno is not a large district: a chain of hills squeezes it against the river, and their summits afford some of the best views over the city.

Once across the Arno, the Medici's catwalk becomes part of the upper façade of **Santa Felicità**, one of Florence's most ancient churches, believed to have been founded by the Syrian Greek traders who introduced Christianity to the city, and established the first Christian cemetery in the small square in front of the church.

Rebuilt in the 18th century, there is one compelling reason to enter, for here, in the first chapel on the right, is the *ne plus ultra* of Mannerism: Pontormo's weirdly luminous *Deposition* (1528), painted in jarring pinks, oranges and blues that cut through the darkness of the little chapel. The composition itself is highly unconventional, with an effect that derives entirely from the use of figures in unusual, exaggerated poses; there is no sign of a cross, the only background is a single cloud. Sharing the chapel is Pontormo's *Annunciation* fresco, a less idiosyncratic work, as well as four tondi of the Evangelists in the cupola, partly the work of Pontormo's pupil and adopted son, Bronzino.

## The Pitti Palace

As the Medici consolidated their power in Florence, they made a point of buying up the most important properties of their former rivals, especially their proud family palaces. The most spectacular example of this was Cosimo I's acquisition of the Pitti Palace, built in 1457 by a powerful banker named Luca Pitti who seems to have had vague ambitions of toppling the Medici and becoming the big boss himself. The palace, with its extensive grounds, now the Boboli Gardens, was much more pleasant than the medieval Palazzo Vecchio, and in the 1540s Cosimo I and his wife Eleanor of Toledo moved in for good.

The palace remained the residence of the Medici, and later the House of Lorraine, until 1868. The original building, said to have been designed by Brunelleschi, was only as wide as the seven central windows of the façade. Succeeding generations found it too small for their burgeoning hoards of bric-a-brac, and added several stages of symmetrical additions, resulting in a long, bulky profile, resembling a rusticated Stalinist ministry, but a landscaped one, ever since the 1996 European Summit.

There are eight separate **museums** in the Pitti (*www.palazzopitti.it*); the ticket office for them all is in the far right corner of the forecourt. They are a tribute to Medici acquisitiveness in the centuries of decadence, from which, in the words of Mary McCarthy, 'flowed a torrent of bad taste that has not yet dried up…if there had been Toby jugs and Swiss weather clocks available, the Grand Dukes would certainly have collected them'. For the visitor who wants to see everything, the Pitti is pitiless; it is impossible to see all in one day.

### Galleria Palatina

*Open Tues–Sun 8.15–6.50; adm.*

The Pitti museum most people see is the Galleria Palatina, containing the Grand Dukes' famous collection of 16th–18th-century paintings, stacked on the walls in enormous gilt frames under the berserk opulence of frescoed ceilings celebrating planets, mythology and, of course, the ubiquitous Medici. The gallery is on the first floor of the right half of the palace; the ticket office is on the ground floor, off Ammannati's exaggerated rustic courtyard, a Mannerist masterpiece.

After the entrance to the Galleria is the neoclassical **Sala Castagnoli**, with the *Tavola delle Muse* in its centre, itself an excellent introduction to the Florentine 'decorative arts'; the table, a paragon of the intricate art of *pietra dura*, was made in the 1870s. The Galleria's best paintings are in the five former reception rooms off to the left, with colourful ceilings painted in the 1640s by Pietro da Cortona, one of the most interesting Italian Baroque artists.

However, the set route takes you through the other part of the palace first, starting with the adjacent **Sala di Prometeo** containing Filippo Lippi's lovely *Tondo of the Madonna and Child* and Baldassare Peruzzi's unusual *Dance of Apollo*. Next you can peek into the **Sala di Bagni**, the Empire bathroom of Elisa Baciocchi, Napoleon's sister, who ruled the Département de l'Arno between 1809 and 1814, and seemingly spent much of those years redecorating the Pitti. Caravaggio's *Sleeping Cupid* is a couple of rooms up, in the **Sala dell'Educazione di Giove**. The next room to this is the pretty **Sala della Stufa**, frescoed with the *Four Ages of the World* by Pietro da Cortona.

The first of the reception rooms, the **Sala dell'Iliade** (frescoed in the 19th century), has some fine portraits by the Medici court painter and Rubens' friend, Justus Sustermans. Two *Assumptions* by Andrea del Sarto, *Philip II* by Titian and a Velazquez equestrian portrait of Philip IV share the room with one of the most unusual residents of the gallery, *Queen Elizabeth*, who seems uncomfortable in such company.

The **Sala di Giove**, used as the Medici throne room, contains one of Raphael's best-known portraits, the lovely and serene *Donna Velata* (1516). The small painting *The Three Ages of Man* is usually attributed to Giorgione. Salviati, Perugino, Fra Bartolommeo and Andrea del Sarto are also represented. The **Sala di Marte** has two works by Rubens, *The Four Philosophers* and the *Consequences of War*, as well as some excellent portraits by Tintoretto and Van Dyck (*Cardinal Bentivoglio*). The newly restored *Annunciation of San Godenzo*, by Andrea del Sarto, is now back in place after a long absence, and there is also Titian's rather dashing *Cardinal Ippolito de' Medici* in Hungarian costume. Ippolito, despite being destined for the Church, was one of the more high-spirited Medici.

In the **Sala di Apollo** there's more Titian – his *Portrait of a Grey-eyed Gentleman*, evoking the perfect 16th-century English gentleman, and his more sensuous than penitent *Mary Magdalene* – as well as works by Andrea del Sarto and Van Dyck. The last reception room is the **Sala di Venere**, with several works by Titian, including his early *Concert*, believed to have been partly painted by Giorgione and a powerful *Portrait of Pietro Aretino*, Titian's close and caustic friend, who complained to the artist that it was all too accurate and gave it to Cosimo I. There are two beautiful landscapes by Rubens, painted at the end of his life, and an uncanny self-portrait, *La Menzogna* ('The Falsehood') by Neapolitan Salvator Rosa. The centrepiece statue, the *Venus Italica*, was commissioned by Napoleon from neoclassical master Antonio Canova in 1812 to replace the *Venus de' Medici* which he 'centralized' off to Paris – a rare case of the itchy-fingered Corsican trying to pay for something he took.

The **Sala di Saturno**, with a newly restored ceiling, is home to several paintings from Raphael's Florence days. These include the *Maddalena and Agnolo Doni* (1506) and the *Madonna 'del Granduca'*, influenced by the paintings of Leonardo. Some 10 years later,

Raphael had found his own style, beautifully evident in his famous *Madonna della Seggiola* ('of the chair'), perhaps the most popular work he ever painted, and one that is far more complex and subtle than it appears. The rounded, intertwining figures of the Madonna and Child are seen as if through a slightly convex mirror, bulging out – one of the first examples of conscious illusionism in the Renaissance.

Some of the more interesting paintings to ferret out in the remainder of the gallery include Filippino Lippi's *Death of Lucrezia* and Raphael's *Madonna dell'Impannata*, both in the **Sala di Ulisse**.

The right half of the Pitti also contains the **State Apartments** (*included as part of the visit to the Galleria Palatina*). These were last redone in the 19th century by the Dukes of Lorraine, with touches by the Kings of Savoy.

## Galleria d'Arte Moderna

*Open 8.30–1.50, closed 2nd and 4th Sun and 1st, 3rd and 5th Mon of month; adm exp; tickets from main ticket office on ground floor.*

On the second floor above the Galleria Palatina has been installed Florence's modern – read late 18th–20th-century – art museum. Though the monumental stair may leave you breathless (the Medici negotiated it with sedan chairs and strong-shouldered servants), consider a visit for some sunny painting of the Italy of your great-grandparents.

The 'Splatterers' or *Macchiaioli* (Tuscan Impressionists) illuminate **Room 16** and the rest of the museum, forming an excellent introduction to the works by Silvestro Lega, Giovanni Fattori, Nicolo Cannicci, Francesco Gioli, Federigo Zandomeneghi and Telemaco Signorini, with an interval of enormous Risorgimento battle scenes. What comes as a shock, especially if you've been touring Florence for a while now, is that the marriage between painting and sculpture that characterizes most of Italian art history seems to have resulted in a nasty divorce in the late 1800s: while the canvases radiate light, statuary becomes disturbingly kitsch, obsessed with death and beauty.

The Galleria was reopened after a major reorganization in 1999 and now consists of over 30 rooms. The most recent paintings on display are those in the last rooms, which cover the years 1900–23. There are plans eventually to open 13 more rooms covering 1923–45.

## Museo degli Argenti

*Open Nov–Feb daily 8.15–4.30; March daily 8.15–5.30; April, May, Sept, Oct 8.15–6.30; June–Aug 8.15–7.30; closed 1st and last Mon of month; adm (combined ticket with Boboli, Museo della Porcellana).*

The ground floor on the left side of the Pitti was used as the Medici summer apartments and now contains the family's remarkable collection of jewellery, vases, trinkets and pricey curiosities. The Grand Duke's guests would be received in four of the most delightfully frescoed rooms to be found anywhere in Florence, beginning with the **Sala di Giovanni di San Giovanni**, named after the artist who painted it in the 1630s. The theme is the usual Medicean self-glorification – but nowhere does such dubious material achieve such flamboyant treatment. Here the Muses, chased from Paradise, find refuge with Lorenzo il Magnifico; Lorenzo smiles as he studies a bust of Pan by Michelangelo. His real passion, a collection of antique vases carved of semi-precious stones or crystal, is displayed in a room off to the left; the vases were dispersed with the rise of Savonarola, but Lorenzo's nephew Cardinal Giulio had no trouble in locating them, as Lorenzo had his initials LAUR.MED. deeply incised into each. The three **Reception rooms** were painted in shadowy blue trompe l'œil by two masterful Bolognese illusionists, Agostino Michele and Angelo Colonna.

The Grand Dukes' treasure hoard is up on the mezzanine. These golden toys are only a fraction of what the Medici had accumulated; despite the terms of Anna Maria's will, leaving everything to Florence, the Lorraines sold off the most valuable pieces and jewels to finance Austria's wars. Among the leftovers here, however, is a veritable apoplexy of fantastical bric-a-brac.

## More Pitti Museums

The **Museum of Costumes** (open daily 8.15–1.50; closed 2nd and 4th Sun and 1st, 3rd and 5th Mon of month) is housed on the second floor of the Palace, near to the Galleria d'Arte Moderna; which has the reconstructed dress Eleanor of Toledo was buried in – the same one that she wears in Bronzino's famous portrait. The **Porcelain Museum** (open same times as Museo degli Argenti) is housed in the casino of Cosimo III, out in the Giardino del Cavaliere in the Boboli Gardens (follow the signs).

## Boboli Gardens

*Open from 9am until one hour before sunset; adm; t 055 265 1838.*

Stretching back invitingly from the Pitti, the shady green of the Boboli Gardens, Florence's largest (and only) central public garden is an irresistible oasis in the middle of a stone-hard city. Originally laid out by Buontalenti, the Boboli reigns as queen of all formal Tuscan gardens, the most elaborate and theatrical, a Mannerist-Baroque co-production of Nature and Artifice laid out over a steep hill, full of shady nooks and pretty walks and beautifully kept. The park is populated by a platoon of statuary, many of them Roman works, others absurd Mannerist pieces.

There are three entrances and exits: through the main courtyard of the Pitti Palace, from Via Romana and in Porta Romana. The main, route, from the Pitti Palace, starts at the **Amphitheatre**, which ascends in regular tiers from the palace, and was designed like a small Roman circus to hold Medici court spectacles. It has a genuine obelisk, of Rameses II from Heliopolis, snatched by the ancient Romans and shipped here by the Medici branch in Rome. The granite basin, large enough to submerge an elephant, came from the Roman Baths of Caracalla. Straight up the terrace is the **Neptune Fountain**; a signposted path leads from there to the pretty **Kaffeehaus**, a boat-like pavilion with a prow and deck offering a fine view of Florence and drinks in the summer. From here the path continues up to the **Belvedere Fort** (newly opened after restoration). Other signs from the Neptune Fountain point the way up to the secluded **Giardino del Cavaliere** (ticket combined with that of Galleria Palatina), located on a bastion on Michelangelo's fortifications. Cosimo III built the casino here to escape the heat in the Pitti Palace; the view over the ancient villas, vineyards and olives is pure Tuscan enchantment. The **Porcelain Museum** here (*see* above) contains 18th- and 19th-century examples of chinawork from Sèvres, Meissen and Vienna.

At the bottom right-hand corner of the garden lies the remarkable **Grotta di Buontalenti** (*ticket combined with that of the Galeria Palatina*), one of the architect's most imaginative works, anticipating Gaudí with his dripping, stalactite-like stone, from which fantastic limestone animals struggle to emerge. Casts of Michelangelo's *nonfiniti* slaves stand in the corners, replacing the originals put there by the Medici, while back in the shadowy depths stands a luscious statue of Venus coming from her bath by Giambologna. The Grotta di Buontalenti has been restored but the fountains are not working yet due to technical problems.

## Casa Guidi

In the old days the neighbourhood around the Pitti was a fashionable address, but during the 19th century rents for a furnished palace were incredibly low. Shortly after their secret marriage, the Brownings found one of these, the **Casa Guidi** at Piazza San Felice 8, the perfect place to settle; during their 13 years here they wrote their most famous poetry. The house is now owned by the Browning Institute, you can visit it at certain times (*open April–Nov Mon, Wed and Fri 3–6; closed Dec–Mar; donations expected*). Dostoevsky wrote *The Idiot* while living nearby, at No.21 Piazza Pitti.

## Stuffed Animals and Wax Cadavers

Past the Pitti on Via Romana 17, is one of Florence's great oddball attractions, the **La Specola** museum (*open Mon–Wed, Fri and Sat 9–1; adm*). The **Zoological Section** has a charmingly old-fashioned collection of nearly everything that walks, flies or swims, from the humble sea worm to the rare Madagascar Aye-Aye or the swordfish, with an accessory case of different blades. The real horror show stuff, however, is kept hidden away in the **Museum of Waxes**. Dotty, prudish old Cosimo III was a hypochondriac and morbidly obsessed with diseases, which his favourite artist, a Sicilian priest named Gaetano Zumbo, was able to portray with revolting realism. His macabre anatomical models were one of the main sights for Grand Tourists in the 1700s.

## Santo Spirito

*Open Mon–Sat 10–12 and 4–5.30, Sun 10.30–12.*

Piazza Santo Spirito, the centre of the Oltrarno, is home to a small market on Monday to Saturday mornings under the plane trees as well as a quiet café or two. In the evening it changes face and the bars fill with people, who meet and chat in the piazza and on the church steps until the early hours. At the southern end, a plain 18th-century façade hides Brunelleschi's last, and perhaps greatest church. He designed Santo Spirito in 1440 and lived to see only one column erected, but subsequent architects were faithful to his elegant plan for the interior. This is done in the architect's favourite pale grey and *pietra serena* articulation, a rhythmic forest of columns with semicircular chapels is gracefully recessed into the transepts and the three arms of the crossing. The effect is somewhat spoiled by the ornate 17th-century *baldacchino*, which sits in this enchanted garden of architecture like a 19th-century bandstand.

The art in the chapels is meagre, as most of the good paintings were sold off over the years. The best include Filippino Lippi's beautiful, restored *Madonna and Saints* in the right transept and Verrocchio's jewel-like *St Monica and Nuns* in the opposite transept. To the left of the church, in the **refectory** (*open Tues–Sat 10–1.30, Sun and hols 10–12.30; adm*) of the vanished 14th-century convent, are the scanty remains of a *Last Supper* and a well-preserved, highly dramatic *Crucifixion* by Andrea Orcagna.

## Santa Maria del Carmine and the Cappella Brancacci

*Open 10–5 (last adm 4.45), Sun and hols 1–5; closed Tues; adm; only 30 people are admitted at a time, for 15 minutes; booking required, t 055 276 8224.*

There is little to say about the surroundings, the piazza-cum-car park, the rough stone façade, or the interior of the Oltrarno's other great church, Santa Maria del Carmine, which burned down in 1771 and was reconstructed shortly after. Miraculously, the **Cappella Brancacci**, one of the landmarks in Florentine art, survived both the flames and attempts by the authorities to replace it with something more fashionable. Three artists worked on the Brancacci's frescoes: Masolino, who began them in 1425, and who designed the cycle; his pupil Masaccio, who worked on them alone for a year before following his master to Rome, where he died at the age of 27; and Filippino Lippi, who finished them 50 years later. Filippino took care to imitate Masaccio as closely as possible, and the frescoes have an appearance of stylistic unity. Between 1981 and 1988 they were subject to one of Italy's most publicized restorations, cleansed of 550 years of dirt and overpainting, enabling us to see what so thrilled the painters of the Renaissance.

Masaccio in his day was a revolution and a revelation in his solid, convincing naturalism; his figures stand in space, without any fussy ornamentation or Gothic grace, very much inspired by Donatello's sculptures. Masaccio conveyed emotion with broad, quick brush strokes and with his use of light, most obvious in the *Expulsion of Adam and Eve*, one of the most memorable and harrowing images created in the Renaissance. In the *Tribute Money*, the young artist displays his mastery of artificial perspective and light effects. The three episodes in the fresco show an official demanding tribute from the city, St Peter fetching it on Christ's direction from the mouth of a fish, and lastly, his handing over of the money to the official.

Other works by 'Shabby Tom' include *St Peter Baptizing* on the upper register, and *St Peter Healing with his Shadow* and *St Peter Enthroned and Resurrecting the Son of the King of Antioch*, the right half of which was finished by Filippino Lippi. The elegant Masolino is responsible for the remainder, except for the lower register's *Release of St Peter from Prison*, *St Peter Crucified* and *St Paul Visiting St Peter in Prison*, all by Filippino Lippi, based on Masaccio's sketches.

Among the detached frescoes displayed in the cloister and refectory is a good one by Filippino's dad, Fra Filippo Lippi, who was born nearby in Via dell'Ardiglione.

# A City with a View

Great Aunt Florence, with her dour complexion and severe, lined face, never was much of a looker from street level, but improves with a bit of distance, either mental or from one of her hill-top balconies: the Belvedere Fort, San Miniato, Piazzale Michelangelo, Bellosguardo, Fiesole or Settignano.

## Belvedere Fort and Arcetri

One of Florence's best and closest balconies is the newly restored **Belvedere Fort**, a graceful, six-point star designed by Buontalenti and built in 1590–5, not so much for the sake of defence but to remind any remaining Florentine republicans who was boss. Since 1958, it has been used for special exhibitions, but you can usually enjoy unforgettable views of Florence and the surrounding countryside from its ramparts. Leading up to it is one of Florence's prettiest streets, **Costa San Giorgio**, which begins in Piazza Santa Felicità, just beyond the Ponte Vecchio.

In this part of Florence, the countryside begins right at the city wall, a rolling landscape of villas and gardens, olives and cypresses. Via San Leonardo winds its way out towards Arcetri; a 10-minute walk will take you to the 11th-century **San Leonardo in Arcetri** (*usually open Sun am*). There is a wonderful 13th-century pulpit, originally built for San Pier Scheraggio, and a small rose window, made according to legend from a wheel of Fiesole's *carroccio*, captured by Florence in 1125. A half-kilometre further on, past the Viale Galileo crossroads, Via San Leonardo changes its name to Via Viviani, where it passes the **Astrophysical Observatory** and the **Torre del Gallo**. Another kilometre further on Via Viviani reaches the settlement of Pian de' Giullari, where Galileo spent the last years of his life, in the 16th-century **Villa il Gioiello**, virtually under house arrest after his encounter with the Inquisition in 1631, and where Milton is believed to have visited him.

## San Miniato

*Open summer daily 8–7.30, winter daily 8–12 and 3–6.*

From Porta San Miniato you can walk up to San Miniato church on the stepped Via di San Salvatore al Monte, complete with the Stations of the Cross, or take the less pious bus 13 up the scenic Viale dei Colli from the station or Via de Benci, near Ponte alle Grazie. High atop its monumental steps, San Miniato's beautiful, distinctive façade can be spotted from almost anywhere in the city, although relatively few visitors take the time actually to visit what is in fact one of the finest Romanesque churches in Italy.

San Miniato was built in 1015, over an earlier church that marked the spot where the head of St Minias, a 3rd-century Roman soldier, bounced when the Romans axed it off. Despite its distance from the centre San Miniato has always been one of the churches dearest to the Florentines' hearts. The remarkable geometric pattern of green, black and white marble that adorns its façade was begun in 1090, though funds only permitted the embellishment of the lower, simpler half of the front; the upper half,

**N**

2.5 miles

**Florence Environs**

Prato

Pratolino ●
*Villa Demidoff* 🏛

Caldine

*R. Mugnone*

Cercina

Fiesole

S. Domenico

Maiano

Settignano

Ponte a Mensola

SS67

Settignano

Arno

S. Donato
in Collina ●

Bagno a Ripoli

Rovezzano

A1

Grassina ●

*VIA BOLOGNESE*

Stibbert Museum 🏛

**Florence**

Stadio
Comunale

Campo di
Marte

Badia a
Ripoli

Ponte a Ema

Villa Careggi 🏛

Fortezza
da Basso

Stazione
Centrale

Belvedere Fort ♜

Gavinana

Firenze
Sud

Rifredi

Villa di Castello 🏛
Villa la Petraia 🏛

Castello 🏛

Daomo ✝

San Miniato ✝

Pian de'
Giullari ●

*AUTOSTRADA DEL SOLE*

Cercina

Quinto

Firenze Nova

Novoli

Boboli Gardens ✿

San Leonardo in Arcetri ✿

Poggio
Imperiale ●

*Ema*

Sesto
Fiorentino

Peretola
Airport ✈

Peretola

Le Cascine

Ippodromo
Ponte della
Vittoria

Bellosguardo ●

Certosa del
Galluzzo ✝

*Firenze
Certosa*

Tavarnuzze ●

*To Siena* →

Settimello

L'Isolotto

Ponte a
Greve

Soffiano

Scandicci

*Greve*

Prato
Calenzano

Firenze
Nord

A11

*AUTOSTRADA FIRENZE-MARE*

Arno

Firenze
Signa

Chiesanuova ●

SS66

**T U S C A N Y**

Campi
Bisenzio

Lastra
a Signa ●

Signa ●

*SS325*

Poggio a Caiano 🏛

*R. Ombrone*

Carmignano ●

Villa d'Artimino 🏛

Montelupo
Fiorentino ●

*To Pisa* ←

full of curious astrological symbolism (someone has written a whole book about it), was added in the 12th century, paid for by the Arte di Calimala, the guild that made a fortune buying bolts of fine wool, dyeing them a deep red or scarlet that no one else in Europe could imitate, then selling them back for twice the price; their proud gold eagle stands at the top of the roof. The glittering mosaic of Christ, the Virgin and St Minias, came slightly later.

The Calimala was also responsible for decorating the interior, an unusual design with a raised choir built over the crypt. As the Calimala became richer, so did the fittings; the delicate intarsia **marble floor** of animals and zodiac symbols dates from 1207. The lower walls were frescoed in the 14th and 15th centuries, including an enormous St Christopher. At the end of the nave stands Michelozzo's unique, free-standing **Cappella del Crocifisso**, built in 1448 to hold the crucifix that spoke to St John Gualberto (now in Santa Trínita); it is magnificently carved and adorned with terracottas by Luca della Robbia.

Off the left nave is one of Florence's Renaissance showcases, the **Chapel of the Cardinal of Portugal** (1461–6). The 25-year-old cardinal, a member of the Portuguese royal family, died in Florence at an auspicious moment, when the Medici couldn't spend enough money on publicly prominent art, and when some of the greatest artists of the quattrocento were at the height of their careers. The chapel was designed by Manetti, Brunelleschi's pupil; the ceiling exquisitely decorated with enamelled terracotta and medallions by Luca della Robbia; the Cardinal's tomb beautifully carved by Antonio Rossellino; the frescoed *Annunciation* charmingly painted by Alesso Baldovinetti; the altarpiece *Three Saints* is a copy of the original by Piero Pollaiuolo.

Up the steps of the choir more treasures await. The marble transenna and pulpit were carved in 1207, with art and a touch of medieval humour. Playful geometric patterns frame the mosaic in the apse, *Christ between the Virgin and St Minias*, made in 1297 by artists imported from Ravenna, and later restored by Baldovinetti. The colourful **Sacristy** on the right was entirely frescoed by Spinello Aretino in 1387, but made rather flat by subsequent restoration. In the **Crypt** an 11th-century altar holds the relics of St Minias; the columns are topped by ancient capitals. The **cloister** has frescoes of the Holy Fathers by Paolo Uccello, remarkable works in painstaking and fantastical perspective, rediscovered in 1925. The monks sing Gregorian chant every afternoon at about 4pm – a magical experience.

The panorama of Florence from San Miniato is lovely to behold, but such thoughts were hardly foremost in Michelangelo's mind during the Siege of Florence. The hill was vulnerable, and to defend it he hastily erected the fortress (now surrounding the cemetery to the left of the church), placed cannons in the unfinished 16th-century campanile (built to replace one that fell over), and shielded the tower from artillery with mattresses. He grew fond of the small church below San Miniato, **San Salvatore al Monte**, built by Cronaca in the late 1400s, which he called his 'pretty country lass'.

With these associations in mind, the city named the vast, square terrace car park below, **Piazzale Michelangelo**, the most popular viewpoint only because it is the only one capable of accommodating an unlimited number of tour buses (though now there are restrictions on the length of time buses are allowed to stop, the situation has improved a bit). On Sunday afternoons, crowds of Florentines habitually make a stop here during their afternoon *passeggiata*. Besides another copy of the *David* and a fun, tacky carnival atmosphere rampant with souvenirs, balloons and ice cream, the Piazzale offers views that can reach as far as Pistoia on a clear day.

## Bellosguardo

Many would argue that the finest view over Florence is from Bellosguardo, located almost straight up from Porta Romana at the end of the Boboli Gardens or Piazza Torquato Tasso. Non-mountaineers may want to take a taxi; the famous viewpoint, from where you can see every church façade in the city, is just before Piazza Bellosguardo. The area is a peaceful little oasis of superb villas and houses gathered round a square – there are no shops, bars or indeed anything commercial.

# Fiesole

Florence liked to regard itself as the daughter of Rome, and in its fractious heyday explained its quarrelsome nature by the fact that its population from the beginning was of mixed race, of Romans and 'that ungrateful and malignant people who of old came down from Fiesole', according to Dante. First settled in the 2nd millennium BC, it became the most important Etruscan city in the region. Yet from the start Etruscan *Faesulae*'s relationship with Rome was rocky, especially after sheltering Catiline and his conspirators in 65 BC. Its lofty position made Fiesole too difficult to capture, so the Romans built a camp below on the Arno to cut off its supplies. Eventually Fiesole was taken, and it dwindled as the camp below grew into the city of Florence, growth the Romans encouraged to spite the old Etruscans on their hill. This easily defended hill, however, ensured Fiesole's survival in the Dark Ages. When times became safer, families began to move back down to the Arno to rebuild Florence. They returned to smash up most of Fiesole after defeating it in 1125; since then the little town has remained aloof, letting Florence dominate and choke in its own juices far, far below.

But ever since the days of the *Decameron*, whose storytellers retreated to its garden villas to escape the plague, Fiesole has played the role of Florence's aristocratic suburb; its cool breezes, beautiful landscapes and belvedere views make it the perfect refuge from the torrid Florentine summers. There's no escaping the tourists, however; we foreigners have been tramping up and down Fiesole's hill since the days of Shelley. A day trip has become an obligatory part of a stay in Florence, and although Fiesole has proudly retained its status as an independent *comune*, you can make the 20-minute trip up on Florence city bus 7 from the station or Piazza San Marco. If you have the time, walk up (or perhaps better, down) the old lanes bordered with villas and gardens to absorb some of the world's most civilized scenery.

## Around Piazza Mino

The long sloping stage of Piazza Mino is Fiesole's centre, with the bus stop, the local tourist office, the cafés and the **Palazzo Pretorio**, its loggia and façade emblazoned with coats of arms. The square is named after a favourite son, the quattrocento sculptor Mino da Fiesole, whom Ruskin preferred to all others. An example of his work may be seen in the **Duomo**, whose plain façade dominates the north side of the piazza. Built in 1028, it was the only building spared by the vindictive Florentines in 1125. It was subsequently enlarged and given a scouring 19th-century restoration, leaving the tall, crenellated campanile as its sole distinguishing feature. Still, the interior has an austere charm, with a raised choir over the crypt similar to San Miniato.

Up the steps to the right are two works by Mino da Fiesole: the *Tomb of Bishop Leonardo Salutati* and an altar front. The main altarpiece in the choir, *Madonna and Saints*, is by Lorenzo di Bicci, from 1440. Note the two saints frescoed on the columns; it was a north Italian custom to paint holy people as if they were members of the congregation. The crypt, holding the remains of Fiesole's patron, St Romulus, is supported by columns bearing doves, spirals and other early Christian symbols.

Located on Via Dupré, the **Bandini Museum** (*open summer daily 10–7, winter Wed–Mon 10–5; adm*) contains sacred works, including della Robbia terracottas and trecento paintings by Lorenzo Monaco, Neri di Bicci and Taddeo Gaddi.

## Archaeological Zone

Behind the cathedral and museum is the entrance to what remains of *Faesulae*. Because Fiesole avoided trouble in the Dark Ages, its Roman monuments have survived in much better shape than those of Florence; although hardly spectacular, the ruins are charmingly set amid olive groves and cypresses.

The small **Roman Theatre** (*open summer daily 10–7, winter Wed–Mon 9.30–6; adm*) has survived well enough to host plays and concerts in the summer; Fiesole would like to remind you that in ancient times it had the theatre and plays while Florence had the amphitheatre and wild beast shows. Close by are the rather confusing remains of two superimposed temples, the baths and an impressive stretch of Etruscan walls (best seen from Via delle Mure Etrusche, below) that proved their worth against Hannibal's siege.

The **Archaeology Museum** (*opening hours as for Roman Theatre*), in a small 20th-century Ionic temple, displays early bronze figurines with flapper wing arms, Etruscan urns and stelae, including the interesting 'stele Fiesolana' with a banquet scene.

## Walking Around Fiesole

From Piazza Mino, Via S. Francesco ascends steeply (at first) to the hill that served as the Etruscan and Roman acropolis. Halfway up is a terrace with extraordinary views of Florence and the Arno sprawl, with a monument to the three *carabinieri* who gave themselves up to be shot by the Nazis in 1944 to prevent them from taking civilian reprisals. The church nearby, the **Basilica di Sant'Alessandro**, was constructed over an Etruscan/Roman temple in the 6th century, reusing its lovely *cipollino* (onion marble) columns and Ionic capitals, one still inscribed with an invocation to Venus. At the top of the hill, square on the ancient acropolis, stands the monastery of **San Francesco**, its church containing a famous early cinquecento *Annunciation* by Raffaellino del Garbo and an *Immaculate Conception* by Piero di Cosimo. A grab-bag of odds and ends collected from the four corners of the world, especially Egypt and China, is displayed in the quaint **Franciscan Missionary Museum** in the cloister (*open summer Mon–Sat 9–12 and 3–7, Sun 3–7; winter Mon–Sat 9–12 and 3–6, Sun 3–6*); it also has an Etruscan collection.

There are much longer walks to be had along the hill behind the Palazzo Pretorio. The panoramic Via Belvedere leads back to Via Adriano Mari, and in a couple of kilometres to the bucolic **Montececeri**, a wooded park where Leonardo da Vinci performed his flight experiments, and where Florentine architects once quarried their dark *pietra serena* from quarries now abandoned but open for exploration.

In Borgunto, as this part of Fiesole is called, there are two 3rd-century BC **Etruscan tombs** on Via Bargellino; east of Borgunto scenic Via Francesco Ferrucci and Via di Vincigliata pass by Fiesole's castles, the **Castel di Poggio**, site of summer concerts, and the **Castel di Vincigliata**, dating back to 1031, while further down is American critic Bernard Berenson's famous **Villa I Tatti**, which he left, along with a collection of Florentine art, to Harvard University as the Centre of Italian Renaissance Studies. The road continues down towards Ponte a Mensola (6km from Fiesole; *see* p.180) and Settignano, with buses back to Florence.

## San Domenico di Fiesole

San Domenico is a pleasant walk from Fiesole towards Florence down Via Vecchia Fiesolana, a steep, narrow road that passes the **Villa Medici** (*Via Beato Angelico 2, privately owned, open Mon–Fri 9–1 though best to call first, t 055 59417, ring the bell*), built by Michelozzo for Cosimo il Vecchio; Lorenzo and his friends of the Platonic Academy would come to escape the world within its lovely gardens; it was also Iris Origo's childhood home.

San Domenico, at the bottom of the lane, is where Fra Angelico first entered his monkish world. The church of **San Domenico** (15th century) contains his *Madonna with Angels and Saints*, in a chapel on the left, and a photograph of his *Coronation of the Virgin*, which the French snapped up in 1809 and sent to the Louvre. Across the nave there's a *Crucifixion* by the school of Botticelli, an unusual composition of verticals highlighted by the cypresses in the background. In the chapterhouse of the monastery (*ring the bell at No.4*) Fra Angelico left a fine fresco *Crucifixion* and a *Madonna and Child*, which is shown with its sinopia, before moving down to Florence and San Marco.

## Badia Fiesolana

The lane in front of San Domenico leads to the Badia Fiesolana (*open Mon–Fri 9–5, Sat 9–12*), Fiesole's cathedral, built in the 9th century by Fiesole's bishop, an Irishman named Donatus, with a fine view over the rolling countryside and Florence beyond. Though later enlarged, it preserves its original elegant façade, a charming example of the geometric black and white marble inlay decoration that characterizes Tuscan Romanesque churches, while the interior is adorned with *pietra serena* in the style of Brunelleschi. The ex-convent next door now houses the European University Institute.

# Settignano

The least touristic hill above Florence is under the village of Settignano (bus 10 from the station or Piazza San Marco). The road passes **Ponte a Mensola**, Boccaccio's childhood home; it is believed he set scenes of the *Decameron* at the Villa Poggio Gherardo. A Scottish Benedictine named Andrew founded its church of **San Martino a Mensola** in the 9th century and was later canonized. The church was rebuilt in the 1400s, it has three trecento works: Taddeo Gaddi's *Triptych*, his son Agnolo's paintings on St Andrew's casket, and high altar triptych by the school of Orcagna. Quattrocento works include Neri di Bicci's *Madonna and Saints* and an *Annunciation* by a follower of Beato Angelico.

Settignano is one of Tuscany's great cradles of sculptors, producing Desiderio da Settignano and Antonio and Bernardo Rossellino; Michelangelo too spent his childhood here, at Villa Buonarroti. Strangely, they left behind no work as a reminder; the good art in **Santa Maria** church is by Andrea della Robbia (an enamelled terracotta *Madonna and Child*) and Buontalenti (the pulpit). However, there are more splendid views from Piazza Desiderio, and a couple of places to quaff a glass of Chianti.

# Medici Villas

Like their Bourbon cousins in France, the Medici dukes liked to while their time away acquiring new palaces for themselves. In their case, however, the reason was less self-exaltation than simple property speculation; the Medici always thought several generations ahead. As a result the countryside around Florence is littered with Medici villas, most of them now privately owned, though some are at least partly open to the public.

## Villa Careggi

*Open Mon–Fri 9–6, Sat 9–12; but you can stroll through the grounds for free.*

Perhaps the best-known is Careggi (Viale Pieraccini 17, take bus 14C from the station), originally a fortified farmhouse, but enlarged for Cosimo il Vecchio by Michelozzo in 1434. In the 1460s this villa became synonymous with the birth of humanism.

The greatest Latin and Greek scholars of the day, Ficino, Poliziano, Pico della Mirandola and Argyropoulos, would sometimes meet here with Lorenzo il Magnifico and hold philosophical discussions in imitation of a Platonic symposium, calling their informal society the Platonic Academy. It fizzled out when Lorenzo died. Cosimo il Vecchio and Piero had both died at Careggi and, when he felt the end was near, Lorenzo had himself carried out to the villa, with Poliziano and Pico della Mirandola to bear him company. After Lorenzo died, the villa was burned down by Florentine republicans, though Cosimo I later had it rebuilt, and Francis Sloane had it restored.

## Villa la Petraia

*Open Nov–Feb 8.15–4.30, Mar and Oct until 5.30; Apr, May and Sept until 6.30; June–Aug until 7.30; adm.*

Further east, amid the almost continuous conurbation of power lines and industrial landscapes that blight the Prato road, Villa la Petraia manages to remain Arcadian on its steeply sloping hill. It's very hard to reach on your own. If you don't have a car, it's best to take a taxi or, if you are adventurous, bus 28 from the station, and get off after the wastelands, by Via Reginaldo Giuliano. La Petraia was purchased by Grand Duke Ferdinando I in 1557 and rebuilt by Buontalenti, keeping the tower of the original castle intact.

Unfortunately Vittorio Emanuele II liked it as much as the Medici, and redesigned it to suit his relentlessly bad taste. Still, the interior is worthwhile for its ornate Baroque court, frescoed with a pastel history of the Medici by 17th-century masters Volterrano and Giovanni di San Giovanni; Vittorio Emanuele II added the glass roof in order to use the space as a ballroom. Of the remainder, you're most likely to remember the Chinese painting of Canton and the games room, with billiard tables as large as football fields and perhaps the world's first pinball machine, made of wood. A small room contains a most endearing statue by Giambologna, *Venus Wringing Water from Her Hair*. La Petraia's beautiful gardens and grounds, shaded by ancient cypresses, are open throughout the afternoon.

## Villa di Castello

*Hours as Villa la Petraia; visits to garden only; adm.*

One of Tuscany's most famous gardens is just down the hill from La Petraia, at Villa di Castello (turn right at Via di Castello and walk 450 metres). The villa was bought in 1477 by Lorenzo di Pierfrancesco and Giovanni de' Medici, two cousins of Lorenzo il Magnifico who were Botticelli's best patrons, and they hung the walls of this villa with his great mythological paintings now in the Uffizi. The villa was sacked in the 1530 siege and then restored by Cosimo I; today it is the headquarters of the Accademia della Crusca, founded in 1582 and dedicated to the study of the Italian language. The garden was laid out for Cosimo I by Tribolo, who also designed the fountain in the centre, with a statue, *Hercules and Antenaeus*, by Ammannati.

Directly behind the fountain is the garden's main attraction, an artificial cavern named the **Grotto degli Animali**, filled by Ammannati and Giambologna with marvellous, true-to-life statues of every creature known to man, and lined with mosaics of pebbles and shells. The terrace above offers the best view over the garden's geometric patterns; a large statue by Ammannati of January, or *Gennaio*, emerges shivering from a pool among the trees.

A 20-minute walk north from Villa di Castello to Quinto takes you to two unusual 7th-century BC **Etruscan tombs**. Neither has any art, but the chambers under their 25ft artificial hills bear an odd relationship to ancient cultures elsewhere in the

Mediterranean – domed *tholos* tombs as in Mycenaean Greece, corbelled passages like the *navetas* of Majorca, and entrances that look like the sacred wells of Sardinia.

## Sesto Fiorentino

You can change gear again by heading out a little further in the sprawl to Sesto Fiorentino, a suburb that since 1954 has been home to the famous Richard-Ginori china and porcelain firm. Founded in Doccia in 1735, the firm has opened the **Doccia Museum** on Via Pratese 31 (*signposted*) to display a neat chronological exhibition of its production of Doccia ware, including many Medici commissions (a ceramic *Venus de' Medici*), fine painted porcelain, and some pretty Art Nouveau works (*Wed–Sun 10–1 and 2–6; closed Aug; adm*).

## Villa Demidoff at Pratolino

*Open Mar Sun 10–6; April, Aug and Sept Thurs–Sun 10–8.30; Oct Sun 10–7; closed Nov–Feb; adm. Take bus 25 which leaves about every 20mins from the station.*

The village of Pratolino lies 12km north of Florence along Via Bolognese and it was here that Duke Francesco I bought a villa in the 1568 as a gift to his mistress, the Venetian Bianca Cappello. Francesco commissioned Buontalenti – artist, architect, and hydraulics engineer – to design the enormous gardens. He made Pratolino the marvel of its day, full of water tricks, ingenious automata and a famous menagerie.

Sadly, none of Buontalenti's marvels has survived, but the largest ever example of this play between art and environment has – Giambologna's massive *Appennino*, a giant rising from stone, part stalactite, part fountain himself, conquering the dragon, said to be symbolic of the Medici's origins in the Mugello just north of here. The rest of the park, made into an English garden by the Lorena family and named for Prince Paolo Demidoff who bought it in 1872 and restored Francesco's servants' quarters as his villa, is an invitingly cool refuge from a Florentine summer afternoon.

## Poggio a Caiano

*Open daily Nov–Feb 8.15–3.30; April, May and Sept 8.15–5.30; Mar and Oct 8.15–4.30; June–Aug 8.15–6.30; closed 2nd and 3rd Mon of month; adm. CAP buses, t 055 214637, go past every half-hour, departing from in front of McDonald's on the north side of the station.*

Of all the Medici villas, Poggio a Caiano is the most evocative of the country idylls so delightfully described in the verses of Lorenzo il Magnifico; this was not only his favourite retreat, but is generally considered the very first Italian Renaissance villa. Lorenzo purchased a farmhouse here in 1480, and commissioned Giuliano da Sangallo to rebuild it in a classical style. It was Lorenzo's sole architectural commission, and its classicism matched the mythological nature poems he composed here, most famously 'L'Ambra', inspired by the stream Ombrone that flows nearby.

Sangallo designed the villa according to Alberti's description of the perfect country house in a style that presages Palladio, and added a classical frieze on the façade, sculpted with the assistance of Andrea Sansovino (now replaced with a copy). Some of the other features – the clock, the curved stair and central loggia – were later additions. In the **interior** Sangallo designed an airy, two-storey **Salone**, which the two Medici popes had frescoed by 16th-century masters Pontormo, Andrea del Sarto, Franciabigio and Allori. The subject, as usual, is Medici self-glorification, and depicts family members dressed as Romans in historical scenes that parallel events in their lives. In the right lunette, around a large circular window, Pontormo painted the lovely *Vertumnus and Pomona* (1521), a languid summer scene under a willow tree, beautifully coloured. In another room, Francesco I and Bianca Cappello, his wife, died in 1587, only 11 hours apart; Francesco was always messing with poisons but in fact a nasty virus was the probable killer.

In the **grounds** (*open same hours as villa*) are fine old trees and a 19th-century statue celebrating Lorenzo's 'L'Ambra'.

## Carmignano and Villa Artimino

A local bus continues 5km southwest of Poggio a Caiano to the village of **Carmignano**, which possesses, in its church of **San Michele** (*open daily 7.30–5, until 6 in summer*), Pontormo's uncanny painting *The Visitation* (1530s), a masterpiece of Florentine Mannerism. There are no concessions to naturalism here – the four soulful, ethereal women, draped in Pontormo's customary startling colours, barely touch the ground, standing before a scene as substantial as a stage backdrop. The result is one of the most unforgettable images produced in the 16th century.

Also to the south, at **Comeana** (3km, signposted), is the well-preserved Etruscan **Tomba di Montefortini**, a 7th-century BC burial mound, 35ft high and 260ft in diameter, covering two chambers. A long hall leads to the vestibule and tomb chamber, both covered with false vaulting; the latter preserves a shelf most probably used for gifts for the afterlife. Nearby, the equally impressive **Tomba dei Boschetti** was seriously damaged over centuries by local farmers (*both open Mon–Sat 8–2*).

The Etruscan city of Artimino, 4km to the west, was destroyed by the Romans and is now the site of a small town and another Medici property, the **Villa Artimino** ('La Ferdinanda'), built as hunting lodge for Ferdinando I by Buontalenti. Its semi-fortified air with buttresses was aimed to fit its sporting purpose, but the total effect is simple and charming, with the long roofline punctuated by innumerable chimneys and a graceful stair, added in the 19th century from a drawing by the architect in the Uffizi.

There is an **Etruscan Archaeological Museum** in the basement, containing findings from the tombs; among them a unique censer with two basins and a boat, bronze vases, and a red figured krater painted with initiation scenes, found in a 3rd-century tomb (*villa open for guided tours only on Tues, t 055 871 8124; museum open Thurs–Tues 9.30–12.30; adm*). There's a convenient place for lunch in the grounds. Also in Artimino is an attractive Romanesque church, **San Leonardo**, built of stones salvaged from earlier buildings.

## Poggio Imperiale and the Certosa del Galluzzo

One last villa open for visits, the **Villa di Poggio Imperiale** (*open Wed 10–12 by request, t 055 220151*), lies south of Florence, at the summit of Viale del Poggio

Imperiale, which leaves Porta Romana with a stately escort of cypress sentinels. Cosimo I grabbed this huge villa from the Salviati family in 1565, and it remained a ducal property until there were no longer any dukes to duke. Its neoclassical façade was added in 1808, and the audience chamber was decorated in the 17th century by the underrated Rutilio Manetti and others. Much of the villa is now used as a girls' school.

The **Certosa del Galluzzo** (also known as the Certosa di Firenze) lies further south, scenically located on a hill off the Siena road (*open Tues–Sun 9–11 and 3–6; closes 5pm in winter; adm by donation; take bus 36 or 37 from the station*). Founded as a Carthusian monastery by 14th-century tycoon Niccolò Acciaiuoli, the monastery has been inhabited since 1958 by Cistercians; there are 12 now living there, one of whom takes visitors around.

The Certosa has a fine 16th-century courtyard and an uninteresting church, though the crypt-chapel of the lay choir contains some impressive tombs. The Chiostro Grande, surrounded by the monks' cells, is decorated with 66 majolica tondi of prophets and saints by Giovanni della Robbia and assistants; one cell is opened for visits, and it seems almost cosy. The Gothic Palazzo degli Studi, intended by the founder as a school, contains five lunettes by Pontormo, painted while he and his pupil Bronzino hid out here from the plague in 1522.

# Chianti and the Mugello

08

# Chianti and the Mugello

10 km
5 miles

N

Roncobilaccio
Firenzuola
Montecarelli
Barberino di Mugello
4 Scarperia
S. Piero a Sieve
Borgo S. Lorenzo
Vaiano
Prato
Sesto Fiorentino
Pratolino
M. Senario
R. Bisenzio
Monti d. Calvana
A11
S65
R. Mugnone
Campi Bisenzio
S325
Florence
Fiesole
Pontassieve
R. Sieve
S555
S67
S. Godenzo
M. Falterona
Pso. d. Calla

Marradi
R. Lamone
S67

EMILIA-ROMAGNA
Dovadola
Predappio
Predappio Alta
Rocca San Casciano
Portico di Romagna
S310
Santa Sofia
Alpe di San Benedetto
Bagno di Romagna
Badia Prataglia
M. Penna

Signa
Scandicci
S. Donato in Collina
R. Pesa
Cerbaia
S. Casciano in Val di Pesa
S. Polo in Chianti
Strada in Chianti
S222
Incisa in Val d'A.
R. Greve
Mercatale in Val di Pesa
Tavarnelle in Val di Pesa
Greve in Chianti
1
S69
A1
Castelfranco di Sopra
TUSCANY
Barberino Val d'Elsa
S. Donato in Poggio
S429
R. Elsa
Pietrafitta
S429
Badia Coltibuono
Poggibonsi
Castellina in Chianti
2
Radda in Chianti
Colle di Val d'Elsa
S222
Monteriggioni
3
S484
Cast. di Brolio
S408
Siena

Stia
Pratovecchio
Casentino
M. Secchieta
Poppi
Bibbiena
Pratomagno
R. Arno
M. Penna
Caprese Michelangelo
S71
Subbiano
Castiglion Fibocchi
S. Giovanni Valdarno
Montevarchi
S69
Arezzo
Ambra
Civitella in Val Chiana
S73
Foce di Scopetone

p.206
p.344
p.366

# Highlights

1 Wine-touring around Greve in Chianti
2 The quattrocento charms of
  Castellina in Chianti
3 The Iron Baron's Castello di Brolio
4 Scarperia: a Florentine outpost
  in the Mugello

SWITZ. AUSTRIA HUNGARY
FRANCE SLOVENIA CROATIA
BOSNIA-HERZ.
Corsica
ITALY
Sardinia
Sicily
TUNISIA

These two regions, Chianti to the south and the Mugello to the north of Florence, one world-famous and one obscure, are delightfully rural and endowed with every Tuscan charm. No Brunelleschi could have designed the grand stone farmhouses that crown every hill, built with an intuitive aesthetic that rarely fails, each different, offering endless variations of arches, loggias and towers, set in an equally endless variety of rolling hills, vineyards, olives and cypresses. Towns are few, monuments scattered and of minor interest, paintings and sculpture very rare. But you'll find few places more enchanting to explore – by car, by bicycle, by foot – in a day or a lifetime.

# Chianti

*From good Chianti, an aged wine, majestic and
imperious, that passes through my heart and chases
away without trouble every worry and grief...*
Francesco Redi, *Bacchus in Tuscany*

In the 17th century, naturalist and poet Francesco Redi was the first to note the virtues of 'Florentine red' from Chianti, and since then the Italians have invested a lot of worry into defining exactly what 'Chianti' means. The name apparently derives from an Etruscan family named Clanti; geographically it refers, roughly, to the hilly region between Florence and Siena, bordered by the Florence–Siena Superstrada del Palio and the A1 from Florence to Arezzo. The part within Siena province is known as *Chianti Storico* or *Chianti Geografico*, once the territories of the Lega del Chianti, a consortium of barons formed in 1385 to protect their interests (and their wine), who adopted a black cockerel as their emblem.

But Chianti is an oenological name as well as a geographical one and, as such, first became official in 1716, when Grand Duke Cosimo III defined which parts of Tuscany could call their vintage Chianti, in effect making wine history – it was the first time that a wine had its production area delimited. The Lorraine grand dukes promoted advances in wine-making techniques and the export of Chianti. Yet the Chianti as we know it had yet to be developed, and it was largely the creation of one man – the 'Iron Baron', Bettino Ricasoli, briefly the second prime minister of unified Italy. The baron was very wealthy but not handsome, and Luigi Barzini, in *The Italians*, recounts how jealous he became when his new bride was asked to dance at a ball. Without ado, he ordered her into their carriage and told the driver to take her to the ancient family seat at Brolio in the Monti del Chianti – an isolated castle that the poor woman rarely left ever after.

To pass the time the baron began to experiment with different vines and processes, eventually hitting upon a pleasing mix of red Sangiovese and Canaiolo grapes, with a touch of white Malvasia, twice fermented in the old Tuscan manner. Meanwhile, the famous dark green flask was invented, the *strapeso*, with its straw covering woven by the local women. The end product took the Paris Exhibition of 1878 by storm; imitators soon appeared and, in 1924, the boundaries of Chianti Storico were more than doubled to create Chianti Classico, drawn by local producers to protect the wine's name, adopting the now familiar black cockerel as its symbol. In 1967 Chianti Classico, along with Tuscany's six other Chianti vinicultural zones, was given its *denominazione di origine* status, and production soared, but quality and sales declined. To improve it, the Chianti Classico Consortium was upscaled to a DOCG rating to guarantee that all wines bearing the black cockerel would be tested and approved by a panel of judges.

But it was tales of Elizabeth Barrett Browning quaffing Chianti and finding her inspiration in its ruby splendour, as well as the sunny rural elegance of the region, that attracted first the English and Dutch, then the Swiss, Americans, French and Germans, especially in the 1960s and 1970s; they form one of Italy's densest foreign colonies, wryly nicknamed 'Chianti-shire'. The newcomers brought more money than Chianti's mouldering barons and contessas had seen since the Renaissance; property prices shot to the moon. But the presence of so much money has begun to cast a shadow over the heart of this ancient, enchanting region; snobbery and pretensions threaten to poison the pleasurable plonk of yesteryear. Some vintners offer limited-edition numbered bottles; designer-label Chianti is upon us. The old vines, following the contours of the hills, are being pulled out to make room for specialized vines in geometric straight lines. And as any old-timer will tell you, the modern DOCG Chianti Classico sniffed and gurgled by wine professionals isn't anything like the joyous, spontaneous wine that made Chianti famous in the first place.

Some 800 farms and estates (only a selection of the most historic are listed below) produce wine in the 70,000 hectares of the Chianti Classico zone, and one of the chief pleasures is trying as many labels as possible – with the different mixtures of grapes, different soils and bottling methods, each should be, or at least strives to be, individual. Nor do estates limit themselves to Chianti; many produce *vin santo*, a white wine called Bianca della Lega, and many reds, as well as Chianti's other speciality, a delicate *extra-vergine* olive oil. Before setting out, call to check hours.

# Western Chianti: Florence to Tavarnelle Val di Pesa

Chianti begins 10km south of Florence, but on the way you may want to follow the sign west off SS222 just past the *autostrada*, for **Ponte a Ema** and the prettily sited 14th-century chapel of the Alberti, Santa Caterina dell'Antella (*closed Sun*) with contemporary frescoes on St Catherine's life, one of Spinello Aretino's greatest works. Further along, at Grassina, there's a turn-off to **Impruneta**, a large town on a plateau noted for its terracotta tiles (including those on Brunelleschi's dome) and pottery, very much on sale, especially during St Luke's Horse and Mule Fair in October. The fair takes place in the main piazza, in the shadow of Impruneta's pride and joy, the **Collegiata**, built to house a miraculous icon of the *Madonna and Child* attributed to St Luke, dug up by a team of oxen in the 10th century. After the Collegiata was bombed in the last war, restorers brought it back to its Renaissance appearance to match its two beautiful chapels, both designed by Michelozzo and richly decorated with enamel terracottas by Luca della Robbia. One houses the icon and the other a piece of the True Cross. In an adjacent chapel is a marble relief, the *Finding of the Icon*, by the school of Donatello; the bronze crucifix in the nave is attributed to

# Getting Around

The two main north–south **routes** through Chianti, the old Roman Via Cassia (SS2) and the Chiantigiana (SS222), rival one another in beauty. An ideal motoring wine tour would take in the east–west SS429 between the Badia a Coltibuono and Castellina. The distances aren't very great, though the single-lane winding routes make for fairly leisurely travel.

Public transport is fairly easy in Chianti and all by **bus**, though you may not always find connections between two towns very commodious; from Florence SITA buses will take you to Greve (25km/45min), Gaiole (55km/1½hrs), Castellina in Chianti (44km/1hr), Mercatale, S. Casciano in Val di Pesa (17km/25min), Tavarnelle Val di Pesa (29km/40min), Panzano, Strada, and Radda (42km/1hr); CAP buses run frequently from Florence to Impruneta (14km/20min).

From Siena TRA-IN buses go to Castellina (20km/25min), Radda (30km/40min), Tavarnelle (38km/50min) and S. Casciano (49km/1¼hrs), Tavarnuzze and Strada.

# Tourist Information

**Impruneta**: Piazza Buondelmonti 29, t/f 055 231 3729, *www.proimpruneta.rtd.it*.
**San Casciano in Val di Pesa**: Piazza della Repubblica, t/f 055 822 9558, *prosanca@ftbcc.it*.
**Barberino Val D'Elsa**: Via Cassia 31a, t/f 055 807 5622. *Open April–Oct.*
**Greve in Chianti**: Viale G. da Verrazzano 33, t/f 055 854 6287.
**Castellina in Chianti**: Via Ferruccio 40, t 057 774 1392.
**Radda**: Piazza Ferrucci 1, t 0577 738494.

# Where to Stay and Eat

In this part of Chianti, hotels tend to be small and usually annexed to restaurants. It is worth noting that many of the larger wine estates have a few rooms or apartments to let. For these you will need to call ahead to see what's available.

## Candeli ✉ 50100
**\*\*\*\*\*Villa la Massa**, Via della Massa 6, t 055 62611, f 055 633102, *villamassa@galactica.it*, *www.villalamassa.com* (*luxury*). A large hotel, recently and spectacularly renovated, with a swimming pool and 39 rooms.

## Impruneta ✉ 50023
**\*\*\*La Vallombrosina**, Via Montebuoni 95, t/f 055 202 0491, *www.lavallombrosina.it* (*moderate, with bath*). A comfortable roof over your head.
**B&B Benedetta Bianchi**, Via Paolieri 26, t/f 055 231 2558 (*moderate*). A spacious new B&B just off the main piazza, with nicely furnished rooms and apartments, and lovely views over the surrounding hills.
**I Falciani**, Via Cassia 245, t 055 202 0091 (*moderate*). A rustic place full of locals, where you may dine with the TV for company on tasty *crostini ribolliti* and, in autumn, on the hunters' roast meat platter.

## Bagno a Ripoli ✉ 50012
**Centanni**, Via Centanni 7, t 055 630122 (*expensive*). Exceptionally pleasant, set among olive groves, where you can dine on a delicious array of *antipasti*, and Renaissance recipes like *brasata dei Medici*, a sweet and sour braised beef dish dating from the 17th century. *Closed Sun.*

## Località I Falciani ✉ 50029
**Antica Trattoria dei Cacciatori**, Via Chiantigiana 22, t 055 232 6327 (*moderate*). Offers sturdy dishes, such as *rognone al ginepro*, kidneys with juniper. *Closed Wed.*

## Tavarnuzze ✉ 50029
**\*\*Gli Scopeti**, Via Cassia 183, t 055 202 2008, f 055 237 3015 (*cheap*). A cheaper alternative.

## Sant'Andrea in Percussina ✉ 50029
**Albergaccio di Machiavelli**, t 055 828471 (*moderate*). Machiavelli's old tavern, now owned by the Conti Serristori Wine Company, serves simple Tuscan meals – in summer, try the refreshing *panzanella* – and fine wines from the estate. You can also buy bottles to take home. *Closed Mon and Tues.*

Giambologna. The campanile dates from the 13th century, and the fine portico from 1634. Among the many terracotta shops, **Artenova** (*Via della Fonte 76, t 055 201 1060*) has creative designs and a good selection of gifts.

## Machiavelli in Exile

From the SS222 south of Florence, a byroad leads west from Tavarnuzze (8km) to **Sant'Andrea in Percussina**, long the country fief of the Machiavelli. Here Niccolò spent his tedious exile, which he described in a letter as whiling away the day in the tavern 'playing at *cricca* and tric-trac, and this gave rise to a thousand arguments and endless exchanges of insults, most of the time there is a fight over a penny...and so surrounded by these lice, I blow the cobwebs from my brain and relieve the unkindness of my fate'. In the evening he would retire to work on *The Prince*.

His old tavern is still a tavern and his home, the Albergaccio (literally, 'nasty little inn'), contains a small museum devoted to his life. Near Chiesanuova, to the north, there's the 16th-century **Palazzo al Bosco**, attributed by some to Michelangelo, a villa built atop a 13th-century structure. The stately, theatrical 15th-century **Villa Tattoli** to the west (on the Chiesanuova–Cerbaia road) features two levels of arcades. Near Cerbaia, 5km from San Casciano, Villa Talente is the former property of the artists who built Orsanmichele in Florence (*t 055 825 9484; offers Chianti, white wine and olive oil*).

# Along the Via Cassia (SS2)

Up-to-date **San Casciano in Val di Pesa**, 17km south of Florence, is the largest and busiest town in Chianti. Long an outpost of Florence, it suffered numerous vicissitudes until its walls were begun by the ill-fated Duke of Athens in 1342. Within these, near the gateway, the church of Santa Maria del Prato (1335) has retained its trecento interior and trecento art: a fine pulpit by Giovanni Balducci da Pisa, a pupil of Andrea Pisano, a crucifix attributed to Simone Martini, a triptych by Ugolino di Neri, and framed paintings on the pilasters by Giotto's pupil, Taddeo Gaddi. The recently opened **Museum of Sacred Art** (*open Sat 5–7, Sun 10.30–12 and 4–7*) includes the *Madonna and Child*, considered to be the first work by Ambrogio Lorenzetti.

In the vicinity of San Casciano, Florentine merchants and noblemen dotted the countryside with villas: the late Renaissance Fattoria Le Corti, 2km east on the Mercatale road, owned by the princely Corsini family for the past six centuries (*t 055 829 0105; own Chianti on sale*) and the 17th-century Poggio Torselli, just off the SS2, approached through a long avenue of cypresses and surrounded by a lovely garden.

## Mercatale, Bargino and Barberino Val d'Elsa

**Mercatale**, 5km east of San Casciano, grew up around its *mercato* (market), protected in the old days by the Castle of the Florentine Bishops, now a ruin fit only to protect the odd lizard. More muscular, just east on the road to Passo dei Pecorai, is the **Castello di Greve** (*t 055 821 101; tastings and lunches with advance notice, own Chianti, vin santo and olive oil on sale*), bound by four round towers. The Bardi put it up in the

# Where to Stay and Eat

Most of the district's lodgings are here, as well as some of Chianti's best restaurants.

## Cerbaia ✉ 50026

**La Tenda Rossa**, Piazza del Monumento 11, t 055 826132 (*very expensive, but worth it*). A family-run abode of haute cuisine: pumpkin-filled *tortellini* or lettuce crêpes filled with artichoke hearts, followed by chicken with grated *porcini* mushrooms, or duck in balsamic vinegar. Save room for one of the innovative desserts. *Closed Mon lunch and Aug.*

## San Casciano ✉ 50026

★★★**Villa Il Poggiale**, Via Empolese 69, t 055 828311, f 055 829 4296, *www.villailpoggiale.it* (*expensive*). This lovely Renaissance villa overlooking a cypress-bordered lawn has elegant rooms, decorated in pastel shades; some have four-poster beds. The atmosphere is of a grand but un-stuffy private country home. Breakfasts are hearty and there is a nice pool. There are self-catering apartments too. Excellent value for money.
**Nello**, Via IV Novembre 66, t 055 820163 (*moderate*). The menu features fresh fish, plus such Tuscany staples as *ribollita pasta* with *funghi porcini*, beef braised in 'Chianti' classico. *Closed Wed eve and Thurs.*
★★★**L'Antica Post**, Piazza Zannoni 1/3, t 055 822313, f 055 822278 (*inexpensive*). Ten rooms with bath, and an excellent, Persian carpet-strewn restaurant. Try *taglierini* with razor clams and asparagus, pheasant with thyme, or rabbit in a sauce of creamed mussels; the wine list is superb. *Reservations necessary.*

## Bargino ✉ 50024

★ **Bargino**, Via Cassia 122, t 055 824 9055 (*inexpensive*). Seven rooms in a garden along the old Roman road, with an excellent fish restaurant, **La Trattoria del Pesce** (*moderate*).

## Mercatale ✉ 50026

★**Soggiorno Paradiso**, Piazza V Veneto 28, t 055 821327, f 055 821281 (*inexpensive*). Simple, but with TVs and electric kettles in the rooms.
**Il Salotto del Chianti**, Via Sonnino 92, t 055 821 8429 (*moderate*). Well-established on the local culinary scene; *ravioli con formaggio, pappardelle alla lepre* and wild boar are extraordinary. *Closed lunch and Wed.*

## Tavarnelle ✉ 50028

**La Gramola**, Via delle Fonti 1, t 055 8050321 (*moderate*). A pleasantly rustic restaurant in the heart of the town, serving variations on traditional Tuscan dishes. The mixed *antipasto* plate is always tasty, ravioli stuffed with pumpkin and flavoured with local truffles are earthy. *Dinner only (except Sun); closed Tues.*
**Youth Hostel**, Via Roma 137, t 055 807 7009 (*inexpensive*). One of the pleasant Chianti hostels, with 60 beds. *Open all year.*

## Barberino Val d'Elsa ✉ 50021

★★**Primavera**, Via della Republicca 27, t/f 055 805 9223 (*moderate*). A pleasant, simple hotel.

## San Donato in Poggio ✉ 50028

**Villa Francesca**, Strada Monestiero 12, t 055 807 2849 (*moderate*). Tasty roasts, risotto with porcini mushrooms and *bistecca*. *Open Thurs–Sun; Thurs, Fri dinner only.*

11th century, before they moved to Florence and founded the greatest pre-Medici bank. Other villas worth visiting near Mercatale are Villa Caserotta, once property of the Strozzi, and the fortified Villa Palagio, on the Mercatale–Campoli–Montefiridolfi road, adapted from a 14th-century castle. The Mercatale–Panzano road will bring you to **La Torre a Luciana**, an unspoiled medieval hamlet once belonging to the Pitti family.

The Via Cassia, between San Casciano and Bargino, passes the ancient **Castle of Bibbione**, once residence of the Buondelmonte family, who owned much of this territory in the days when they were throwing fat on the Guelph and Ghibelline fires in Florence. Near **Bargino**, in the same bellicose spirit, is the impressive fortified hamlet of **Montefiridolfi**, just east of the Via Cassia. This road, meanwhile, rolls south through lovely hills towards **Tavarnelle Val di Pesa**, of mostly 19th-century origin, and medieval **Barberino Val d'Elsa**, with some Etruscan finds in the town hall and a good 10th-century Romanesque church, the Pieve di Sant'Appiano. From here the Via Cassia continues to **Poggibonsi** (*see* pp.347–9), with a possible detour to **La Paneretta**, a sturdy 15th-century fort amid olive groves, with Baroque frescoes inside.

# Central Chianti: Along the Chiantigiana (SS222)

From Florence the scenic Chiantigiana (SS222) passes the Ugolino Golf Course (*see* p.86) and offers its first tempting detour at Petigliolo: turn left after 4km for the ivy-covered Santo Stefano a Tizzano, a Romanesque church built by the Buondelmonti, not far from an 11th-century castle-villa, the **Castello di Tizzano** (*t 055 855 5040; offers Chianti Riserva, vin santo naturale and prize-winning olive oil*). The same road continues for 2km to **San Polo in Chianti**, the centre of Tuscany's iris industry, celebrated in an Iris Festival in May. On a hill from San Polo you can see a lonely building once belonging to the Knights Templar; an equally ancient church, San Miniato in Robbiana, was reconsecrated in 1077 by the Bishop of Fiesole, according to a still legible inscription. San Polo's **Antico Toscano** is a wine shop with offerings from all over the region.

**Strada**, 14km from Florence along the Chiantigiana, is thought to take its odd name from an old Roman road. In the Middle Ages, the road to the south, towards the Valdarno was protected by the **Castello di Mugano**, one of the best preserved in the region, polished up by a recent restoration. The rolling countryside is the dominant feature until **Vicchiomaggio**, with a distinctive castle where Leonardo da Vinci once stayed. This is now the British-run Fattoria Castello di Vicchiomaggio (*t 055 854079; own-label Chianti, vin santo, olive oil, honey and upmarket accommodation*).

New Yorkers will recognize the name of nearby **Verrazzano** at once, thanks to Giovanni da Verrazzano, a captain who, in the service of François I of France, discovered New York harbour and Manhattan island in 1524. He disappeared on his second voyage to Brazil, but surely smiles down on the bridge named in his honour. His birthplace, the **Castello di Verrazzano** (*call t 055 854243; tastings with a week's notice*), offers wines and olive oils. East of the Chiantigiana, 1.5km north of Greve, stands the 13th-century **Castello di Uzzano** (*t 055 854032; tastings with one day's notice*), built by the Bishop of Florence, which was gradually converted into one of Chianti's most impressive villa estates.

## Greve in Chianti and Environs

The biggest **wine fair** in Chianti occurs in September in the medieval town of **Greve** (pop. 10,800), which is seen as the region's capital. Located on the banks of the river, it is celebrated for its charming, arcaded, funnel-shaped **Piazza del Matteotti**, studded with a statue of Verrazzano. And that's about all – its castle was burned down in 1387, and its Franciscan convent became a prison in the 19th century. In the church of **Santa Croce** there's a triptych by Lorenzo di Bicci and a painting by the 'Master of Greve'.

# Where to Stay

## Greve ✉ 50022

***Del Chianti**, Piazza Matteotti 86, t/f 055 853763, *www.albergodelchianti.it* (*expensive*). Pleasantly refurbished; near the centre, with comfortable, stylish air-conditioned rooms, and a pool and garden in the back.

***Giovanni da Verrazzano**, Piazza Matteotti 28, t 055 853189, f 055 853648, *www.verrazzano.it* (*expensive*). Eleven elegant rooms overlooking the pretty main square.

**Villa Vignamaggio**, Via Petriolo 5, t 055 854 4840, f 055 854 4468, *www.vignamaggio.it* (*expensive*). 5mins' drive from Greve on the Panzano road. You can stay in buildings in the grounds or in the historic villa (see p.196). Tennis and a pool are available. Mona Lisa was born here in 1479, and *Much Ado About Nothing* was filmed here in 1992.

## Panzano ✉ 50022

****Villa le Barone**, Via S. Leolino 19, t 055 852621, f 055 852277, www.villalebarone.it (*luxury half-board only*). Just south of Greve is the 16th-century villa of the della Robbia family, who still own it: it's a lovely, intimate hotel, a great base for visiting the region, or for lounging in the pretty garden by the pool (bring the children). Many rooms are decorated in della Robbia blue and white. *Open April–Oct; min. stay 3 nights.*

**Villa Rosa** Via San Leolino 59, t 055 852577, f 055 856 0835, *www.resortvillarosa.it* (*expensive*). On the road between Panzano and Radda, Villa Rosa has a pleasant, relaxed atmosphere; there is a shady terrace at the back and a pool on the hillside, which enjoys beautiful views.

## Monte S. Michele ✉ 50020

**Villa San Michele**, t 055 851034 (*inexpensive*). The youth hostel, with beds for 60. *Closed Nov–Mar.*

## Castellina ✉ 53011

****Tenuta di Ricavo**, t 0577 740221, f 0577 741014, *www.ricavo.com* (*very expensive*). 3km north of Castellina, this is more than a hotel – it's an entire medieval hamlet of stone houses, wonderfully isolated in the pines and with a large garden and pool. Many rooms are situated in the old houses, ideal for families. *Open April–Oct.*

****Villa Casalecchi**, t 0577 740240, f 0577 741111, *www.villacasalecchi.com* (*very expensive*). A comfortable if rather sombre old house, set among trees and vineyards on a slope, with some elegant rooms full of antiques and some not so elegant, but a big pool and enchanting views over the hills. *Open April–Oct.*

***Salivolpi**, Via Fiorentina, t 0577 740484, f 0577 740998, *www.hotelsalivolpi.com* (*moderate*). Two old farmhouses have been combined to create this smart establishment just outside Castellina; a garden and pool are added attractions.

# Eating Out

## Greve ✉ 50022

**Bottega del Moro**, Piazza Trieste 14r, t 055 853753 (*expensive–moderate*). Right in the heart of Greve, a simple *trattoria* where you can eat typical Tuscan dishes. *Closed Wed.*

**Osteria di Passignano**, Via Passignano 33, Badia a Passignano, t 055 807 1278 (*expensive*). Set in the old wine cellars of a monastery on the famous Antinori wine estates just south of Florence, this is one of the best country restaurants in the area. The atmosphere is elegant rustic and the creative food is firmly rooted in Tuscan and Italian traditions. *Closed Sun and most of Jan.*

**La Cantinetta di Rignana**, Via Rignana, Greve, t 055 852601 (*moderate*). This *trattoria* is situated in idyllic countryside between

Greve is awash with wine, so seek out the specialized wine shops (*see* 'Wine-tasting in and around Greve', p.195). Meat-lovers flock to the **Macelleria Falorni** (*Piazza Matteotti 69/71*, *t 055 853029*), one of the region's most famous butchers, acclaimed for its cured hams and *finocchiona* salamis flavoured with fennel seeds. In a nearby hamlet, **Cintoia**, east of Chiocchio, there is the little church of

Greve and Badia in Passignano (to the south), and has a panoramic terrace ideal for long, lazy lunches. Whet the appetite with a *bruschetta* doused in local oil; pastas come with mushrooms, truffles or traditional meat sauces. *Closed Tues.*

**Giovanni da Verrazzano**, Piazza Matteotti 28, **t** 055 853189 (*moderate*). This is one of Greve's most charming restaurants, furnished with antiques and with a lovely terrace overlooking the piazza. The main meat dishes are especially good – *nana in sugo* (duck in wine sauce), turkey with olives, and a varied mixed grill. *Closed Mon.*

There are also a number of good places in the following villages close to Greve:

## Montefioralle ✉ 50022

**Taverna del Guerrino**, Via di Montefioralle 39, **t** 055 853106 (*moderate*). A rustic place surrounded by a panoramic garden, offering good Tuscan home cooking, including *panzanella*, *ribollita* (Tuscan bread soup), sausage and beans *all'uccelletto* and wines from the local *fattoria*. *Closed Mon–Wed.*

## Spedaluzzo ✉ 50027

**La Cantinetta**, on the Chiantigiana 93, **t** 055 857 2000 (*moderate*). Good home-made pasta and country specialities like stuffed rabbit, pigeon, stuffed artichokes and grilled meats. *Closed Mon.*

## Località Lucolena ✉ 50020

**Borgo Antico**, **t** 055 851024 (*moderate*). Worth trying for tasty *pappardelle* made with chestnut flour with wild boar or duck sauce. Porcini mushrooms in season. Also rooms for rent. *Closed Mon–Thurs in winter.*

## Panzano ✉ 50022

**Montagliari**, Via di Montagliari 28, **t** 055 852184 (*moderate*). Decorated in the style of an old Tuscan farmhouse, with tables in the panoramic garden. Dishes include ravioli filled with walnuts, boar *alla cacciatora* and *pollastro Montagliari al vino bianco* (chicken with white wine and black olives). *Booking obligatory.*

## Castellina ✉ 53011

**Albergaccio di Castellina**, Via Fiorentina 35, on the road to San Donato, **t** 0577 741042 (*expensive*). On the outskirts of town, this serves 'creative' fare. *Closed Sun.*

**Antica Trattoria La Torre**, Piazza del Comune 1, **t** 0577 740236 (*moderate*). A popular, family-run place, with a cosy atmosphere and tasty dishes like risotto with mushrooms and an exceptional *fagiano alla torre*, prepared to an ancient Chianti recipe. *Closed Fri.*

**Pietrafitta Ristoranti in Chianti** Località Pietrafitta 41, **t** 0577 741123 (*moderate*). This is slightly cheaper, owned by an American with an Australian cook, offering surprisingly good regional and international dishes. Imaginative Italian–Mediterranean food. *Closed Tues.*

# Wine-tasting in and around Greve

**Bottega del Chianti Classico**, Via Cesare Battisti 4, **t** 055 853631.

**Castello di Querceto**, just outside Greve on the Figline Val d'Arno road, **t** 055 85921. A lovely place offering a wide variety of wines, including Sangiovese aged in *barriques*, and olive oil (*tastings with one week's notice*).

**Enoteca del Chianti Classico**, Piazzetta S. Croce 8, **t/f** 055 853297.

**Fontodi**, Via S. Leolino 87, on the Chiantigiana, near Sant'Eufrosino, **t** 055 852005. Also has wine aged in *barriques*, Chianti, Bianco della Lega and olive oil (*tastings with one week's notice*).

Santa Maria a Cintoia which has a beautiful 15th-century panel attributed to Francesco Granacci.

The ancient village and castle of **Montefioralle**, 1km west of Greve, is where the people of Greve lived in the bad old days. Recently restored, it is an interesting place to poke around in, with its octagonal walls intact, its old tower houses, and two

Romanesque churches: Santo Stefano, housing early Florentine paintings, and the porticoed Pieve di San Cresci a Montefioralle, just outside the walls. A minor road to the west passes the ruined castle of **Montefili**, built in the 900s as the eastern outpost of one of Chianti's most powerful religious institutions, the **Badia a Passignano**, a fortified complex, converted since into a villa. You can visit the old abbey church, **San Michele**, which contains paintings by Ghirlandaio, Alessandro Allori and Domenico Cresti (better known as Passignano) and a bust of San Giovanni Gualberto, founder of the Vallombrosan Order, who arrived here in the mid-11th century. Most buildings date from the 14th century, with a few 17th- and 19th-century remodellings.

Just east of Greve, the beautiful villa **Vignamaggio** was built by the Gherardini family, whose most famous member, Lisa, was born here. She married Francesco del Giocondo before posing for the world's most famous portrait. More recently, in 1992 it was the setting for Kenneth Branagh's film, *Much Ado About Nothing*. **Panzano**, an agricultural centre 6km south of Greve on the Chiantigiana, played an important role in the Florence–Siena squabbles, but retains only part of its medieval castle. Its famous butcher, Dario Cecchini, is known for his protests when 'beef on the bone' was banned in 2001. He holds court in his shop (Via XX Luglio 11) on the outskirts of town on Sunday mornings, while playing loud music and reciting Dante. Panzano is best known for its embroidery, and for the **Pieve di San Leolino**, 1km south, with its pretty 16th-century portico on a 12th-century Romanesque structure; inside there's a triptych by Mariotto di Nardo. Another Romanesque church south of Panzano, Sant'Eufrosino, just off the SS222, enjoys especially fine views. Near Panzano is the **Fattoria Montagliari** (*sells a wide variety of its own wines, grappa, olive oil, cheese, salami, honey, etc.*). **Pietrafitta**, 9km further south and 4km from Castellina, is a lovely hamlet hidden in the woods.

## Castellina in Chianti

One of Chianti's most charming hill-top villages, Castellina (pop. 2,700) was fortified by Florence as an outpost against Siena, and for centuries its fortunes depended on who was on top in their endless war. It was lost to a combined Sienese-Aragonese siege in 1478, though after the fall of Siena itself in 1555 both cities lost interest in Castellina, and today it looks much as it did in the quattrocento: the circuit of walls is almost intact, complete with houses built into and on top of them. The **Rocca**, or fortress, is in the centre, its mighty donjon now home to the mayor; and the covered walkway, Via delle Volte, is part of the 15th-century defensive works. Less historic but worth visiting is the Bottega del Vino Gallo Nero, Via della Rocca 10 (*sells wines and olive oils*). You can explore the **Ipogeo Etrusco di Montecalvario**, a recently restored 6th-century BC Etruscan tomb. West of Castellina on the SS429, **Granaio** is home to one of Chianti's most renowned wineries, the **Melini Wine House**, established in 1705.

There are many splendid old farmhouses and villas around Castellina, nearly all formerly fortifications along Chianti's medieval Maginot line, like the **Villa La Leccia** just southwest of Castellina, and the **Castello di Campalli** near **Fonterutoli**, an ancient hamlet south on the Chiantigiana. In the 13th century Florence and Siena often met here to work out peace settlements, none of which lasted long. Since 1435 the Mazzei family at the **Fattoria di Fonterutoli** (*t 0577 740476*) has produced wine in traditional oak casks, including Chianti and Bianco della Lega, as well as lavender products, honey and Tuscany's finest *extra vergine*. Further south, **Quercegrossa**, 10km from Siena, but now practically a suburb of the city, was the birthplace of quattrocento sculptor Jacopo della Quercia. A road forks northeast for Vagliagli, site of the medieval **Fattoria della Aiola** (*t 0577 322509; with wines, grappa, olive oil, honey and vinegar*).

# Monti del Chianti: Radda and Gaiole

East of Castellina lies the more rugged region of the Monti del Chianti. Here in the ancient capital of the Lega del Chianti, **Radda in Chianti** (pop. 1,650), the streets follow a medieval plan, radiating from the central piazza and its stately, heraldry-encrusted Palazzo Comunale, with a 15th-century fresco *Madonna, St Christopher and St John the Baptist* in the atrium. Just outside town is the Franciscan **Monastero,** a pretty 15th-century church. Two medieval villages are nearby: **Ama**, with its castle 8km to the south, near the attractive Romanesque church of San Giusto; and **Volpaia**, 7km to the north, with another ancient castle and walls, and an unexpected 'Brunelleschian' church, La Commenda. Also near Radda is the **Fattoria Vigna Vecchia** (*t 0577 738090, www. vignavecchia.com; offers Chianti, grappa, vin santo, olive oil and tastings with 3 days' notice*).

On the way to Gaiole, 10km east of Radda, you pass the ancient **Badia a Coltibuono**, one of the gems of Chianti. Set among centuries-old trees and gardens, the abbey is believed to have been founded in 770, passing to the Vallombrosan Order in the 12th century. The Romanesque church, San Lorenzo, dates from 1049. The monastery was converted into a splendid villa, owned in the 19th century by the Poniatowski, one of Poland's greatest noble families, and now occupied by a wine estate, **Fattoria Badia a Coltibuono.** You can visit the cellars and Italianate garden (*t 0577 74481, f 0577 749235; open May–Oct, Mon–Sat 2.30–6.30*) and restaurant (*see* 'Where to Stay and Eat', p.198).

**Gaiole in Chianti** (pop. 4,780) is an ancient market town: the **Agricoltori Chianti Geografico** (*Via Mulinaccio 10, t 0577 749489; sells Chianti, Vernaccia di San Gimignano, vin santo and olive oil*) is the headquarters of a local cooperative; the **Enoteca Montagnani**, Via B Bandinelli 9, specializes in Chianti Classico. Beside wine tasting Gaiole has little to offer, but it is a good base for visiting the impressive castles between the Arno and Siena. Just to the west are the walls and imposing donjon of the well-preserved 13th-century **Castello di Vertine**, one of the most striking sights in Chianti. To the east of Gaiole is the ancient fortified village of **Barbischio**, and 3km south on the SS408 is the impressive medieval **Castello di Meleto** with its sturdy cylindrical towers. From here the road continues 4.5km up to the mighty **Castello di Castagnoli**, guarding a fascinating little medieval town in a commanding position.

Most majestic of all is the Iron Baron's isolated **Castello di Brolio** (*open daily 9–12 and 3–sunset*) some 10km south of Gaiole along the SS484, high on a hill with views for miles around. Donated to the monks of the Badia in Florence in 1009, by Matilda of Tuscany's father Bonifacio, it passed to the Ricasoli in 1167. In 1478 the castle was

# Where to Stay and Eat

## Radda ✉ 53017

**La Locanda,** Località Montanino, Vilpaia,
**t** 0577 738833, *www.locanda.it* (*luxury*). Set on
a wooded hillside overlooking the hamlet of
Volpaia, this little hotel, housed in a collection of restored stone farm buildings, enjoys
perfect peace and the atmosphere of a private house. Rooms are rustic but stylish,
views from the terraced garden are stunning,
the food is good and there is a small pool.

**Antica Trattoria Botteganova,** Via Chiantigiana 29, **t** 0577 284230 (*very expensive*).
Known for fish and meat in interesting
combinations – *tortelli* with truffle and
Parmesan sauce, clams with aniseed, and
sweet and sour pigeon. Leave space for the
wonderful desserts. *Closed Mon.*

**\*\*\*\*Relais Vignale,** Via Pianigiani 8, **t** 0577
738300, **f** 0577 738592, *www.vignale.it* (*very
expensive*). Thirty rooms in a charming old
house, with some fine views and a pool for
hotter days. Their excellent restaurant is
320m down the road. *Open April–Dec.*

**Il Vignale,** Via XX Settembre 23, **t** 0577 738094
(*very expensive*). A family-run restaurant,
featuring refined Tuscan home cooking, very
popular locally. *Closed Thurs.*

**Badia a Coltibuono,** next to the old abbey of
the same name between Radda and Gaiole,
**t** 0577 749031 (*expensive*). Delicious *tortelloni, tagliatelle ai porcini*, meats roasted on a
spit, and tempting desserts.

**Podere Terreno,** on road to Volpaia, **t/f** 0577
738312 (*expensive – half-board*). A working
wine-producing farm and *agriturismo*, 5km
north of Radda. Rooms are simple, the
atmosphere relaxed, with meals served at a
communal table in a cluttered living room.

**\*Il Girarrosto,** Via Roma 41, **t** 0577 738010
(*inexpensive*). In the village centre, nine simple
rooms annexed to this very popular restaurant
(*moderate*). Ideal if you're in the mood for a
roast meat and wine debauch. *Closed Wed.*

**Il Carlino d'Oro,** Via Brolio, San Regolo, **t** 0577
747136 (*cheap*). Enjoying an idyllic setting in
the shadow of the great Castello di Brolio,
this small, family-run *trattoria* is very popular, so be sure to book at weekends.
Excellent *minestra di fagioli* (bean soup) or
*pappardelle* with hare sauce, grilled meats

and delicious deep-fried chicken and rabbit.
*Open lunch only, plus dinner Fri–Sun in
summer. Closed Mon.*

## Gaiole ✉ 53013

**\*\*\*\*Castello di Spaltenna, t** 0577 749483,
**f** 0577 749269, *www.spaltenna.it* (*very
expensive–expensive*). Beautifully located
in an old fortified monastery in Spaltenna,
just above Gaiole, with some theatrical
medieval touches. The 21 delightful, comfortable bedrooms, furnished with antiques,
have stunning panoramic views over the
valley or courtyard. There is also an indoor
pool, sauna and beauty centre. *Closed mid-
Jan–Mar.* The restaurant (*very expensive*) in
the ancient castle refectory serves both traditional and creative Tuscan dishes.

**Castelnuovo Berardenga,** Relais Borgo San
Felice, Loc. Borgo San Felice, **t** 0577 359260,
**f** 0577 359089, *www.relaischateaux.fr/
borgofelice* (*very expensive*). A lovely renovated
hilltop hamlet, entirely occupied by this
hotel; beautifully furnished rooms are dotted
around various buildings in the village. There
is an excellent restaurant, gym, pool and
tennis court. Surrounded by vines of the
famous San Felice estate. *Closed Nov–Easter.*

**Castello di Tornano,** Loc. Lecchi, **t/f** 0577
746067, *www.castelloditornano.it* (*rooms –
very expensive; apartments – moderate*).
A restored, fortified farmhouse and castle
with a 1,000-year-old tower commanding
views of steep wooded hills. The outbuildings have been converted into self-catering
apartments in rustic style sleeping 2–4. The
castle and tower now house nine luxurious
double rooms and suites, all furnished with
original antiques; they also have use of the
grand public rooms in the castle. There is a
restaurant, pool and tennis court.

## Brolio ✉ 53013

**Castello di Brolio** (*call the tourist office for
contact details*). Three large apartments
available in this famous site, near to Gaiole.
*Reserve far in advance.*

**Osteria del Castello, t** 0577 747277 (*expensive*).
This osteria has now been transformed into
a delightful restaurant, serving understated,
elegant food in surroundings to match.
*Closed Thurs.*

bombarded for weeks by the Aragonese and Sienese, who later demolished it so 'the walls levelled with the earth'. Florence rebuilt it, and in the mid-19th century Baron Ricasoli converted it into a splendid fortified residence, while experimenting with the modern formula for Chianti. You can sample the famous wines and olive oil and visit the cellars 10km south at the **Cantine Barone Ricasoli** (*call ahead* **t** *0577 7301*). The **Fattoria dei Pagliaresi** (**t** *0577 359070; offers older wines as well as new, and olive oil*) is near Castelnuovo Berardenga, between S. Gusmé and Pianella. To the south, Castelnuovo Berardenga is an agricultural centre with the remains of a 14th-century castle, and from here it's 16km to **Monteaperti**, where Florence almost went down the tubes (to continue south, *see* 'Monte Oliveto Maggiore and Around', p.368).

# The Mugello

Over the years, as their ambitions became less discreet, the Medici concocted a pretty story of how they were descended from knights of Charlemagne. In truth they came down to Florence from the Mugello, the hilly region just to the north – as did Giotto and Fra Angelico. As far back as Boccaccio's time, the Mugello was considered the loveliest region of the Florentine *contada*, and its bluish-green hills are dotted with elegant weekend and summer retreats, rather smarter than the typical stone *fattorie* of the Chianti. The Florentines come here whenever they can, and if you find

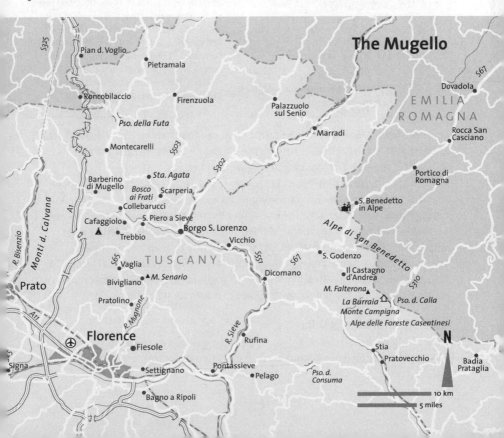

# Getting Around

The Mugello lies to the east of the A1 and north of Pontassieve. It has two exits off the A1: at Barberino (28km from Florence) and Roncobilaccio (47km) near the Passo della Futa.

The two main **roads** north from Florence, the SS65 (Via Bolognese) to the Medici Villas and Passo della Futa and the SS302 to Borgo San Lorenzo (28km), are pretty drives. North of the river Sieve, mountain roads slow travelling – allow at least two hours from Florence to Firenzuola (51km), more to Marradi (64km).

You can also do a loop by **train** through the Mugello from Florence, passing through Pontassieve, Dicomano, Vicchio, Borgo San Lorenzo, San Piero a Sieve, and Vàglia. SITA **buses** are more scenic and just as infrequent; check times before setting out (most pass through the junction at San Piero). Better still, hire a car.

# Tourist Information

For the Mugello: Borgo San Lorenzo, Via P. Togliatti 45, t 055 845271, f 055 845 6288, *wwww.mugellotoscana.it.*

# Where to Stay and Eat

The Mugello has quite a few hotels, most fairly pricey and nearly all in the countryside, so you need a car to reach them.

## Bivigliano ✉ 50030

**★★★Giotto Park Hotel/Giotto Park Hotel Dipendenza,** Via Roma 11, t 055 406608, f 055 406730, *www.giottoparkhotel.it* (*expensive*). This small, restful villa, along with the cheaper *dipendenza*, is a comfortable option, set in a garden with a tennis court.

## Borgo San Lorenzo ✉ 50032

**★★★Locanda degli Artisti**, Piazza Romagnoli 2, t 055 845 5359, f 055 845 0116, *www.locandartisti.it* (*moderate*). In the centre and next to the excellent Ristorante degli Artisti (different owners), this neat little guest house has eight simple but pretty rooms.

**Ristorante degli Artisti**, Piazza Romagnoli 1, t 055 845 7707 (*moderate*). Elegant, serving Mugello cooking in the *centro storico* of Borgo, with a pretty courtyard terrace. Just about everything is home-made. *Closed Wed.*

## Marradi ✉ 50034

**Palazzo Torriani**, Via Fabroni 58, t 055 804 2363, f 055 804 2835, *www.palazzotorriani.it* (*moderate*). Housed in a beautifully restored 16th-century palazzo in the centre of the town, this '*residenza d'epoca*' consists of 3 self-catering apartments one of which can be rented as two separate bedrooms. The rooms are graced with early 20th century frescoes and are furnished with family antiques. Meals available on request.

yourself stewing with them in the traffic gridlocks approaching Piazza della Libertà, know that all you have to do is turn up the Via Bolognese or Via Faentina and in 10 minutes you'll be in a cool, enchanting world immersed in green.

North of Florence altitudes rise appreciably towards the central Apennine spine that divides Tuscany from Emilia-Romagna. Tucked in these hills lies the Mugello basin, a broad valley along the river Sieve and its tributaries, which, in the Miocene era, held a lake. Most of the towns of the Mugello are here, surrounded by a sea of vines; olive groves cover the slopes, but soon give way to deep forests of pines, chestnuts and oaks, cool and refreshing, dotted with small resorts. And like any fashion-conscious Florentine, the Mugello changes colours with the seasons, and is strikingly beautiful any time of year, a place to return to, again and again.

## The Original Medici Villa

Following Via Bolognese (SS65) north, past the gardens of **Pratolino**, one of the last Medici villas (*see* **Florence**, 'Medici Villas', p.180), it's a panoramic and winding 30km to

## Scarperia ✉ 50038

**✶✶Hotel Cantagallo**, Viale Kennedy 17, t 055 843 0442, f 055 843 0443 (*moderate*). A tidy little hotel overlooking a shady garden.

**Teatro dei Medici**, Loc. La Torre 12, t 055 845 9876 (*moderate*). Set in an old house that once belonged to the Medici, this is the place to go for Mugello cooking – and everyone does – so in summer it's worth booking ahead. Country *antipasti*, good pasta dishes and wild game in season.

## Locanda Senio ✉ 50035

**✶✶✶Palazzuolo sul Senio**, Borgo dell'Ore 1, t 055 8046019, f 055 8043949, *www. locandasenio.it* (*very expensive*). The eight pretty bedrooms and suites at this hotel, which occupies a series of ancient buildings in the medieval town of Palazzuolo, are furnished with antiques. The food is excellent, there is a heated pool and a small health spa, which you can use free of charge.

## Vicchio ✉ 50039

**Villa Campestri**, Via de Campestri 19, t 055 849 0107, f 055 849 0108, *www.villa campestri.it* (*very expensive*). On a hill south of Vicchio stands one of the most beautiful hotels in the region: an elegant Tuscan villa set in a 300-acre park, boasting a pool with a view, exquisitely furnished rooms and a good restaurant.

**Antica Porta di Levante**, Piazza Vittorio Veneto 5, t 055 840050 (*moderate*). A young enthusiastic team run this interesting little restaurant just outside Vicchio's old eastern gate. Dishes are creative Tuscan, using seasonal ingredients (some work better than others), and the wine list is comprehensive. There's a pretty vine-covered terrace too. *Closed Mon.*

**La Casa di Caccia**, t 055 840 7629 (*moderate*). An isolated old hunting lodge, about 20mins of winding, climbing road north of Vicchio, with stunning views across the valley. Game, home-made pasta, grilled meats.

## Sagginale ✉ 50032

**Trattoria Sagginale**, t 055 849 0130 (*cheap*). Between Borgo San Lorenzo and Vicchio, a family-run restaurant known locally as 'Da Giorgione' at the back of a shop, serving excellent rustic food in a simple setting – try the fabulous home-made ravioli rolled, stuffed rabbit. *Closed Thurs, and Mon–Wed lunch.*

## Ponte a Vicchio ✉ 50039

**Casa del Prosciutto**, t 055 844031 (*moderate*). Part-grocer, part-*trattoria*, specializing in local dishes including good char-grilled chicken and potato-stuffed *tortelli* (takeaway as well). *Lunch only, closed Mon.*

two of the very first. On the way, a slight detour east (from Pratolino or Vaglia) ascends to **Monte Senario** (820m/2,680ft) where, in 1233, seven Florentine noblemen founded the mendicant Servite Order, living in grottoes and building simple cells in the woods. The Servites later built Santissima Annunziata in Florence. Rebuilt in the 16th century, the monastery here has amazing views over the Arno valley and Mugello.

North, towards San Piero a Sieve, there's a turn-off west on an untarred road for the Medici **Castello di Trebbio**, a family estate remodelled in 1461 by Michelozzo into a fortified villa with a tower. It has a formal Italian garden, which you can visit. For groups ring t 055 845 6230.

A bit further up looms the even grander **Villa Cafaggiolo** (*www.villacafaggiolo.it*; *open Wed and Fri 2.30–6.30, Sat–Sun 10.30–12.30 and 2.30–6.30*), favoured by Cosimo il Vecchio and Lorenzo il Magnifico, who spent as much of the summer as possible in its cool halls. Cosimo had Michelozzo expand and transform this ancient family seat into an imposing castellated villa, its entrance protected by a bulging tower, adorned with an incongruous clock. To the east, a minor road leads up to the wooded **Bosco ai**

## Deluxe Virgins

Some day, on a trip to one of the fancier Italian food shops, you may pause near the section devoted to condiments and wonder at the beautiful display of bottles of unusually dark whiskies and wines, with corks and posh, elegant labels – why, some is even DOC, though much of it is far more costly than the usual DOC vintages. A closer look reveals these precious bottles are full of nothing but olive oil. Admittedly *olio extra vergine di oliva* from Tuscany and Umbria makes a fine salad dressing – according to those in the know the oil of the Chianti brooks few rivals, Italian or otherwise. Its delicate, fruity fragrance derives from the excellent quality of the ripe olive and the low acidity extracted from the fruit without any refinements. The finest, Extra Virgin, must have less than 1 per cent acidity (the best has 0.5 per cent acidity). Other designations are Soprafino Virgin, Fine Virgin, and Virgin (each may have up to 4 per cent acidity) in descending order of quality.

As any Italian will tell you, it's good for you – and it had better be, because Tuscan or Umbrian chefs put it in nearly every dish, as they have for centuries. The only difference is that it now comes in a fancy package for a fancy price, a victim of the Italian designer label syndrome and Tuscan preciosity. Not only does the olive oil have corks, but the trend in the early 1990s was for some of the smarter restaurants to offer an olive oil list similar to a wine list – one restaurant in Tuscany even had an oil sommelier. Many of these, perhaps fortunately, seem to have gone out of business.

**Frati**, with a simple porticoed church also by Michelozzo; inside there's a fine crucifix by Donatello, and another attributed to Desiderio da Settignano.

Beyond Cafaggiolo, towards Barberino (about 4km from Barberino) is the huge artificial **Lago di Bilancino**. The lake, which is dammed (the dam controls the water of the Sieve river) occupies nearly five square kilometres, has a beach with sunbeds and umbrellas and is good for water sports: sailing, windsurfing, fishing and canoeing. Bars, restaurants and other leisure facilities are also being developed. There have been many problems and lots of controversy over the plans, but all is now going ahead.

## To the Passo della Futa

Just off the *autostrada*, the largest town on the western rim of the Mugello basin is **Barberino di Mugello**, a market town spread under the **Castello dei Cattani**. Its 15th-century Palazzo Pretorio, like many others, is emblazoned with coats of arms; the open Loggie Medicee is another work by Michelozzo. On the SS65, 5km away at Colle Barucci, is one of the grandest estates in the Mugello, the **Villa delle Maschere** ('of the masks').

Continue 14km north for the breathtaking views from the **Passo della Futa** (903m/2,962ft), a pass on the principal Apennine watershed; below, the whole Mugello is spread out like a relief map. In 1944, the pass was the Germans' strong point on the Gothic Line – until the Allies rendered it useless by capturing Firenzuola to the north. Beyond the pass the road winds under the craggy **Sasso di Castro** (1,276m/4,185ft); at La Casetta you can turn off for Firenzuola (*see* opposite) or hotfoot it over the mountains in time for dinner in Bologna, the culinary capital of Italy.

## Scarperia and Around

Standing at the major crossroads of the SS503 north and the SS551 along the Sieve, **San Piero a Sieve** is a busy little town defended by a mighty Medici citadel, the **Fortezza di San Martino**, designed by Buontalenti in 1571. Its Romanesque parish church, with a façade from 1776, contains a remarkable octagonal baptismal font in polychrome terracotta, by Luca della Robbia. From here it's 4km to **Scarperia**, the most charming town in the Mugello, perched high above the valley. Florence fortified it in 1306, and laid out its simple rectangular plan, with one long main street.

The **Palazzo dei Vicari** (*open 15 Sept–1 June Sat–Sun and hols 10–1, 3–6.30; 1 June– 15 Sept: Wed–Fri 3.30–7.30, Sat–Sun and hols 10–1, 3.30–7.30*), dating from 1306, is so heavily decorated with stone and ceramic coats of arms that it resembles a page from a postage stamp album. Its atrium and upper halls have 14th- and 15th-century frescoes, the earliest ones by the school of Giotto. The palazzo also houses the **Museo dei Ferri Taglienti** (*same hours as Palazzo dei Vicari*), a small museum dedicated to knife-making and cutting tools. The oratory of the **Madonna di Piazza** has an attractive Renaissance front and a cinquecento fresco of the Madonna and Child, attributed to Iacopo del Casentino; the church dedicated to Our Lady of the Earthquakes has a fresco that some attribute to Filippo Lippi.

From the 16th century, Scarperia supplied the duchy of Tuscany with knives, forks and scissors, as well as daggers and swords. By 1900 there were 46 thriving firms, though machine-made competition has reduced this. Firms still making knives, where you can buy bone- or horn-handled cutlery (at high prices) include Conaz (Via Roma 8), Saladini (Via Solferino 15), Berti (Via Roma 37) and Giglio (Via delle Oche). Scarperia is now better known for the **Autodromo Internazionale del Mugello**, a 5km track built by Florence's Auto Club in 1976, which is fairly well hidden in the hills east of town.

The Mugello's most fascinating historical relic, 4km northwest of Scarperia, is the 11th-century parish church of **Sant'Agata** (*open daily 7.30–5*), restored after an earthquake in 1919, with an unusual apse and a pulpit from 1175, decorated with white and green marble intarsia designs and animals. The chapel to the right of the altar houses Bicci di Lorenzo's painting, *The Mystical Marriage of St Catherine*. **Firenzuola** is 22km north of Scarperia and is famous for its production of 'Pietra Serena', the pale grey stone you see in buildings all over Tuscany. A small holiday resort, cool even in August, it was devastated in the Second World War and rebuilt along the lines of the original street plan between the Porta di Bologna and the Porta di Firenze. Four kilometres west, in Cornacchiaia is a church believed to date back to Carolingian times.

## Borgo San Lorenzo and Vicchio

Borgo San Lorenzo (pop. 16,300) on the river Sieve is the boom town of the Mugello, partly due to its fast-train rail link to Florence. It's surrounded by new residential neighbourhoods with gardens full of little chameleons; and indeed they are fond of animals here, as evidenced by the **Statue of Fido** in honour of man's best friend, in Piazza Dante. Otherwise, the main sights are two Romanesque churches: San Lorenzo, with an unusual hexagonal campanile built in 1263, and 3km north, the parish church of San Giovanni Maggiore, with a bell tower that is square at the base but octagonal on top, and a lovely 12th-century pulpit in marble intarsia. To the north the road divides into the SS477 to **Palazzuolo sul Senio** (which has an annual medieval festival in July) and the SS302 to **Marradi**, also small resorts; Palazzuolo has a small **Ethnographic Museum** (*open Mar–June and Sept–Dec Sun 3–6; July–Aug Tues 8–11pm, Thurs, Sat, Sun 4–7*) in the 14th-century Palazzo dei Capitani.

**Vicchio**, east of San Lorenzo, is a sleepy little town, birthplace of the Blessed Fra Angelico (Giovanni da Fiesole, 1387–1455) and often a home from home for Benvenuto Cellini. The Palazzo Pretorio contains the **Museo Comunale Beato Angelico** (*t 055 844 8251; open Sat–Sun 10–12 and 4–7, also Thurs 10–12 in summer; adm*), with detached frescoes, Etruscan finds from nearby Poggio alla Colla, and a 13th-century holy water stoup. Not to be outdone, the nearby hamlet of **Vespignano** was the birthplace of Giotto di Bondone (1267–1337). The simple stone cottage where the father of Renaissance painting is said to have been born has been carefully restored as the **Casa di Giotto** (*open Sat–Sun 10–12 and 4–7, also Thurs 10–12 in summer; adm*). According to tradition, Cimabue discovered Giotto near the old (restored) bridge over the Enza, where the young shepherd was sketching his sheep on a stone.

## The Valdisieve

The lower Sieve valley is mostly industrial: **Dicomano** can boast of an interesting fresco by the school of Piero della Francesca, but little else besides a big Saturday-morning market and the junction for the SS67, which climbs east into a pretty range of mountains called the Alpi di San Benedetto. **San Godenzo**, 10km up the SS67, is the largest village, site of an 11th-century Benedictine abbey; its plain church has a raised presbytery and a polyptych by the school of Giotto.

From San Godenzo a road continues up to the birthplace of Andrea del Castagno, now called **Il Castagno d'Andrea** ('Andrew's chestnut') (1,022m/3,355ft), a small holiday village. Wind a further 18km up to **San Benedetto in Alpe**, with a 9th-century Benedictine abbey that sheltered Dante (*Inferno*, Canto XVI, 94–105), and where you can hire horses to visit the enchanting Valle dell'Aquacheta with its pretty waterfall. In the old town of **Portico di Romagna** 11km further north, the Portinari family, including the beautiful Beatrice, spent their summers – their house still stands in the main street. Deeper into Romagna lie the fascinating medieval town of **Brisighella**, the ceramic city of **Faenza**, and **Ravenna**, not only filled with ravishing Byzantine mosaics from the time of Justinian but also the site of Dante's real tomb.

There is little along the lower Sieve. **Rufina**, 10km south of Dicomano, is dominated by the 16th-century Villa Poggio Reale, producing *Chianti Rufina* and *Pomino* wines. Continuing east along the SS70 beyond Pontassieve, turn left after a few kilometres for **Castello di Nipozzano** (*for opening times call t 055 27141*), one of the great Frescobaldi wine estates, producing prize-winning oak-aged red wines. For white wines, climb into the hills to the north and visit **Castello di Pomino**, another Frescobaldi property. **Poggio Reale** has a small wine museum (*call ahead, t 055 839 5078*). From **Pontassieve** the scenic SS70 leads up to the dramatic Passo della Consuma (1,022m/3,355ft) before descending into the Casentino (*see pp.396–400*).

# The Valdarno, Prato and Pistoia

09

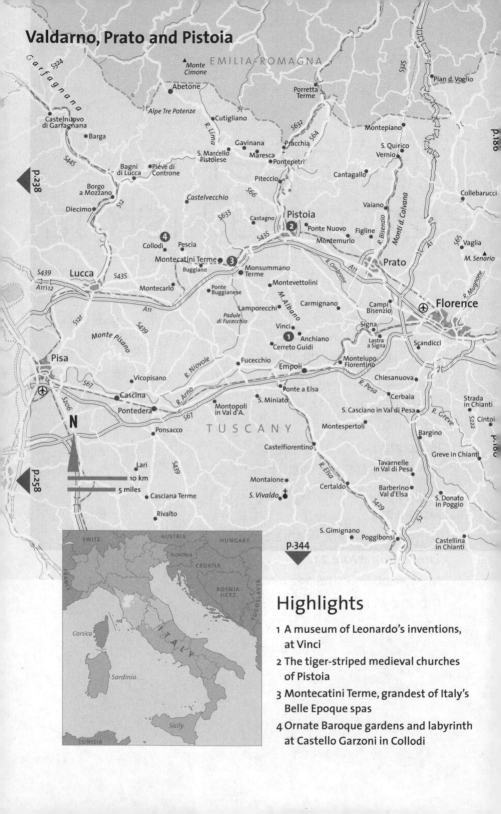

# Valdarno, Prato and Pistoia

## Highlights

1 A museum of Leonardo's inventions, at Vinci

2 The tiger-striped medieval churches of Pistoia

3 Montecatini Terme, grandest of Italy's Belle Epoque spas

4 Ornate Baroque gardens and labyrinth at Castello Garzoni in Collodi

Whether you travel by car, bus or train, there are two routes between Florence and Pisa. The route along the Arno, often hemmed in by the hills, has always been historically and economically the least important and carries less traffic. The large cities of Prato, Pistoia and Lucca grew up in an arc north of the Monte Albano hills, where there's more fertile land and room to grow, and the route takes in the nearby Florentine towns of Vinci, Castelfiorentino and Certaldo.

# Down the Arno to Pisa

## Florence to Empoli

The old Florentine satellite town of **Scandicci** (6km west), once in the business of renting villas to foreigners like Dylan Thomas and DH Lawrence (who finished *Lady Chatterley's Lover* here), has since found more profit in industry. Most towns along the Arno specialize in certain products; in **Lastra a Signa** it's straw goods, sold in numerous village shops. Lastra retains its 14th-century walls and the **Loggia di Sant'Antonio**, all that survives of the hospital founded by Florence's Silk Guild in 1411; many believe Brunelleschi was the architect, and that the work was a prototype of Florence's Spedale degli Innocenti, funded by the same guild. Just outside Lastra, the church of **San Martino a Gangalandi** has a beautiful, semicircular apse with *pietra serena* articulation designed by Alberti. In **Signa**, the next village, the Romanesque **San Lorenzo** houses a remarkable 12th-century marble pulpit and trecento frescoes.

After Signa the road and river continue 12km through a gorge before **Montelupo Fiorentino**, celebrated since the Renaissance for its terracottas and delicately painted ceramics. The town hosts a ceramics fair at the end of June, which also features Renaissance music and costumes, demonstrations and exhibitions. The **Museo Archeologico e della Ceramica**, Via Baccio Sinaldi 45 (*t 0571 51352; open Tues–Sun 10–6; adm*), has examples from nearly every period, and a display on the lower Valdarno's prehistory, while Montelupo's shops sell more recent ceramic creations. The old **castle** here was built in 1203 by the Florentines, during the wars against Pisa; the church **San Giovanni Evangelista** contains a lovely *Madonna and Saints* by Botticelli and his assistants. On the outskirts of Montelupo, you can see Buontalenti's **Villa Ambrogiana** (1587) from the outside, though you'll probably want to avoid being invited in – it's a mental hospital. From Montelupo a road leads southeast 20km to the town of San Casciano in Val di Pesa, in Chianti (*see* p.191).

### Empoli

The modern market town of **Empoli**, 32km from Florence, was witness to one of the turning points in Tuscan history: in 1260, the Ghibellines of Siena, fresh from their great victory over Florence at Monteaperti, held a parliament in Empoli to decide the fate of their arch enemy. Everyone was for razing Florence to the ground once and for all, and waited for the approval of their leader, Farinata degli Uberti.

The Uberti were Florentine gangster nobles famous for their hatred of their fellow citizens, and Farinata surprised all when he announced that, even if he had to stand alone, he would defend Florence for as long as he lived. The Sienese let their captain have his way, and lost their chance of ever becoming *numero uno* in Tuscany.

The prosperous new Empoli (pop. 45,000) produces green glass and raincoats. You'll find little to recall the days of Farinata, until you reach the piazza named after him; here is the palace where the parliament convened, across from the gem of a Romanesque church, the **Collegiata Sant'Andrea**, with its green and white marble geometric façade in the style of Florence's San Miniato. The lower portion dates from 1093; the upper had to wait until the 18th century, but it harmonizes extremely well.

## Museo della Collegiata

Empoli has its share of 13th- and 14th-century Florentine art, much of it now in the small but choice **Museo della Collegiata** (*open Tues–Sun 9–12 and 4–7; adm*) in the Collegiata's cloister. The most celebrated work is Masolino's *Pietà* fresco, with its poignant faces; upstairs there's an elegant relief of the *Madonna and Child* by Mino da Fiesole and his brother Antonio's painted tabernacle of St Sebastian. Lorenzo Monaco contributes a long-eyed *Madonna and Saints*; Lorenzo di Bicci's scene of San

Nicola da Tolentino shielding Empoli from a rain of plague arrows is a quattrocento view of the city. There is a rare series of frescoes by Masolino's master, Starnina, as well as two saints by Pontormo, who was born nearby, and the fine *Tabernacle of the Holy Sacrament* by Francesco Botticini and his son Raffaello, with a good predella.

The upper Loggia has works by Andrea della Robbia, and the suspended wooden wings of the donkey that flies down on a wire from the church tower on *Corpus Domine* (although a papier-mâché donkey has of late replaced the original one). Empoli's **Santo Stefano** church (*open Tues–Fri 9–12 by appt – enquire at the Museo della Collegiata*), restored after damage during the Second World War, has more beautiful frescoes by Masolino and a marble *Annunciation* by Bernardo Rossellini.

## Around Empoli

Northwest of Empoli, in the Monte Albano, lies the old hill townlet of **Cerreto Guidi**, former property of the Counts of Guidi, taken over by Florence in 1237. It is known these days for its *Chianti Putto*, and for the **Villa Medicea** (*www.villamedicea. it; open daily 9–6.30; closed 2nd and 3rd Mon of month; adm*), rebuilt for Cosimo I by Buontalenti in 1564, relatively simple as Medici villas go, but approached by the 'Medici bridges', a grand double ramp of bricks. In 1576 Cosimo I's daughter Isabella was murdered here by her husband Paolo Orsini for her infidelities; look carefully and you will see the unhappy couple among the scores of Medici portraits in the villa. From the terrace there are fine views of the Monte Albano.

From Cerreto it's 5km to **Vinci**, a tiny town most famous as the home of Leonardo, who was born in a humble house in Anchiano on 15 April 1452, the illegitimate son of the local notary and a peasant girl. In his honour, the town's landmark Conti Guidi Castle has been converted into the **Museo Leonardiano** (*www.museoleonardiano.it*; *open Nov–Feb daily 9.30–6; Mar–Oct daily 9.30–7; adm*), full of models of inventions he designed in his *Codex Atlanticus* notebooks, most of which this supreme 'Renaissance man' never had the time or attention span to build. There are descriptions in English for the hundred or so machines, including some inspired by those invented by Brunelleschi to build Florence's cathedral dome. More speculative designs

## Getting Around

If you're **driving**, persist: the Florentine sprawl finally gives way at Signa and after that the Arno road (S67) becomes even scenic in stretches. LAZZI **buses** take the main route to Pisa; SITA goes directly from Florence to Castelfiorentino or Certaldo; for Vinci, COPIT. **Trains** at least once an hour follow the Arno between Florence and Pisa, and at Empoli turn off for Castelfiorentino, Certaldo, Poggibonsi and Siena. Note that San Miniato and Fucecchio share a railway station; local buses commute from there to both centres.

## Tourist Information

**Vinci**: Via delle Torri 11, t 0571 568012. (Also serves Empoli.)
**San Miniato**: Piazza del Popolo 3, t 0571 42745.
**Castelfiorentino**: c/o the Station, Via Ridolfi, t/f 0571 629049. *Open April–Oct.*
**Certaldo**: Via Cavour 32, Viale Fabbiano 5, t 0571 656721.

## Where to Stay and Eat

The lower Arno Valley isn't exactly awash with pleasure domes, but you won't starve.

### Santa Maria a Marciola ✉ 50018
**Fiore**, Via di Marciola 112, near Scandicci, t 055 768678 (*moderate*). A good place to stop if it's time to eat just as you're leaving or approaching Florence, not only for its

delicious crêpes and mixed meats on the grill, game, *bistecca*, etc., but for its lovely garden setting and pine-clad slopes. *Open for dinner daily and Sun and Sat lunch.*

### Vinci ✉ 50059
**★★★Alexandra**, Via dei Martiri 36, t 0571 56224, f 0571 567972 (*moderate*). Vinci's one hotel; quiet and comfortable.

As for restaurants, there isn't much choice.
**Antica Cantina di Bacco**, Piazza Leonardo da Vinci 3, t 0571 568041 (*cheap*). A cosy wine bar with an attractive terrace, serving the usual *enoteca* fare; toasted *crostoni* with various toppings, a few pasta dishes, cheeses, desserts and, of course, wine.

### Empoli ✉ 50053
Empoli isn't a posh town by any means, but it can be an agreeable place to stay over. It also has some good places to eat.
**★★★Sole**, Piazza Don Minzoni, t 0571 73779 (*moderate*). A good bargain, by the station.
**Cucina Sant'Andrea**, Via Salvagnoli 43, t 0571 73657 (*expensive–moderate*). On the remains of the city walls, this *trattoria* run by a brother and sister serves creative versions of local dishes: pigeon terrine, courgette flan, risotto with artichokes, wild boar and game.
**La Panzanella**, Via dei Cappucini 10, t 0571 922182 (*cheap*). An old-fashioned *trattoria*, also by the station, which does an unusual artichoke soup and wonderful things with porcini mushrooms in season. Also a few fish dishes. *Closed Sun.*

include a flying machine, a paddle boat, a spring-driven mechanical car, an almost perfect modern bicycle, diving gear, a parachute and a device to walk on water. Also present are Leonardo's famous tank, machine gun and helicopter. This gentle fellow once said, 'I'll do anything for money', which must be one of the most startling quotes of the Renaissance. On the other hand, nothing could be more typical of the age than brilliance combined with immorality; while he often neglected his art, Leonardo was happy to help the bellicose princes who employed him with their military problems. We should probably be thankful that these gadgets never escaped from his notebook. Leonardo was baptized in the font in **Santa Croce**, next to the museum.

From Vinci it's a 3km walk (or drive) southeast to **Anchiano**, where the simple stone house where Leonardo was born has been restored (*open Nov–Feb daily 9.30–6, in summer until 7; adm*).

### San Miniato ✉ 56027
★★★**Miravalle**, Piazza Castello 3, t 0571 418075, f 0571 418075, *www.albergomiravalle.com* (*moderate*). Frederick II's 12th-century imperial palace, near the top of town.
**Il Canapone**, Piazza Bonaparte 5, t 0571 418121 (*moderate*). A simple place where you can try the local truffles on spaghetti, in risotto, or with veal *scaloppine*; in the spring there's risotto with asparagus. *Closed Mon.*

### Certaldo ✉ 50052
★★★**Osteria del Vicario**, Via Rivellino 3, t/f 0571 668228 (*moderate*). A beautiful 12th-century ex-monastery with a garden, surrounded by a Romanesque courtyard. Rooms are simple, with terracotta floors, and the restaurant (*expensive*) serves creative fresh local fare. *Restaurant closed Wed.*
★★**Il Castello**, Via della Rena 6, t/f 0571 668250, *www.albergocastello.it* (*expensive–moderate*). One of the more interesting of the three small hotels in town.
One place in Certaldo can satisfy all your little vices at once:
**Dolci Follie**, Piazza Bocaccio t 0571 668188 (*moderate–cheap*). A fancy *pasticceria*, a wine bar and a fine little restaurant, where the cuisine (both fish and meat dishes) is more than a prelude to the exquisite desserts.

### Artimino ✉ 50040
**Paggeria Medicea**, t 055 871 8081, f 055 871 8080, *www.artimino.com* (*very expensive*). An interesting place, located in the Medici Villa Artimino near Carmignano. A former country residence of the famous family, the stables have been converted into a very comfortable hotel with pool and tennis.
**Da Delfina**, t 055 871 8074 (*expensive*). Boasts a Michelin star and a well-deserved reputation. There's Tuscan food (ravioli stuffed with potato), and a terrace for dining out.

### Fucecchio ✉ 50054
**Le Vedute**, Via Romana-Lucchese 121, t 0571 297498 (*expensive*). A good inland seafood restaurant, pleasantly situated in the country. Serves good meats as well, especially in autumn. In summer you can linger on the veranda. *Closed Mon.*
★★★**La Campagnola**, Viale Colombo 144, t 0571 260786, f 0571 261781 (*moderate*). 25 air-conditioned rooms.

### Montopoli in Val d'Arno ✉ 56020
★★★**Quattro Gigli**, Piazza Michele 2, t 0571 466 878, f 0571 466 879, *www.quattrogigli.it* (*moderate*). In this little place across the Arno, the old town hall has been converted into an inn with 28 rooms of varying quality. The restaurant, beyond the permanent display of Montopoli's painted ceramics, has a delightful terrace and features an imaginative menu. Some of the dishes are based on centuries-old recipes, such as tripe with eggs and saffron. Others are more creative, such as fresh tuna soufflé with artichokes, *pici* with baby squid, sea bass cooked with *aceto balsamico* or duck with dried fruit. *Closed Mon, also Sun eve in winter.*

# South of Empoli

## San Miniato

Just southwest of Empoli, the river Elsa flows into the Arno near **San Miniato** (pop. 23,000), a hill town that grew up at the crossroads of the Via Francigena (the main pilgrimage route from France to Rome) and the Florence–Pisa road. On a clear day the view takes in everything from Fiesole to the sea. Its strategic location made it the Tuscan residence of the Emperors, from Otto IV to Frederick II; Matilda of Tuscany was born here in 1046, and in the 12th century it was an important imperial fortress, protecting the crossroads and levying tolls on travellers and merchandise.

Of the citadel, only two towers survive: the present campanile of the cathedral and the taller 'Torrione', in the shady Prato del Duomo that crowns San Miniato, with its peculiar chimney-like structures on top. It was from the top of this tower that Frederick II's secretary and court poet Pier della Vigna, falsely accused of treason, leapt to his death, to be discovered by Dante in the forest of suicides, as described in the *Inferno* XIII. Also in the Prato del Duomo stand the 12th-century **Palazzo dei Vicari dell'Imperatore** and the **Duomo** itself, with a Romanesque brick façade, incorporating pieces of sculpted marble and 13th-century majolica that catch the light as the sun sets. Most of the art in the interior is Baroque, except for a fine 13th-century holy water stoup; most of the earlier artworks from the region have been placed in the **Museo Diocesano d'Arte Sacra**, to the left of the cathedral (*open Tues–Sun 10–12.30 and 3–6.30*). Among the prizes are the fresco of the *Maestà* by the 'Maestro degli Ordini' from Siena, a bust of Christ attributed to Verrocchio, Neri di Bicci's *Madonna con Bambino* and a *Crucifixion* by Filippo Lippi. Since 1968, the Prato del Duomo has also been the site of the **National Kite Flying Contest** (*1st Sun after Easter*).

In the Piazza del Popolo's 14th-century church of **San Domenico** you can see minor works by Masolino, Pisanello and the della Robbias. Bernardo Rossellino carved the fine 15th-century tomb of Giovanni Chiellini, the Florentine founder of San Miniato's Hospital of Poor Pilgrim Priests. The tomb is modelled after Rossellino's famous tomb of Leonardo Bruni in Florence's Santa Croce. The beautiful church of **San Francesco** has fresco fragments by a follower of Masolino. Napoleon paid a visit in 1797, to visit his relatives in the **Palazzo Bonaparte**. In the surrounding countryside are rich caches of white truffles, sought fervently in the autumn for the large market on the last Sunday in November; and many of what appear to be plain-looking Romanesque churches around San Miniato are actually tobacco-curing barns from the 1900s.

## Castelfiorentino and San Vivaldo

Some 12km south along the Valdelsa from San Miniato, **Castelfiorentino** (pop. 18,000) is another old hill town, though much rebuilt after damage in the Second World War. Castelfiorentino's church of **Santa Verdiana** dates from the 18th century and houses the **Museo di Arte Sacra Santa Verdiana** (*open Sat 4–7, Sun and hols 10–12 and 4–7*), with some excellent trecento paintings, including a *Madonna* attributed to Duccio da Buoninsegna, another by Francesco Granacci, and a triptych by Taddeo Gaddi. In the **Biblioteca Comunale**, Via Tilli 41 (*open Mon, Wed and Sat 9–1; Tues and Thurs 3.30–7; adm*) are frescoes by Benozzo Gozzoli that were originally in the Tabernacle of the Madonna della Tosse, 'the coughing Madonna', in a nearby village, and also from the Cappella della Visitazione.

One of the more unusual sights in Tuscany, the **Monastery of San Vivaldo**, lies to the southwest of Castelfiorentino, beyond the village of Montaione. Vivaldo, a hermit from San Gimignano, lived in a hollow chestnut tree where he was found dead in 1301, still in the attitude of prayer. A Franciscan community grew up in his footsteps, and in 1500, when the monastery was being rebuilt, one member, Fra Tommaso da Firenze, designed a 'New Jerusalem' in the monastery's wooded hills, with 34 chapels representing the sites of Christ's Passion. To render the symbolic journey more realistic for pilgrims, the 34 chapels combined polychrome terracottas by Giovanni della Robbia and other artists, set in frescoes – Pope Leo X immediately granted a fat indulgence to anyone who did the whole route. Today only 17 of the chapels survive (*Oct–Mar guided tours Sun and hols 3.30; April–Sept guided tours Sun and hols 5pm; to visit outside these hours, call t 0571 699252 for an appointment*).

## Certaldo

**Certaldo** (pop. 16,000), former seat of Florence's deputy, or Vicariate of the Valdelsa, is synonymous with Giovanni Boccaccio, who spent the last 13 years of his life up in the old town, known as Castello Aldo, which could be a set for the *Decameron* itself (don't confuse it with the ugly sprawl of the new town at the bottom of the hill). Everything here is of good, honest brick, from the pavements to the palazzi, of which the most striking is the 14th-century castellated **Palazzo Pretorio**, studded with the arms of the former Vicars. Inside it has a beautiful courtyard and museum (*open summer daily 10–7, winter Tues–Sun 10.30–4.30; adm*) containing Etruscan artefacts, frescoes and, in the annexed church and cloister, Gozzoli's *Tabernacle of the Punished*, not one of his more cheerful works. The walls of the old jail bear the forlorn graffiti of past prisoners.

The house traditionally associated with Certaldo's great author is the **Casa di Boccaccio**, on Via Boccaccio 18, which has been restored and is now the seat of the International Centre of Boccaccio Studies (*open April–Sept daily 10–7; Oct Mon, Wed–Fri 10.30–4.40, Sat and Sun 10–7; Nov–Mar Wed–Mon 10.30–4.30*). Boccaccio died here in 1375 and lies buried in **Santi Michele ed Iacopo**, under an epitaph he penned himself; a 16th-century monument erected in his honour was destroyed by prudes in 1783. Boccaccio himself, in his later years, regretted the racy frivolity of his most famous book, wishing he had spent his time on serious Latin works – not a regret too many people have ever shared. From Certaldo you can follow a pretty road to the south which leads to **San Gimignano** (*see* pp.348–53), about 13km away.

# Empoli to Pisa

There is no compelling reason to stop in the lower Valdarno unless you're low on petrol. If you're spending more time here, consider a visit to **Fucecchio** for its panoramic views, or better yet for the **Padule di Fucecchio** (*open all year; guided nature tours in spring by Centro di Ricerca, Documentazione e Promozione del Padule di Fucecchio t 0573 84540*), claimed to be Italy's biggest inland swamp and certainly an excellent place for bird-watching.

Next comes **Montopoli in Val d'Arno**, a tiny medieval town dating from the 11th century on the south bank. Further down-river lies industrial **Pontedera**, where the Piaggio Company produces most of Italy's motor scooters. Here you may detour south on the SS439 to Volterra (*see* pp.353–61), by way of **Ponsacco** and the four-towered **Villa di Camugliano**, built by Alessandro and Cosimo I, an example of Medici real estate speculation. Between here and Volterra roll the Pisan Hills, some of the quietest, most rural countryside in Tuscany; the main attraction may be precisely its lack of art and history. Alternatively, from Ponsacco, you can head southwest to tiny **Lari**, with the remains of a Medici fortress, and for your rheumatism, to Casciana Terme, famous for its cures in Roman times, and rebuilt by the Pisans in the 14th century. The hamlet of **Rivalto**, 6km south of the spa, has almost perfectly preserved its medieval character.

**Vicopisano**, north of the Arno, defended the eastern frontier of Pisa from Lucca's ambitions, and its impressive *castello* was remodelled by Brunelleschi after the Florentine conquest of Pisa; vineyards now surround its walls and towers. Across the bridge, **Cascina** still has most of its medieval walls and Roman grid plan. It also has three churches that are worth a visit: **San Casciano**, an unusual 12th-century Roman-esque church, with blind arches and some fine sculptural details; Romanesque **San Benedetto a Settimo**, adorned with a 14th-century alabaster altarpiece of Irish origin; and **San Giovanni Evangelista**, built by the Knights of St John, with trecento Sienese frescoes, recently restored after the church was used as a barn for several centuries. Further west lies the Certosa di Pisa (8km; *see* p.280) and Pisa itself (14km; *see* p.267).

# Prato

**Prato** is only 18km from Florence but a world away in atmosphere; this is a city that works for its living, where the population has doubled since the Second World War to 145,000, third largest in Tuscany after Florence and Livorno. And a vibrantly, joyously proletarian city it is, fond of Henry Moore, comic books, avant-garde theatre and heavy-metal bars, full of people wanting you to sign petitions or buy encyclopaedias, all proud to live in 'the Manchester of Tuscany'. Living in Florence's shadow for the past thousand years has not dampened Prato's spirits; as in the days of the famous Francesco di Marco Datini, immortalized in Iris Origo's book *The Merchant of Prato*, this city still earns its keep from the manufacture of textiles, and especially the recycling of wool and rags. In the Renaissance, Prato made enough profit from these rags to hire the greatest artists of the day to embellish its churches and palaces.

## History

In the 9th century Prato was known as Borgo al Cornio. Outside the town was a meadow, or *prato*, the site of the market and fortifications, which gradually became

# Getting Around

Prato is easily reached by **train** from Florence but better by LAZZI bus (25mins), Pistoia (25mins) or Bologna (55mins), and has two stations: the main Stazione Centrale, facing a pretty green square on the other bank of the river Bisenzio; and the Stazione Porta al Serraglio (not all trains stop), just north of the walls and closer to the centre, on the Florence–Pistoia line. This was one of Italy's first railways, built in 1848 for the Lorraine grand dukes by an Englishman, Ralph Bonfield, who so pleased the grand duke that he was made Count of St George of Prato. All Bonfields take note! The Prato tourist office is searching for his descendants, to claim the title and supply a likeness of Bonfield so they can erect a proper monument in his honour.

**Buses** from Prato depart from Piazza Ciardi or the Stazione Centrale; all pass through Piazza San Francesco (CAP or LAZZI buses, every half-hour to Florence with connections to the Mugello; also LAZZI buses to Pistoia, Montecatini, Lucca, Pisa and Viareggio).

Prato has two exits on the *autostrada* A11 between Florence and Pisa (from Florence get on at Peretola). The centre is closed to traffic: Piazza Mercatale is a convenient place to park.

# Tourist Information

**Prato**: Piazza Santa Maria delle Carceri 15, t 0574 24112, *www.prato.turismo.toscana.it*.

# Shopping

Prato still makes its living from fine fabrics and clothing, and people from all over Tuscany come to visit the **factory outlets** where these are available at discount prices. Clothing designers from all over the world, including some of the biggest names, buy their fabric in Prato. One of the specialities is **cashmere**.

**Maglificio Denny**, Zia Zarini 261, t 0574 592350. Cashmere, wool and cotton knitwear.

**Anngorelle**, Via Vella, t 0574 467275. For Cashmere and mohair.

**Tessiture Cecchi & Cecchi**, Via delle Calandre 53. Does covers, scarves and such in cashmere, wool and silk.

There are also some good **clothing** outlets:

**M-Wear-Milior**, Via Pistoiese 755D, t 0574 818288. Women's clothing and accessories.

**Maglificio Pratesi**, Via Baccheretana 83, Seano, t 055 870 5467. Clothing for men, women and children.

# Where to Stay

## Prato ✉ 50047

Prato's hotels mostly cater for businessmen, but can be a good bet in the summer when Florence is packed to the gills.

**\*\*\*Flora**, Via Cairoli 31, near S. Maria dei Carceri, t 0574 33521, f 0574 400289, *www.prathotels.it* (*expensive*). Old-fashioned but decent modernized rooms. All rooms have a video machine and there is a small video library.

**\*\*\*Hotel Giardino**, Via Magnolfi 2, t 0574 26189, f 0574 606591, *www.giardinohotel.com* (*expensive*). This smartly modernized and friendly hotel on Piazza del Duomo has a pleasant bar, a reading room and a private garage.

so important that the whole town took the name. It was first ruled by the Alberti, one of the region's more ambitious feudal families, who conquered lands all the way from the Maremma to the Mugello. In 1107 Countess Matilda personally led a combined Tuscan army against Prato in order to humble the Alberti; then, in 1140, the Pratesi rid their counts of most of their power and ran their city as a free *comune*. In 1193, at the height of the city's power, it even managed to snatch some of Florence's own *contado*. By this time Prato had also become one of the most important manufacturers of woollen goods in Europe, and was so wealthy that the University of Paris created a special college for students from Pratesi.

★★★**Villa Santa Cristina**, Via Poggio Secco 58, t 0574 595 951, f 0574 572 623 (*expensive*). A relaxing spot with a garden, pool and most other comforts, over the river in the hills to the east of Prato.

★★★**San Marco**, Piazza San Marco 48, t 0574 21321, f 0574 22378, *www.hotelsanmarco prato.com* (*moderate*). A pleasant place between the Stazione Centrale and the Castello, convenient if you arrive by train.

★★★**Villa Rucellai**, Via di Canneto 16, 4km northeast of town, t 0574 460392 (*moderate*). A delightful B&B in a Renaissance villa, with pool. Despite being surrounded by Prato's industrial sprawl, its formal gardens and the wonderful atmosphere of the house (filled with the family's books, pictures and furniture) is an oasis. What's more, it's good value.

★★**Toscana**, Piazza Ciardi 3, t 0574 28096, f 0574 25163 (*moderate*). More economical, on a quiet square on the far side of the Stazione Porta al Serraglio.

# Eating Out

One reason for staying in Prato is the food, especially if you like fish.

**Osvaldo Baroncelli**, Via Fra Bartolomeo 13, t 0574 23810 (*very expensive–expensive*). À small establishment with an innovative chef. The set menu is good value. A la carte options include fricassée of salt cod, Tuscan bean and spelt soup with fish and frizzled leeks, pasta with fish and artichoke hearts, and fish couscous. There is a fabulous array of Italian and French cheeses. *Closed Sun.*

**Enoteca Barni**, Via Ferrucci 22, t 0574 607 845 (*expensive*). Has an excellent wine list; the food is good with simpler, cheaper lunch menus and more interesting choices at night, in a more elegant setting – asparagus soufflé with foie gras sauce, red mullet with basil, black olives and tomato, bean and cabbage soup with lobster, lamb in a herb crust. *Closed Sat lunch, Sun and Mon dinner; Aug.*

**Il Pirana**, Via Valentini 110 (south of Viale Vittorio Veneto, between the central station and Piazza San Marco), t 0574 25746 (*expensive*). Maintains a justified reputation for some of the best seafood in inland Tuscany. An elegant place, hidden behind reflecting glass windows. Try the *gran piatto* of raw marinated fish, *gnocchetti* with scampi and zucchini flowers, or fish ravioli in lobster sauce. *Closed Sat lunch and Sun.*

**Maffei**, Via Ricasoli 22. The distinctive bright blue bags displayed in the window of this *biscotteria* and bar contain the best *biscotti* (or *cantucci) di Prato* around. Don't settle for anything less.

**Osteria Cibbé**, Piazza Mercatale 49, t 0574 607509 (*cheap*). A small, family-run *osteria* with marble-topped tables set in a brick-vaulted room, serving delicious rustic dishes such as *pappa al pomodoro, garganelli* with aubergine and wild mushrooms, stock fish *in zimino* (spicy sauce with Swiss chard), and meatballs with ricotta cheese. *Closed Sun.*

**La Vecchia Cucina di Soldano**, Via Pomeri 23, t 0574 34665 (*cheap*). A very gratifying *trattoria* for something less elaborate, with a traditional menu cooked and served on red-checked cloths by the Mattei family, that's full of *ribollita* and *pasta e fagioli*, stuffed celery and all the other old-fashioned soups and stews, including the house speciality, a hearty beef and onion stew known as *francesina*. *Closed Sun.*

Florence, however, could not countenance so near and ambitious a rival, and in 1350, on charges of fomenting rebellion in the Valdelsa, Florence besieged Prato. An honourable peace was made; the next year Florence cemented its hold over its neighbour by purchasing it for the sum of 17,500 florins from its nominal overlord, the Angevin Queen of Naples.

Despite the ignominy of being bought, Prato functioned more as Florence's ally than its possession, retaining a certain amount of local autonomy. The late 14th century was the day of Francesco di Marco Datini, the Merchant of Prato, one of the richest men in Europe and history's first recorded workaholic businessman. However, although he built his palace in his home town of Prato, the big profits were to be had in Florence, and Datini spent most of his time there. Under the influence of Savonarola's preaching, Prato joined Florence in rebelling against Medici rule, but was soon to play the role of whipping boy, when the Spaniards, at the instigation of the Medici Pope Leo X, besieged and sacked the city with unheard-of brutality. Since that dark day, Prato's history has followed that of its imperious neighbour, until a few years ago, at least. You can't keep a good town down for ever, and Prato and its hinterlands have finally wriggled out from Florentine control and become a province in their own right – one of Italy's newest, and smallest.

## Frederick's Castle

*Open Wed–Sun 9–1 and 4–7; winter: am only; adm.*

Most people, whether arriving by car, bus, or at the Stazione Centrale, approach the walled core of Prato through the Piazza San Marco, embellished with a white puffy sculpture by Henry Moore from 1974. Viale Piave continues to the defiantly Ghibelline swallowtail crenellations of the **Castello dell'Imperatore**. Built in 1237 by Frederick II, Holy Roman Emperor and heir to the Norman kingdom in southern Italy and Sicily, it marks a strange interlude in Prato's past. Frederick, unlike his grandfather Frederick Barbarossa, never spent much time in Tuscany, preferring his more civilized dominions in Apulia and Sicily, where he could discuss poetry, philosophy and falconry (in Arabic or Latin) with his court scholars. When he did come, it was in magnificent progress featuring dancing girls, elephants and the Muslim Imperial bodyguard. His Tuscan taxpayers were not impressed; nor did they much appreciate Frederick's tolerant, syncretistic approach to religion. The popes excommunicated him twice. He built this castle here because he had to, not so much to defend Prato, but to defend his Imperial *podestà* from the Pratesi, and perhaps impress the locals with its design – its clean lines must have seemed very sharp and modern in the 13th century.

Don't doubt for a minute that this castle is quite intentionally a work of art. The design, by a Sicilian named Riccardo da Lentini, is perfectly in tune with the south Italian works of the 'Hohenstaufen Renaissance' of Frederick's reign, a reminder of a rare age when artistically the south was keeping up with northern Italy, and often a little in advance. There isn't much inside the castle now, though the city often uses the space for special exhibitions. Usually it is possible to walk up along its walls for a bird's-eye view of Prato.

## Santa Maria delle Carceri

Next to the castle stands the unfinished black and white marble façade of **Santa Maria delle Carceri**, begun in 1485 by Giuliano da Sangallo. Brunelleschian architecture was always a fragile blossom, as is clearly shown by the failure of this sole serious attempt to transplant it outside the walls of Florence. Santa Maria always merits a mention in architectural histories. It was an audacious enterprise: Sangallo, a furiously diligent student of Vitruvius and Alberti, attempted to create a building based entirely on philosophical principles. Order, simplicity and correct proportion, as in Brunelleschi's churches, were to be manifest, with few frills allowed. Sangallo, the favourite of Lorenzo il Magnifico, unfortunately proved to be a better theorist than he was an architect. Santa Maria was a clumsy tombstone for the sort of theoretical architecture that was a fad in the 1400s, one more often expressed in paintings than actual buildings. The interior is better than the exterior; a plain Greek cross in the Brunelleschian manner with a decorative frieze and *tondi* of the four Evangelists by Andrea della Robbia. The church's name – *carceri* means prisons – refers to a local miracle, a speaking image of the Virgin painted on a nearby prison wall, that occasioned the building of the church. Behind the church is Prato's grand 1820's **Teatro Metastasio**, home to some of the most innovative theatre in Italy and also to frequent concerts.

## Piazza San Francesco and Datini

From Santa Maria delle Carceri you can see the apse of Prato's huge brick church of **San Francesco**, dating from the end of the 13th century, and embellished in front with white and green marble stripes. Inside, on the left wall is the Tomb of Gemignano Inghirami, one of Europe's crack lawyers of the quattrocento, the design attributed to Bernardo Rossellino (1460s); near the altar is the **tomb slab of Francesco di Marco Datini** (1330–1410) by Niccolò di Piero Lamberti. Off the elegant Renaissance cloister you'll find the entrance to the **Cappella Migliorati**, beautifully frescoed in 1395 by Niccolò di Pietro Gerini, one of the period's finest draughtsmen; here he depicts the Lives of Saints Anthony Abbot and Matthew.

Niccolò also frescoed the **Palazzo Datini**, nearby on Via Mazzei 33 (*open Mon–Sat 9–12 and 4–6*), the showplace palace built in the 1390s by the Merchant of Prato. If there were an Accountants' Hall of Fame, Francesco di Marco Datini would surely be in it; he helped invent that dismal science. Nor did he ever let anyone throw anything away, leaving to posterity 150,000 documents, ledgers (all inscribed: 'For God and Profit') and private letters that are stored in the archives in this palace; these formed the basis for Iris Origo's fascinating account of his life and times. Datini left nearly all of his indecent fortune to the Ceppo, a Pratese charity he founded in 1410 and which now has its headquarters on the first floor of this palace; in gratitude the city had the façade frescoed with scenes of his life, unfortunately now much faded.

## Galleria Comunale

*Currently closed. The most important works have been moved temporarily to the Museo di Pittura Murale (see p.221).*

Just north lies Prato's charming civic centre, the **Piazza del Comune**, decorated with a 19th-century **statue of Datini** with bronze reliefs of the merchant's life, and a pretty fountain by Tacca nicknamed 'Il Bacchino', or Little Bacchus (1659). The city's **Palazzo Comunale**, behind the portico, retains only traces of its medieval heritage; drop in to see its **Sala di Consiglio** with its coffered ceiling, two quattrocento frescoes and portraits of the grand dukes. The rugged **Palazzo Pretorio** is entirely medieval, a relic of the days when Prato governed itself without any help from the Medici; the stair on the façade leads up to the **Galleria Comunale** with a good collection of mostly Florentine art. There's a tabernacle by Filippino Lippi, painted for his mother and later restored after damage in the war; up in the grand **Salone Udienza** with the fine wood ceiling is Bernardo Daddi's *Story of the Holy Girdle*, a predella telling the tale of Prato's most famous relic, the Virgin Mary's belt. According to tradition she gave it to Doubting Thomas, from whom it was passed down until it became part of the dowry of a woman who married Michele, a knight from Prato during the First Crusade. Michele returned to Prato and hid the precious relic under his mattress; angels lifted him off, and the girdle was given into the care of the cathedral. In the same hall are fine 14th-century works by Giovanni di Milano, Michele di Firenze, Lorenzo Monaco, and a *tondo* attributed to Luca Signorelli. In an adjoining room is *Noli me tangere* by Battistello, a follower of Caravaggio; this curious work portrays Christ wearing a fedora at a rakish angle, doing a quick dance step to evade the Magdalene's touch.

For a celebration of Prato medieval and modern textile industry visit the **Museo del Tessuto** (*open Mon and Wed–Sun 10–6*) which has a unique collection of fabrics and looms dating back to the 5th century AD. It is housed in a stunning 19th-century textile mill at Via Santa Chiara 24, where the full collection of fabrics (some 6,000 pieces, including contemporary textiles) is on display.

## Cathedral of Santo Stefano

In the centre of Prato rises its cathedral, like a faded beauty who never recovered from the blow of a broken engagement. It was begun with great promise in the 13th century, and added to on and off for the next 200 years, with ever-dwindling passion and money. The best features are an exotic, almost Moorish campanile, a rather dirty Andrea della Robbia lunette of the *Madonna and St Stephen* over the door, a big clock on the half-striped façade that makes you smile when you notice it sitting where the rose window ought to be and, above all, the circular **Pulpit of the Sacred Girdle**, projecting from the corner of the façade. Perhaps no other church in Italy has such a perfectly felicitous ornament, something beautiful and special that the Pratesi look at every day as they walk through the piazza. Michelozzo designed it in 1428 and Donatello added the delightful reliefs of dancing children and *putti* along the lines of his *cantoria* in Florence's cathedral museum (the bas-reliefs are only casts, but you can see the originals in the Museo dell'Opera). The Holy Girdle (*see* above) is publicly displayed here five times a year on Easter Day, 1 May, 15 August, 8 September and Christmas Day.

The Duomo's interior continues the motif of green and white stripes in its Romanesque arcades and ribs of the vaulting. The **Chapel of the Sacred Girdle**, just to the left as you enter, is protected by a screen, and the inside is covered with frescoes by Agnolo Gaddi on the legend of the girdle, and adorned with a beautiful marble statue, the *Madonna and Child*, by Giovanni Pisano. In the left aisle there's a masterful **pulpit** carved by Mino da Fiesole and Antonio Rossellino, with harpies around the base. Filippo Lippi's celebrated frescoes on the *Lives of Saints John the Baptist and Stephen* (1452–66) are undergoing restoration and work is expected to continue for several years (*to visit the chapel and see the work in progress contact the* *tourist office for a guided tour, Sat at 10, 11, 4 and 5, Sun at 10 and 11; adm).* While painting these frescoes, his first major work, Lippi fell in love with a brown-eyed novice, Lucrezia Buti, who according to tradition posed for his magnificent *Herod's Banquet*, either as the melancholy Salome herself or as the figure in the long white dress, second from the right; Fra Filippo placed himself among the mourners for St Stephen, third from right, in a red hat. The less lyrical frescoes in the next chapel are by Uccello and Andrea di Giusto. There's a lovely, almost Art Nouveau, candelabra on the high altar by Maso di Bartolomeo (1440s), closely related to his work in Pistoia cathedral.

The **Museo dell'Opera del Duomo** *(open Mon and Wed–Sat 9.30–12.30 and 3–6.30, Sun 9.30–12.30; adm)* is located next door in the cloister, one side of which retains its 12th-century geometric marble decorations and rambunctious capitals. The museum is currently undergoing long-term restoration work to enlarge it and only two rooms are open. The most important works are now at the Museo di Pittura Murale *(see below)*. The tragic star of the museum is the original pulpit of the Sacred Girdle, with Donatello's merry *putti* made lepers by car exhaust. Lippi's *Death of San Girolamo* was painted to prove to the bishop that he was the man to fresco the cathedral choir. Other works include his son Filippino's *St Lucy*, blissfully ignoring the knife in her throat, and another full-length portrait, of *Fra Jacopone di Todi*, believed to be an early work by Uccello. More dancing *putti* adorn the *Reliquary of the Sacred Girdle* (1446) by Maso di Bartolomeo, which was stolen but recovered at the Todi antique fair. Also worth seeing are the saccharine *Guardian Angel* by Carlo Dolci, a sophisticated *Madonna with Saints* by the quattrocento 'Master of the Nativity of Castello', and a strange reliquary that resembles a mushroom.

## Walking through Prato

Most of Prato's old streets are anonymous, self-effacing Tuscan. Sadly, some areas suffered bomb damage in the war, notably the great pear-shaped **Piazza del Mercatale** on the banks of the Bisenzio. This was long the working core of the city, surrounded entirely by porticoes and workshops; it was and is the site of Prato's big market and fairs. A few faded, peeling, porticoed buildings remain, overlooking the river that has laundered the products of Prato's principal industry for eight centuries.

Sunday is a good day to visit sturdy brick **San Domenico** on the west side of town, a large Gothic church begun in 1283 and completed by Giovanni Pisano, one side of it lined with arcades. There's not much to see inside, but the adjacent convent, the home of painter Fra Bartolommeo and Pratese address of Savonarola, holds the **Museo di Pittura Murale** *(open Mon, Wed, Thurs and Sat 9–1; Fri–Sat 9–1 and 3–6; adm)*, housing a collection of detached frescoes from surrounding churches, and currently holding some of the works of Prato's other museums while they undergo reorganization. There are charming quattrocento graffiti court scenes from the Palazzo Vaj, a sinopia from the cathedral attributed to Uccello, and Niccolò di Piero Gerini's *Tabernacle of the Ceppo*. Filippo Lippi painted the *Madonna del Ceppo* for the Ceppo offices in the Palazzo Datini; it portrays the tycoon himself, with four fellow donors, who contributed less and thus get portrayed as midgets.

Just north of San Domenico, **San Fabiano**, Via del Seminario 30, has an enchanting pre-Romanesque mosaic pavement, depicting mermaids, birds and dragons biting their own tails; north of San Fabiano, 15th-century **Sant'Agostino** contains Prato's most ridiculous painting, the *Madonna della Consolazione* (attributed, naturally, to Vasari), who does her consoling by distributing belts from heaven.

Despite all its artistic treasures, Prato doesn't sit on its Renaissance laurels. In 1988 the ambitious **Centro per l'Arte Contemporanea Luigi Pecci** opened on Viale della Repubblica in the suburbs (*www.centropecci.it; open Wed–Mon 9–7; adm exp*), with a collection of modern works from artists around the world. The only place to see contemporary art on this scale in Tuscany, it holds temporary exhibitions by important artists, and also summer concerts in the amphitheatre. Since the successful reception of Henry Moore's big lump by the train station in the 1970s, Prato has also accumulated outdoor abstract sculpture in a big way. Two that stand out, if only for their breathtaking pretentiousness, are Barbara Krueger's billboard *Untitled* (Viale da Vinci), and Anne and Patrick Poirier's *Exegi Monumentum Aere Perennius*, in the grounds of the Centro Luigi Pecci. A regular season of concerts is held here.

## North of Prato: the Val di Bisenzio

Prato's river begins some 40km up in the Apennines, and along its valley runs the SS325, a secondary highway towards Bologna. This valley was long the fiefdom of the Alberti counts, whose fortifications dot its sides. **Vaiano**, the first town on the main route, has a Romanesque abbey church and green-striped campanile as its landmark; just beyond are the ruins of the Alberti's **Rocca di Cerbaia** (12th century). The highway continues to **Vernio** and **San Quirico**, with another ruined Alberti castle up above.

From San Quirico's neighbour to the west, **Cantagallo** ('cock's crow'), a lovely walking path leads up to the **Piano della Rasa** in little over an hour, which is a panoramic valley with an alpine refuge (*open April–Oct*). Further north on the SS325, at the small resort of **Montepiano**, the waters destined for the Tyrrhenian and Adriatic split and go their own ways. There is another ancient abbey here, the Vallombrosan **Badia di Santa Maria**, with good 13th- and 14th-century frescoes. From the abbey begins another fine walking path up to **Alpi di Cavarzano** (1,008m/3,306ft), and from there, it is another hour or so's walk up to the highest peak in the region, **Monte La Scoperta** (1,278m/4,192ft).

## Figline and Montemurlo

The old road between Prato and Pistoia passes near **Figline di Prato**, a medieval village well-known for its terracotta vases. Figline has a 14th-century parish church with contemporary mural paintings, including a 'primitive' Last Supper and also a St Michael with a finely detailed background; a small parish museum contains other 'primitives'. **Montemurlo**, on its hill over the plain of Prato, is also medieval; in 1537 its castle, a stronghold of the Guidi counts, was the Alamo for the anti-Medici republican oligarchs of Florence, led by Filippo Strozzi, who were defeated here once and for all by the troops of Cosimo I. The old walled town is interesting, with an impressive and rather stylish **Rocca** for its crown, approached these days by a Mannerist ramp. The Romanesque church of 'Beheaded John' (**San Giovanni Decollato**) has a pretty campanile and some good art in its baroqued interior, including a miraculous Byzantine crucifix and a 16th-century painting by Giovanni da Prato illustrating its story.

# Pistoia

You know **Pistoia** (pop. 94,000) is near when the road plunges into a Lilliputian forest of umbrella pines and cypresses, all in tidy rows. These are Italy's most extensive ornamental nurseries, a gentle craft that thrives in the rich soil at the foot of the Apennines. But Pistoia wasn't always content to cultivate its own garden peacefully;

## Getting Around

Pistoia lies along the A11, and at the foot of two important routes north over the Apennines, the SS64 towards Bologna and SS633 to Abetone. From the station, just south of the city walls at the end of Via XX Settembre, there are frequent **trains** along the main Florence–Lucca line. COPIT **buses** for Vinci and Empoli (37km/2hrs – a beautiful, twisting road over the Monte Albano), Cutigliano (37km/1hr 45min), Abetone (50km/2½hrs), the zoo, Montecatini (16km/30min), and other destinations in Pistoia's little province depart from Piazza San Francesco. LAZZI buses depart for Florence (35km/1hr), Prato, Lucca (43km/1½hrs), Montecatini, Viareggio and Pisa (65km/2hrs) from Viale Vittorio Veneto, near the train station. **Cars** are banned from most of the city centre (in theory, anyhow) but there's plenty of parking around the Fortezza di Santa Barbara in the southeast corner of the walls.

## Tourist Information

**Pistoia**: Piazza del Duomo, in the bishop's palace, t 0573 21622, f 0573 34327, *www.pistoia.turismo-tuscany.it*.
**Post office**: Via Roma 5.

### Festivals

**Giostra dell'Orso** (Joust of the Bear), *25 July*. The culmination of a month of concerts, fairs and exhibits. The Joust began in the 14th century, pitting 12 knights against a bear dressed in a checked cloak. The bear has been replaced by two wooden dummies, but the pageantry remains the same.

## Where to Stay

### Pistoia ✉ 51110

Pistoia gives the impression that it's more accustomed to lodging and feeding business travellers than pleasure-seekers. On balance, it might be better to make this city a day trip, or stay in nearby Montecatini Terme instead.

There are a couple of options if you travel a few kilometres outside town.

**\*\*\*Il Convento**, Via S. Quirico 33, 5km east at Pontenuovo, t 0573 452651, f 0573 453578, *www.ilconventohotel.com* (*expensive*). A former convent, preserving its exterior if not all of its interior. The setting is quiet, with views over Pistoia; there's a pool and one of the city's better restaurants.

**Villa Vannini**, about 6km north of town, t 0573 42031, f 0573 26331, *www.volpe-uva.it* (*moderate*). Even more rural is this delightful, if slightly fading villa among the fir trees, where you can relax with wonderful hill walks on the doorstep; elegant, comfortable, good-value rooms, and a fantastic restaurant.

There are a few reasonable options if you do need somewhere in Pistoia itself.

**Tenuta di Pieve a Celle**, Via Pieve a Celle, t 0573 913087 (*expensive*). A stylish *agriturismo*

this is the place, after all, that gave us the word 'pistol' – which originally referred to the surgical knives made in the city, but later came to mean daggers, and finally guns.

Today it specializes in light rail trains (the Breda works built the cars for the Washington DC metro), mattresses, cymbals and baby trees. Although seldom sampled by the moveable feast of tourism, the historic centre of Pistoia is almost perfectly intact, and behind its medieval walls there is some fine art to be seen, part Pisan, part Florentine, reflecting its position between the two great rivals.

## History

*...Proud you are, envious, enemies of heaven,*
*Friends to your own harm and, to your own neighbour,*
*The simplest charity you find a labour.*
      'Invective against the People of Pistoia', a sonnet by Michelangelo

right next to the zoo, this farmhouse has been converted into five guest rooms with great taste and style. The setting is lovely (the only sound that might disturb the peace is the odd animal roar) and there is a fine pool. Guests can order dinner.

***Hotel Patria**, Via Crispi 8, t 0573 25187, f 0573 368168, *www.patriahotel.it* (*moderate*). Situated near San Domenico, this hotel has recently been revamped so is a bit more cheerful than the other hotels in town. You can even have bacon and eggs for breakfast.

***Leon Bianco**, Via Panciatichi 2, t 0573 26675, f 0573 26676, *www.hotelleon bianco.it* (*moderate*). A bit dated, but reasonably comfortable, with views over the campanile.

***Piccolo Ritz**, Via Vannucci 67, t 0573 26775, f 0573 27798 (*moderate*). A newer place near the station – nice, but somewhat noisy.

****Firenze**, Via Curtatone e Montanara 42, t/f 0573 23141, *www.hotelfirenze.it* (*moderate*). The closest thing to inexpensive accommodation, near Piazza del Duomo, but it's a bit woebegone.

# Eating Out

Pistoia has many simple *trattoria*s and pizzerias, and also several places offering delicious local cuisine.

**La Bottegaia**, Via del Lastrone 17, t 0573 365602 (*moderate*). Tucked away behind the baptistry, occupying a beautifully appointed vaulted room and a lovely terrace, this wine bar/restaurant serves snacks (selections of cheeses and meat, *bruschette* and salads) and full meals from a short, but ever-changing menu. The *menu degustazione* is excellent value and features such dishes as celery soup with pecorino cheese, leek flan, pesto lasagne, and duck breast with wild fennel. There are some 600 wines to choose from too. *Closed Sun lunch, Mon.*

**San Jacopo**, Via Crispi 15, t 0573 27786 (*cheap*). A pleasant *trattoria*, serving top-quality traditional food (both fish and meat dishes) on crisp white cloths; Tuscan soups, spaghetti with clams, tripe, *baccalà*, rabbit with olives and, in season, porcini mushrooms. *Closed Tues lunch, Mon.*

**Trattoria dell'Abbondanza**, Via dell' Abbondanza 10, t 0573 368037 (*cheap*). There is an abundance of tempting dishes at this cheerful *trattoria* near the Duomo. The food is rustic and delicious: porcini soup, *gnocchi all'Abbondanza* (with tomatoes, pesto and pecorino cheese), octopus and potato stew, and roast pork spiked with rosemary and garlic. *Closed Thurs lunch, Wed.*

And outside the town itself:

**Rafanelli**, Via Sant'Agostino 47, Sant'Agostino, t 0573 532046 (*moderate*). Local dishes, including *maccheroni* with duck, game dishes and lamb, served in a pretty country villa setting, also does a great *bistecca*, grilled over a wood fire. *Closed Sun eve, Mon and Aug.*

Pistoia's fellow Tuscans have looked askance at her ever since Roman times, when the city was called *Pistoria* and saw the death struggle of the Catiline conspiracy, the famous attempted coup against the Roman Republic in 62 BC, which ended when the legions tracked down the escaped Catiline and his henchmen near Pistoia. Its position on the Via Cassia helped it prosper under the Lombards, who elevated it to a royal city. In 1158 Pistoia became a *comune*, and was seen as enough of a threat for Florence and Lucca to gang up against it twice. In the 13th century Pistoia's evil reputation gave it credit for having begun the bitter controversy between Black and White Guelphs that so obsessed Florence; Dante, himself a victim of that feud, made sure that in writing the *Divina Commedia* he never missed an opportunity to curse and condemn the fateful city. In 1306 Florence exacted revenge by capturing Pistoia, and as usual she adapted her politics to the nature of her conquest: Prato she made an ally, Pisa she held with fortresses, but Pistoia she controlled with factions. The only interlude came between 1315 and 1328, when Lucca's Castruccio Castracani held Pistoia as part of his empire; it was a short-lived respite, however: after his fall the Florentines soon returned. Pistoia, preoccupied with its own quarrels, carried on happily ever after, making a good living from its old speciality, ironworking. It proudly supplied the conspirators of Europe with fine daggers, and later, keeping up with technological advances, with pistols.

## Piazza del Duomo

Pistol-Pistoia no longer packs any heat, but it packs in the heart of its 16th-century diamond-shaped walls one of the finest squares in Italy, a lesson in the subtle medieval aesthetic of urban design, an art lost with the endless theorizing and compulsive regularity of the Renaissance. The arrangement of the buildings around the L-shaped **Piazza del Duomo** seems at first to be haphazard. The design is meant to be experienced from street level; if you try walking into the piazza from a few of its surrounding streets, you'll see how from each approach the monuments reveal themselves in a different order and pattern, like the shaking of a kaleidoscope; the windows of the Palazzo del Comune echo those on the Palazzo del Podestà, and the striped decoration of the baptistry is recalled in the campanile and Duomo. The piazza provides the perfect setting for Pistoia's great annual party in July, the colourful *Giostra dell'Orso* (Joust of the Bear, *see* 'Festivals', p.64).

The **Duomo**, dedicated to San Zeno, dates from the 12th century; the Pisan arcades and stripes of its façade, combined over the geometric patterns of the Florentine Romanesque and polychrome terracotta lunette by Andrea della Robbia, strike an uneasy balance between the two architectural traditions. The outsize **Campanile**, originally a watchtower, tips the balance towards Pisa, with exotic, almost Moorish candy-striped arches at the top added in the 14th century when it was converted to church use – though you can still see the old Ghibelline crenellations on top. Inside the cathedral is a wealth of art – on the right a **Font** with quaint medieval heads, redesigned by Benedetto da Maiano, the **Tomb of Cino da Pistoia** (1337), a close friend of Dante, shown lecturing to a class of scholars, and a 13th-century painted crucifix by Coppo di Marcovaldo. The cathedral's most precious treasure is in the **chapel of St James** (*contact the sacristan to view; adm*): a fabulous altar made of nearly a ton of silver, comprising 628 figures, begun in 1287 and added to over the next two centuries; among the Pisan, Sienese and Florentine artists who contributed to this shining *tour de force* was Brunelleschi, who added the two half-figures on the left before he decided to devote all his talents to architecture. Some of the oldest art, fine medieval reliefs of the Last Supper and Gethsemane, have been relegated to the dim and ancient crypt. By the altar there's a fine painting by Caravaggio's pupil, Mattia Preti, and Maso di Bartolomeo's bronze candelabra. On the left the **chapel of the Sacrament** contains a bust of a Medici archbishop attributed to Verrocchio, who also added the statues of Faith and Hope to the weeping angels on the **tomb of Cardinal Forteguerri**, just left of the main entrance.

Next to the Duomo stands the partly striped and partly brick **Palazzo dei Vescovi**, mangled by remodellings over the centuries. The tourist information office is here, and the restorations undertaken to install it uncovered some Etruscan *cippi* (gravestones), and the foundations of Pistoia's original cathedral. The Etruscan finds, along with relics of Roman Pistoia, have been arranged in an **Archaeological Itinerary** in the Palazzo's basement, and the old cathedral is now included in the **Museo San Zeno** (*open Tues, Thurs and Fri plus 2nd and 4th Sun of the month, 10–1 and 3–5*), along with some paintings and a fine reliquary by Lorenzo Ghiberti.

Across from the Duomo stands Pistoia's octagonal zebra of a **baptistry** (*open Tues–Sat 10–12.30 and 3–6, Sun 9.30–12.30*), whose proper name is San Giovanni in Corte. Built over the site of a Lombard-era royal palace (the *corte*), it was finished in 1359, to a design by Andrea Pisano. It is one of the few outstanding Gothic buildings in Tuscany, embellished with fine sculptural details on the outside. The interior has a remarkable conical ceiling of brick and a beautifully decorated font dating from 1226, designed by Lanfranco da Como. In Piazza della Sala, behind the baptistry, is a medieval well, topped by a Florentine *Marzocco*.

## Museo Civico

*Open Tues–Sat 10–7, Sun 9.30–12.30; adm.*

The Piazza del Duomo's other two palaces are civic in nature. The 14th-century **Palazzo Pretorio** on the west side has a decorated courtyard and an old stone bench where the judges once sat and where they often condemned malefactors to a unique punishment – they were ennobled. Not that Pistoia wanted to reward them; rather, to become noble meant losing one's rights as a republican citizen. The tower near here is known as the tomb of Catiline, who according to tradition was secretly buried here.

On the other side of the piazza stands the elegant **Palazzo Comunale**, begun in 1294, and prominently embellished with the usual Medici balls and the more unusual black marble head, believed to be that of a Moorish king captured by a captain from Pistoia on a freebooting expedition to Mallorca. Besides the town council and offices, the palazzo houses the **Museo Civico**, an excellent collection of great and odd paintings to suit even the most jaded of palates. Pistoiese patrons were uncommonly fond of 'Sacred Conversations' – group portraits of saints around the Madonna, and there are good ones by Mariotto de Nardo, Beccafumi, Lorenzo di Credi and Pistoia's own Gerino Gerini (1480–1529), a follower of Raphael. From the 15th-century 'Maestro delle Madonne di Marmo' there's a sweetly smiling marble relief of the Madonna and child; then two fancy St Sebastians with flowing curls, who precede the *Madonna della Pergola*, by local painter Bernardino di Antonio Detti (1498–1554), whose flaccid charwoman of a Madonna holds a child with a large housefly on his chubby arm before a crazy quilt of confusing iconography – children with dolls, the Judgement of Solomon, a child with a fruit-bowl, a floor littered with flowers, amulets, spoons and rags. On the mezzanine is the document centre of the great 20th-century Pistoiese architect Giovanni Michelucci; a comprehensive collection of models and drawings, as well as photos of his buildings and the media reaction to them. One example of his work is the large, angular Santa Maria Novella station in Florence, another is the restaurant in the Parco Collodi (*see* p.235).

Plod up another flight of stairs to see some screamingly lurid paintings from the 17th and 19th centuries, with enough historical canvases of murder and mayhem to suggest the local taste for violence lingered on for some time, at least within the confines of art. There are two mythological paintings swathed in Caravaggiesque darkness by Cecco Bravo; a 17th-century *Young Woman with a Flower*, bathed in ghostly light; a sensuous, pouting St Sebastian, disdainfully plucking arrows from his chest; an absurd allegory of Medici rule in Pistoia, with *putti* scattering the family's lily symbol like flowers over the city; a Magdalene fondly patting a skull; as well as two rather nightmarish imaginary battle scenes by a 17th-century Neapolitan named Francesco Graziani.

Just off the Piazza del Duomo on Ripa del Sale, the 16th-century Palazzo Rospigliosi houses two small museums, the **Museo Rospigliosi**, with a collection of its original furniture and paintings *in situ*, the paintings mostly by a Pistoiese artist named Giacinto Gimignani, and the **Museo Diocesano** (*both open Tues, Thurs and Fri 10–1 and 4–7, Wed and Sat 10–1; joint adm*), displaying crosses and reliquaries from the early Middle Ages.

## Ospedale del Ceppo and Sant'Andrea

In medieval Tuscany, it was customary to collect alms in a hollowed-out log (or *ceppo*) left in a public place, to be gathered and distributed to the poor at Christmas-time. *Ceppo* became synonymous with the word charity, as in Datini's famous foundation in Prato, and even earlier here in Pistoia, when the **Ospedale del Ceppo** (*a working hospital; call the tourist office to arrange a visit*) was founded in the 13th century. Still functioning at the same address (walk down Via Filippo Pacini from the Palazzo Comunale), the building was given a fine arcaded porch in the 1500s, in the style of the famous Spedale degli Innocenti in Florence. And, as in Florence, the della Robbias were called upon to provide the decoration, in this case the usually insipid Giovanni, who with the help of his workshop and other artists, created not only the typical della Robbian *tondi*, but a unique terracotta frieze that spans the entire loggia in resplendent Renaissance Technicolor, with scenes of the acts of mercy and theological virtues. Inside there's a small **Museo dei Ferri Chirurgici** dedicated to Pistoia's old iron industry, especially surgical knives.

A short walk west of the hospital on Via Sant'Andrea is the 12th-century church of **Sant'Andrea** (*open daily 8–12.30 and 3.30–6*), with a Pisan façade and over the door, a charming bas-relief of the Journey of the Magi, dated 1166, and a pair of ghastly, leering lions. The real jewel is inside: Giovanni Pisano's hexagonal **pulpit** (1297), exquisitely carved in stirring high relief with scenes of the Nativity, Massacre of the Innocents, Adoration of the Magi, Crucifixion and Last Judgement, with sibyls in the corners and pedestals in the forms of the four Evangelists – one of the masterpieces of Italian Gothic. Sant'Andrea contains three other crucifixions: Giovanni Pisano's wooden crucifix in the right aisle, a medieval version over the main altar, portraying Christ crowned and dressed in a kingly robe, and in the right nave, a large, rather mysterious painting of the saint crucified on a tree.

## San Francesco and the Madonna dell'Umiltà

Pretty striped churches circle the centre of Pistoia like zebras on a merry-go-round. The two plain ponies in the lot lie to the west. The large **San Francesco al Prato** in Piazza San Francesco d'Assisi, plain and Gothic like most Franciscan churches, has some notable 14th-century frescoes, especially in the chapel to the left of the altar, with Sienese scenes portraying the Triumph of St Augustine. On the side of the church there's an ancient olive tree and a memorial to assassinated prime minister Aldo Moro, a stark contrast with the heroic Fascist-era war monument in the piazza itself. South along Corso Gramsci is Pistoia's main theatre, the 1694 **Teatro Manzoni**; further south, on Via della Madonna, towers Pistoia's great experiment in High Renaissance geometry, the octagonal, unstriped **Basilica della Madonna dell'Umiltà** begun in 1518 by local architect and pupil of Bramante, Ventura Vitoni, who graced it with an imposing barrel-vaulted vestibule. In the 1560s Giorgio Vasari was called upon to crown Vitoni's fine start; not content to limit his mischief to Florence, he added a dome so heavy that the basilica has been threatening to collapse ever since. More work to shore it up is currently under way.

## San Giovanni Fuorcivitas and San Domenico

To the south of the Piazza del Duomo (Via Roma to Via Cavour) lies the tiny **Piazza San Leone**, the ancient Lombard centre of Pistoia; its stubby tower once belonged to the nastiest Pistoian of them all, a 13th-century noble thug and church robber named Vanni Fucci whom Dante found in one of the lower circles of Hell, entwined in a serpent, cursing and making obscene gestures up at God. Around the corner of Via Cavour, the 12th-century **San Giovanni Fuorcivitas** claims the honour of being the most striped church in all Christendom, its green and white flank an abstract pattern of lozenges and blind arches that out-Pisas anything in Pisa. The gloomy interior holds a dramatic pulpit (1270) by Fra Guglielmo da Pisa, a pupil of Nicola Pisano, a holy water stoup supported by caryatids by Giovanni Pisano and a white, glazed terracotta group of the Visitation by Luca or Andrea della Robbia.

Piazza Garibaldi, also to the south, is adorned with a good equestrian statue of Garibaldi, some florid street lamps, and **San Domenico**, begun in the late 13th century. In its spacious, airy interior, there's a splendid Baroque organ from 1617 and two Renaissance tombs: that of Filippo Lazzari, by the Rossellino brothers, portraying the deceased lecturing to his pupils (one of whom can't help yawning), and the other of Lorenzo da Ripafratta, with a fine effigy. In 1497, Benozzo Gozzoli died of the plague in Pistoia and is buried somewhere in the cloister of San Domenico; you can see a fresco he began of the Journey of the Magi nearby. Although the monastery is still in use, you can ring to see the frescoes in the chapter house, among them good Sienese works and a Crucifixion with its sinopia, dating back to the mid-13th century. Even more interesting are the frescoes across the street in the little **Cappella del Tau** (*open Mon–Sat 9–2*), so named after the blue 'T' its priests wore on their vestments. The vividly coloured scenes of Adam and Eve and assorted saints are attributed in part to Masolino. The convent of the chapel has become the **Marino Marini centre** (*open Tues–Sat 9–1 and 3–7, Sun 9–12.30; adm*). The collection traces the career of this

Pistoiese artist, who died in 1980, in both paint and sculpture; it includes the bronze *Young Girl* which recalls the antique tradition not only in her facial features but also her truncated arms. Next to it, at No.72, note the coat of arms over the pretty window of two dancing bears, recalling the Giostra dell'Orso. There's another good Gothic façade on **San Paolo**, a block to the east, with broader stripes and a statue of St James on the very top, attributed to Orcagna.

There are more old churches in central Pistoia, but only one other worth going out of your way to visit: **San Bartolomeo in Pantano** (St Bart in the Bog), on the east side of town, built on marshy land in the 8th century and sinking gently into the ground ever since. It has an attractive, partially completed façade, and contains a carved marble lectern of 1250 by Guido da Como.

## The Zoo, the Medici and some Iron

The newest stripes in Pistoia may well be on the zebras in the **Pistoia Zoo** (*open summer 9–7, winter 9–5; adm exp*), 4km northwest of the city in Via Pieve a Celle. Though the Medici always kept big menageries, modern Italians don't usually care for zoos; this is one of the best in the country, even though it's only just over 30 years old. Polar bears, kangaroos, giant turtles, reptiles, and other zoo favourites are in attendance.

Thirteen kilometres to the southeast, off the SS66, is yet another Medici villa, the **Villa della Magia in Quarrata** (*closed for restoration; call t 0573 7710 for info*), begun in 1318. Its grand hall has 18th-century frescoes, and in 1536 Charles V and Alessandro de' Medici met there. In Pistoia itself you can visit one of the city's wrought-iron 'laboratories', **Bartoletti** (*open Mon–Sat; t 0573 452784*), in Via Sestini 110.

# The Mountains of Pistoia

North of Pistoia rises a fairly unspoiled stretch of the central Apennines, luxuriantly forested and endowed with some lovely mountain escape routes, deep green in the summer and ski white in the winter. Main routes include the beautiful Bologna road (SS64) known as the 'Porrettana', which follows the Bologna–Pistoia railway through the sparsely settled mountains, and the equally beautiful, parallel SS632, less encumbered with traffic. The main mountain resorts up to Abetone are along the SS66 and SS12, as easily reached from Lucca as from Pistoia.

Due north of Pistoia, 10km along a byroad towards Piteccio, is the ancient hamlet of **Castagno**, now converted into a unique open-air art gallery. Its lanes are embellished with 20th-century frescoes on the 12 months; modern statues pose in the nooks and crannies; and Castagno's ancient church and oratory dedicated to St Francis, both with interesting frescoes, have recently been restored. A 4km backtrack takes you to the main SS66; at Pontepetri (20km) the SS632 veers north to the formerly popular little mountain resort of **Pracchia**.

Most visitors continue along the SS66 for the newer summer–winter resorts by way of the lovely state forest of Teso, at the fine old villages of **Maresca** and **Gavinana**. The latter is notorious in Florentine history for the defeat of its army by the imperial

# Tourist Information

**San Marcello Pistoiese**: Via Marconi 28,
t 0573 630145, f 0573 622120.
**Cutigliano**: Via Roma 25, t 0573 68029.
**Abetone**: Piazza Piramidi, t 0573 60231.

# Where to Stay and Eat

There's nothing posh about this pretty but neglected corner of Tuscany – nearly all hotels are good bargains. In the mountains, many open only during the ski season and in July and Aug. There are some economical holiday villas near the towns and alpine refuges in the mountains nearby; the tourist office has a complete list.

## San Marcello Pistoiese ✉ 50128

**★★★Il Cacciatore**, Via Marconi 87, t 0573 630533, f 0573 630134 (*moderate*). Pleasant, green and quiet. *Open all year.*

**La Vecchia Cantina**, Via Risorgimento 4, t 0573 64158 (*moderate*). Menus are seasonal and dishes are rooted in local traditions; ravioli with goat's cheese, home-made pasta with courgette flowers and prosciutto, mushrooms or artichokes, boar stewed with wine and chestnuts and pork fillet with apple sauce. Good cheese and wine too. *Closed Tues in winter.*

## Cutigliano ✉ 50124

**★★★Hotel Miramonte**, Piazza Catilina 12, t 0573 68012, f 0573 68013 (*inexpensive*). Quiet with a nice garden and restaurant.

**L'Osteria**, Via Roma 6, t 0573 68272 (*cheap*). Top-class mountain food in the centre of town. Hearty soups, local lamb and pecorino cheeses. *Closed Tues lunch, Mon.*

## Abetone ✉ 51021

This ski resort is somewhat fancier.

**★★★★Il Granduca**, Via Brennero 289, t 0573 60067, f 0573 60585 (*moderate*). More elegant than most. *Open July–Aug and Dec–April.*

**★★★Regina**, Via Uccelleria 5, t 0573 60007, (*expensive–moderate*). On a quieter street. *Open July–mid-Sept and Dec–April.*

**Ostello Renzo Bizzarri**, Via Brennero at Cosuma, t 0573 60117 (*cheap*). The youth hostel, with room for 92. *Open Dec–Mar and July–Aug, longer on demand.*

**Da Pierone**, Via Brennero 556, t 0573 60068 (*moderate*). Rustic family-run restaurant serving local dishes, veal escalope with truffles, excellent choice of wine. *Closed Thurs.*

**La Capannina**, Via Brennero 520, t 0573 60562 (*moderate*). Good choice: rustic décor, local dishes and a wide selection of wines. *Closed Mon and Tues outside high season.*

forces of Charles V, a battle that cost the lives of both commanders. The Florentine leader, Francesco Ferrucci, was knifed in the back, and has his own little museum in the main piazza. The SS66 continues to **San Marcello Pistoiese**, 29km from Pistoia, the 'capital' of the mountains, in a lovely setting, where since 1854 the inhabitants have launched a hot-air balloon each year on 8 September as a farewell to summer. You can walk over the 720ft **suspension bridge of Mammiano** all year round, however. **Cutigliano**, a growing winter resort 7km north, has 27km of ski trails and a cable car up to its highest peak, Doganaccia (1,175m/3,854ft). In the village itself, the **Palazzo Pretorio** fairly bristles with the coats of arms of its former governors.

Near the northern border of Tuscany, through a lush and ancient forest, lies **Abetone** (1,400m/4,592ft), one of the most famous resorts in the central Apennines. Named after a huge fir tree, it grew up in the late 18th century, when Grand Duke Pietro Leopoldo built the road to the Duchy of Modena, designing it not to pass through the detested Papal States (the modern province of Bologna). Two milestones at Abetone mark the old boundary. The closest ski resort to Florence, it is highly developed, with 35km of trails, a new cable car and 23 chairlifts; in summer its cool climate, pools and other facilities make it popular, especially at weekends. In other seasons, rain is not exactly unknown.

# The Valdinievole

## Montecatini Terme

West of Pistoia lies the Valdinievole, the 'Valley of Mists', a land obsessed with water, though mostly of the subterranean, curative variety, available in Italy's most glamorous thermal spa, **Montecatini** (pop. 21,500). Leonardo da Vinci's first known drawing was of a view towards Montecatini from Lamporecchio, near his home town of Vinci (*see* pp.210–11), and it is believed that his lifetime fascination with canals, locks, currents and dams and the misty, watery backgrounds of his most famous paintings come from a childhood spent in the Valdinievole. He even designed a fountain for the baths of Montecatini in one of his notebooks, which after 380 years is now being built of Carrara marble as his monument.

Even in these days of holistic medicine, preventive medicine, herbal cures and pharmaceutical paranoia, the Montecatini tourist board despair that Anglo-Saxons from both sides of the Atlantic refuse to believe that soaking in or drinking mere water can do anything as beneficial for them as imbibing a pitcher of Chianti.

## Getting Around

Montecatini is easily reached by **train** from Florence (51km/1½hrs), Pistoia (16km/25mins) and Lucca (27km/45mins). The station, t 0572 78551, is on Via Toti, as is the LAZZI **bus** terminal, t 0572 911781, with hourly connections (at least until evening) to Florence, Lucca, Pisa, Viareggio and Montecatini Alto; also to Collodi via Pescia (6 daily).

## Tourist Information

Montecatini: Viale G Verdi 66, t/f 0572 772244.

## Where to Stay

### Montecatini Terme ✉ 51016

Even if you don't care to take the waters, you'll have no difficulty finding a room. Italy's choicest spa has no fewer than six hotels that claim the title of 'Grand' and a half-dozen others that only decline to for discretion's sake. **Full board**, not counting breakfast, is the rule in most places; outside high season they might not require it, but ring ahead to make sure. The **APIA hotel association** on Via delle Saline 88, t/f 0572 72603, helps with bookings.

★★★★★**Grand Hotel Bellavista**, Viale Fedeli 2, t 0572 78122, f 0572 73352, *www.pancioli hotels.it* (*luxury*). Among the grandest, offering golf, tennis, indoor pool, luxurious rooms, sauna, health club, and an infinite number of chances for self-indulgence. *Open April–Nov.*

★★★★★**Grand Hotel & La Pace**, Corso Roma 12, t 0572 75801, f 0572 78451, *www.grandhotel lapace.it* (*luxury*). Renowned throughout the rest of Europe for its genuine *belle époque* charm, this hotel has similarly impressive luxuries as the Bellavista; and the restaurant is unquestionably elegant, if expensive. *Open April–Oct.*

★★★★**Grand Hotel Plaza e Locanda Maggiore**, Piazza del Popolo 7, t 0572 75831, f 0572 767985, *www.hotelplaza.it* (*expensive*). This was apparently Verdi's favourite; it has a pool and air-conditioned rooms. *Open all year.*

★★★**Belvedere**, Viale Fedeli 10, t 0572 70251, f 0572 70252, *www.gallinganihotels.it* (*expensive*). One of the more charming choices, featuring an indoor pool, tennis courts and friendly service, next to the Parco delle Terme. *Open April–Oct.*

**Villa Pasquini**, in Massa e Cozile, 8km from Montecatini, t 0572 72205, f 0572 910888, *www.villapasquini.it* (*expensive*). Charming,

Unlike so many continental enthusiasts, we defy the wisdom of the ancients – especially the Romans, who spent the plunder accumulated from conquering the world on ever more fabulous baths. But taking the waters, no matter how hot, radioactive, or chock-full of minerals, is only half the cure; the other is simply relaxation; the chance to stroll through gardens, listen to a little music, linger in a café, to indulgein a bit of the old *dolce far niente*. In Montecatini you can do just that without touching a blessed, unfermented drop, surrounded by *belle époque* nostalgia from the days when the spa seethed with dukes, politicians, literati and actresses; you may recognize it from the film *Dark Eyes* (*Oci Ciornie*), starring Marcello Mastroianni.

## Parco delle Terme

*Baths open May–Oct, exc the Excelsior, which stays open all year.*
*Tickets for a day or subscriptions are available from the central office in*
*Viale Verdi 41, t 0572 778428, f 0572 778444, www.termemontecatini.it.*

A short stroll from the station, past Montecatini's trendy boutiques, cafés, cinemas and some of its 200 hotels up to Viale Verdi, will take you to the town's mineral

friendly and old-fashioned, set in lush gardens with rooms verging on the grand (some of them have frescoes), and a good restaurant.

***Corallo**, Viale Cavallotti 116, t 0572 78288, f 0572 79512, *www.golfhotelcorallo.it* (*moderate*). Small but refined, with a pool and garden, on a quiet side street near the park. *Open all year.*

Il Salotto di Gea, Via Talenti 2, t 0572 904318 (*moderate*). A small hotel (only 8 rooms) in the heart of the old town, a delightful and good-value alternative to some of the rather overblown hotels in Montecatini. Rooms are decorated with unfussy good taste. Breakfast is served on the piazza in summer. The restaurant offers tempting fish and meat dishes: warm octopus salad, spaghetti with mullet roe, aubergine ravioli with pesto, and fillet of beef with a Chianti sauce.

# Eating Out

### Montecatini Terme ✉ 51016

Most guests dine in their hotels, but there are some places that are well worth making the effort to leave the hotel and get there for.

**Enoteca da Giovanni**, Via Garibaldi 25, t 0572 71695 (*very expensive*). Break loose at least once for the imaginative fare at this unique and much-honoured place, where game dishes – hare, venison, wild duck – and fish turn into impeccably *haute cuisine* in the hands of a master chef. *Closed Mon.*

**Ristorante il Cucco**, Via Salsero 3, t 0572 72765 (*expensive*). Elaborate Tuscan cooking, both meat and seafood, at more reasonable prices: try the spaghetti with fresh anchovies and breadcrumbs. *Closed Wed lunch, Tues.*

**Cucina da Giovanni**, Via Garibaldi (*moderate*). Next door to the *Enoteca da Giovanni* (*see above*), offering simple fare at more modest prices (try the wonderful *antipasti* and fabulous *maccheroncini* with duck sauce).

**La Torre**, Piazza Giusti, t 0572 70650 (*moderate–cheap*). A wine bar/restaurant, up in the old town. If you want a full meal (rather than a drink and a snack), there are soups, good pastas and simple meat dishes.

When you get tired of immersing yourself in the health-giving waters, why not dip into the vintages at a wine bar instead? Either of the following should do the trick:

**Enoteca**, Via Forini 13.
**Antinori 'Degustazione Vini'**, Viale Verdi 35.

water Elysium, the immaculately groomed **Parco delle Terme**, where the high temples of the cult dot the shaded lawn. The Lorraine grand dukes, spa-soaks like their Habsburg cousins, were behind the initial development of Montecatini's springs, and many of the baths, or *terme*, are neoclassical pavilions – monumental, classical and floral architecture that lent itself nicely to the later Liberty-style embellishments of the 1920s. You can take in some of these Art Nouveau fancies in Montecatini's Municipio, on Viale Verdi opposite the park, or in the most sumptuous and ancient of its nine major bathing establishments, **Tettuccio**. In the 1370s a group of Florentines attempted to extract mineral salts from the spring and built a little roof (*tettuccio*) over it; and although they failed it was soon discovered that the water had a good effect on rotten livers – one of the first to come here was Francesco Datini, the Merchant of Prato, in 1401. By the 18th century, Tettuccio was in a state of ruin, and Grand Duke Leopold I had it splendidly rebuilt. His façade remains, while the interior was redone by Montecatini's greatest architect, Ugo Giovanozzi, in the 1920s, and embellished with paintings by Italy's Art Nouveau master, Galileo Chini, and ceramic pictures by Cascella in the drinking gallery; there's an elegant café, fountains, a reflecting pool and rotunda, writing hall, music rooms, a little city within a city – all adorned with scenes from an aquatic Golden Age of languid nymphs – surely the perfect place to sip your morning glass of liver-flushing water.

Other establishments, each with their special virtues, are nearby – the Palladian-style arcade of the **Regina** spring; the **Terme Leopoldine**, another grand ducal establishment, with mud baths housed in a temple-like building dedicated to Aesculapius, the god of health; the half-neo-Renaissance, half-modern **New Excelsior baths**; the pretty Tuscan rustic **Tamerici**, in its lush garden; the **Torretta**, with its phony medieval tower and afternoon concerts in the loggia.

## During Digestion

While the water works its way through your system, you can work your way through Montecatini's diversions. The **Art Academy** consists solely of donations from Montecatini's admirers – the piano Verdi used during his annual stays in the Locanda Maggiore, where he composed *Otello*, and art by Salvador Dalí, Galileo Chini, Fattori and many others. Just behind the Parco delle Terme is **Le Panteraie**, a wooded park with a swimming pool, where deer roam freely.

You can play a round at the **Montecatini Golf Course** (*t 0572 62218*), among olive groves and cypresses, or a game of tennis at the centrally situated courts of La Torretta, (*t 0572 78161*). Alternatively you can try to win back your hotel bill at the trotting races at the **Ippodromo**. The **Kursaal**, with cinema, nightclub and games, is a popular meeting place. One of the prettiest excursions is to take the funicular up to **Montecatini Alto**, the original old hill town, with breathtaking views over the Valley of Mists and a charming little piazza with a small theatre; nearby you can visit the stalactites in the **Grotta Maona** (*open April–Oct*).

# Around Montecatini Terme

## Monsummano and Serravalle

Narrow lanes crisscross the Valdinievole landscape, offering a wealth of tempting excursions further afield. Approximately 5km east of Montecatini is its sister spa, **Monsummano Terme**, which as its speciality offers vapour baths in natural grottoes. The first of these was discovered by accident in 1849, when the Giusti family moved a boulder and found the entrance to a stalactite cave. The **Grotta Giusti**, which is 325ft deep, has three small lakes fed by hot springs. These caves, including the steamy **Grotta Parlanti** (*open May–Oct; info t 0572 953029*), are only open to visitors seeking serious thermal treatment.

Monsummano meanwhile hasn't rested on its vapours, but has transformed itself into one of Italy's biggest shoe-making towns; like Montecatini it has an old antecedent atop a hill, **Monsummano Alto**, today all but abandoned, but with a pretty Romanesque church, a romantically ruined castle and splendid views. Another panoramic view may be had from **Montevettolini**, 4km from Monsummano, site of a villa built by Ferdinando I in 1597.

## Where to Stay and Eat

**Monsummano Terme** ✉ 51015
★★★★**Grotta Giusti**, Via Grotta Giusti 171, t 0572 51165, f 0572 51269, *www.grotta giustispa.com* (*luxury*). Near the vaporous grottoes, the villa of the family of the poet Giuseppe Giusti. Recently upgraded and now a very comfortable hotel filled with antiques, rich fabrics, etc. Half or full board obligatory in high season (Aug and Sept, Christmas, Easter). *Open Mar–Nov.*

**Montevettolini** ✉ 51015
**Villa Lucia**, Via dei Bronzoli 144, t 0572 617790, *www.bboftuscany.com* (*very expensive*). An English-style B&B (the *padrona* is American/Italian), in a delightful setting on a hillside, with garden and pool.
**San Michele**, Piazza Bargellini 80, Montevettolini, t 0572 617 547 (*cheap*). A café-bar-restaurant with a tempting array of *antipasti* (smoked salmon, caviar, *carpaccio* with truffles), followed by spaghetti with lobster, perhaps, and prawns. *Closed Mon.*

**Pescia** ✉ 51017
★★★**Villa delle Rose**, Via del Castellare 21, t 0572 4670, f 0572 444 003,

*www.rthotels.com* (*moderate*). Just outside Pescia, with a pleasant garden and pool and comfortable, modern rooms.
**Cecco**, Via Forti 96/98, t 0572 477955 (*moderate*). Fine dining on seasonal dishes starring Pescia's famous asparagus, or wild mushrooms, truffles or zucchini flowers; for dessert, there's *torta di Cecco*, prepared according to an ancient recipe. *Closed Mon.*
**Monte a Pescia**, Via del Monte Ovest 1, Monte a Pescia, t 0572 476887 (*moderate*). A rustic restaurant in a tiny, hilltop hamlet just outside Pescia, with a terrace overlooking the Valdinievole. Home-made pasta is served with asparagus, porcini or game sauce and meat is grilled over an open fire.

**Collodi** ✉ 51014
**All'Osteria del Gambero Rosso**, Parco Collodi, t 0572 429 364 (*moderate–cheap*). Set in the grand Parco Collodi, this restaurant has made a name for its food as much as for its attractive surroundings. The building was designed by Giovanni Michelucci, arguably one of Italy's greatest 20th-century architects. Tuck into cannelloni, *tagliolini* with porcini mushrooms and prosciutto, and excellent crêpes stuffed with seafood or spinach. *Closed Mon eve and Tues.*

Continuing east, the old fortress at **Serravalle Pistoiese** 'locks the valley' between the Apennines and Monte Albano. Its old Lombard tower and 14th-century additions saw considerable action in Tuscany's days of inter-urban hooliganism.

## Pescia

To the west of Montecatini, there's another attractive old hill town, **Buggiano Castello**, and for those who imagine that frescoes went out of fashion years ago, there's San Michele in nearby **Ponte Buggianese**, freshly frescoed in stark colours by Pietro Annigoni. The colours are even more dazzling in **Pescia** (pop. 20,000), Italy's capital of flowers, a title snatched from San Remo on the Riviera. Some three million cut flowers are sent off every summer's day from Pescia's giant market; besides the gladioli, it is celebrated by gourmets for its tender asparagus and *fagioli*.

Pescia has several interesting monuments, beginning with a 14th-century church of **San Francesco**, containing Bonaventura Berlinghieri's 1235 portrait of St Francis with scenes from his life, considered to be one of the most authentic likenesses of the saint; also take a look at the *Crucifixion* by Puccio Capanna in the sacristy. The **Duomo** was rebuilt in the 1600s, but has a fine Romanesque campanile sporting a little cupola, and a late terracotta triptych by Luca della Robbia. On the long, narrow Piazza Mazzini stands the imposing **Palazzo del Vicario**; in nearby **Sant'Antonio**, from the 1360s, look up the 'Ugly Saints', a 13th-century wooden *Deposition from the Cross*.

The green, hilly region of prosperous villages north of Pescia in the upper Valdinievole is known as 'Little Switzerland'. In its cheerful core, some 12km from Pescia, stands one of Italy's most bizarre churches, the 12th-century **Pieve di Castelvecchio**, decorated with grinning and grimacing stone masks.

## Collodi and Pinocchio

Just west of Pescia is **Collodi**. As a child, Florentine writer Carlo Lorenzo (1826–90) often visited his uncle who worked in the castle, and took the name Collodi as his own when he published his *Adventures of Pinocchio*. In his honour the town has built the **Parco di Pinocchio** (*open 8.30–sunset; adm*), with a bronze statue of the character by Emilio Greco and a piazza of mosaics with scenes from the book by Venturino Venturi, as well as other figures, all very much in the angular style of the late 1950s and early 60s; there's a lawn maze, a museum dedicated to the book, a playground and other amusements for the kids. Adults, meanwhile, can try to work their way through a much older labyrinth in the magnificent, recently restored hillside gardens of the **Castello Garzoni** (*gardens open mid-Nov–mid-Mar, Sun only, 9–one hour before sunset; adm*), designed in the 17th century by Ottaviano Diodati of Lucca and considered one of the finest late Italian gardens, ornate with a labyrinth, fountains and statuary. The castle 'of a hundred windows' has a few grand rooms, and the kitchen where young Carlo sat and dreamed up Pinocchio.

# Lucca, the Garfagnana and Lunigiana

10

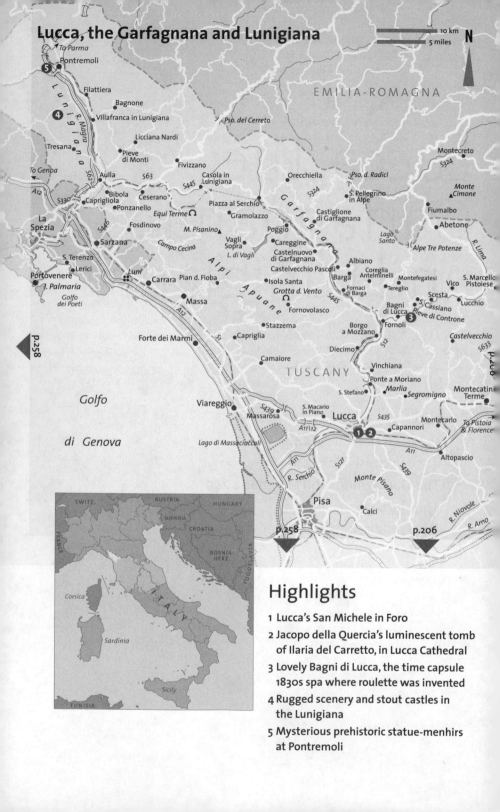

# Lucca, the Garfagnana and Lunigiana

10 km
5 miles

N

**EMILIA-ROMAGNA**

**5** Pontremoli
To Parma

Filattiera

Bagnone

Villafranca in Lunigiana

Pso. del Cerreto

Montecreto
S324

Licciana Nardi

**4** Tresana

Pieve di Monti

Fivizzano

Casola in Lunigiana

Orecchiella

Pso. d. Radici

S. Pellegrino in Alpe

Monte Cimone

Fiumalbo

R. Magra

Lunigiana

To Genoa

Aulla
S63
S445

Piazza al Serchio

Castiglione di Garfagnana

Abetone

S62

Bibola
Caprigliola
Ponzanello

Ceserano

Gramolazzo

Garfagnana

Lago Santo

Alpe Tre Potenze

R. Lima

S330
S446

La Spezia

Fosdinovo

Equi Terme

M. Pisanino

Poggio

Careggine

Castelnuovo di Garfagnana

S324

Albiano

Coreglia Antelminelli

Montefegatesi

S. Marcello Pistoiese

Vico

Sarzana

Campo Cecina

Vagli Sopra
L. di Vagli

Castelvecchio Pascoli

Barga

Fornaci di Barga

Tereglio

Scesta

Lucchio

S. Terenzo
Lerici

Luni

Carrara

Pian d. Fioba

Alpi

Isola Santa

Grotta d. Vento

S445

Bagni di Lucca
**3**

S. Cassiano
Pieve di Controne

Portovenere

I. Palmaria

Golfo dei Poeti

A12

Massa

Apuane

Fornovolasco

Borgo a Mozzano

Fornoli

Castelvecchio

S633

p.416

p.258

Forte dei Marmi

Stazzema

Capriglia

S1

Diecimo

S12

Vinchiana

Montecatini Terme

Camaiore

**TUSCANY**

Ponte a Moriano

S. Stefano

Marlia

Segromigno

Golfo

Viareggio

S439

Massarosa

S. Macario in Piano

Lucca

S435

Montecarlo

To Pistoia & Florence

di Genova

Lago di Massaciuccoli

A11/12

**1** **2**

Capannori

A11

Altopascio

A11

R. Serchio

S12r

Monte Pisano

S439

R. Niovole

p.258

**Pisa**

Calci

p.206

R. Arno

SWITZ.
AUSTRIA
HUNGARY

FRANCE

SLOVENIA

CROATIA

BOSNIA-HERZ.

YUGOSLAVIA

Corsica

ITALY

Sardinia

Sicily

TUNISIA

# Highlights

1 Lucca's San Michele in Foro

2 Jacopo della Quercia's luminescent tomb of Ilaria del Carretto, in Lucca Cathedral

3 Lovely Bagni di Lucca, the time capsule 1830s spa where roulette was invented

4 Rugged scenery and stout castles in the Lunigiana

5 Mysterious prehistoric statue-menhirs at Pontremoli

# Lucca

*Nowhere in Lucca*
*will you see the face of a Philistine.*
Heine, *Travels in Lucca*

Of all Tuscany's great cities, Lucca (pop. 92,500) is the most cosy, sane and domestic, a tidy gem of a town encased within its famous walls. Yet even these hardly seem formidable, more like garden walls than something that would keep the Florentines at bay. The old ramparts and surrounding areas, once the outworks of the fortifications, are now full of lawns and trees; on the walls, where the city's soldiers once patrolled, citizens ride their bicycles, walk their dogs, and stop to admire the view.

Like paradise, Lucca is entered by way of St Peter's Gate. Once inside you'll find tidy, well-preserved Romanesque churches and medieval towers that destroyed Ruskin's romantic notion that a medieval building had to be half-ruined to be beautiful, a revelation that initiated his study of architecture. Nor do Lucca's numerous Liberty-style shop signs show any sign of rust; even the mandatory peeling ochre paint and green shutters of the houses seem part of some great municipal housekeeping plan. Bicycles have largely replaced cars within the walls. At first glance it seems too bijou, but after its long and brave history it has earned the right to a little quiet. The hordes of tourists leave Lucca alone for the most part, though a small number of discreet visitors, many of them German and Swedish, come back every year. They don't spread the word, apparently trying to keep one of Italy's most beautiful cities to themselves.

## History

Lucca's rigid grid of streets betrays its Roman origins; it was founded as a colony in 180 BC as *Luca*, and it was here in 56 BC that Caesar, Pompey and Crassus met to form the ill-fated First Triumvirate. It was converted to Christianity early on by St Peter's disciple Paulinus, who became first bishop of Lucca. The city did especially well in the Dark Ages; in late Roman times it was the administrative capital of Tuscany, and under the Goths managed to repulse the murderous Lombards; its extensive archives were begun in the 8th century, and many of its churches were founded shortly after. By the 11th and 12th centuries Lucca emerged as one of the leading trading towns of Tuscany, specializing in the production of silk, sold by colonies of merchants in the East and West, who earned enough to make sizeable loans to Mediterranean potentates. A Lucchese school of painting developed, and beautiful Romanesque churches were erected, influenced by nearby Pisa. Ghibellines and Guelphs, and then Black and White Guelphs made nuisances of themselves as they did everywhere else, and Lucca often found itself pressed to maintain its independence from Pisa and Florence.

In 1314, at the height of the city's wealth and power, the Pisans and Ghibellines finally managed to seize it. But Lucca had a trump card: a remarkable adventurer named Castruccio Castracani, an ambitious noble who lived for years in exile – part of it in England. When he heard the bad news he at once set forth to rescue his home town. Within a year he had chased the Pisans out and seized power for himself,

to Bagni di Lucca

VIALE AGOSTINO MARI

VIALE BARSANTI

VIALE P. BATONI

PIAZZALE MARTIRI
DELLA LIBERTÀ

BALUARDO
SAN
MARTINO

P

BALUARDO
CESARE
BATTISTI

PASSEGGIATA DELLE MURA URBANE

D. CAVALLERIZZA

PIAZZA MARIA
DEL BORGO

P

VIA MICHELE ROSI

VIALE GUGLIELMO MARCONI

P

VIA FILLUNGO

VIA BUSDRAGHI

VIA SANTA GEMMA GALGANI

VIA DELLA ZECCA

VIA DEL FOSSO

P

Roman
Amphitheatre

San Pietro
Somaldi

San Francesco

A DELL'ANFITEATRO

PIAZZA
S. PIETRO
SOMALDI

P

VIA
D. FRATTA

Santa Maria
dello Stellario

PIAZZA
S. FRANCESCO

VIA DELLA QUARQUONIA

BALUARDO
SAN
SALVATORE

VIA ANTONIO MORDINI

Museo Nazionale
Guinigi

to Florence,
Montecatini Terme

PIAZZA DEL
CARMINE

VIA DI CHIAVI D'ORO

Torre
Guinigi

VIA GUINIGI

VIA DEL'ANGELO CUSTODE

VIA SAN NICOLAO

VIA DEL FOSSO

Villa
Bottini
Gardens

VIA SANTA CHIARA

VIA BRUNERO PAOLI

SANT' ANDREA

VIA FATINELLI

PIAZZALE DON
ALDO MEI

VIALE G. PACINI

Porta
San Gervasio

VIA ELISA

PIAZZA
BERNARDINI

VIA SANTA CROCE

Santa Maria
Forisportam

Santa
Trinità

PIAZZA
DEI SERVI

P

PIAZZA
SANTA MARIA
FORISPORTAM

BALUARDO
CAIROLL

VIA A. VALLISNERI

VIA DELLA ROSA

VIA DEL GIARDINO

Botanico

VIA SAN NICOLAO

Giardino
Botanico

PIAZZA
NTELMINELLI

VIA DEL
DUOMO

Duomo

Santa Maria
della Rosa

VIA DEL FOSSO

PASSEGGIATA DELLE MURA URBANE

BALUARDO
SAN REGOLO

P

BALUARDO
SAN
COLOMBANO

VIALE GIUSEPPE GIUSTI

N

PIAZZALE
RICASOLI

Train
Station

200 metres
200 yards

leading Lucca into its most heroic age, capturing most of western Tuscany to form a Luccan empire, subjugating even Pisa and Pistoia. After routing the Florentines at Altopascio in 1325, Castracani was planning to snatch Florence too, but died of malaria just before the siege was to begin. Bickering between the powerful local families soon put an end to Lucca's glory days, though in 1369 the city managed to convince Emperor Charles IV to grant it independence as a republic, albeit a republic ruled by oligarchs like Paolo Guinigi, the sole big boss between 1400 and 1430.

But Lucca continued to escape being gobbled up by its voracious neighbours, surviving even after the arrival of the Spaniards – perhaps due not so much to its

## Getting Around

The **railway** station is just south of the walls on Piazza Ricasoli, with lots of trains on the Viareggio–Pisa–Florence line, t 0583 892021. **Buses** leave from Piazzale Verdi, just inside the walls on the western end: LAZZI buses to Florence, Pistoia, Pisa, Prato, Bagni di Lucca, Abetone, Montecatini and Viareggio (t 0583 584876); and CLAP (that's right, CLAP) buses to towns within Lucca province, including Collodi, Marlia and Segromigno, as well as the Serchio valley (t 0583 587897). Get around Lucca itself like a Lucchese by hiring a **bicycle** from Poli (t 0583 493787) or Bizzarri (t 0583 496031), both in the Piazza Santa Maria.

## Tourist Information

**Lucca**: Vecchia Porta San Donato, Piazzale Verdi, t 0583 583150, *www.carismalucca.it*. **Piazza S. Maria**: t 0583 919931, *www.luccaturismo.it*.

## Where to Stay

### Lucca and Around ✉ 55100

Lucca can be less than charm city if you arrive without booking ahead; there simply aren't enough rooms (especially inexpensive ones) to meet demand.

*****Locanda l'Elisa**, Via Nova per Pisa, Massa Pisana, t 0583 379 737, *www. locandalelisa.com (luxury)*. Part of the Relais et Châteaux group, this bright blue, French-style 18th-century villa is set in a glorious mature garden. Public rooms and bedrooms are luxuriously appointed and

furnished with antiques and elegant fabrics, with canopies over the beds. There is a conservatory restaurant (*expensive*) and a pool. *Closed Jan.*

****Alla Corte degli Angeli**, Via degli Angeli 23, t 0583 469204, f 0583 991989, *www. allacortedegliangeli.com (very expensive)*. Modern B&B with attractive, comfortable rooms; bathrooms have jacuzzis.

****Ilaria**, Via del Fosso 20, t 0583 476158, *www.hotelilaria.com (very expensive)*. Recently upgraded to a four-star hotel, smart comfortable rooms and car park.

***La Luna**, Corte Compagni 12, t 0583 493634, f 0583 490021, *www.hotellaluna. com (expensive)*. A cosy place, recently renovated, in a quiet part of the centre, with a private garage for your car.

***Universo**, Piazza Puccini, t 0583 493678, f 0583 954854, *www.hoteluniverso.it (expensive)*. Within the walls, a slightly frayed, green-shuttered and delightful hotel, in the centre. Ruskin slept here, paving the way for nearly everyone else who followed him to Lucca. Some rooms are better than others.

***Piccolo Hotel Puccini**, Via di Poggio 9, t 0583 55421, f 0583 53487, *www.hotel puccini.com (moderate)*. A central, small, comfortable hotel with 14 rooms.

**Diana** Via del Molinetto 11, t 0583 592202, f 0583 47795 (*moderate*). Friendly and well run, with some of the nicest inexpensive rooms in Tuscany, some with bath. Now has a more up-market annexe nearby.

**Villa Casanova**, Via Casanova, just outside the city at Balbano, t 0583 548429, f 0583 368955 (*moderate*). This has simple rooms but a pleasant garden, as well as tennis and a swimming pool to lounge by.

great walls as to its relative insignificance. Amazingly enough, after the Treaty of Câteau-Cambrésis, Lucca stood together with Venice as the only truly independent states in Italy. And, like Venice, the city was an island of relative tolerance and enlightenment during the Counter-Reformation, its walls proving stout enough to deflect the Inquisition. In 1805 Lucca's independence ended when Napoleon gave the republic to his sister Elisa Baciocchi, who ruled as its princess; it was given later to Marie-Louise, Napoleon's widow, who governed well enough to become Lucca's favourite ruler and earn a statue in the main Piazza Napoleone. Her son sold it to Leopold II of Tuscany in 1847, just in time for it to join the Kingdom of Italy.

**Affittacamere S. Frediano**, Via degli Angeli 19, t 0583 469630 (*moderate*). Six spotless, nicely furnished rooms (not all with private bath) near the Anfiteatro.

**Da Elisa alle Sette Arti**, Via Elisa 25, t 0583 494539, f 0583 471609, *www.daelisa.com* (*inexpensive*). This good value guest house offers nine pretty and airy rooms in the centre of town with use of kitchen. Breakfast is taken at a neighbouring bar.

**Locanda Buatino**, Borgo Giannotti 508, t 0583 343207, f 0583 343298 (*inexpensive*). Just outside the city walls to the north, with five simple but welcoming rooms above a restaurant of the same name (*see* below).

# Eating Out

Within the walls:

**Il Giglio**, Piazza del Giglio, t 0583 494058 (*expensive*). Lucca's best seafood place, in Hotel Universo – river trout is a speciality. *Closed Tues eve and Wed.*

**La Buca di Sant'Antonio**, Via della Cervia 3, t 0583 55881 (*moderate*). An inn since 1782, offering old recipes like smoked herring and kid on a spit, newer dishes like ravioli with ricotta and sage. *Closed Mon.*

**Da Giulio in Pelleria** Via Conce, t 0583 55948, (*moderate*). Less expensive, surprisingly sophisticated twists on 'peasant' fare. Booking advised. *Closed Sun and Mon.*

**Vineria dei Santi**, Vineria I Santi, Via dell'Anfiteatro 29a, t 0583 496124 (*moderate*). Tucked behind Piazza dell'Anfiteatro, this restaurant/wine bar has a pretty terrace. You can order a glass of good wine and snack on a selection of cheeses and salamis and hams or go for something more substantial from the daily menu: honey-glazed turkey breast or baby squid (*moscardini*) soup.

**Buatino**, Via Borgo Giannotti 508, t 0583 343207 (*cheap*). Here you can enjoy good-value, excellent meals in lively surroundings: there's *zuppa di farro*, delicious roast pork, salt cod with leeks, and more. *Closed Sun.*

**Da Leo**, Via Tegrini 1, t 0583 492236 (*cheap*). Pretty chaotic, full of both locals and tourists. Rabbit stewed with olives, and veal with green peppers; fish only on Fridays. *Closed Sun.*

**Gli Orti di Via Elisa**, Via Elisa 17, t 0583 491241 (*cheap*). This cheerful *trattoria* is great for an inexpensive meal. Pizzas, salads, plus good pastas, etc. *Closed Thurs lunch, Wed.*

**Caffé di Simo**, Via Fillungo 58. Come here for a drop of java in a classic turn-of-the-century *gran caffé*.

Lucca's table service will be particularly memorable if you have the horsepower to get out to some of the villages in its immediate surroundings:

**La Mora**, Via Sesto di Moriano 104, Ponte a Moriano, t 0583 406402 (*expensive*). North of Lucca, in an old posthouse with four cosy rooms inside and dining outside under a pergola in the summer. According to the season, choose delicious ravioli flavoured with marjoram, roast lamb, pigeon or local freshwater fish.

**Vipore**, in nearby Pieve Santo Stefano, t 0583 394065 (*expensive*). Located in a 200-year-old farmhouse, with views over the fertile plain of Lucca. Top-quality prime ingredients go into fresh pasta and meat dishes. *Closed Mon.*

## The Walls

Lucca's lovely bastions evoke the walled rose gardens of chivalric romance, enclosing a smaller, more perfect cosmos. They owe their charm to Renaissance advances in military technology. Prompted by the beginning of the Wars of Italy, Lucca began to construct the walls in 1500. The councillors wanted up-to-date fortifications to counter new advances in artillery, and their (unknown) architects gave them state-of-the-art examples, a model for the new style of fortification soon to transform the cities of Europe. Being Renaissance Tuscans, the architects also gave them a little more elegance than was strictly necessary. The walls were never severely tested. Today, with the outer ravelins, fosses and salients cleared away (such earthworks usually took up as much space as the city itself), Lucca's walls are just for decoration; under the peace-loving Duchess Marie-Louise they were planted with a double row of plane trees to create a 4km elevated garden boulevard, offering a continuous bird's-eye view over Lucca. They are among the best preserved in Italy. Of the gates, the most elaborate is the 16th-century **St Peter's Gate**, near the station, its portcullis still intact, with Lucca's motto of independence, LIBERTAS, inscribed over the entrance. One of the best ways to explore the walls is by bicycle; hire one (see p.242) and do a circular tour.

## San Martino Cathedral

*Open summer Mon–Fri 9.30–5.45, Sat 9.30–6.45, Sun 9–9.50, 11.30–11.50 and 1–5; winter Mon–Sat 9.30–5.*

Through St Peter's Gate (Porta San Pietro), and then to the right, Corso Garibaldi leads to Lucca's cathedral (Duomo), perhaps the most outstanding work of the Pisan style outside Pisa, begun in the 11th century and completed only in the 15th. Above the singular porch, with three different-sized arches, are three levels of colonnades, with pillars arranged like candy sticks, while behind and on the arches are exquisite 12th- and 13th-century reliefs and sculpture – the best work Lucca has to offer. Look out especially for the *Adoration of the Magi* by Nicola Pisano, for the column carved with the Tree of Life, with Adam and Eve crouched at the bottom and Christ on top, and a host of fantastical animals and hunting scenes, the months and their occupations, mermaids and dragons (see Pienza, p.374), and a man embracing a bear, even *Roland at Roncevalles*, all by unknown masters. There is also a medieval maze on the right side of the portico, which you can trace with your finger. Walk round the back, where the splendidly ornate apse and transepts are set off by the green lawn. The crenellated **Campanile** dates from 1060 and 1261.

The dark interior offers an excellent introduction to the works of Lucca's one and only great artist, **Matteo Civitali** (1435–1501), a barber until his mid-30s, when he decided he'd much rather be a sculptor. He deserves to be better known – but may never be, since everything he made is still in Lucca. His most famous work is the octagonal **Tempietto** (1484), a marble tabernacle in the middle of the left aisle, containing Lucca's most precious holy relic, the world-weary *Volto Santo* (Holy Image), a cedar-wood crucifix said to be a true portrait of Jesus, sculpted by Nicodemus, an eye-witness to the crucifixion. Saved from the iconoclasts, it was set adrift in an empty boat and floated to Luni, where the bishop was instructed by an angel to place it in a cart drawn by two white oxen, and where the oxen should halt, there should the image remain. They lumbered to Lucca, where the *Volto Santo* has remained. Its likeness appeared on the republic's coins, and there was a devoted cult of the image in medieval England; Lucca's merchant colony in London cared for a replica in old St Thomas's, and according to William of Malmesbury, King William Rufus always swore by it, '*per sanctum vultum de Lucca*'. Long an object of pilgrimage, the image goes out for a night on the town in a candlelight procession each 13 September.

Further up the left aisle a chapel contains Fra Bartolommeo's *Virgin and Child Enthroned*. Here, too, is an altarpiece by Giambologna, *Christ with SS. Peter and Paul*. Civitali carved the cathedral's high altar, and also two tombs in the south transept. A door from the right aisle leads to the sacristy (*adm*), where you can see Lucca's real icon, the remarkable **Tomb of Ilaria del Carretto** (1408), perhaps Jacopo della Quercia's most beautiful work, a tender, effigy of the young bride of boss Paolo Guinigi, with a dog at her feet, waiting for his mistress to awaken. The city has always had a strange love–hate relationship with this lovely statue. Right after her husband was over-thrown they hustled her out of the cathedral, and she didn't come back for centuries. Near the statue is a *Madonna Enthroned with Saints* by Domenico Ghirlandaio.

A side altar near the sacristy has a typically strange composition from the Venetian Tintoretto, a *Last Supper* with a nursing mother in the foreground and cherubs floating around Christ. In the centre, unfortunately often covered up, is a particularly fine section of the inlaid marble floor; on the entrance wall, a 13th-century sculpture of St Martin has been brought in from the façade.

An **Antiques Market** takes place in the cathedral's Piazza di San Martino the third Saturday and Sunday of each month. Next to the cathedral is the **Museo della Cattedrale** (*open mid-Mar–Oct daily 10–6, Nov–mid-Mar Mon–Fri 10–2, Sat and Sun 10–5; adm*). Its treasures, include the crown and garments of the *Volto Santo*, some good 13th-century reliquaries and pyxes, tapestries and paintings from Lucca's ancient cathedral, San Giovanni, and della Quercia's *St John the Evangelist*. The museum's upstairs windows afford a close-up view of some of the wonderful sculpture on the cathedral.

Across Piazza San Martino from the cathedral, **San Giovanni e Santa Reparata** (*open daily 10–6; adm*) was Lucca's original cathedral. The exterior has only parts of an 1187 portal to show for its old distinction, but inside there are some surprises. Excavations during the 1970s uncovered a series of buildings: the site of a 5th-century basilica, adjacent to it a huge, square **baptistry** from the 1300s, and under this the original Roman font – a walk-in model for total immersion baptisms – with bits of its mosaics, as well as later Romanesque pavements and a bishop's chair. San Giovanni also has a superb painted coffered ceiling and, above the main door, an attractive organ case, though the pipes have been removed. Lucca was once a city of organ builders, and many of the churches have beautifully crafted instruments with elaborate cases.

## Piazza Napoleone and Piazza San Michele

San Giovanni lies on the Via del Duomo between Piazza San Martino and Lucca's shady twin squares, **Piazza del Giglio** and **Piazza Napoleone**, the focus of the Lucchesi evening *passeggiata*. The architectural hotchpotch of a palace on Piazza Napoleone, formerly seat of the republican council, has been called the **Palazzo Ducale** ever since it was used by Lucca's queen for a day, Elisa Bonaparte Baciocchi. In the 16th century, Ammannati had a go at it, and the courtyard, at least, still preserves signs of his Mannerist handiwork. One of Matteo Civitali's most beautiful works, the tomb of San Romano, is in the rarely opened church of **San Romano**, behind the Palazzo.

Via Vittorio Veneto leads from Piazza Napoleone into Piazza San Michele, with a church many people mistake for Lucca's cathedral. Built about the same time, and with a similar Pisan façade, it is almost as impressive. The full name, **San Michele in Foro** (*open daily 7.30–12 and 3–6*), stems from its location on what was Roman Lucca's forum. The ambitious façade rises high above the level of the roof, to make the building look even grander. Every column in the Pisan arcading is different; some doubled, some twisted like corkscrews, inlaid with mosaic Cosmati work, or carved with fanciful figures and beasts, exquisite work similar to the cathedral's, and recently completely restored. The whole is crowned by a giant statue of the Archangel – note the bracelet on his arm, set with real jewels. On the corner of the façade is a Madonna by Civitali; the graceful, rectangular campanile is Lucca's tallest and loveliest.

Inside, there's a glazed terracotta *Madonna and Child* attributed to Luca della Robbia, a striking 13th-century *Crucifixion* over the high altar and a painting of plague saints by Filippino Lippi. Giacomo Puccini began his musical career as a choirboy in San Michele (his father and grandfather had been organists in the cathedral) – he didn't have far to go, as he was born in Via di Poggio 30, just across the street. The house is now a little **Puccini Museum** (*entrance in Corte San Lorenzo 9; open summer Tues–Sun 10–1 and 3–7*), with manuscripts, letters, mementos, the overcoat and odds and ends of the great composer, as well as the piano he used to compose *Turandot*.

## Pinacoteca Nazionale

The quarter west of San Michele is perfumed by the big state tobacco factory, which produces Toscanelli cigars, the world's vilest smokes. Via San Paolino (the Roman *decumanus major*) leads to the church of **San Paolino** where little Puccini played the organ to earn some pin-money. It contains two beautiful works: a 13th-century French *Madonna and Child* brought back by Lucchese merchants from Paris, and an anonymous quattrocento Florentine *Coronation of the Virgin*, with Mary hovering over a city of pink towers; unusually she is crowned by God the Father instead of Christ.

The **Pinacoteca Nazionale** (*open Tues–Sat 8.30–7, Sun 8.30–1; adm*) is housed in the 17th-century Palazzo Mansi, in Via Galli Tassi. Most of the art, as well as the rich furnishings, dates from the 17th century. Portraits by Pontormo and Bronzino hang in the Prima Sala after the large hall: the Salone has a dark, damaged Veronese, and a follower of Tintoretto's *Miracle of St Mark Freeing the Slave*, showing the saint dive-bombing from heaven to save the day. There is also a set of neoclassical reliefs from the Palazzo Ducale of the *Triumphs of Duchess Maria Luisa*. The 1600s frescoes are more fun than the paintings, especially the *Judgement of Paris*, which Venus wins by showing a little leg. And one can't help but wonder what rococo dreams tickled the fancy of the occupants of the amazing bedroom.

## San Frediano and the Amphitheatre

East of San Michele, medieval **Via Fillungo** and its surrounding lanes make up the busy shopping district, a tidy grid of straight and narrow alleys where Lucca's contented cheerfulness seems somehow magnified. Along Via Fillungo you can trace the old loggias of 14th-century palaces, now bricked in, and the ancient **Torre delle Ore** (tower of hours), which since 1471 has striven to keep the Lucchesi on time, and perhaps now suggests that it's time for a coffee in Lucca's historic **Caffè di Simo** at Via Fillungo 58. At Via Fillungo's northern end stands the tall church and taller campanile of **San Frediano**, built in the early 1100s, and shimmering with the colours of the large mosaic on its upper façade, showing Christ and the Apostles in elegant flowing style. The 11th-century bronze Arabian falcon at the top is a copy – the original is kept in a safe. The palatial interior houses Tuscany's most remarkable baptismal font, the 12th-century *Fontana lustrale* carved with reliefs, and behind it, a lunette of the *Annunciation* by Andrea della Robbia. On the left are several chapels, one with frescoes by Aspertini. The last chapel on the left has an altarpiece and two tomb slabs by Jacopo della Quercia and his assistants. The bedecked mummy is St Zita, patroness of maids and ladies-in-waiting; even in England maids belonged to the Guild of St Zita. The Lucchesi are very fond of her, and on 26 April they bring her body out to caress.

Next to San Frediano, on Via degli Asili, the **Palazzo Pfanner** (*open Mar–Oct daily 10–6; Nov–Feb by appt only, t 340 923 3085*) has an 18th-century garden, a fine staircase, a collection of silks made in Lucca, and 17th- to 19th-century costumes. In the other direction, skirting Via Fillungo, narrow arches lead into something most visitors miss, the **Roman Amphitheatre**. Only outlines of its arches are still traceable in the outer walls, while within the inner ring only the form remains – the marble was probably carted off to build San Michele and the cathedral – but the outline has been perfectly preserved. The foundations of the grandstands now support a perfect ellipse of medieval houses. Duchess Marie-Louise cleared out the old buildings in the former arena, and now, where gladiators once slugged it out, boys play football and the less active while away the time in cafés and shops around the piazza.

The streets in this quarter have scarcely changed in the past 500 years. Along Via Sant'Andrea and narrow Via Guinigi, you'll pass a number of resolutely medieval palaces, including that of the Guinigi family. Their lofty stronghold, the **Torre Guinigi** (*mid-Sept–Feb daily 9.30–6; Mar 9.30–7; April 9.30–8; summer 9–midnight; adm*), stands next to their palace and is one of Lucca's landmarks, with a tree sprouting out of its top – the best example of that quaint Italian fancy. The tower has been restored and it's worth the stiff climb up for the view over the city and the Apuan Alps.

## The East Side

Roman Lucca ended near the Guinigi palace, and when a new church was built in the early 12th century it was outside the gate, hence the name of **Santa Maria Forisportam** in Via Santa Croce, a pretty church in the Pisan style with blind arcades. Inside, it not only looks but smells terribly old, and contains two paintings by the often esoteric Guercino. Beyond the church is the best-preserved gate of 1260, the **Porta San Gervasio** giving on to the former moat, now a picturesque little canal running along Via del Fosso. Just across the canal from the gate is **Santa Trinità** (*if closed, ask for the key in the convent next door*), home of Civitali's *Madonna della Tosse* (Our Lady of the Cough), a bit too syrupy sweet, but perhaps that helped the cure. Nearby on Via Elisa is the entrance to the **Villa Bottini gardens** (*open Sun–Fri 9–7*), one of the few green oases inside the city walls.

At the northern end of Via del Fosso stands a 17th-century column dedicated to another Madonna, and to the east, the church of **San Francesco**, a typical 13th-century Franciscan preaching church with the tombs of Castracani and Lucchese composer Luigi Boccherini (d. 1805) – he of the famous *minuet* – and some detached frescoes of the Florentine school. Beyond San Francesco stands the palatial brick Villa Guinigi, built in 1418 by the big boss Paolo Guinigi in his glory days. Now the **Museo Nazionale Guinigi** (*open Tues–Sat 8.30–7, Sun 8.30–1; adm*), its ground floor houses a collection of Romanesque reliefs, capitals and transennas, some of which are charmingly primitive – St Michael slaying the dragon, Samson killing the lion, a 9th-century transenna with birds and beasts, spirals and daggers. Upstairs, room XI has a lovely *Annunciation* by Civitali. The painting gallery contains intarsia panels from the cathedral, each with scenes of Lucca as seen from town windows, some trecento works by the Lucca school and a charming quattrocento *Madonna and Child* by the 'Maestro della Vita di Maria'. Other rooms contain oversized 16th-century canvases, some by Vasari.

## Villas around Lucca

In 16th-century Lucca, as elsewhere in Italy, trade began to flounder, and merchants turned to the joys of property, where they could decline genteelly in a little country palace and garden. For the Lucchesi, the preferred site for such pleasure domes was in the soft, rolling country to the north and northeast of the city. Three of these villas or their grounds are open for visits. In Segromigno, 10km from Lucca towards Pescia, there's the charming, mid-16th-century but often modified **Villa Mansi** (*open summer 10–1 and 3–6, winter 10–1 and 3–5; adm*), embellished with a half-Italian (geometric) and half-English (not geometric) garden by the Sicilian architect Juvarra.

Nearby in Camigliano, the even more elaborate **Villa Torrigiani** (*villa and park open Mar–mid-Nov Wed–Mon 10–1 and 3–sunset; in winter call ahead t 0583 928041; adm exp*), also begun in the 16th century , was celebrated for its fabulous parties and entertainments. Set in a lush park of pools and trees, it has 16th–18th century furnishings. Elisa Bonaparte Baciocchi combined a villa and a summer palace to make her country retreat, now called the **Villa Pecci-Blunt ex-Villa Reale** in Marlia. Only the park and the Giardino Orsetti are open, but they are worth the trip (*tours by appt, t 0583 30108; Mar–Nov Tues–Sun at 10, 11, 12, 3, 4, 5 and 6; Dec–Feb call ahead; adm*).

## The Lucchese Plain

East and west of Lucca, what was swampland in the Middle Ages has been reclaimed to form a rich agricultural plain. One of its features are its 'courts' – farm hamlets not constructed around a central piazza, but with houses in neat rows. At one time there were 1,100 such courts on the plain. Among the highlights of the area is curious **Castello di Nozzano** just to the west, built by Matilda of Tuscany on a hill, its pretty tower now incongruously topped by a large clock. To the east, one of the first villages, **Capannori**, is the head town of several courts and has a couple of interesting Romanesque churches, especially the 13th-century **Pieve San Paolo**, around which a small village incorporated itself, using the campanile for defence. The most imposing monument nearby is the 19th-century **Acquedotto del Nottolini**, which is also visible from the *autostrada*. Just south is the pretty hill-top village of **Castelvecchio**, its tall houses forming an effective circular wall. **Altopascio**, on the Lucca–Empoli road, was built around an 11th-century hospice run by an obscure chivalric order called the Hospitaller Knights of the Order of Altopascio, who originally occupied themselves with rescuing travellers from the swamps. Only the campanile of their church remains in the village today. **Montecarlo** gives its name to a very good dry white wine produced in the immediate area.

# The Garfagnana and Lunigiana

The rugged northern finger of Tuscany encompasses the region's 'Alps', the tall and jagged **Alpi Apuane**, which like the real Alps wear brilliant white crowns, though not made of snow – that's marble up there, the 'tears of the stars', the purest and whitest in Italy. Historically the land is divided into two mini-regions: along the bank of the Serchio river, between the Apuan Alps and the Apennines, is the **Garfagnana**; while the region north of the village of Piazza al Serchio is the **Lunigiana**, former hinterland of the ancient Roman port of Luni.

The Garfagnana and Lunigiana are relatively undiscovered, and threaten to dispel many people's typical image of Tuscany; the mountains are too high, the valleys are too narrow, and you're more likely to find yourself amidst pine forests than vineyards and olive groves. However, a spell in this striking mountain scenery can be just what you need when the thought of cathedrals or art galleries begins to pall.

## The Garfagnana

For many years the chief export of the Garfagnana has been Italians; the green hills and mountains, the narrow valley of the Serchio, between the Apennines and the Apuan Alps, the stone villages perched on slopes that look so picturesque on postcards were simply never generous enough to provide a sufficient livelihood for their inhabitants. The chief staple of the district until recently was flour made from chestnuts, and chestnut groves still cover much of the region.

### Lucca to Bagni di Lucca

North of Lucca, the first tempting detour off the SS12 is to one of the many Romanesque churches in the region, **San Giorgio di Brancoli**, near Vinchiana, as

# Getting Around

CLAP **buses** from Lucca connect the city to Bagni di Lucca (27km/40min), Barga (37km/1hr), and Castelnuovo di Garfagnana (50km/1½hrs). The **railway station** is just south of the walls on Piazza Ricasoli. **Trains** on the scenic Lucca–Aulla line go up the Serchio valley, though beware that the stations for Bagni di Lucca and Barga are quite a distance from their centres and don't always have buses that connect; you'd be better off taking the bus to begin with.

If you're **driving** from the south, the most convenient way into these mountains begins at Lucca; both the SS12 and SS445 routes follow the river Serchio.

# Tourist Information

**Bagni di Lucca**: Viale Umberto I, 139, t 0583 805745 (*summer only*).
**Barga**: Piazza Angelo, t 0583 724745.
**Castelnuovo di Garfagnana**: Rocca Loggiato Porta 10, t/f 0583 641007, *www.corriere digarfagnana.com*.
The Visitors' Centre for the Parco Regionale delle Alpi Apuane is at Piazza delle Erbe 1, t 0583 644242.

# Where to Stay and Eat

There's nothing exceptional in Garfagnana, but the Italians firmly believe the further north in Tuscany you go, the better the cooking, graced by the kindly influences of Liguria and Emilia-Romagna; the pasta dishes in the region are especially good. Specialities include *torte di erbe* (vegetable pies), chestnut puddings and *pattona* (chestnut biscuits).

## Bagni di Lucca ✉ 55022

Bagni di Lucca is wonderfully genteel, with a score of quiet, modest Victorian hotels.
**\*\*\*Regina Park Hotel**, Viale Umberto I 157, t 0583 805508, *www.coronaregina.it* (*expensive*). A smart hotel with all mod cons housed in a Renaissance palazzo in the centre of Bagni. A lovely loggia overlooks the ample grounds, which back onto the river Lima. *Closed mid-Oct–Easter.*
**\*\*\*Corona**, Via Serraglia 78, t 0583 805151, *www.coronaregina.it* (*moderate*). Under the same ownership as the Regina, this is cheaper, but still very comfortable. The restaurant serves imaginative dishes such as *zucchini, taleggio* and truffle timbale, gnocchi with baby squid and chickpeas, and duck breast cooked with blackcurrants.

notable for its lovely setting as for its 12th-century pulpit. **Diécimo**, across the river, has a name that survives from Roman times – it lies 10 Roman miles (18km) from Lucca. The town's main landmark is the mighty Romanesque campanile of the 13th-century church of **Santa Maria**, standing out starkly against the surrounding hills. **Borgo a Mozzano**, 4km further upstream, is famous for its beautiful little hump-back bridge, with arches in five different shapes and sizes, which is dedicated to the Magdalene, or to the Devil. According to legend, he built it one dark and stormy night in exchange for the first soul to cross – the clever villagers outwitted him by sending a dog over in the morning. The real builder in this case was the slighty less lethal 11th-century Countess Matilda who, besides the bridge, endowed the villages around Borgo with a number of solid Romanesque parish churches. Inside Borgo's church you can see a wooden *San Bernardino* by Civitali.

To the north, just above the confluence of the Serchio river and the Torrente Lima, lie the long and narrow riverside hamlets that make up **Bagni di Lucca**, Lucca's once-grand old spa, first mentioned in the days of Countess Matilda. In the early 1800s, under the patronage of Elisa Bonaparte Baciocchi, it enjoyed a moment in high society's favour – long enough to build one of Europe's first official gambling casinos (1837; roulette was invented here), an Anglican church in an exotic Gothic Alhambra

*Roma, Via Umberto I 110, t/f 0583 87278 (*inexpensive*). Toscanini, Puccini and Caruso all stayed here, a small, old-fashioned place with a shady garden at the back, also in Villa di Bagni. Most rooms have a bathroom.

Circolo dei Forestieri, Loc Ville, t 0583 86038 (*moderate–cheap*). Slightly smarter, where you can eat *filetto al pepe verde* and *crêpes ai funghi*. Closed Mon and Tues lunch.

Da Vinicio, Via del Casino, t 0583 87250 (*cheap*). A chaotic and popular pizzeria a block west of Bagni's bridge, also good roast pigeon and seafood.

### Barga ✉ 55051

****Il Ciocco in Castelvecchio, 6km north at Pascoli, t 0583 7191, f 0583 723197, www. ciocco.it (*expensive*). A huge resort hotel with some 260 rooms plus self-catering chalets. heliport, restaurant, bars, tennis court – in short, the works.

***Villa Libano, Via del Sasso 6, t 0583 723774, f 0583 724185, www.hotelvillalibano. com (*inexpensive*). A lovely place in a courtyard, set next to Barga's city park; there's a restaurant with tables out in the garden.

Terrazza, 5km north at Albiano, t 0583 766155 (*cheap*). The best restaurant, featuring the specialities of the region. Closed Wed.

### Castelnuovo di Garfagnana ✉ 55032

***Da Carlino, Via Garibaldi 15, t 0583 644270 f 0583 62616, www.dacarlino.it (*moderate–cheap*). A rustic old place with an Alpine feel to it, now run by Carlino's grandson. Excellent restaurant serves home-made and organic produce, also pizzas baked in a wood oven.

La Geragetta, Capanne di Careggine, t 0583 667065 (*cheap*). For a rustic feast with the majestic backdrop of the Apuanian Alps, seek out this Alpine chalet-style restaurant just above Isola Santa. You will be hard-pressed to pay more than €17 for everything, from the *aperitivo* at the start to the *grappa* at the finish of your meal. In between, your digestion will be challenged by a vast range of *antipasti*, home-made pastas, game and roast meats, mushrooms in season, good solid desserts and unlimited wine. Closed Mon.

Osteria Vecchio Mulino, Via Vittorio Emanuele 12, t 0583 62192 (*cheap*). This atmospheric wine bar, just outside the city walls, is a great place for a snack accompanied by some wonderful wines. Eat cold meats and superb cheeses from wooden boards at long tables surrounded by bottles, or try one of the excellent flans, with delicious marinated picked vegetables. Closed Mon.

style, and an unusual 1840 suspension bridge (the **Ponte alle Catene**) – before sinking into obscurity. In Bagni's heyday, though, Byron, Browning, Shelley and Heine came to take the sulphur and saline waters, and perspire in a natural vapour bath. Heine was particularly enthusiastic: 'A true and proper sylvan paradise. I have never found a valley more enchanting,' he wrote; even the mountains are 'nobly formed' and not 'bizarre and Gothic like those in Germany'. Little has changed, and these days Bagni di Lucca is a sleepy but charming little place, with some pretty villas, elegant thermal establishments that spring into action every summer, a miniature pantheon, and a fancy Circolo dei Forestieri, or foreigners' club (now a restaurant), on the river-front.

## Up the Lima Valley

From Bagni di Lucca, the SS12 leads towards San Marcello Pistoiese and the ski resort of Abetone (*see* p.231), following the lovely valley of the Lima. A byroad beginning at Bagni leads to picturesque, rugged stone hamlets like **Pieve di Controne** and **Montefegatesi** which only appear on the most detailed maps; from Montefegatesi, an unsealed road continues to the dramatic gorge of **Orrido di Botri** at the foot of the Alpe Tre Potenze (1,939m/6,363ft). As the byroad winds back towards the SS12 at

Scesta, it passes **San Cassiano**, site of a fine 13th-century Pisan-style church with a delicately carved façade, in an isolated setting. Other byroads from the SS12 lead to tiny hamlets like **Vico Pancellorum** to the north and **Lucchio** to the south.

## To Barga and the Cave of the Wind

The Garfagnana proper begins where the Lima flows into the river Serchio at Fornoli. In the 14th century this area was ruled by the kinsmen of Castruccio Castracani; one of their prettiest mountain hamlets is **Tereglio**, along the scenic northeast road to the **Alpe Tre Potenze**, before it meanders on to Abetone. The Castracani had their base at **Coreglia Antelminelli**, high above the Serchio and the main SS445 (turn off at Piano di Coreglia). Coreglia's church contains a magnificent 15th-century processional cross, and there's a **Museo della Figurina** (*open summer Mon–Sat 8–1, Sun 10–1 and 4–7; winter Mon–Sat 8–1; adm*) devoted to the Garfagnana's traditional manufacture of plaster figures. To the north, the hill town of **Barga** (pop. 11,000) stands above its modern offspring, Fornaci di Barga on the main SS445. Barga was astute enough to maintain its independence until 1341, when it decided to link its fortunes with Florence. At the very top of town stands Barga's chief monument, its **cathedral**, begun in the year 1000 on a terrace, with a panoramic view over the rooftops and of surrounding hills apparently clad in green velvet, and bare mountains scoured with white marble. Built of a blonde stone called *alberese di Barga*, its square façade is discreetly decorated with a shallow pattern, charming reliefs and two leering lions; on the side the campanile is incorporated into the church; over the portal, there's a relief of a feast scene with a king and dwarfs. There's yet another dwarf inside, supporting one of the red marble pillars of the **pulpit** by the idiosyncratic 13th-century Como sculptor, Guido Bigarelli. The other pillars required a pair of lions, one grinning over a conquered dragon, one being both stroked and stabbed by a man. Less mysterious are the naive reliefs around the pulpit itself, startlingly sophisticated versions of familiar scriptural scenes. In the choir note the venerable polychrome wood statue of St Christopher (early 1100s) and a choir screen with strange medieval carvings, including a mystic mermaid (*see* pp.375–6). Around the back, the cathedral's garden has a magnificent Lebanon cedar. Next to the cathedral stands the **Palazzo Pretorio**, with a small **Museo Civico,** and 14th-century **Loggetta del Podestà**; if you go down the stairs towards the dungeon you can see Barga's old corn measures – a medieval Trading Standards Office.

The rest of Barga is a photogenic ensemble of archways and little palazzi piled on top of each other, with walls, gates and a ravine planted with kitchen gardens. Things get lively in July and August with the classes and performances of **Opera Barga** in the old Dei Differenti Theatre, founded in 1600. Between Barga and Fornaci di Barga, you can measure the showy success of the city's emigrants who returned to build modern palaces in the suburb of Giardino.

From Barga you can take a 17km potholing detour to Fornovalasco in the Apuan Alps to see Tuscany's best cave, the **Grotto del Vento** (*open daily all year; guided 1hr tours at 10, 11, 12, 2, 3, 4, 5 and 6, 2-hour tours for real cave fiends daily April–Oct; winter Sun and hols only at 11, 3, 4 and 5pm; sometimes only part of the cave is visited; less crowded in* *the mornings; call t 0583 722 024, f 0583 722 053 for details; adm exp*), a long cavern of fat stalactites, bottomless pits and abysses, and subterranean lakes and streams, set in a barren, eerie landscape.

## Castelnuovo di Garfagnana

Hanging over the Serchio, 11km north of Barga, is **Castelnuovo di Garfagnana**, the region's lively 'capital', guarded by its **Rocca**. Its most famous commander was Ludovico Ariosto, author of the epic poem of chivalry and fantasy, *Orlando Furioso*. Ariosto was employed by the Este Dukes of Ferrara to chase bandits and collect tolls here in the 1520s, but didn't take to it. 'I'm not a man to govern other men,' he wrote, 'I have too much pity, and can't deny the things they require me to deny.'

Castelnuovo makes a handy base for excursions into its often wild surroundings. Northeast, past the small resort of **Castiglione di Garfagnana,** a tortuous mountain road continues through 16km of magnificent scenery to the **Foce delle Radici** (the pass into Emilia-Romagna) and **San Pellegrino in Alpe**, with magnificent views, an ancient monastery and a good little museum, the **Museo Etnografico Campagna** (*t 0583 649072, open April–May Tues–Sun 9–12 and 2–5; June–Sept Tues–Sun 9.30–1 and 2.30–7; daily July and Aug; winter Mon–Sat 9–1, Sun 9–12 and 2–5; adm*). West of Castelnuovo a scenic road leads over the Apuan Alps to Carrara and the coast, through the desolate Turrite Secca, its sombre features relieved by the romantic oasis of **Isola Santa** (13km) – a tiny, slate-roofed village amid trees on a lake, once a hideout for medieval renegades; now it is abandoned, save for a few old folks and the sheep who lives behind the altar of the church.

North of Castelnuovo the road enters Garfagnana Alta, one of the least-known corners of Tuscany. Just north of town lies the **Parco Naturale dell'Orecchiella**, with eagles, mouflons, deer and a botanical garden, its mountains crisscrossed by paths; pick up a map at the visitor centre in Orecchiella. At Poggio, back on the Serchio, there's a turn-off for **Careggine**, a lofty old hamlet with commanding views, and the artificial **Lago di Vagli**. Creating this lake submerged the village of Fabbriche; the campanile may still be seen sticking stubbornly out of the water. There are more stunning views from **Vagli Sopra**, village of old marble quarries and an 18th-century road, deteriorated into a footpath, which leads into the Valle di Arnetola. Towering over all is **Monte Pisanino** (1,945m/6,380ft), the tallest of the Apuan Alps; the road up to the summit and the alpine refuge of Donegani, passing the lakelet of Gramolazzo, begins at **Piazza al Serchio**, leaving the Serchio and the Garfagnana behind.

# The Lunigiana

Even less populous and less visited than the Garfagnana, the Lunigiana, separating Liguria and Emilia-Romagna from the rest of Tuscany, has traditionally been a tough nut for its would-be governors to crack. The Romans of Luni (founded in 180 BC to contain the fearsome Ligurians) found it a wild place; even in the 7th century, missionaries were still bashing revered ancient idols. This rugged territory of chestnut

# Getting Around

If you're approaching from the north, **trains** and *autostrade* from Genoa (A12) and Parma (A15) merge near Aulla. From here there are frequent trains to Massa-Carrara, Viareggio and Pisa, Pontremoli or Lucca. From Lucca, trains to Aulla take over 2hrs (85km) and to Pontremoli 2½ hrs (108km). CAT **buses** serve the Lunigiana, with Aulla as the main depot; there are services to Massa and Carrara, and to Bagnone, Filattiera, Fivizzano, Fosdinovo, Licciana Nardi, Pontremoli and Villafranca.

# Tourist Information

**Fivizzano**: Via Roma, t 0585 92017.
**Pontremoli**: Piazza della Repubblica, t 0187 833701.

# Where to Stay and Eat

### Equi Terme ✉ 54022

*****La Posta in Via Provinciale**, t 0585 97937 (*inexpensive*). Friendly little place with a bright restaurant and attractive rooms. Eat ravioli stuffed with ricotta and nettles or the house special 'La Spagnola' (a kind of cheesy strudel). *Closed Feb.*

### Bagnone ✉ 54021

**I Fondi**, Via della Repubblica 26, t 0187 429086 (*cheap*). Up in fortified Bagnone, you can fortify yourself with good, solid country cooking – lasagne with pesto or mushrooms, ravioli filled with gorgonzola and *radicchi*, *testeroli* in pesto, duck cooked with herbs, wild boar, local sausages.

### Fivizzano ✉ 54013

**\*\*Il Giardinetto**, Via Roma 151, t 0585 92060 (*moderate*). A delightful, old-fashioned place overlooking Piazza Medicea. Rooms are comfortable, and there's a little garden. The

*antipasti* are especially tempting, as well as the pasta and game (try the pasta with venison sauce, polenta with mushrooms, and venison stewed with juniper). *Closed Oct.*

### Pontremoli ✉ 54027

Pontremoli is rich in good restaurants, and has several hotel options.

**\*\*\*Golf Hotel**, Via Pineta, t 0187 831573, f 0187 831591, *www.golfhotel.it* (*moderate*). New, out of town in a pine wood, offering a restaurant and 80 very comfortable rooms, all with bath and TV.

**Da Bussé**, Piazza del Duomo 31, t 0187 831371 (*moderate*). An age-old restaurant featuring Pontremoli's special *pasta testaroli* with pesto, *involtini* (little meat parcels) in tomato sauce, stuffed pigs' trotters, and a delicious Swiss chard and ricotta pie. A sign on the door announces that they don't cook mushrooms. Finish with *spongata*, a local chocolate tart. *Open lunch only Mon–Thurs, lunch and dinner Sat, Sun; closed Fri.*

**Osteria Caveau del Teatro**, Piazza Santa Cristina, t 0187 833328, *www.caveau delteatro.it* (*moderate*). Elegant yet cosy cellar restaurant offering a change from rustic fare. The menu features such dishes as pâté of foie gras with port, potato *tortelli* with a Parmesan cream, roast pork with orange, and chocolate mousse with apricot coulis. The adjoining 17th-century tower houses 7 delightful bedrooms, beautifully furnished with antiques.

**La Manganella**, Via Garibaldi 20, t 0187 830653 (*moderate*). If you want mushrooms, here they do them every way under the sun: grilled, raw in salad, *trifolati* (sautéed), with pasta... *Closed Mon.*

**Trattoria del Giardino da Bacciottini**, Via Ricci Armani 13, t 0187 830120 (*cheap*). In the old town, you'll find *fritelle* of salt cod, marinated herrings and excellent *testaroli* with pesto and lamb.

forests is crowded with the castles of would-be rulers and other toll-collecting gangsters. In the early 1900s the Lunigiana was a stronghold of rural anarchism, and in 1944 its partisans made it one of the bigger free zones in the north. Since then life has been fairly tranquil; rocky, forested landscapes, ruined castles (many bombed in the last war) and simple Romanesque churches form the main attractions.

## Piazza al Serchio to Aulla

Beyond **Piazza al Serchio**, the first town of consequence along the SS445 is fortified **Casola in Lunigiana** (20km); just beyond, a road veers south for the spa of **Equi Terme**, a tiny place where the medieval town is spectacularly perched on a rock above the new town. Equi is less known these days for its waters than for its cave, **La Buca del Cane**, or Dog's Hole (*closed to visitors*) after its relics of prehistoric man's best friend. Our ancestors also apparently socialized with bears (or ate them), judging by the bones that have been found here. **Fivizzano** to the north (on the SS63 or by road from Casola) belonged to the Malaspina of Massa until the Medici snatched it and fortified it as a grand ducal outpost. The main square, **Piazza Medicea**, has a grand fountain paid for by Cosimo III, a few Florentine-style palaces, and the 13th-century parish church with the inevitable Medici balls on the front. There are two interesting Romanesque chapels in the vicinity, **Santa Maria Assunta**, 3km towards Pognana, in a lovely isolated setting, and 12th-century **San Paolo a Vendaso** with carved capitals inside, on the SS63 towards the Passo di Cerreto.

From Ceserano, just south of the SS445, the SS446 heads southwest over the mountains to Sarzana, passing **Fosdinovo**, where the Malaspina castle that hosted Dante in 1306 is one of the most beautiful and majestic in the Lunigiana (*t 0187 68891, guided tours winter Wed–Mon 10–11 and 4–5; summer Wed–Mon 10–11 and 4–6; adm*). Inside is a collection of arms and ornaments found in local tombs.

## Aulla

**Aulla** grew up at the Lunigiana's hotly contested crossroads, guarding access into the Magra valley. The powerful, 16th-century **Fortezza della Brunella** was built by the Genoese, who bought Aulla in 1543; Napoleon gave it to his sister Elisa in Lucca; it now contains a natural history museum (*t 01867 400252; open Tues–Sun 9–12 and 3–6, summer until 7; adm*). Nearby are the citadels of two other rivals for the town – the Bishop of Luni's **Caprigliola**, a fortified village still inaccessible to cars (6km southwest on the SS62) and the Malaspinas' fortified hamlet of **Bibola** and their romantically ruined **Ponzanello**, both due south of Aulla. The Malaspina also fortified the strategic road to the pass, to the northeast at **Licciana Nardi** (surrounded by immensely thick 11th century walls with only narrow passageways giving access to its centre), and especially at **Bastia**, 4km further on.

From Aulla you can tuck down into Liguria and the **Italian Riviera** to visit the 'Gulf of the Poets' (or, more prosaically, the Gulf of La Spezia), named after Byron, who swam across it, and Shelley, who last lived in San Terenzo near the Pisan town of **Lerici**. On the gulf's western shore (in Liguria) lies enchanting old **Portovenere**, named after the goddess of love herself. Near Carrara are the excavations of ancient Luni (*see p.261*).

North of Aulla is **Villafranca in Lunigiana**, along the Via Francigena, the pilgrimage route from France; here you can visit the 16th-century church of **San Francesco** and an **Ethnographic Museum** (*open Tues–Sun 9–12 and 3–6, in summer until 7; adm*) devoted to rural life in the Lunigiana, especially the chestnut industry. Yet another mighty castle beckons further up at **Bagnone**, 5km to the east.

## Prehistoric Mysteries

This hidden corner of Italy holds a genuine prehistoric mystery. To learn about it, climb up the narrow medieval lanes above Pontremoli to the gloomy, 14th-century Castello del Piagnaro and its **Museo delle Statue-stele della Lunigiana** (*open Tues–Sun 9.30–12.30 and 2.30–6; adm*). This small museum holds over a score of large, carved statue-*steles* of an unknown culture that flourished in the Lunigiana between the 3rd millennium BC and the 2nd century BC. The *steles*, rather like menhirs with personality, include stylized warriors with daggers or axes, and women with little knobbly breasts. They are displayed in semi-darkness, which adds to their mystery. The oldest (3000–2000 BC) have a U for a face and a head hardly distinguishable from the trunk; the middle period (20th–8th century BC) sport anvil heads and eyes; the last group (7th–2nd century BC) are mostly warriors, with a weapon in each hand, just as Virgil described the Gauls who invaded Lazio. They were often discovered near sources of water, and some scholars think they may have symbolized the heavens (the head), the earth (the arms and weapons) and the underworld (the lower third, buried in the ground). Similar *steles* turn up in southern Corsica and other places around the Mediterranean. Some of the *steles* had their heads knocked off, a sure sign that the pope's missionaries in the 8th century were doing their job. Curiously, in the nearby hamlet of Vignola, a folk memory survives of the destruction of idols; during the patron saint's festival they make little wooden idols strangely similar to Pontremoli's statue-*steles* and burn them to celebrate the triumph over the pagans.

## Pontremoli

Long and low-key, stretched lazily along the river Magra and the Torrente Verdi, is **Pontremoli** (pop. 11,000), chief town of the Lunigiana and the northernmost in Tuscany. The Via Francigena passes through the middle. Pontremoli is full of wonderful *belle époque* details – lamp-posts, shop fronts and interiors, even the marble street names. The historical Liberty-style Caffè Fratelli Aichta in Piazza della Repubblica, with its old carved wood cabinets and counters, is well worth a visit. The town wasn't always so peaceful: in 1322 Guelph and Ghibelline quarrels led Castruccio Castracani to build a fortress, called *Cacciaguerra* ('drive-away war'), in the town centre to keep the two parties apart until they made peace. Of this noble effort only the **Torre del Campanone** and what is now the campanile of the **Duomo** survive. The Duomo itself has a fine, ballroom interior hung with dozens of glittering chandeliers, unusual for Tuscany. Over the Torrente Verdi, the church of **San Francesco** contains a lovely polychrome relief of the Madonna and Child attributed to Agostino di Duccio. Between the centre and the station the oval 18th-century church of **Nostra Donna** is a rare example of Tuscan rococo.

In 1471 the Virgin made an appearance a mile south of Pontremoli, and to honour the spot the **church of Santissima Annunziata** was built with a lovely marble **Tempietto** by Jacopo Sansovino, a quattrocento fresco of the *Annunciation* by Luca Cambiaso, an elegant triptych of uncertain hand or date, and some fun trompe l'œil frescoes by a Baroque painter from Cremona named Natali.

# The Tuscan Coast

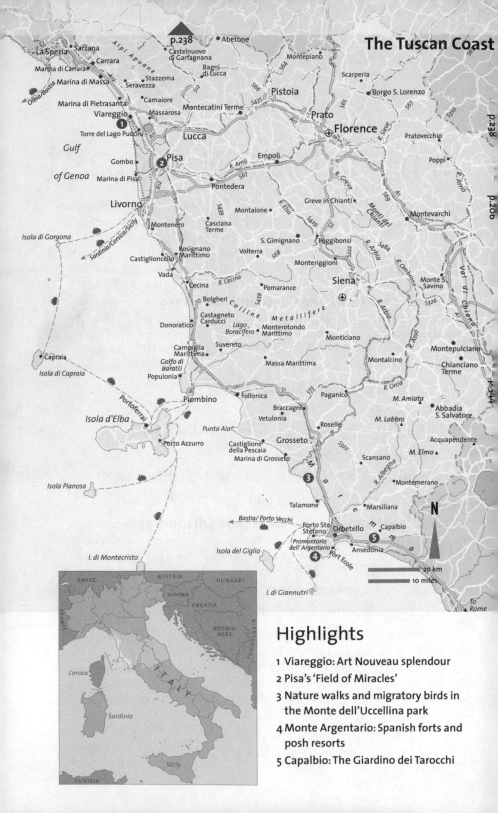

# The Tuscan Coast

p.238

Abetone
Castelnuovo
di Garfagnana
Montepiano
Scarperia
Borgo S. Lorenzo

La Spezia  Sarzana
Carrara
Marina di Carrara
Marina di Massa
Stazzema
Seravezza
Camaiore
Marina di Pietrasanta
Viareggio **1**
Massarosa
Montecatini Terme
Pistoia
Bagni
di Lucca

Alpi Apuane

Torre del Lago Puccini
Lucca
Prato
Florence
Pratovecchio

*Gulf*
Gombo
*of Genoa*
Marina di Pisa
Pisa **2**
R. Arno
Empoli
Poppi

Pontedera
R. Arno
R. Greve

Livorno
Montaione
Greve in Chianti
Montevarchi

Montenero
Casciana
Terme
Volterra
S. Gimignano
Poggibonsi
Monteriggioni
Monte S.
Savino

Isola di Gorgona
Rosignano
Marittimo
Castiglioncello
Vada
Cecina
R. Cecina
Pomarance
Siena

*Sardinia/Corsica/Sicily*

Bolgheri
Colline    Metallifere
Castagneto
Carducci
Lago
Boracifero
Monterotondo
Marittimo
Monticiano
Montepulciano
Chianciano
Terme

Capraia
Donoratico
Campiglia
Marittima
Suvereto
Massa Marittima
Montalcino

Isola di Capraia
Golfo di
Baratti
Populonia

Portoferraio
Piombino
Follonica
Braccagni
Paganico
M. Amiata
Abbadia
S. Salvatore

*Isola d'Elba*
Vetulonia
Roselle
M. Labbro
Acquapendente

Punta Ala
Grosseto
Scansano
M. Elmo

Porto Azzurro
Castiglione
della Pescaia
Marina di Grosseto

Isola Pianosa
Montemerano

Talamone
Marsiliana

Bastia/ Porto Vecchi
Porto Sto.
Stefano
Orbetello
Capalbio **5**

I. di Montecristo
Isola del Giglio
Promontorio
dell' Argentario **4**
Port'Ecole
Ansedonia

I. di Giannutri
To
Rome

20 km
10 miles

SWITZ.  AUSTRIA  HUNGARY
SLOVENIA
CROATIA
FRANCE
BOSNIA-
HERZ.
YUGOSLAVIA
Corsica
ITALY
Sardinia
Sicily
TUNISIA

# Highlights

1 Viareggio: Art Nouveau splendour

2 Pisa's 'Field of Miracles'

3 Nature walks and migratory birds in
the Monte dell'Uccellina park

4 Monte Argentario: Spanish forts and
posh resorts

5 Capalbio: The Giardino dei Tarocchi

The Etruscan Riviera, the Tyrrhenian shore, Tuscany by the sea – most of it is flat, straight, dull (apart from the incredible backdrop of marble mountains behind) and endowed with wide, usually crowded, sandy beaches. The sea isn't as clean as it might be, and the closer you get to the mouth of the Arno and Livorno, the less savoury it becomes. For a spell on the beach, you may find Tuscany's archipelago of seven islands more congenial – the sea is cleaner and the coast and beaches prettier.

Harder to escape, unless you go to the smallest islands, is Italian beach culture. Much of the shore is privately owned and you must pay for access to a veritable wall of deck chairs and beach umbrellas, packed as densely as possible; behind this there's inevitably a busy road, where the traffic is mainly vans with loudspeakers and motorcycles; behind the busy road is another wall of hotels, and perhaps a few pine woods. As always, you'll find it more pleasant and less frenzied outside July and August.

The most beautiful and fashionable section of the Tuscan coast is the Argentario, around Porto Santo Stefano, but it's also the most expensive. Elba, the largest island, is rugged and beautiful, but a busy Euro-holiday destination. Other places are an acquired taste: Viareggio, with more character than most, and the Puccini opera festival in nearby Torre del Lago, or Livorno, one of Italy's largest ports, famous for its seafood restaurants. The mellow old city of Pisa, an ancient maritime republic long ago silted up by the Arno, needs no introduction. In Carrara you can learn about marble in the Apuan Alps, in the Maremma you can learn about Italian cowboys and discover the lovely old town of Massa Marittima.

# North of Livorno: The Coast and Inland

## The Riviera della Versilia: Carrara to Viareggio

### Carrara

In the centre of dynamic, up-to-date **Carrara** (pop. 69,000) there's a garden square called Piazza Gramsci with an unusual fountain, consisting of a large, snow-white sphere of marble that revolves hypnotically, glistening with water, while the Apuan Alps tower in the background, streaked with the white quarries from where the sphere was 'liberated'. Carrara means marble; its name is believed to come from 'kar', the Indo-European word for stone. The Romans were the first to extract it 2,000 years ago; they drove wooden wedges soaked in water into the natural cracks in the stone, and when the wedges swelled, the marble broke off, and was rolled away on iron balls and sent to Rome to become Trajan's column or Apollo Belvedere.

The same techniques were still being used when Carrara began its revival in 1502, when Pope Julius II sent Michelangelo to find the marble for his tomb. These mountains are haunted by the memory of the 'divine' sculptor, in his old clothes and smelly goatskin boots, going to the most inaccessible corners to discover new veins of perfect, white stone. Michelangelo thought quarrying just as serious an art as sculpture; he loved to spend time here with his rock, and he claimed with his usual modesty to have 'introduced the art of quarrying' to Carrara. Marble has also made the Carraresi traditionally a breed apart – although their official past is dominated by the rule of godfatherish noble clans like the Malaspina and Cybo-Malaspina, the undercurrents were always fiercely independent, leaning strongly towards anarchism.

Some of Carrara's marble went into its one outstanding monument, the **cathedral**, a distinctive Romanesque church begun in the 11th century with marble stripes and an arch of marble animals, and later embellished with an exquisite 14th-century rose window made of marble lace, and marble art and statues inside, including a huge marble bowl in the baptistry. In the little piazza there's a bulky sculpture by the Florentine hack Bandinelli, generally known as the Giant, although it is supposed to be *Andrea Doria in the Guise of Neptune*. Next to Piazza Gramsci, on Via Roma 1, is the **Accademia delle Belle Arti**, set in a medieval castle. It was converted into a palace in the 16th century by Alberico Cybo-Malaspina, the Marchese di Massa, whose descendants ruled Massa and Carrara until they died out in 1829, when the state joined the Duchy of Modena until unification. The courtyard contains sculptures from Luni and the *Edicola dei Fantiscritti*, a Roman tabernacle from the Fantiscritti quarry, with bas-reliefs of Jove, Hercules and Bacchus, arm-in-arm like old chums, surrounded by graffiti by Giambologna and other sculptors who visited the quarries.

## Marble Quarries and Roman Ruins

Even though Carrara exports half a million tons of different marbles a year, there is little danger of it running out soon; though they will gravely tell you that there are only a few cubic kilometres of good stone left. The **quarries** surrounding Carrara are an unforgettable sight; usually they extend straight up to the sky, a blinding white scar down the mountain with a narrow access road zigzagging perpendicularly to the top. Signs from the centre of Carrara direct you to the quarries, or *Cave di Marmo* – **Colonnata** (8km, founded as a colony of Roman slaves and famous for *lardo di Colonnata*, a fat bacon salted in marble vats), **Fantiscritti** (a Roman quarry still in use) and **Ravaccione** (with fine views over the mountains). The **Museo Civico del Marmo** on Viale XX Settembre, the main road between Carrara and the train station (*open May, June and Sept 10–6; Oct–April 9–5; July and Aug 10–8; closed Sun and hols; adm*), takes you through the history with remarkable photographs of the marble-workers of a century ago and the surreal world of the quarries; halls of polished slabs introduce the amazing variety of marbles and travertines from the area, and the rest of the world; and there's marble art and a room of modern marble to prove it's not just limited to churches.

The Apuan Alps, only a few kilometres from the sea, give this coast a certain majesty. The beach at **Marina di Carrara** is divided in two by the marble port, which sends the big blocks all over the world; in July and August the port-resort puts on a big show of marble arts and crafts. Just to the north, on the border of Liguria near Marinella, you can visit the site of Roman **Luni**, a colony built as a bulwark against the fierce Ligurians. The city survived until the Middle Ages; the power-hungry Bishop of Luni survived even longer, until 1929, when the bishopric was combined with that of La Spezia. Excavations have brought to light a sizeable amphitheatre, forum, houses, temples, etc.; on the site is the **Museo Nazionale di Luni** (*open Tues–Sun 9–7 daily in summer; adm*), with an interesting collection of marble statuary, coins, jewellery, portraits and so on, as well as a display of modern archaeological techniques used in the excavation of the site, which can be toured with a guide. To the east off the SS446, 20km in the mountains, there is an extraordinary panoramic view over the marble quarries from **Campo Cecina**. The city of Carrara has an alpine refuge here, a good base for exploring the network of trails across the Apuan Alps (the tourist office can provide a map).

## Massa

**Massa** (pop. 66,200), nearly the same size as Carrara and co-capital of the province, was the principal seat of the Cybo-Malaspina dukes. They were never great builders or patrons, except when it came to their own digs – the polychrome 17th-century **Palazzo Cybo-Malaspina**, on central Piazza degli Aranci, with its orange trees and obelisk, and the **Castello Malaspina** up the hill on Via della Rocca (*open Sept–June Sat 9–12, Sun 3.30–6; July–Aug Tues–Sun 9.30–12.30 and 5–11.30pm; adm*), an 11th-century

# Getting Around

Transport is very easy along the coast, by **train** or especially by **bus**, with three companies – CAT, CLAP and LAZZI. CAT buses link the Marinas of the coast with Massa and Carrara, and the towns of the Lunigiana; CLAP links Forte dei Marmi and Viareggio with Lucca; LAZZI connects the coast with Lucca, Montecatini, Pistoia and Florence.

There are regular **trains** along the coastal rail line, which hugs the shore except at the mouth of the Arno and the Maremma. Trains to Massa or Carrara leave you between the beach and the centre, but CAT bus connections to either are frequent. The stations at Pietrasanta and Camaiore are inland, not at the marinas.

By **car** you can whip through the dull stretches on the A12, or follow the Via Aurelia (SS1), the main Roman route, though both keep their distance from the sea.

# Tourist Information

**Marina di Carrara**: Viale Galileo Galilei, t 0585 631925, www.aptmassacarrara.it.
**Marina di Massa**: Viale Vespucci 24, t 0585 240063, f 0585 869015.
**Forte dei Marmi**: Via Franceschi 8b, t 0584 80091, f 0584 83215.
**Pietrasanta**: Piazza Duomo, t 0584 795560.
**Marina di Pietrasanta**: Via Donizetti 14, t 0584 20331.

# Where to Stay and Eat

If you are planning a camping trip, there are a lot of campsites stretched out along the public beach between the marinas of Massa and Carrara.

At many hotels in coastal resorts, half-board is obligatory in high season (mid-July–mid-Aug); most of the hotels have a restaurant.

## Carrara ✉ 54033

**★★★Michelangelo**, Corso F Rosselli 3, t 0585 777161, f 0585 74545 (*moderate*). Considered the best hotel, with modern rooms and parking facilities.
**Ostello Apuano**, Viale delle Pinete 237, Marina di Massa e Carrara, t 0585 780034, f 0585 74266 (*very cheap per head, price inc. breakfast*). The youth hostel, for anyone who's game. *Open mid-Mar–Sept*.

Most of the good places to eat are outside town. Look out for Candia, the white wine eked from Carrara's mountain terraces.
**Da Venanzio**, amid the quarries in Colonnata, t 0585 758062 (*expensive–moderate*). Here you can try the local speciality, *lardo* – a delicately flavoured pork fat lard preserved in salt and rosemary in large marble vats. Also recommended are lasagne with mushrooms, snails in a tomato and garlic sauce, delicious *tordelli*, or pigeon in balsamic vinegar. *Closed Thurs, and Sun eve*.
**Locanda Apuane**, Colonnata, t 0585 768017 (*moderate*). A cheaper option, serving delicious *antipasti* and excellent *tordelli* (meat, spinach and ricotta-filled ravioli). *Closed Mon, Sun eve*.

A good town-centre option is;
**Roma**, Piazza Battisti, t 0585 70632 (*moderate–cheap*). A favourite for simple Tuscan cooking; also worth trying are the delicious stuffed mussels and the very good *fritto misto* of fish. *Closed Sat lunch*.

## Forte dei Marmi ✉ 55042

Don't expect to find anything cheap in Forte, though many places reduce their prices

---

castle with Renaissance additions, including a beautiful, ornate courtyard, loggias, and frescoed rooms. From Massa there are other marble quarries to visit, near **Pasquilio** 11km east, a balcony with views over the Gulf of La Spezia; in the same area, the **Pian della Fioba**'s botanical garden features the flora of the Apuan mountains, more stunning views, and another alpine refuge open all year.

**Marina di Massa**, on a marsh drained in the last century, is a lively proletarian resort with lots of pine trees; its neighbour, **Cinquale**, the 'Marina' of the old hill town of Montignoso, is smaller and prettier, and between it and Forte dei Marmi there's a greatly in June and September. For budget accommodation, look in adjacent Marina di Pietrasanta or Torre del Lago.

*****Augustus**, Viale A Morin 169, t 0584 787200, *augustus@versilia.toscana.it, www.versilia.toscana.it/augustus* (*luxury*). The best in town: a lovely old villa in extensive grounds, set back from the sea. Inside, it is elegant and luxurious. The numerous facilities include a heated pool and chic private beach.

***Hotel Mignon**, Via G Carducci 58, t 0584 787495, *info@hotelmignon.it, www.hotel mignon.it* (*expensive*). A pleasant hotel, a couple of blocks from the sea. Bright and airy rooms, a garden and private beach with a pool.

**Da Lorenzo**, Via Carducci 61, t 0585 89671 (*very expensive*). Serves beautifully and imaginatively prepared seafood: be sure to reserve. *Closed Mon.*

### Pietrasanta

A busy place, full of great places to eat and one of the nicer places to stay in the area.

****Albergo Pietrasanta**, Via Garibaldi 35, t 0584 793727, *info@albergopietrasanta.com, www.albergopietrasanta.com* (*luxury*). An upmarket hotel in a 17th-century palazzo in old town pedestrian zone. Luxurious accommodation, a conservatory for cold-weather breakfasts and a pretty courtyard garden. It has a unique collection of contemporary Italian art hung throughout public rooms and bedrooms. From the top floor, you can see the sea.

***Hotel Franceschi**, Via XX Settembre 19, t 0584 787114, *www.hotelfranceschi.it* (*luxury*). Don't let the 3-star rating deceive: this is another upmarket hotel. A lovely villa set in a shady garden; many of the

comfortable bedrooms have a balcony. The restaurant (*expensive*) is excellent; try the house speciality *pesce in pane* (whole fish baked in a bread crust). Prices are almost halved out of season.

***Palagi**, Piazza Carducci 23, t 0584 70249, *info@hotelpalagi.com, www.hotelpalagi.com* (*expensive*). Just outside the old town walls; newly decorated, with comfortable rooms, some of which have wood-beamed ceilings.

**Da Sci**, Vicolo Porta a Lucca 3, t 0584 790983 (*moderate*). A simple, traditional *trattoria* down a narrow lane, serving vegetable flans, grilled vegetables, *pappa al pomodoro*, spinach and ricotta gnocchi and stewed rabbit. *Closed Sun.*

**Enoteca Marcucci**, Via Garibaldi 40, t 0584 791962 (*moderate*). More a restaurant with a fabulous wine list than a wine bar, the Marcucci is very popular (frequented by the rich and famous), so be sure to book. If you don't want a full meal, you can sample various starters: duck terrine, fresh tuna and tomato soup, cabbage stuffed with potatoes and porcini, Parmesan and pear ice cream. Then there are a few pasta dishes and grilled meats (the duck breast with herbs is delicious). *Open for dinner only, closed Mon.*

### Camaiore ✉ 55043

**Locanda delle Monache**, Piazza XXIX Maggio 36, t 0584 989258 (*moderate*). An excellent hotel and restaurant housed in a former convent in the old part of Camaiore; clean and simple.

**Emilio e Bona**, Località Candalla, Via Lombrice 22, t 0584 989289 (*expensive*). Just outside Camaiore, offering excellent fare, including duck breast with herbs, or steak with almonds. *Closed Mon.*

long stretch of free beach. Near Montignoso stand the picturesque ruins of the **Castle of Aghinolfi**, a Lombard outpost built in AD 600 by King Agilufo.

## Around Forte dei Marmi

**Forte dei Marmi** is one of the larger and smarter resorts on the coast. Full of very chic shops, bars, clubs and restaurants, it is definitely a playground for the rich and famous. Founded in 1788, when Grand Duke Leopoldo constructed the fortress and seaport to serve the marble quarried from Seravezza, its old loading pier is now used as a promenade. In the 1860s the first holiday villas were built, and today alongside the popular white sandy beach you'll find chi-chi designer boutiques and an excellent market on Piazza Marconi on Wednesday mornings. The public stretch is to the north of the town. **Marina di Pietrasanta** isn't quite so up-market, but in its **Parco della Versiliana** is the last section of the coastal forest, lush with parasol pines, holm oaks and myrtles. This was a favourite haunt of Gabriele D'Annunzio; in the summer La Versiliana arts festival features concerts, plays and ballets in its small outdoor theatre. **Lido di Camaiore**, the last resort before Viareggio, caters mainly for families, and differs from its neighbours in its elevated garden terrace along the beach front.

Inland from Forte dei Marmi is the important marble town of **Seravezza**, where Michelangelo lived in 1517 during his marble pilgrimage to Monte Altissimo, rich in statue stone known as *statuario*. Not long afterwards, Duke Cosimo I commissioned Ammannati to build the **Villa Medicea** with its Mannerist courtyard. The **cathedral** contains works by Florentine goldsmiths, including a crucifix attributed to one of the Pollaiuolo brothers; 5km away, the **Pieve alla Cappella** has a fine rose window nicknamed the 'Eye of Michelangelo'. Another pretty place is **Stazzema**, with a Roman-esque church and more stunning views. The quarries nearby produce the blue and white streaked 'flowered' marble used in the Medici's Princes' Chapel. Among the mountains is the curious Monte Forata (1,212m/3,975ft), with a hole near its summit.

## Pietrasanta

**Pietrasanta**, near the coast, is a mellow old town rich in marbly traditions. It has undergone something of a revolution in the past five years and is now a chic resort patronized by well-heeled Italian holiday-makers. It is also home to a permanent sub-culture of foreign artists, attracted by its proximity to one of the world's greatest sources of marble and by the facilities around it, from marble studios to bronze foundries. Bottero still lives here part of the year, Henry Moore and Mitoraj, among others, have been temporary residents, using local craftsmen for their work.

The town's walls date from 1255, though its regular street plan suggests a Roman origin. Life centres around the large central Piazza del Duomo, with its Florentine *Marzocco* on a pillar (1514) and the **Duomo di San Martino**, begun in 1256 and restored in 1630 and 1824, with a rose window carved from a single block of marble. There is more marble inside, as well as a bronze crucifix by Tacca and a 13th-century fresco by the school of Giotto. Its Renaissance campanile looks half-finished. It shares the piazza with the **Palazzo Pretorio** and **Sant'Agostino** (14th century) with an attractive minimalist Pisan façade. From here a road leads up to the citadel, or **Rocca Arrighina**, built in the 1300s by Castruccio Castracani and lit up at night, which often hosted emperors on their way to Rome. Cosmave (*t 0584 791297, f 0584 790885*) can give information about the work of local artists. Alternatively turn right from the main gate for the central market building, its parking area adorned with an erotic statue of a woman *en déshabillé* pulling a young bull after her. There is often a sculpture exhibition set up in the pretty piazza or the cloisters of Sant'Agostino.

## The Mountains Beyond Pietrasanta

From Pietrasanta a road heads inland towards **Valdicastello Carducci** (birthplace of the poet Giosuè Carducci) passing the 9th-century **Pieve di Santi Giovanni e Felicità**, the oldest church in the Versilia, with 14th-century frescoes. The road winds up into the mountains giving lovely views, particularly at **Capezzano** and **Capriglia**.

**Camaiore** (from the Roman *Campus Major*, pop. 31,000) is an industrial town on the road to Lucca, with two Romanesque churches – the **Collegiata, Santi Giovanni e Stefano** (with a stately bell tower and Roman sarcophagus for a font), and **Badia dei Santi Benedettini**, 8th century with 11th-century additions. In Via IV Novembre, the **Museo d'Arte Sacra** (*open summer Tues, Thurs and Sat 4–7.30, Sun 9–12; winter Thurs and Sat 3.30–6, Sun 10–12*) has good Flemish tapestries. A road from Camaiore leads up to **Monteggiori**, with more fine views. Other destinations include the beautiful **Valle Freddana** and Monte Magno; and **Pieve a Elici**, near Massarosa, with a fine Romanesque church, 12th-century **San Pantaleone**. From here a minor road continues up through chestnut groves to **Montigiano**, one of the best balconies in the Apuans.

# Viareggio to the Parco Naturale Migliarino

## Viareggio

Up until the 1820s **Viareggio** (pop. 59,000), Tuscany's biggest seaside resort, was little more than a fishing village, named after the medieval royal road, the 'Via Regia' between Migliarino and Pietrasanta. After the 14th-century battles with Pisa, Genoa and Florence, this village was the republic of Lucca's only port. Fortifications were built – Forte del Motrone (lost in 1441), the Torre del Mare and Torre Matilde near the canal (*open on request*). Lucca's beloved Duchess Marie-Louise drained the swamps, developed the shipyards and fishing and resort industries, and laid out the neat grid of streets; by the 1860s the first cabanas and beach umbrellas had arrived.

By 1900 Viareggio was booming. Playful, intricate wooden Art Nouveau buildings lined its promenade, the Passeggiata Viale Regina Margherita. A massive fire in 1917 led to major rebuilding in the 1920s; the most important buildings were designed by Galileo Chini and the eclectic Alfredo Belluomini. Chini (1873–1956) was one of the founders of Italian Art Nouveau, or the Liberty Style, and especially well known for florid ceramics. He also designed stage sets for the New York Metropolitan Opera's premières of his friend Puccini's operas: *Turandot, Manon Lescaut* and *Gianni Schicchi*, as well as the throne room of the King of Siam (1911–14). With Belluomini he produced what has become the symbol of Viareggio, the colourful, twin-towered **Gran Caffè Margherita**, in a kind of Liberty-Mannerism; as well as the **Bagna Balena** and what is now the Supercinema, all on the Passeggiata. You can compare their work with the 1900 **Negozio Martini**, the only wooden building to survive the 1917 fire. Chini and Belluomini also designed a number of hotels (*see* p.266) as well as Puccini's villa on Piazza Puccini and the buildings at Piazza D'Azeglio 15 and Viale Manin 20.

Viareggio is also famous for its **Carnival**. Begun in the 1890s, it has grown to rival the much older carnivals of Rome and Venice, and in pure frivolity has surpassed

# Tourist Information

**Viareggio**: Viale Carducci 10, **t** 0584 962233, **f** 0584 47336, *www.versilia.turismo.toscana. it*. In season, there is an office at the station.
**Torre del Lago**: Viale Kennedy 1, **t** 0584 359893. Viale Margherita 1, **t** 0584 427242

# Where to Stay

**Viareggio** ✉ 55049
**\*\*\*\*Grand Hotel Excelsior**, Viale Carducci 88, **t** 0584 50726, **f** 0584 50729 (*very expensive*). One of their most extravagant ventures, built in 1923. The public rooms preserve their original décor. *Open April–Oct.*
**\*\*\*\*Plaza e de Russie**, Piazza d'Azeglio 1, **t** 0584 44449, *www. plazaederussie.com* (*very expensive*). Elegant and luxurious, with marble and Murano glass in the public rooms, and a lovely roof-top breakfast room and restaurant.

Some Liberty villas survive by the seafront, and several of these are modest hotels:
**\*\*Apollo**, Viale Caducci 76, **t** 0584 407 2823 (*moderate*). Simple and caught in a time warp. Bedrooms are spartan, but the house has original *belle époque* features: lamps, mosaic floors, painted ceilings, plaster moulding, carved wood and wrought iron. Also a garden and a restaurant (*cheap*).
**\*\*Al Piccolo Hotel**, Via Duilio 16, **t** 0584 51014 (*moderate*). An old villa a few blocks from the sea, now a modest hotel. *Closed winter.*
There are lots of hotels along the beach, especially *inexpensive* ones – you won't have trouble finding a room.

# Eating Out

Viareggio has numerous good restaurants.

## Very Expensive
**L'Oca Bianca**, Via Coppino 409, **t** 0584 388477. South of the centre, by the port, the restaurant overlooks the yacht harbour and has 180 champagnes on its wine list. Sample Mediterranean lobster (*aragosta*), all kinds of fish and other gourmet concoctions. For a cheaper meal try the Taverna dell'Oca next door. *Dinner only.*
**Romano**, Via Mazzini 122, **t** 0584 31382. An elegant restaurant, reputedly the best, with an interior garden. Creative cooking and delicious seafood *à la toscana*. Book in advance. *Closed Mon.*

## Moderate
**Al Porto**, Via Coppino 118, **t** 0584 383878. In stunning new premises, with a huge roof terrace overlooking the port. Well-known for its *carpaccio di mare* (raw seafood), lobster *alla catalana* (steamed and served on a bed of raw vegetables), plus excellent pasta with giant prawns, scampi, mixed seafood and crab. *Closed Mon lunch and Sun.*
**Piccolo Tito**, Lungomolo del Greco, **t** 0584 962016. A lively and popular restaurant with a big, sunny verandah overlooking the canal, where fish stalls thrive in the mornings. The menu offers no-nonsense, reasonably priced fish dishes; *antipasto di pesce*, big fishy salads, seafood pastas and risottos and grilled catch of the day. There are pizzas too; it's a good place for lunch.
**La Darsena**, Via Virgilio 154, **t** 0584 392785. Although the Darsena is no longer the Darsena it once was, it is hugely popular. Crowds flock in for an endless variety of antipasti, pasta with red mullet or with fresh anchovies, and fish baked with potatoes and black olives or a fabulous *fritto misto. Closed Sun.*
**L'Imbuto**, Via Fratti 308, **t** 0584 48906 (*moderate*). This informal, lively restaurant serves innovative fish dishes such as anchovy *'sformato'*, a tangy 'tartar' of grey mullet, spaghetti with scampi, baby quid and courgettes, rolled stuffed sole with caramelised onions and (a nod to carnivores) duck breast with pears and red wine. The interesting wine list lives up to the food. *Closed Mon.*

them all. At the centre of the action are large, papier-mâché floats, often lampooning public figures and politicians. If you can't make the massive parade on *Martedì Grasso* (Shrove Tuesday, and also on the four previous Sundays), you can see the floats all year round at the **Citadella del Carnivale**, Via Maria Goretti, near the Aurelia in the northwest of the town. This vast new workshop and performance space houses the carnival floats and is the setting for concerts (mostly jazz and rock) in the summer. It is closed during much of the winter while floats are being made. (*Call* *t 0584 46 2568 to arrange a visit*.) Viareggio also has an open-air **flea market** around Piazza Manzoni on the fourth Saturday and Sunday of each month.

## Torre del Lago and Puccini

Puccini spent most of his later years in his villa at **Torre del Lago**, 6km south of Viareggio along Via dei Tigli (buses from Piazza D'Azeglio). The villa, now the **Museo Pucciniano** (*www.giacomopuccini.it*; *open Mar–April 10–12.30 and 3–5.30; May–Oct 10–12.30 and 3–6.30; Dec–Feb 10–12.30 and 2.30–5; closed Mon and all Nov; adm*), is on the banks of Lake Massaciuccoli, where he could practise 'my second favourite instrument, my rifle' on passing coots. The villa contains its original furnishings, old photos, the piano on which Puccini composed many of his operas, his rifles and other mementos. The maestro, along with his wife and son, is buried in the adjacent chapel.

In July and August the Torre del Lago **opera festival** presents both famous and more obscure works by the great composer. The stage is built out on the lake and the audience sit on the lakeside – beware the mosquitoes. (*For tickets contact the Festival Pucciniano, Piazzale Belvedere Puccini, Torre del Lago, t 0584 359322, www.puccinifestival.it.*)

Most of Lake Massaciuccoli and the *macchia* (marshlands) and beaches to the south are part of the **Parco Naturale Migliarino San Rossore Massaciuccoli** (*open Tues, Thurs, Sat and Sun 8–2; guided tours arranged, to book call t 050 530101/533751*). To get there, catch one of the boats that run from Torre del Lago, or drive to the tiny village of Massaciuccoli. The wild beaches between Viareggio and Torre del Lago, with their low dunes and scrubby pine forest, are free and undeveloped. The forest of San Rossore, dating from Roman times, is today threatened by the spray blowing in from the polluted sea nearby, which is gradually killing the pines.

# Pisa

**Pisa** (pop. 104,000) is at once the best-known and the most mysterious of Tuscan cities. Its most celebrated attraction has become a symbol for all Italy; even the least informed recognize the 'Leaning Tower of Pizza'. Tour buses disgorge thousands of people every day into the Field of Miracles, to spend a couple of hours 'doing' the sights before leaving again for Florence, Elba or Rome. At night even the Pisani make a mass exodus into the suburbs, as if they sense that the city is too big for them, not physically, but in terms of unfulfilled ambitions, of past greatness nipped in the bud.

Yet in 1100, Pisa was 'the city of marvels', the 'city of ten thousand towers', with a population of 300,000 – or so it seemed to the awed writers of that century, who, at least outside Venice, had never before seen such an enormous, cosmopolitan city in Christian Europe since the fall of Rome. Pisan merchants travelled all over the

to Genoa

VIALE DELLE CASCINE

LARGO COCCO GRIFFI

VIA CAMMEO

Stazione San Rossore

VIA CONTESSA MATILDE

Camposanto

Baptistry

Duomo

Leaning Tower

Museo del Duomo

VIA PIETRO MAFFI

PIAZZA ARCIVESCOVADO

VIA ANDREA PISANO

PIAZZA MANIN

PIAZZA DUOMO

Museo delle Sinopie

VIA ANDREA PISANO

VIA BONANNO PISANO

VIA DELLA FAGGIOLA

Botanical Gardens

VIA PAOLO SAVI

VIA ROMA

VIA SANTA MARIA

VIA MILLE

VIA PAOLI

DON BOSCHI

VIA GABBA

VIA DERNA

VIA VOLTA

VIA ARANCIO

VIA RISORGIMENTO

PIAZZA DANTE

VIA NICOLA PISANO

San Nicola

PIAZZA CARRARA

VIA E FERMI

Museo Nazionale di Palazzo Reale

LUNGARNO PACINOTTI

VIA VOLTURNO

PIAZZA SOLFERINO

PONTE SOLFERINO

Santa Maria della Spina

VIA BONANNO PISANO

Arsenal

LUNGARNO SIMONELLI

PIAZZA A. SAFFI

VIA SANT'ANTONIO

Citadel

LUNGARNO SONNINO

Sant'Agata

San Paolo a Ripa d'Arno

VIA FRANCESCO CRISPI

PONTE DELLA CITTADELLA

PIAZZA SAN PAOLO A RIPA D'ARNO

VIA F NIOSI

PONTE FERROVIA

LUNGARNO COSIMO

Arno

VIA NINO BIXIO

APT Buses

VIA CESARE BATTISTI

VIA S GIOVANNI AL GATANO

VIA CONTE FAZIO

VIA ALDO MORO

VIA LIVORNESE

to Livorno

# Getting Around

## By Air

Pisa's international **airport**, Galileo Galilei, (*t 050 500707, www.pisa-airport.com*), 3km to the south, is linked to the city by CPT bus no.1 which arrives at Piazza Stazione in front of the main station on the south side of the Arno – the airport and the station are only 10mins apart. The Pisa Aeroporto rail station also has a few daily trains to the centre as well as a special train service to Florence (1hr, every 1–2hrs daily).

## Car Hire at the Airport

**Hertz, t** 050 43220.
**Maggiore, t** 050 42574.
**Avis, t** 050 42028.
**Easycar, t** 050 220 1219.

## By Train

Pisa has three train stations: some coastal trains stop at **San Rossore**, close to the Campo dei Miracoli (visible from the window, as in the famous adverts Federico Fellini made for Pisa's Campari liquor). Some trains from Florence stop at **Pisa Aeroporto** (*see* above). You would be better off planning your trips through the **Stazione Centrale** south of the Arno, where all trains call; train information **t** 892021.

## By Bus

All intercity buses depart from near Piazza Vittorio Emanuele II, the big roundabout just north of the central station: CPT buses for Volterra, Livorno and the coastal resorts (to the left on Via Nino Bixio, **t** 800 012773) and LAZZI buses to Florence, Lucca, La Spezia (on Via d'Azeglio, **t** 050 46288). Many of these buses also stop at Piazza D Manin, just outside the walls of the cathedral. The Natural Park Migliarino San Rossore Massaciuccoli may be reached by city bus no.11 from Piazza Vittorio Emmanuele.

## By Bicycle

Pisa lends itself well to **bicycles**; you can hire one at **A Ruota Libera**, Via Galli Tassi 6, near the Leaning Tower.

# Tourist Information

**Pisa**: Piazza Duomo 1, **t** 050 560464, *www.pisa.turismo.toscana.it*.
Piazza Vittorio Emanuele II 16, **t** 050 42291.
Also an office at the airport.

# Festivals

**Gioco del Ponte**, Ponte de Rezzo, *last Sun in June*. A tug-of-war dating from the 13th century, played out on the bridge, with costumes, processions and music (*see* p.277).
**Regatta and lights festival of San Ranieri**, *16–17 June*. The banks of the Arno glimmer magically with tens of thousands of candles.
**San Sisto**, *6 Aug*. Features folklore displays.
**Old Maritime Republics boat race** (next one 2006). Hotly contested each year between four old sea rivals: Pisa, Venice, Genoa and Amalfi; hosted by Pisa every four years.

# Shopping and Activities

Pisa is the best place in Tuscany for tacky **souvenirs**, and the best selection is around the

Mediterranean, bringing back new ideas and new styles in art, as well as riches. Pisa contributed much to the rebirth of Western culture: Pisan Romanesque, with its stripes and blind arcades, which had such a wide influence in Tuscany, was inspired by the Moorish architecture of Andalucía; Nicola Pisano, first of a long line of great sculptors, is as important to the renaissance of sculpture as Giotto is to painting.

Pisa has put all its efforts into one fabulous spiritual monument, while the rest of the city wears a decidedly undemonstrative, almost anonymous face, a little run-down. It is a subtle place, a little sad perhaps, but strangely seductive if you give it a chance. After all, one can't create a Field of Miracles in a void.

Campo dei Miracoli. Light-up Leaning Towers in all sizes are an amazingly good buy; some have pens attached for the scholar, or plastic kittens for the kids' room, or naked ladies for your favourite uncle. Other specialities are medieval weapons – crossbows, cudgels, maces, whips – and plastic skulls, reptiles and insects. If it is the **boutiques** you're after head down Via Oberdan and Corso Italia.

You can go **horse-riding** at the Cooperativa Agrituristica in Via Tre Colli in Calci, **swim** in the pool in Via Andrea Pisano, or have a drink in Pisa's best cake shop and bar, Pasticceria Federico Salza in Bargo Stretto 46.

## Where to Stay

### Pisa ✉ 56100

Pisa isn't known for fine hotels, but there's usually enough room for the visitors who elect to stay overnight. Many of the *moderate* hotels are around the train station, south of the Arno.

Inexpensive hotels are spread throughout town and are often full of students, particularly around the start of the university term; it's always best to call ahead, or else go up to the Campo dei Miracoli.

*****Relais dell'Orologio**, Via della Faggiola 12–14, **t** 050 830361, *www.hotelrelais orologio.com* (*luxury*). Housed in what was, until quite recently, the owner's 13th-century family home, the Orologio is Pisa's only five-star hotel. While it is the most comfortable place in town, the bedrooms are rather small, but the swish public rooms make up for that.

****Grand Hotel Duomo**, Via S. Maria 94, **t** 050 561894, **f** 050 560418, *www.grand hotelduomo.it* (*very expensive*). Near the Campo dei Miracoli, this is rather dreary.

***Giardino**, Piazza Manin, **t** 050 562101, **f** 050 831 0392, *www.pisaonline.it/giardino* (*expensive*). This little hotel just outside the walls off Piazza dei Miracoli, has just been upgraded to a smart three-star establishment. Rooms and baths are modern and stylish and there is a pleasant terrace.

***Royal Victoria**, Lungarno Pacinotti, **t** 050 940111, **f** 050 940180, *www.royalvictoria.it* (*expensive*). A hotel since 1839, overlooking the Arno and full of atmosphere. The spacious rooms (still very much in 1930s style) are sparsely furnished with heavy antiques. Dickens and Ruskin stayed here.

***Verdi**, Piazza Repubblica 5, **t** 050 598947, **f** 050 598944 (*expensive*). Another good choice in this price range, in the centre, set in a well-restored historic palace.

**Villa Kinzica**, Piazza Arcivescovado 2, **t** 050 560419 (*expensive*). You can practically touch the Leaning Tower from the rooms of this hotel just off the Campo dei Miracoli. The bedrooms are fairly basic and rather worn at the edges, but the staff are friendly.

***Di Stefano**, Via Sant'Apollonia 35, **t** 050 553559, **f** 050 556038, *www.hoteldi stefano.pisa.it* (*moderate*). Nice and central, this hotel has recently been upgraded, with TVs in all the rooms, but not all have private bath.

*****Helvetia**, Via Don Boschi 31, **t** 050 553084 (*moderate*). Clean and cheap. Some rooms have private bath.

**Youth hostel**, Via Pietrasanta 15, **t** 050 890622 (no.3 bus). As hostels go, this isn't far out: just 1km from the Campo dei Miracoli; it also provides cooking facilities.

## History

Pisa used to like to claim that it began as a Greek city, founded by colonists from Elis. Most historians, however, won't accept anything earlier than around 100 BC, when a Roman veterans' colony was settled there. Records of what followed are scarce, but Pisa, like Amalfi and Venice, must have had an early start in building a navy and establishing trade connections. By the 11th century, the effort had blossomed into opulence; Pisa managed to build itself a small empire, including Corsica, Sardinia, and for a while the Balearics. Around 1060, work was begun on the great cathedral complex and many other buildings, inaugurating the Pisan Romanesque.

# Eating Out

Apart from Sunday night, when it's hard to find food, at other times, walks on the wild side of the Tuscan kitchen seem more common than elsewhere – you can find eels and squid, *baccalà*, tripe, wild mushrooms, 'twice-boiled soup' and dishes that waiters cannot satisfactorily explain.

**Ristoro dei Vecchi Macelli**, Via Volturno 49, **t** 050 20424 (*expensive*). A gourmet stronghold on the north bank of the Arno, near Ponte Solferino, with highly imaginative dishes based on coastal Tuscan traditions. *Closed Wed*.

**Cagliostro**, Via del Castelletto 26–30, **t** 050 575413 (*moderate*). It's hard to believe that you are in Italy at this extraordinary restaurant /caffè/enoteca/art gallery/night club and general trendy hang-out; the cooking is 'Tuscan Creative' but throws in other dishes from all over Italy. Lunch is a somewhat more modest (and cheaper) affair. *Closed Tues*.

**Osteria dei Cavalieri**, Via San Frediano 16, **t** 050 580858 (*moderate*). Offers several fixed-price menus featuring seafood, meat and vegetarian dishes, and good game dishes such as rabbit with thyme, gnocchi with courgette flowers and pistachios and rabbit with oregano, plus an excellent wine list. *Closed Sun and sat lunch*.

Pisa has plenty of unpretentious *trattorias*, which are popular with its student population; many are in the area near the university.

**Il Nuraghe**, Via Mazzini 58, **t** 050 44368 (*moderate*). Offers specialities such as ricotta ravioli and snails. The chef is Sardinian, so Tuscan and Sarde specialities rub shoulders. *Closed Mon*.

**La Mescita**, Via D Cavalca 2, **t** 050 554294 (*moderate*). In the heart of the Vettovaglie market area, this has a huge wine list but unfortunately, the food is inconsistent in quality. *Open Tues–Sun for dinner, Fri–Sun for lunch as well*.

**Osteria La Grotta**, Via San Francesco 103, **t** 050 578105 (*moderate*). A cosy place with a simulated grotto and comforting, traditional dishes, imaginatively prepared and without pretensions. Meat-lovers are well catered for. Menu changes regularly. *Closed Sun*.

**Re di Puglia**, Via Aurelia Sud 7, Loc Mortellini, **t** 050 960157 (*moderate*). Occupying a converted farmhouse, 1km from the Pisa Sud *autostrada* exit, this restaurant is famous for its local organic meat, much of which is cooked over an open grill. The speciality is home-reared mutton, but there is beef, too. *Dinner only, also lunch on Sun. Closed Mon and Tues*.

**Pasticceria Salza**, Borgo Stretto 46, **t** 050 580144 (*moderate*). Pisa's most elegant bar/pasticceria has tables under Borgo Stretto's portico, an excellent vantage point to watch the world go by. Come for morning coffee, a light lunch, delicious afternoon pastry or an evening aperitif. *Closed Mon*.

**Trattoria S. Omobono**, Piazza S. Omobono 6, **t** 050 540847 (*cheap*). A simple, rustic *trattoria* in a little square just off the main market place. Sample risotto with porcini, spaghetti *alla marinara*, *stoccafisso* (stockfish) with potatoes, and a wonderful fish *fritto misto*. *Closed Sun*.

**Vineria di Piazza**, Piazza delle Vettovaglie 13 (no telephone) (*cheap*). The food here is simple and very tasty; bean soup with *pioppini* mushrooms, fish soup, risotto with radicchio and gorgonzola. Tables right in the market. *Closed Sun*.

In 1135 Pisa captured and sacked Amalfi, its greatest rival. The First Crusade, when Pisa's archbishop led the entire fleet in support of the Christian knights, turned out to be an economic windfall for the city. And when the Pisans weren't fighting the Muslims of Spain and Africa, they were learning from them: much of medieval Arab science, philosophy and architecture came into Europe through Pisa. Pisa's architecture, the highest development of the Romanesque in Italy, saw its influence spread from Sardinia to Puglia in southern Italy; when Gothic arrived in Italy Pisa was one of the few cities to take it seriously, and the city's accomplishments in that style rank with Siena's. In science, Pisa contributed a great if shadowy figure, the mathematician Leonardo Fibonacci, who either rediscovered the principle of the Golden Section or learned it from the Arabs, and also introduced Arabic numerals to Europe. Pisa's scholarly tradition was crowned in the 1600s by its most famous son, Galileo Galilei.

Pisa was always a Ghibelline city, the greatest ally of the emperors in Tuscany if only for expediency's sake. But the real threat eventually came from the rising mercantile port of Genoa. After years of constant warfare, the Genoese devastated the Pisan navy at the Battle of Meloria (an islet off Livorno) in 1284. All chance of recovery was quashed by an even more implacable enemy: the Arno. Pisa's port was gradually silting up, and when the cost of dredging became greater than the traffic could bear, the city's fate was sealed. The Visconti of Milan seized the economically enfeebled city in 1396, and nine years later Florence snatched it from them.

Excepting the period 1494–1505, when the city rebelled and kept the Florentines out despite an almost constant siege of 15 years, Pisa's history as a key locale was ended. The Medici dukes did the city one big favour, in supporting the university and even removing Florence's own university to Pisa. In the last 500 years of Pisa's pleasant twilight, this institution has helped the city stay alive and vital, and in touch with the modern world; one of its students was the nuclear physicist Enrico Fermi.

# The Field of Miracles

*For the museums and monuments on the Field of Miracles, you can save by getting a joint ticket; the Leaning Tower costs €15 extra.*

Almost from the time of its conception, this was the nickname given to medieval Italy's most ambitious building programme. Too many changes were made over two centuries of work to tell exactly what the original intentions were, but of all the unique things about this complex, the location is most striking. Whether their reasons had to do with aesthetics or land values, the Pisans built their cathedral on a broad expanse of green lawn at the northern edge of town, just inside the walls. The cathedral was begun in 1063, the famous Leaning Tower and the baptistry in the middle 1100s, at the height of Pisa's fortunes, and the Campo Santo in 1278.

## The Baptistry

*Open April–Sept daily 8–8; Oct daily 9–7; Nov–Feb daily 10–5; Mar daily 9–6; adm.*

The biggest of its kind in Italy; those of many other cities would fit neatly inside. The original architect, Master Diotisalvi ('God save you'), saw the lower half done in the Pisan-style stripes-and-arcades. A second colonnade was intended, but as the Genoese gradually muscled Pisa out of trade routes, funds ran short. In the 1260s, Nicola and Giovanni Pisano redesigned and completed the upper half in a harmonious Gothic crown of gables and pinnacles. The Pisanos also added the dome over Diotisalvi's original prismatic dome, still visible from the inside. Both domes were impressive for their time, among the largest attempted in the Middle Ages.

Inside, the austerity of the simple, striped walls and heavy columns of grey Elban granite is broken by two superb works of art. The great **baptismal font** is the work of Guido Bigarelli, the 13th-century Como sculptor who made the crazy pulpit in

Barga. Its 16 exquisite marble panels are finely carved in floral and geometrical patterns of inlaid stones, an almost monochrome variant on the Cosmati work of medieval Rome and Campania. Nicola Pisano's **pulpit** (1260) was one of that family's first, and established the form for their later pulpits, the columns resting on fierce lions, the relief panels crowded with intricately carved figures in New Testament episodes – a style that seems to owe much to the reliefs on Roman triumphal arches and columns. The baptistry is famous for its uncanny acoustics; if you have it to yourself, try singing a few notes from as near the centre as they will allow you to go. If there's a crowd the guards will just be waiting for someone to bribe them to do it.

## The Cathedral

*Open April–Sept Mon–Sat 10–8, Sun 1–8; Oct Mon–Sat 9–7, Sun 1–7;*
*Nov–Feb Mon–Sat 10–5, Sun 1–5; Mar Mon–Sat 9–6, Sun 1–6.*

One of the first and finest works of the Pisan Romanesque, the cathedral façade, with four levels of colonnades, is a little more ornate than Buscheto, the architect, planned back in 1063. These columns, with similar colonnades around the apse and the Gothic frills later added around the unique elliptical dome, are the only showy features on the calm, restrained exterior. On the south transept, the late 12th-century **Porte San Ranieri** has a fine pair of bronze doors by Bonanno, one of the architects of the Leaning Tower. The biblical scenes are enacted among real palms and acacia trees; the well-travelled Pisans would have known what they looked like.

On the inside, little of the original art survived a fire in 1595, and a coffered Baroque ceiling and some poor painting were added during the reconstruction. Some fine works remain: a few patches of the Cosmati pavement; the great mosaic of Christ Pantocrator in the apse by Cimabue; and some portraits of the saints by Andrea del Sarto in the choir and his *Madonna della Grazia* in the right nave.

The **pulpit** (*c.* 1300), by Giovanni Pisano, is that family's acknowledged masterpiece, and one of the greatest achievements of Pisan sculpture. After the 1595 fire it was left unassembled in crates until the 20th century. It show a startling mix of classical and Christian elements as never before. St Michael, as a telamon, supports the pulpit with Hercules and the Fates, while prophets, saints and sibyls look on. The relief panels, full of expressive faces, are equal to the best work of the Renaissance. Notice particularly the Nativity, the Massacre of the Innocents, the Flight into Egypt, and the Last Judgement.

## The Leaning Tower

*Open April–Sept daily 8.30–8.30 (until 11pm mid-June–mid-Sept); Oct daily*
*8.30–7.30; Nov–Feb daily 9.30–5; Mar daily 9–6. A maximum of 30 people are*
*allowed up at a time, accompanied by a guide. Book well in advance on*
*www.opapisa.it. Children under 8 not permitted, 8–12 year-olds must be hand-*
*held by an adult, 12–18 year-olds must be accompanied by an adult. There are*
*300 steps to the top. Adm.*

The stories claiming the tilt was accidental were most likely pure fabrications, to account for what must have seemed a great civic embarrassment. The argument isn't very convincing. It seems hard to believe that the tower would start to lean when only 33ft tall; much of the weight would still be in the foundations. The argument then insists that the Pisans doggedly kept building it after the lean commenced. The architects who measured the stones in the last century concluded that the tower's lean was intentional when it was begun in 1173. Mention this to a Pisan, and he will be as offended as if you had suggested lunacy is a problem in his family.

The leaning campanile is not the only strange thing in the Field of Miracles. The more time you spend here, the more you will notice: little monster-griffins, dragons and such, peeking out of every corner of the oldest sculptural work, skilfully hidden, or the big bronze griffin sitting on a column atop the cathedral apse (a copy) and a rhinoceros by the door, Muslim arabesques in the Campo Santo, perfectly classical Corinthian capitals in the cathedral nave and pagan images on the pulpit. The elliptical cathedral dome, in its time the only one in Europe, shows that the Pisans had not only the audacity but the mathematical skills to back it up. You may have noticed that the baptistry too is leaning – about 5ft, in the opposite direction. And the cathedral façade leans outwards about a foot, hard to notice but disconcerting if you see it from the right angle. This could hardly be accidental. So much in the Field of Miracles gives evidence of a very sophisticated, strangely modern taste for the outlandish. Perhaps the medieval master masons in charge here simply thought that plain perpendicular buildings were becoming just a little trite.

Whatever, the campanile is a unique and beautiful building – also a very expensive bit of whimsy, with some 190 marble and granite columns. It has also been expensive to the local and national governments who have tried to shore up the tower – $80 million since 1990, when rescue operations began. In the first phase counterweights (800 tons of lead ingots) were stacked at the base of the tower's leaning side, supporting the tilt. Then the lead ingots were replaced by an underground support: a ring of cement was laid around the foundations and anchored to 10 steel cables attached to the bedrock 164ft underground. But digging under the 14,000-ton tower is perilous; in September 1995, while workers were freezing the ground to mute vibrations, they found a ring of cement from the last century, when suddenly to their horror the tower groaned and tipped another tenth of an inch.

To prevent similar scares, in 1998 the tower was given a girdle of plastic-coated steel braces, attached by a pair of 72ft steel cables to a counterweight system hidden among the buildings on the north end of the Campo dei Miracoli. The final stage involved removing soil from under the north, east and west sides of the tower from a depth of about 20ft below ground level. This seems to have worked; the tower is not only stable but has actually righted itself about 16 inches (to a lean of about 15ft). It was finally re-opened to the public in December 2001.

## Campo Santo

*Opening hours as Baptistry; adm.*

If one more marvel in the Campo dei Miracoli is not excessive, then there is this remarkable cloister, as unique in its way as the Leaning Tower. Basically, the cemetery is a rectangle of gleaming white marble, unadorned save for the blind arcading around the façade and the beautiful Gothic tabernacle of the enthroned Virgin Mary over the entrance. With its uncluttered, simple lines, the Campo Santo seems more like a work of our own century than the 1300s.

The cemetery began, according to legend, when the battling Archbishop Lanfranchi, who led the Pisan fleet into the Crusades, came back with boatloads of soil from the Holy Land for extra-blessed burials. Over the centuries an exceptional hoard of frescoes and sculpture accumulated here. Much of it went up in flames on a terrible night in July 1944, when an Allied incendiary bomb hit the roof and set it on fire. Many priceless works of art were destroyed and others, including most of the frescoes, were damaged beyond hope of ever being perfectly restored. The biggest loss, perhaps, was the set of frescoes by Benozzo Gozzoli – including the *Tower of Babylon*, *Solomon and Sheba*, *Life of Moses* and the *Grape Harvest*; in their original state they must have been as fresh and colourful as his famous frescoes in Florence's Medici Palace. Even better known, and better preserved, are two 14th-century frescoes of the Triumph of Death and the Last Judgement by an unknown artist (perhaps Buffalmacco, who is described by Boccaccio in the *Decameron*) whose failure to sign his work unfortunately passed him down to posterity with the Hallowe'en name, 'Master of the Triumph of Death'. In this memento of the century of plagues and trouble, Death (in Italian, feminine: *La Morte*) swoops down on frolicking nobles, while in the *Last Judgement* (which has very little heaven, but plenty of hell) the damned are variously cooked, wrapped up in snakes, poked, disembowelled, banged up and chewed on; still, they are some of the best paintings of the trecento, and somehow seem less gruesome and paranoid than similar works of centuries to come (though good enough to have inspired that pop classic, Lizst's *Totentanz*).

Another curiosity is the *Theological Cosmography* of Piero di Puccio, a vertiginous diagram of 22 spheres of the planets and stars, angels, archangels, thrones and dominations, cherubim and seraphim, etc; in the centre, the small circle trisected by a T-shape was a common medieval map pattern for the known earth. The three sides represent Asia, Europe and Africa, and the three lines the Mediterranean, the Black Sea and the Nile. Among the sculpture in the Campo Santo, there are sarcophagi and Roman bath tubs and, in the gallery of pre-war photographs of the lost frescoes, a famous Hellenistic marble vase with bas-reliefs.

## Museo delle Sinopie and Museo del Duomo

*Opening hours are the same as the Baptistry; adm.*

There are two museums around the Campo dei Miracoli. Opposite the cathedral, the **Museo delle Sinopie** contains the pre-painting sketches on plaster of the frescoes lost in the Campo Santo fire. Many of these are works of art in their own right, which, though faint, help to give an idea of how the frescoes once looked. The **Museo del Duomo**, near the Leaning Tower in Piazza Arcivescovado, has been arranged in the old chapterhouse, with descriptions in English available for each room. The first rooms contain the oldest works – beautiful fragments from the cathedral façade and altar; two Islamic works, the very strange, original bronze **Griffin** from the top of the cathedral, believed to have come from Egypt in the 11th century, and a 12th-century bronze basin with an intricate decoration. Statues by the Pisanos from the baptistry were brought in from the elements too late; worn and bleached, they resemble a convention of mummies.

Other sculptures in the next room survived better: Giovanni Pisano's grotesque faces, his gaunt but noble *St John the Baptist* and the lovely *Madonna del Colloquio*, so named because she speaks to her child with her eyes; and in the next room are fine works by Tino di Camaino, including the tomb of San Ranieri and his sculptures from the tomb of Emperor Henry VII, sitting among his court like some exotic oriental potentate. In Room 9 are works by Nino Pisano, and in Rooms 11–12 the Cathedral Treasure. Giovanni Pisano's lovely ivory *Madonna and Child* steals the show, curving to the shape of the elephant's tusk; there's an ivory coffer and the cross that led the Pisans on the First Crusade. Upstairs are some extremely large angels used as candlesticks, intarsia and two rare illuminated 12th- and 13th-century scrolls (called exultet rolls), perhaps the original visual aids; the deacon would unroll them from the pulpit as he read so the congregation could follow the story with the pictures. The remaining rooms have some Etruscan and Roman odds and ends (including a good bust of Caesar) and prints and engravings of the original Campo Santo frescoes made in the 19th century. The courtyard has a unique view of the Leaning Tower, which seems to be bending over to spy inside.

# North Pisa

With the cathedral on the very edge of town, Pisa has no real centre. Still, the Pisans are very conscious of the division made by the Arno; every year in June the neighbourhoods on either side of the river fight it out on the Ponte di Mezzo in the *Gioco del Ponte*, a medieval tug-of-war where the opponents try to push a big decorated cart over each other. From the Field of Miracles, Via Cardinale Pietro Maffi leads east to the ruins of some **Roman Baths** near the Lucca Gate; two interesting churches in the neighbourhood are **San Zeno**, in a corner of the walls, with some parts as old as the 5th century, and **Santa Caterina**, a Dominican church with a beautiful, typically Pisan façade. Inside there is an *Annunciation* and a sculpted Saltarelli tomb by Nino Pisano, and a large painting from the 1340s of the *Apotheosis of St Thomas Aquinas*, with Plato and Aristotle in attendance and defeated infidel philosopher Averroes below, attributed to Francesco Traini.

One long street near the Campo dei Miracoli begins as Via della Faggiola, leading into the **Piazza dei Cavalieri**. Duke Cosimo I started what was probably the last crusading order of knights, the Cavalieri di Santo Stefano, in 1562. The crusading urge had ended long before, but the duke found the knights a useful tool for placating the anachronistic fantasies of the Tuscan nobility – most of them newly titled bankers – and for licensing out freebooting expeditions against the Turks. Cosimo had Vasari build the **Palazzo della Carovana** for the order, conveniently demolishing the old Palazzo del Popolo, the symbol of Pisa's lost independence. Vasari gave the palace an outlandishly ornate *graffito* façade; the building now holds the Scuola Normale Superiore, founded by Napoleon in 1810. Next door, **Santo Stefano**, the order's church, is also by Vasari, though the façade was designed by a young Medici dilettante; inside are some war pennants which the order's pirates captured from the Muslims in North Africa. Also on the piazza, the **Palazzo dell'Orologio** was built around the 'Hunger Tower' (right of the big clock), famous from Dante's story in the *Inferno* of Ugolino della Gherardesca, the Pisan commander who was walled in here with his sons and grandsons after his fickle city began to suspect him of intrigues with the Genoese. The **University**, founded by his family in 1330 and still one of Italy's most important, is just south of here, while Via dei Mille leads west to the **Botanical Gardens**, created by Ferdinando I de' Medici for the university in 1595; the institute, in the grounds, has an extraordinary façade entirely covered with shells and mother-of-pearl.

From Piazza dei Cavalieri, Via Dini takes you south into the twisting alleys of the lively market area, around **Piazza Vettovaglie** ('victuals square') where every morning except Sunday the city's ancient mercantile traditions are renewed. Tucked in the main street, old arcaded **Borgo Stretto**, you'll see one of the most gorgeous façades in the city, belonging to **San Michele in Borgo**, a 10th-century church redone in the 14th century, with three tiers of arcades. Much of the interior collapsed during the bombing raids of 1944. Off to the west, Via S. Francesco leads to the church of **San Francesco**: Gothic, with a plain marble façade, but containing some good paintings – a polyptych over the altar by Tommaso Pisano, frescoes by Taddeo Gaddi, Niccolò di Pietro Gerini (in the chapterhouse) and in the sacristy, *Stories of the Virgin* by Taddeo di Bartolo (1397). The unfortunate Count Ugo and sons are buried in a chapel near the altar.

## Museo Nazionale di San Matteo

*Open Tues–Sat 8.30–7.30, Sun 8.30–1.30; closed Mon; adm.*

On the Lungarno Mediceo, an old convent which once also served as a prison, now immures much of the best Pisan art from the Middle Ages and Renaissance. It has works by Giunta Pisano, believed to be the first artist ever to sign his work (early 1200s), and an excellent and well-arranged collection of 1300s paintings by Pisans and other schools gathered from the city's churches; a polyptych by Simone Martini, paintings by Francesco Traini, Taddeo di Bartolo, Agnolo Gaddi, Antonio Veneziano and Turino Vanni; some sculptures by the Pisanos (especially the *Madonna del Latte* by Andrea and Nino); and medieval ceramics from the Middle East, brought home by old Pisan sea dogs. In Room 7, after all the trecento works, the Early Renaissance comes as a startling revelation, as it must have been for the people of the 15th century: here is Neri di Bicci's wonderfully festive *Coronation of St Catherine* bright with ribbons, a *Madonna* from the decorative Gentile da Fabriano, a sorrowful *St Paul* by Masaccio, with softly moulded features and draperies, an anonymous *Madonna with Angel Musicians*, and a beautifully coloured *Crucifixion* by Gozzoli that looks more like a party than an execution. The last great work is Donatello's gilded bronze reliquary bust of *San Lussorio*, who could pass for Don Quixote.

## Along the Lungarno

Take time to head up the Lungarno Mediceo, where Pisa's **Prefettura** is housed in the lovely 13th-century stone, brick and marble Palazzo Medici, once a favoured residence of the magnificent Lorenzo. Nearby is the beautiful 16th-century **Palazzo Toscanelli** (which was once attributed to Michelangelo), where Byron lived from 1821–2 and wrote six cantos of *Don Giovanni*. Behind it, picturesque **Via delle Belle Torri** is lined with houses from the 12th and 13th centuries, which rub shoulders with a lot of new constructions that fill in the gaps left by bombs.

Further down the Lungarno is the former Palazzo Reale, begun in 1559 by Cosimo I, which has recently found a new life as the **Museo Nazionale di Palazzo Reale** (*entrance at Lungarno Pacinotti 46; open Mon–Fri 9–3, Sat 9–2; adm*), an annexe to the Museo di San Matteo, housing a collection of old armour which gets dusted off every June for the *Gioco del Ponte*, as well as some 900 other pieces from the 15th–17th centuries. A new section is planned to concentrate paintings, sculptures and collectables (mostly from the 15th–18th centuries) from the Medici and Lorraine archducal hoards.

Just behind the Palazzo Reale, look at Pisa's other famous bell tower, belonging to the 12th-century church of **San Nicola**: cylindrical at the bottom, octagonal in the middle, and hexagonal on top. Designed by Nicola Pisano, it has exactly the same kind of tilt as the Leaning Tower itself, built to lean forward before curving back again towards the perpendicular. Ask the sacristan to show you the famous spiral stair inside, claimed by Vasari to have inspired Bramante's Belvedere stair in the Vatican. The church contains a fine *Madonna* by Traini, a wooden sculpture, also of the Madonna, by Nino Pisano, and a painting from the quattrocento of St Nicholas of Tolentino shielding Pisa from the plague (in the fourth chapel on the right).

# South of the Arno

After the Campo dei Miracoli, the thing that has most impressed Pisa's visitors is its languidly curving stretch of the Arno, an exercise in Tuscan gravity, the river lined with two mirror-image lines of blank-faced yellow and tan buildings, all the same height, with no remarkable bridges or any of the picturesque quality of Florence. Its uncanny monotony is broken by only one landmark, but it is something special.

Opposite the Palazzo Reale, **Santa Maria della Spina** sits on the bank like a precious Gothic jewel box. Although its placement on the Lungarno Gambacorti is perfect, it was built at the mouth of the Arno, where it suffered so many floods that it was on the point of vanishing in 1871, when it was dismantled and rebuilt by the city on this new site. Although it's an outstanding achievement of Italian Gothic, it wasn't originally Gothic at all. Partially rebuilt in 1323, its new architect – perhaps one of the Pisanos – turned it into an extravaganza of pointed gables and blooming pinnacles. All of the sculptural work is first class, especially the figures of Christ and the Apostles in the 13 niches facing the streets. The chapel takes its name from a thorn of Christ's crown of thorns, a relic brought back from the Crusades. Inside the luminous zebra interior, the statues of the Madonna and Child, St Peter and St John are by Andrea and Nino Pisano. A few blocks west, near the walls where the famous 'Golden Gate' – medieval Pisa's door to the sea – once stood, remains of the old brick Citadel and Arsenal are still visible across the river. Just down from Santa Maria della Spina, the church of **San Paolo a Ripa del Arno** has a beautiful 12th-century façade similar to that of the cathedral. San Paolo stands in a small park, and is believed to have been built over the site of Pisa's original cathedral; perhaps building cathedrals in open fields was an old custom. Behind it, the unusual and very small 12th-century chapel of **Sant'Agata** has eight sides and an eight-sided prismatic roof like an Ottoman tomb.

Down the Arno, the monotony is briefly broken again by the arches of the 17th-century **Logge di Banchi**, the old silk and wool market, at the Ponte di Mezzo and at the head of Pisa's main shopping street, the Corso Italia. A bit further down is another octagonal church, **San Sepolcro**, built for the Knights Templar by Diotisalvi.

Behind it, picturesque **Via San Martino** was Pisa's old casbah, the main street of the Chinizica, the medieval quarter of Arab and Turkish merchants. At No.19 a Roman relief was incorporated into the building, known since the Middle Ages as Kinzica, after a maiden who saved Pisa when the Saracens sailed up to the Golden Gate. At the east end of the Lungarno, there's a shady park, **Giardino Scotto**, in the former Bastion Sangallo. Shelley lived nearby, in the Palazzo Scotto (1820–22), where he wrote *Adonais* and *Epipsychidion*.

## Around Pisa

A couple of kilometres up river to the east stands 'Pisa's second leaning tower', the campanile of the Romanesque **San Michele dei Scalzi**. Under the slopes of Monte Pisano, **Calci** has a good 11th-century church and an eroded giant of a campanile; 11km from here, in a prominent site overlooking the Arno, is the ornate **Certosa di Pisa** (*open Tues–Sat 8.30–6.30, Sun 8.30–12.30; adm*), founded in 1366, but then completely baroqued in the 18th century, in a kind of 1920s Spanish–Californian exhibition style with three fine cloisters. There are some lavish pastel frescoes by Florentine Baroque artist Bernardo Poccetti and his school, and a giraffe skeleton, some stuffed penguins, Tuscan minerals, even wax intestines – all part of the university's **Natural History Collections**, founded originally by the Medici and housed in the Certosa since 1981 (*open winter Tues–Sat 9–5, Sun and hols 10–6; summer Tues–Fri 10–7, Sat– Sun and hols 4–midnight; adm*).

Towards the coast, 6km from Pisa, is the beautifully isolated basilica of **San Piero a Grado**. According to tradition it was founded in the first century by St Peter himself, and in the Middle Ages it was a very popular pilgrimage destination. Although first documented in the 8th century, the current buildings are 11th century, embellished with blind arcades and ceramic *tondi*. Like many early churches and basilicas, it has an apse on either end, though of different sizes; the columns were brought in from a variety of ancient buildings. The altar stone, believed to have been set there by St Peter, was found in recent excavations that uncovered the remains of several previous churches. Frescoes in the nave by a 14th-century Lucchese, Deodato Orlandi, tell the *Story of St Peter* with effigies of the popes up to the turn of the first millennium AD (John XVIII) and a view of heaven.

In 1822, a strange ceremony took place on the wide, sandy beach of **Gombo**, near the mouth of the Arno, described in morbid detail by Edward Trelawny: 'The brains literally seethed, bubbled, and boiled as in a cauldron, for a very long time. Byron could not face this scene, he withdrew to the beach and swam off to the *Bolivar*.' Such was Shelley's fiery end, after he drowned sailing from Livorno.

Gombo, and Pisa's other beaches, the **Marina di Pisa** and **Tirrenia**, are often plagued by pollution, although Marina di Pisa makes a pretty place to stroll, with its Liberty-style homes and pine forests.

# The Coast of Livorno and its Islands

## Livorno

*...There is plenty of space; it is a fully registered cemetery with an attendant keeper. So, if any of you have the intention of retiring to this very interesting part of Tuscany you will be well taken care of!*
                    Horace A. Hayward, on the British cemetery in Livorno

Right from its founding in 1577, the English spent so much time in this city and grew so fond of it that they decided to rename it. It's time that the bizarre anglicization, *Leghorn*, be put to sleep. The city that Duke Cosimo founded to replace Pisa's silted-up harbour is named **Livorno**. It hasn't much in common with the other Tuscan cities – full of sailors and African pedlars, blissfully unafflicted with architecture and art, as picturesque and romantic as Buffalo, New York. Instead of frescoes, Livorno has perhaps the best seafood on the Tyrrhenian coast. Instead of rusticated palazzi and marble temples, it has canals, docks and a very lively citizenry famous for freethinking and tolerance. And instead of winding country lanes, there are big white ferries to carry you off to the Tuscan Islands, Corsica or Sardinia.

### History

The site had always been a safe harbour, and in the Middle Ages there was a small fortress here. It's odd no one thought of making a port here long before Cosimo. The Pisani considered it briefly in the 1300s, when it was becoming clear that Pisa's own port would ultimately fill up with the sands of the Arno. Eventually the fortress fell into the grasp of the Genoese, who sold it to Florence in 1421. Cosimo I, in his attempts to build Tuscany into a modern state, first saw the advantage of having a good port to avoid trading at the mercy of the Spaniards and Genoese. Cosimo expanded the fortress, but it was not until the reign of his successors, Francesco and Ferdinando, that Livorno really got off the ground. The first stone was laid on 28 March 1577, and a regular gridiron city soon appeared, designed by Buontalenti, and surrounded by fortresses and canals.

Almost from the beginning there was an English connection. Sir Robert Dudley, Queen Elizabeth's favourite, and illegitimate son of the Earl of Leicester, left England in 1605 after failing to prove his legitimacy in the Star Chamber court. (Perhaps he had other reasons; immediately upon arrival he converted to Catholicism and obtained a papal divorce from the wife he had abandoned back home.) Dudley built warships for the grand dukes, fortified the port of Livorno and drained the coastal swamps, making the region healthy and inhabitable for the first time.

In 1618, Livorno was declared a free port, free not only for trade but for the practice of any faith and for men of whatever nationality. It was a brilliant stroke, designed to fill out the population of this very rough and dangerous new town, and it is, to the eternal credit of the Medici dukes, an act of tolerance almost unthinkable in the Catholic Mediterranean of the 1600s. Before long, Livorno was full of persecuted Jews, Greeks, English Catholics, Spanish Muslims and loose ends from around Europe. As the only safe trading port in a sea full of Spaniards, the port acquired thriving communities of English and Dutch merchants. In the 1700s progressive, tolerant Livorno was a substantial city, a breath of fresh air in the decadent Mediterranean and a home away from home for British travellers. Shelley wrote *The Cenci* here, as well as 'To a Skylark'; he bought his fatal sailing boat in Livorno's port.

Livorno declined a little once the same low tariffs and trading advantages became available in other Mediterranean ports. The Austrian dukes, especially Leopold II, helped keep Livorno ahead of its rivals; nevertheless, true to its traditions, the city contributed greatly to the mid-century revolutionary movements and the wars of the Risorgimento. After unification it was still a lively place, full of men of many nations; it also began to make its first cultural contributions to the new Italy – the operatic composer Mascagni, the painter Modigliani, and several other artists of the Macchiaioli school. The Second World War and its bombers hit Livorno harder than anywhere in Tuscany, but the city rebuilt itself quickly. Long before other ports, Livorno realized the importance of container shipping. As the Mediterranean's first big container port, Livorno today has become the second city of Tuscany, and Italy's second-largest port after Genoa.

## Four Moors, Inigo Jones and the American Market

There isn't a lot to see in Livorno. You may enjoy the place and stay for a day or two, or you may be ready to bolt after five minutes. Though the streets are usually brimming, a combination of the prevailing north Tuscan austerity and an excess of dreary architecture make Livorno a disconcertingly anonymous city. It would have been a perfect setting for a German Expressionist film of the 1920s; unfortunately, such

# The Coast and Islands

*Gulf*

*of Genoa*

Isola di Gorgona

Golfo Aranci/ Olbia/
Portoferraio/ Caprala/
Bastia/ Porto Torres/
Palermo

a di Capraia

Capraia
Sto. Stefano

Isola d'Elba

Portoferraio

Isola Pianosa

I. di Montecristo

Tirrenia
To Pisa
Ponsacco
Livorno
Lari
Montaione
Ardenza
Casciana Terme
Antignano
Montenero
Rosignano
Marittimo
Castiglioncello
Montecatini
Val di Cecina
Volterra
Rosignano Solvay
Vada
Cecina
Guardistallo
R. Cecina
Pomarance
Marina di Cecina
Bolgheri
Castelnuovo
di Val di Cecina
Colline
Donoratico
Metallifere
Lago
Boracifero
Castagneto
Carducci
Monterotondo
Marittimo
S. Vincenzo
Campiglia
Marittima
Suvereto
Massa Marittima
Golfo di
Baratti
Populonia
To
Grosseto
Piombino
Follonica
Rio Marina
Punta Ala
Porto Azzurro
Isola del Giglio

A12
S206
S61
S439
S206
S1
S68
S439
S1
S68
S439
S439
S398
S1
S439
S322

N

10 km
5 miles

# Getting Around

Livorno's **train** station is on the edge of the city, with plenty of trains to Pisa, Florence and along the Tyrrhenian coast. Some trains to Pisa go on to Lucca–Pistoia–Florence. There are some connections to Volterra, with a change down the coast at Cecina. The station is well over a mile from the city centre; take the no.1 bus (most other city buses also pass through the centre, though routes are circuitous).

**Buses** for all villages in Livorno province (the strip of coast down as far as Follonica) leave from Piazza Grande. LAZZI buses for Florence depart from Scali A Saffi, on the Fosse Reale, just off Piazza Cavour.

Livorno is the main port for **ferries** to Corsica, with daily departures (Corsica Ferries, t 0586 881380) from late March to early November; it's a 4-hour trip to Bastia, a very pleasant town; some Corsica Ferries call at Porto Vecchio and Elba on the way.

Compagnia Sarda Navigazione/Linea dei Golfi, t 0586 409925, has daily ferries to Olbia in Sardinia (a depressing town on a wonderful island) from April until September. There are other departures on the Sardinia Ferries line (t 0586 881380) from Easter to October; these go to Golfo Aranci on the Costa Smeralda. A newcomer, with its striking, psychedelic-painted ships, is Moby Lines, which in summer take you to Bastia or Olbia (Via Veneto 24, Livorno, t 0586 899950).

For the Tuscan Islands, services are handled by TOREMAR (t 0586 896113): they do a daily trip to Capraia, and a daily afternoon run to Portoferraio, Elba, from 16 June until 30 September. The main Elba services go from Piombino down the coast.

All ticket offices are in the port area. For departure information in a pinch, call the Capitaneria del Porto, t 0586 826011.

# Tourist Information

**Livorno**: Piazza Cavour 6 (2nd floor), t 0586 204611, f 0586 896173; in summer, there are two booths in the port, on the Porto Mediceo, t 0586 895320, *www.livorno. turismo.toscana.it*.

# Where to Stay

## Livorno ✉ 57100

As it's a port town, there's an abundance of inexpensive hotels. Many, though none especially distinguished, are across the piazza from the train station. Dozens more crowd the area around the port and Via Grande. Some are real dives, but Corso Mazzini, a few blocks south of the Fosso Reale, has some nice ones.

★★★**Gran Duca**, Piazza Micheli 16, t 0586 891024, f 0586 891153, *www.granduca.it* (*expensive*). Livorno's most interesting hotel, built into a section of the walls right on the piazza near the harbour. Inside it's modern; some rooms overlook the Quattro Mori and the port.

★★★**La Vedetta di Montenero**, Via della Lecceta 5, t 0586 579957, *www.hotellavedetta.it* (*expensive*). A new hotel in the suburb of Montenero, overlooking the sea. It is a good alternative to the rather grim hotels in the

cinematic possibilities have not so far been exploited. There's nothing disconcerting about the **port**, a busy, fascinating jumble of boats, cranes, docks and canals. Close to the port entrance on Piazza Micheli, the **Fortezza Vecchia** conceals the original Pisan fortress and an 11th-century tower built by the famous Countess Matilda. Piazza Micheli, Livorno's front door to the sea, is decorated with Livorno's only great work of art, the **Quattro Mori** by the Carraran sculptor Pietro Tacca (1623). The monument's original design became somewhat mangled, and Tacca's brilliant figures now sit in chains under a silly earlier statue of Duke Ferdinando I. The four Moors are a symbol of Sardinia, but the statue's original intent was to commemorate the successes of the great Tuscan pirates, the Order of Santo Stefano, against North African shipping.

From here, the arcaded **Via Grande** leads into the city centre; every original building on this street was destroyed in the bombings of 1944. **Piazza Grande**, the centre of town centre and has comfortable rooms (many with sea views) and a restaurant.

**★★Giardino**, Piazza Mazzini 85, t/f 0586 806330 (*moderate*). Near the port.

# Eating Out

The main purpose of a trip to Livorno is to eat seafood. The Livornese have their own ways of preparing it, now much copied throughout Tuscany, and restaurants usually prove easier on your budget than elsewhere. Besides lobster and grilled fish, pasta dishes with seafood figure on all the local menus, as does the Livornese dish, *cacciucco*, the famous fish stew.

After a rich meal, try a *bomba livornese*: the local answer to Irish coffee is made with equal quantities of coffee and rum served hot.

**Ciglieri**, Via Franchini 38, Ardenza, t 0586 508194 (*very expensive*). This highly regarded restaurant – elegant, with soft lighting and only a few tables – serves high-quality fish dishes such as scampi ravioli, tagliatelle with lobsters, broad beans and deep-fried parsley, sea bass with artichokes or giant prawns in a citrus sauce, and boasts a comprehensive wine list. *Closed Wed*.

**La Barcarola**, Viale Carducci 39, t 0586 402367 (*expensive*). A big, noisy place towards the train station, serving up *zuppa di pesce*, penne with scampi, and everything else the Tyrrhenian has to offer, all in the old Livornese style. Try the *Pesce alla Nonna Virginia* (Aunt Virginia's Fish), baked in the oven with vegetables. *Closed Sun and Aug*.

**La Chiave**, Scali della Cantine 52, t 0586 888609 (*moderate*). One of Livorno's better restaurants, serving elegant fish dishes: spaghetti with clams, smoked mullet roe and courgettes, oysters, caviar, risotto with crustacea flavoured with gin and meat dishes, such as quails stuffed with figs and rice. *Eves only, closed Wed*.

**Da Motorino**, Via Oberdan 30, t 0586 896485 (*moderate*). Don't be put off by the rather spartan appearance of this *trattoria* and the brusqueness of the owner; this is one of the best places to eat *cacciucco* in town. Booking is essential.

**Vecchia Livorno**, Via Scali delle Cantine 34, t 0586 884048 (*moderate*). In the *centro storico*, this lively *trattoria* serves interesting variations on traditional dishes; *linguine* with salt cod and leeks, penne with *zucchini* flowers, red mullet and saffron, stuffed mussels and a delicious *fritto misto*. If you want to try their *cacciucco* (thick, spicy fish soup) order it in advance. *Closed Tues*.

**Cantina Nardi**, Via L. Cambini 6, t 0586 808006 (*cheap*). This wine bar is a pleasant surprise for lunch when a few tables are laid, surrounded by wine bottles – who could want better company? The day's menu is written on a blackboard. *Closed eves and Sun*.

Many of the best restaurants are to the south in the seaside suburb of Ardenza.

**Da Oscar**, Via Franchini 78, t 0586 501258 (*expensive–moderate*). A favourite for decades, with a good selection of wines to accompany *linguine* and clams, risottos, and grilled *triglie* and *orate*. *Closed Mon*.

Livorno, features the **cathedral**, designed on a bad day by Inigo Jones in 1605; the present building is a complete post-war reconstruction. Jones spent some time in Tuscany as a student of Buontalenti, and he took a little bit of Livorno home with him. His plan for Covent Garden (originally arcaded all round, without the market) is a simple copy of this piazza, with St Paul's in place of the cathedral. Via Grande continues on to **Piazza della Repubblica**, contender for the title of the most ghastly square in Italy. There are no trees on it, because the piazza is really a paved-over section of the **Fosso Reale**, the curving canal that surrounded the original city of Livorno. Just off to the north, the sprawling, brick **Fortezza Nuova** stands on an island in the canal, now landscaped as a park and a popular resort for the Livornese on Sundays. Nearby, on Via della Madonna, three adjacent churches (now recycled for other uses) make a fitting memorial of Livorno's career as a truly free city. The first is

Greek Orthodox, the second Catholic, and the next Armenian. On the other side of Piazza della Repubblica, Piazza XX Settembre is the site of the Saturday **American Market**, so called for the vast stores of GI surplus sold here after the war, and still Livorno's street market for clothes and odd items.

## Little Venice and the Museo Civico

By now, you may be entirely despairing of finding anything really uplifting in Livorno. But just off Piazza della Repubblica is a neighbourhood unlike anything outside Venice. In fact, they call it 'Nuova Venezia', or 'Piccola Venezia', and for picturesque tranquillity it may outdo its famous precursor. **Little Venice** is a quarter only a few blocks square, laced with quiet canals that flow between the Fortezza Nuova and the port, lined with sun-bleached tenements hung with the week's wash. The pseudo-Baroque **Santa Caterina** church is typical of the ungainly, functional buildings of early Livorno. If you're here in late July or August you'll find a livelier Little Venice than usual as the restaurants stay open late for the *Effetto Venezia*, a 10-day summer festival featuring evening shows and concerts and foodstalls selling *cacciucco*, the hearty, locally made fish soup.

Leading out eastwards from the Piazza della Repubblica, Viale Carducci is Livorno's *grand boulevard*, heading towards the railway station. Along the way it passes the **Cisternone**, a neoclassical palace built to house the water works Leopold II had constructed in the 1830s. Just next to this is the **Parterre**, a city park with a rather sad zoological garden.

Along the coast south of the centre, Viale Italia leads past the **Terrazza Mascagni**, a grandiose overlook on the sea. A few streets inland, in a park called the Villa Mimbelli, Livorno has just completed a new building for the **Museo Civico Giovanni Fattori** (*open Tues–Sun 10–1 and 4–7; adm*). This contains a good collection of works by the Macchiaioli, Italy's late 19th-century Impressionists. The museum is on the third floor of the city library, housing a small collection that includes only one work by Modigliani, but a wealth of paintings that lead up to his art. The painters represented include Ulivi Liegi, Mario Puccini, that rare blossom Lodovico Tommasi and Livorno's own Giovanni Fattori, one of the leading figures of the Macchiaioli. Together, they make a natural progression from the Biedermeier art of the 1860s – including stirring scenes of Italian volunteers leaving for the front – to the sweet haziness of the *belle époque* 1890s.

South of Terrazza Mascagni, Viale Italia continues past the **Italian Naval Academy** (where you might just get a glimpse of one of the exquisite old sailing ships the Navy uses for training), and then through some neighbourhoods full of surprisingly blatant neo-Gothic and Art Nouveau villas dating from the 1890s, on the way to **Ardenza**, with its seafront park and marina.

## The English Cemeteries and Montenero

For a sentimental journey into Livorno's cosmopolitan past, pay a visit to the **English Cemeteries** on Via Pisa and Via Adua, situated next to the Anglican Church (*ask at Via Adua's Archiconfraternità della Misericordia*). Crotchety old Tobias Smollett, who never stopped crabbing about Italy and never quite got around to leaving it, is interred here, along with numerous members of the British trading community and quite a few Americans. Many of the tombs (dating back to 1670) are truly monumental, some with inscriptions from Scripture or Shakespeare; some are charmingly original. Many of those among the British community, including Byron and Shelley, chose to pass their time not in Livorno itself, but up on the suburban hill of **Montenero** to the south. Byron and Shelley spent six weeks in 1822 at Villa delle Rose (*open by request of the owner, Signor Varvaro di Valentina at No.57*), a fascinating romantic ruin of a place. There is a charming, old-fashioned funicular railway to take you to the top, where there has been a sanctuary and pilgrimage site since an apparition of the Virgin Mary there in the 1300s. The present church, full of *ex votos*, is the work of an 18th-century architect named Giovanni del Fantasia; there are also a small museum, an ancient pharmacy and a number of caves, the Grotte del Montenero.

# Tuscan Islands

The Tuscan Archipelago is a broad arch of islets stretching from Livorno to Monte Argentario and enclosing Elba, the only large and heavily populated member of the group. Fate has not been kind to these islands: what with deforestation, Saracen and Turkish pirates, and finally the Italian government, not much is left. Two of the islands are still prison camps, while another is a nature reserve where no one is allowed to stay overnight. Gorgona and Capraia get a daily boat from Livorno – and are in fact administratively part of Livorno. The others will be dealt with later (*see* pp.290–8 and 309–10). Elba is most conveniently reached from Piombino; Giglio and Giannutri from Porto Santo Stefano.

## Gorgona

To see **Gorgona**, 37km from Livorno, you'll either have to get permission from the Ministero di Grazia e Giustizia in Rome (quite difficult) or else punch a *carabiniere*. Gorgona, a hilly, rectangular square mile, was first used as a prison by Pope Gregory the Great, 15 centuries ago. A later Carthusian monastery lasted until the new Italian state expropriated the entire island in 1869; it was to be a 'model prison' with workshops and vineyards, but it soon deteriorated into just another lock-up. There's nothing to see on Gorgona, except maquis and a handful of olive trees, and you'll have to be content with the view from the boat, which stops daily on the way to Capraia to drop off new cons and supplies. Ambitious plans are afoot to close the prison and turn Gorgona into a wildlife reserve, but so far nothing has been decided.

## Capraia

**Capraia**, 65km from Livorno, is the third largest of the islands, after Elba and Giglio. It measures about 10km by 5km, and has some 400 inhabitants. Like Elba, it is mountainous, but has fewer trees; most of the island is covered with scrubby *macchia*.

# Tourist Information

**Capraia Isola**: Pro Loco, Via Roma 2,
t 0586 905138.
**Castiglioncello**: Via Aurelia 967, t 0586 754890.
**San Vincenzo**: Via Aliata, t 0565 701533.
**Piombino**: Via Ferruccio, t 0565 225639.
*Open summer only.*
**Suvereto**: Piazza dei Giudici 3, t 0565 829304.

# Where to Stay and Eat

## San Vincenzo ✉ 57027

**Gambero Rosso**, Piazza della Vittoria 13,
t 0565 701021 (*very expensive*). Widely
considered to be one of Italy's top restaurants. It's earned its name not only for its
fish, but also for serving devilishly perfect
and delicate crustacea, pasta, pheasant and
pigeon with foie gras; there's an equally
thorough wine list. If you can't decide, take
the easy way out and order the *menu degustazione*. The restaurant overlooks the sea, so
it's a wonderful place to eat and watch the
sun go down. *Closed Mon, Tues*.

## Bibbona ✉ 57020

**Podere Le Mezzelune**, Località Mezzelune 126
t 0586 670266, *www.lemezzelune.it*
(*expensive*). This four-roomed B&B between
Livorno and Piombino has charming Italian
owners. There are antique furnishings, a
welcoming open fire for colder weather and
a shady terrace for hot days. There's no
restaurant, which is a good excuse for a
meal at the Gambero Rosso San Vincenzo.

## Donoratico ✉ 57022

**Enoteca Maestrini**, Via Aurelia 1 (on the SS1),
near Castagneto Carducci. A wine bar
serving Tuscany's best, along with light
dinners, local cheeses and home-made
desserts. *Closed Mon and Sept*.

In Roman times Capraia seems to have been a private estate, and the ruins of an
extensive villa can be seen. In the days of the Empire, the island was occupied by a
colony of Christian monks. Such a setting was perfect for the Christian ideal of
withdrawal and contemplation, but it also prevented the Church authorities from
keeping a close watch on the colony, and the monks slipped into unorthodoxy and
loose behaviour; an armed mission from Pope Gregory the Great was needed to force
them back in line in the late 6th century.

When Saracen pirates began to infest the Tyrrhenian Sea, Capraia, like most of the
group, became deserted. The Pisans thought it important enough to repopulate and
fortify in the 11th century. Genoa eventually gained control, as she did in Corsica only
32km away. This proximity gave Capraia its one big moment in history; in 1767 the
revolutionary forces of the Corsican nationalist leader, Pasquale Paoli, and the
weakness of the Genoese, resulted in, of all things, an independent Capraia, which
soon learned to support itself by piracy. However, French occupation put an end to
that four years later.

A decade or so ago tourist accommodation on Capraia consisted of one hotel and
two tiny *pensioni*. Today, by a miracle of 21st-century Euro-tourism, these have all
grown into three-star hotels, and two more have sprouted to join them. It helps
that Capraia is an island, and a pretty one, but its real attraction is its natural
setting, its deep-sea diving and marine grottoes. In the last century the northern
quarter of the island was put to use as an agricultural penal colony, which is what
it is today. The civilian population is almost entirely concentrated in the port and
only town, **Capraia Isola**.

The port is actually 500m from the town, connected by the island's only tarmac road. In the town are the Baroque church and convent of **Sant'Antonio**. Used as a barracks in the last century, it is now crumbling and abandoned. On the outskirts are the ruins of the **Roman villa**, apocryphally the abode of Augustus' profligate daughter Julia, and an 11th-century Pisan chapel dedicated to the **Vergine Assunta**. Overlooking it all is the large and impressive fortress of **San Giorgio**, begun by the Pisans and completed by the Genoese. The well-preserved **watchtower** at the port was built by the Genoese Bank of St George.

On the eastern side of town there is a beach under the cliffs with an interesting tower, built by the Pisans, and connected to the cliff by a natural bridge. A visiting Californian at the turn of the century was so struck by it that he built a copy of it on a beach near San Diego.

From Capraia Isola a road leads southwest across the island, passing another Pisan church, that of **Santo Stefano**, built on the ruins of a 5th-century church used by the early monks and destroyed by the Saracen pirates. Near Monte Pontica is a cave, the **Grotta di Parino**, a sacred spot used as a place of meditation by the monks. The road ends at a lighthouse on the western coast. Just south is a sea cave, the **Grotta della Foca**, where Mediterranean seals are still reported to live. At the southern tip of the island is another Genoese watchtower, the **Torre dello Zenobito**.

# Livorno's Coast

Livorno's clever tourist office has taken to calling this shore the 'Etruscan Riviera', conjuring up the irresistible idea of Etruscans lounging in beach chairs the way they do on their funerary urns. Beyond Antignano, the shoreline becomes jagged and twisting, dotted with beaches that are usually more than well exploited. **Castiglioncello** is a pretty corner of the coast, but the beaches are narrow and packed with Italians throughout the summer. Nearby **Rosignano** is a similar resort, graced with a gargantuan chemical plant. **Vada** and **Marina di Cecina** are a little better; both at least have stretches of free beach. Marina di Cecina, 36km from Livorno, is a suburb of Tuscany's newest city, **Cecina**, founded only a century ago, now an unkempt town populated by dissipated factory hands and motorcycle-heads. **San Vincenzo** is a booming, awful resort, but it has miles of good beaches on either side, perhaps your best chance on this strip of coast for a little seaside peace and quiet.

Next is the half-moon **Golfo di Baratti**, with more tranquil beaches and some Etruscan tombs from the once mighty town of **Populonia**. Modern Populonia has an impressive medieval castle and a small archaeological museum; ask there about visiting the ruins of the Etruscan city and tombs, which include a so-called 'arsenal' where the Etruscans turned Elban iron into armaments (**t** *0565 29436*). **Piombino**, at the tip of this stubby peninsula, is Tuscany's Steel City, mercilessly flattened during the war, and mercilessly rebuilt afterwards. The government might close the obsolete steelworks at any time, but Piombino will at least remain the major port for Elba. Towns of interest up in the hills include **Bolgheri**, near Cecina, centre of a DOC wine area (Bolgheri is a little-known dry white wine); **Castagneto Carducci**, a pretty town where strawberries are grown; and finally **Suvereto**, a seldom-visited medieval village with an arcaded Palazzo Comunale and the 12th-century Pisan church of San Giusto.

# Elba

When the government closed the steel mills on **Elba** after the war, the national and local governments sought to make up the lost income by promoting tourism on the island. They have been singularly successful: Elba has become one of Europe's most popular holiday playgrounds, and with tourists approaching some two million every year, prosperity has returned to its 30,000 inhabitants.

Tourist Elba, however, is no glamour-puss. It is a comfortable place attracting mainly families. Germans in particular are fond of the island; they have bought up most of the southern coast, and many of them return every year. There is no single big, crowded tourist ghetto, as on some other Mediterranean islands, but plenty of quiet, small resorts all around the coast. The lives of the Elbans themselves have adjusted to the cyclical rhythms of tourist migrations. In winter the island seems empty; much of the population stays only to work during the season. Other activities do exist to supplement tourism, such as fishing and mining, but the old iron mines have finally given out after thousands of years. The last of them closed in 1984.

In an unspectacular way, Elba is beautiful. Pink and green predominate – pink for the granite outcrops and houses, green because the island is heavily forested. Like its neighbour Corsica, it is a chain of mountains rising out of the sea, the tallest of which are to the west, grouped around Monte Capanne (1,080m/3,546ft). For a mineralogist, Elba is a holiday dream – besides iron ore, dozens of common and rare minerals are found there, everything from andalusite to zircon. For most people, however, Elba's greatest attraction is its wealth of beaches and particularly mild climate – it hardly ever rains. The coastline, all bays and peninsulas, is over 150km in length, and there are beaches everywhere, large and small, sand or pebbles. Even in the crush of August, there's plenty of Elba-room for all, and if you look carefully, you just might find a beach that's not too crowded.

## History

*Able was I ere I saw Elba*
        The Napoleonic palindrome

Elba is close enough to the Italian mainland to have been inhabited from the earliest times. When Neanderthal Man was tramping through the neighbourhood about 50,000 years ago, Elba may still have been linked to the peninsula. Later peoples, a seemingly unending parade of them, colonized the island after 3000 BC, drawn by Elba's treasure hoard of metals. In the Copper Age they mined its copper; in the Bronze Age they alloyed the copper into bronze. The copper gave out just in time for the Iron Age, and Elba, conveniently, had vast deposits of this as well.

Competition was fierce: the Etruscans and Greeks fought over the island and established colonies of miners to extract the iron, but archaeologists have not been able to find evidence of any permanent settlements.

For Rome, which was expanding across the Italian peninsula in the 4th century BC, Elba was seen as an important prize. After conquering the island at the end of the century, the Romans founded towns to consolidate their hold on it. From then on, whenever the Roman legions ran their swords through Teutons, Persians, Gauls, Carthaginians or each other, those swords were usually made from Elban iron. The mines and forges, then as now, were concentrated on the eastern third of the island, while the beautiful beaches in the rest of the island became a holiday spot for wealthy Romans, as demonstrated by the archaeological remains of large villas discovered near Portoferraio.

The fall of Rome brought invasions, disorder, depopulation and pirates to Elba; the Lombards in the 6th century, under the murderous Gummarith, subjugated the island with their usual bloodshed; Saracens and adventurous barons from Italy fought for the scraps. By the 11th century Pisa had assumed complete control, as the island lay across its most important trade route. It held Elba for almost 500 years, constructing fortresses at Luceri and Volterraio and exploiting the mineral resources. At the time the capital was called *Ferraia*, of which the modern capital of Portoferraio was only the port. Nowadays not a trace remains of the medieval city, and archaeologists are still trying to locate its site.

From the 13th century on, Genoa contested Pisa's possession of the island. In the 16th century, Duke Cosimo I saw his opportunity and seized it for Florence. He built Portoferraio and the walls around it, but soon had to contend with the growing power of Spain in the western Mediterranean, and after some inconclusive skirmishes, Elba was partitioned between Tuscany and Spain. Spain built the town and fortress of Porto Azzurro as a counter to Portoferraio, an arrangement that lasted throughout the 18th century, despite French efforts to grab the island.

# Getting There and Around

You'll never have to wait long for a **ferry** to Elba, especially during the summer. Apart from the scant services from Livorno (*see* p.284), gritty Piombino is the point of departure. Any train going down the Tyrrhenian coast will take you as far as the station called Campiglia Marittima; from there the FS operates a regular shuttle train to Piombino (don't get off at the central station; the train has a short stop there and continues to the port). Two companies run services to Elba: TOREMAR (head office: Via Calafati 6, Livorno, t 0586 896113; on Elba, Calata Italia 23, t 0565 918080; in Piombino, Piazzale Premuda, t 0565 31100); NAVARMA (head office: Piazzale Premuda, Piombino, t 0565 221212).

The most frequent passage is the 1hr Piombino–Cavo–Portoferraio trip, and there are also TOREMAR hydrofoils that go from Piombino to Rio Marina and then to Porto Azzurro (2hrs). Services to Elba can be as frequent as every half-hour in July, down to two or three a day in winter. TOREMAR also has a daily Livorno–Portoferraio run (5hrs) by way of Gorgona and Capraia in the summer. Note that the NAVARMA service in summer carries on from Portoferraio to Bastia, in Corsica. To keep up with demand in the summer, Elba Ferries runs hydrofoils from Piombino to Portoferraio; these only take 25mins, but are more expensive.

Elba has just room enough for an **airport** (t 0565 976011), and there are plenty of flights in the summer – mainly to Germany, Switzerland and Austria, with an infrequent service to Pisa, Florence and Milan.

Elba has an efficient **bus** service to every corner of the island and buses depart frequently. Portoferraio is the hub of the system, with buses leaving and returning to the terminal by the Grattacielo, facing the harbour.

There are plenty of **car hire** agencies on the island, in all the principal towns; you can hire scooters and bicycles everywhere too, and the tourist office has itineraries for bicycle and mountain bike trips around the island.

# Tourist Information

**Elba**: Grattacielo building, Calata Italia 26, Portoferraio, across from the ferry dock, t 0565 914671/2.

# Where to Stay

## Elba ✉ 57037

With more than 150 hotels on the island, Elba has something for everyone. The emphasis is on the not-too-expensive resort, attractive to family holiday-makers. Many hotels stay open all year, with substantial off-season discounts. Beware, however: Elba is a big package-tour destination, and despite its scores of lodgings, you'll need to book ahead. Note that many hotels require half-board in high season (mid-June–mid-Sept). For a wide choice of self-catering accommodation across the island, visit *www.charmingvillas.com*.

\*\*\*\***Villa Ottone**, at Ottone, t 0565 933042 (*expensive*). A 19th-century villa on the beach, brought up-to-date, with a shady garden and tennis court.

**The Hermitage**, Località Biodola, Portoferraio, t 0565 9740 (*expensive*). This sprawling resort hotel sits back forma white sandy beach and, having lots of facilities, it is popular with families. Rooms are quite luxurious. *Closed mid-Oct–Easter.*

\*\***L'Ape Elbana**, Salità de' Medici 2, t/f 0565 914245 (*moderate*). In Portoferraio, one interesting possibility is the 'Elban Bee', the oldest hotel on the island; it entertained Napoleon's guests.

The resorts begin where Portoferraio's suburbs end. Some areas within a few km offer good value in lovely settings.

# Portoferraio

**Portoferraio** (pop. 11,000) is the capital and indeed the only city of Elba. The massive walls built by Duke Cosimo remain, though Portoferraio has spilled out west along the bay. Here the ferries dock at the Calata Italia, where the visitor's introduction to Elba is the **Grattacielo** (skyscraper), a 10-storey pile of peeling paint built in the 1950s,

**Tirrena**, at Magazzini, t 0565 933002, f 0565 933452, *www.elbahotelelba.com* (*moderate*).

At Cavo, on the east coast, prices tend to be slightly lower, and there are plenty of campsites and holiday apartments. The same is true of most beaches on the southeastern peninsula around Capoliveri.

**La Conchiglia**, Cavoli, t 0565 987010, *www.laconchigliacavoli.it* (*moderate – half-board only*). Small, with air-conditioning.

**La Voce del Mare**, Naregno beach, t 0565 968455 (*moderate – half-board only*). One of many nice hotels on the beach. The best beach may be at Cavoli, west of Campo nell'Elba.

Among the resorts to the west, there are some smart places near Procchio, more modest hotels at Sant'Andrea and Pomonte, and a few that are blissfully out of the way.

***Hotel Ilio**, Capo Sant'Andrea 24, t 0565 908018, *www.ilio.it* (*very expensive – half-board obligatory April–mid-Oct*). With only 19 rooms, in a modern white-washed villa and its outbuildings, this has an intimate feel. The pretty bedrooms are pretty with rattan furniture. Breakfasts are huge and the obligatory evening meals are excellent.

# Eating Out

There are many restaurants on Elba, but few that really stand out. Elba's DOC wines, *Elba rosso* and *Elba bianco,* complement any meal.

## Piombino (Mainland)

**Ristorante Terrazza**, Piazza Premuda, t 0565 226135 (*moderate*). Somewhere to wait for the ferry, above the bar in the port, with delicious *spaghetti alle vongole* and a picture window with a good view of Piombino's steel mills.

## Portoferraio

**La Barca**, Via D. Guerrazzi, t 0565 918036 (*moderate*). A good honest *trattoria* a few steps from Piazza della Repubblica, with all sorts of seafood *antipasti* and pastas galore. Friendly service. *Closed Wed.*

**La Ferrigna**, Piazza della Repubblica 22, t 0565 914129 (*moderate*). One of the most popular places in Portoferraio, offering extravagant seafood *antipasti*, stuffed roast fish, and an Elban version of *Livornese cacciucco*, at tables on the convivial piazza. *Closed Tues.*

## Porto Azzurro

**Tavernetta**, Lungomare Vitaliani 42, t 0565 95110 (*cheap*). One of many seafood places on the beach in southern Elba, built over the sea for a fine view. *Closed Thurs.*

## Capoliveri

**Chiasso**, Via Nazario Sauro 20, t 0565 968709 (*expensive*). Offers a local dish – stuffed fresh anchovy spaghetti with fish roe and an Elban favourite, *risotto al nero di seppia* (with cuttlefish in its own ink). *Closed Tues.*

**Solemar**, outside Capoliveri at Loc. Lacona, t 0565 964248 (*cheap*). Nice *trattoria* with the best pizzas on Elba. *Closed Mon in winter.*

## Poggio

**Osteria del Noce**, Via della Madonna 27, Marciana Alta, t 0565 901284 (*moderate*). Beautifully situated in the hilltop village of Marciana Alta with fabulous views to the sea. Sit at tables carved from old wine barrels for dishes with flavours of Elba, Liguria and Sardinia; bean and mussel soup, pasta with clams and courgettes or fresh tuna and rocket, grilled tuna steaks and the catch of the day baked on a bed of potatoes and black olives. Booking is essential.

## Marciana Marina

**Rendezvous**, Piazza della Vittoria, t 0565 99251 (*very expensive*). Famous for a curious dish of baked potato stuffed with seafood, but the crustacea and mollusc soup is also excellent. *Closed Wed in winter.*

which is surely one of the most endearingly hideous buildings in the Mediterranean. It contains tourist information, most of the ferry offices, and the Portoferraio bus terminal at the back, the hub of connections to all the towns and resorts on the island.

Follow Calata Italia and its various pseudonyms under the walls, next to the old U-shaped harbour. On the far side rises the **Torre del Martello**, from which in the old days a chain was stretched across the harbour in times of danger. The main gate of the city is the **Porta a Mare** at the base of the U, over which can be seen the inscription of Duke Cosimo reminding us with the usual Medicean vanity how he built the whole town 'from the foundations upwards'; the new town had originally been dubbed Cosmopolis.

Directly inside the Porta a Mare is **Piazza Cavour**. Portoferraio is a big natural amphitheatre; from the piazza the town slopes upwards in all directions towards the walls on the high cliffs. North of the piazza, Via Garibaldi leads up to the main attraction, Napoleon's house, the **Villa dei Mulini** (*open Wed–Mon 9–7; joint adm with the Villa di San Martino,* see *below*), yellowing, unloved, unchanged since Napoleon had it built according to his own simple tastes; inside you can see his furnishings, books

## Napoleon on Elba

During the Napoleonic wars Elba was occupied for a time by the English, and Portoferraio was unsuccessfully besieged for over a year by Napoleon's troops in 1799. Napoleon finally annexed it in 1802, with no premonitions that the 1814 Treaty of Fontainebleau would put a temporary end to the First Empire and send him there.

Napoleon himself chose Elba, from the variety of small Mediterranean outposts offered him, for 'the gentleness of its climate and its inhabitants'. Also, perhaps, because on clear days he could see his own island of Corsica. No one, however, seems to have consulted the Elbans themselves on the matter, and they can be excused for the cold indifference with which they received their new ruler.

On 4 May 1814, he arrived at Portoferraio with some 500 of his most loyal officers and soldiers and a British Commissioner charged with keeping an eye on him. But Napoleon soon won over the hearts of the Elbans by being the best governor they had ever had. New systems of law and education were established, the last vestiges of feudalism abolished, and what would today be called economic planning was begun; he reorganized the iron mines and started work on Elba's modern network of roads.

Not that Napoleon ever really took his stewardship seriously. Remaking nations and institutions was a reflex by then, after doing it all across Europe for 20 years. It was the return to France that occupied his attention. The atmosphere was thick with intrigues and rumours, and secret communications flowed incessantly between Napoleon and his partisans on the Continent. On 20 February 1815, just nine months after his arrival, the Elbans and the embarrassed British watchdog awakened to find the emperor missing. The 'Hundred Days' had begun. Later, after Waterloo, a smaller, gloomier and more distant island would be found to keep Napoleon out of trouble.

Elba was returned to Tuscany, and soon after it joined the new Kingdom of Italy. It was hit hard by the Second World War; Portoferraio and its environs were bombed in 1943–4, first by the Allies, and then by the Germans. In 1944, in one of the more disgraceful episodes of the war, Elba was 'liberated' by Free French and African troops, with more murder, pillage and rape than had been seen in the Mediterranean since the days of the pirates.

and other paraphernalia, including the flag with three golden bees that he bestowed on the Elbans. It's worth the trip just to see the contemporary political cartoons mocking him. The gardens, equally uncared for, offer fine views over the city walls. On either side you can see the two Medici fortresses dominating the highest points in the city: **Forte Falcone** to the west (*open daily Easter–Sept 9–6, July–Aug 9–midnight; adm*), which you can visit, and **Forte Stella** to the east, now used as housing.

On the way down Via Garibaldi are two parish churches: the **Holy Sacrament**, which has a copy of Napoleon's death mask, or the **Misericordia**, which on 5 May holds a procession to commemorate Napoleon's death, complete with a replica of his coffin. The **Town Hall**, originally a bakery for Cosimo's troops, was the boyhood home of Victor Hugo, whose father was the French military commander in Elba. There's a Roman altar in the courtyard; inside, the **Biblioteca Foresiana** (*closed for renovation; call t 0565 937111 for information*) has a library of books about Elba and a small picture collection.

Two blocks west is the tiny but surprisingly grand **Teatro dei Vigilanti**, rebuilt by Napoleon from an abandoned church, while east of Via Garibaldi lies the **Piazza della Repubblica**, the throbbing heart of Portoferraio, with its crowded cafés, 18th-century **cathedral** (not really a cathedral at all these days) and the nearby market. Outside the walls, on the eastern side of the port, an salt warehouse has been converted into the **Museo Civico Archeologico** (*Tues–Sun 10–1 and 4–7.40, afternoon hours vary in winter; adm*), with items from the Roman patrician villas, one of which was discovered here.

## Around Portoferraio

Most of Portoferraio's hotels and restaurants are in the modern extension outside the city walls. There's a pebble beach, **Le Ghiaie**, on the north side, and another, **Le Viste**, under the walls near Forte Falcone. One of the two roads from the capital leads along the northern coast to the small resorts of **Acquaviva** and **Viticcio**, and to **Capo d'Enfola**, a lovely headland rising sheer out of the sea, barely connected to the rest of the island.

The second road runs south to the junction of **Bivio Boni**, where it branches to the east and west. Nearby is a thermal spa at **San Giovanni**, and the ruins of a Roman villa at **Le Grotte**, on the south shore of the Gulf of Portoferraio, more interesting for its view than its scant remains. There are beaches here at Ottone, Magazzini and **Bagnaia**, the latter the site of the simple, beautiful 12th-century **church of Santo Stefano**, the best Pisan monument in the archipelago. At **Acquabona** you can shoot some bogeys at one of Elba's two golf courses (nine holes), or continue west from Bivio Boni to the resort at **Biodola Bay** and the **Villa Napoleone di San Martino** (*same hours as Villa dei Mulini in Portoferraio but closed Mon; joint adm*). The emperor soon tired of life in Portoferraio and built this house as his country retreat. In later years the husband of his niece (daughter of Jérome) purchased the place and added a pretentious neoclassical façade with big Ns pasted everywhere; it's now another Napoleonic museum, with a little art gallery including a *Galatea* by Canova.

## Eastern Elba

**Rio nell'Elba** is the old mining centre, though it's not what one would expect – it's as pleasant and pastel as any other Elban town, set in the hills overlooking the eastern coast. Archaeological sites, the scanty remains of mines and Etruscan mining camps dot the neighbourhood. There are many undeveloped beaches on the western side of Rio's peninsula, including Nisporto and Nisportino. The road between Portoferraio and Rio passes the steep hill of **Volterraio**, where you can make the long climb to the 11th-century Pisan castle perched on the summit. **Rio Marina**, as its name implies, is the port for Rio nell'Elba. Here, the **Mineralogical Museum** (*open 15 Mar–15 Oct daily 9.30–12.30 and 3.30–6.30; but hours are likely to vary in high summer; adm*) in the Palazzo Comunale has displays of the island's unusual rocks and minerals – few places on earth have such a variety. Devoted rock hounds will continue on to the **Parco Minerario** (*visits at 6pm in summer; for guided visit, call* **t** *0565 962088*) in an old mine. Rio Marina has a busy harbour, its many small fishing boats under the vigilant eye of an octagonal Pisan watchtower. The eastern side of this peninsula, like the western side, has some fine beaches where you can sometimes escape the crowds – Ortano, Porticciolo, Barbarossa among others. On the northern tip stands **Cavo**, an older resort town on a tiny port.

## Porto Azzurro and Capoliveri

South of Rio, the road passes through some difficult terrain towards **Porto Azzurro**, built by the Spaniards and now a large holiday town. Until 1947 it was called *Porto Longone*. The fortress, built in 1603 to withstand the Austrians and French, was later converted into a famous Italian calaboose that hosted many political prisoners and criminal celebrities.

Besides the town beach, there are several others nearby, including a bizarre one at **Terrenere**, where a yellow-green sulphurous pond festers near the blue sea in a landscape of pebble beach and ancient mine debris – for those jaded travellers seeking something beyond Elba's mass tourism. During the season, day excursions run from Porto Azzurro to the island of Montecristo.

Just north of Porto Azzurro is the **Sanctuary of Monserrato**, a famous shrine with an icon known as the 'Black Madonna'. The Spanish governor built this here in 1606 because the mountain (Monte Castello) reminded him of the peculiar mountain of Monserrat near Barcelona. Similar Black Madonnas are revered from Portugal to Poland; over the centuries the oxidization of yellow paint has darkened them. South of Porto Azzurro is another Spanish fortress at **Capo Focardo**, on a large oval-shaped peninsula consisting of Monte Calamita and the rough hill country around it.

On this peninsula is **Capoliveri**, one of the oldest inhabited sites on the island. The town takes its name from the Roman *Caput Liberi*, which may refer either to the worship of Liber, an Italian equivalent of Dionysus (this has always been a wine-growing area) or to the free men (*liberi*) who lived there. In Roman times Capoliveri was a refuge for any man who could escape to it. It has had a reputation for independence ever since, giving a bad time to the Pisans, the Spanish and even Napoleon. Today it is peaceful, with fine views from its hilltop over the surrounding countryside and sea, though much of its scenic coast is privately owned. South of Capoliveri, near the coast, is the **Sanctuary of the Madonna delle Grazie**, with a painting of the Madonna and Child by the school of Raphael, miraculously saved from a shipwreck. The coast west of Capoliveri is marked by two lovely broad gulfs, **Golfo Stella** and **Golfo di Lacona**, separated by a steep, narrow tongue of land. Both are developed resort areas, with centres at Lacona and Lido Margidore.

## Western Elba

Beyond Biodola, the scenic corniche road west from Portoferraio passes through the adjacent resorts of **Prócchio** and **Campo all'Aia**; the former is larger and one of the more expensive resorts on Elba. **Marciana Marina**, 7km west, is another popular resort, with a 15th-century Pisan watchtower, the **Torre Saracena**. This is the port for **Marciana**, the oldest continuously inhabited town on Elba.

In the 14th and 15th centuries, when life near the coast wasn't safe, Marciana was the 'capital' of the feudal Appiani barons, the most powerful family on the island. Today, high in the forests on the slopes of Monte Capanne, it is surprisingly beautiful, characterized by narrow streets, stone stairs, archways and belvederes. Sections of the old city wall and gate are still intact, and the old Pisan **fortress** hangs over the town (*opening hours vary – usually mornings, and evenings 6–11pm; closed Nov–Easter; t 0565 901215; adm, joint ticket with Archaeology Museum*). The palace of the Appiani may be seen on a narrow *vicolo* in the oldest part of town. Marciana's **Archaeology Museum** (*opening hours as for fortress, above*) has a small collection of prehistoric and Roman objects found in the area. In season, a cable lift (*departs daily April–Oct at 10, 12, 2.45 and 5; fare exp*) climbs to the summit of Elba's highest peak, **Monte Capanne** (1,019m/3,342ft), with stupendous views over Corsica, the Tuscan archipelago and the mountains of Tuscany itself.

Three churches outside Marciana are of interest: the ruined Pisan **San Lorenzo**, the **Sanctuary of San Cerbone**, who escaped here from the troublesome Lombards (later his body was buried in a rainstorm, so they wouldn't see), and the **Sanctuary of the Madonna del Monte**, dating from the 11th century and one of the island's most important shrines, with a Madonna painted on a lump of granite. Pagan Elbans may have worshipped on this site as well, as did Napoleon for two weeks, after a fashion, with his Polish mistress, Maria Walewska. Another mountain village is **Poggio**, just to the east, with a natural spring where the Elbans bottle their *acqua minerale* – called Napoleone, of course. It's very good, but the Elbans keep it all to themselves.

On the rugged coast to the west and south of Marciana, there are more beaches and resorts: **Sant'Andrea**, **Patresi**, **Chiessi**, **Pomonte**, **Fetovaia** (a lovely stretch, protected by a rocky promontory), **Seccheto** and **Cavoli**. Seccheto has ancient granite quarries from which the stone was cut for the Pantheon in Rome.

Elba's pocket-sized plain, the **Campo nell'Elba**, stretches 7km east of Marciana, extending from Procchio to Marina di Campo and separating the western mountains from the central range. Elba's airport is here – the only place they could put it. Two old towns lie on the edge of the plain: **Sant'Ilario in Campo** and **San Piero in Campo**. San Piero's parish church of San Niccolò has interesting frescoes; it was built on the ruins of an ancient temple to Glaucus. Halfway between the towns are the ruins of the Pisan church of **San Giovanni**, along with a watchtower (*closed; may be viewed from outside*). On the coast is **Marina di Campo**, Elba's first, perhaps largest resort, with the largest beach. The harbour watchtower was built by the Medici.

## Pianosa and Montecristo

Two other members of the Tuscan archipelago are included in Livorno province: one you won't want to visit, and the other you usually can't. **Pianosa** is the black sheep of the chain. Its name, taken from the Roman *Planasia*, explains why – it's as flat as a pool table. Like Gorgona, Pianosa's unhappy fate was to serve as a prison island, although it has been closed for many years. There are some substantial ruins of a Roman villa, from the days when Pianosa was the playground of Cornelius Agrippa, Emperor Augustus' great general, but to see them you'll need special permission from the prison authorities in Rome.

Likewise, don't count on visiting **Montecristo**, which lies 40km south of Elba. Once the hunting preserve of King Vittorio Emanuele III, this tiny island, in fact the tip of an ancient volcano, has now been declared a nature reserve. Private boats and day trips organized from Porto Azzurro on Elba may dock at Cala Maestra, but visitors are only allowed to stay on the cove and its beach; the mountain, ruins of a medieval monastery and royal villa (now the custodian's house) are out of bounds. In Roman times this was an important religious site, *Mons Jovis*, with a famous temple of Jupiter; not a trace remains. The early Church wasted no time Christianizing the place, renaming it Montecristo. The first monastic community was founded in the 6th century by San Mamiliano (*see* pp.308–9), who reportedly killed a dragon upon arrival. None of *The Count of Monte Cristo* is really set here; like the Count himself, seeing the place on a map is probably as close to it as Alexandre Dumas ever got.

## South of Piombino: The Coast and Offshore

## The Maremma

In a sense, this flat, lonely stretch of coast really belongs to Italy's south. History has been unkind to the Maremma, domain first of the Etruscans, later of the anopheles mosquito. Like many southern coastal regions, the Maremma was a prosperous agricultural region until Roman times. The Romans gave it its name: the 'maritime' zone (as names such as Massa Marittima), gradually mangled into Maremma.

Historians sometimes give the Romans too much credit for capable governance; on the contrary, their grasping, bureaucratic state slowly corroded and eventually destroyed the Italian economy. Many centuries of Roman misgovernment – impossible taxes, cheap imported grain and especially, in this case, neglect of the Etruscans' system of drainage canals – doomed the Maremma to a slow death.

# South of Piombino: Maremma to Lazio

When the drainage canals failed, much of the land was abandoned and reverted to swamps, breeding the malarial mosquitoes that made the Maremma of the Middle Ages a place of suffering and death, inhabitable only by the *butteri*, tough Tuscan cowboys who tended the herds in the abandoned marshy pastures. A considerable body of folklore has grown up around the *butteri*, and the Maremma's proudest moment came in the last century when some of them went to Rome and defeated Buffalo Bill and his travelling Wild West show in a test of cowboy know-how. The first work of reclamation began with the Austrian Grand Dukes. The Italian Kingdom that followed them forgot all about the Maremma, and it was not until after the Second World War that the task was completed. The Maremma today is back on its feet, a new region and a little rough around the edges, but prosperous once more.

# Tourist Information

**Follonica**: Via Giacomelli II, **t** 0566 52012, **f** 0566 53833.

**Castiglione della Pescaia**: Piazza Garibaldi, on the harbour, **t** 0564 933678.

# Where to Stay and Eat

## Castiglione della Pescaia ✉ 58043

Castiglione may lack appealing beaches, but it has a wide range of inexpensive hotels – rare along this coastline. Most offer only half or full board from mid-July to mid-Sept.

**\*\*Rossella**, Via Fratelli Bandiera 18, **t** 0564 933832, *www.albergorosella.it* (*expensive*; June–mid-Sept half-board only). Near the beaches.

**Hotel Miramare**, Via Vittorio Veneto 27, **t** 0564 933524, *www.hotelmiramare.info* (*moderate*). Home to an excellent seafood restaurant (*expensive*). Try the *tesoro di Montecristo*, a delicious mixed grill of fish. Innovative dishes, such as crêpes filled with prawns and baked *spaghetti al cartoccio*.

**Osteria nel Buco**, Via del Recinto 11. **t** 0564 934460 (*moderate*). A cosy and friendly *trattoria*, offering good food and sometimes a musical contribution to the evening. Local fish dishes include anchovies marinated in pesto, crab soup, and fresh catch of the day. There are meaty alternatives too. *Tues–Sat dinner only, Sun lunch and dinner; open Mon also in July and Aug*.

## Follonica and Punta Ala

After Piombino, the coast bends eastwards into a broad arc, the Golfo di Follonica. There are some wonderful beaches between Piombino and Follonica, notably La Sterpaia, which partially backs on to a nature reserve. Since the Second World War, new resort towns have been popping up like toadstools all along the Tuscan coast. One of the biggest and least likeable is **Follonica**, 21km east of Piombino, partially redeemed by the long pine groves that follow its crowded beaches. Follonica has other enchantments, notably the **Museum of Iron and Cast Iron** (*open Wed and Fri 4.30–7.30, Sat 10–12.30; for visits outside these hours, contact t 0566 59391/59380*) in an old foundry of the 1830s where Elban iron was once smelted. There is also **CARAPAX** (*t 0566 940083, www.carapax.org; open Mar Mon–Fri 9–5; April–20 June daily 9–6; 21 June–20 Sept daily 9–7; 21 Sept–31 Oct daily 9–5; Nov–Feb closed; feeding time 9am*), the European Centre for the Protection of Turtles and Tortoises. No fooling. They study turtles, save endangered ones and reintroduce them into the wild. Visitors are welcome to look at the turtle clinic and nursery, and see exotic species from as far as the Amazon and the Sahel. The centre is also working to reintroduce the stork to Italy, and has a colony of them in Italy's biggest aviary.

On the promontory that closes the gulf, 14km to the south, **Punta Ala** is a new, entirely synthetic resort, built in the suburban style of the Costa Smeralda. It's an attractive location, with a fine sandy beach and views around the gulf, and it attracts a very well-heeled clientele with unusual (for Tuscany) diversions like golf (*at the Golf Hotel, Via del Gualdo*) and polo (*Polo Club*).

**Castiglione della Pescaia**, to the south, is just the opposite: much less exclusive, attached to an attractive, ancient fishing village. The beach isn't great, but the town on its hill, with trees and ivy-covered walls, is one of the more pleasant detours on this coast. The Spanish left a 16th-century castle, the Rocca Aragonese, and the church of

San Giovanni has an interesting tower that could pass for a minaret. From the harbour, Navimaremma offers summer island cruises; the tourist office has details.

## Grosseto

For the original edition of this book, years ago, we enjoyed writing the following:

*When Duke Cosimo I gobbled up Grosseto in 1559, along with the rest of the Sienese republic, he resolved to make it into a fortress town, guarding his southern borders against Spain and the pope. Following the manic geometry of the age, Cosimo's architects enclosed Grosseto in a nearly perfect hexagon of walls. But as any good Chinese geomancer (or reader of Doris Lessing's* Shikasta*) could have told the Duke, one can't take such matters lightly. Maybe it was the wrong polygon for the prevailing telluric forces, but Grosseto (pop. 70,000) has certainly been suffering from some strange vibrations. Come to Grosseto, and you will find a city of Art Nouveau buildings and perverse teenagers, a city conducive to hallucinations, its streets alive with swirls of dust and flying plastic bags. Its citizens have a penchant for punk music and American football (the Grosseto 61ers), also, so they claim, the highest rate of drug addiction in Italy. It is the only city in Italy, outside Calabria, where you cannot buy a decent slice of pizza.*

God knows where the flying bags, the hallucinations and the 61ers have gone, and today the teenagers look no more perverse than anywhere else in Europe. Under the prevailing prosperity, the natural Tuscan sense of order and propriety has slowly been asserting itself here. Instead of punk music, there is a busy *assessorato della cultura* in the town hall laying on dance and chamber music concerts and scholarly conferences. Italy's Most Improved Town, always a likeable place, grows steadily more normal, even pleasant – though the *pizza a taglio* situation still needs some work.

### Around La Vasca

Via Carducci leads you from the station towards the fearful hexagon, passing Mussolini's contribution to the city, the circular Piazza Fratelli Rosselli that is really known to one and all as **La Vasca** (which can mean 'tub' or 'toilet bowl'); here the starring role is played by an exuberant Mussolini **post office**, with heroic statuary in travertine. The main gate is only a block away. Cosimo's walls are perfectly preserved, done in tidy, reddish brick festooned with Medici balls. Much of the old city looks very Spanish; the Art Nouveau pharmacies and shoe shops along the main street, Corso Carducci, contribute to the effect, as does the arcaded Piazza del Duomo, very like a Spanish *Plaza Mayor*. The **Duomo**, built 1190–1250, suffered grievously from over-ambitious restoration in the 1840s; the façade looks more like a Hollywood prop than a genuine cathedral. Have a look inside for a genuinely lovely painting, Matteo di Giovanni's *Madonna delle Grazie* (1470). Around the side of the Duomo there is an interesting sundial, and in the piazza an allegorical monument to the Maremma's benefactor, the Lorraine Grand Duke Leopold II; the woman he is raising up represents the suffering Maremma, and the snake he's crushing is Malaria.

Around the corner in Piazza Baccarini, two museums, collectively called the **Museo Archeologico e d'Arte della Maremma** (*t 0564 488750; open summer Tues–Sun 10–1*

# Getting Around

**Trains** depart regularly for Siena, via Roccastrada and Buonconvento (7 a day, some of which continue on to Florence), and on the coastal line for Livorno, or Orbetello and Rome. RAMA **buses (t** 0564 25215) have connections to Siena (7 a day) and every town in Grosseto province, including Massa Marittima (twice daily, *see* **Hill Towns West of Siena**, p.362), Arcidosso and Pitigliano (5 daily, *see* **Southern Tuscany**, pp.386 and 390). Everything leaves from the train station.

# Tourist Information

**Grosseto**: Viale Monterosa 206, **t** 0564 462611, *www.lamaremma.info.*

# Where to Stay and Eat

## Grosseto ✉ 58100

Hotels here tend to be simple. In the unlikely event that you can't find anywhere, the city's *Consorzio Albergatori* might be able to help (**t** 0564 415446).

**\*\*\*\*Bastiani Grand Hotel**, Via Gioberti 64, **t** 0564 20047, **f** 0564 29321, *www.hotel bastiani.com* (*expensive*). One exception to the rule is this city-centre hotel, housed in a gracious 1890s palazzo.

**\*\*\*Leon d'Oro**, Via San Martino 46, **t** 0564 22128, **f** 0564 22578 (*moderate*). Offers double rooms with bath, and the restaurant's not bad either. *Closed Sun.*

**Buca di San Lorenzo**, Via Manetti 1, **t** 0564 25142 (*moderate*). Dug into the Medicean walls. Menus depend on what is available at the market; only the freshest fish is used. All pasta is home-made. *Closed Sun.*

**Il Canto del Gallo**, Via Mazzini 29, **t** 0564 414589 (*moderate*). A tiny *trattoria* in the centre of the old town. The owner will advise you on what to eat and then prepare it personally. Home-made pasta with wild boar, spelt soup, wild boar stew and other local specialities; fish if you order in advance. Booking essential. *Closed lunch and Sun.*

**Da Remo**, Rispescia Stazione, **t** 0564 405014 (*moderate*). A few km south of Grosseto, just off the Aurelia. Mixed *antipasti* include a superb *insalata di mare* and grilled oysters while the sea bass cooked *al cartoccio* (in foil) with mussels, clams and local herbs is sublime. *Closed Wed.*

**La Taverna Etrusca**, Vetulonia (*cheap*). If you're going up to visit Vetulonia, try this good inexpensive *trattoria* at the top of town; it also has some reasonably priced rooms.

and 5–8; Nov–Feb Tues–Fri 9–1, Sat and Sun 9.30–1 and 4.30–7; Nov and April Tues–Sun 9.30–1 and 4.30–7) want to show you something of life in this region before there ever was a Grosseto. Some parts of this coastline just can't stand still. Thousands of years ago, Grosseto and most of its surrounding plain were under water; by the time of the Etruscans, the sea had receded, leaving a large lake on the plain. Two wealthy Etruscan cities, *Vetulonia* and *Roselle* (*see* below), stood on the hills above the lake, and they contributed most of the items here: cinerary urns with scenes from Homer, architectural fragments and delicate terracottas, some preserving bits of their original paint. The collection is not a rich one, though well organized and relentlessly didactic. Up on the third floor, the city **Pinacoteca** (*recently reopened after restoration, same opening hours as the Archaeology Museum*) houses some good Sienese art, including an amazing, very Byzantine *Last Judgement* by the 13th-century artist Guido da Siena.

Just north of the museum, the church of San Francesco has an early work by Duccio di Buoninsegna, the crucifix above the high altar, and also some good 13th-century frescoes. From here, you can start a walk around the Medicean walls. After Italian unification, the bastions were landscaped into beautiful semi-tropical gardens; some are still well kept, while others have decayed into spooky jungles. The liveliest parts of Grosseto are the shopping streets around Piazza del Mercato; nearby, just outside the walls, mornings see a large, almost picturesque street market.

## Roselle and Vetulonia

You can learn more about these two Etruscan towns from the Grosseto museum than from visiting the ruins, although this can be fun. **Roselle**, 7km north of the city, is the mother city of Grosseto. It survived Roman rule better than many other Etruscan cities, but by the 5th century it was almost abandoned. Nevertheless, the bishops of Roselle hung on until 1178, when the seat was transferred to Grosseto.

Like many other Etruscan towns, Roselle stands atop a high plateau and is surrounded by over 3km of walls. A Roman road leads up to the complex where there are still a few building foundations, remains of the baths, the imperial forum and the outline of the Roman amphitheatre, a medieval tower, and necropolises. North of the site are the ruins of a **Roman villa** (*open daily 9–dusk*) with parts of its original mosaic floor paving. The last occupant operated a forge here to melt down bronze statues.

**Vetulonia**, 17km from Grosseto, above the Via Aurelia west of Braccagni, lives on in its worthy successor, Massa Marittima (*see* pp.361–3). On the site itself, a miniature hill town survives, set in rugged but lovely countryside with occasional views over the Tyrrhenian and the islands. Like Roselle, it lasted until the Middle Ages, and was probably destroyed in a 14th-century revolt against its Pisan overlords.

Bits of old Vetulonia can be seen in the **Aree Archeologiche** (signposted) and the nearby **museum** (*open daily winter 9–5; summer 9–7.30; joint adm for both*). The scanty ruins are more Roman and medieval than Etruscan, but on the periphery are some interesting tombs (also signed): the massive **Tomba della Pietrera** and the unique **Il Diavolino** (7th century BC). Both have a long corridor under a tumulus, with an arched burial chamber in the centre; the Diavolino has a window to the sky.

## Monti dell'Uccellina: The Maremma Nature Park

*Open daily from 8 until 1 hour before sunset; adm. The visitors' centre is at Alberese, west of the coastal Via Aurelia/SS1; park and take the regular shuttle service into the park. During the summer some areas can only be visited by guided tour. Adm limited; during busiest times – Easter, 29 April–1 May, July and August – it's best to call ahead, t 0564 407098; ask about guided tours in English during the summer.*

One effect of the Maremma's history of abandonment is a beautiful, unspoiled coast. In the 1950s and 1960s developers followed in the wake of DDT wherever they could, but the government managed to set aside a few of the best parts. The **Monti dell'Uccellina**, a ragged chain of hills south of Grosseto, largely covered with umbrella pines, is an important pit stop for migratory birds between Europe and Africa, hence the name.

The park has some pretty strict rules. Only 500 people a day, and no cars and no dogs, are allowed to enter. Nine walks have been laid out, lasting 2–6 hours, and visitors are expected to keep to them. Note that one of the walks begins from a separate park entrance at Talamone, further south, but it doesn't connect to the others.

The visitors' centre recommends you bring good shoes and some water, and if you like they can book you an experienced guide for about €12 an hour.

For such a small area (roughly 5km by 15km), the park has a lot to see: nine old defence towers, dozens of caves and the ruins of an 11th-century monastery, **San Rabano**, that belonged to the Knights of Malta. It retains its campanile and some early medieval stone-carving. Where the park meets the sea there is a strip of fabulous beaches. Despite the park status, some people still make their living here, herding cattle, cutting cork oak and gathering pine nuts for Italy's pastry cooks.

The park's landscape ranges from swamps to heather and scented *macchia* (mixed Mediterranean scrub) to pine groves, and includes among its fauna wild horses, deer and boar, along with the *uccellini* themselves – herons, eagles and falcons, ospreys and kingfishers, every sort of duck, and that most overdressed of all waterfowl, the *cavaliere d'Italia*. Some peripheral areas can be toured on horseback, and Il Rialto at Albarese (*t 0564 407 1020*) can fix you up with a steed; they also rent bikes and canoes.

## Talamone

The Sienese Republic never really had a port, gravely hampering its foreign trade. Now and then, it tried to make one out of **Talamone**, a fishing village at the tip of the Monti dell'Uccellina. Unfortunately, the little harbour couldn't be kept clear, a continuing embarrassment for the republic; even Dante dropped a jibe about foolishly 'hoping from Talamone'. Garibaldi had better luck: when in 1860 he and his 'Thousand' chose to stop here rather than Sardinia, they avoided the orders for their arrest that had been sent by the treacherous Count Cavour; Garibaldi also found a cache of weapons in Orbetello, which came in handy during the conquest of Sicily.

Today the walled village on its rock has become a discreet, laid-back resort with a small marina. Above, a 16th-century Spanish castle sits like an abstract modern sculpture, set to house a new museum devoted to nature in the Monti dell'Uccellina.

# Monte Argentario

In the last decade or so, this curiosity of the Tuscan coast has grown popular. It has much going for it: some attractive old towns, a genuine Mediterranean feeling and matching scenery, a noticeable attraction on the humdrum Tuscan coast. Once, long ago, Argentario was an island, the member of the Tuscan archipelago closest to the shore. No one seems able to explain how it happened, but the Tyrrhenian currents gradually built up two symmetrical sand bars, connecting the rugged, mountainous island to the mainland. In between, there was a peninsula with the Etruscan, then Roman city of Orbetello; the Romans built a causeway on to Argentario that split the natural lagoon in half. It is said that sailors named the Argentario in classical times, noticing the bright flashes of silver from the olive trees that still cover its slopes.

Most books describe Porto Santo Stefano and Porto Ercole as 'exclusive', even 'posh'. Not true. The Argentario attracts its share of the high life, particularly the yachting crowd from Rome, and it's a bit pricier than other resorts. But the peninsula has not become an overcrowded beach Babylon like Elba. The beaches are not special, and Tuscany's art and other attractions are far away, but on balance, if you're after the best place for a seaside holiday in the region, the Argentario presents a strong case.

## Orbetello

Go to the northern tip of **Orbetello**'s peninsula, near the causeway, and look over the water; below the modern breakwater, you can see bits of ancient wall in huge irregular blocks. These are the sole remnants of Etruscan Orbetello, probably the biggest port on the Etruscan coast, and defensible enough to give the city a minor historical role over the centuries. The Byzantines held out longer here than anywhere else on this coast; the city then fell into the hands of the Three Fountains Abbey in Rome, who handed it to the Pope – until 1980 the pope was also bishop of Orbetello. After the treaty of Câteau-Cambrésis in 1559, Orbetello became capital of a new province – the Spanish military *Presidio*, from which imperialist Spain could menace both Tuscany and the Pope, ruled by a viceroy directly responsible to the King.

The Spanish Presidio lasted only until 1707, but it had a strong impact on the area's buildings and its people. Orbetello was briefly something of a resort, but passed this role on to Porto Ercole and Porto Santo Stefano, and its most recent flash of glory came in the 1930s when Mussolini made it Italy's main seaplane base. Fascist hero Italo Balbo began his famous transatlantic flight from the lagoon in 1933, landing at the opening of the Chicago World's Fair.

Confined on its peninsula, with its palm trees and sun-bleached Spanish walls, Orbetello (pop. 13,500) is a charming town, where buses barely squeeze through the main gate. Viale Italia, the main street, runs down the centre of the peninsula; just north on Piazza della Repubblica, the **cathedral**'s façade has a sculpted portal and rose window from 1376, though its interior was rebuilt in the 1600s.

Orbetello's **lagoons**, on average about 3ft deep, are partially used for fish farms, but most of the northern half has been declared a nature reserve, run by the World Wide Fund for Nature. Like the Monti dell'Uccellina, the area is a breeding ground for marine birds, and also storks and a species of eagle, not to mention the stilt plover, the bee-eater and the lesser hen harrier. Their nesting period lasts from April to October, and from May to September the reserve is closed to humans. The **visitors' centre** is on the coast road between Orbetello and Albinia (*open Oct–April for guided tours, Thurs, Sat and Sun, 10 and 3; t 0564 820297 for info; adm*).

## Porto Ercole and Porto Santo Stefano

Over the causeway from Orbetello on to Monte Argentario, you can go either north or south to begin the *gita panoramica*, the 24km road that circles the island (it offers some exceptional views, but it's not surfaced the whole way and you won't get round unless you have a jeep). To the south, **Porto Ercole** wraps itself around a yacht-filled harbour, guarded on either side by Spanish fortresses. Forte Stella and Forte San Filippo were probably the last word in 16th-century military architecture, with low, sloping walls and pointed bastions draped over the cliffs; today they are an ominous, surreal sight. San Filippo is the more interesting, though you can't visit – it has been

# Getting Around

Orbetello is the centre for public transport around the Argentario, with a bus station just off Piazza della Repubblica. There are regular **buses** for Porto Ercole, Porto S. Stefano, Grosseto, and the **railway station**, about 2km east of town, on the Grosseto–Rome coastal line, plus daily buses to Capalbio and Pitigliano.

# Tourist Information

Orbetello: Piazza della Repubblica,
t 0564 860447.
Porto Santo Stefano: Corso Umberto 55,
t 0564 814208.
Capalbio: Capalbio Scalo, t 0564 8638.

# Where to Stay and Eat

Orbetello ⊠ 58035

★★★San Biagio Relais, Via Dante 34, t 0564 860543, f 0564 867787, www.sanbiagio relais.com (*very expensive*) A good choice in the centre of town; this new, classy hotel (housed in an elegant palazzo) has 17 comfortable, individually furnished rooms and suites decorated in warm colours and furnished with antiques.

★★★Hotel Relais Presidi, Via Mura di Levante 34, t 0564 867601, f 0564 860432, www.ipresidi.com (*expensive*). The best in Orbetello, with lagoon views and a restaurant. Most rooms have balconies.

★Piccolo Parigi, Corso Italia 169, t 0564 867233 (*inexpensive*). Delightful, very friendly and very Mediterranean, in the middle of town, ideal if you're travelling on a budget.

Osteria del Lupacante, Corso Italia 103, t 0564 867618 (*moderate*). Wonderful fresh seafood, from octopus and potato salad to spaghetti with sea urchin or *zucchini* flowers stuffed with baby squid. *Closed Tues in winter.*

I Pescatori, Via Leopardi 9, t 0564 860611 (*cheap*). Opened by the local fisherman's co-op, and featuring only fish caught in the lagoon, this simple restaurant (where you eat off plastic plates) is delightful. Housed in a former warehouse on the lagoon, you select your fish and pay at the cash desk then sit down to smoked mullet roe, pasta with John Dory or mullet, roast catch of the day or eel. The local wine is cold and cheap. *Open daily for dinner mid-June–mid Sept, Fri–Sun for dinner in winter.*

Porto Ercole ⊠ 58018

★★★★Il Pellicano, Cala dei Santi, a cove near Porto Ercole, t 0564 858111, f 0564 833418,

converted into holiday flats. Above the souvenir shops and seafood restaurants of the harbour, there is a fine old town, entered through a Gothic gate constructed by the Sienese. Little Piazza Santa Barbara is the centre, with the dignified 17th-century palace of the Spanish governor, and a view over the harbour below. Caravaggio was buried in the church of Sant'Erasmo in 1609 after dying of malaria in a tavern nearby; the artist was on his way back from Malta to Rome, where he had hoped the Pope would pardon him for a tennis-court murder committed years before. Beyond Porto Ercole, the coast road twists and turns under the slopes of Il Telegrafo, Argentario's highest peak (635m/2,083ft). One feature of the *gita panoramica* is the many defence towers, some built by the Sienese, others by the Spaniards.

On the northern side of the Argentario, **Porto Santo Stefano** makes a matching bookend for Porto Ercole. Larger than its sister town, this one also began as a sleepy fishing village. Now the fishing boats are elbowed off to the side of the port by speedboats, big shiny yachts and the Giglio ferries, and the old town has become lost in the agglomeration of hotels and villas on the surrounding hills. However, it remains less exclusive than Porto Ercole and more of a real community than an exclusive yachting port. There are really two harbours: the first, larger one has the *www.pellicanohotel.com (luxury – half-board obligatory mid-June–Sept)*. If you've bushels of money and like swilling gin with yachtsmen and Italian TV stars, this Relais et Châteaux hotel provides every imaginable amenity. There's a beach, a pool, windsurfing and every other water sport, plus tennis – not to mention a first-class restaurant.

★★★★**Torre di Calapiccola, t** 0564 825111, **f** 0564 825235, *www.torredicalapiccola.com (luxury)*. An apartment complex spectacularly set high above the sea, with a beach and activities, or for peace and quiet on the western tip of the peninsula.

★★★**Don Pedro,** Via Panoramica, **t** 0564 833914, **f** 0564 883129, *www.hoteldonpedro.it (very expensive)*. Above the town, but some way from the nearest beach.

★**La Conchiglia,** Via della Marina, **t** 0564 833134 *(moderate)*. One of the few moderate places on Argentario proper.

**Osteria I Nobili Santi,** Via dell'Ospizio 8, **t** 0564 833015 *(moderate)*. This excellent little fish restaurant serves up elegant dishes of the freshest of fish (and only fish) in an elegant setting. The mixed *antipasto* (comprising at least ten dishes) is superb as is the pasta – try sea bass ravioli or gnocchi with a scampi cream. Follow this with a tasty *fritto misto* or baked fish with potatoes and black olives. *Open Tues–Sun; closed for lunch in summer.*

**Porto Santo Stefano** ✉ 58019

★★★**La Caletta,** Via Civinni 10, **t** 0564 812939, **f** 0564 817506, *www.hotelcaletta.it (expensive)*. Pleasant rooms overlooking the sea.

★★★**Filippo II, t** 0564 811611, *www.filippo secondo.it (expensive)*. Recently refurbished, this is doubtless the best in town; close to the beaches at Poggio Calvella.

I **Due Pini,** Loc. La Soda, **t** 0564 814012 *(expensive)*. A wood-panelled restaurant in a stunning beachside setting, on the coast road into Porto Santo Stefano. The food is good (although pricy) too; a fabulous array of *antipasti*, pasta with lobster or clams, and fish and crustacea.

**Dal Greco,** Via del Molo 1, **t** 0564 814885 *(expensive)*. An elegant establishment on the yacht harbour, pricy but worth it. *Terrina di pesce* with vegetables, and lobster, are the star attractions. *Closed Tues.*

★★**Alfiero,** Via Cuniberti 12, **t** 0564 814067 *(moderate)*. A simple, less expensive hotel at the centre of the action around the harbour.

**Orlando,** Via Breschi 3, **t** 0564 812788 *(moderate)*. Popular and lively, with a terrace overlooking the sea. The mixed seafood *antipasto* is generous, 'Pirates' spaghetti is delicious, as are the sautéed prawns. Honest prices and a relaxed atmosphere. *Closed Wed.*

ferries and the fish markets; the yachts – and some real dreadnoughts they are – call at the western harbour, at the other side of a small promontory.

The two spits of land joining Argentario to the mainland are made up of two long beaches, the Giannella and the Feniglia. The latter is backed by a beautiful protected pine forest (a nature reserve) with a path running right along it. You can hire bikes and ride the 7km of its length, branching on to the beach at various points. The Giannella is backed by the main road, but faces west so you get lovely sunsets.

# Giglio and Giannutri

## Giglio

Giglio is the largest of the Tuscan islands after Elba, measuring about 21km by 8km. It is also second in population, with about 1,600 souls, almost all in its three little villages: Giglio Porto, Giglio Castello and Giglio Campese. Like many Italian islands, Giglio suffered grievously from deforestation and abandonment of the land in the 18th and 19th centuries. Though much of it remains green and pretty, large expanses

## Getting There and Around

Porto S. Stefano is the **port** for Giglio, a one-hour run; the ferry service is shared by the TOREMAR line (**t** 0564 810803) and Maregiglio, (**t** 0564 812920), both in Porto S. Stefano; boats run at least twice daily, and more frequently in the summer.

The **railway station** for Porto S. Stefano, along the main Livorno–Rome line, is Orbetello Scalo; buses meet the trains to carry passengers to the port. Giannutri can be reached regularly only in July and August, on a daily boat from Porto S. Stefano. On Giglio, buses run fairly regularly from the ferry dock to Giglio Castello and Giglio Campese.

## Tourist Information

**Giglio Porto**: Via Umberto I 48, **t** 0564 809400 (*summer only*).

## Where to Stay and Eat

### Giglio ✉ 58012

The number of tourists, and hotels (12) on Giglio seems to have stabilized, leaving it not entirely overcrowded even in the summer.
**\*\*\*Arenella**, Via Arenella 5, **t** 0564 809340, **f** 0564 809443 (*expensive*). Persevere until you leave the Porto to enjoy something rather more serene; this is near the beach, with a pretty garden and a good restaurant.
**\*\*\*Demo's**, Via Thaon De Revel, **t** 0564 809235, **f** 0564 809319, *www.hoteldemos.com* (*expensive*). Right in the port, in the 1960s Miami Beach style.

**\*\*La Pergola**, next door, **t** 0564 809051 (*moderate*). Smaller and cosier.

If you really want to get away from it all, your best chance is in Cala degli Alberi:
**\*\*Pardini's Hermitage**, Cala degli Alberi, **t** 0564 809034, **f** 0564 809177 (*luxury – full board*). In its quiet cove, this can only be reached by boat (ask at the Giglio Sub shop on the port, but with only 11 rooms it's best to book). Sports and nature activities if you want, or just enjoy the sea and mountains. Only full or half-board in the summer.

### Giglio Campese ✉ 58012

**\*\*\*Campese**, Via della Torre 18, **t** 0564 804003, **f** 0564 804093, *www.hotelcampese.com* (*very expensive* – half-board). A good, modern beach hotel.

### Giglio Porto

**La Margherita**, **t** 0564 809237 (*moderate*). One of the most popular of the seafood restaurants around the harbour; good fish and a terrace on the beach. *Closed Mon*.

### Giglio Castello

**Da Maria**, Via Casamatta 12, **t** 0564 806062 (*very expensive*). A real find, with good seafood (stuffed squid or lobster flambé) and game dishes like the house speciality, wild rabbit *alla cacciatora*. *Closed Wed*.
**Da Santi**, Via Marconi 20, **t** 0564 806188 (*expensive*). Those 'in the know' go to Santi's in the old town. An ex-ship's cook, he cooks good fresh food in his simple old-fashioned restaurant. Specialities include sea bass ravioli and game. Sample, too, the local white wine, which is rarely on sale. *Closed Mon off season*.

are now almost barren. Recently, however, a remarkable change in Giglian environmental consciousness seems to have occurred; if the big signs all over the harbour are any indication, they've gone to the opposite extreme – no camping, no noise, no riding over the wild flowers (and no collecting rocks – they're part of the island too).

The word *Giglio* means lily, and the lily has become the island's symbol, although it has in fact nothing to do with its name. The Romans called it *Aegilium* or *Gilium*. Under them, Giglio like most of the other Italian islands was a resort for the very wealthy. Pisa, Aragon and various feudal families held the island in the Middle Ages. Duke Cosimo seized it for Tuscany in the 16th century, but did little to protect it against its greatest danger, pirates. Fortunately, the Giglians had the holy right arm of San Mamiliano to protect them. This 6th-century Sicilian bishop, fleeing from the

Arian heretics, became a hermit on Montecristo. When he died, a divine signal alerted fishermen from Elba, Giglio and even Genoa, who arrived at the same time and began to fight over the remains. In the true tradition of Christian brotherhood, they struck a deal and cut Mamiliano in three pieces. Giglio got the arm, which proved its worth by chasing away Turkish pirates in 1799. On other occasions it wasn't so helpful. The redoubtable pirate Barbarossa carried off most of the population in 1534, and his understudy Dragut came back for the rest in 1550.

**Giglio Porto**, the island's metropolis, is a colourful place, with red and green light-houses to welcome the ferries, and pink and beige houses straggling up the hills. There are two beaches south of the town, at **Cala delle Canelle** and **Cala delle Caldane**, one to the north at **Punta Aranella**, all more or less developed, and in the town itself, the world's smallest beach, tucked behind the houses on the left side of the port. From Giglio Porto a difficult mountain road leads up to **Giglio Castello**, the only secure refuge in pirate days, and until recently the only real town. The fortress itself was begun by the Pisans and completed under the grand dukes. The picturesque town inside, all medieval alleys and overhanging arches, has plenty of gulls and swallows, a few German tourists, and a small Baroque church with an odd tower and the famous arm of San Mamiliano.

From Giglio Castello, a road leads southwards past **Poggio della Pagana**, the island's highest peak (498m/1,633ft), through land largely reforested with pines to Punta del Capel Rosso, at the southern tip, then back along the coast to Giglio Porto. The main road from Giglio Castello continues on to **Giglio Campese**, a growing resort area with an old watchtower and a large sandy beach.

## Giannutri

**Giannutri**, the southernmost island of the Tuscan archipelago, is a rocky crescent about 5km long, with little water and no fertile ground, and little history to speak of. The ancient Greeks knew it as *Artemisia*, and the Romans as *Dianium*; perhaps the associations with the moon goddess came from the island's crescent shape. In Roman times it was an estate of the noble Ahenobarbus family, and there are the substantial ruins of a **Roman Villa** (1st century AD) near Cala Maestra, which are a popular destination for daytrippers from Porto Santo Stefano in the summer months. Though Giannutri has no permanent population, there is a tourist village and some holiday cottages near the well-protected bay, **Cala Spalmatoio**, on the eastern coast.

# Capalbio and the Giardino dei Tarocchi

Back on the coast south of Orbetello, almost nothing is left of **Ansedonia**, destroyed by the Sienese in 1330. There's a beach, a few hotels, and an unusual Etruscan attempt to stop Cosa's harbour from silting up: deep channels hewn from the solid rock. For ruins you must climb up to **Cosa**, settled by Romans in the 3rd century BC to keep an eye on the restless Etruscan cities – and maybe accelerate their decline by draining off trade. Cosa was sacked by Visigoths in the 5th century, but the ruins give a fair idea of the Roman city: a typical rectangular circuit of walls with three gates, a strict street grid, a 'Capitoline' temple, and cisterns for rainwater. Remains of the port are visible from Ansedonia harbour and there is also a small museum on the site.

Before the Via Aurelia (SS1) passes from Tuscany into Lazio, it skirts another World Wide Fund for Nature project, a nature reserve at the **Lago di Burano** (*tours Sept–April Sun at 10 and 3; in summer you can book, t 0564 898829; adm*). Though small, the lagoon attracts all the same birds as the Monti dell'Uccellina and Orbetello lagoons; including, in summer, perhaps the only cranes left on the Italian mainland.

**Capalbio**, 6km inland, is one of the loveliest villages in southern Tuscany. It's a circular, hill-top enclave built around a castle, with a pretty 12th-century church. Head a few kilometres east, though, by the Lazio border, for a sneak preview of what may some day be one of Tuscany's best-known sights. They don't want any publicity, and it isn't signed, but if you turn off the SS1 to Capalbio, and turn right just before the first petrol station, you'll get a surprise. The **Giardino dei Tarocchi** (*open mid-May–late Oct daily 12.30–7.30; adm exp; winter 1st Sat of each month for group visits, min. 15 people, adm free, request by fax f 0564 895700 or email tarotg@tin.it*) is the project of French artist Niki de Saint-Phalle (who died in 2002), known for her works at the Pompidou Centre and the Bastille Opera in Paris, and for the colossal, humorous figures she calls 'nanas' scattered over Europe. In this garden, created for abstruse meditation, monumental sculptures represent each of the 22 key arcana of the Tarot deck: mad, brilliant works in concrete, bright ceramics and mirrors that hark back to Antoni Gaudí. A few are over 50ft tall, glittering over the Maremma coast like some interplanetary Lunar Park. Their symbolism is often obscure, but some, like the broken *Tower*, are unmistakable.

# Over the Border

If you're bound for Rome, there are a few attractions in Lazio to distract you along the way. The wealthiest Etruscan cities were here rather than Tuscany, and so the finest painted tombs are on the north Lazio coast at **Tarquinia** and **Cervetri**. Inland are the remains of the Etruscan town of **Vulci**, the fortress of Castello dell'Abbadia holds an Etruscan museum, and an Etruscan bridge spans the gorge. Not much has happened here since Etruscan times, but **Tuscania** has two extremely unusual early medieval churches in the style of medieval southern Italy. Further inland is a chain of lakes, including tranquil **Lake Vico**, and the city of **Viterbo**, once home to the popes.

# Siena

12

# Siena

VIALE LIPPO MEMMI

VIALE PIETRO TOSELLI

VIA DUCCIO DI BONINSEGNA

VIA BALDASSARRE PERUZZI

San Francesco

Oratorio di San Bernardino

TERZO DI CAMOLLIA

Fonte di Follonica

V. ILLUSTRIO BANDINI

TERZO DI SAN MARTINO

Logge del Papa

VIA DI PANTANETO

VIA BALDASSARRE PERUZZI

Santo Spirito

VIA DEI PISPINI

Porta Pispini

V. ARETINA

SS NO. 73

to Arezzo, Perugia and Motorway

A DEL PORRIONE

VIA SAN MARTINO

A DI SALICOTTO

VICOLO DELL'ORO

V. PAGLIARESI

PIAZZETTA A. FRANCHI

San Raimondo

VIA ROMA

VIA DELLE CANTINE

VIA DEI SERVI

VIA DI PORTA GIUSTIZIA

VIA GIROLAMO GIGLI

P

Basilica di Santa Maria dei Servi

VIA DI FONTANELLA

Porta Romana

N

250 metres

250 yards

# Getting Around

## By Car

The fastest route from Florence to Siena (68km) is the toll-free Superstrada del Palio (1hr); the most scenic routes are the Chiantigiana (SS222) through the heart of Chianti and the Via Cassia (SS2), which weave amongst the hills. Both of these take 2hrs.

From the south, there are two possible approaches from the A1: the SS326 by way of Sinalunga (50km) or the more scenic and winding SS73 by way of Monte Sansovino (44km). Cars are forbidden to enter the centre – and you wouldn't want to try it anyway – but there are clearly defined **parking areas** along all entrances to the city, especially around Piazza San Domenico, the Fortezza and along Viale dello Stadio.

Computerized signs on the approaches direct you to the city-run car parks and garages, and tell you whether or not they're full. Beware though: the rates are expensive enough, especially if you stay overnight. Look out for free car parks along the way – you'll just have to walk a little further.

## Car Hire

**Avis**, Via Simone Martini 36, t 0577 270305.

## By Train

Siena's station is located below the city, 1½km from the centre down Viale G. Mazzini, and is linked to the centre by frequent buses. Siena's main line runs from Empoli (on the Florence–Pisa line) to Chiusi (Florence–Rome).

There are trains roughly every hour, with frequent connections to Florence from Empoli (97km/1hr), less frequently to Pisa from Empoli (125km/2hrs), and to Chiusi towards Umbria and Rome (65km to Chiusi, 1hr). A secondary line runs towards Grosseto (70km/1hr) – 8 a day, of which 3 go on to Orbetello. Information and tickets are available at the **Il Caroccio Agency**, Via Mortanini 73, t 0577 226964.

## By Bus

Almost every town in southern Tuscany can be reached by bus from **Piazza San Domenico**, the big transport node on the western edge of Siena, with tourist information and hotel information booths. A board is posted with all departure times and the exact location of the stop; the ticket office (with a fancy, computer-operated information dispenser) is in the little building next to the San Domenico church. The name of the company serving the whole of Siena province is TRA-IN, t 0577 204246, *www.trainspa.it*, causing endless difficulties, according to the local tourist office, with

---

Draped on its three hills, Siena (pop. 59,000) is the most beautiful city in Tuscany, a flamboyant medieval ensemble of palaces and towers cast in warm, brown, Siena-coloured brick. Its soaring skyline is its pride, dominated by the blazing black and white banner of a cathedral and the taut needle of the Torre di Mangia; yet the Campo, the very centre of Siena, is only four streets away from olive groves and orchards. The contrast is part of the city's charm: dense brick urbanity, neighboured by a fine stretch of long Tuscan farmland that fills the valleys within the city's walls.

Here art went hand-in-hand with a fierce civic pride to make Siena a world of its own, and historians go so far as to speak of 'Sienese civilization' in summing up the achievements of this unique little city.

## History

Everywhere in Siena you'll see the familiar Roman symbol of the she-wolf suckling the twins. This is Siena's symbol as well; according to legend, the city was founded by the sons of Remus, Senius and Ascius. One rode a black horse, the other a white, and the simple *comunal* shield of black and white halves (the *balzana*) has been the other most enduring symbol of Siena over the centuries. It is most likely that some people were living on these three hills long before this mythological pair;

English tourists looking for TRA-INs in the train station; for some of the closer villages, look for TRA-INs on Viale F. Tozzi, just north of San Domenico.

Other companies depart for other cities like Florence (SITA, about once every hour, also to Rome, Perugia, Pisa, etc.), but all leave from San Domenico. Within the walls, there is now a bus service run by the TRA-IN, using what they call the *pollicini* or Tom Thumbs: little buses designed to get around narrow streets. Regular buses to the **train station** and everywhere else in the modern suburbs depart from **Piazza Matteotti**, north of the Campo.

## Tourist Information

**Siena**: Piazza del Campo 56, **t** 0577 280551, **f** 0577 270676, *www.comune.siena.it/ turismo, www.terresiena.it*
**Post office**: Piazza Matteotti 37.

## Shopping

Siena, with its population of only 60,000, is blissfully short of designer boutiques; even the usual tourist trinkets seem to be lacking – illuminated plastic models of the cathedral are harder to find every year. Nevertheless, a thorough search of the back streets will turn up plenty of unpretentious artisan workshops – almost all of which are so unconcerned with the tourist industry that they don't even bother hanging out a sign. The following are just some examples.

**Stained glass**: Vetrate Artistiche Toscane, Via Galuzza 5, just off Piazza Indipendenza, *www.glassisland.com*. Creations (most of them portable) in a distinctive modern style. The artist is also available to give informal talks about his work.

**Ceramics**: Via di Città 94. Selling a range of interesting pieces.

**Libreria Senese**, Via di Città 62–64. Siena's best bookshop, just down the street.

**Antica Drogheria Manganelli**, Via di Città 71–73, **t** 0577 280002. One-hundred-year-old original wooden shelving lines the walls of this gourmet's treasure trove, jammed full of delicious regional foods and wines. Worth a visit.

**Morbidi**, Via Banchi di Sopra 73/75. For delicious picnic treats; a multitude of cheeses, hams, salamis, prepared dishes, wines and breads.

**La Fattoria Toscano**, Via di Città 51. Those gastronomic goodies.

excavations have found traces of Etruscan and even Celtic habitation. The almost impregnable site, dominating most of southern Tuscany, would always have been of interest. Roman-era *Sena Julia*, refounded by Augustus as a colony for his veterans, never achieved much importance, and we know little about the place until the early 12th century, when the emerging *comune* began keeping written records. In 1125, an increasingly independent Siena elected its first consuls. By 1169, the *comune* had wrested political control away from the bishop, and some 10 years later, Siena developed its own written constitution.

The political development of the city is complex, and with good reason. Twelfth-century Siena was a booming new city: having control over its rich countryside, supplying some of the best wool in Italy, helped start an important cloth industry, and a small silver mine, acquired from Volterra in the 1160s, provided seed capital for what was to become one of the leading banking towns of Europe. Like so many other Italian cities, Siena was able early on to force its troublesome rural nobles to live within its walls, where they built scores of tall defence towers, fought pitched battles in the streets and usually kept the city divided into armed camps. In the narrowest part of the city, the *comune* once had to lay out new streets parallel to Via Camollia because of one particularly boisterous nobleman whose palace most

## Market Days

Markets are held around the Fortezza and Via XXV Aprile. *Wed.*

# Where to Stay

## Siena ✉ 53100

Until the opening of the luxurious Grand Hotel Continentale a few years ago, Siena's finest and most interesting hotels were all outside the walls, in the countryside or near the city gates. With the exception of the Continentale, what's left in the centre is simple but comfortable enough. In summer, rooms are in short supply and it's best to book ahead. If you come without a reservation, it is worth contacting the following organizations: **Hotel Information Centre**, Piazza San Domenico, t 0577 288084, f 0577 280290, *www.hotel siena.com*. Make this your first stop. Run by the city's innkeepers, it's conveniently located at the terminus of all intercity bus routes. If you arrive by train, take the city bus up from the station to Piazza Matteotti and walk a block down Via Curtatone. Even at busy times, they should be able to find you something – except during the Palio when you should book several months in advance. *Open Mon–Sat 9–7, until 8 in summer.*

## Luxury

If you have a car, there are a number of hotels outside the walls that offer rural Tuscan charm and views of the city that more than make up for the slight inconvenience of getting there.
**\*\*\*\*\*La Certosa di Maggiano**, 1km southeast of the city, near the Porta Romana, t 0577 288180, f 0577 288189, *www.certosadi maggiano.com*. This must be one of the most remarkable establishments in Italy, set in a restored 14th-century Carthusian monastery. There are 18 rooms, a heated pool, air conditioning that works, a quiet chapel and cloister, a salon where guests can play backgammon and chess, tennis courts, an excellent restaurant and a library fit to feature in any antiquarian's dream. It doesn't come cheap, but it is lovely.
**\*\*\*\*\*Continentale**, Via Banchi di Sopra 85, t 0577 56011/44204, f 0577 560 1555, *www. grandhotelcontinentalesiena.it*. Over 50 rooms, all furnished with fine fabrics and antiques.
**\*\*\*\*Villa Scacciapensieri**, on Strada Scacciapensieri 10, 3km north of the city, t 0577 41441, f 0577 270854, *www.villa scacciapensieri.it*. Come here to marvel at glorious sunset views over Siena. This is a quiet country house divided into 28 spacious rooms; besides the view, it has a pool and a good restaurant with an outdoor terrace.

---

Sienese were afraid to pass. Yet Siena was never completely able to bring its titled hoodlums under control. The businessmen made the money, and gradually formed their city into a sophisticated self-governing republic, but the nobles held on to many of their privileges for centuries, giving an anachronistically feudal tinge to Siena's life and art.

Like its brawling neighbours, medieval Siena enjoyed looking for trouble; in the endless wars of the 13th century, they never had to look very far. Originally a Guelph town, Siena changed sides early to avoid being in the same camp with arch-rival Florence. Along with Pisa, Siena carried the Ghibelline banner through the Tuscan wars with varying fortunes. Its finest hour came in 1260, when a Florentine herald arrived with the arrogant demand that Siena demolish its walls and deliver up its large population of Ghibelline exiles from Florence. If not, the armies of Florence and the entire Guelph League – some 40,000 men – were waiting outside to raze the city to the ground. Despite the overwhelming odds, the Sienese determined to resist. They threw the keys of the city on the altar of the as yet unfinished new cathedral, dedicating Siena to the Virgin Mary (a custom they have repeated ever since when the city is endangered, most recently just before the battle for liberation in 1944). In

**Very Expensive**

**★★★Park Hotel**, Via Marciano 18, **t** 0577 44803, **f** 0577 49020, *www.parkhotelsiena.it*. A 16th-century building designed by Peruzzi, on the hill that dominates Siena, with great views.

**Hotel Garden** Via Custoza 2, **t** 0577 47056, *www.gardenhotel.it*. This renovated 18th-century villa stands about 1km from town in a big garden. Rooms are in the main villa (where there are antiques and original frescoes) or in one of three annexes. There is a pool, a good restaurant and the staff are helpful.

**Expensive**

**★★★Antica Torre**, Via di Fieravecchia 7, **t/f** 0577 222255. Siena's most popular small (only eight rooms) hotel; a restored 16th-century tower, with marble floors, antiques and beamed ceilings.

**★★★Duomo**, Via Stalloreggi 34, **t** 0577 289088, **f** 0577 43043, *www.hotelduomo.it*. A friendly, comfortably old-fashioned place south of the Duomo. Rooms are a bit stark but clean.

**★★★Palazzo Ravizza**, Pian dei Mantellini 34, near the Porta Laterina, just inside the walls, **t** 0577 280462, **f** 0577 221597, *www.palazzoravizza.it*. An elegant 19th-century palazzo with up-market rooms furnished with antiques. There is a lovely garden at the back and a restaurant, too.

**★★Il Giardino**, Via Baldassare Peruzzi 35, **t** 0577 285290, **f** 0577 221197, *www.hotelilgiardino.it*. Highly recommended in readers' letters, near the Porta Pispini, with views and a swimming pool.

**★★Piccolo Hotel Il Palio**, Piazza del Sale 19, **t** 0577 281131, **f** 0577 281142, *www.piccolohotelilpalio.it*. A little way from the centre, but it has the advantages of a quiet location and a friendly, English-speaking owner.

**Villa Liberty**, Viale V. Veneto 11, **t** 0577 44966, **f** 0577 44770, *www.villaliberty.it*. A pleasant and elegant 'Liberty-style' villa near San Domenico and set in a garden. Rooms are well-furnished; two have private terraces.

**Moderate**

Many of Siena's two- and three-star hotels are around the entrances to the city, but there are also a number of options closer to the centre.

**★★Canon d'Oro**, Via Montanini 28, **t** 0577 44321, **f** 0577 280868. Near the bus station; nice, friendly and good value. Rooms have all been renovated in the last couple of years.

**★★Centrale**, Via Angiolieri 26, **t** 0577 280379, **f** 0577 42152. Very near to the Campo. The seven rooms are spacious and comfortable.

**★★Piccolo Hotel Etruria**, Via delle Donzelle 3, **t** 0577 288088, **f** 0577 288461. Friendly, clean

the morning, they marched out to the **Battle of Monteaperti** and beat the Florentines so badly that they captured their *carroccio*.

After the battle, Siena had Florence entirely at her mercy and, naturally, was anxious to level the city and scatter the ground with salt. One of the famous episodes in the *Inferno* relates how the Florentine exiles, who made up a substantial part of the Sienese forces, refused to allow it. Unfortunately for Siena, within a few years Florence and the Tuscan Guelphs had the situation back under control and Siena was never again to come so close to dominating Tuscan affairs. Nevertheless the city would be a constant headache to Florence for the next three centuries.

When things were quiet at the front, the Sienese had to settle for bashing each other. The constant stream of anti-Siena propaganda in Dante isn't just Florentine bile; medieval Siena thoroughly earned its reputation for violence and contentiousness. The impressive forms and rituals of the Sienese Republic were merely a façade concealing endless, pointless struggles between the various factions of the élite. Early on, Siena's merchants and nobles divided themselves into five *monti*, syndicates of self-interest that worked like political parties only without any pretence of principle. At one point, this Tuscan banana republic had and a good bargain. Four rooms in the annexe opposite. Restaurant (*cheap*) next door also owned by the hotel.

# Eating Out

Sitting between three of Italy's greatest wine-producing areas, the Chianti, the Brunello of Montalcino and the Vino Nobile of Montepulciano, Siena always has something to wash down the simple dishes of its table. This city's real speciality is sweets, and visitors often find they have no room for a meal after repeated slices of *panforte*, a heavy but indecently tasty cake laced with fruits, nuts, orange peel and secret Sienese ingredients or *panpepato*, similar but containing pepper.

They are all artists – shop windows flaunt gargantuan creations of cake and crystallized fruit, several feet high and as colourful as a Lorenzetti fresco, set out proudly for all to see before they are carted off to a wedding party.

The *Enoteca* inside the Medici fortress (*see* p.341) is another distraction; at times, special tastings are organized, concentrating on a particular region of Italy.

As a university town, Siena is never short on snacks and fast food; try *cioccina*, their special variation on pizza; or *pici* (thick south Tuscan spaghetti) with a sauce prepared from ground pork, *pancetta*, sausages and chicken breasts, added to tomatoes cooked with Brunello wine, which is the city's favourite pasta dish.

### Expensive

**Antica Trattoria Botteganova**, Via Chiantigiana 29, t 0577 284230. A few km northeast of Siena on the SS408 to Montevarchi. Meats such as the stuffed rabbit are earthy, or try the more delicate fish choices such as the tomato flan with basil-flavoured sturgeon fillets. *Closed Sun*.

**Certosa di Maggiano**, Via di Certosa 82, t 0577 288180. In an exquisite setting: part of a luxury hotel housed ina former Carthusian monastery, with 14th-century cloisters. Modern, *haute cuisine* dishes served with some pomp.

**Compagnia dei Vinattieri**, Via delle Terme, t 0577 236568. The many wines on offer in this basement restaurant/*enoteca* are stored in a 14th-century cellar – ask to have a look before you leave. You can pop in for just a drink and a snack, but that would mean missing out on excellent dishes, such as ravioli with a mild goat's cheese and basil sauce, stuffed chicken neck(!) with a pungent 'salsa verde', rabbit stewed with black olives and chocolate and coffee mousse.

10 constitutions in 27 years, and more often than not, its political affairs were settled in the streets. Before the Palio was invented, Siena's favourite civic sport was the *Gioco del Pugno*, a general, 300-a-side fist fight in the Campo. Sometimes tempers flared and the boys would bring out the axes and crossbows.

## Siena's Golden Age

The historical record leaves us with a glaring paradox. For all its troubles and bad intentions, Siena often managed to run city business disinterestedly and with intelligence. An intangible factor of civic pride always made the Sienese do the right thing when something important was at hand, like battling with the Florentines or selecting a new artist to work on the cathedral. The Battle of Monteaperti may have proved a disappointment in terms of territorial ambitions, but it inaugurated the most brilliant period of Sienese culture, and saw the transformation of the hilltop fortress town into the beautiful city we see today. In 1287, under pressure from the Guelphs and their Angevin protectors, Siena actually allied itself with Florence and instituted a new form of government: the '**Council of the Nine**'. Excluding nobles from office, as Florence would do six years later, the rule of the Nine was to last until 1355, and it gave Siena a more stable regime than it knew at any other period.

**Da Enzo**, Via Camollia 49, **t** 0577 281277.
A traditional restaurant with a long, varied menu, offering plenty of choice between fish and meat. The cutlets of wild boar in a sweet and sour sauce and fish baked in a potato crust are delicious. *Closed Sun*.

**Ai Marsili**, Via del Castoro 3, **t** 0577 47154.
An elegant setting and a wide choice of excellent Sienese dishes. Among them, Catherine de' Medici's famous dish, *faraona alla Medici*, guinea fowl roasted with pine nuts, almonds and plums. *Closed Mon*.

**Osteria Le Logge**, Via del Porrione 33, **t** 0577 48013. The high-ceilinged and airy main room of this restaurant must be one of the most pleasant places to eat in Siena. A tempting choice of *antipasti* precede such dishes as wild boar with juniper berries and lasagne with turbot, mozzarella and pesto. *Closed Sun*.

## Moderate

**Guido**, Vicolo Pier Pettinato 7, **t** 0577 280042.
A central, traditional Sienese restaurant with a somewhat medieval feel. The grilled lamb, veal and *bistecca* are excellent.

**Osteria di Castelvecchio**, Via Castelvecchio 65, **t** 0577 49586. The décor here is original and modern, but this building was once the stable block of one of Siena's oldest *palazzi*. Traditional recipes (penne with *salsiccia* and peppers, risotto with fresh herbs) with an emphasis on vegetarian dishes. The *menu degustazione* is good value. *Closed Tues*.

**Osteria di Ficomezzo**, Via dei Termini 71, **t** 0577 222384. Lunch is a simple affair here. In the evenings there are more inventive dishes, such as guinea fowl cooked with tarragon, served alongside the more traditional *pici*, hearty soups and stews. *Closed Sun*.

## Cheap

**Il Grattacielo**, Via dei Pontani 8, **t** 0577 289326. Another popular student hangout. The simple dishes are good value for money and the wine flows freely. *Closed Sun*.

**Osteria La Chiacchiera**, Via Costa di Sant' Antonio 4, **t** 0577 280631. This friendly, highly recommended little *trattoria* serves excellent local dishes: *pici*, *rilbollita*, kidneys, cockscombs (*cibreo*), stews or a simple *bistecca*. There are outdoor tables for summer dining.

**Pizzeria Carlo e Franca**, Via Pantaneto 138, **t** 0577 284385. *Antipasti* and pizzas at reasonable prices, and not far from the centre. *Closed Wed*.

**La Torre**, Via Salicotto 17, **t** 0577 287548.
A fun, lively place; popular with students. *Closed Thurs*.

Business was better than ever. The city's bankers came to rival Florence's, with offices in all the trading centres and capitals of Europe. A sustained peace, and increasing cultural contacts with France and Naples, brought new ideas and influences into Siena's art and architecture, just in time to embellish massive new building programmes like the **cathedral** (begun in 1186, but not substantially completed until the 1380s) and the **Palazzo Pubblico** (1295–1310). Beginning with Duccio di Buoninsegna (1260–1319), Sienese artists took the lead in exploring new concepts in painting and sculpture and, throughout the 1300s, contributed as much as or more than the Florentines in laying the foundations for the Renaissance. Contemporary records betray an obsessive concern on the part of bankers and merchants for decorating Siena and impressing outsiders. At the height of its fortunes, in the early 14th century, Siena ruled most of southern Tuscany. Its bankers were known in London, in the Baltic and in Constantinople, and its reputation for beauty and culture was matched by few cities in Europe.

The very pinnacle of civic pride and ambition came in 1339, with the fantastical plan to expand the still-unfinished cathedral into the largest in all Christendom. The walls of that effort, a nave that would have been longer than St Peter's in Rome, stand today as a monument to the dramatic event that snapped off Siena's career in

## Ancient Rivals

Few rivalries have been more enduring than that between Florence and Siena; to understand Tuscany, take a moment to compare the two. Long ago, while Florence was off at university busily studying her optics and geometry, Lady Siena spent her time dancing and dropping her scarf for knights at the tournament. Florence thought she had the last laugh in 1555, when Duke Cosimo and his black-hearted Spanish pals wiped out the Sienese Republic and put this proud maiden in chains. It's frustrating enough today, though, when Florence looks up in the hills and sees Siena, an unfaded beauty with a faraway smile, sitting in her tower like the Lady of Shalott.

For two towns built by bankers and wool tycoons, they could not have less in common. Siena may not possess an Uffizi or a David, but neither does it have to bear the marble antimacassars and general stuffiness of its sister on the Arno, nor her smog, traffic, tourist hordes and suburban squalor. Florence never goes over the top. Siena loves to, especially in the week around the race of the Palio, the wildest party in Tuscany, a worthy successor to the fabulous masques and carnivals, the bullfights and bloody free-for-alls of the Sienese Middle Ages. In fact, Florence has been clicking its tongue at Siena since the time of Dante, who refers sarcastically in his *Inferno* to a famous club called the *Brigata*, made up of 12 noble Sienese youths who put up 250,000 florins for a year of nightly feasting; every night they had three sumptuously laid tables, one for eating, one for drinking and the third to throw out the window.

But there's more to Siena than that. This is a city with its own artistic tradition (*see* **Art and Architecture**, p.14); in the 1300s, Sienese painters were giving lessons to the Florentines. Always more decorative, less intellectual than Florence, Siena fell behind in the quattrocento. By then, fortunately, the greatest achievement of Sienese art was already nearing completion – Siena herself.

full bloom. The **Black Death** of 1348 carried off one-third of the population – a death toll perhaps no greater than in some other Italian cities, but it struck Siena at a moment when its economy was particularly vulnerable, and started a slow but irreversible decline that was to continue for centuries. Economic strife led to political instability, and in 1355 a revolt of the nobles, egged on by Emperor Charles IV who was then in Tuscany, overthrew the Council of the Nine. Then in 1371, seven years before the Ciompi revolt in Florence, the wool workers staged a genuine revolution. Organized as a trade union of sorts, the **Compagnia del Bruco** seized the Palazzo Pubblico and instituted a government with greater popular representation.

The decades that followed saw Siena devote more and more of its diminishing resources to buying off the marauding mercenary companies that infested much of Italy at this time. By 1399 the city was in such dire straits that it surrendered its independence to **Giangaleazzo Visconti**, the tyrant of Milan, who was then attempting to surround and conquer Florence. After his death, Siena reclaimed its freedom. Political confusion continued throughout the century, with only two periods of relative stability. One came with the pontificate (1458–63) of Pius II, the great Sienese scholar **Aeneas Silvius Piccolomini**, who exerted a dominating influence over his native city while he ruled at Rome. In 1487, a nobleman named **Pandolfo Petrucci** took over the government; as an honest broker, regulating the often murderous ambitions of the *monti*, he and his sons kept control of the republic until 1524.

## The Fall of the Republic

Florence was always waiting in the wings to swallow up Siena and finally had its chance in the 1500s. The real villain of the piece, however, was not Florence but that most imperious Emperor, **Charles V**. After the fall of the Petrucci, the factional struggles resumed immediately, with frequent assassinations and riots, and constitutions changing with the spring fashions. Charles, who had bigger prey in his sights, cared little for the fate of the perverse little republic; he feared, though, that its disorders, religious toleration and wretched financial condition were diseases that might spread beyond its borders. In 1530, he took advantage of riots in the city to install an imperial garrison. Yet even the Emperor's representatives, usually Spaniards, could not keep Siena from sliding further into anarchy and bankruptcy on several occasions, largely thanks to Charles's war taxes. Cultural life was stifled as the Spaniards introduced the Inquisition and the Index. Scholars and artists fled, while poverty and political disruptions meant that Siena's once proud university ceased to function.

In 1550, Charles announced that he was going to build a fortress within the city walls, for which the Sienese were going to pay. Realizing that the trifling liberty still left to them would soon be extinguished, the Sienese ruling class began intrigues with Charles' great enemy, France. A French army, led by a Piccolomini, arrived in July 1552. Inside the walls the people revolted and locked the Spanish garrison up in its own new fortress. The empire was slow to react but, inevitably, in late 1554, a huge force of imperial troops, along with those of Florence, entered Sienese territory. The siege was prosecuted with remarkable brutality by Charles's commander, the **Marquis of Marignano**, who laid waste much of the Sienese countryside (which did not entirely recover until this century), tortured prisoners and even hired agents to start fires inside the walls. After a brave resistance, led by a republican Florentine exile named **Piero Strozzi** and assisted by France, Siena was starved into surrendering in April 1555. Two years later, Charles's son Philip II sold Siena to Duke Cosimo of Florence and the republic was consumed by the new Grand Duchy of Tuscany.

If nothing else, Siena went out with a flourish. After the capture of the city, some 2,000 republican bitter-enders escaped to make a last stand at Montalcino. Declaring 'Where the *Comune* is, there is the City', they established what must be the world's first republican government-in-exile. With control over much of the old Sienese territory, the '**Republic of Siena at Montalcino**' held out against the Medici for another four years.

With its independence lost and its economy irrevocably ruined, Siena withdrew into itself. For centuries there was to be no recovery, little art or scholarship, and no movements towards reform. The Sienese aristocracy, already decayed into a parasitic *rentier* class, made its peace with the Medici dukes early on; in return for their support, the Medici allowed them to keep much of their power and privileges. The once-great capital of trade and finance shrank rapidly into an overbuilt farmers' market, its population dropping from a 14th-century high of 60–80,000 to around a mere 15,000 by the year 1700. This explains largely why medieval and Renaissance Siena is so well preserved – for better or worse, nothing ever happened to change it.

By the Age of Enlightenment, with its disparaging of everything medieval, the Sienese seem to have quite forgotten their own history and art, so it is no surprise that the rest of Europe forgot them too. During the first years of the Grand Tour, no self-respecting northern European considered visiting Siena. Few had probably ever heard of it and those who stopped overnight on the way to Rome were usually dismayed at the 'inelegance' of its medieval buildings and art.

It was not until the 1830s that Siena was rediscovered, with the help of *literati* like the Brownings, who spent several summers here, and later that truly Gothic American, Henry James. The Sienese were not far behind in rediscovering it themselves. The old civic pride that had lain dormant for centuries yawned and stretched like Sleeping Beauty and went diligently back to work.

Before the 19th century was out, everything that could still be salvaged of the city's ancient glory was refurbished and restored. More than ever fascinated by its own image and eccentricities, and more than ever without any kind of economic base, Siena was ready for its present career as a cultural attraction, a tourist town.

## Orientation: *Terzi* and the *Contrade*

The centre of Siena, the site of the Palio and, importantly to the Sienese, the 'farthest point from the world outside', is the piazza called **Il Campo**. The city unfolds from it like a three-petalled flower along three ridges. It has been a natural division since medieval times, with the oldest quarter, the **Terzo di Città**, to the southwest; the **Terzo di San Martino**, to the southeast; and the **Terzo di Camollia**, to the north.

Siena is tiny, barely over a square mile in size. The density, and especially the hills, make it seem much bigger when you're walking. There are no short cuts across the valleys between the three *terzi*. Although there are few cars in the centre, taxis and motorbikes will occasionally try to run you down.

### Contrade

The Sienese have taken the *contrade* for granted for so long that their history is almost impossible to trace. Basically, the word denotes the 17 neighbourhoods into which Siena is divided. Like the *rioni* of Rome, they were once the original wards of the ancient city – not merely geographical boundaries but self-governing entities; the ancients with their long racial memories often referred to them as the city's 'tribes'. In Siena, the *contrade* survived and prospered all through classical times and the Middle Ages. More than anything else, they maintained the city's traditions and sense of identity through the dark years after 1552. Incredibly enough, they're still there now, unique in Italy and perhaps all Europe. Once Siena counted over 60 *contrade*. Now there are 17, each with a sort of totem animal for its symbol:

# The Palio

The thousands of tourists who come twice a year to see the Palio, Siena's famous horse race around the Campo, probably think the Sienese are doing it purely for their benefit. Yet, like the *contrade* which contest it, the Palio is an essential aspect of Sienese culture, as significant to the city today as it was centuries ago. Here are the plain facts on Italy's best-known annual festival.

The oldest recorded Palio was run in 1283, though no one knows how far the custom goes back. During the Middle Ages, besides the horse races there were violent street battles, bloody games of primeval rugby and even bullfights. (Bullfights were also common in Rome and there's an argument to be made that Italy is actually the place where the Spaniards got the idea, back in the 16th and 17th centuries when Spain's own medieval passion for such things was all but forgotten.) At present, the course comprises three laps around the periphery of the Campo, although in the past the race has been known to take in some of the city's main streets.

The *palio* (Latin *pallium*) is an embroidered banner offered as a prize to the winning *contrade*. Two races are held each year, on 2 July and 16 August, and the *palio* of each one is decorated with an image of the Virgin Mary; after political violence, the city's greatest passion has always been Mariolatry. The course has room for only 10 horses in each race, so some of the 17 *contrade* are chosen by lot each race to ensure that they all have a fair chance. The horses, too, are selected by lot, but the *contrade* are free to select their own jockeys.

Although the race itself lasts only a minute and a half, there's a good hour or two of pageantry preceding it; the famous flag-throwers or *alfieri* of each participating *contrada* put on a dazzling show, while the medieval *carroccio*, drawn by a yoke of white oxen, is pressed into service to circle the Campo, bearing the prized *palio* itself.

The Palio is no joke; baskets of money ride on each race, not to mention the sacred honour of the district. To obtain divine favour, each *contrada* brings its horse into its chapel on race morning for a special blessing (and if a little horse manure drops during the ceremony, it's taken as a sign of good luck). The only rule stipulates that you can't seize the reins of an opponent. There are no rules against bribing opposing jockeys, making alliances with other *contrade* or ambushing jockeys before the race.

The course around the Campo has two right angles. Anything can happen; recent Palii have featured not only jockeys but *horses* flying through the air at the turns. The Sienese say no one has ever been killed at a Palio. There's no reason to believe them. They wouldn't believe it themselves, but it is an article of faith among the Sienese that fatalities are prevented by special intervention of the Virgin Mary. The post-Palio carousing, while not up to medieval standards, is still impressive; in the winning *contrada* the party might go on for days on end, while the losers shed bitter tears.

No event in Italy is as infectiously exhilarating as the Palio. There are two ways to see it, either from the centre of the Campo, packed tight and always very hot, or from an expensive (€130–260) seat in a viewing stand, but book well in advance if you want one of these. Several travel agencies offer special Palio tours (*see* **Travel**, pp.57–9); otherwise make sure you book by April.

*Aquila* (Eagle), *Onda* (Dolphin), *Tartaruga* (Turtle), *Pantera* (Panther), *Selva* (Rhinoceros) and *Chiocciola* (Snail): all southwest of the Campo in Terzo di Città.

*Leocorno* (Unicorn), *Torre* (Elephant), *Civetta* (Owl), *Nicchio* (Mussel shell) and *Valdimontone* (Ram): in Terzo di San Martino southeast of the Campo.

*Oca* (Goose), *Drago* (Dragon), *Giraffa* (Giraffe), *Lupa* (Wolf), *Bruco* (Caterpillar) and *Istrice* (Porcupine): all in the north in the Terzo di Camollia.

Sienese and Italian law recognize each of these as legally chartered communities; today a *contrada* functions as a combination of social-and-dining club, neighbourhood improvement organization, religious confraternity and mutual assistance fund. Each elects its own officials annually in May. Each has its own chapel, museum and fountain, its own flag and colours, and its own patron saint who pulls all the strings he can in Heaven twice a year to help his beloved district win the Palio.

Sociologists, and not only in Italy, are becoming ever more intrigued with this ancient yet very useful system, with its built-in community solidarity and tacit social control. (Siena has almost no crime and no social problems, except of course for a lack of jobs.) The *contrade* probably function much as they did in Roman or medieval times, but it's surprising just what up-to-date, progressive and adaptable institutions they can be, and they are still changing today. Anyone born in a *contrada* area, for example, is automatically a member; besides their baptism into the Church, they also receive a sort of 'baptism' into the *contrada*. This ritual isn't very old and it is conducted in the pretty new fountains the *contrade* have constructed all over Siena in recent years as centrepieces for their neighbourhoods.

To learn more about the *contrade*, the best place to go is one of the 17 little *contrada* museums. The tourist office can give you a list of addresses. One of the best is that of the Goose in the Terzo di Camollia. Though the caretakers usually live close by, most of them ask visitors to contact them a week in advance. The tourist office also has details on the dates of the annual *contrada* festivals and the other shows and dinners they are wont to put on; visitors are always very welcome.

## Walking in Siena

If you keep your eyes open while walking the back streets of Siena, you'll see the city's entire history laid out for you in signs, symbols and a hundred other clues. You usually won't have trouble guessing which *contrada* you're in. Little ceramic plaques with the *contrada* symbol appear on buildings and street corners, not to mention flags in the neighbourhood colours, bumper stickers on cars and the fountains, each with a modern sculptural work, usually representing the *contrada*'s animal.

Look for noblemen's coats of arms above the doorways; aristocratic, archaic Siena will show you more of these than almost any Italian city. In many cases, they are still the homes of the original families, and often the same device is on a dozen houses on one block, a reminder of how medieval Siena was largely divided into separate compounds, each under the protection (or intimidation) of a noble family. One common symbol is formed from the letters IHS in a radiant sun. Siena's famous 15th-century preacher, San Bernardino, was always pestering the nobles to forget their contentiousness and enormous vanity; he proposed that they replace their heraldic symbols with the monogram of Christ. The limited success his idealism met with can be read on the buildings of Siena today.

They don't take down their old signs in Siena. One, dated 1641, informs prostitutes that the Most Serene Prince Matthias (the Florentine governor) forbids them to live on his street (Via di Salicotto). Another, a huge 19th-century marble plaque on the Banchi di Sotto, reminds passers-by that 'in this house, before modern restorations reclaimed it from squalidness, was born Giovanni Caselli, inventor of the pantograph'. A favourite, to be found on Via del Giglio, announces a stroke of the rope and a 16-lira fine for anyone throwing trash in the street, with proceeds to go to the accuser.

# The Campo

There is no lovelier square in Tuscany and none more beloved by its city. The Forum of ancient *Sena Julia* was on this spot, and in the Middle Ages it evolved into its present fan shape, rather like a scallop shell or classical theatre. The Campo was paved with brick as early as 1340; the nine sections into which the fan is divided are in honour of the Council of the Nine, rulers of the city at the time. Thousands crowd over the bricks every year to see the Palio run on the periphery.

For a worthy embellishment to their Campo, the Sienese commissioned for its curved north end the **Fonte Gaia** from Jacopo della Quercia, their greatest sculptor, though what you see now is an uninspired copy from 1868. He worked on it from 1408 to 1419, creating the broad rectangle of marble with reliefs of Adam and Eve and allegorical virtues. It was to be the opening salvo of Siena's Renaissance, an answer to the baptistry doors of Ghiberti in Florence (for which della Quercia himself had been one of the contestants). Perhaps it was a poor choice of stone, but the years have been incredibly unkind to this fountain; the badly eroded remains of the original can be seen up on the loggia of the Palazzo Pubblico.

No one can spend much time in Siena without noticing its fountains. The republic always made sure each part of the city had access to good water; medieval Siena created the most elaborate engineering works since ancient Rome to bring the water in. Fonte Gaia, and others such as Fontebranda, are fed by underground aqueducts that stretch for miles across the Tuscan countryside. Charles V, when he visited the city, is reported to have said that Siena is 'even more marvellous underground than it is on the surface'.

The original Fonte Gaia was completed in the early 1300s; there's a story that soon afterwards some Sienese citizens dug up a beautiful Greek statue of Venus signed by Praxiteles himself. The delighted Sienese carried it in procession through the city and installed it on top of their new fountain. With the devastation of the Black Death, however, the preachers were quick to blame God's wrath on the indecent pagan on the Fonte Gaia. Throughout history, the Sienese have always been ready to be shocked by their own sins; in this case, with their neighbours dropping like flies around them, they proved only too eager to make poor Venus the scapegoat. They chopped her into little bits, and a party of Sienese disguised as peasants smuggled the pieces over the border and buried them in Florentine territory to pass the bad luck on to their enemies.

## Palazzo Pubblico

If the Campo is like a Roman theatre, the main attraction on stage since 1310 has been this brick and stone palace, the enduring symbol of the Sienese Republic and still the town hall today. Its façade is the face of Siena's history, with the she-wolf of Senius and Ascanius, Medici balls, the IHS of San Bernardino, and squared Guelph crenellations, all in the shadow of the tremendous **Torre di Mangia** (*open daily, Nov–mid-Mar 10–4; mid-Mar–Oct 10–7; July and Aug 10am–11pm; adm €6 (€5 if you pre-book*)), the graceful, needle-like tower that Henry James called 'Siena's Declaration of Independence'. At 332ft, the tower was the second-tallest ever raised in medieval Italy (only the campanile in Cremona beats it). At the time, the cathedral tower up on its hill completely dominated Siena's skyline; the Council of the Nine wouldn't accept that the symbol of religious authority or any of the nobility's fortress-skyscrapers should be taller than the symbol of the republic, so its Perugian architects, Muccio and Francesco di Rinaldo, made sure it would be hard to beat.

There was a practical side to it, too. At the top hung the *comune*'s great bell, which had to be heard in every corner of the city tolling the hours and announcing the curfew, or calling the citizens to assemble in case of war or emergency. One of the first men to hold the job of bell-ringer gave the tower its name, a fat, sleepy fellow named *Mangiaguadagni* (eat the profits) or just Mangia for short; there is a statue of him in one of the courtyards. Climb the tower's endless staircase for the definitive view of Siena – on the clearest days, you'll also be able to see about half of the medieval republic's territory, a view that is absolutely, positively worth the slight risk of cardiac arrest. At the foot of the tower, the marble **Cappella della Piazza**, with its graceful rounded arches, stands out clearly from the Gothic earnestness of the rest of the building. It was begun in 1352, in thanks for deliverance from the Black Death, but not completed until the mid-15th century.

Most of the Palazzo Pubblico's ground floor is still used for city offices, but the upper floors have been made into the city's **museum** (*open Nov–mid-Mar 10–6.30, mid-Mar–Oct 10–7; adm*).

Here the main attraction is the series of state rooms done in frescoes, a sampling of the best of Sienese art throughout the centuries. First, though, come the historical frescoes in the **Sala del Risorgimento**, done by an artist named A.G. Cassioli in 1886: the meeting of Vittorio Emanuele II with Garibaldi, his coronation, portraits, epigrams of past patriots and an 'allegory of Italian Liberty', all in a colourful and photographically precise style.

Next, on the same floor is the **Sala di Balia** with frescoes depicting the life of Alessandro VII and some vigorous battle scenes by the Sienese Spinello Aretino (1300s) and the *Sixteen Virtues* by Martino di Bartolomeo. The adjoining **Anticamera del Concistoro** has a lovely *Madonna and Child* by Matteo di Giovanni. In the **Sala del Concistoro**, Gobelin tapestries adorn the walls while the great Sienese Mannerist

Beccafumi contributed a ceiling of frescoes in the 1530s celebrating the political virtues of antiquity; that theme is continued in the **vestibule to the chapel**, with portraits of ancient heroes from Cicero to Judas Maccabeus, all by Taddeo di Bartolo. These portrayals, along with more portraits of the classical gods and goddesses and an interesting view of ancient Rome, clearly show the extent of a real fascination with antiquity even in the 1300s.

Intruding among the classical crew, there's also a king-sized St Christopher covering an entire wall. Before setting out on a journey, it was good luck to catch a glimpse of this saint, and in Italy and Spain, he is often painted extra large so you won't miss him. In a display case in the hall, some of the oldest treasures of the Sienese Republic are kept: the war helmet of the Captain of the People, and a delicate **golden rose**, a gift to the city from the Sienese Pope, Pius II.

The chapel (**Cappella del Consiglio**) is surrounded by a lovely wrought-iron grille designed by Jacopo della Quercia; when it is open, you can see more frescoes by Taddeo di Bartolo, an altarpiece by Il Sodoma and some exceptional carved wood seats by Domenico di Nicolò (*c.* 1415–28). In the adjacent chamber (**Sala del Mappamondo**), only the outline is left of Lorenzetti's cosmological fresco, a diagram of the universe including all the celestial and angelic spheres, much like the one in the Campo Santo at Pisa. Above it, there is a very famous fresco by Simone Martini (*c.* 1330), showing the redoubtable *condottiere* **Guidoriccio da Fogliano** on his way to attack the castle of Montemassi, during a revolt against Siena. Also by Martini is an enthroned Virgin or *Maestà*, believed to be his earliest work (1315).

## The Allegories of Good and Bad Government

When you enter the **Sala dei Nove** (or Sala della Pace), meeting room of the Council of the Nine, you'll understand at a glance why they ruled Siena so well. Whenever one of the councillors had the temptation to skim some cream off the top, or pass a fat contract over to his brother-in-law the paving contractor, or tighten the screws on the poor by raising the salt tax, he had only to look up at Ambrogio Lorenzetti's great frescoes to really feel like a worm. There are two complementary sets, with scenes of Siena under good government and bad, and allegorical councils of virtues or vices for each. Enthroned Justice rules the good Siena, with such counsellors as Peace, Prudence and Magnanimity; bad Siena groans under the thumb of one nasty piece of work, sneering, fanged Tyranny and his cronies: Pride, Vainglory, Avarice and Wrath, among others. The good Siena is a happy place, with buildings in good repair, well-dressed folk who are dancing in the streets, and well-stocked shops where the merchants appear to be making a nice profit. Bad Siena is almost a mirror image, only the effects of the Tyrant's rule are plain to see: urban blight, crime in broad daylight, buildings crumbling and abandoned, and business bad for everybody – a landscape which for many of us modern city dwellers will seem all too familiar.

Lorenzetti finished his work around 1338, probably the most ambitious secular painting ever attempted up to that time. The work has been recently cleaned and restored; fittingly, Good Government has survived more or less intact, while Bad Government has not aged so well and parts have been lost. In the next room is

Guido da Siena's large *Madonna and Child* (mid-1200s), the earliest masterpiece of the Sienese school. If you're not up to climbing the tower, at least take the long, unmarked stairway by the Sala del Risorgimento, leading up to the **loggia**, with the second-best view over Siena and disassembled pieces of della Quercia's reliefs from the Fonte Gaia, not particularly impressive in their worn and damaged state.

## Around the Campo

Part of the Campo's beauty lies in the element of surprise; one usually enters from narrow arcades between the medieval palaces that give no hint of what lies on the other side. Two of Siena's three main streets form a graceful curve around the back of the Campo; where they meet the third, behind the Fonte Gaia, is the corner the Sienese call the **Croce del Travaglio** (a mysterious nickname: the 'Cross of Affliction').

Here, the three-arched **Loggia della Mercanzia**, in a sense Siena's Royal Exchange, was where the republic's merchants made their deals and settled their differences before the city's famed commercial tribunal. The Loggia marks the transition from Sienese-Gothic to early Renaissance style – begun in 1417, it was probably influenced by Florence's Loggia dei Lanzi. The five statues of saints on the columns are the work of Antonio Federighi and Vecchietta, the leading Sienese sculptors after della Quercia.

The three streets that meet here lead directly into the three *terzi* of Siena. All three are among the city's most beautiful, in particular the gracefully curving **Banchi di Sotto**, main artery of the Terzo di San Martino. Just beyond the Campo, this street passes Siena's most imposing *palazzo privato*, the **Palazzo Piccolomini** (*library open (to view the* Tavolette della Biccherna) *Mon–Sat with entrance at 9.30, 10.30 or 11.30*), done in the Florentine style by Rossellino in the 1460s. This palace now houses the old Sienese state archive – not a place you might consider visiting but for the presence of the famous *Tavolette della Biccherna* (the account books of the *Biccherna* or state treasury). Beginning in the 1200s, the republic's custom was to commission the best local artists to decorate the covers of the *tavolette*, portraying such prosaic subjects as medieval citizens coming to pay their taxes, city employees counting their pay and earnest monks trying to make the figures square – all are Cistercians from San Galgano (*see* pp.363–4), the only people medieval Siena trusted to do the job. Among other manuscripts and documents you'll find Boccaccio's will.

# Terzo di Città

Southwest from the Croce del Travaglio, Via di Città climbs up to the highest and oldest part of Siena, the natural fortress of the Terzo di Città. Among the palaces it passes is the grandiose **Palazzo Chigi-Saracini**, with a wretched old tree, barely surviving, hanging over the street from its stony courtyard. The palace contains an internationally important music school, the Accademia Musicale Chigiana, and a large collection of Sienese and Florentine art (*open to the public for limited periods of the year; call* **t** *0577 246928 for information*). Next door is yet another reminder of the Piccolomini, the **Palazzo delle Papesse**. The family, along with the Colonna of Rome and the Correr of Venice, was one of the first to really exploit the fiscal possibilities of the papacy; Aeneas Silvius (Pius II) built this palace, also designed by Rossellino, for his sister, Caterina Piccolomini.

## The Duomo

All approaches from Via di Città to Siena's glorious **cathedral**, spilling over the highest point in the city, are somewhat oblique. Easiest, perhaps, is Via dei Pellegrini, which winds around the back, past the unusual crypt-baptistry tucked underneath (*see* pp.334–5), up the steps to the Piazza del Duomo, and through a portal in a huge, free-standing wall of striped marble arches, a memorial to that incredible ill-starred 1339 rebuilding plan confounded by the plague. The cathedral the Sienese had to settle for may not be a transcendent expression of faith, and it may not be a great landmark in architecture, but it is certainly one of the most delightful, decorative ornaments in Christendom.

Begun around 1200, one of the first Gothic cathedrals in central Italy, it started in the good medieval tradition as a communal effort, not really a project of the Church. There doesn't seem to have been much voluntary labour – even in the Middle Ages, Italians were a little too blasé for that – but every citizen with a cart was expected to bring in two loads of marble from the quarries each year, earning him a special indulgence from the bishop. One load must have been white and the other black for, under the influence of Pisa, the Sienese built themselves one thoroughly striped cathedral – stripes darker and bolder than Pisa's or even Pistoia's. The campanile, with its distinctive fenestration, narrowing in size down six levels, rises over the city like a giant ice cream parfait. Most of the body of the church was finished by 1270, and 14 years later, Giovanni Pisano was called in to create the sculpture for the lavish **façade**, with statues of biblical prophets and pagan philosophers. The upper half was not begun until the 1390s and the glittering mosaics in the gables are, like Orvieto's, the work of Venetian artists of the late 19th century.

### The Cathedral Interior: the Marble Pavement

*Open winter Mon–Sat 10.30–6.30, Sun and hols 1.30–5.30;*
*summer Mon–Sat 10.30–7.30, Sun and hols 1.30–6.30.*

This is a virtual treasure box, fit to keep a serious sightseer busy for an entire day. Upon entering the main portal, the ferociously striped pilasters and the Gothic vaulting, a blue firmament painted with golden stars, inevitably draw the eye upwards. The most spectacular feature, though, is at your feet – the marble pavement, where the first peculiar figure smiling up at you is **Hermes Trismegistus** (*see* p.332), the legendary Egyptian father of alchemy, depicted in elegant *sgraffito* work of white and coloured marble. In fact, the entire floor of the cathedral is covered with almost 12,000 square metres of virtuoso *sgraffito* in 56 scenes, including portraits, mystical allegories and Old Testament scenes. Like the Biccherna covers in the Palazzo Piccolomini, they were a tradition carried on over centuries. Many of Siena's best artists worked on them, beginning in 1369 and continuing into the 1600s; Giorgio

Piazza San Giovanni

# Siena Cathedral

Via Monna Agnese

Piazza
Jacopo della Quercia

Piazza
del Duomo

1 Pisano's Pulpit
2 Chapel of San Giovanni Battista
3 Tomb of Cardinal Pecci (Donatello)
4 Tomb of Cardinal Petroni (Tino da Camaino)
5 Stained Glass of Duccio
6 High Altar
7 Piccolomini Altar (della Quercia, Michelangelo)
8 Campanile
9 Sacristy
10 Cantorie
11 Choir
12 Piccolomini Library
13 To Cathedral Museum
14 Cathedral Extension
15 Baptistry (lower level)

A *Hermes Trismegistus*
B *Allegory of Virtue*
C *Wheel of Fortune*
D *Massacre of the Innocents*
E *Judith Liberating Bethulia*
F *Seven Ages of Man*
G *Allegories of Faith, Hope and Charity*
H *Story of Absalom*
I *Emperor Sigismund on his Throne*
J *Sacrifice of Elias, Execution of the False Prophets*
K *Samson and the Philistines*
L *David the Psalmist*
M *Sacrifice of Abraham*
N *Moses Receives the Commandments*
O *Story of Jephta*

Vasari claimed that Duccio di Buoninsegna himself first worked in this medium, though he has none among the pictures here.

Even in a building with so many marvels – the Piccolomini Library, Nicola Pisano's pulpit, Duccio's stained glass, works by Donatello, della Quercia, Pinturicchio, Michelangelo, Bernini and many others – this pavement perhaps takes pride of place. The greatest limitation of Sienese art was always the conservatism of its patrons, accustomed to demanding the same old images in the same old styles. Commissions from the Office of Cathedral Works, controlled by the state, were usually more liberal, allowing the artists to create such unique, and in some cases startling images, one of the greatest achievements of Renaissance Siena.

The Hermes on the cathedral pavement, by Giovanni di Stefano, was completed in the 1480s, a decade after Ficino's translation; he is shown with Moses, holding a book with the inscription 'Take up thy letters and laws, O Egyptians'. On either side, all 10 prophetic *Sibyls*, done by various artists at the same time, decorate the aisles. Nor are Hermes and the sibyls the only peculiar thing on this floor. Directly behind him begins a series of large scenes, including a *Wheel of Fortune*, with men hanging on to it for dear life, another wheel of uncertain symbolism, and emblems of Siena and other Tuscan and Latin cities. Oddest of all is a work by Pinturicchio, variously titled the *Allegory of Virtue* or the *Allegory of Fortune*; on a rocky island full of serpents, a party of well-dressed people has just embarked, climbing to the summit where a figure of 'Socrates' accepts a pen from a seated female figure, and another, 'Crates', empties a basket of gold and jewels into the sea. Below, a naked woman with a gonfalon stands with one foot in a boat and another on land.

Unfortunately, many of the best scenes, under the crossing and transepts, are covered to protect them. You'll need to come in the peak tourist season to see the visionary works of Alessandro Franchi – the *Triumph of Elias* and other events in that prophet's life – and Domenico Beccafumi's *Sacrifice of Elias* and the *Execution of the False Prophets of Baal*, which are usually uncovered for a couple of months in late summer (*Sept–Oct; call tourist office for confirmation*). Other works that are uncovered all year include *The Seven Ages of Man* by Antonio Federighi, *Scenes From the Life of Moses* by Beccafumi, Matteo di Giovanni's *Massacre of the Innocents* (always a favourite subject in Sienese art), and, best of all, the beautifully drawn *Judith Liberating the City of Bethulia*, a collaboration of Federighi, Matteo di Giovanni and Urbano da Cortona.

## Elsewhere in the Cathedral

Perhaps the greatest attraction above floor level is the great Carrara marble **pulpit** done by Nicola Pisano in the 1280s. Pisano started on it directly after finishing the one in Pisa; one of the assistants he brought here to help with the work was the young Arnolfo di Cambio. The typical Pisano conception is held up by allegorical figures of the seven liberal arts – more sibyls, prophets, Christian virtues and saints tucked away in the odd corners, and vigorous, crowded relief panels from the Passion as good as the ones in Pisa. Nearby, in the left transept, the **chapel of San Giovanni Battista** has frescoes by Pinturicchio and a bronze statue of St John the

## Hermes Trismegistus

Hermes Trismegistus is someone rarely seen in art, though he is a mysterious protagonist in a great undercurrent of Renaissance thought. 'Thrice-great Hermes', mythical author of a series of mystic philosophical dialogues from the 2nd century AD, had a profound influence on Greek and Arabic thought, gradually becoming associated (correctly or not) with the Egyptian god Thoth, inventor of writing and father of a deep mystical tradition that continues up to this day.

In the 1400s, the Hermetic writings were introduced in the West, thanks largely to the work of Greek scholars fleeing the Ottoman conquest of Constantinople and Trebizond. These writings made quite a splash, prompting a number of key figures to take action. So great was its impact that Marsilio Ficino, the Florentine Humanist and friend of Cosimo de' Medici, completed the first Latin translation of the Hermetic books in 1471 – Cosimo specifically asked him to put off his translations of Plato to get this more important work finished!

To the men of the Renaissance, Hermes was a real person, an Egyptian prophet, who lived in the time of Moses and may perhaps have been his teacher. They saw, revealed in the Hermetic books, an ancient, natural religion, prefiguring Christianity and complementary to it – and, in fact, much more fun than Christianity, for the magical elements in it were entirely to the taste of neo-Platonists like Ficino. From a contemporary point of view, the recovery of Hermes Trismegistus was one of the main intellectual events of the century, one that witnessed a tremendous revival of natural magic, alchemy and astrology.

The memorable Hermes in Siena is depicted surrounded by a bevy of 10 Sibyls: those of Cumae and Tivoli (the Italian contingent), Delphi, Libya, the Hellespont, Phrygia and others. These ladies, part of a pan-Mediterranean religious tradition even older than Hermes Trismegistus, are far more common in Tuscan religious iconography (as seen in the Baptistry and Santa Trinità in Florence, or most famously, on Michelangelo's Sistine Chapel ceiling), for the belief that they all in some way foretold the birth of Christ.

Baptist by Donatello, who also contributed the **Tomb of Giovanni Pecci**, a 1400s Sienese bishop. Another tomb worth a look is that of Cardinal Petroni, an influential early Renaissance design from 1310 by Tino di Camaino.

Some of the **stained glass** in the cathedral is excellent, especially the earliest windows, in the apse, designed by Duccio, and the rose window with its cornucopia. Over the high altar is a bronze **baldachin** by Vecchietta, and in the north aisle the **Piccolomini Altar** includes four early statues of saints by Michelangelo, and one by Torrigiano, the fellow who broke Michelangelo's nose and ended up in exile, working in Westminster Abbey. There is also a *Madonna* by Jacopo della Quercia. Throughout the cathedral, as everywhere else in Siena, be sure to keep an eye out for details – like the tiny, exquisite heads of the popes that decorate the clerestory wall. The Office of Works never settled for anything less than the best, and even such trifles as the holy water fonts, the choir stalls, the iron grilles and the candlesticks are works of genuine artistic merit.

## Piccolomini Library

*Open winter Mon–Sat 10.30–6.30, Sun and hols 1.30–5.30;*
*summer Mon–Sat 10.30–7.30.30, Sun and hols 1.30–6.30; adm.*

This is the room with the famous frescoes by Pinturicchio, built to hold the library of Aeneas Silvius, the greatest member of Siena's greatest noble family. The entrance is off the left aisle, near the Piccolomini altar.

Aeneas Silvius Piccolomini, eventually to become Pope Pius II, was the very definition of a Renaissance man. He was probably the greatest geographer of his age: his works were studied closely by Columbus. Beyond that, and his activities as a poet, diplomat and historian, founder of Pienza and an important patron of artists and humanist scholars, he had, of course, a busy clerical-political career, working fitfully to reform the Church of Rome and the constitution of his native city. In 1495, 31 years after his death, Cardinal Francesco Piccolominii, the man who would become Pope Pius III, decided his celebrated uncle's life would make a fine subject for a series of frescoes. He gave the job to Pinturicchio, his last major commission; among his assistants was the young, still impressionable Raphael – anyone who knows his *Betrothal of the Virgin* will find these paintings eerily familiar.

The 10 scenes include Aeneas Silvius' attendance at the court of James I in Scotland – a Scotland with a Tuscan fantasy landscape – where he served with an embassy. Later he is shown accepting a poet laureate's crown from his friend Emperor Frederick III and presiding over the meeting of Frederick and his bride-to-be, Eleanor of Aragon. Another fresco depicts him canonizing St Catherine of Siena. The last, poignant one portrays a view of Ancona, and its cathedral up on Monte Guasco, where Pius II went in 1464, planning a crusade against the Turks. While waiting for the help promised by the European powers, help that never came, he fell ill and died.

Art historians and critics, following the sniping biography of the artist by Vasari, are not always kind to Pinturicchio. As with Gozzoli's frescoes for the Medici Palace in Florence, the consensus seems to be that this is a less challenging sort of art or perhaps just a very elevated approach to interior decoration. Certainly Pinturicchio seems extremely concerned with the latest styles in court dress and coiffure. However, the incandescent colour, fairytale backgrounds and beautifully drawn figures prove irresistible. These are among the brightest and best-preserved of all quattrocento frescoes; the total effect is that of a serenely confident art, concerned above all with beauty for beauty's sake, even when chronicling the life of a pope. Aeneas Silvius' books have all been carted away somewhere but one of his favourite things remains, a marble statue of the *Three Graces*, a copy of the work by Praxiteles that was much studied by the artists of the 1400s.

## Museo dell'Opera Metropolitana

*Open daily Nov–mid-Mar 9–1.30; summer 9–7.30; Oct 9–6; adm.*

Around the side of the cathedral, off the right transept, Piazza Jacopo della Quercia is the name the Sienese have given to the doomed nave of their 1330s **cathedral extension**. All around this square, heroic pilasters and arches rise, some incorporated into the walls of later buildings. Beyond the big, blank façade, a little door on the right allows entrance to the **Museo Metropolitana**, built into what would have been one of the cathedral transepts. This is the place to go to inspect the cathedral façade at close range. Most of the statues on the façade today are modern copies, replacing the works of great sculptors like Nicola Pisano, Urbano da Cortona and Jacopo della Quercia. The originals have been moved to the museum for better preservation and you can look the cathedral's marble saints right in the eye – if you care to; many of these remarkable statues, fairly alive with early Renaissance *prontezza* (alertness), seem ready to hop off their pedestals and start declaiming if they suspect for a minute you've been skipping Sunday Mass.

Besides these, there are architectural fragments and leftover pinnacles, as well as some bits of the marble pavement that had to be replaced. On the first floor, a collection of Sienese paintings includes Duccio di Buoninsegna's masterpiece, the *Maestà* that hung behind the cathedral's high altar from 1311 until 1505. Painted on both sides, the main composition is a familiar Sienese favourite, the enthroned Virgin flanked by neat rows of adoring saints – with expressive faces and fancy clothes set against a glittering gold background. Among the other paintings and sculptures are works by Pietro and Ambrogio Lorenzetti, Simone Martini, Beccafumi and Vecchietta.

Among the works on the top floor is the *Madonna dagli Occhi Grossi* ('of the Big Eyes') by an anonymous artist of the 1210s, a landmark in the development of Sienese painting and the original cathedral altarpiece. There's a hoard of golden croziers, reliquaries and crucifixes from the cathedral treasure, including another lovely golden rose from the Vatican – probably a gift from Aeneas Silvius. A stairway from here leads up to the top of the **Facciatone**, the 'big façade' of the unfinished nave, where you can contemplate vain ambitions and enjoy a view over the city.

## Baptistry

*Open summer daily 9–7.30; Oct daily 9–6; winter daily 10.30–1 and 2–5; adm.*

Outside the unfinished cathedral nave, a long, steep set of stairs leads down around the back of the church to Piazza San Giovanni. In this lower but prominent setting, the Office of Works architects squeezed in a baptistry, perhaps the only one in Italy situated directly under a cathedral apse. Behind its unfinished 1390s Gothic façade, this baptistry contains yet another impressive hoard of art. It's hard to see anything in this gloomy cellar, though; bring plenty of coins for the lighting machines. Frescoes by Vecchietta, restored to death in the 19th century, decorate much of the interior. The crown jewel, however, is the **baptismal font**, a king-sized work embellished with some of the finest sculpture of the quattrocento. Of the gilded reliefs around the sides, *Herod's Feast* is by Donatello, and the *Baptism of Christ* and *St John in Prison* by Ghiberti. The first relief, with the *Annunciation of the Baptist's Birth*, is the work of Jacopo della Quercia, who also added the five statues of prophets above. Two of the statues at the corners of the font, the ones representing the virtues Hope and Charity, are also by Donatello.

Just across the street from the baptistry, the Renaissance **Palazzo del Magnifico** was the family headquarters of the Petrucci, Sienese power-brokers (and perhaps would-be tyrants) in the late 15th and early 16th centuries.

## Ospedale di Santa Maria della Scala

*Open Mar–Oct daily 10.30–6.30, Nov–Feb daily 10.30–4.30; adm.*

Opposite the old cathedral façade, one entire side of the piazza is occupied by the great **Ospedale di Santa Maria della Scala**. Believed to have been founded in the 9th century and for centuries one of the largest and finest hospitals in the world, it is now an exciting museum project. According to legend, the hospital had its beginnings with a pious cobbler named Sorore, who opened a hostel and infirmary for pilgrims on their way to Rome. (Siena was an important stop on medieval Europe's busiest pilgrimage route, the Via Francigiana). Sorore's mother, it is said, later had a vision here – of babies ascending a ladder (*la scala*) into heaven and being received into the arms of the Virgin Mary – and consequently a foundling hospital was soon added. A meticulous attention to the health of its citizens was always one of the most praiseworthy features of Siena; even in the decadence of the 1700s, advances in such things as inoculation were being made here. In the 14th century, it insisted on such revolutionary practices as the washing of hands by doctors and nurses, meals adapted to each patient's illness, and the use of iron beds (to prevent the spread of bed bugs). To encourage donations, laws were passed allowing wealthy Sienese to deduct gifts from their taxes (remember, this was the 14th century) and not a few left huge sums in their wills; after the plague of 1348, the hospital was up to its ears in gold.

In recent years, the hospital functions have been gradually moved out to more accessible locations (one of the last to die here was novelist and folktale compiler Italo Calvino). As the place closed up, there was talk of converting it into a museum. Now they're doing it, and in a big way. The Sienese say that their new museum, dedicated to all the arts and the city's history, will be one of the largest in the world, with three times the exhibition space of the Pompidou Centre. Don't ask when it will be finished; the point of this innovative exercise is that it will *never* be finished. An international competition was held to plan the new complex; the winner, Professor Guido Canali of Parma, came up with the idea of a *cantiere didattico*, a kind of 'educational construction site', where the process of museum-building itself is part of the attraction. They should have many of the permanent exhibits in place in 10 years or so, along with shops, temporary exhibits and restoration workshops. In a typical gesture of Sienese pride, the *comune* declined to ask for state help in completing this project; they mean to keep control by paying the whole bill themselves.

For now, it's definitely worth the price of admission just to see the big frescoes in the **Sala dei Pellegrini**, the hospital's main reception hall. Another pioneering fresco-cycle devoted to a secular subject, like those in the Palazzo Pubblico, this is a tribute to old Siena's advanced, humanistic outlook; all the scenes are devoted to the history of the hospital, including the vision of Sorore's mother and everyday views of the hospital's activities. In the best of them, Domenico di Bartolo shows how Sienese art was still keeping up with the Florentines in 1441 with his *Reception, Education and Marriage of a Daughter of the Hospital*; care of abandoned children, the *gettatelli* (literally, 'little ones thrown away'), was one of the hospital's impor-tant functions. Other frescoes, by different Sienese artists, portray in loving detail the caring for the sick, the distribution of alms to the poor, and the paying of the wet-nurses of the *gettatelli*. All are lively, crowded scenes of life in a unique institu-tion, and an insight into a side of old Siena you might not have thought existed.

Already, there is plenty to see, including a collection of precious golden reliquaries and other church paraphernalia, some of it from medieval Constantinople, in refurbished chambers cheerfully marked *isolamento dei contagiosi*. Some other original features of the hospital include the **Cappella del Sacro Chiodo**, with damaged frescoes by Vecchietta, the elaborate **Cappella SS. Annunziata**, and the thoroughly spooky **Cappella di Santa Caterina**, which begins with a leering skull and ends with an altarpiece by Taddeo di Bartolo. Old views and relics of the hospital are displayed in many of the long hallways; in some of the oldest, you can see how the façade was originally covered with frescoes (by Pietro and Ambrogio Lorenzetti), a colourful counterpoint to the cathedral façade across the way. Another part of the complex now houses the **Museo Archeologico** (*open daily winter 10.30–4.30, summer 10–6; joint adm with Santa Maria della Scala*) with an Etruscan and Roman collection.

## The Pinacoteca

The ancient quarter of steep narrow streets north of the cathedral is the *contrada* of the *Selva* (forest) – Rhinoceros country. In its heart, Piazza della Selva, one of the most charming of the new *contrada* fountains has a bronze statue of the neighbourhood's Rhinoceros symbol. Leaving the cathedral in the opposite direction, south down Via del Capitano, will lead you into the haunts of the Dolphin and Turtle (*Onda* and *Tartaruga*). Where the street meets Via di Città, it changes its name to Via San Pietro, passing the 14th-century Palazzo Buonsignori, one of the most harmonious of the city's noble palaces, now restored as the home of the **Pinacoteca Nazionale** (*open Mon 8.30–1.30, Tues–Sat 8.15–7.15, Sun and hols 8.15–1.30; adm*).

This is the temple of Sienese art, a representative sampling of this inimitable city's style; many of the works have been recently restored. The collection is arranged roughly chronologically, beginning on the top floor with Guido da Siena and his school in the mid-13th century (Room 2), continuing through an entire room of delicate, melancholy Virgins by Duccio and his followers, before reaching a climax with Duccio's luminous though damaged *Madonna dei Francescani* in Room 4. Madonnas and saints fill room after room, including important works by Siena's greatest 14th-century artists. One of the most famous is Simone Martini's *Madonna and Child*; the story goes that this Madonna was a great Palio fan. When everyone had gathered in the Campo for the event, she would wander out in the empty streets and tiptoe over for a look. One day, she lingered too long in the Campo and had to run back home, losing her veil in her haste. She has yet to find it, and according to the Sienese, she weeps sweetly during the Palio, probably because she can't get through the Pinacoteca's security system. Other Madonnas that stand out are those of Pietro and Ambrogio Lorenzetti (*Madonna Enthroned* and the *Annunciation*, both in Room 7) and Taddeo di Bartolo (*Triptych*, in Room 11), with their rosy blooming faces and brilliant colour, a remarkable counterpoint to the relative austerity of contemporary painting in Florence. One element that is clearly evident in many of these paintings is Sienese civic pride; the artists take obvious delight in including the city's skyline and landmarks in the background of their works – even in Nativities.

Sienese Renaissance painters are well represented, often betraying the essential conservatism of their art and resisting the new approaches of Florence: Domenico di Bartolo's 1433 *Madonna* in Room 9; Nerocchio and Matteo di Giovanni of the 1470s (Room 14); Sano di Pietro, the leading painter of the 1440s (Rooms 16 and 17). The first floor displays some of Il Sodoma's most important works, especially the great *Scourging of Christ* in Room 31 (1514); in Room 37 the *Descent into Hell* is one of the finest works by Siena's greatest Mannerist, Beccafumi.

### Around the Terzo di Città

Next to the Pinacoteca, the church of **San Pietro alle Scale** contains *The Flight into Egypt*, an altarpiece by Rutilio Manetti, the only significant Sienese painter of the Baroque era, a follower of Caravaggio. **San Giuseppe**, at the end of Via San Pietro, marks Siena's uneasy compromise with the new world of the 1600s. One of the city's first Baroque churches, it was nevertheless built not in Baroque marble or travertine but good Siena brown brick. This is the church of the *Onda* (Dolphin) district; the *contrada*'s fountain is in front. Just around the corner, the gloomy bulk of **Sant'Agostino** conceals a happier rococo interior of the 1740s by Vanvitelli, the Dutchman (born Van Wittel) who was chief architect for the Kings of Naples. Most of the building dates back to the 13th century, however, and there are surviving bits of trecento frescoes and altarpieces all around. In the north aisle, the Piccolomini chapel (*usually shut*) has a fine painting by Il Sodoma, an *Epiphany* and a *Massacre of the Innocents* by Matteo di Giovanni.

Via Piero Andrea Mattioli leads from here to the city walls and the Porta Tufi, passing along the way a path that leads to Siena's small **Botanical Gardens** (*open Mon–Fri 8–12.30 and 2.30–5.30, Sat 8–12; book in advance for guided tours, t 0577 232874*). Further west, the *contrada* of the *Chiocciola* (Snail) is centred on the church of **Santa Maria del Carmine**, a 14th-century church remodelled by Baldassare Peruzzi in 1517; inside there is a painting of *St Michael* by Beccafumi and a rather grimly Caravaggiesque *Last Judgement* by an anonymous 16th-century artist.

## Terzo di San Martino

Beginning again at the Croce del Travaglio and the Palazzo Piccolomini (*see* p.328), Banchi di Sotto leads into the quiet eastern third of the city, passing the **Loggia del Papa**, a Renaissance ornament given to Siena by Aeneas Silvius Piccolomini in 1462.

The most intriguing parts of this neighbourhood are found on the hillside behind Piazza del Mercato, old streets on slopes and stairs in the *contrada* of the *Torre* (Elephant) – one of the 'unlucky' *contrade* that hasn't won a Palio in decades. Nevertheless they have a fine fountain with their elephant-and-tower emblem on pretty Piazzetta Franchi. One of the more characteristic streets in this part of town is **Via dell'Oro**, an alley of overhanging medieval houses, much like the ones in the Palazzo Pubblico's frescoes of Good and Bad Government (*see* p.327). For a change, **Via Porta Giustizia** will lead you on a country ramble within the city's walls, along the valley that separates Terzo San Martino and Terzo di Città.

Among the noteworthy churches in this Terzo are **Santo Spirito** on Via dei Pispini, with further frescoes by Il Sodoma in the first chapel on the right; and **Santa Maria dei Servi**, to the south on Via dei Servi in the *contrada* of *Valdimontone* (Ram). Here, in the north transept, is one of the earliest and finest Sienese nativities, the altarpiece in the second north chapel, by Taddeo di Bartolo. Good paintings include a *Madonna* by Coppo di Marcovaldo and the *Madonna del Popolo* by Lippo Memmi. An interesting comparison can be made between two versions of that favourite Sienese subject, the *Massacre of the Innocents*: one from the early trecento by Pietro Lorenzetti, and another from 1491 by Matteo di Giovanni.

Nearby at Via Roma 7, the *Società Esecutori Pie Disposizioni* keeps an **oratory** and a small but good collection of Sienese art (*call ahead, t 0577 284300; open Mon and Fri 9–1, Tues and Thurs 3–5.30*). This Terzo also has two of the best surviving city gates, the **Porta Romana** at the end of Via Roma, and the elegant **Porta Pispini** on the road to Perugia. The latter was once embellished with a *Nativity* by Sodoma, of which only traces are still visible.

## Terzo di Camollia

Leading north from the Campo, the **Via Banchi di Sopra** is a most aristocratic thoroughfare, lined with the palaces of the medieval Sienese élite. It forms the spine of this largest and most populous of the *terzi*. The first important palace is also one of the oldest, that of the Tolomei family, a proud clan of noble bankers who liked to trace their ancestry back to the Greek Ptolemies of Hellenistic-era Egypt. The **Palazzo Tolomei**, begun in 1208, is the very soul of Sienese Gothic; it gave its name to Piazza Tolomei in front, the space used by the republic for its assembly meetings before the construction of the Palazzo Pubblico.

Just a few blocks down Banchi di Sopra, **Palazzo Salimbeni** on Piazza Salimbeni was the compound of the Tolomeis' mortal enemies; their centuries-long vendetta dragged Sienese politics into chaos on more than a few occasions. Together with the two adjacent palaces on the square, the Salimbeni is now the home of the *Monte dei Paschi di Siena*, founded by the city as a pawnshop in 1472, now a remarkable savings bank with a medieval air about it that has a tremendous influence over everything that happens in southern Tuscany, and branches as far away as Australia – they also have a good art collection, sometimes open to the public along with special exhibitions. The national government is currently trying to privatize the Monte dei Paschi, which makes the Sienese hopping mad. A little further up the street, the plain brick **Oratory of Santa Maria di Nevi** is almost always locked up; if you should chance to see it open, stop in to see the altarpiece, the finest work of the late 1400s painter Matteo di Giovanni.

East of these palaces, in the neighbourhood of the *Giraffa* (Giraffe), is one of the last important churches built in Siena, the proto-Baroque **Santa Maria di Provenzano** (1594), at the end of Via del Moro. This particular Virgin Mary, a terracotta image said to have been left by St Catherine (*see* below), has had one of the most popular devotional cults in Siena since the 1590s; the annual Palio is in her honour. The quiet streets behind the church, Siena's red-light district in Renaissance times, lead to **San Francesco**, begun in 1326, one of the city's largest churches. It's a sad tale; after a big fire in the 17th century, this great Franciscan barn was used for centuries as a warehouse and barracks. Restorations began in the 1880s and the 'medieval' brick façade was completed only in 1913. The interior is still one of the most impressive in Siena, a monolithic rectangle with vivid stained glass (especially in late afternoon) and good transept chapels in the Florentine manner. A little artwork has survived, including traces of frescoes by both the Lorenzettis in the north transept. To the right is the fine Renaissance cloister.

Next to San Francesco is the equally simple **Oratorio di San Bernardino** (*open mid-Mar–Oct daily 10.30–1.30 and 3–5.30; adm*), begun in the late 1400s in honour of Siena's famous preacher and graced with the preacher's heart. Its upper chapel, a monument of the Sienese Renaissance, contains frescoes by Beccafumi, Il Sodoma and the almost forgotten High Renaissance master Girolamo del Pacchia, few of whose works survive. The areas west of San Francesco, traditionally a solid working-class quarter, make up the *contrada* of *Bruco* (Caterpillar); their fountain is under the steps on Via dei Rossi. On the wall of the house opposite is a curious marble relief of a woman at a window peering at a pomegranate from behind half-closed curtains. Caterpillars are everywhere.

*Bruco*'s name recalls the Compagnìa del Bruco, the trade union that initiated the revolt of 1371, temporarily reforming Siena's faction-ridden government. The workers paid a terrible price for it; while the revolution was under way, some young noble *provocateurs* started a fire that consumed almost the entire *contrada*. Today *Bruco* fares worst of the 'unlucky' neighbourhoods; it hasn't won a Palio since 1955.

## St Catherine, St Dominic and the Goose

Unlike the poor caterpillar, the equally proletarian *Oca* (Goose) seems the best organized and most successful *contrada*. On occasion during the Napoleonic Wars, with Tuscan and city governments in disarray, the *Oca*'s men took charge of the city.

The goose's most famous daughter, Caterina Benincasa, was born here on Vicolo del Tiratoio in 1347. She was the last but one of 25 children born into the family of a wool-dyer. At an early age the visions started. By her teens, she had turned her room at home into a cell and, while she never became a nun, she lived like a hermit, a solitary ascetic in her own house, sleeping with a stone for a pillow. After she received the stigmata, like St Francis, her reputation as a holy woman spread across Tuscany; popes and kings corresponded with her, and towns would send for her to settle their disputes. In 1378 Florence was under a papal interdict, and the city asked Catherine to plead its case at the papal court at Avignon. She went, but with an agenda of her own – convincing Pope Gregory XI to move the papacy back to Rome where it belonged. As a woman, and a holy woman to boot, she was able to tell the pope to his face what a corrupt and worldly Church he was running, without ending up dangling from the top of a palace wall.

Talking the pope (a French pope, mind you) into leaving the civilized life in Provence for turbulent, barbaric 14th-century Rome is only one of the miracles with which Catherine was credited. Political expediency probably helped more than divine intervention – much of Italy, including anathemized Florence, was in revolt against the absentee popes. She followed them back and died in Rome in 1380, aged only 33.

Canonization came in 1460, and in the 19th century, she was declared co-patron of Italy (along with St Francis) and one of the Doctors of the Church. She and St Teresa of Avila are the only women to hold this honour – given in acknowledgement of their inspired devotional writings and their practical, incisive letters encouraging church reform.

The *contrada* of the Goose stretches down steeply from Banchi di Sopra to the western city walls. At its centre, on Vicolo di Tiratoio, St Catherine's house is preserved as a shrine; the **Santuario e Casa di Santa Caterina** (*open daily 9–12.30 and 3–6*) includes the whole of the Benincasa home and the dyer's workshop, each room converted into a chapel, many with frescoes by 15th- and 16th-century Sienese artists. The adjacent oratory is now the *Oca's contrada* chapel (note the goose in the detail of the façade).

Via Santa Caterina, the main street of the *Oca*, slopes down towards the city walls and **Fontebranda**, a simple pointed-arched fountain of the 13th century. It doesn't seem much now, but medieval and Renaissance travellers always remarked on it, and it was an important part of Siena's advanced system of fountains and aqueducts. The church of **San Domenico**, on the hill above Fontebranda, similarly fails to impress, at least when you see it close up from the bus depot on Piazza San Domenico. From Fontebranda, however, the bold Gothic lines of the apse and transepts give a great insight into the straightforward, strangely modern character of much Sienese religious architecture. It's a long climb up to the church from here. Inside, the church is as big and empty as San Francesco; among the relatively few works of art is the only existing portrait of St Catherine, on the west wall, painted by her friend, the artist Andrea Vanni. In this church, scene of so many incidents from the saint's life, you can see her head in a golden reliquary, though the real attraction is the wonderfully hysterical set of murals by Il Sodoma in the **Cappella Santa Caterina**, representing the girl in various states of serious exaltation.

The open, relatively modern quarter around San Domenico offers a welcome change from the dark and treeless streets of this brick city, in a shady park called **La Lizza** and the green spaces around the **Fortezza Medicea**. Though the site is the same, this is not the hated fortress Charles V compelled the Sienese to build in 1552;

as soon as the Sienese chased the imperial troops out, they razed it to the ground. Cosimo I forced its rebuilding after annexing Siena, but to make the bitter pill easier to swallow, he employed a Sienese architect, Baldassare Lanci, and let him create what must be the most elegant and civilized, least threatening fortress in Italy. The Fortezza, a long, low rectangle of Siena brick profusely decorated with Medici balls, seems more like a setting for garden parties or summer opera than anything designed to intimidate a sullen populace.

The Sienese weren't completely won over; right after the Italian reunification, they renamed the central space of the fortress **Piazza della Libertà**. The grounds are now a city park, and the vaults of the munition cellars have become the **Enoteca Nazionale** (*open Tues–Sat 12pm–1am, Mon 12pm–8pm, closed Sun*), the 'Permanent Exhibition of Italian Wines'. Almost every variety of wine Italy produces can be bought here, by the glass or by the bottle. The Enoteca's purpose is to promote Italian wines – it ships thousands of bottles overseas each year and hosts an annual *Settimana dei Vini* featuring regional wines in the first half of June.

East of the fortress, beyond the Lizza and the city stadium, lie the twin centres of modern Siena, **Piazza Gramsci**, terminus for most city bus lines, and **Piazza Matteotti**. Continuing northwards towards the Camollia Gate, you pass the little Renaissance church of **Fonte Giusta**, just off Via di Camollia on Vicolo Fontegiusta. Designed in 1482 by Urbano da Cortona, this church contains a fresco by Peruzzi (another sibyl) and a magnificent tabernacle over the main altar; there is also a whalebone, left here, according to local legend, by Christopher Columbus. The **Porta Camollia**, in the northernmost corner of Siena, underwent the Baroque treatment in the 1600s. Here you will see the famous inscription 'Wider than her gates Siena opens her heart to you'. Old Siena was never that sentimental. The whole thing was added in 1604 – undoubtedly under the orders of the Florentine governor – to mark the visit of Grand Duke Francesco I, who wasn't really welcome at all.

# Peripheral Attractions

From Porta Camollia, Viale Vittorio Emanuele leads through some of the modern quarters outside the walls. Beyond the gate it passes a column commemorating the meeting of Emperor Frederick III and his bride-to-be Eleanor of Aragon in 1451 – the event captured in one of the Pinturicchio frescoes in the Piccolomini Library. Next looms a great defence tower, the **Antiporto**, erected just before the Siege of Siena and rebuilt in 1675. Further down, the **Palazzo dei Diavoli** (1460) was the headquarters of the Marquis of Marignano during the siege.

There isn't much on the outskirts of the city – thanks largely to Marignano, who laid waste lovely and productive lands for miles around. Some 2km east (take Via Simone Martini from the Porta Ovile), in the hills above the railway station, the basilica and monastery of **L'Osservanza** has been carefully restored after serious damage in the last war. Begun in 1422, a foundation of San Bernardino, the monastery retains much of its collection of 13th- and 14th-century Sienese art.

To the west of the city, the road to Massa Marittima passes through the hills of the Montagnola Sienese, an important centre of monasticism in the Middle Ages (*see* San Galgano, pp.363–4). Near **Montecchio** (6km), the hermitage of **Lecceto**, one of the oldest in Tuscany, has been much changed, but still has some Renaissance frescoes in the church and a 12th-century cloister; nearby, the hermitage of **San Leonardo al Lago** is mostly in ruins but the 14th-century church survives, with masterly frescoes (*c.* 1360) by Pietro Lorenzetti's star pupil, Lippo Vanni. Just outside the village of **Sovicille** (13km), there is a 12th-century Romanesque church, the **Pieve di Ponte alla Spina**.

The village of **Rosia** (17km) has another Romanesque church, and just south is the Vallombrosan **Abbey of Torri** (*open Mon–Fri 3.30–6*), with much from its original foundation in the 1200s; it has a rare three-storey cloister, with three types of columns.

# Hill Towns West of Siena

# Hill Towns West of Siena

## Highlights

1 San Gimignano's skyline of medieval skyscrapers
2 Volterra: Etruscan relics and alabaster
3 The spectacular cathedral of Massa Marittima
4 The sword in the stone at San Galgano

In the late Middle Ages, this dramatically diverse, often rugged countryside was a border region, both culturally and politically, its people alternately subject to the strong pull of Florence and Siena. Its towns do not have that much in common: Poggibonsi is almost all new, while Volterra goes back to the Etruscans. San Gimignano presents its famous skyline of medieval skyscrapers, while parts of the Metal Hills show outlandish silhouettes of cooling towers from the ubiquitous geothermal power plants. San Gimignano and Volterra are the main attractions, both beautiful cities containing some remarkable works of art. Massa Marittima, often overlooked, has one of the finest cathedrals in Italy.

Beyond that there is a doll-sized walled city, bubbling sulphurous pits, alabaster souvenirs, a Roman theatre, lonely moors and a sword in a stone (not King Arthur's but someone else's).

# Monteriggioni, Colle di Val d'Elsa and Poggibonsi

## Monteriggioni

The SS2 passes a genuine curiosity 11km north of Siena, the tiny fortified town of **Monteriggioni**. For much of Siena's history, this was its northernmost bastion, often in the frontlines in the wars with Florence after its construction in 1219. Now it sits like a crown on its roundish hill, a neat circle of walls with 14 towers, with just enough room inside for two oversized piazzas, a few houses and their gardens, and the inevitable bars and restaurants. In late July, the town hosts a medieval festival – a re-enactment of medieval life with food, drink, music and dancing – the highlight is the third weekend in July. Some 3km further towards Colle di Val d'Elsa, there is a turn-off to the left for the 12th-century Abbey of Santi Salvatore and Cirino, better known as the **Abbadia dell'Isola**. The Cistercians began it in 1101 on an 'island' among the marshes, hence the name. Inside this stark Romanesque building is a restored fresco by Taddeo di Bartolo and a Renaissance altarpiece.

## Colle di Val d'Elsa

**Colle di Val d'Elsa** (pop. 16,300), a striking, ancient town up on a steep hill, presents an impressive silhouette if you see it from the right angle – it's long enough but at most only three blocks wide. Though probably as old as the Etruscans, Colle first became prominent in the 12th century, a safe, fortified stronghold that attracted many migrants from the surrounding plains. In later centuries, it was known for the manufacture of wool, paper and ceramics; today, Colle is Italy's largest producer of fine glass and crystal, and there are lots of shops selling it. There is also a new museum, the **Museo del Cristallo** (*Via dei Fossi, t 0577 924135; open April–Oct Tues–Sun 10–12 and 4–7.30; Nov–Mar Tues–Fri 3–7, Sat and Sun 10–12 and 3–7; adm*) in a 19th-century crystal factory in the 'new' town (down the hill). The Collegiani will never allow the world to forget that their town was the birthplace of Arnolfo di Cambio, the great architect who built Florence's Palazzo Vecchio and began its cathedral.

# Getting Around

The main routes between Florence and Siena – the Via Cassia (SS2) or the parallel Superstrada del Palio – have exits for Colle di Val d'Elsa (27km/35mins from Siena, 49km/1hr from Florence) and Poggibonsi, 7km further north on SS68.

Poggibonsi is a major **bus** junction in south Tuscany, with easy connections to Florence, Siena, San Gimignano, Volterra and Colle di Val d'Elsa (TRA-IN buses if you're coming from Siena, SITA from Florence). Poggibonsi is also on the Empoli–Siena **railway** line, with a branch or bus beyond to Colle in 15mins.

# Tourist Information

**Monteriggioni**: Largo Fontebianda 5, t/f 0577 304810.
**Colle di Val d'Elsa**: Via Campana 43, t 0577 922791, f 0577 922621.

# Where to Stay and Eat

## Monteriggioni ✉ 53035

If you're heading from Florence to Siena, or from Siena out to the west, a good place to stop for lunch is the little castle village of Monteriggioni.

**Hotel Monteriggioni**, t 0577 305009, f 0577 305011, *www.monteriggioni.net* (*very expensive*). If you want to keep within the walls, you can have a very comfortable stay at the Monteriggioni, made up of two old stone houses, a garden and even a tiny pool.

**Il Pozzo**, Piazza Roma 2, t 0577 304127 (*expensive*). Here they do some of the simpler dishes very well – bean soup and roast meats – but their real forte is fancy desserts (they even serve *crêpes Suzette*). *Closed Sun eve and Mon.*

## Colle di Val d'Elsa ✉ 53034

**★★★Villa Belvedere**, Località Belvedere, t 0577 920966, f 0577 924128, *www.villabelvedere.com* (*expensive*). Located 1km or so east of the town, near the Siena highway, this pretty, old villa has a good restaurant, a big garden, swimming pool and 15 simple rooms.

**★★★Arnolfo**, in the Borgo at Via Campana 8, t 0577 922020, f 0577 922324, *www.hotel arnolfo.it* (*moderate*). Simple and comfortable, in the town itself.

**Arnolfo Restaurant**, Via XX Settembre 52, t 0577 920549 (*expensive*). This occupies a Renaissance palace, the perfect setting for what is widely considered one of the top restaurants in all Italy. Menus change with the seasons, but you can always choose from two *menu degustazioni* – one 'traditional', one 'creative'. *Closed Tues and Wed.*

**Osteria di Sapia**, Via del Castello 4, t 0577 921453 (*moderate*). The décor in this elegant osteria (yellow and blue walls and lots of ethnic bits and pieces) situated in the old town is a refreshingly far cry from typical Tuscan rustic. The food, too, is a bit different. Creative variations on the Tuscan theme include vegetarian lasagne and pork tenderloin cooked with peaches and *vin santo*. The two set menus are good value and there is a lovely terrace. *Closed Mon, lunch Nov–Feb.*

**Fattoria di Mugnano**, 7km along the Colle–Volterra road, t 0577 959023 (*cheap*). An old farm, now a thriving business, out among the olive groves in the nearby hamlet of Mugnano. The delightful restaurant offers local and Sicilian cuisine; they'll sell you some of the wine and olive oil. They also offer a few spartan rooms (*inexpensive*). *Closed Thurs.*

**L'Oste di Borgo**, Via Gracco del Secco 58, t 0577 922499 (*cheap*). A nice little *osteria* with a terrace and a few marble-topped tables in a wood-panelled room and background jazz. You can eat a light meal (choose from an interesting selection of pastas and salads), or snack on *bruschette*, local cheeses, hams and salamis. *Closed Wed.*

## Poggibonsi ✉ 53036

**★★★Alcide**, Via Marconi 67a, t 0577 937501, f 0577 981729 (*moderate*). If you're spending time in Poggibonsi this offers doubles with air conditioning. Their restaurant (*expensive*) is one of the better places for seafood in this landlocked province, featuring dishes with a South Italian slant, like Apulian *orecchiette* in a sauce with cuttlefish and several varieties of maritime risotto. *Closed Sun eve, Mon.*

Down on the plain below the citadel, the modern part of the town surrounds the arcaded **Piazza Arnolfo di Cambio**. Via Garibaldi or Via San Sebastiano will take you up to old Colle – but for a proper introduction you'll need to come on the road from Volterra, passing through a grim Renaissance bastion called the **Porta Nuova**, designed by Giuliano da Sangallo, and then across the medieval-Renaissance suburb known as the **Borgo**. Between the Borgo and the old town, called the **Castello**, there is a picturesque narrow bridge and the **Palazzo di Campana** (1539, by Giovanni di Baccio d'Agnolo); the arch in its centre is the elegant gateway to the town.

Via del Castello runs straight up the centre, with narrow medieval alleys on both sides. Here you'll find the **cathedral**, built in 1603 (Colle only got its own bishop in 1592) with a Victorian-era façade, a few Renaissance palaces, and some museums. Beside the cathedral, in the Palazzo Pretorio, a small **Museo Archeologico** (*open Oct–April Tues–Fri 3.30–5.30, Sat, Sun and hols 10–12 and 3.30–6.30; May–Sept Tues–Sun 10–12 and 4.30–7.30; adm*) displays Etruscan objects; there is a small picture collection in the nearby **Museo Civico** (*same hours as Museo Archeologico; adm*). The best is the **Museo d'Arte Sacra** (*same hours as Museo Archeologico; adm*) in the old episcopal palace, with a few Sienese and Florentine paintings and the frescoes commissioned by some jolly 14th-century bishop – scenes of the hunt and from the Crusades, believed to be the work of Ambrogio Lorenzetti.

Near the end of Via del Castello, the Collegiani claim an old tower-fortress as the **House of Arnolfo di Cambio**. Arnolfo's father, a gentleman and an architect, probably came to Colle di Val d'Elsa from Lombardy in the 1230s, bringing the great tradition of the Lombard master masons into Tuscany. He may have received his initiation into the new (for Italy) Gothic style from studying works in Siena or the new Cistercian abbey at San Galgano. He worked for Nicola Pisano on the Siena cathedral pulpit, and for Giovanni Pisano on the Fonte Maggiore in Perugia, and probably moved to Florence in the 1270s.

South of Colle, many of the villages in the hills retain their simple Romanesque churches from the 11th and 12th centuries, beginning with the isolated **Badia a Coneo**, a Vallombrosan foundation of the 1120s (5km from Colle on an unpaved lane off the road to Casole). At **Casole d'Elsa** (15km south, local bus), a town that took hard knocks in the last war, there is an interesting **Collegiata** church begun in the 12th century, with Sienese frescoes, two fine, late 14th-century sepulchres by Gano da Siena, and terracottas by Giovanni della Robbia. Casole's Sienese **Rocca** held out into the 16th century, long after the rest of the Valdelsa flew the Florentine flag. South from Casole, the road winds through pleasant, green countryside leading up to the Colline Metallifere, the 'metal hills', and you can seek out more Romanesque churches in **Mensano** (7km) and **Radicondoli** (15km, the church of **San Simone**).

## Poggibonsi

If you spend enough time in Tuscany, sooner or later you are bound to pass through **Poggibonsi** (pop. 25,700), a major knot on the SS2, SS429 and Superstrada del Palio roads linking Siena to Florence and Pisa. These days, residents of the pretty tourist towns of central Tuscany are not above having a laugh at the expense of this homely, hard-working industrial centre. Poor Poggibonsi! Founded only in 1156, the original *Poggiobonizzo* grew rapidly. By 1220, it was probably one of the largest cities in Tuscany, with a population of some 15,000; in that year, Emperor Frederick II declared it a *Città Imperiale* with special rights and privileges. Ghibelline politics and its imperial favour, however, were to prove Poggiobonizzo's undoing. In 1270, San Gimignano and Colle di Val d'Elsa, along with the Florentines and the troops of Charles of Anjou, besieged and conquered the city, then razed it to the ground. Some of the poorer citizens stayed behind, refounding the town as a market village on the plain. Poggibonsi was thoroughly wrecked again during the battles of 1944, but has grown tremendously since to become the biggest town between Florence and Siena.

There isn't much to see; the 14th-century Palazzo Pretorio and the collegiate church on the main street recall something of the appearance of pre-war Poggibonsi. Close by, the **Castello della Magione** is a small complex from the 1100s; the Romanesque chapel and outbuildings form a little closed square, a fortified pilgrims' hospice said to have been built by the Templars. Above the town, an unfinished fortress begun by Lorenzo de' Medici covers much of the original city of Poggiobonizzo.

Just 2km south of town near the SS2, is the austerely Franciscan **Basilica of San Lucchese**; inside are some good frescoes, including works by Taddeo Gaddi and Bartolo di Fredi. Not surprisingly, this strategically important corner of Tuscany is scattered with castles, including the 13th-century **Castello della Rochetta**, once the home of the famous *condottiere* Sir John Hawkwood, and the romantically ruined **Rocca di Staggia** (5km south of Poggibonsi on the SS2), built by the Florentines in the 1430s – a counterpart to Sienese Monteriggioni, just a few kilometres further on.

# San Gimignano

In the miniaturist landscape of this corner of Tuscany, **San Gimignano**, Italy's best-preserved medieval city, is an almost fantastic landmark. Seen from Poggibonsi or the Volterra road its medieval towers, some of them over 50m tall, loom over the surrounding hills. Once, almost every city in central Italy looked like this; more than just defensive strongholds in the incessant family feuds, these towers served as status symbols for the families and the cities themselves, a visible measure of a town's power and prosperity. By the 16th century, most of Italy's towers had succumbed to age, decay and the efforts of the urban *comuni*, which pruned and destroyed these symbols of truculent nobility at every opportunity. Oddly, this did not happen in San Gimignano, famous even in the 1300s as the '*città delle belle torri*'. Originally there were at least 70 towers (in a town one-eighth of a square mile in size). Only 15 remain, but in conjunction with the beautiful streets, churches and public buildings, they are enough to give you the impression that the town has been hermetically sealed in a time-capsule since the Middle Ages.

## History

According to legend, the town was originally called Castel della Selva. When the Gothic army of Totila passed through in the 550s, the townsfolk for some reason chose to pray to an obscure saint named Gimignano, a martyred bishop of Modena,

## Getting Around

The railway station is 11km away and is an infrequent stop on the Empoli–Siena line. Buses to the town *usually* coincide with the **trains**, but from either Siena or Florence you'll be better off taking the bus, which leaves you right at the Porta San Giovanni, the main entrance to the town.

TRA-IN **buses** from Siena (38km/45mins – the same bus that goes to Colle di Val d'Elsa) are very frequent, though for most, you will need to change in Poggibonsi. Several daily SITA buses arrive from Florence (54km/1hr 15mins) and there are four buses a day to nearby Certaldo.

If you're **driving**, San Gimignano is 11km west of Poggibonsi, 13km south of Certaldo or 14km from Colle di Val d'Elsa, each route more scenic than the last. Within the walls, San Gimignano is usually closed to traffic; the main car park is outside Porta San Giovanni. Get a pass from the police to park at one of the hotels inside.

## Tourist Information

**San Gimignano**: Piazza del Duomo 1, t 0577 940008, f 0577 940903, www.sangimignano.com.

### Admission

If you plan to visit all the key sights, it is worth buying the cheaper joint ticket (*biglietto cumulativo* €7.50) which covers the four museums, the tower of Palazzo del Popolo and the Capella di Santa Fina, but not the Collegiata.

## Shopping

There isn't any particular artisan tradition here, but so many tourists visit that enterprising shop owners have assembled a host of interesting things – the town hasn't quite turned into a great trinket bazaar, but it's getting there.

**Linea Oro**, Via San Giovanni. Among the good buys are pretty things in alabaster from nearby Volterra.

**Via San Matteo 85**, north of Piazza del Duomo. One of the best shops for alabaster is here.

**La Stamperia**, Via San Matteo 88. Sells original prints including views of Tuscan towns and countryside.

**Ceramics** are everywhere; some of the local work is quite good and inexpensive.

Just within Porta San Giovanni is a 13th-century church now converted to a shop for local wine, olive oil and other farm products.

San Gimignano's other specialities are a formidable white wine called Vernaccia (*see* p.352) and a sweet called *mandorlato*, very like the *panforte* of Siena. Many local vineyards would be glad to sell you a bottle of *Vernaccia*. One such is **Cantine Baroncini**, Casale, t 0577 940600.

## Activities

If you want to explore the surrounding countryside on horseback, there is a riding centre close by.

**Vecchio Maneggio**, Sant'Andrea 22, Ulignano, t 0577 950232, 5km along the road to Certaldo. Also an *agriturismo* offering rooms (*moderate*).

---

for their salvation from a near-guaranteed sacking. Gimignano came through in style, looming down from the clouds in golden armour to scare away the besiegers.

Although it must have been an important and prosperous place, San Gimignano does not cut much of a figure in the medieval chronicles. The city was an independent republic from the early 1100s until 1353, when it came under the rule of Florence. It certainly participated in the Guelph–Ghibelline strife, and in all the other troubles of the period, though today it is probably best remembered as the home town of the poet Folgore of San Gimignano (*c.* 1250), famous for his lovely sonnets to the months of the year. San Gimignano has the air of a false start, a free *comune* that could build a wall and defend itself, yet lacked the will or the money to make itself into a Siena

# Where to Stay

## San Gimignano ✉ 53037

In the summer, you may want a hand finding a place to sleep.

**Hotel Association**, just inside the gate on Via S. Giovanni, **t/f** 0577 940809.

★★★**Antico Pozzo**, Via San Matteo 87, **t** 0577 942014, **f** 0577 942117, *www.anticopozzo.com* (*expensive*). Next to the main square, this is a stylish hotel with wonderful views from rooms at the top of the house. The building dates from the 1500s – several of the rooms even have delicately frescoed ceilings.

★★★**La Cisterna**, **t** 0577 940328, **f** 0577 942080, *www.hotelcisterna.it* (*expensive*). If the Leon Bianco is full, this is in the same square and also comes highly recommended.

★★★**Le Renaie**, Loc Pancole, about 7km towards Certaldo, **t** 0577 955044, **f** 0577 955126, *www.hotellerenaie.com* (*expensive*). If you prefer the tranquillity of the very lovely Tuscan countryside, head north of town to find this attractive modern building, with a garden, pool and tennis court.

★★★**Leon Bianco**, Piazza della Cisterna, **t** 0577 941294, **f** 0577 942123, *www.leon blanco.com* (*moderate*). An excellent hotel with modern rooms.

To fill the vacuum of inexpensive accommodation, a score of San Gimignesi rent out rooms. The tourist office can give you a list.

# Eating Out

San Gimignano may entertain a good many visitors, but it makes a fine host.

**Dorando**, Vicolo del Oro 2, **t** 0577 941862 (*expensive*). For the more adventurous. The chef attempts to recreate authentic Renaissance and Medieval cuisine – *cibreo* (a chicken liver pâté so rich Caterina de' Medici nearly died from a surfeit of it), boned guinea fowl with honey and black sesame seeds, maccheroni with duck and mushroom sauce and a truffle glaze, crème caramel flavoured with coriander, and things stranger still. Readers have praised it highly. *Closed Mon in winter*.

**Osteria delle Catene**, Via Mainardi 18, **t** 0577 941966 (*moderate*). Good regional food. *Closed Wed*.

**Le Terrazze**, in Hotel La Cisterna (*see left*), **t** 0577 940328 (*moderate*). Popular for its panoramic views as well as the cuisine. The *medaglione al vin santo* is a surprise treat or else the *osso buco alla toscana* following old house specialities like *zuppa sangimignese* and *pappardelle alla lepre* (wide noodles with hare sauce). *Closed Wed lunch, Tues*.

**Osteria del Carcere**, Via del Castello 13, **t** 0577 941905 (*moderate–cheap*). A tiny restaurant that serves unusual cold cuts and terrines, a delicious saffron-flavoured goats' cheese mousse, soups, roast guinea fowl with chestnuts and lamb with pecorino cheese. *Closed Thurs lunch, Wed*.

**Enoteca Gustavo**, Via San Matteo 29, **t** 0577 940057 (*cheap*). A good choice for a glass of local Vernaccia and a snack, this wine bar serves all sorts of sandwiches and *crostoni* (a rustic toasted open sandwich), cheeses and meats. *Closed Tues*.

**Gelateria di Piazza**, Piazza della Cisterna, **t** 0577 942244. Truly wonderful ice cream in a myriad of flavours. *Closed Nov–Feb*.

or a Florence. When it lost the wealth or the fierceness that briefly made it an important player on the Tuscan stage, the city crystallized into its medieval form, a perfect preparation for its role as a tourist town. Today San Gimignano has a population of some 7,700. On a good day in July or August, it may see several times that in day-trippers. Even during the Renaissance, the town was a resort for the Florentines: Dante, Machiavelli and Savonarola all spent time here, and artists like Ghirlandaio and Gozzoli were happy to come up for a small commission. Don't let the prospect of crowds keep you from visiting. San Gimignano handles them gracefully; its fine art, elegant medieval cityscapes and the verdant rolling countryside right outside its gates make this one of the smaller towns of Tuscany most worth seeing.

## Piazza del Duomo and the Palazzo del Popolo

From the southern gate, Porta San Giovanni, the street of the same name leads towards the town centre, passing the little churches of **San Giovanni**, built by the Knights Templar, and **San Francesco**, with a good Pisan-Romanesque façade, now deconsecrated and converted into a wine shop. Another ancient gate, the Arco dei Bacci, leads into the triangular **Piazza della Cisterna** and the adjacent **Piazza del Duomo** – a superbly beautiful example of asymmetrical, medieval town design. Piazza della Cisterna contains the town's well and some of its towers.

On Piazza del Duomo, two stout, Gothic public buildings with Guelph crenellations and lofty towers compete with the Collegiata church for your attention. The **Palazzo del Podestà**, with its vaulted *loggia*, was begun in the 1230s by Emperor Frederick II at the height of imperial power. Above it stands the Torre della Rognosa, with a small cupola; at 167ft it once marked the height limit for private towers – the *podestà* didn't want anyone putting him in the shade. Later, when the *comune* was able to wrest effective self-government from the emperors, it built an even taller tower for the **Palazzo del Popolo** across the piazza; the 177ft Torre Grossa was completed about 1300 and the rest of the Palazzo about 20 years later.

Underneath this tower, an archway leads into the charming, thoroughly medieval **Cortile**, or courtyard, with bits of frescoes (one by Il Sodoma) and the painted coats of arms of Florentine governors from after 1353. A stairway leads up to the **Museo Civico** (*open Mar–Oct daily 9.30–7; Nov–Feb daily 10–5; adm*), with an excellent collection of art from both Florentine and Sienese masters. One of the oldest works is a remarkable painted crucifix by Coppo di Marcovaldo (*c.* 1270) that predates (and some might say surpasses) the similar, more famous crucifixes of Giotto. There are also two sweet Madonnas by Benozzo Gozzoli, a pair of *tondi* by Filippino Lippi portraying the Annunciation, and a big, colourful enthroned Virgin by Pinturicchio, famous for the Piccolomini chapel in Siena. Taddeo di Bartolo's paintings depict the story of San Gimignano; he is pictured calming the sea, exorcizing a devil who had been inhabiting the daughter of Emperor Jovian, and succumbing to the flesh while saying Mass (he has to pee, but on sneaking out of the church, a winged devil attacks him; fortunately, he has a crucifix to hand, and drives it away).

To the San Gimignanese, the biggest attraction of the museum is the Sala del Consiglio, or **Sala di Dante**, where the poet spoke in 1299 as an ambassador of Florence, seeking to convince the *comune* to join the Guelph League. The frescoes on its walls include more works by Gozzoli, a glittering company of angels and saints in the *Maestà* of the Sienese artist Lippo Memmi, and some trecento scenes of hunting and tournaments. After this, contemplate a climb up the **Torre Grosso** (*same hours as Museo Civico; adm*) – several hundred steps, but the view is worth the effort.

### The Collegiata

The name Piazza del Duomo is misleading: San Gimignano no longer has a cathedral, but a **Collegiata**, begun in the 12th century and enlarged in the 15th, which would make an impressive seat for any bishop. It turns a blank brick façade to the world, but the interior is a lavish imitation of Siena Cathedral, with its tiger-striped arches and

## Local Wine

San Gimignano has its own wine, *La Vernaccia di San Gimignano* (makes one think of varnish), a dry, light yellow white, with a pungent bouquet and a slightly bitter aftertaste. It is generally drunk with fish dishes and as an *aperitivo*, but it's also good to try with typical San Gimignano dishes such as liver, tripe, rabbit and *panzanella*.

The wine is made only in the hills around San Gimignano and has been around since antiquity. It gets a mention in Dante's *Purgatory*: Pope Martin IV apparently drowned eels in Vernaccia before roasting them over a charcoal fire. It has recently been awarded the DOCG.

vaults painted with golden stars. Its walls, however, outshine the larger cathedral with first-class frescoes of the 14th and 15th centuries, mostly by artists from Siena.

In the north aisle, Bartolo di Fredi painted the Old Testament scenes in the 1360s. Note *Noah with the Animals* and *The Torments of Job* (also how each scene is accompanied by a neat explanation in simple Italian, a fascinating example of the artists and the Church coming to terms with a newly literate public). Some of Bartolo's best work is in the lunettes off the north aisle: a medieval cosmography of the Creation, scenes of Adam naming the animals and a graphic view of the creation of Eve. New Testament pictures by Barna da Siena (about 1380) cover the south wall; his *Crucifixion* is an exceedingly fine work. On the west wall, over the entrance, is a well-punctured *Saint Sebastian* by Gozzoli and the most perverse *Last Judgement* in Italy. What moved Taddeo di Bartolo – a painter of rosy Sienese Virgins – to this madness isn't recorded. You may think you have seen the damned suffering interesting tortures and indignities before; Italy has plenty of such scenes. This is the first time that delicacy forbids us to describe one. It's a little faded, unfortunately, but you'll find it near two wooden figures depicting an *Annunciation* by Jacopo della Quercia.

Off the south aisle, the **Chapel of Santa Fina** (*open 1–20 Jan and Mar Mon–Sat 9.30–5, Sun and hols 12.30–5; April–Oct Mon–Fri 9.30–7, Sat 9.30–5, Sun 12.30–5; 21 Jan–28 Feb open only for religious functions; adm*) offers a delightful introduction to one of the most irritating hagiographies in Christendom. Little Fina was going to the well for water, when she accepted an orange from a young swain. Upon returning home, her mother told her how wicked she was to take it, whereupon the poor girl became so mortified over her great sin that she lay down on the kitchen table and prayed for forgiveness without ceasing for the next five years. Finally, St Anthony came to call her soul up into heaven, and the kitchen table and all the towers of San Gimignano burst into bloom with violets. Domenico Ghirlandaio got the commission to paint all this; he did a splendid job (1475) in the brightest springtime colours. In the last scene, note San Gimignano's famous towers in the background.

Just to the left of the Collegiata there is a lovely small courtyard where musicians sometimes play on summer weekends. Here, on the wall of the baptistry, you will see another fine fresco by Ghirlandaio, an *Annunciation* that has survived reasonably well for being outside for 500 years. The town's two other museums are housed here, in the same building as the **Museo Archeologico**: the **Museo Etrusco** has a small collection of local archaeological finds and the **Museo d'Arte Sacra** has some good painted wood statues from the late Middle Ages (*open Mar and Nov–20 Jan Mon–Sat 9.30–5, Sun 12.30–5; April–Oct Mon–Fri 9.30–7, Sat 9.30–5, Sun 12.30–5; closed Jan and Feb; adm*).

### Around the Town

From Piazza del Duomo, it's not too difficult a climb up to the **Rocca**, a ruined fortress of the 1350s, offering one of the best views of this towered town. In the summer, it's the site of an outdoor cinema. Down Via di Castello, at the eastern end of town, the **Oratory of San Lorenzo in Ponte**, now unused, has quattrocento Florentine frescoes and an exhibition of finds from the pharmacy of the Hospital of Santa Fina in the 16th to 18th centuries. The busiest and finest street of San Gimignano heads north from Piazza del Duomo: Via San Matteo, lined with shops and modest Renaissance palaces. It begins by passing the three truncated **Salvucci Towers**, once the fortified compound of the Ghibelline Salvucci, one of the town's most powerful families (the towers of their enemies, the Guelph Ardinghelli, are the ones on the west side of Piazza della Cisterna).

In the quiet streets on the north side of town is the church of **Sant'Agostino**, famous for a merry series of frescoes by Gozzoli on the *Life of St Augustine*. Many of the frescoes are faded and damaged, but not the charming panel where the master of grammar drags sullen little Augustine off to school. Another well-preserved scene shows the saint in Rome, with most of the city's ancient landmarks visible in the background. Gozzoli also painted the *St Sebastian* on the left aisle. There is a haunting altarpiece (1483) by Piero Pollaiuolo, with an anticipatory touch of the El Greco to it, and some good trecento Sienese painting in a chapel off to the right. Across the piazza from Sant'Agostino, the little church of **San Pietro** has more trecento Sienese painting. Via Folgore di San Gimignano leads to the northeast corner of the town; **San Jacopo** stands under the town wall, another simple but interesting building left by the Templars.

Around much of San Gimignano, the countryside begins right outside the town's wall. Pleasant walks or picnics can be had in any direction, with a few landmarks to visit along the way: the **Fonti**, arched, medieval well-houses much like Siena's, are just outside the Porta dei Fonti, south of San Jacopo. Further away, there is the **Pieve di Cellole,** a pretty 12th-century church in a pleasant, peaceful setting, 4km west of the Porta San Matteo; its harmonious serenity amid the cypresses inspired Puccini's opera *Suor Angelica*. There are a number of ruined castles and monasteries around the town, each offering a different view of San Gimignano's remarkable skyline.

# Volterra and Around

On a good day in spring or summer, the sunshine illuminates Volterra's elegant streets and *piazze* full of locals, and bouncing holiday-makers come to buy alabaster cups and lampshades. A cloudy, windy day may remind you of fate and of the Etruscans, who arrived here some 2,700 years ago. Like so many of their other cities, the Etruscans founded Volterra on top of a steep hill with a flat top; from afar, you see only a silhouette looming over an eerie, empty landscape. The soil around

## Getting Around

Volterra lies 81km/2½hrs southwest of Florence by way of Colle di Val d'Elsa and the winding SS68; it's 50km/1½hrs west from Siena; and 61km/2hrs southeast of Pisa by way of Cascina and the SS439. It isn't the easiest town to reach if you don't have a car.

The only **train** service gets as far as Saline di Volterra, 10km southwest of the city. This is an infrequent branch line that goes to Cecina, 30km to the west on the coast south of Livorno. Some trains continue on from Cecina to Pisa. (It wasn't like this in the old days: as late as the 1920s, a little steam train used to climb right up to the town.) Buses connect the Saline station with Volterra, but not always when you need them.

All **buses** leave from Piazza Martini della Libertà, which is just inside the walls. You can get information, timetables and buy tickets from the tourist office. There are plenty of buses which go direct to Pisa and Montecatini Terme, 4 a day to Florence and Siena via Colle Val d'Elsa, and a few to Poggibonsi and San Gimignano; 3 a day go to Livorno via Cecina; there are also 2 to Massa Marittima (usually with a change at Monterotondo).

**Cars** aren't allowed within Volterra's walls, but lots of parking space is provided all around the walls and at the gates. Strangely enough there are also some street parking spaces inside, and you can usually sneak your car into one that's near your hotel in the evening; it's best to check out the situation on foot beforehand.

## Tourist Information

**Volterra**: Via Turazza 2, t 0588 86150, f 0588 90350, *www.provolterra.it*.
Palazzo dei Priori 19–20, t/f 0588 87257, *www.volterratur.it*.

## Alabaster

Archaeological evidence has the Villanovan culture in Tuscany finding creative uses for the *pietra candida*, alias $CaSO_42H_2O$, as early as 800 BC. The Etruscans made good use of this luminous, easily worked mineral in their funeral urns and everyday objects. It appears that the locals forgot all about it during the Dark Ages, though now and then, some artist would turn a chunk into a vase or cup (the Medici, with their insatiable lust for dust magnets, bought quite a few). The craft of carving alabaster revived dramatically in the last two centuries. Volterra today is full of small workshops, and even a few large firms that turn the stone into vases, figurines, ashtrays and everything else that's serviceable or collectable.

Many of the alabaster-workers are genuine artists, turning out one-of-a-kind pieces at high prices; the city runs a contest each year for the best. Others produce vast numbers of attractive little baubles from €3 and up.

There are shops selling alabaster in every corner of Volterra; it's best to seek these out, and avoid the temptations of the big glossy establishments in the most prominent places.

**Via Porta all'Arco 45**. The shop of Paulo Sabatini, who has won several prizes in the annual competition, with some of the most original creations in town.

**Via Porta all'Arco 26**. Stocks some more unusual alabaster miniatures.

More can be found along Via di Sotto.

**Via di Sotto 2**. Simple, elegant vases and lamps.

**'Come una Volta'**, Via di Sotto 6.

**Via Antonio Gramsci 20** and **53**. Two of the more interesting shops among many.

**Via Guarnacci 26**. More avant-garde, with some splashy modern work in coloured alabaster.

Volterra (pop. 12,796) is a thin clay, not much good for vines or olives. Few trees grow here. It makes good pasture land – not as barren as it looks, but disconcerting enough among the green woods and well-tended gardens of this part of Tuscany.

### History

Etruscan **Velathri**, one of the largest and most powerful cities of the Dodecapolis, grew up in the 9th or 8th century BC from an even earlier settlement of the

**City Artisans' Cooperative**, Piazza dei Priori.

For really serious alabaster – say, complete bathrooms or life-size copies of the Trevi Fountain – try the big shops with big car parks around the outskirts of town.

If Auro Bongini's workshop on **Via Don Minzoni** 54 is open, it's well worth taking a look. He makes doll's house furniture from local olive wood in 19th-century style. His exhibition work fills the small workshop, but there are also a few individual pieces for sale. If you are interested, you can call in advance to make an appointment, **t** 0588 88040.

# Where to Stay and Eat

## Volterra ✉ 56048

Volterra does not see as many tourists as San Gimignano, but is nevertheless just as expensive – at least, inexpensive rooms are hard to find.

**\*\*\*\*San Lino**, Via San Lino 26, near Porta San Francesco, **t** 0588 88053, **f** 0588 80620, *www.hotelsanlino.com* (*moderate*). More upscale, with tastefully remodelled rooms in an old cloister, standing out only for being the only place with parking.

**\*\*\*Nazionale**, Via dei Marchesi 11, **t** 0588 86284, **f** 0588 84097, *www.albergo nazionalevolterra.it* (*moderate*). A pleasant old hotel, situated within the walls of the town.

**\*\*\*Villa Nencini**, Borgo S. Stefano, **t** 0588 86386, **f** 0588 80601, *www.villanencini.it* (*moderate*). A 16th-century house with beautiful views, located just north of the city centre.

**L'Etrusca**, Via Porta all'Arco 37, **t/f** 0588 84073 (*moderate*). This has small apartments with kitchenettes just off Piazza del Popolo. Guests may use the pool at the sister hotel/restaurant **Sant'Elisa** (*see right*).

**Ostello della Gioventù**, Via Don Minzoni, **t** 0588 887257. Students aren't entirely out of luck: there's the youth hostel, providing an institutional atmosphere but at rock-bottom rates.

Many restaurants in Volterra specialize in roast boar and the like, medieval cuisine entirely in keeping with the spirit of the place.

**Del Duca**, Via di Castello 2, **t** 0588 81510 (*expensive*). Volterra is distinctly lacking in good restaurants, but this new one stands out. The set *menu degustazione* is good value, or choose from the full menu: rabbit with black olives cooked in Vernaccia, duck breast or *foie gras*, and a delicious chocolate soufflé to finish. *Closed Tues.*

**Il Porcellino**, Vicolo delle Prigioni 16, **t** 0588 86392 (*moderate*). Lots of different set menus, combining seafood and familiar Tuscan favourites with local treats like roast pigeon and boar with olives. *Closed Oct–Mar.*

**Il Sacco Fiorentino** (the name refers to Lorenzo de' Medici's massacre of the citizens of Volterra in 1472), Piazza XX Settembre 18, **t** 0588 88537 (*cheap*). Combines a vast range of *crostini*, gnocchi with baby vegetables, penne with Tuscan cheeses, roast pork with black olives, rabbit cooked in garlic and *vin santo* and pigeon with red radicchio and *vin santo*, an imaginative menu that changes with the seasons. *Closed Wed.*

**Sant'Elisa**, about 3km away on the SS68, **t** 0588 80034, **f** 0588 87284 (*cheap*). One of the restaurants most popular with the Volterrans. Superb simple, homecooked food; it serves lots of game, such as *pappardelle* with wild boar or deer sauce, or wild boar stew with black olives. Also a 3-star hotel with pool. *Closed Tues.*

**Taverna dei Priori**, Via G. Matteotti 19, **t** 0588 86180 (*cheap*). Good for a quick bite: it's essentially a *tavola calda*, serving sandwiches, salads and cooked food. *Closed Wed.*

Villanovan culture; it is undoubtedly one of Italy's oldest cities. The attraction that has kept this hill continuously occupied for so many centuries is easily explained – sulphur, alum, salt, alabaster, lead and tin; the town is at the centre of one of the richest mining regions in Italy. In Etruscan days, there was iron, too, and the people of Velathri did a thriving trade with the Greeks and Carthaginians.

Velathri reached the height of its prosperity in the 5th and 4th centuries BC, leaving as testimony three great circuits of walls; the largest is over 8km in length, enclosing an area three times the size of the present city. The Romans captured it some time in the 3rd century and Velathri began to decline. Along with most of Etruria, the city chose the populist side in the Social Wars, and was punished with a siege and sacking by Sulla in about 80 BC. Yet Roman *Velaterrae* remained an important town. It was the home of Saint Linus, successor to St Peter and the second pope.

Even though many of the mines were giving out, Volterra managed to survive the Dark Ages intact. The Lombards favoured it, and for a time it served as their capital. Medieval Volterra was ruled by its bishops, who were increasingly finding themselves in conflict with the rising middle class. An independent *comune* was established late in the 12th century, a good Ghibelline town that participated in most of the factional wars of the period, before finally coming under the nominal control of Florence in 1361.

The Florentines were content with an annual tribute until the 'affair of the alum' in the 1470s, that wonderfully Italian ruckus that caused Pope Sixtus IV to plot the murder of Lorenzo de' Medici, excommunicate him and finally declare war on him. Lorenzo had taken over a syndicate to mine here for alum, a key material used in dyeing cloth, on which the popes had a monopoly from their mines at Tolfa. Besides alarming the pope, Lorenzo also caused the Volterrans to revolt when they realized that he wanted to keep production down and prices high without letting any profit trickle down to them (the Medici Bank, not surprisingly, also controlled the sale of the pope's alum). Lorenzo eluded the pope with some difficulty (*see* **Florence**, History, pp.110–11) and then hired the mercenary captain Federico da Montefeltro – none other than the famous broken-nosed Duke of Urbino, patron of artists and scholars – to subdue the Volterrans. This he did with a brutality quite unbecoming to the 'ideal Renaissance prince'. Lorenzo wept some crocodile tears over Volterra; after extinguishing the city's independence once and for all, he offered it the magnificent sum of 2,000 florins in damages.

Fortunately for the Volterrans, the mining business was picking up again. Between 1400 and 1800, many pits that had been abandoned since Roman times were reopened. In particular, Volterra became Europe's largest centre for the mining and working of alabaster, a craft tradition that is still the city's biggest business today.

## A Little Archaeology

Coming from Florence or Siena, the entrance to Volterra will be the eastern gate, the **Porta a Selci**, with a moving tribute to the *partigiani* of Volterra killed in 1944–5. Inside the gate, Via Don Minzoni leads towards the bus terminal at Piazza XX Settembre, passing along the way at No.15 the **Museo Etrusco Guarnacci** (*open mid-Mar–Oct daily 9–7; 5 Nov–15 Mar daily 9–2; adm exp, a joint ticket covers Volterra's other museums*), the repository for finds from the Velathri necropolises. Over 600 sculpted alabaster, travertine or terracotta cinerary urns make up the core of the collection. Exhibits are arranged in chronological order, except for the original Guarnacci collection which is grouped by subject matter. These tend to be conventional – an Etruscan family would ask the artist for a scene from Greek mythology, from the Trojan War perhaps, or something like the death of Actaeon, or a daemon conducting the souls of the dead down to the underworld. Perhaps the artist already had one in stock. One rule of Etruscan art is its lack of rules. Expect anything: some of the reclining figures of the dead atop the urns are brilliant portraiture, while others could be the first attempts of a third-grade craft class. All, holding the little cups or dishes they carry down into Hades, look as serene and happy as only a defunct Etruscan can.

As always, the Etruscans do their best to make you laugh. One terracotta, the *Urna degli Sposi*, portrays a hilariously caricatured couple who look as if they are about to start arguing over whose turn it is to do the dishes. Another Etruscan joke is the *Ombra della Sera* (evening shadow), quite a celebrity around Volterra, a small, carefully detailed bronze of a man with a quizzical expression and spidery, grotesquely elongated arms and legs. There are also prehistoric finds, Roman mosaics from the baths, artefacts discovered in the theatre, and some fine pieces of Etruscan jewellery.

The museum lies a stone's throw from Piazza XX Settembre, the bus terminal; from here Via Gramsci leads towards the town centre. Climb any of the alleys to the south of the museum, however, and you'll reach Volterra's **Parco Archeologico** (*open Nov–mid-Mar Sat 10.30–4, Sun 10.30–5; summer daily 10.30–5.30*) just inside the walls. There isn't much that's archaeological about it – some Etruscan foundations and a huge ancient cistern called the *Piscina Romana* – but the park is a marvel, a lush English garden of manicured lawns and shady groves unlike anything else in Tuscany. Above the park stretches an exceptionally long and elegant castle, the **Fortezza Medicea**, begun in 1343 and completed by Lorenzo de' Medici in 1472. You can't get in; it has been a prison almost from the day it was built, perhaps the fanciest in this nation of fancy calabooses.

## Piazza dei Priori

This is a fine little republican piazza, surrounded by plain, erect palazzi that discreetly call your attention to the sober dignity of the *comune*. The **Palazzo dei Priori**, of 1208, is said to be the oldest such building in Tuscany, the model for Florence's Palazzo Vecchio and many others. Its tower has long been closed, but if you ever find it re-opened, climb up for a view that literally takes in all of Tuscany; on a clear day, you'll see Monte Amiata, all the coast from La Spezia to the Argentario, and Corsica and Elba as well.

Across the square, the simple **Palazzo Pretorio** is almost as old. Next to it, the rakishly leaning **Porcellino Tower** takes its name from the little pig sculpted in relief near the base, just barely visible after seven centuries.

## The Cathedral and the Etruscan Arch

Just to the right of the Palazzo dei Priori, a bit of green and white striped marble façade peeks out between the palaces. This is the back of the Archiepiscopal Palace, located around the corner in the **Piazza del Duomo**. Quiet and dowdy, the contrast of this square with the well-built Piazza dei Priori is striking, a lasting memory of the defeat of Volterra's medieval bishops by the *comune*. Its octagonal **baptistry**, begun in 1283, has its marble facing completed only on one side. Within, there is a fine baptismal font sculpted by Andrea Sansovino in the early 1500s, an altar by Mino da Fiesole, and a holy water dish carved out of an Etruscan boundary stone.

The plain **cathedral** façade has a good marble doorway. This forlorn mongrel of a building was begun in the Pisan-Romanesque style in the 1200s, and worked on fitfully for the next two centuries. The campanile went up in 1493, and the interior was entirely redone in the 1580s when the blatant Medici coat of arms was placed over the high altar. Do not pass this old Duomo by; the works of art inside are few in number, but of an exceptionally high quality. Fittingly, as this is Volterra, some of the windows are made of thin-sliced alabaster, a stone that was also used in the intricate, Renaissance **tabernacle** by Mino da Fiesole over the high altar.

The chapels on either side have excellent examples of Tuscan woodcarving: a 15th-century piece attributed to a local artist named Francesco di Domenico Valdambrino off to the left, the *Madonna dei Chierici*, and to the right, a polychromed *Deposition* with five separate, full-sized figures, certainly ranked among the best of 13th-century Pisan sculpture, shining immaculately after a recent restoration. Another chapel off to the right contains fragments of unusually good anonymous trecento frescoes of the *Passion of Christ*, very much ahead of their time in composition, in the figures and the folds of the draperies – even Giorgio Vasari might have liked them.

In the left aisle, the ***pergamo*** (pulpit) is one of the lesser-known works of the Pisani, less spectacular than the ones in Pisa, Siena and Pistoia, but still showing something of the vividness and electric immediacy seen in the best Pisan sculpture. Guglielmo Pisano did the fine relief of the *Last Supper* (note the faces of the Apostles and the sly metaphorical monster sneaking under the table). The pulpit's supporting columns rest on two lions, a bull and one unclassifiable beast, all by Bonamico Pisano. In the oratory, off the left aisle near the entrance, behind a 16th-century wooden statue group of the *Adoration of the Magi*, is a small fresco said to be by Benozzo Gozzoli, though perhaps because of its deterioration or early date, it lacks Gozzoli's usual charm. Close by in the Archiepiscopal Palace, a small **Museo d'Arte Sacra** (*open mid-Mar–Oct 9–7; 5 Nov–15 Mar 9–2; adm exp*) displays sculpture and architectural fragments, and a della Robbia terracotta of St Linus, Volterra's patron.

From the Duomo, if you retrace your steps back towards Piazza dei Priori and turn down Via Porta all'Arco, you'll find the quaintest old relic in Volterra, the **Arco Etrusco**. The Etruscans built the columns at least, though the arch above them was rebuilt in Roman times. Set into this arch are three primeval black basalt sculpted heads from the original gate, *c*. 600 BC, believed to represent the Etruscan gods Tinia (Jupiter), Uni (Juno) and Menvra (Minerva). Some of the features of Juno are barely traceable; 2,700 years of wind and rain have worn all three into great black knobs – carved out of the voussoirs, they resemble nothing so much as garden slugs.

## The Pinacoteca

*Open mid-Mar–Oct daily 9–7, 5 Nov–15 Mar daily 9–2; adm exp, joint ticket valid 1 year covers Volterra's other museums, no single tickets.*

Just off Piazza dei Priori, the intersection of Via Roma and Via Buonparenti is one of the most picturesque corners of Volterra, with venerable stone arches and tower houses such as the 13th-century Casa Buonparenti. Via Buonparenti leads into Via dei Sarti; the elder Antonio da Sangallo's Palazzo Solaini (note the elegant arcaded courtyard) has been restored to hold Volterra's **Pinacoteca**, another small but choice collection. Trecento Sienese painting is well represented, including a glorious altarpiece of the *Madonna and Child* by Taddeo di Bartolo. To complement the remarkable 14th-century wood sculptures in the Duomo, the Pinacoteca has two figures portraying the *Annunciation* by Francesco di Valdambrino. Neri di Bicci was a quattrocento Florentine, but his *St Sebastian* here looks entirely Sienese – probably at the request of the customer. Among other Tuscan works, there is a shiny altarpiece by Ghirlandaio, and two by Luca Signorelli (or his workshop): a *Madonna and Saints* and an *Annunciation*. Only tantalizing fragments are left of another altarpiece by Giuliano Bugiardini (1475–1554), a little-known Florentine with a very distinctive style.

For all that, the prize of the collection is the Rosso Fiorentino *Deposition*, dated 1521 and perhaps his greatest work in all Italy. Even out in the boondocks of Volterra, it attracts considerable attention from the art scholars, being a seminal work and one of the thresholds from the Renaissance into Mannerism, with all the precision and clarity of the best quattrocento work, yet also possessing an intensity that few works had ever achieved. The *Descent from the Cross* is a starkly emotional subject; in Rosso's work it is terror and disarray, a greenish Christ and a small, nearly hysterical crowd dramatically illuminated against a darkening deep blue sky. You'll find little that this painting has in common with Rosso's contemporaries, not even with his fellow madman Pontormo (who did his own, quite different, *Deposition* in Florence's Santa Felicità) – but oddly enough, it could almost be mistaken for a work of Goya. Many of the best paintings are currently covered with little bits of what looks like sticking plaster, the result of a blunder by the administration who, it is said, turned the heating up too high. As a result the paint bubbled on the canvases and they are being restored.

## San Francesco and the Roman Theatre

On the corner east of the Pinacoteca, the church of **San Michele** has a Pisan Romanesque façade. In the other direction, towards the Porta San Francesco on the western edge of town, you pass through back streets dusty with alabaster workshops, before finally arriving at the church of **San Francesco** on Via San Lino. Here the attraction is off to the right of the altar, the **chapel of the Holy Cross**, completely frescoed in 1410 by a Florentine artist whose name seems to be Cenni di Francesco di Ser Cenni – a rare soul, indeed, with a sophisticated, wonderfully reactionary, medieval sense of composition and his own ideas about Christian iconography, done in a bold style that in places almost seems like modern poster art. The *Legend of the Cross* frescoes generally follow those of Gaddi at Santa Croce in Florence (*see* p.163), and there are also scenes of *St Francis*, the *Passion*, and the *Massacre of the Innocents*, many with fantasy city backgrounds. Note the *Dream of Constantine* (or of Heraclius), in his tent adorned with the imperial eagle; naturally the artist had never seen a Roman eagle, but he painted a very nice medieval German one instead.

Just to the right of San Francesco, a pedestrian passage under the walls takes you out to Viale Francesco Ferrucci, home to a lively outdoor **market** on Saturday mornings. Beneath the walls, ancient Velaterrae's large **Roman theatre** (*open Nov–mid-Mar Sat 10.30–4, Sun 10.30–5; summer daily 10.30–5.30*) has been excavated. Enough marble slabs and columns have survived for the archaeologists to reconstruct part of the stage building, an impressive testimony to the past importance of the city. Behind the theatre are ruins of baths and a large rectangular *palaestra*, a yard for exercise and gymnastics.

## The *Balze*

Leaving Volterra from San Francesco Gate, you pass the Borgo San Giusto and its ruins of the 12th-century Pisan-Romanesque church of **Santo Stefano**. The road to Pisa exits through the outer **Etruscan walls**; though barely more than foundations, they are traceable for most of their length around the city and easily visible here.

Some 2km beyond, decorating the moors, are the *balze*: barren clay-walled gullies that may have begun as Etruscan mining cuts. They've a life of their own; medieval chronicles report them gobbling up farms and churches around the city, and no one has yet found a way to stop their inexorable growth. In the 1700s they tried to atone for their appetite, revealing some of the most important Etruscan necropolises yet discovered, and contributing urns to the Guarnacci Museum. Now even the necropolises are all but gone, though on the edge of one cliff you can see the **Badia**, an 11th-century Camaldolensian abbey, now half-devoured.

## The Val di Cecina and the Metal Hills

There are few attractions in the romantic emptiness of the Volterran Hills. If you take the SS68 west from Volterra along the Cecina Valley to Guardistallo, you reach a rolling valley with pines and cypresses in just the right places – a suitable Tuscan backdrop for any Renaissance painting. **Montecatini Val di Cecina**, in the hills to the north, is quiet and medieval, with a 12th-century castle. Further west, a big wine area extends around **Montescudaio** (Montescudaio, red and white, is a distinguished though lesser-known dry variety with a DOC label).

The most unusual road from Volterra, the SS439, leads south over the Colline Metallifere towards Massa Marittima and the coast. These 'metal hills', along with the iron mines of Elba, did much to finance the gilded existence of the Etruscans. Several mines operate today, though driving through the hills you may see little but oak forests and olive groves. **Pomarance** holds few surprises, but wait for **Larderello**, the self-proclaimed 'World Centre of Geothermal Energy'. This is the north boundary of volcanic Italy; that extinct volcano, Monte Amiata, and the ancient crater lakes of Umbria and Lazio are not far away. This far north, the only manifestations of a subterranean nature are benign little geysers and gurgling pools of sulphurous mud. Larderello is a growing town; huge ugly cooling towers of the type that signify a nuclear power plant anywhere else can be spotted wherever there is a geothermal source worth tapping. Near the centre, there is a strange, postmodernist church designed in the 1950s by Michelucci, the architect of Florence's rail station, and the **Museo della Geotermia** (*t 0588 07724, open daily 8–12.30 and 1.30–5.30; closed Sat in winter; adm*), which may explain something of this overheated little town's career.

After Larderello, and almost as far as Monterotondo, the landscape is downright uncanny. It smells bad, too; geysers and steam vents (*soffioni*) whistle and puff by the roadside, while murky pits bubble up boric salts amidst yellow and grey slag piles. Follow the yellow signs of the *'itinerario dei soffioni'* to see the best of it. Despite the sulphur and borax, the cooling towers and occasional rusting hulks of old mining equipment, the Metal Hills are quite winsome, especially south of Larderello (still on the SS439) around the medieval village of Castelnuovo di Val di Cecina, surrounded by chestnuts and the Ala dei Diavoli (Devils' Wing) pass at the crest of the hills. Monterotondo Marittimo, further south, has more than its fair share of subsurface curiosities; nearby Lago Boracifero is Italy's centre for borax mining. In some places, the ground is covered with strange webs of steam pipes, built since the *comune* discovered its unique resource could power almost everything in town for free.

# Massa Marittima

This lovely, rugged area is part of the coastal Maremma district only in name; even in Roman times it was considered part of the 'maritime' province. And for just as long, **Massa Marittima** has been making its living from the mines, though today its 10,000 people are not enough to fill the space within its medieval walls. Albeit small, its brief prosperity left it beautiful, and well worth visiting: firstly, to see the second city of the Sienese Republic, a lesson in urban refinement within a small place; and secondly, to see its exquisite cathedral, one of Tuscany's great medieval monuments.

This town appeared as a free *comune*, the *Repubblica Massetana*, around 1225, just coinciding with a dizzying period of prosperity owing to its discovery of new silver and copper deposits nearby. Unfortunately, this wealth proved fatally attractive to Massa's bigger neighbours. Pisa and Siena fought over it for a century and it finally fell to the latter in 1337. Soon after, the mines gave out, putting Massa into centuries of decline. Malaria was a problem from the 1500s, and not until the Lorraine dukes drained the wet places and re-opened some of the mines, did things start looking up.

## The Duomo

It's quite a sight, rising incongruously on its pedestal, its effect heightened by its setting above and at an angle to Massa's **Piazza Garibaldi**, a true *tour de force* of medieval town design. Reconstruction of an earlier cathedral began around 1200 and finished in 1250, though some additions were made; note the contrast between the original Pisan-Romanesque style, with blind arches and lozenges, and the Sienese campanile, added about 1400. Its best features include Gothic windows, capitals and the carvings of animals protecting humans on the façade and the left side.

# Getting Around

Massa is only 22km off the coastal Via Aurelia at Follonica, absolutely worth the diversion if you are passing that way; direct from Siena it's a not particularly captivating 65km/1hr 20mins **drive** on the SS73 (passing by San Galgano) and the SS441.

There are 3 or 4 **buses** a day from Volterra (change at Monterotondo), 5 to nearby Follonica, and frequent buses and **trains** from there to Grosseto (Massa is in Grosseto province); also 2 a day to Florence and Siena, and 1 direct to Grosseto. Information and tickets from *Agenzia Massa Veterensis* opposite the Duomo. Most buses stop on Via Corridoni, behind and a little downhill from the Duomo.

# Tourist Information

**Massa**: Via Todini 3/5, **t** 0566 902756, **f** 0566 940095.

# Where to Stay and Eat

**Massa Marittima** ✉ 58024

Massa becomes ever more popular and its room capacity is often stretched to the limit.

**★★Duca del Mare**, Via D. Alighieri 1/2, **t** 0566 902284, **f** 0566 901905, *www.ducadelmare.it* (*moderate*). One of the town's three hotels, just below the town centre on the Via Massetana, in a lovely setting with a garden and views over the countryside (Massa lies on a rather steep hill); it's set in a modern building and has a simple *trattoria*. Pool, too!

**★★Girifalco**, Via Massentana, **t/f** 0566 902177, *www.ilgirifalco.com* (*inexpensive*). Offers similar amenities (but no pool) and the same views as Duca del Mare, but cheaper.

Dining in Massa is uncomplicated.

**Da Bracolì**, Località Ghirlanda, **t** 0566 902318 (*very expensive*). Offers *haute cuisine* variations on local dishes and a formidable wine list in an elegant setting. *Closed Mon and Tues.*

**Taverna del Vecchio Borgo**, **t** 0566 903950 (*expensive*). This comes highly recommended, not only for its food – game dishes including pheasant, boar and venison – but for its long list of grappas. *Closed Sun eve and Mon.*

**Da Tronca**, Vicolo Porta 5, **t** 0566 901991 (*cheap*). This rustic *trattoria* with its rough stone walls and arches has something of a medieval atmosphere. The food is local and delicious; anchovies in pesto, *tortelli maremmani* (stuffed with chard and ricotta), pasta with courgettes and ricotta, mushroom soup, wild boar, rabbit and tripe. *Closed Wed and lunch.*

The interior, under massive columns with delicate capitals, each one different, has a few trecento and quattrocento frescoes, including one of St Julian tending the sick near the main entrance. On the left, there is a luminous *Madonna* by Duccio (1318) and unique reliefs from the original 11th-century church: staring priests and apostles in vigorous, cartoon-like style. On the right hangs the *Nativity of Mary* by that most peculiar Sienese artist, Rutilio Manetti (d. 1639): woebegone ladies and a jellicle cat attend a pug-nosed, thumb-sucking, very unbeatific baby Mary. Nearby is a fine font with reliefs by Giraldo da Como (*c.* 1250) and a Renaissance tabernacle added in 1447. A wooden crucifix by Giovanni Pisano hangs over the high altar; in the Gothic apse is the *Ark of San Cerbone* with more reliefs (1324) on the life of Massa's patron saint.

## Up and Down Massa

Next to the cathedral on Piazza Garibaldi, the 1230 **Palazzo del Podestà** holds Massa's **Museo Archeologico** (*open Nov–Mar Tues–Sun 10–12.30 and 3–5; April–mid-July Tues–Sun 10–12.30 and 3.30–7; 21 July–31 Aug Tues–Sun 10–1 and 4–10; Sept and Oct Tues–Sun 10–12.30 and 3.30–7; adm*), with a well-organized if a little uninspiring archaeological collection – the Medici dukes carried the best finds to Florence. The museum also houses the offices of La Coop Colline Metallifere (*t 0566 902289*), which runs all Massa's museums.

In the small Pinacoteca, the best work is a *Maestà* by Ambrogio Lorenzetti, aglow with rosy faces, flowers and golden trim. Note the angel with the distaff and spindle in the centre – a sure sign that the local wool guild paid for the painting. Today the city offices are in the **Palazzo Comunale** across the square, formed from a group of connected tower-houses from the 13th and 14th centuries. Note the inscription above the door of another old building there: MASSA VETERNENSIS CELEBRIS VETULONIA QUONDAM (Massa was once famed Vetulonia).

Just as Grosseto sees itself as successor to Etruscan *Roselle*, Massa is heir to lost Vetulonia, the once-great city of the Dodecapolis near the coast (*see* p.303). Piazza Garibaldi is lively, often crowded with Teutons perching on the steps of the Duomo or swilling beer in the café-pizzerias. Via Libertà leads into the older quarter, a nest of arches and alleys barely changed over centuries. Like Siena, Massa is divided into three *terzi*; this is the *terzo* of Civitavecchia. Via Moncini climbs to the **Città Nuova**, a 14th-century suburb behind unusual Sienese fortifications; the street ends at Piazza Matteotti, with the 1330 **Torre del Candaliere** (Torre dell'Orologio), linked to the fortifications by the **Sienese Arch**, a slender walkway; it's a beautiful ensemble, more for show than any military consideration (*open Nov–Mar Tues–Sun 11–1 and 2.30–4.30; April–Oct Tues–Sun 10–1 and 3–6; adm*). Up Corso Diaz, **Sant'Agostino** church (completed 1313) has works by Rutilio Manetti.

Finally, no visit to Massa is complete without a trip to a mining museum (ask politely at the city library and they may show you the city's treasure, the 1310 *Codice Minerario Massetano*, modern Europe's first code of laws concerning mining rights). The **Museo di Arte e di Storia della Miniera** on Piazza Matteotti (*open April–Sept Tues–Sun 3–5.30; adm*) is very small, but there's another one, the **Museo della Miniera** on Via Corridoni (*open for guided tours only, leaving regularly: in summer between 10.15 and 5.45; in winter between 10.15 and 4.15; closed Mon; call t 0566 902289 for exact times; visits in English on request; adm*). Here the entrance leads into nearly half a mile of tunnels, with exhibits to show how the job was done from medieval days to the present.

# San Galgano and the Sword in the Stone

The SS73 east from Massa to Siena skirts the southern Colline Metallifere, through lands that saw a great medieval flowering of monasticism. The monks are mostly long gone, but they left one of the most unusual, least-visited sights in Tuscany – the ruined Cistercian **Abbey of San Galgano** (*open daily 8am–11pm*), some 2km north of Palazzetto. In some of the older paintings in Siena's Pinacoteca, you will see the oddly Arthurian figure of a man apparently drawing a sword from a stone. This is San Galgano and, in fact, he is putting the sword in.

Galgano Guidotti, from nearby Chiusdino, was a dissolute soldier who one day had a vision of St Michael on the slopes of Montesiepi, ordering him to change his ways.

Thrusting his sword into a rock to symbolize his new life, Galgano became a holy hermit; an ensuing career of miracles ensured his rapid canonization in 1181.

Almost from the start, the community he founded here was associated with the Cistercian Order, attracting monks from France as well as from around Siena. For centuries they played a vital role in the community, draining swamps, building mills and starting up a small textile industry. The Republic of Siena found them indispensable as architects, administrators – and as accountants. Many of the *Biccherna* covers in the Siena archives show Cistercians puzzling over the books or handing out pay. With its immense wealth, and its French architects eager to initiate the backward Italians in the glories of the new Gothic style, the order began its great **Abbey Church** in 1218. The Cistercians were already in a bad way when the abbey was dissolved in 1600; soon after their departure the roof, the façade and the campanile collapsed, leaving the grandest French-Gothic building in Tuscany a ruin. Its beautiful travertine columns and pointed arches remain, with the sky as roof and green lawns as carpet. Parts of the monastery survive, now in the care of Olivetan nuns.

After Galgano's death, St Michael appeared again on a hill above the abbey to command his followers to build the **Cappella di Montesiepi** over the sword in the stone. The curious round chapel, one of very few in Italy, was begun in 1185. The sword is still there, protruding from its rock right in the centre. As with all the sites associated with St Michael, it is a reminder of a branch of medieval mysticism that, while not entirely lost, is hardly well understood. It's a very curious place – during a recent visit, a beautiful woman in black entered, carrying a gleaming silver sword, and went off to a side room with the caretaker (we didn't ask). Note the pair of human hands in a glass box, with a card explaining how they were bitten off by wolves. The altar has a cross of the type often seen on buildings of the Knights Templar, and the ceiling dome, patterned in 22 concentric stripes, may be a representation of the heavenly spheres of medieval cosmology (as in the famous fresco in Pisa's Campo Santo). In a side chamber is a series of frescoes by Ambrogio Lorenzetti on the life of the saint, an *Annunciation* and a *Coronation of the Virgin*.

In the silent countryside around town, possible detours include **Chiusdino** (8km west), the dense, sleepy birthplace of San Galgano, or the aged **Monticiano**, south on the SS73, where a Romanesque church has trecento frescoes by Bartolo di Fredi.

## South Along Route 223

Possibly the least interesting route south from Siena leads to Grosseto, passing through the fertile, but nearly empty, valley of the river Merse. Once into Grosseto province it becomes even emptier, though there are a few towns worth a visit: old, walled **Bagni di Petriolo**, with thermal springs to relieve your gout; **Civitella Marittima**, a hill town with the Romanesque church of San Lorenzo al Lanzo, and **Paganico**, a charming village retaining its Sienese walls. Its church, San Michele, has well-preserved frescoes by trecento and quattrocento Sienese artists.

# Southern Tuscany

14

# Southern Tuscany

p.392
Southern Tuscany

10 km
5 miles

N

Siena

Monteaperti

R. Ombrone

To Arezzo

Val di Chiana

Castiglion Fiorentino

Monte S. Savino

Cortona

Montecchio

Rapolano Terme

Lucignano

S223

Ponte a Tressa

R. Arbia

Pievina

Asciano

Tuoro sul Trasimeno

S326

Sinalunga

Lucignano d'Arbia

Fatt. d'Amorosa

Bettolle

Trequanda

Lago Trasimeno

Murlo

Abbazia di M. Oliveto Maggiore

S. Giovanni d'Asso

Montisi

Torrita di Siena

Buonconvento

R. Asso

Montefollonico

S146

Castiglione del Lago

Montepulciano

S146

S. Biagio

Pienza

Pieve di Corsignano

L. di Montepulciano

Pari

Montalcino

S. Quirico d'Orcia

Monticchiello

Chianciano

Macchie

L. di Chiusi

Bagno Vignoni

Chianciano Terme

S. Antimo

Ripa d'Orcia

Chiusi

Paciano

S. Angelo in Colle

Castiglione d'Orcia

UMBRIA

Civitella Marittima

R. Orcia

Sarteano

Città della Pieve

Paganico

S73

Seggiano

S323

Vivo d'Orcia

Campiglia d'Orcia

Bagni S. Filippo

Cetona

S223

**TUSCANY**

M. Amiata

S2

S478

Radicofani

Castel d. Piano

Arcidosso

Abbadia S. Salvatore

S. Casciano dei Bagni

Fabro

Roselle

Piancastagnaio

To Rome

Grosseto

M. Labbro

Sta. Fiora

Castell' Azzara

**LAZIO**

Orvieto

S322

Roccalbegna

S323

Semproniano

M. Elmo

Sorano

S74

S71

Scansano

R. Albegna

Saturnia

Sovana

Monti Volsini

Bolsena

Magliano in Toscana

S. Bruzio

Montemerano

Manciano

Pitigliano

Lago di Bolsena

Talamone

S323

Marsiliana

Poggio Buco

p.258

Albinia

Capalbio

Laguna di Orbetello

Orbetello

To Rome

p.344

# Highlights

1 **Monte Oliveto Maggiore:** Siena's élite Renaissance hermitage

2 **Pienza:** Pope Pius II's Renaissance city

3 **Montepulciano:** Vino Nobile and fine art

4 **Chiusi:** underground Etruscan mysteries

Not counting the coastal Maremma around Grosseto, the old territories of the Sienese Republic make a complete and coherent landscape, rolling hills mostly given over to serious farming and pastureland. It isn't as garden-like as some other parts of Tuscany, though tidy vineyards and avenues of cypresses are not lacking. Hill towns, ready landmarks, poke above the horizon – Montepulciano off to the east, Pienza a bit to the left, while that castle on the left of the road must be Castiglione d'Orcia. At times, it seems the whole region is laid out before you, bounded on one side by the hills around Siena, on the other by the cones of Monte Amiata and Radicofani.

In the little tourist offices in these towns, they remark that not too many English or Americans pass through, which is a pity. It's beautiful countryside, the food and wine are among the best in Tuscany, and there are delightful towns with souvenirs from the Renaissance and Middle Ages.

# Asciano and the *Crete*

The SS326 from Siena heads east; its main purpose is to get you out to Cortona (*see* pp.414–9) and then to Umbria. Before it leaves Siena province, the road passes the village of **Monteaperti**, where the Sienese won their famous victory over Florence in 1260, and **Rapolano Terme** (27km), a small spa that retains some of its medieval walls. Besides the hot springs there is a surplus of natural gas in the area, some of it pumped out from wells, and some just leaking out of the ground – don't drop any matches. **Asciano**, 10km south of Rapolano, has walls built by the Sienese in 1351 and a good collection of Sienese art. The **Museo d'Arte Sacra** and the **Museo Etrusco** are now united in the same building, Palazzo Corboli at Corso Matteotti 122 (*open Mar–Oct Tues–Sun 10–1 and 3–7; Nov–Feb Thurs–Sat 10–1 and 3–5.30, Sun 10–1 and 2.30–6*). In a house at Via del Canto 11, there are some recently discovered Roman mosaics; ask at the pharmacy on Corso Matteotti to arrange a visit.

Southeast of Siena, the valleys of the Ombrone and the Asso enclose the country of the *crete*. Like the *balze* of Volterra, the *crete* are uncanny monuments to the power of erosion. The countryside around Asciano is dotted with them, exposing chalk cliffs where the soil above has eroded; they often appear in the backgrounds of 14th- and 15th-century Sienese and Florentine paintings (similar eroded chalk hills are called *biancane*). This is sheep country and it suffered a great deal after the Second World War, when many of the local men left the area to seek work in the cities. Today, immigrants from Sardinia make up a sizeable minority of the population, born shepherds who are trying to get the business back on its feet.

Old **Sinalunga**, up on its hill, is next (22km west), but offers little to detain you; the main square is named after Garibaldi, to commemorate his arrest here in 1867 on the orders of King Vittorio Emanuele, who was afraid his volunteers were about to attack Rome. **Torrita di Siena**, an old Sienese border fortress 6km southwest of the junction with the A1 from Florence to Rome, owes its name to the tall towers of its walls, some of which remain.

## Tourist Information

**Rapolano Terme**: Piazza Matteotti 9,
t 0577 724079.
**Asciano**: Corso Matteotti 18, t 0577 719510.
**Buonconvento**: Via Soccini 32, t 0577 807181.
**San Giovanni d'Asso**: Via Piazza Gramsci 1,
t 0577 803101.
**Trequanda**: Via Roma 4, t 0577 662296.

## Where to Stay and Eat

Accommodation isn't always easy to find in
this quiet corner of Tuscany. Villages may only
have one real hotel, or none. However, there
are plenty of rooms in the various *agriturismo*
farmhouses dotted around; either follow signs
on the road, or ask at the local tourist office.
Some restaurants, too, have rooms to rent and
there are always a few private homes with
rooms to rent that don't advertise. Don't be
shy; ask around and you'll find something.

### Asciano ✉ 53041

**Da Miretta**, near Asciano at Loc. La Pievina on
the Laurentana road, t 0577 718368 (*expensive*).
A very friendly place, serving regional dishes
and seafood – save some room for the
home-made desserts. The enormous set
meal (€35–45 for the fish meal; meat costs

less at €35) involves at least three hours,
delicious dishes (including *antipasti* and up
to six desserts) and local wine. *Closed Mon,
Tues. Only open for dinner plus Sun lunch.*

### Buonconvento ✉ 53022

**★★Albergo Ristorante Roma**, Via Soccini 14,
t 0577 806021, f 0577 807284 (*inexpensive*).
The closest rooms to Monte Oliveto
Maggiore are in Buonconvento, on the main
street of the old town. Simple and
old-fashioned, the Roma also has a very
good restaurant, a nice place to have a snack
after visiting Monte Oliveto Maggiore.

### Sinalunga ✉ 53048

**★★★★Locanda dell'Amorosa**, 2km south of
Sinalunga at Loc. L'Amorosa, t 0577 677211,
f 0577 678216, *www.amorosa.it* (*luxury*).
This is something really special, though you
need to reserve long in advance. It is an
entire medieval hamlet, complete with a
manor house and frescoed church. There are
16 beautiful rooms and a swimming pool.
The restaurant (*very expensive*) gets mixed
reviews. The seasonal menu usually includes
some freshwater fish dishes (Lake Trasimeno
isn't far away) such as *ravioli di pesce*; for
seconds, try stuffed pigeon or the big
Florentine steaks. *Closed Tues lunch, Mon.*

# Monte Oliveto Maggiore and Around

South of Siena, the SS2 wends towards Rome, roughly following the Roman Via
Cassia and the medieval pilgrims' path to Rome, the *Via Francigena*. Along the way, it
passes **Lucignano d'Arbia** (16km), a charming, tiny village with a medieval church, and
**Buonconvento** (27km), a gritty industrial town that hides a miniature walled medieval
centre – it would make a pretty hill town, if it only had a hill. The walls, no longer very
proper or military, are peppered with windows of the houses that have been built
against them. There are two fine gates at either end of the main street, and in the
middle, the 14th-century parish church with an altarpiece by Matteo di Giovanni.

In the broken, jumbled hills south of Asciano, austere green meadows alternate with
ragged gullies and bare white cliffs. At the centre of these *crete*, in the bleakest and
most barren part, there is a grove of tall, black cypresses around the monastery of
**Monte Oliveto Maggiore** (*open daily but times are not reliable; it is advisable to call to
check, on* t 0577 707611), 9km from Buonconvento on the SS451. Gentlemen from
Siena's merchant élite founded Monte Oliveto, including Giovanni Tolomei and
Ambrogio Piccolomini, both jaded merchants and sincere Christians who retired here

in 1313 to escape the fatal sophistication of the medieval city. Their new Olivetan Order was approved by the pope only six years later. With such wealthy backers, the monastery became a sort of élite hermitage for central Tuscany. An ambitious building programme in the 1400s made it a marvel of Renaissance clarity and rationality, expressed in simple structures and good Siena brick. The beautiful, asymmetrical **gatehouse**, decorated with a della Robbia terracotta, makes a fitting introduction to the complex. Inside, the well-proportioned brick **Abbey Church** (finished in 1417) has an exceptional set of wooden intarsia **choir stalls** by the master of the genre, Fra Giovanni da Verona, among the best work of this kind in all Italy. Note also the unusual dome with an octagon of interlocking arches, an Islamic-Andalucian design that made its way here via Spanish Christian churches and the chapel of the Castel Nuovo in Naples.

The monastery's greatest treasure, however, is the **Great Cloister**, embellished with 36 frescoes of scenes from the life of St Benedict (whose original rule Tolomei and the Olivetans were trying to restore). All 36 are currently undergoing restoration; the first nine are by Luca Signorelli, with formidable ladies and bulky, white-robed monks in the artist's distinctive balloonish forms and sparing use of colour. All the rest are the work of Il Sodoma (1505–8) – some of his best painting, ethereal scenes of Pre-Raphaelite ladies and mandarin monks, with blue and purple backgrounds of ideal landscapes and cities. If you are of the persuasion, popular enough a century ago, that it was with Raphael and Michelangelo that the Renaissance started to go wrong, you should visit here. Il Sodoma, not a Florentine nor really even a Sienese (he was from Vercelli in the north), wrote the last word to the mainstream tendency of Tuscan painting before the excesses of Mannerism. Mr Sodomite himself appears in the scene *'Come Benedetto risaldò lo capistero che era rotta'* ('How Benedict repaired the broken sieve'); he's the dissipated fellow on the left with the white gloves. Look carefully – not only did Sodoma paint himself in, but also his pet badgers, of which he was very fond. They and others of Sodoma's many pets appear in various other frescoes.

Unlike so many great Tuscan art shrines, Monte Oliveto, isolated here in the Sienese hills, retains something of its original aloof dignity. Although Napoleon himself suppressed the monastery in 1810, a group of talented brothers still works here, specializing in the restoration of old books. They won't be telling you much about the place – they're vowed to silence – but there is a monkish gift shop outside that sells home-made wine and honey, as well as other products from the monasteries around Tuscany.

In the *crete* around Monte Oliveto, the village of **San Giovanni d'Asso** (8km southeast) is built around a Sienese fortress; the church of San Pietro in Villore is from the 12th century, with an ambitious, unusual façade. From here, unsignposted byroads lead east to **Montisi** (7km) and **Trequanda** (12km), two fine villages, seldom visited because they're hard to find; the latter has a 13th-century castle and a Romanesque church. You might even find **Sant'Anna in Camprena**, between Montisi and Pienza, an ambitious medieval monastery complex that time forgot – until the location scouts from *The English Patient* arrived. The place is now being fitfully restored, and if you liked Sodoma's work in Monte Oliveto, stop in here to see another of his frescoes, portraying Christ with children, small dogs and fantasy Roman monuments.

# Montalcino and Around

Situated on a lofty hill inhabited since Etruscan times, swathed in vineyards and olive groves, the walled village of **Montalcino** (pop. 5,400) dominates the serene countryside 14km south of Buonconvento. Its major attraction is liquid – Brunello di Montalcino, a dark pungent red proudly holding its own among Italy's finest wines.

Every year at the Palio in Siena, there is a procession of representatives from all the towns that once were part of the republic. The honour of leading the parade belongs to Montalcino, for its loyalty and for the great service it rendered in 1555 after the fall of Siena (*see* **Siena**, History, p.321). During the siege, diehard republicans escaped from Siena to the impregnable fortress of Montalcino, where they established the 'Republic of Siena at Montalcino', holding out against the Medici until 1559. Today, Montalcino tries hard to be up-to-date (it was the first town in Tuscany to declare itself a 'denuclearized zone'); in reality, it's a friendly, resolutely sleepy town.

## Within the Walls

Right on Piazza Cavour is one of Montalcino's modest museums: the small **Archaeology Museum**, set in a former hospital pharmacy with detached frescoes by a student of Il Sodoma. Via Mazzini leads west to the Piazza del Popolo, and the attractive **Palazzo Comunale**, begun in the late 13th century, with a slender tower that apes the Torre di Mangia in Siena. Nearby, **Sant'Agostino** is a simple Sienese church, preserving some original frescoes from the 1300s. The **Diocesan and Civic Museum** around the corner (*open Tues–Sun 10–1 and 2–5.30; adm*), has a collection of Sienese painting and polychromed wood statues, including Madonnas by three great Sienese artists (Martini, Pietro Lorenzetti and Il Vecchietta), and some of the earliest successes of Sienese art, an illuminated Bible and painted crucifix, both from the 12th century. Besides some minor works of the 14th- and 15th-century Sienese masters, there is a collection of locally produced majolica from the same period.

Just down Via Ricasoli, at the east end of Montalcino, the impressive 14th-century **Rocca** (*open daily summer 9–8, winter 9–6; free, but adm to go up on the walls*) was the centre of the fortifications that kept the Spaniards and Florentines at bay. This citadel means a lot to Italian patriots; it was the last stronghold of the Sienese and a symbol of all the medieval freedoms of the Italian cities blotted out in the reactionary 1500s. Near the entrance is a plaque with a poem from the 'Piedmontese Volunteers of Liberty', extolling Montalcino's bravery in 'refusing the Medici thief'. Now a city park, the Rocca contains the last battle standard of the Sienese Republic and an **Enoteca**, where you can become better acquainted with Montalcino's venerable Brunello and other local wines, such as Moscadello and Rosso di Montalcino.

Following the town walls on the north side, you pass through neighbourhoods largely made up of orchards and gardens – Montalcino isn't nearly as busy a place as it was in the 1400s. The **cathedral**, on Via Spagni, was mostly rebuilt in the 1700s. Follow that street past the Baroque church of the Madonna del Soccorso, and you come to the city park, the 'Balcony of Tuscany', with views over Siena and beyond.

# Getting Around

There are regular **buses** from Siena (41km/1hr), a few of which involve a change at Buonconvento, near the SS2 crossroads for Montalcino. Buses stop at Piazza Cavour at the eastern end of town; you can obtain tickets and perhaps information at the bar on the piazza. Unfortunately, there are no convenient buses to take you to Sant'Antimo.

Besides wine, Montalcino is known for its honey and in early September hosts the **National Honey Fair.**

# Tourist Information

**Montalcino**: Costa del Municipio 8, **t/f** 0577 849331.

# Where to Stay and Eat

**Montalcino** ✉ 53024

★★★★**La Vecchia Oliviera**, Porta Cerbaia, **t** 0577 846028, **f** 0577 846029, *www.vecchiaoliviera. com* (*very expensive*). As the name suggests, this hotel occupies what was once an olive press. Offering the most luxurious accommodation in Montalcino, it is situated by the old gate into the town. The 13 comfortable and elegant rooms are prettily decorated; the swimming pool has a jacuzzi.

★★★**Dei Capitani**, Via Lapini 6, **t/f** 0577 847227, *www.deicapitani.it* (*expensive*). This old palazzo is your best bet in the centre. It has wonderful views, a small pool and (a rarity here) a car park.

**Boccon Divino**, Loc. Colombaio Tozzi, **t** 0577 848233 (*expensive*).Sit on the terrace and enjoy some of the best food in the area, such as saffron ravioli with black truffles, *gnocchetti* with truffles, meat roasted *sotto sale* (in a salt crust) with a delicious lettuce sauce and marvellous *bistecca alla fiorentina. Closed Tues.*

★★★**Il Giglio**, Via Soccorso Saloni 5, **t/f** 0577 848167, *www.gigliohotel.com* (*moderate*). Similarly central.

★★★**Bellaria**, Via Osticcio 19, **t** 0577 849326, **f** 0577 848668, *www.hotelbellaria montalcino.com* (*moderate*). A farmhouse hotel, a short walk through a pine wood to town. Some rooms, and the pool, have fabulous views.

**Osteria Osticcio**, Via Matteotti 23, **t** 0577 848271 (*moderate–cheap*). Magnificent views from the back of this pleasant wine bar. Good for a glass of wine and a snack: meats, cheeses *crostini* and salads. *Closed Tues.*

**Locanda Sant'Antimo**, near the church in Sant'Antimo. A good pizzeria which also has rooms (*inexpensive*).

**Il Pozzo**, Piazza del Pozzo, Loc S. Angelo in Colle, **t** 0577 844015 (*cheap*). Worth the detour for a cheap, traditional meal. *Closed Tues.*

## Sant'Antimo

*Open daily 6am–9pm; adm.*

A few of the vineyards that produce the famous Brunello di Montalcino are on the road south for **Sant'Antimo**. Two of them welcome visitors (*call before visiting*): the **Azienda Agricola Greppo** (*t 0577 848087*) and the **Cantine dei Barbi** (*t 0577 841111*). Sant'Antimo itself, about 10km south of Montalcino, is worth the detour. One of the finest Romanesque churches in Tuscany, it originally formed part of a 9th-century Benedictine monastery founded, according to legend, by Charlemagne himself. The present building, begun in 1118, incorporates parts of the Carolingian works, including the crypt. This half-ruined complex, reached by a long, winding avenue of cypresses, could easily serve as the set for *The Name of the Rose*. An important monastic community once flourished here, and there are still some monks about; they'll sell you a CD of their Gregorian chant, which you can hear them sing at Mass (*Mon–Sat 9.15am and 7pm, Sun 11am and 6.30pm*). The church is exquisite, with its elegant tower and rounded apse. Some of the stone inside, on the capitals and elsewhere, is luminous alabaster from Volterra. The sophistication of the architecture is impressive – in particular, the Byzantine-style women's gallery, and the ambulatory behind the apse with its radiating chapels.

# The Val d'Orcia

**San Quirico d'Orcia**, a humble little agricultural centre where the SS146 from Pienza joins the SS2, still has some of its medieval walls. Once on the pilgrim route of the Via Francigena, the town was endowed with hospices and hospitals built to accommodate pilgrims en route to Rome. The magnificent **Collegiata**, rebuilt in the 12th century over an earlier 8th-century church, has an exceptional façade built from local travertine and three portals from the 1200s, sculpted with lions and telamons, the finest of their kind in the area. Just behind it is the newly restored and somewhat forbidding 17th-century **Palazzo Chigi** – a surprisingly grand presence for such a tiny town. Since its restoration, the frescoed rooms are open to visitors (*open daily 8–6.30; adm*). There are a couple more attractive churches in the town: **Santa Maria di Vitaleta**, with a Gothic façade and an enamel *Annunciation* by Andrea della Robbia on the high altar, and the pretty little 11th-century **Santa Maria Assunta**. You

## Tourist Information

**San Quirico**: Via Dante Aligheri 33, t 0577 897211. *Closed Oct–Easter.*
**Castiglione d'Orcia**: Viale G. Marconi 13, t 0577 887363.
**Radicofani**: Via R. Magi 57, t 0578 55684.

## Festivals

**'Incontri in Terra di Siena'**: t 0578 69101, *www.lafoce.com* for details, *late July.*
A chamber music festival based at *La Foce*, home of the writer Iris Origo, on the Monte Amiata road from Chianciano.
**Festival del Val d'Orcia**: *late July–Aug.*
A month of music, theatre and dance.

## Where to Stay and Eat

**Bagno Vignoni** ✉ **53027**
**La Locanda del Loggiato**, Piazza del Maretto 30, t 0577 888925, f 0577 888370, *www.loggiato. it* (*expensive*). A B&B on the main square. Its six rooms occupy the first floor of a lovely medieval house. Eat in the wine bar that takes over the breakfast room in the evening.

**Hotel Posta Marcucci**, Via Ara Urcea, t 0577 887112, f 0577 887119, *www.hotelposta marcucci.it* (*expensive*). On a hillside, with a thermal pool and terraces enjoying stunning views over the Val d'Orcia. The restaurant serves rather dismal food though.
**Osteria del Leone**, Via dei Mulini 4, t 0577 887300 (*moderate*). A very good restaurant. Specialities include traditional *bruschetta*, *pici*, *tagliata* (steak) topped with rocket, vegetarian options and fish, too. *Closed Mon.*

**San Quirico d'Orcia** ✉ **53027**
**Hotel Palazzo del Capitano**, Via Poliziano 18, t 0577 89028, *www.palazzodelcapitano.com* (*very expensive*). This elegant 15th-century palazzo is in the medieval heart of town. The 11 rooms are tastefully done in pastel colours with linen fabrics and some romantic four-posters. There is a pretty terrace and garden and an excellent restaurant in the old bakery.

**Radicofani** ✉ **53040**
**La Palazzina**, Loc Le Vigne, t 0578 55771, *www.fattorialapalazzina.com* (*moderate*). A 200-year-old villa located just outside the village, with a few rooms and a pool. Set in lovely grounds. Min. 3 nights in high season.

can also visit the **Horti Leonini** (*open daily, dawn to sunset*), a lovely garden designed in the late 15th century by Diomede Lioni as a resting place for pilgrims.

There are a couple of points of interest nearby: **Ripa d'Orcia**, a hamlet with a stately castle of its own (*now a hotel, call t 0577 897376, www.castelloripadorcia.com*), 7km to the south, and **Bagno Vignoni**, a small spa town just south off the SS2, where the piazza has a '*vasca termale*' built by Lorenzo de' Medici, who came for the waters. There used to be three of these pools – one for men, one for women and one for horses. The one pool that remained was fed by a spring that has dried up. Once this pool has been cleaned and restored, water from a new spring will be redirected to it. If you long for a bathe, it is possible to buy day tickets for the hot springs at the Hotel Posta Marcucci (*see* 'Where to Stay and Eat', opposite).

Before the modern SS2 was built, the old Via Francigena traversed the valley of the Orcia, passing a patch of castles and fortified towns that began in the early Middle Ages. **Castiglione d'Orcia** (9km south of San Quirico) is as medieval-looking a town as you could ask for (though its cobbled piazza and fountain are from the 1600s) with two parish churches. The ruined fortress overlooking the town was built by the Aldobrandeschi family, who controlled much of southern Tuscany as late as the 1200s. Just outside to the north a pretty road winds up through olive groves to **Rocca d'Orcia**, another well-preserved medieval village clustered below its impressive castle, the **Rocca di Tentatenno**, which is open to visitors and used for art exhibitions. Another 15km south of Castiglione is the village of **Vivo d'Orcia**, which began as a Camaldolensian monastery in 1003; when the monastery withered the village grew instead, leaving only the pretty Romanesque **Cappella dell'Ermicciolo** in the woods above the town.

**Bagni San Filippo**, some 8km east of Vivo, circling back towards the SS2, may go into the books as the world's smallest thermal spa – a telephone booth, a few old houses and one small hotel. It takes its name from San Filippo Benizi, a holy hermit of the Middle Ages who hid here when he heard there was a movement to elect him pope. Gouty old Lorenzo Il Magnifico used to come here, too, though he didn't leave any embellishments like the piazza in Bagno Vignoni. You can stop here for a swim in the natural terraced pools of the **Fosso Bianco**, a glistening limestone formation – a sort of stone waterfall – created by the flowing sulphurous waters.

## Radicofani

Some wonderfully rugged countryside lies in the valley of the Orcia, east of this chain of villages, especially along the roads approaching **Radicofani**, a landmark of southern Tuscany, with its surreal, muffin-shaped hill topped by a lofty tower. The ruined fortress around it, originally built by Pope Adrian IV (the Englishman Nicholas Breakspear), served in the 1300s as headquarters for the legendary bandit Ghino di Tacco, solid citizen of Dante's *Inferno* and subject of a story in the *Decameron* (Day 10, Number 2), about how he imprisoned the Abbot of Cluny in this tower. The elegant loggias on the highway, just outside town, belong to the 17th-century Palazzo La Posta, once the only good hotel between Siena and Rome; most of the famous on the Grand Tour stopped on their way through.

# Pienza

Some 50km south of Siena on the SS2, you'll come across a perfect, tiny core of Renaissance order and urbanity, surrounded by a village of about 2,500 souls. **Pienza** is a delightful place, even if it does get more than its share of tourists. Like Monte Oliveto Maggiore, it is a small dose of the best of the Renaissance, a jewel set among some of the most glorious and archetypal of Tuscan landscapes.

During a period of political troubles, common enough in Renaissance Siena, the great family of the Piccolomini chose to exile itself temporarily in one of its possessions, the village of Corsignano. Aeneas Silvius Piccolomini (*see* p.333) was born there in 1405; later, as Pope Pius II, he became determined to raise his country birthplace into a city. No historian has ever discovered any compelling economic or military reason for a new town here. Architect Bernardo Rossellino designed it, with some help from Pius, the pennies of the faithful paid for it, and Pius named it after himself: Pienza. Perhaps fortunately, after the first wave of papal patronage Pienza was nearly forgotten. The strict grid of streets that was to extend over the Tuscan hills never materialized, and only the central piazza with a new cathedral and a Piccolomini palace was ever completed – enough to reveal something of the original intention.

## Pienza's Piazza Pio II

Piazza Pio II, the heart of Rossellino's design scheme, is simple and decorous; it displays the chief buildings of the town without any of the monumental symmetry of the later Renaissance, relying on proportion alone to tie it all together. Such a square shows how, despite all its paintings of ideal buildings and streetscapes, the Early Renaissance still followed the 'picturesque' urban design of the Middle Ages; Piazza Pio was made to be a stage set for daily life or the background of a painting.

Rossellino designed a truly elegant façade for the **cathedral** (1462), capturing the spirit of the times by omission – there is no hint anywhere that it belongs to a Christian building, though the arms of the Piccolomini and the papal keys are carved on the pediment. The interior, though equally elegant, is surprisingly tame Gothic – as if this bold Renaissance architect were a slightly embarrassed humanist who believed that only Gothic truly suited a church. Rossellino also carved a marble altar and baptismal font in the lower church; there are also altarpieces by other leading Sienese artists: Sano di Pietro, Matteo di Giovanni, Vecchietta and Giovanni di Paolo. Nothing in this cathedral has been changed, or even moved, since the day it was completed; Pius' papal bull of 1462 expressly forbade it. See it while it lasts: the cathedral, built on the edge of a slight cliff, has been subsiding almost since it was built. Occasionally sulphurous fumes seep from the floor. If you walk around the left side of the building, there is a fine view over the countryside, and also a glimpse of the fearfully large cracks that have been developing in the apse. No one has yet discovered a way to shore it up permanently, and even though restoration work has been done it could still collapse, at least partially, at any time. This collection has been rehoused in the **Museo Diocesano** (*see opposite*).

Next to the cathedral, the columned **well**, a favourite sort of Renaissance urban decoration, is also by Rossellino. So is the newly restored **Palazzo Piccolomini**, a rehash

# Tourist Information

**Pienza**: Pro Loco, Piazza Pio II, t 0578 749 071.
Offers occasional guided tours of town.

# Shopping

Corso Rossellino leads from the centre of the village to Porta Murello and the bus terminus, passing trendy artisan shops selling ceramics and leatherwork, antique shops and health food stores. Pienza for some reason has dozens of these, offering among other things the very good, locally made honey and preserves. And if Renaissance architecture leaves you cold, you can at least come for the sheep's cheese, maybe Italy's best. Pienza's variety of pecorino has a delicate taste, available in different strengths depending on how long it has been aged. This 'capital of sheep's cheese' has been making it at least since the time of the Etruscans.

# Where to Stay and Eat

**Pienza** ✉ 53026

If you are on a low budget, a number of private houses in the town offer rooms for rent; the tourist office has a full list.

**★★★Il Chiostro**, Corso Il Rossellino 26, t 0578 748400, f 0578 748440, www.relaisilchiostro dipienza.com (very expensive). As the name implies this is an old cloister, in the centre just off Piazza Pio II; modernized rooms have been stylishly restored with all the amenities, beautiful gardens, a small pool, and a good restaurant.

**La Saracina**, about 7km from Pienza on the road to Montepulciano, t 0578 748022, www.lasaracina.it (expensive). Five suites and rooms in an old farmhouse with beautiful gardens, pool and tennis, out in the countryside.

**★★★Corsignano**, Via della Madonnina 9, t 0578 748501, f 0578 748166 (moderate). Modern and comfortable.

**Latte di Luna**, Via S. Carlo 2/4, t 0578 748606 (moderate). Popular with the locals, serving home-made pasta with truffles, duck with olives, wild boar and local grappa. Closed Tues.

**La Pergola**, Via dell'Acero 2, t 0578 748051. (moderate). The building (just outside town on the road to San Quirico) that houses this excellent restaurant may be uninspiring, but the food is anything but that and prices are reasonable. Carefully prepared versions of local dishes are served up plus the odd surprise; an amazing olive oil ice cream, for example. There is a fine selection of cheeses and an interesting wine list, too.

**Sperone Nudo**, Via G. Marconi, t 0578 748641. (cheap). This is a great stop for lunch, where you can get a glass of wine and bruschette, sandwiches or other snacks. Closed Mon.

of the more famous Palazzo Rucellai in Florence, whose design follows Alberti. The best bit is at the rear, where a three-storey loggia overlooks a 'hanging garden' on the cliff edge. The interior of the palace and gardens are open to visitors (open winter Tues–Sun 10–12.30 and 4–7; summer Tues–Sun 10–12.30 and 3–6; adm). Other buildings on the piazza include the **Archbishop's Palace** and the Gothic **Palazzo Comunale**. Behind the Palazzo Piccolomini, the church of **San Francesco** predates the founding of Pienza; there are some 14th–15th-century frescoes inside including one attributed to Luca Signorelli. The **Museo Diocesano di Pienza** (open Wed–Mon 10–1 and 3–6.30; Nov–Mar Sat, Sun and hols 10–1 and 3–6, or by pre-booking t 0578 749905; adm), in the sumptuously restored 15th-century Palazza Borgia in Corso Rossellino, boasts a collection of objects from nearby churches, several paintings (some by Signorelli), as well as Flemish tapestries.

Few people visit the 11th-century **Pieve** of old Corsignano, 1km west of the town (signposted from the car park/piazza at the entrance to the central pedestrian zone). This unusual church, where Aeneas Silvius was baptized, has some even more peculiar carvings over its entrance. Mermaids, or sirens, turn up with some frequency in Romanesque tympana and capitals, in Tuscany and Apulia especially, as well as many other places in Italy and France. Here there are several – one spreading its forked tail to display the entrance to the womb, flanked by others, and a dancer and a musician, with dragons whispering into their ears. Such symbols are steeped in medieval mysticism, not entirely inaccessible to the modern imagination. One scholar interprets this scene as a cosmic process: the sirens, representing desire, as the intermediary by which nature's energy and inspiration (the dragons) are conducted into the conscious world. It has been claimed that they betray the existence of an ecstatic cult, based on music and dance and descended from the ancient Dionysian rituals.

# Montepulciano

Another graceful hill town lingers south of Siena, also with a distinguished past and best known for wine. **Montepulciano** is larger (pop. 14,500) and livelier than Montalcino, with some fine buildings and works of art. Old Montalcino was a home from home for the Sienese, while Montepulciano usually allied itself with Florence. Its Vino Nobile di Montepulciano, while perhaps not as celebrated as Montalcino's Brunello, was praised by connoisseurs over 200 years ago, and can certainly contend with Italy's best today.

Inhabitants of Montepulciano, which began as the Roman *Mons Politianus*, are called *Poliziani*, and that is the name of its most famous son – Angelo Ambrogini, or Poliziano, was one of the first Renaissance Greek scholars, an accomplished poet and critic and scholar at the court of Lorenzo de' Medici and tutor to his children. Botticelli's mythological paintings may have been inspired by his *Stanze per la Giostra*. Today's Poliziani are a genteel and cultured lot, still capable of poetic extemporization and singing. The *Bruscello*, a partly improvised play on medieval and Renaissance themes in music and verse, acted by the townspeople in the Piazza Grande each August, is the town's biggest festival. A second August festival, the *Bravio delle Botti*, requires no poetry but plenty of sweat, when neighbourhood teams race up the steep main street pushing huge barrels.

## Palazzi and Pulcinello

Entering the city through the **Porta al Prato**, you will first encounter a stone column bearing the *marzocco*, a symbol of Montepulciano's long attachment to Florence. Though nominally under Florentine control, the city was allowed a sort of independence up to the days of Cosimo I. The main street, called here Via di Gracciano del Corso, climbs and winds in a circle up to the top of the city (if you follow it all the way, you'll walk twice as far as you need to, and end up thinking Montepulciano is a major metropolis). This stretch is lined with noble palaces: those at No.91 and No.82 are both the work of the late Renaissance architect Vignola, famous for his Villa Giulia in Rome and the Farnese Palace in Caprarola (Lazio). Up at No.73, **Palazzo Bucelli** has the most unusual foundation in Italy – made almost entirely of Etruscan cinerary urns, filled with cement and stacked like bricks, many still retaining their sculpted reliefs. Montepulciano was once Etruscan, though the urns probably came from Chiusi.

Piazza Michelozzo, where the street begins to ascend, is named after the Florentine architect of **Sant'Agostino** church, with an excellent, restrained Renaissance façade, similar to the cathedral in Pienza though more skilfully handled. Michelozzo also contributed the terracotta reliefs over the portal. Across the piazza, note the figure atop the old **Torre del Pulcinello**. To anyone familiar with Naples, the white *Commedia dell'Arte* clown banging the hours on the town bell will be an old friend. It is said that a Neapolitan bishop was once exiled here for indiscretions back home, and when he returned, he left this bit of Parthenopean culture as a souvenir to thank the Poliziani.

Continuing along the main street, you pass a dozen or so more palaces, reminders of the city's aristocratic past. There is one florid Baroque interior, in the **Gesù Church** by Andrea Pozzo. Further down, the street curves around the medieval **Fortezza**, now partly residential, within the oldest part of town, a fascinating quarter of ancient alleys.

## Piazza Grande

These days, when even the stalwart citizens of hill towns are a little too spoiled to walk up hills, the old centres of towns sometimes become quiet and out-of-the-way. So it is in Montepulciano, where the **Piazza Grande** is city's highest point. On one side, Michelozzo added a rusticated stone front and tower to the 13th-century **Palazzo Comunale** to create a lesser copy of Florence's Palazzo Vecchio. Opposite, a Renaissance well stands in front of the **Palazzo Contucci**, built by the elder Antonio da Sangallo. On the west side, a tremendous pile of bricks, a sort of tenement for pigeons, proclaims the agonizing unfinishability of the **cathedral**, sad victim of a doomed rebuilding project begun in 1592. Like the toad, believed by medieval scholars to conceal a precious jewel in its brain, this preposterous building hides within its bulk a single transcendent work of art. Atop a marble Renaissance altar adorned with *putti* stands an *Assumption of the Virgin* by Taddeo di Bartolo, one of the greatest of all 14th-century Sienese paintings. Set in glowing, discordant colours – pink, orange, purple and gold – this is a very spiritual Madonna, attended by a court of angel musicians. Don't miss the predella panels beneath; each is a serious, inspired image from the Passion, including one panel of the *Resurrection* that can be compared to Piero della Francesca's more famous version in Sansepolcro.

The **Museo Civico**, holding the **Pinacoteca Crociani** just down Via Ricci (*open Tues–Sun 10–1 and 3–6; in summer until 8; Dec–Mar Sat–Sun 10–1 and 3–6; adm*), houses several collections under one roof. On the first and second floors are some della Robbia terracottas from the dissolved convent that was once downstairs, and the Crociani collection of paintings. The old collection, with a *Crucifixion* from Filippino Lippi's workshop, an *Assumption* by the Sienese Jacopo di Mino, an odd work by Girolamo di Benvenuto – baby Jesus as an *objet d'art* – and, even more peculiar, an inexplicable *Allegory of the Immaculate Conception* by one Giovanni Antonio Lappoli (d. 1552), has gained additions from other collections in Montepulciano. However, the key improvement is the archaeological section on ground level, now rearranged to include the contents of five locally discovered Etruscan tombs previously housed in the Uffizi. Artefacts include Bucchero ware, ceramics and bronzes dating from the 5th to the 2nd century BC.

Continue down Via Ricci and you will find the church of **Santa Lucia**, with a small *Madonna* by Luca Signorelli in a chapel off to the right.

## Antonio da Sangallo's San Biagio

One of the set pieces of Renaissance architecture was the isolated temple, a chance to create an ideal building in an uncluttered setting, often on the edge of a city. Giuliano da Sangallo's Santa Maria delle Carceri in Prato was the first and worst, followed by Bramante's San Pietro in Montorio in Rome and the Tempio della Consolazione in Todi (Umbria). Montepulciano's example of this genre lies south of the city (a lengthy walk downhill and back, if you don't have a car) near the road junction for Chianciano; a stately avenue of cypresses, each over a small marker commemorating a local soldier who died in the First World War, leads to the site.

Antonio da Sangallo, long in the shadow of his less talented brother Giuliano, left his masterpiece here. **San Biagio** stands in a small park, a central, Greek cross church of creamy travertine. As with so many other Renaissance churches, there is more

## Getting There and Around

Montepulciano is situated 12½km/20mins east of Pienza on the SS146, 66km/1½hrs from Siena, and 16km/30mins west of the Chiusi exit on the A1.

The **train** station (Florence–Rome line) is way out in the countryside, irregularly served by buses to town, and it tends to be only local trains that stop; a better possibility is to use the station at Chiusi-Chianciano, which has bus connections up to Chiusi town, to Chianciano Terme, Montepulciano and occasionally Pienza.

The **bus** station in Montepulciano is just outside the Porta al Prato, the main gate into the city. There are very regular buses to Chianciano Terme–Chiusi–Chiusi station; slightly fewer to Pienza; one each in the morning and afternoon for Siena (via Pienza and San Quirico), also daily connections to Abbadia San Salvatore, Montalcino, Perugia and Arezzo.

There is an LFI bus information booth inside the train station at Chiusi; outside, besides the buses mentioned above, there are rather infrequent LFI connections to Cortona, Arezzo, Perugia, Orvieto and Città della Pieve.

If you aren't up to climbing up to the top of Montepulciano, the LFI runs a handy **minibus** service up the Corso to Piazza Grande.

## Tourist Information

**Montepulciano**: Via Gracciano nel Corso 59a, off Piazza Grande, t 0578 757341. Open daily 9–12.30 and 3–6.

## Where to Stay and Eat

### Montepulciano ✉ 53045

Montepulciano puts out the welcome mat at a few very amiable hotels.

***Borghetto**, Borgo Buio t 0578 757535, *www.ilborghetto.it* (*expensive*). Just around the corner, with pleasant rooms, some of which have great views over the edge of the town.

***Marzocco**, Via G. Savonarola 18, t 0578 757262, f 0578 757530, *www.albergoil marzocco.it* (*moderate*). An airy, serendipitous establishment, family-run, and located next to the *Marzocco* itself, just inside the main gate.

***Il Riccio**, Via Talosa 21, t/f 0578 757713, *www.ilriccio.net* (*moderate*). Tastefully furnished rooms in a renovated medieval palazzo, with a pleasant rooftop terrace for catching the sun.

If you can't find a room in the town, there are lots of *agriturismo* places in the surrounding countryside, and hundreds of rooms just a few km south at Chianciano architecture than Christianity in the design, a consciously classical composition, using an adaptation of the 'Tuscan' order on the ground level, Ionic on the second and Corinthian on the upper storeys of the campanile, gracefully fitted into one of the corners of the Greek cross. The interior, finished in marble and other expensive stone, is equally symmetrical, rational and impressive. Over the handsome altar, a Latin inscription proclaims, '*Hinc deus homo et home Deus. Immensum Concept – Aeternum Genuit*' (Hence God is Man, and for humanity, he created Eternity). The beautiful **Canon's House**, with its double *loggia*, is also the work of Sangallo.

## Around Montepulciano

Among some beautiful villages on the hills around Montepulciano, **Montefollonico** (8km northwest), has a frescoed church and Palazzo Comunale, both 13th century. **Monticchiello**, 7km southwest on a back road towards Pienza, hangs languorously on its hilltop; it too has a 13th-century church, with a rose window, an altarpiece by Pietro Lorenzetti and Sienese frescoes (late 14th century).

Terme (*see* p.380). If you go to Sant'Albano, 3km from Montepulciano, you'll find seven more hotels, all in the inexpensive range, stuck in the middle of nowhere – presumably because there are more thermal baths nearby.

The best restaurants are outside town.

**La Chiusa**, Via Madonnina, Montefollonico, **t** 0577 669668, *www.ristorantelachiusa.it* (*very expensive*). Located in an old *frantoio* or olive press, on the edge of the village of Montefollonico, with panoramic views back towards Montepulciano. La Chiusa has been acclaimed as the best restaurant in southern Tuscany, and though its reputation has wobbled slightly in recent years, you're guaranteed at the very least an incredible seven-course *menu degustazione* and an exhaustive wine list. It also has some very luxurious suites and rooms. *Closed Tues.*

**La Grotta, t** 0578 757607 (*expensive*). In the shadow of the dramatic San Biagio, serving traditional Tuscan dishes with a creative twist, with the likes of smoked goose breast, ravioli stuffed with pigeon and saffron, pigeon stuffed with truffles or duck breast with juniper berries and orange peel. *Closed Wed.*

**Osteria Borgo Buio**, Via di Borgo Buio 10, **t** 0578 717497 (*moderate*). This excellent *osteria* not only offers local dishes such as *pici* and other home-made pasta dishes,

but also historical dishes such as *pepposo*, a peppery beef stew cooked in *vino nobile*. *Closed Thurs.*

**Caffè Poliziano**, on the Corso. Montepulciano's old-fashioned *gran caffè*; worth visiting at least for a cup of coffee.

Alternatively, why not have a picnic? Stock up on some of the fine local products – honey and preserves, pecorino cheese, ham or boar salami and a case of *vino nobile*; any of the back roads off the SS146 will lead you at some point to an ideal spot.

### Monticchiello ✉ 53020

**L'Olmo, t** 0578 755133, **f** 0578 755124, *www. olmopienza.it* (*luxury*). Just below Montichiello is an elegant guesthouse in a beautifully restored stone post-house, with gardens and a pool overlooking the Val d'Orcia. Bedrooms are supremely comfortable and decorated in sophisticated rustic style; dinner is available on request. *Closed mid-Nov–Easter.*

**La Porta**, Via del Piano 1, **t** 0578 755163. An excellent *osteria/enoteca*, with wonderful views over Pienza and the valley from its panoramic terrace. Here you can have anything from a sandwich or a plate of local cheeses with a glass of wine, to a pasta dish or a succulent *tagliata* of tender steak topped with rocket leaves. *Closed Thurs.*

### *Vino Nobile* and Other Delights

Montepulciano and its environs are full of *cantine*, and each of these is full of people ready for long discussions on the virtues of this famous wine.

After two years, it carries the bouquet of unknown autumn blooms, a perfume that confounds melancholy; its colour is a mystery of faith. Certain writers are known to be very fond of it. A wine tour of Montepulciano should begin with the **Cantine Cantucci**, on the Piazza Grande, where they might show you the salon with frescoes by Baroque artist Andrea Pozzo. The **Cantina Gattavecchia**, next to the church of Santa Maria at the southern end of town, has a *cantina* dating back to the 1500s; don't neglect the venerable cellar built into the embankment beneath Piazza Grande, next to the Teatro Poliziano.

Vino Nobile isn't the only variety of wine made in these parts. There is a version of Chianti – Chianti Colli Senesi, a creditable white Valdichiana and a sweet dessert *vin santo*. And on those evenings when quantity means more than quality, try any of the mass-produced Montepulciano reds; more honourable plonk is hard to find.

Besides wine, Montepulciano has some local surprises to offer – jams, preserves, honey and other farm specialities have all recently become prominent in this corner of Tuscany, where the ideology of natural food has become just as popular as in the trendiest neighbourhoods of New York. You'll find them in almost any grocer's. Montepulciano has some very good antique stores on its back streets, and a sound crafts tradition, especially in woodcarving. On Piazza Grande, there is a School of Mosaics; take a peek at the mosaic fountain in the courtyard.

## Chianciano Terme

*'Chianciano – Fegato Sano'* – this is the slogan you see everywhere in **Chianciano Terme** (pop. 7,500): on the signs that welcome you, on the municipal buildings, even on the garbage trucks: 'Chianciano, for a healthy liver'. And after rotting yours on too much Montepulciano wine, how convenient to have a spa close at hand to flush it out and get it pumping again. The waters here were known to the Etruscans, but have only been exploited in a big way in the last 50 years. There is an old walled town, Chianciano Vecchio, with a medieval clocktower and a Museo d'Arte Sacra; at the gate is the bus station and information booth. Just outside the old town, the **Museo Civico Archeologico delle Acque** (*open April–Oct Tues–Sun 10–1 and 4–7; Nov–Mar Sat and Sun 10–1 and 4–7; other days by appt only, call t 0578 30471; adm*) occupies an old granary, displaying mainly Etruscan and Roman exhibits excavated locally since 1986. Among the usual bronzes and ceramics are finds from Poggio Bacherina, an Etruscan farm uncovered between 1986 and 1989. The newest display has reconstructions of tombs, built in the hollows that were originally carved out to hold wine barrels in the granary. These 'tombs' contain finds from the excavation of the Tolle Necropoli at neaby La Foce, arranged more or less as they were found at the site.

Beyond, modern Chianciano stretches for miles down Viale della Libertà, passing hundreds of hotels, gardens with clipped lawns, and bathhouses in a clean, modern style from the 1950s. Besides repairing your liver, Chianciano has mineral mud packs for your acne, hot aerosol douches and plenty of other medically respected treatments for your every ailment. They'll lock you in a room full of gas for a collective dry nebulization, throw you in the hydro-gaseous bath and then hand you over to the *masseuses* (this for patients suffering from trauma), or put you face-to-face with the sulphurous sonic aerosol spray. 'Ah,' said the despairing Italians, 'the English never come. They simply do not understand the baths...'

## Around Chianciano: La Foce and Castelluccio

Southwest of Chianciano lies **La Foce**, a large estate on the hills overlooking the Val d'Orcia. Its strategic position on the Via Francigena has long attracted settlers; recent excavations brought to light a burial place from the 7th century BC.

Antonio and Iris Origo bought the property in 1924 when it was barren and poverty-ridden, working throughout their lives to regenerate the area; they set up a school, a day clinic and a nursery, also an orphanage during the war. Iris Origo's autobiographical books *Images and Shadows* and *War in the Val d'Orcia* make fascinating reading: the former covers the estate's development, while the latter focuses on the war years.

The villa was built in the late 15th century as a hostel for pilgrims and merchants, and restored by the Origos under the guidance of English landscape architect Cecil Pinsent, who designed the delightful gardens (*gardens only open Wed 3–dusk; t 0578 69101*). Nearby, on the road to Montepulciano, is the medieval **Castelluccio**, also part of the estate and open to visitors. As well as exhibitions, it holds concerts in the summer, as a venue for the **Incontri in Terra di Siena** music festival (*see p.372*).

## Tourist Information

**Chianciano Terme**: Piazza Italia 67,
t 0578 671122.

## Where to Stay and Eat

### Chianciano Terme ✉ 53042

Whether or not you feel ready to entrust yourself to the thermal torture of the spa, Chianciano can be useful in the summer when hotels are booked solid everywhere else. **Azienda Autonima di Cura**, Viale Roma 67. Offers help with accommodation.

Most of Chianciano's hotels were built in the last 30 years – nothing is outstanding, but you will find a fair amount of choice within every price range. As in most spa towns, people tend to dine in their hotels, but a few restaurants have cropped up, too.

**La Foce**, Casella Postale 55, t 0578 69101, *www.lafoce.com* (*luxury–expensive*). Several of the farmhouses on this estate have been turned into up-market self-catering apartments, sleeping 2–14 guests. Furnishings are elegant rustic in style, with plenty of antiques, and each house has use of a pool and private garden. Meals available on request.

**L'Oasi**, Loc La Foce, t 0578 755 077 (*moderate*). A useful stop-off just below La Foce on the road to Monte Amiata, this is a rustic, family-run bar/restaurant, serving *panini* with slabs of the local pecorino or heartier fare, such as *pici* and wild boar.

**La Rosa del Trinoro**, on the road between La Foce and Sarteano, at Castiglioncello del Trinoro, t 0578 265 529, *www.larosadel trinoro.it* (*expensive*). It's worth climbing the 11km of 'white road' from La Foce (turn left just after the villa towards Chiarentana) for the view alone, but also for the 'other worldliness' of this tiny hamlet. The menu features creative and elegant versions of local and not-so-local dishes; there are also nine pleasant rooms (*moderate*).

# Chiusi and Around

If anyone ever read you Macaulay's rouser *Horatio at the Bridge*, you will remember the fateful Lars Porsena of Clusium leading the Etruscan confederation and their Umbrian allies to attack Rome in brave days of old. Thanks to Horatio, Rome survived and made a name for itself; here you can see what happened to Clusium – or *Camars*, as the Etruscans called it. Most of its 9,500 citizens live in the new districts by the railway station, but the hill town on the site of Lars Porsena's capital still thrives.

## Archaeological Museum

*Open daily 9–8; adm.*

From those brave days of old, Chiusi retains at least an excellent **Archaeological Museum**, beautifully laid out and well-labelled. As with so many Etruscan collections, the main attraction is the large number of cinerary urns, and as usual, the Etruscans are able to produce a bewildering variety of styles and themes. Large urns with thoughtful, reclining figures are common, as well as mythological battle scenes with

# Tourist Information

**Chiusi**: Pro Loco, Via Porsenna 67, t 0578 227 667.

# Where to Stay and Eat

**Chiusi** ✉ 53043

Most of the hotels are down by the railway station in Chiusi Scalo, and unremarkable.

**\*\*\*Centrale**, Piazza Dante 3, t 0578 20118 (*moderate*). A typical offering, with several modern rooms.

There are a couple of options out of town.

**\*\*\*La Fattoria**, Conciarese al Lago, t 0578 21407, *www.la-fattoria.it* (*moderate*). An old farmhouse with views over the lake; there are eight nice rooms and a very good restaurant specializing in fresh fish from the lake, plus every sort of roast and pasta dish made with porcini mushrooms. *Closed Mon*.

**Le Anfore**, Via Chiusi 30, just outside town on the road to Sarteano, t/f 0578 265521, *www.balzarini.it* (*moderate*). An attractive and beautifully restored farmhouse providing good value family accommodation with pool, tennis and riding – there's even a restaurant.

**Da Gino**, Via Cabina Lago 42, t 0578 21408 (*moderate*). On the shores of the Lago di

Chiusi. The speciality is fresh lake fish, grilled over bamboo fire (also from the lake) and *tegamaccio* (fish soup) and eel. *Closed Wed*.

**Zaira**, Via Arunte 12, t 0578 20260 (*moderate*). Italians in the know make the detour off the Rome–Florence *autostrada* up to the oldest part of Chiusi, heading for this restaurant with its speculative 'Etruscan cuisine'. Every restaurant that tries to reconstruct an Etruscan menu comes up with something different. No matter; it's a harmless fancy, and with dishes such as *pasta del lucumone* (with ham and three different cheeses), duck cooked in *vino nobile* and guinea fowl *al cartoccio*, it's hard to complain. Zaira takes special pride in the wine list, having one of Tuscany's largest cellars. It's good value, too. *Closed Mon in winter*.

**La Solita Zuppa**, Via Porsenna 21, t 0578 21006 (*moderate*). The name is too modest – not really the 'same old soup', but their speciality: four or five different kinds on any given day, along with home-made *pici* and good meat dishes; in a warm, old-fashioned *osteria* atmosphere up in the Old Town. *Closed Tues*.

**Sarteano** ✉ 53047

**Residenza Santa Chiara**, Piazza S. Chiara, t 0578 265412, f 0578 266849, *www. conventosantachiara.it* (*expensive*). Nice old winged gods. Not all the tombs contained the well-known rectangular urns; some Etruscans chose to be buried in 'canopic' jars, surmounted by a terracotta bust of the deceased. Camars was a wealthy town, and the excavations at its necropolises unearthed a large amount of Greek pottery – note the urn with Achilles and Ajax playing at dice, and the Dionysian scenes with sexy maenads and leering satyrs. Many Etruscan imitation vases are on display; it's easy to believe the local talent could have done as well as the Greeks, had they only possessed thinner paintbrushes. To end the collection, there is a glittering hoard of nice barbaric trinkets from some 6th- and 7th-century Lombard tombs on the Arusa hill just outside town.

## Etruscan Tombs and Tunnels

If you're interested in seeing some of the Etruscan tombs (5th–3rd century BC) where these items were discovered, mention it to the museum guards, who arrange guided tours – in fact, they'll probably ask you first. These are the only good painted tombs in Tuscany; the best one, the **Tomba della Scimmia**, contains paintings of wrestlers and warriors, in addition to the monkey that gives the tomb its name.

building at the top of the town with a cool, shady garden, simple but perfectly adequate rooms, and an excellent restaurant.

**La Giara**, Viale Europa 2 (6km southwest of Chiusi), **t** 0578 265511 (*expensive*). Usually crowded with Sartanese, and with good reason, lured in by the home-made pasta, pizza, roast duck and lamb chops. *Closed Mon.*

**Osteria Da Gagliano**, Via Roma 5, **t** 0578 268022 (*moderate*). A simple *osteria* with wooden tables and benches. Excellent local dishes include gnocchi (on Thursdays), tripe or pecorino *al forno. Closed Tues.*

### Cetona ✉ 53040

★★★★**La Frateria**, Convento di San Francesco, **t** 0578 238015, *www.mondox.it* (*very expensive*). The most unusual hotel in the area, in the buildings of a 13th-century monastery founded originally by St Francis. It's now run by a community of young people who have managed to preserve a feeling of peace and tranquillity in keeping with the setting, despite the lavish physical comforts on offer. Among the luxuries is an excellent, if somewhat overpriced, restaurant. *Closed Jan.*

**La Locanda di Anita**, Piazza Balestrieri 5, **t** 0578 237075, *www.lalocandadianita.it* (*expensive*). A tiny *locanda* with four beautiful rooms and a suite, and a pretty breakfast terrace. You can enjoy good, home-cooked food in

the nearby **L'Osteria Vecchia**, under the same management.

### San Casciano dei Bagni ✉ 53040

★★★★**Fonteverde**, Loc Terme 1, **t** 0578 58023, **f** 0578 58013, *www.fonteverdespa.com* (*luxury*). A new luxury spa hotel built in and around a Medici villa with extensive gardens on the site of the restored thermal baths. B&B or a package including full board and a huge range of beauty therapies and treatments.

★★★**Sette Querce**, Viale Manciati 2, **t** 0578 58174, **f** 0578 58172, *www.settequerce.it* (*expensive, suites very expensive*). A delightful hotel furnished in a riot of colour. Comfortable rooms have their own sitting area and some have kitchenette. Breakfast is served in your room, other meals are available at **Da Daniela** (*see* below).

**La Fontanella**, Via Roma 6, **t** 0578 58300, *www.albergolafontanella.com* (*expensive*). Good value, and with an excellent restaurant (*moderate–cheap*).

**Da Daniela**, Piazza Matteotti 7, **t** 0578 58041 (*moderate*). Serves interesting variations on local themes in a lovely, brick-vaulted room. Sample bean soup, ravioli stuffed with pigeon, fricassée of lamb with artichokes or rich, bubbling pecorino with truffles. Leave room for *mousse di marrons glacés* topped with forest fruits. *Closed Wed in winter.*

The **Tomba della Pellegrina** and the **Tomba del Granduca** are also interesting, as is the **Tomba Bonci Casuccini**, in a different necropolis east of town.

## The Cathedral

Across the street from the museum, Chiusi's cathedral is the oldest in Tuscany. Only parts of it – the recycled Roman columns in the nave – go back to the original 6th-century building. The cathedral was rebuilt in the 12th century and again in the 19th. Have a look at the mosaics that cover the walls inside. At first glance, they seem astounding, an unknown chapter in early Christian art. Then you'll notice they have a touch of Art Nouveau about them – and finally, you realize they aren't mosaics at all, but skilfully sponged-on squares of paint, a crazy masterpiece of mimicry completed in 1915. The small **cathedral museum** (*open 15 June–Sept Mon–Fri 9.30–12.45 and 4–7; Oct–14 June 9.30–12.45 only; adm*) contains Roman fragments and some beautiful 15th-century illuminated choir books. The best part, though, is that your admission includes a climb up the campanile, and a descent into the mysterious network of tunnels and galleries underlying the town, bits of which go back to the time of the Etruscans. Whatever their original purpose, some were converted into catacombs by early Christian communities; there's also an underground cistern from Roman times.

## Around Chiusi: Lakes, Sarteano and More *Crete*

Just northeast of Chiusi, the **Lago di Chiusi** and the **Lago di Montepulciano** are pretty patches of blue on the border between Tuscany and Umbria, smallest in the chain of lakes that begins with Lago Trasimeno. Lago di Chiusi, in particular, is nice for a picnic, close to the *autostrada* if you're headed from Florence to Rome or Orvieto.

**Sarteano** is a smaller resort spa, 9km south of Chianciano or Chiusi, attached to a fine old hill town with some Renaissance palaces, a squarish medieval fortress, and the church of **San Martino in Foro**, with an *Annunciation* that is one of the best works of the Sienese Mannerist Beccafumi. A small and delightful Etruscan museum – the **Museo Civico Archeologico** – has opened in the impressive Palazzo Gabrielli, containing some wonderful funerary accoutrements. Most striking of all are the magnificent urns containing bones and other anthropomorphic paraphernalia.

Another 6km south of Sarteano, off the ruggedly scenic SS321, lies **Cetona**, a small, untouristic gem, with a growing population of discerning foreign residents who have rejected Chianti country and all that it implies. The Palazzo Comunale has a **Museo Civico per la Preistoria del Monte Cetona**, documenting archaeological discoveries since the 1920s, including a massive bear some believe to be 50,000 years old.

Take the road to Sarteano, and after 6km or so you'll reach the **Parco Archeologico Naturalistico di Belvedere**, with remains from one of the most important Bronze Age sites in Italy. On the approach to Sarteano, you can visit the 14th-century ex-convent of Santa Maria a Belvedere, now inhabited by the same community who run the up-market La Frateria di Padre Egidio (*see* 'Where to Stay and Eat', p.383), but also housing frescoes attributed to Petruccioli and Andrea di Giovanni.

The SS478 from Sarteano towards Monte Amiata passes one of the loneliest, most barren regions of *crete* en route to the Val d'Orcia (*see* p.372), while the road south from Cetona takes you on a beautiful, winding drive skirting Monte Cetona, punctuated with dramatic views as you pass through woods and olive groves towards **San Casciano dei Bagni**, a pretty spa town on the borders of Umbria and Lazio. There are a couple of ancient churches and a castle; the hot springs are just outside to the south. The resort's heyday was in the Renaissance, when Grand Duke Ferdinand built a villa there and developed the spa; the baths have been restored and the Medici villa transformed into a luxury hotel (*see* 'Where to Stay and Eat', p.383).

# Monte Amiata and Around

**Monte Amiata**, the rooftop of southern Tuscany, is an extinct volcanic massif with a central peak over a mile high (1,722m/5,649ft). With no real competition close by, it has become a skiing and hiking centre – the closest to Rome, and as such, popular in both summer and winter. The presence of Europe's second-largest mercury mine (a complex that has been putting dinner on the table for Abbadia San Salvatore since the Middle Ages) does not detract from area's natural beauty. The lower, uncultivated slopes are covered in chestnut and beech trees. Higher up, there are beautiful mature forests, where the leaves catch the early frosts and change colour marvellously in the autumn.

## Abbadia San Salvatore

A thousand years ago, you might have heard of this town, home of the most important monastic centre in Tuscany and a fair-sized city in its own right. History passed by **Abbadia San Salvatore** a long time ago; today it makes a modest living as a mountain resort, the gateway to Monte Amiata. Abbadia (pop. 7,900) appears modern at first, but just behind Viale Roma, a narrow gateway leads into the grey, quiet streets of the **medieval centre**. It isn't very large, and there are no buildings of particular interest, but it is as complete and unchanged as any medieval quarter in Tuscany. Note the symbols carved into many of the doorways: coats of arms, odd religious symbols (a snake, for example) or signs like a pair of scissors that declare the original owner was a tailor.

The **abbey church** is outside the centre, a few blocks north in Via del Monastero; in the Middle Ages it must have been open countryside. According to legend – there's even a document telling the story, dated the Ides of March, 742 – the Lombard King Rachis was on his way to attack Perugia when a vision of the Saviour appeared to him. Rachis not only founded the monastery, but retired to it as a monk. Historians consider the whole business a convenient fabrication, but by 1000, the abbey had achieved considerable wealth and influence, ruling over a large piece of territory and waging occasional wars with the Bishop of Chiusi. In 1036, the present church was begun, an excellent Romanesque work that may seem plain to us, but was undoubtedly one of the grandest sights in Tuscany when it was new.

# Getting Around

Don't try to get to Amiata by **train**; there's a 'Monte Amiata station' on an infrequent branch line from Siena, but it's really some 40km on the northern side of the massif, near Castiglione d'Orcia. It's much easier to get a **bus** from Siena, Chiusi or Grosseto. Buses stop on Viale Roma in the centre of Abbadia San Salvatore (tickets and timetables in the toy store behind the information booth); a few go daily to Buonconvento and Siena (79km/ 2½hrs), Montepulciano–Chiusi (48km/1½hrs); nine a day go from Abbadia to Arcidosso (25km/1hr) and Castel del Piano on the western side of Amiata.

Note that Arcidosso and the other towns on the west slope are in Grosseto province; almost all the buses there go on to Grosseto. There are also at least 2 daily ACOTRAL or SIRA buses that run through Castel del Piano, Arcidosso and Abbadia San Salvatore to Viterbo and on to Rome.

# Tourist Information

**Abbadia San Salvatore**: Via Adua 25, **t** 0577 775811, *info@amiata.turismo. toscana.it*.

**Castel del Piano**: Via G. Marconi 2, **t** 0564 951026.
**Arcidosso**: Piazza Castello 1, **t** 0564 968010.

# Sports and Activities

As one of the few good **skiing** areas close to Rome, Monte Amiata can be a busy place. The pistes begin almost at the summit; there are two chair lifts and 13 ski lifts. The 15 runs (the longest is 1,500m/4,900ft) are connected by paths through the forest. There are also ski schools (**t** 0577 789740 and **t** 0564 959004).

It's also perfect for **cross-country skiing** and **hiking**. A network of hiking trails has been marked as far as Castiglione d'Orcia. The tourist offices can give you a map: ask for the *Cartografia dei Sentieri*.

For snow news and information, call the tourist office in Abbadia San Salvatore, **t** 0577 775811.

# Where to Stay and Eat

**Monte Amiata** ✉ 53021
For skiing, there are pleasant facilities near the summit.
**★★★Rifugio Cantore**, at '*Secondo Rifugio 10*', along the road from Abbadia, **t** 0577 789704

Behind the twin-steepled façade, the church is surprisingly long; the eastern end has a raised chancel, leading to a series of arches over the altar and choir. Here frescoes by Nasino, an early 1700s artist, tell the story of King Rachis. His **crypt**, under the chancel, was the original 8th-century church. The proportions are thoroughly Byzantine, with stone vaulting and oddly carved columns and capitals, no two alike.

South of Abbadia San Salvatore, **Piancastagnaio** is a smaller mountain resort. It has a **castle** of the Aldobrandeschi, housing a small museum, a 17th-century palace and, as its name implies, lots of chestnut trees. Chestnuts and chestnut flour were once the staple food around Amiata; restaurants still occasionally offer chestnut polenta.

### Around Amiata

On the panoramic route around Amiata is **Seggiano**, 20km northwest of Abbadia, with its unusual 16th-century church with a square cupola, the Madonna della Carità. South another 7km is **Castel del Piano**, with an old centre, laid out in *belle époque* parks and boulevards. **Arcidosso**, another 4km south, is the largest town (pop. 4,500) on the Grosseto side of Amiata, with a stately Aldobrandeschi fortress, and one church outside the town, the triple-apsed Santa Maria in Lamula, begun in the 900s and redone in the 12th century.

(*moderate*). Stays open all year to cater for summer mountaineering.

***La Capannina**, Vette Amiata, **t** 0577 789713, **f** 0577 789777 (*moderate*). A cosy place, a little further up. The hotel restaurant is one of the best in the area; lots of dishes with mushrooms (including polenta, that northern Italian alternative to pasta that is also popular around here) and also stuffed pigeon. *Open 15 Dec–Easter, also June–mid-Sept and Oct weekends.*

## Abbadia San Salvatore ✉ 53021

Abbadia San Salvatore is popular, not just for winter skiing, but also as a cool summer retreat. There are a dozen or so hotels in town.

***Adriana**, Via Serdini 76, **t** 0577 778116, (*moderate*). A few blocks north of the centre.

**Relais San Lorenzo**, Loc. San Lorenzo, **t** 0577 785003 (*moderate*). A new hotel/restaurant in an old building on the slopes of Monte Amiata in a wonderful setting, with ample grounds. Eighteen rooms and apartments, all comfortably furnished and with fridges, plus the usual 3-star amenities. The restaurant serves excellent local food.

****San Marco**, Via Matteotti 19, **t/f** 0577 778089 (*moderate–inexpensive*). Newer, with a restaurant serving a *menu fisso* (*cheap*).

## Arcidosso ✉ 58031

An excellent base for Amiata; there are several good modern hotels, many at bargain rates.

***Aiuole**, Loc. Aiuole, **t** 0564 967300 (*moderate*). The restaurant here specializes in porcini mushroom soup, but also other sturdy dishes and excellent local cheeses. *Closed Mon in winter*.

## Castel del Piano ✉ 58033

There are a couple of further options a few kilometres from Arcidosso.

***Contessa**, at Prato della Contessa, **t** 0564 959000, *www.hotelcontessa.it* (*moderate*). This hotel is in a lovely setting above town on the slopes of Monte Amiata and organizes nature walks, cultural tours and more. The restaurant, which is also good, lays on special seasonal menus.

**Albergo Ristorante Silene**, Località Pescina 9, **t** 0564 950805 (*expensive*). Silene has been serving food (and providing a bed – six nice rooms, *moderate*) since 1830. The regularly changing menu features seasonal local produce, offering dishes such as *taglierini* with wild asparagus, *gnocchetti* with truffles and wild boar stew spiked with juniper. The hot chocolate soufflé is divine.

The town is best known, however, for the strange career of David Lazzaretti, a millenarian prophet gunned down by the Carabinieri during a disturbance in 1878. People in this area still talk about Lazzaretti; his movement, combining reformed religion and plain rural socialism (in an age when land reform was Italy's biggest social issue), spread widely in southern Tuscany. Before Lazzaretti's murder, his followers had started to create a sort of commune on **Monte Labbro**, 10km to the south. The tower, bits of buildings and remains of the church they built on Monte Labbro still stand, and a few of the faithful occasionally hold 'Giurisdavidical' services there.

**Roccalbegna**, 20km south on the SS323, has another Aldobrandeschi castle, and some Sienese art in SS. Pietro e Paolo and the nearby Oratorio del Crocifisso. For a landmark Roccalbegna has one very conspicuous rock, a bizarre conical mass looming over the village called simply 'La Pietra'. The Aldobrandeschi also built at **Santa Fiora**, a pleasant town 7.5km south, with della Robbia terracottas in its three churches. Just south of Arcidosso, on the northern slopes of Monte Labbro, is a nature reserve, the **Parco Faunistico del Monte Amiata** (*open Tues–Sun dawn–sunset; t 0564 966867*). Hiking trails offer a look at various kinds of deer, mountain goats, and maybe wolves – there is a project to reintroduce these here.

Amiata's summit, decorated with the obligatory iron crucifix (made in the Victorian foundries of Follonica, like the bandstands and even some of the fountains you will see locally), lies about halfway between Abbadia and Arcidosso; roads reach almost to the top. The skiing area is here, too, at the point called **Vetta Amiata**.

# The Lost Corner of Tuscany

Only a true connoisseur of regional obscurity would appreciate the inland reaches of Grosseto province, the largest stretch of territory in Italy north of the Abruzzo without a single well-known attraction. Once part of the Etruscan heartland, these towns have been poor and usually misgoverned ever since – by the Romans, the noble Aldobrandeschi, the popes and the Tuscan dukes. Some don't even consider the area part of Tuscany, and it's true that in many ways, it has more in common with the haunted, empty expanses of northern Lazio across the border.

## Sorano

Southeast 20km from Santa Fiora, **Castell'Azzara** takes its name from a medieval game of dice (the word similar to our *hazard*); one of the Aldobrandeschi won it in a crap shoot. **Sorano**, a grim, grey town to the south, clings tenaciously to its rock, almost hidden between two deep and lovely wooded canyons. Bits of the town have been crumbling down into the surrounding valleys for centuries; many houses were destroyed in a landslide 80 years ago. It is still inhabited, though more houses have been abandoned as younger people move away to find work. Sorano is dominated by two equally grim castles; the larger is the 15th-century **Rocca degli Orsini**. Outside town on the road to Sovana is a strange natural rock formation called the **Mano di Orlando**, the 'Hand of Roland'.

## Sovana and the Vie Cave

**Sovana**, 10km to the west, with a population of about 190, is another medieval time capsule, a town almost perfectly preserved in its 13th- or 14th-century appearance, perched dramatically on a ridge overlooking the surrounding countryside. Sovana was an important Etruscan city, and in the 11th century it thrived as the family headquarters of the Aldobrandeschi. This powerful clan, controlling much of southern Tuscany and northern Lazio, had a political role on a European level. The zenith of its influence came with the election to the papacy of one of its members in 1073. Gregory VII (his common name *Hildebrand* betrays the Aldobrandeschi's Teutonic origins) made a great reforming pope, but he also took care of the family interests.

On Sovana's humble main street, the Via di Mezzo, you can see the 13th-century Palazzo del Pretorio, with only a clock and *bifore* windows to betray its civic dignity. There is some interesting early Christian and medieval sculpture preserved in the 12th-century church of **Santa Maria** in the village centre, including a remarkable 9th-century *ciborium* in bold barbaric arabesques and floral motifs, along with Renaissance frescoes. The **Duomo**, just outside the village, has an octagonal dome

# Tourist Information

**Sorano**: Piazza Busatti 8, t/f 0564 633099.
**Pitigliano**: Piazza Garibaldi 51, off the main
piazza, t/f 0564 617111.
**Saturnia**: in the old town, Piazza Vittorio
Veneto 8, t 0564 601280, f 0564 601257.
**Manciano**: Via Marsala, t 0564 620532, f 0564
621877. *Winter open Fri–Sun only*.

# Where to Stay and Eat

Real pioneers will be able to find reasonable
accommodation and good food throughout.
The region produces some good but
little-known wines, notably Morellino di
Scansano, a severe dry variety with a beautiful
deep red colour, and also a delicious, crisp
Bianco di Pitigliano.

## Pitigliano ✉ 58017

**\*\*Corano**, Loc. Corano on the SS74,
t/f 0564 616112 (*moderate*). Just outside
Pitigliano, with 35 modern rooms and also a
swimming pool.
**Il Tufo Allegro**, Vicolo della Costituzione, t 0564
616192 (*moderate*). A wonderful restaurant
in a great setting carved out of tufa. The menu
is seasonal: in winter hearty dishes include
rabbit stewed in locally made Morellino or
*pappardelle* with lamb and artichoke sauce;
in summer *tagliolini* with marinated vegetables. There's a good wine list, too. *Closed Tues*.
**\*\*Guastini** on Piazza Petruccioli 4,
t 0564 616065, f 0564 616652 (*moderate–
inexpensive*). Central, with a restaurant
(*inexpensive*) specializing in home-made
pasta, Bianco di Pitigliano wine and
'Etruscan-style' dishes like *buglione
d'agnello*; well worth the price.
**Trattoria dell'Orso**, Piazza San Gregorio, t 0564
614273 (*cheap*). Offers a wide range of the
local *cucina tipica*: tagliatelle with truffles,
boar *alla cacciatora*, and plenty of roast
meats and an excellent-value menu, well
within the cheap range for *à la carte*.

## Sovana ✉ 58010

**\*Scilla**, Via del Duomo 5, t 0564 616531, f 0564
614329 (*moderate*). Also a restaurant
(*moderate*) with terrace, serving ravioli with
ricotta and asparagus, pork with porcini
mushrooms and thyme, and delicious local
cheeses. *Closed Tues*.
**Hotel della Fortezza**, Piazza Cairoli, t 0564
632010, f 0564 632012, *www.fortezzahotel.it*
(*moderate*). Partly occupies the 11th-century
Orsini fortress on the edge of the town.
Antique-filled rooms with fabulous views.
**\*\*\*Taverna Etrusca**, Piazza Pretorio,
t 0564 616183, f 0564 614193 (*moderate*).
Soak up the ambience of the Dark Ages in
this square, sampling roast boar and the
other south Tuscan favourites. Seven newly
renovated rooms upstairs.

## Saturnia ✉ 58050

Saturnia has plenty of accommodation.
**\*\*\*\*Hotel Terme di Saturnia**, Strada
Provinciale della Follonata, t 0564 601061,
f 0564 601266 (*luxury*). The best in town,
and very popular. The restaurant (*moderate*)
merits a visit with fresh seafood, including a
good *risotto marinaro*, besides game dishes
like quail with olives.
**Villa Clodia**, Via Italia 43, t 0564 601212,
f 0564 620013, *www.laltramaremma.it*
(*moderate*). A friendly little place with its
pleasant rooms and great views.
**Locanda Laudomia**, Poderi di Montemerano,
7km south of Saturnia, t 0564 620062,
f 0564 620013 (*inexpensive*). Peace and quiet
in the countryside, with 12 pretty bedrooms
offering lovely views. Its restaurant, over
the road, is good.

## Montemerano ✉ 58050

**Da Caino**, Via Canonica 3, t 0564 602817, f 0564
602807 (*very expensive*). An elegant restaurant
for a small village, where the menu varies
regularly according to the availability of
fresh ingredients. *Closed Thurs lunch and
Wed in winter; open daily in summer*.

from the 900s, a crypt 200 years older, and some sculptural work on the façade that
may have been recycled from a pagan temple.

The **Vie Cave**, which you will see signposted all around this area, are sacred ways of
the Etruscans, carved for part of their length out of the *tufa* and often lined with

tombs. In many cases, they follow modern roads, as with the pretty road from Sovana to Saturnia. Here you can stop to see the **Tomba della Sirena**, where the pediment is carved with a much-eroded fork-tailed mermaid – possibly the original of the mermaids on the Pieve di Corsignano and elsewhere around Tuscany.

Not far from here is the 3rd-century BC **Tomba Ildebranda**. This elaborate tomb once had the façade of a Greek temple, though little of the colonnade survives. It resembles the rock-cut tombs of the same era common in Lycia, on the south coast of Turkey, built by people who may have been the Etruscans' cultural cousins.

## Pitigliano

Just 8km away is **Pitigliano**, another ominous-looking place that could be Sorano's twin. It makes a memorable sight, perched along the edges of the cliffs; underneath are countless holes in the cliff faces that were once Etruscan tombs, now used as stables or storehouses. Once inside, you'll find the hill town itself as attractive as any of the better-known ones further north. Piazza della Repubblica has a big fountain and the 14th-century **Palazzo Orsini**, stronghold of the powerful Roman family that aced the Aldobrandeschi out of many of their holdings in south Tuscany. The castle has a small **museum** of Etruscan finds, and an analemmic sundial with a Latin inscription reminding us the hours are 'for work, not for play'.

Pitigliano has a picturesque medieval centre, and a 16th-century **aqueduct**, running across Via Cavour. The alleys around Vicolo Manin, where parts of **synagogue** still stand, were once Pitigliano's **Jewish ghetto** (*open summer Sun–Fri 10–12 and 4–6.30; winter mornings and some afternoons, check with tourist office*); the centuries-old Jewish community was decimated in 1945. Other Jewish relics can be visited on the International Day of Jewish Culture, usually the first Sunday in September. On the cliffs underneath the town, along the road for Sovana, is a Christian **cave chapel** (*c*. 400 AD). They claim it's the oldest in Italy.

## Saturnia

Little **Saturnia**, 25km west of Sovana, sits all alone above the Val d'Albegna. One of the most ancient centres in Italy, it claims to be the first city ever founded there – by the god Saturn himself, in the Golden Age. This attractive hill town, was originally Roman, but fragments of pre-Etruscan walls can be seen, and aerial photography has discerned traces of an older city beneath the Roman level. There are hot springs in the neighbourhood, still in use; ruins are everywhere, including an Etruscan necropolis to the north, and **Poggio Buco** on the road to Pitigliano.

To the west on SS323, the walled city of **Magliano in Toscana** has a Sienese-style Palazzo dei Priori, and the church of San Giovanni Battista, with a Renaissance façade. Its best-known attraction is the **Ulivo della Strega** (the witch's olive tree), a gnarled tree over 1,000 years old, said to be the site of ritual dances in pagan days, and still haunted today. The tree is just outside the Porta San Giovanni, near the Romanesque **Annunziata** church, containing Sienese frescoes. About 2km southeast, on the Marsiliana road, are the ruins of the 12th-century abbey of **San Bruzio**.

# Arezzo and its Province

# Arezzo Province

Florence

**N** 10 km — 5 miles

EMILIA ROMAGNA

MARCHES

TUSCANY

Siena

UMBRIA

Perugia

p.186

To Orvieto

*Lago Trasimeno* p.366

## Highlights

1 Medieval mountain villages of the Casentino
2 La Verna: St Francis' rugged hermitage
3 Piero della Francesca's masterpiece frescoes in San Francesco, Arezzo
4 The surprising Renaissance art town of Cortona

Between Florence and Umbria lies a lovely region of nature and art, most of which is included in the province of Arezzo. Watered by the newly born Arno and Tiber rivers (which at one point flow within a mere 15 kilometres of each other), it occupies a keystone position in Italy, not only geographically but as amazingly fertile ground for 'key' Italians: Masaccio and Cosimo Il Vecchio's humanist Greek scholar and magician, Marsilio Ficino, were born in the Arno Valley; Petrarch, Michelangelo,

Piero della Francesca, Paolo Uccello, Luca Signorelli, Andrea Sansovino, Vasari, the great satirist Aretino, Guido Monaco (inventor of the musical scale), Pietro da Cortona and the Futurist Gino Severini were born in Arezzo or its province. Because of its strategic location battlefields and castles dot the countryside, yet here, too, is St Francis's holy mountain of La Verna, where he received the stigmata.

There are two possible routes between Florence and Arezzo: the quick one, following the trains and Autostrada del Sole down the Valdarno, or the scenic route, through the Passo della Consuma or Vallombrosa, taking in the beautifully forested areas of Pratomagno and the Casentino.

# The Valdarno and Casentino

## Florence to Arezzo

If a Tuscan caveman ever yearned for the ideal Neolithic home, he would have wanted to live in what is now the Arno Valley. In the Pliocene Age, the valley was a lake, a popular resort of ancient elephants, and farmers are not surprised when their ploughs collide with fossils. The typically Tuscan towns of the Valdarno, however, are hardly fossilized. On the contrary, it is a highly industrialized region: lignite and felt hats are stand out in particular, but new factories and power lines seem to be going up all the time.

Besides the *autostrada*, the main valley routes are the old SS69, and the beautiful 'Strada dei Sette Ponti', following the old Etruscan road of 'Seven Bridges' from Saltino by Vallombrosa to Castiglion Fibocchi, along what was once the upper shore of the ancient lake, between the Valdarno and the Pratomagno ridge. Along it are areas strikingly eroded into pyramids, around Pian di Scò and Castelfranco. By public transport the Valdarno's peripheral attractions are harder to reach; buses from Arezzo to Loro Ciuffenna and Castelfranco di Sopra take in much of the Strada dei Sette Ponti.

The most scenic route from Florence to the Valdarno follows the A1 down to Incisa (23km), although it's worth turning west at Torre a Cona for **Rignano sull'Arno**, with sculptures by Mino da Fiesole and Bernardino Rossellino in the church of San Clemente, and for **Sanmezzano** (2km across the Arno). Here a medieval castle was converted into a Medici villa and in the 19th century purchased by the Ximenes d'Aragona family, who gave it a Spanish-Moorish fantasy facelift. Down river, at **Incisa Valdarno**, Petrarch spent his childhood. There's an old bridge off which, the Italians claim, Lucrezia Borgia jumped in 1529, fleeing the Prince of Orange, despite the fact that she had died in childbirth 10 years earlier.

**Figline Valdarno** (pop. 15,000), 5km south, was in 1439, the birthplace of Ficino. The historic centre has preserved much of its character: the loggia of the old Serristori Hospital, the Palazzo Pretorio, and the **Collegiata di Santa Maria**, containing among its works of art a beautiful painting of the *Madonna with Child and Angels* by the 14th-century 'Maestro di Figline' and a fresco by the school of Botticelli.

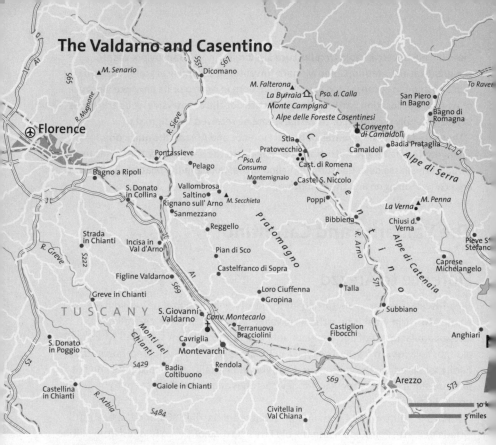

## San Giovanni Valdarno

If you're only planning one stop within the Valdarno, **San Giovanni** (pop. 19,500), although one of the most industrial towns in the region, is also one of the most interesting. The Florentines fortified it in the 13th century against the warlike Aretini and sent Arnolfo di Cambio to lay out the streets and fortifications, and to design the handsome arcaded **Palazzo Comunale**; its arches are echoed by the buildings on to the piazza and are covered with escutcheons left by Florentine governors.

The oft-restored **Basilica di Santa Maria delle Grazie** (1486) has a rich 17th-century interior, though most paintings have been removed to the adjacent **Museo della Basilica** (*open summer 10.30–12.30 and 4–7; winter 10.30–12.30 and 3.30–6.30; closed Sun am and Wed; adm*): a *Madonna, Child and Four Saints*, attributed to Masaccio (1401–28), an *Annunciation* by Jacopo di Sellaio, Baroque paintings by Giovanni di San Giovanni (born here, 1592–1636), and a fresco of a local miracle, in which a grandmother is suddenly able to give milk to her starving grandchild (14th century). Best of all is Fra Angelico's *Annunciation*, in deep, rich colours, seemingly a model for the *Annunciation* in Florence's San Marco, though here Adam and Eve are off to the left, fleeing the Garden of Eden. Earlier frescoes adorn the Gothic church of **San Lorenzo**.

Some 2.5km south of San Giovanni is the Renaissance **Convento di Montecarlo**. From here the road continues up to the Monti del Chianti by way of **Cavriglia**; the hills around are scarred with open lignite mines. Cavriglia is also a natural park, where modern deer and buffalo roam with other animals from around the world.

The Valdarno also offers a look at older species of animal, especially the *elephas meridionalis* in the **Museo Paleontologico** (*open Tues–Sat 9–12.30 and 4–6, Sun 10–12; adm*) in **Montevarchi**. Montevarchi is a major marketing centre of the region, famous for hats and chickens; in its ancient core, you can trace the oval medieval street plan. In the centre stands the old **Collegiata di San Lorenzo**, which had a complete facelift in the 18th century. Within it is an unusual reliquary 'of the holy milk', brought from a cave in the Holy Land where the Holy Family is said to have rested and where a fountain of milky water flows; a small museum holds a quattrocento **Tempietto** covered inside and out with Andrea della Robbia's cherub friezes. Across the Arno, **Terranuova Bracciolini** is an old Aretine fortress town, its walls still standing.

# Tourist Information

**San Giovanni Valdarno**: Palazzo d'Arnolfo, Piazza Cavour 1, **t** 055 9121123.

# Where to Stay and Eat

**Figline Valdarno** ✉ 50063
★★★**Hotel Masaccio**, **t** 055 954 4851, **f** 055 954 4322, *www.hotelmasaccio.it* (*inexpensive*). Changed hands and totally refurbished in April 2004. Thirteen rooms and a garden cater for a comfortable stay.

**San Giovanni Valdarno** ✉ 52027
★★★**La Bianca**, Viale Don Minzoni 38, **t** 055 912 3402 (*moderate*). San Giovanni doesn't get many tourists, so accommodation is limited. However this will provide an agreeable stay.
**Adriano**, Piazza Masaccio 15, **t** 055 912 2470 (*moderate*). A tiny place where you can dine well on the local stew, called *stufato alla sangiovannese*, or home-grown roast chicken, home-made desserts, and wines from across Tuscany.
**Da Giovanni**, Piazza della Libertà 24, **t** 055 912 2726 (*cheap*). A family-run place with typical Tuscan fare. *Closed Wed*.

**Montevarchi** ✉ 52025
**L'Osteria di Rendola**, Via di Rendola, Loc. Rendola, **t** 055 970 7491 (*expensive*). A wonderful restaurant, serving creative Tuscan dishes such as marinated salmon with fennel risotto with pumpkin and

saffron and scampi chicken stuffed with artichokes. There is also an interesting wine list. The *agriturismo* next door offers horse-riding. *Closed Thurs lunch, Wed*.
★★★**Delta**, Via Diaz 137, **t** 055 901213, **f** 055 901727, *www.hoteldelta.it* (*moderate*). The best that Montevarchi has to offer, complete with a garage, air conditioning and TV in all the bedrooms.

**Terranuova Bracciolini** ✉ 52028
**Il Canto del Maggio**, Loc. Penna Alta, near Loro Ciuffenna, **t** 055 970 5147 (*moderate*). This delightful restaurant occupies a stone village house with a pretty garden, in the tiny hamlet of Penna Alta. Adjacent buildings house a number of apartments to let and a wine bar. The menu is based on local dishes using fresh ingredients; *gnudi* (spinach and ricotta gnocchi) with truffles, *papardelle* with hare sauce, wild boar stew and good, local steaks. Desserts are delicious, too. Meals are served under the olive trees in summer. *Closed Mon; Oct–May also Tues. Open for dinner Tues–Sat, Sun also lunch*.
**Hosteria Costachiara**, Via Santa Maria 129, **t** 055 944318 (*moderate*). Follow the signs from the Valdarno *autostrada* exit, and you will come upon this wonderful, family-run country restaurant, well worth the detour. A table laden with help-yourself *antipasti* provides a tempting start to any meal, but so do the *pici* with guinea fowl sauce or *pappardelle* with wild boar. Follow this with roast meats or quail cooked in wine. There are also a few pleasant rooms for rent. *Closed Mon eve and Tues*.

## Along the Road of Seven Bridges

East of the Arno, the panoramic Strada dei Sette Ponti passes several medieval towns en route to Arezzo. **Reggello** (8km east of Sanmezzano) stands amid its famous olive groves; some streets retain their medieval arcades, and the 12th-century parish church of **San Pietro a Cascia** has good, early Romanesque columns with carved capitals depicting lively scenes. **Castelfranco di Sopra**, 12km south, was another Florentine military town laid out by Arnolfo di Cambio, and to the north at **Pulicciano** the landscape is eroded into pyramidical forms, or *balze*, like those at Volterra. **Loro Ciuffenna** offers some picturesque medieval corners, a Romanesque bridge and tower, and a triptych by Lorenzo di Bicci in **Santa Maria Assunta**.

Best of all is the tiny 12th-century parish church of **Gropina** (from the Etruscan *Kropina*), 2km away, an excellent example of rural Romanesque. Although it was referred to in the 8th century, the current church was built in the early 1200s. Dominated by its huge campanile, the façade is simplicity itself, while the three naves and little semicircular apse have never been altered. The columns are carved with primitive tigers, eagles, etc., while the round marble **pulpit** is a bizarre relic of the Dark Ages, carved with archaic figures raising their arms over a marble knot; over them is a kind of totem pole, geometrical and floral decorations, and a sexy siren with a snake whispering in her ear. **Castiglion Fibocchi**, 13km from Arezzo, is another typical town where little has changed, except for the industry on its outskirts.

# The Pratomagno and Vallombrosa

The Strada dei Sette Ponti skirts the west of the **Pratomagno**, a wrinkled, forested mountain ridge. Its highest peak, Croce di Pratomagno (1,592m/5,222ft), is due north of Loro Ciuffenna; winding roads from Loro go through tiny mountain hamlets, while the Loro–Talla route crosses over into the Casentino.

Further to the north, the two routes from Florence into the Casentino, both take in fine, wooded scenery. The SS70 over the **Passo della Consuma** (1,025m/3,362ft) is a favourite Italian rest stop; the secondary route passes through **Vallombrosa**, famous for its abbey founded by San Giovanni Gualberto of Florence, and headquarters of his Vallombrosan order. The abbey has undergone several remodellings in the 15th and 17th centuries and is mainly of interest for its splendid position. **Saltino**, 1km away, is a small summer resort, an excellent base for a walk or a drive. One of the most beautiful routes leads up to the Monte Secchieta (1,449m/4,753ft), with views over most of north-central Italy; in the winter, the skiing facilities spring into action. For a longer outing, follow the **Panoramica del Pratomagno**, which crosses nearly the entire Pratomagno to join the Strada dei Sette Ponti near Castiglion Fibocchi.

# The Casentino: North to South

The Casentino's blue mountains, pastoral meadows and velvet valleys have long been Tuscany's spiritual refuge. Since the 18th century, travellers have trickled into the area, attracted initially by its famous monasteries, then charmed by one of the loveliest and most peaceful regions in Tuscany.

The Arno, such a turgid, unmannerly creature in its lower reaches ('the emblem of Despair', Norman Douglas once called it), is a fair, sparkling youth near its source at

## Getting Around

A **car** is the only way of conveniently seeing the sights, but in the Casentino you might enjoy getting around on the LFI narrow-gauge **rail** line that passes through Stia, Poppi and Bibbiena on its way to Arezzo.

## Tourist Information

**Stia**: Pro Loco, Piazza Tanucci 65, **t** 0575 504106 **f** 0575 581122.
**Badia Prataglia**: Piazza 13 Aprile, **t** 0575 559054.
**Bibbiena**: Via Berni 25, **t** 0575 593098.

## Where to Stay and Eat

**Stia** ✉ 52017
**★★★ Albergo Falterona**, Piazza Tanucci 85, **t** 0575 504982, *www.casentino.net/ falterona* (*moderate*). In the *centro storico*, recently renovated in an upmarket rustic style; 15 rooms, one adorned with pretty frescoes.
**★★La Foresta**, Via Roma 27, **t** 0575 504650 (*inexpensive*). Basic but comfortable.
**Ristorante Filetto**, Piazza Tanucci 28, **t** 0575 583631 (*cheap*). Offers *pappardelle* with wild boar and other hearty fare.

**Poppi** ✉ 52010
**★★★Casentino**, Piazza Repubblica, **t** 0575 529090, *www.albergocasentino.it* (*moderate*). Recently revamped and upgraded, and right opposite the castle. The popular restaurant offers tortellini, ravioli, game, truffles and mushrooms.
**★★★Il Rustichello**, Via del Corniolo 14, **t/f** 0575 556 046 (*moderate–inexpensive*). A small modern resort hotel, a great place to bring the kids. with tennis, mini golf and walks in the woods. The restaurant (*moderate*) serves great pasta dishes from

Emilia-Romagna, grilled meats and Casentino cheeses.
**★★Campaldino**, Via Roma 95, **t** 0575 529008, **f** 0575 529032 (*moderate–inexpensive*). An inn at Ponte a Poppi, established in 1800, offering 10 simple guest rooms. The restaurant (*cheap*) offers tasty local prosciutto, ravioli stuffed with vegetables and ricotta, or succulent lamb and chicken, and for dessert, home-made *semifreddi* and *biscotti*.

**Pratovecchio** ✉ 52015
**La Tana degli Orsi**, Via Roma 1, **t** 0575 583377 (*moderate*). This restaurant/*enoteca* (The Bears' Den) is one of the more interesting places to eat and drink in this remote area. You can enjoy a bottle of wine (chosen from some 600 labels from all over Italy) and a snack, or pick from the restaurant menu, where imaginative variations on local dishes are on offer: pear and pecorino flan, potato *tortelli* with black truffles, venison or rabbit cooked with blackcurrants and porcini. Leave room for delicious home-made desserts. *Closed lunch and Wed.*

**Camaldoli** ✉ 52010
**★La Foresta**, **t** 0575 556015 (*moderate*). This simple hotel/restaurant is stuck in a time warp. The spartan bedrooms have their original wood-panelled ceilings and rustic wood floors while the furniture is of rickety 1930s vintage. The restaurant serves up wholesome local food. Half-board only.

**Passo della Consuma**
**★★★Miramonti**, **t** 055 830 6566 (*inexpensive*). This modern hotel enjoys a spectacular setting and long views at the top of the Passo della Consuma (1,058m/3,480ft above sea level). Bedrooms are functional, but the grounds are lovely and there is a tennis court. The restaurant (*moderate*) is a popular truck stop, serving vast portions of local fare such as *pappardelle* with venison sauce and huge steaks.

**Monte Falterona** (1,658m/5,438ft); one of the classic excursions is to take the trail up and spend the night, to witness the sunset over the Tyrrhenian Sea and dawn over the Adriatic. **Stia** (pop. 3,000), the first town the Arno meets, is pretty and medieval, centred about large porticoed Piazza Tanucci and **Santa Maria Assunta**. The 17th-century façade hides a fine Romanesque interior, with some curious primitive capitals, a triptych by Lorenzo di Bicci and a Madonna by Andrea della Robbia. Wool – the thick, heavy, brightly coloured *lana del Casentino* – is the main industry; in the old days, Stia was the market for the Guidi counts, whose ruined **Castello di Porciano** (*open mid-May– mid-Oct Sun 10–12 and 4–7; call* **t** *0575 582626 to visit out of season; adm*) guarded the narrow Arno Valley from the 10th century. Near this (4km north of Stia) is the **Sanctuary of Santa Maria delle Grazie**, a 14th-century church containing frescoes, works attributed to Luca della Robbia, and a painting by Lorenzo di Niccolò Gerini. This road continues into the Mugello (*see* p.199), while the SS310 from Stia skirts Monte Falterona towards the **Passo la Calla** and Emilia-Romagna. Near the pass, the alpine pasture **Burraia** (15km from Stia) is ideal for a cool summer picnic.

Down the Arno, **Pratovecchio** was the birthplace of Paolo Uccello in 1397 and he would still recognize its narrow, porticoed lanes. Just 2km from the centre is the most beautiful Romanesque church of the Casentino, **Pieve di Romena**, founded in 1152, which has retained its original lines in spite of several earthquakes and subsequent repairs (*to visit, call the custodian in advance* **t** *0575 583725*). The façade is plain, but the apse has two tiers of blind arcades, pierced by narrow windows. Inside, the capitals are decorated with a medieval menagerie. Among the works of art, dating back to the 1200s, is a Madonna by the Maestro di Varlungo. Nearby, the Guidi's **Castello di Romena** was one of the most powerful in the Casentino, with three sets of walls and 14 towers (now reduced to three), and wide-ranging views. It now houses a small archaeological museum and armour collection (*to visit, call* **t** *0575 582520; adm*). Dante mentioned it in the *Inferno*, and the **Fonte Branda**, the ruins of which are close by.

Dante knew this region well; at 24, he fought with the Guelphs against the Ghibellines of Arezzo and their allies at the **Battle of Campaldino** (1289), just south of Pratovecchio. The victory made Florence the leading power in Tuscany, and from there, she went on to conquer Pisa and Arezzo. A column commemorating the battle was erected near the crossroads in 1921. At the head of the plain, just off the SS70, Countess Matilda's **Castel San Nicolò**, the wee medieval hamlet of **Strada** and its little Romanesque church form a picturesque ensemble in the wooded hills.

## Poppi and Camaldoli

Between 1000 and 1440, the Casentino was ruled by the Counts Guidi, whose headquarters were at **Poppi** (pop. 5,700). From miles around, you can see their stalwart **Castello** (*open Nov–mid-Mar Thurs–Sun 10–5; mid-Mar–June daily 10–6; July–Oct daily 10–7; adm*), modelled on the Palazzo Vecchio in Florence. The best-preserved medieval castle in the region, it has a magnificent courtyard and stairs that zigzag to and fro with a touch of Piranesi. If you ask, the custodian will show you the grand hall with Florentine frescoes of the 1400s, the chapel with frescoes by Taddeo Gaddi, restored about 10 years ago, and the commanding views from the tower.

The centre of Poppi has ancient porticoed lanes, winding around a small domed chapel; at the end of the main street is the Romanesque church of **San Fedele**, with a 13th-century *Madonna and Child*. Shops selling locally made copperware line the main street of lower Poppi, and there's the little **Zoo Fauna Europea** for the kids.

A beautiful road runs northeast through the Forest of Camaldoli, part of the Parco Nazionale delle Foreste Casentinesi, with a huge variety of trees, wild deer and ideal for walking. The road leads to the hermitage and monastery of **Camaldoli**, founded in 1012 by St Romualdo, a Benedictine monk. He was given this forest by Count Maldolo (hence 'Camaldoli') to found a community of hermits, similar to those of the early Christians. A conflict soon arose, for the piety of the hermits soon attracted pilgrims and visitors who interfered with their solitary meditations. Romualdo's solution was ingenious: he founded another monastery lower down, with a more relaxed rule, to entertain visitors and care for the forest domains. The Camaldolese are self-sufficient vegetarians whose rule orders them to plant at least 5,000 new trees every year. Little remains of San Romualdo's original foundation, except for portions of the 11th-century cloister, the rich library and the 16th-century pharmacy, where the monks sell their balsams, herbal remedies and liqueurs. Part of the monastery is now a *foresteria*, providing accommodation in simple rooms; you can also eat here (*call t 0575 556013 for information*). Some 3km further up, a beautiful hour's walk, is the **Eremo**, with its 20 cottages set in an amphitheatre of pines, each with its own chapel and walled kitchen garden, where the hermits live in silence and solitude, meeting only on certain feast days and in the church, which was decorated inside by Vasari and has two marble tabernacles by Desiderio da Settignano. The church and St Romualdo's cell are open to visitors, but you may not go past the gate to the hermits' cottages.

**Badia Prataglia**, 10km from Camaldoli, is the region's most popular secular retreat, a summer resort spread out among the trees and hills, with beautiful walks along streams and waterfalls leading off in all directions.

## Bibbiena and La Verna

As chief town of the modern Casentino, **Bibbiena** has been enveloped in sprawl and lacks Poppi's quaint charm, though in its heart it retains its old Tuscan feel. Few buildings stand out – a good Renaissance palace, **Palazzo Dovizi**, and the church of **San Lorenzo**, where there are some excellent polychrome terracottas by Andrea della Robbia. From Bibbiena, the SS208 crosses east over into a range of hills bravely called the Alpe di Catenaia, which divides the Arno from the Tiber Valley, to the famous Franciscan monastery of **La Verna**, high up on a bizarre rocky outcrop, which, according to one of St Francis's visions, had been rent and blasted into its wild shape at the moment of the Crucifixion. The land was given to Francis in 1213 by another pious nobleman, Count Orlando, and the saint at once built some mud huts here for a select group of his followers. He found La Verna a perfect spot for meditation and came to his holy mountain on six occasions. During the last, on 14 September 1224, he became the first person ever to receive the stigmata – an event pictured in the frescoes of Assisi and elsewhere – after which he could only walk in extreme pain.

The churches, chapels and convent at La Verna are simple and rustic, though the main church, the chapel of Stigmata and St Francis's tiny church of **Santa Maria degli Angeli** are decorated by the most transcendently beautiful blue, green and white terracottas that Andrea della Robbia ever made, especially the *Annunciation*. You can also visit the **Sasso Spicco**, Francis's favourite retreat under a huge boulder, and **La Penna** (1,283m/4,208ft), on a sheer precipice, with views of the Arno and Tiber valleys.

# Arezzo

Strategically located on a hill at the convergence of the Valdarno, Casentino and the Valdichiana valleys, ancient **Arezzo** (pop. 92,000) was one of the richest cities of the Etruscan Dodecapolis. Nor is modern Arezzo a loser in the money game – it has one of the biggest jewellery industries in Europe, with hundreds of small firms stamping out gold chains and rings, and bank vaults full of ingots. Its second most notable industry, one that fills the shops around its main Piazza Grande, is furniture-making and marketing antiques; on the first weekend of each month, the entire square becomes an enormous antique curiosity shop.

Arezzo is a bit of a curiosity shop itself. It had only a brief, though remarkable, bask in the Renaissance sunshine, although in the Middle Ages, it was a typical free *comune*, a Ghibelline rival to Florence and a city of great cultural distinction. Around the year 1000, it gave birth to Guido Monaco (or Guido d'Arezzo), inventor of musical notation and the musical scale; in the 13th century, it produced Margarito, or Margaritone, an important painter in the transition from the Byzantine to the Italian styles. In 1304 Petrarch, the 'first modern man', was born here into a banished Florentine Black Guelph family; his Arezzo contemporary was Spinello Aretino, one of Tuscany's trecento masters. Arezzo was at its most powerful in the early 1300s, when it was ruled by a remarkable series of warrior bishops. One died in the Battle of Campaldino; another, the fierce Guido Tarlati, ruled the city from 1312 to 1327. He expanded its territory, built new walls, settled internal bickerings, renewed warfare with Florence and Siena, and was excommunicated. After Bishop Guido came the deluge – his brother sold the city for a brief period to Florence, family rivalries exploded, the plague carried away half the population and, to top it all, in 1384 the French troops of Louis d'Anjou sacked the city and brought it to its knees, refusing to move on until Arezzo paid 40,000 florins. Florence came up with the ransom money, and in effect purchased Arezzo's independence. Although henceforth an economic backwater, on the fringe of the Renaissance, it managed to produce two leading personalities: Giorgio Vasari and Pietro Aretino, the uninhibited writer and poet whose celebrated poison pen allowed him to make a fortune by *not* writing about contemporary princes and popes – the most genteel extortionist of all time.

## San Francesco

If you arrive by train or bus, Via Guido Monaco leads up to the old centre of Arezzo by way of a stern statue of musical monk Guido, and passes on the left one of Italy's prettiest post offices, with an ornate ceiling, before ending in Piazza San Francesco, site of **San Francesco** (*call* **t** *0575 900404 or see www.pierodellafrancesca.it for details; open winter Mon–Fri 9–5.30, Sat 9–5, Sun 1–5.30; summer Mon–Fri 9–7, Sat 9–6, Sun 1–6*). This dowdy barn of a Franciscan church contains Arezzo's star attraction: Piero della Francesca's frescoes on the popular pseudo-classical/Christian subject of the Legend of the True Cross (*see* **Florence**, p.165), the most riveting cycle of frescoes of the 1400s and the gospel of Renaissance painting. Piero literally wrote the book on the new science of artificial perspective, and yet as strictly as these frescoes obey the dictates of the vanishing point they make no concessions to realism; simplified and drawn with geometrical perfection, Piero's beings are purely spiritual creatures. It is intriguing that Piero and Uccello, the two artists most obsessed with perspective and space, should have created the most transcendent art; few compositions are as haunting as Piero's *Dream of Constantine*, a virtuoso demonstration of lighting, colouring and perspective, the angel swooping down from the upper left-front of the scene – and yet all is uncannily still; the soldiers stand guard, woodenly unaware; the sleeping emperor's attendant gazes out with a bored expression. Note, too, the *Annunciation* in which Gabriel announces both the birth and death of her son to Mary.

The fact that the frescoes exist at all is nothing short of a miracle. The walls have been damaged by an earthquake, struck by lightning, burned twice and shot at by Napoleon's troops, who also scratched the eyes of the figures. To keep the church standing after so much abuse, the first restorers injected tons of cement into the

# Getting Around

From Florence (75km/1½hrs), Perugia (73km/1½hrs) and Cortona (32km/45mins), the **train** is the easiest way to reach Arezzo; the station is at the southern end of town, where Via Guido Monaco meets the old city walls.

The LFI light-gauge rail line from Arezzo to the Casentino gives a picturesque ride up to Subbieno, Bibbiena, Poppi and Stia (about 17 daily); another LFI line heads south for Monte San Savino, Lucignano and Sinalunga, with connections to Chiusi and Siena. **Buses** for Cortona and other towns in Arezzo province, as well as for Siena (7 a day) and Florence (4 a day), leave from the station directly opposite on Viale Piero della Francesca, t 0575 382647/382651.

# Tourist Information

**Arezzo**: Piazza della Repubblica, in front of the train station, t 0575 377678, f 0575 20839, *www.apt.arezzo.it*; *info@arezzo.turismo.toscana.it*, *www.arezzocitta.com*.

# Where to Stay

**Arezzo** ✉ 52100

No hotels in Arezzo really stand out – the forces of tourism have yet to convert old villas into modern accommodation. What the city does have is comfortable and up-to-date.

**★★★★Minerva**, Via Fiorentina 4, t 0575 370390, f 0575 302415, *www.hotel-minerva.it* (*expensive*). Convenient if you're travelling by car. A few blocks west of the city walls in ugly modern suburbs, but with pleasant rooms, TV, air conditioning and parking places. It also has an excellent restaurant (*moderate*).

**★★★★Hotel Patio**, Via Cavour 23, t 0575 401962, *www.hotelpatio.it* (*very expensive*). This new hotel, just a few steps from San Francesco, is a bit like a tasteful theme park. The seven rooms are each decorated in the style of a country visited by Bruce Chatwin, so if you were to stay a week, you could sleep in China, India, Africa, Morocco and so on. It's stylish and fun and there is an American-style bar/restaurant in the basement.

In town, most rooms are close to the station.
**★★★Continentale**, Piazza Guido Monaco 7, t 0575 20251, f 0575 350485, *www.hotel continentale.com* (*expensive–moderate*). A fine, older hotel, with a lovely roof terrace.
**★★Truciolini**, Via G. Ferraris 29, t 0575 984104, f 0575 984137, *www.truciolini.it* (*moderate*). Less expensive, with parking and air con.
**★★★Casa Volpi**, Via Simone Martini 2, t 0575 354364, *www.casavolpi.it* (*moderate*). A few kilometres to the southeast of the city, Casa Volpi is a pleasant old villa set above the road in a large garden. The comfortable bedrooms are furnished with antiques and

walls, which, combined with humidity, nearly ruined the frescoes once and for all. Although the frescoes were cleaned in the 1960s, no attempt was made to protect them from further damage. Now, after 15 years of painstaking and complex work, they have at last been fully restored and, hopefully, saved.

During the restoration, it was discovered that the 'night' the art historians always referred to in Piero's *Dream of Constantine* is not actually night after all. After removing layers of dirt, it became obvious that the artist had portrayed a magnificent dawn. So much for the most famous nighttime painting in the history of art.

## Piazza Grande

Few piazzas in Italy have the eclectic charm of Arezzo's **Piazza Grande**, the perfect backdrop for both the *Giostra del Saracino* in early September and the monthly antiques fair. On this occasion, the town sports from the four quarters of Arezzo don 13th-century costume to re-enact an event first documented in 1593, a celebration of have lots of character. There is an excellent restaurant (*evenings only*), which serves a range of local dishes, home-made from prime ingredients.

**La Foresteria**, Via Bicchieraia 32, t 0575 370474, f 0575 324219 (*inexpensive*). This must be Arezzo's best bargain. Twelve simple rooms are housed in a 14th-century ex-Benedictine convent, which you approach through a marvellous cloister. Most of the rooms have beautiful frescoes and, although simple, they are not without style. Meals are served in the refectory.

Budget hotels do exist out of the centre. The following are near Porta San Lorentino.

**★Toscana**, Via Pirennio 56, t 0575 21692 (*inexpensive*).

**Ostello Villa Severi**, Via Francesco Redi 13, t 0575 299047. The local youth hostel. Take bus number 4 from the station. *Open all year*.

# Eating Out

**Buca di San Francesco**, Via S. Francesco 1, t 0575 23271 (*moderate*). This is a tourist favourite, but it has an honest-to-goodness medieval atmosphere and tasty Tuscan fare, if adapted for the uninitiated. *Closed Mon eve and Tues, also July.*

**Vino Divino**, Corso Italia 53, t 0575 299598 (*moderate*). On the first floor of a 14th-century palazzo, this restaurant offers an interesting menu of local and not-so-local dishes: *taglierini* with truffles or with prawns and cherry tomatoes, wild boar with prunes. Cheeses come from all over Europe while excellent wines come from the *enoteca* (same owners) round the corner. *Closed Mon.*

**Osteria La Capannaccia**, Loc. Campriano 51c, t 0575 361759 (*moderate–cheap*). One of the best, serving specialities of the Aretine countryside – *minestra di pane*, roast meats, including an excellent *bistecca alla fiorentina* and Colli Aretini wines. *Closed Sun eve and Mon.*

**Da Guido**, Via Madonna del Prato 85, t 0575 23760 (*moderate–cheap*). A cosy *trattoria* not far from the station, serving *pappardelle* with hare sauce, *orecchiette* with courgettes, duck wrapped in roast pork and rabbit with baby onions and white grapes.

**Torre di Gnicche**, Piaggia San Martino 8, near Piazza Grande, t 0575 352035 (*cheap*). A tiny wine bar facing out on to Piazza Vasari, where you can enjoy a glass of wine from an interesting list, plus snacks or dishes of the day; there's no formal menu. The onion soup is excellent or you can be adventurous and go for tripe or *baccalà* (salt cod). *Closed Wed.*

**Antica Osteria Agania**, Via Mazzini 10, t 0575 295381 (*cheap*). Rustic, popular and excellent value. Try tripe, *baccalà*, rabbit, duck or fried eggs with truffle shavings.

the feats of arms against Saracen pirates who menaced the Tyrrhenian coast in the 16th century and penetrated inland as far as Arezzo. Revived in 1932, the festival begins with a parade of costumes and flag-tossing by the *sbandieratori*, and is followed by a test of individual prowess between eight knights, two representing each quarter, who tilt against a wooden figure named 'Buratto, King of the Indies' for the prize of a golden lance.

The **Fiera Antiquaria** attracts hundreds of vendors from all over the country, selling everything from Renaissance ceramics to 1950s junk; it takes place on the first Saturday and Sunday of each month (Sunday is the big day), but ring the tourist office in advance to make sure. The piazza and surrounding streets are also lined with antique shops. On one side of the piazza is the **Loggia del Vasari**, a large building Vasari designed for his home town in 1573, with the idea of replicating a Greek stoa, with little shops, workshops, expensive bars and restaurants under the portico. Vasari also designed the clocktower of the **Palazzetto della Fraternità dei Laici**, an ornate building, half Gothic and half by Renaissance master Bernardo

Rossellino. Although it looks like a town hall, the palazzo is really the home of a lay brotherhood founded in the 1200s. The old Palazzo del Popolo exists only in ruins, behind Vasari's loggia on Via dei Pileati. Like Pisa's, it was destroyed by the Florentines after they captured the city.

## Santa Maria della Pieve

Perhaps most impressive on Piazza Grande is the round, Romanesque arcaded apse of Arezzo's great 12th-century church of **Santa Maria della Pieve**; it turns its back on the piazza, while directing its unusual Pisan-Lucchese façade towards narrow Via dei Pileati, where it's hard to see well. Each tier of arches is successively narrower, in a unique rustic style with no two columns or capitals alike. The campanile 'of a hundred holes' has so many neat rows of double-mullioned windows that it resembles a primitive skyscraper. Under the arch of the front portal, note the restored early medieval *Reliefs of the Twelve Months*: April with her flowers, February with his pruning hook and the pagan two-headed god Janus for January. The dim interior has an early Romanesque relief of the *Three Magi* on the entrance wall and decorated capitals in the nave. Like many early churches, the presbytery is raised above the low crypt, the most ancient part of the church, with primitive capitals – human faces mingling with rams, bulls and dragons. On the left wall there's another primitive relief of the *Nativity* and *Christ's Baptism*, while above in the choir is a beautiful polyptych by Pietro Lorenzetti (1320), featuring the *Madonna and Saints* modelling the latest Tuscan fashions and fabrics.

Below Santa Maria descends Corso Italia, Arezzo's main evening parade, while above, Via dei Pileati continues into the oldest quarter of the city, passing by way of **Petrarch's House** (*open Mon–Fri 10–12 and 3–5; Sat 10–12; adm*), a replacement for the original bombed in the last war; it stands near the picturesque 14th-century Palazzo del Pretorio, decked with coats of arms of imperial and Florentine governors.

## The Duomo

From the Piazza Grande, narrow streets lead up to the **Passeggio del Prato**, an English-style park with lawns, trees, a café and a big white elephant of a Fascist monument to Petrarch. All of Arezzo slopes gradually upwards from the railway station, ending abruptly here; from the cliffs on the edge of the Prato there is a memorable view over the mountains towards Florence and Urbino. Overlooking the park is a half-ruined Medici fortress of the 1500s and at the other end is the back of the **Duomo**, with a lovely Gothic bell tower from the 19th century.

The cathedral, built in bits and pieces over two and a half centuries (1276–1510), has a nondescript façade but several great works of art in its dimly lit Gothic naves. Its stained-glass **windows**, created by the greatest 16th-century master, Frenchman Guillaume de Marcillat, seem almost like illuminated frescoes by Gozzoli or Luca Signorelli. The magnificent marble Gothic High Altar is dedicated to San Donato and there are impressive tombs – the first is of Pope Gregory X (1205–76) with a canopy and 4th-century sarcophagus, holding the mortal dust of the pope who holds the record for taking the longest to be elected; the enclave, in Viterbo, lasted from 1268 to 1271, and only ended when the Viterbans starved the cardinals into deciding. The second, even more impressive, is the 1327 **Tomb of Bishop Guido Tarlati**, an early predecessor of the heroic sculptural tombs of the Renaissance, perhaps designed by Giotto. The tomb is divided into three sections, with a relief resembling a miniature theatre and a Ghibelline eagle on top; below lies the battling bishop's effigy; and below that, 16 fine relief panels that tell the story of his life, his battles and his good works. Beside it is Piero della Francesca's fresco of the Magdalene holding a crystal pot of ointment. The **Museo del Duomo** (*open Thurs–Sat 10–12; adm*) contains detached frescoes by Spinello Aretino and his son Parri di Spinello, a terracotta depicting the *Annunciation* by Bernardo Rossellino and paintings by 13th-century master Margarito d'Arezzo, Signorelli and Vasari.

## Museo d'Arte

*Open Tues–Sun 8.30–7.30; adm.*

Diagonally opposite the cathedral stands Arezzo's Ghibelline **Palazzo del Comune** with its distinctive tower; from here Via Ricasoli descends past the birthplace of Guido Monaco (with a plaque of Guido's do-re-mi), to the **Museo d'Arte Medioevale e Moderna**, where you can get to know some local medieval and Renaissance artists not often seen elsewhere. The collection is housed in a medieval palace, remodelled in the Renaissance, perhaps by Bernardo Rossellino, and later used as a customs house. All is arranged chronologically: the attractive courtyard contains medieval columns and capitals, a fine sculpted horse's head and gargoyles, while the two rooms on the ground floor contain sculptural details from the cathedral façade and a fine 10th-century *pluteo* carved with peacocks.

Among the works on the first floor are a stylized Byzantine *St Francis* by Margarito d'Arezzo, painted just after the saint's death and an *Enthroned Virgin* by Guido da Siena, studded with chunky, plasticky gems. Next you'll find detached frescoes by Spinello Aretino, the city's greatest trecento artist, and by his son Parri di Spinello (1387–1453), whose ghostly battle scene *Sconfitta di Massenzio* was discovered in the Badia after the war; the museum also has one of his beautifully dressed Madonnas. Another native of Arezzo, Bartolomeo della Gatta, painted the plague saint Rocco praying to liberate the city from the Black Death. Also on the first floor is a fresco attributed to Signorelli; a huge busy canvas by Vasari of *Esther's Wedding Banquet*; a collection of small Renaissance bronzes, including a bear with a monkey on his head; beautiful ceramics from Urbino, Deruta and Montelupo; and a plate by Master Giorgio of Gubbio with his secret red. On the second floor, there's a strange painting by Angelo Cacoselli (d. 1652) called the *Maga*, of an enchantress with her animals, a small room of 18th-century Neapolitan *presepi* figurines, and some splashy Mannerist canvases by Vasari, Allori and the great Rosso Fiorentino.

## Vasari, Cimabue and More Vasari

Around the corner, at Via 20 Settembre 55, is the **Casa del Giorgio Vasari** (*open Mon and Wed–Sat 8.30–7.30, Sun 8.30–1; adm*). Vasari was so fond of his own brand of spineless Mannerism that he wasn't about to leave it all for Duke Cosimo, but decorated his own house with the same fluff. Mediocrity attracts mediocrity; besides the frescoes there are several rooms of nondescript paintings, of which three stand out: the most repugnant St Sebastian ever committed to canvas, a terracotta portrait of Galba, one of Rome's ugliest mugs, by Sansovino, and a painting by a follower of Santi di Tito, of Christ and the Apostles dining in the 17th-century equivalent of a greasy spoon.

From Vasari's house, Via San Domenico will take you to the 13th-century church of **San Domenico**, with a simple asymmetrical exterior and a fine stone Gothic chapel (1360s) on the right wall, while the rest of the walls are covered with frescoes that overlap like pages on the bottom of a canary cage. The main altar has a crucifix by Cimabue (*c.* 1265); the chapel to the left contains a fine triptych of the Archangel Michael by the 'Maestro del Vescovado'.

Via Garibaldi from the art museum returns to the centre by way of **Santissima Annunziata**, Arezzo's late response to the Florentine Brunelleschi, begun by Bartolomeo della Gatta in the 1490s and completed by Antonio da Sangallo; the fourth altar has a painting by Pietro da Cortona and in the choir there's a stained-glass window by Marcillat. Further up, off Via Porta Buia, stands **Santissime Flora e Lucilla in Badia**, a 13th-century church with an unusual interior remodelled by Vasari. He also designed the two-sided altar, with reliefs from the Gospel of St Matthew on the front and St George slaying the dragon on the back. Over the presbytery the impressive cupola is a masterful fake by 17th-century *trompe-l'œil* master Andrea Pozzo. At the entrance there's a good fresco of St Lawrence by della Gatta; the fine cloister is by Giuliano da Maiano, a student of Brunelleschi (entrance No.2, Piazza della Badia).

On the southern edge of Arezzo, near the station on Via Margaritone, the remains of a small **Roman amphitheatre** have become a quiet city park. The former Olivetan monastery, built on a curve over the amphitheatre's foundations, has been restored to house the **Museo Archeologico** (*open daily 8.30–7.30; adm*). Not much has survived of the thriving Etruscan and Roman city of *Arretium*, but there are some mosaics and sarcophagi, Etruscan urns and Greek vases, examples of the Roman era red *corallino* vases and an excellent portrait of a rather jaded-looking, middle-aged Roman worked in gold.

## Santa Maria delle Grazie

Finally, you can take a 15-minute walk from Viale Mecenate out through Arezzo's auto-clogged southern suburbs to see a simple but exceptionally pretty Renaissance church, **Santa Maria delle Grazie**, finished in 1444 and given a jewel of a porch by Benedetto da Maiano, in 1482. With its subdued, delicate decoration, and round arches braced with slender iron bars, this could be the archetypal creation of early Renaissance architecture – certainly it will call to mind the backgrounds of any number of Tuscan paintings. The interior has an early Renaissance delight to match, a colourful terracotta altarpiece full of coloured fruit and *putti* by Andrea della Robbia, surrounding Parri di Spinello's *Madonna della Misericordia* (1430).

# The Valtiberina and the Valdichiana

## The Valtiberina

The Valtiberina, or upper valley of the Tiber, is a luminous patchwork of glowing pasturelands and pine and beech woodlands, birthplace of Michelangelo and Piero della Francesca.

### Arezzo to Sansepolcro

While Michelangelo took fresh air and stone-flavoured milk from his native place, Piero della Francesca carried the light and luminous landscape along the Tuscan-Umbrian frontier with him throughout his career, and left more behind in his native haunts than Michelangelo.

From Arezzo, it's a pretty 41km drive to Sansepolcro, especially along the SS73, which ascends through the Foce di Scopetone (with panoramic views back towards the city) then continues another 17km to the short turn-off for **Monterchi**. Dedicated to Hercules in Roman times, the town is a tiny medieval triangle; while strolling its lanes, don't miss the curious underground passageway around the apse of the parish church, dating back to the Middle Ages but of uncertain purpose. Monterchi is most famous, however, for Piero della Francesca's extraordinary fresco in the little chapel at the cemetery. The *Madonna del Parto* (1445) is perhaps the first (and last?) portrayal of the Virgin in the ninth month of her pregnancy, a mystery revealed by twin angels who pull back the flaps of a tent that is empty but for Mary, who is weary and melancholy, one eyelid drooping, one hand on her hip, the other on her swollen belly, almost painful to see. It is now housed in a former school building on Via della Reglia, well signposted from all directions (*open Tues–Sun 9–1 and 2–7, until 6 in winter; adm*). Details of its restoration are exhibited with the painting.

**Anghiari** (pop. 6,200), between Monterchi and Sansepolcro, is a fine old town located on a balcony over the Valtiberina. Once a property of Camaldoli and later of the Tarlati family, it was the site of a 1440 victory of the Florentines over the Milanese, a decisive victory in corking up Visconti ambitions over Tuscany and the rest of Italy – also a nearly bloodless one, the epitome of Renaissance Italy's civilized chessboard wars; only one man died at Anghiari and that was an accident. Leonardo da Vinci chose it as his subject matter in the Battle of the Frescoes in Florence's Palazzo Vecchio – one of the Renaissance's greatest unhappenings, though the cartoons left behind by the master were often copied and became one of the inspirations of Florentine Mannerism. In Anghiari's Renaissance Palazzo Taglieschi at Via Mameli 16, the **Museo delle Arti e Tradizioni Popolari dell'Alta Valle del Tevere** (*open Tues–Sat 8.30–7, Sun 9–1; adm*) has exhibits relating to traditional crafts of the upper Tiber valley. Just over 1km to the southwest, there's the pretty Romanesque **Pieve di Sovara**, and on the Sansepolcro road, you can still make out the 8th-century Byzantine origins of **Santo Stefano**.

The Valtiberina and Valdichiana

EMILIA-ROMAGNA

To Ravenna

10 km
5 miles

N

M. Falterona
Pso. d. Calla
La Burraia
Bagno di Romagna
S. Leo
Novafeltria
Montefeltro
Pennabilli
R. Marecchia
Stia
Pratovecchio
Camaldoli
Badia Prataglia
Alpe di Serra
Monte Fumaiolo
Balze
M. Carpegna
Montecopiolo
Carpegna
Sassocorvaro
MARCHES
Castel S. Niccolo
Poppi
Bibbiena
La Verna
M. Penna
Chiusi d. Verna
Pieve Sto. Stefano
Badia Tedalda
Sestino
R. Foglia
Piandimeleto
R. Metauro
Pratomagno
R. Arno
Caprese Michelangelo
Alpe d. Luna
Mercatello s. Metauro
S. Angelo in Vado
R. Candigliano
Talla
Subbiano
Sansepolcro
To Florence
Castiglion Fibocchi
Anghiari
Val Tiberina
R. Tevere
Citta di Castello
S257
TUSCANY
Arezzo
S69
Monterchi
S73
Monte Sta. Maria Tiberina
Civitella in Val Chiana
Foce di Scopetone
Morra
R. Nestore
Montone
UMBRIA
Gargonza
Sta. Maria d. Vertighe
Castiglion Fiorentino
Montecchio
le Celle
Umbertide
Monte S. Savino
Marciano d. Chiana
Cortona
Sta. Maria d. Calcinaio
Lucignano
Camuccia
Preggio
Antognola
E45
S326
Foiano della Chiana
Ossaia
Sinalunga
Tuoro sul Trasimeno
Castel Rigone
A1
S75
Val di Chiana
Petrignano di Lago
Lago Trasimeno
To Orvieto
To Perugia

## Sansepolcro

**Sansepolcro** (pop. 15,500) is the largest town of the Valtiberina, famous for lace, pasta (the Buitoni spaghetti works are just outside the city) and Piero della Francesca. The painter was born here *c.* 1410–1420 and given his mother's name as his father had died before his birth. Although he worked in the Marches, Arezzo and Rome, he spent most of his life in Sansepolcro, painting and writing books on geometry and perspective until he went blind at the age of 60. Piero may have had a chance to discuss his theories with a younger son of Sansepolcro, the great mathematician Luca Pacioli

(b. 1440), who wrote his *Divina Proporzione* with some help from Leonardo da Vinci (he also gets credit for the first book on accounting).

Sansepolcro was founded around the year 1000, and like Anghiari, belonged to the monks of Camaldoli until the 13th century. The historic centre, with its crew-cut

# Getting Around

CAT **buses** from Arezzo serve this area efficiently if not especially frequently. Sansepolcro is the terminus of Umbria's FCU light **rail** line, which slowly trundles you down to Città di Castello (16km/25mins), Umbertide, Perugia, Todi and Terni. Buses from Sansepolcro (station just outside the walls) go to Città di Castello, Caprese Michelangelo (26km/45mins), Arezzo (38km/1hr), Florence and Pieve Santo Stefano.

# Tourist Information

**Anghiari**: Corso Matteotti 103, **t** 0575 749279.
**Sansepolcro**: Piazza Garibaldi 2,
  **t/f** 0575 740536.

# Where to Stay and Eat

**Anghiari** ✉ 52031
**Locanda al Castello di Sorci**, near Anghiari at San Lorenzo, **t** 0575 789066 (*cheap*).
A country beanery in a former tobacco barn, in a beautiful setting. You can only eat a set menu, but it's incredible value and includes wine: the fare is simple, rustic and plentiful much of it (wine and meats) coming from the farm annexe. *Closed Mon.*

**Sansepolcro** ✉ 52037
****La Balestra**, Via del Montefeltro 29, **t** 0575 735151, **f** 0575 740370, *www. labalestra.it* (*moderate*). Pleasant, with modern, comfortable rooms, parking and a good restaurant, with delicious home-made pasta; for seconds, try the lamb chops with courgette flowers.
***Fiorentino**, Via L. Pacioli 60, **t** 0575 740350, **f** 0575 740370, *www.albergofiorentino.com* (*moderate*). Situated near the main gate, this has been the town inn since the 1820s; rooms provide all the basics and there's a garage. The restaurant is Sansepolcro's best;

it's a good place to try Italian onion soup and other local specialities, and there's a wide assortment of local cheeses. *Closed Fri.*
**Il Convivio**, Via Traversari 1, **t** 0575 736543 (*moderate*). In a Renaissance palazzo, this restaurant offers interesting dishes from the Valtiberina. Try the tortelloni flavoured with lemon peel, onion soup, saddle of lamb, veal flavoured with tarragon and porcini mushrooms and truffles. *Closed Tues.*
****Orfeo**, Viale Diaz, **t** 0575 742061 (*inexpensive*). Around the corner from the Fiorentino, this will do if the others are full.
**Locanda La Pergola**, Via Tiberina, Pieve Santo Stefano, **t** 0575 797053 (*inexpensive*). 16km north of Sansepolcro on the La Verna road, this inn has recently changed hands and been restored in classy country style with rustic antiques throughout. The restaurant (*cheap*) serves superbly cooked country food including ravioli, freshly made daily with local ricotta.
**Enoteca Guidi**, Via Pacioli 44, **t** 0575 736587 (*cheap*). A cosy wine bar with a small room lined with bottles in front and a larger dining room at the back, this is a good place for a light meal or glass of wine (from a vast choice) and a snack. Choose between various kinds of ravioli or *carpacci*, a selection of cheeses, salads and desserts. *Closed Sun lunch, Wed and Sat.*

# Caprese Michelangelo ✉ 52033
***Il Faggeto**, **t** 0575 793925 (*moderate–inexpensive*). Up in the Alpe Faggeto, above Caprese Michelangelo, this pleasant little mountain hotel and restaurant is set in a lovely forested landscape. The hotel has simple rooms; its restaurant, the **Fonte Galletta** (*moderate*), uses the freshest local ingredients – chestnuts, wild mushrooms, truffles, game, mountain hams – to create tasty dishes. The pasta is excellent, as are the home-made *semifreddi. Closed Tues and Wed Easter– Christmas; in winter open weekends only.*

towers, has plenty of character, though it's a bit dusty and plain after several earthquakes and rebuildings. It is enclosed within well-preserved walls, built by the Tarlati and given a Renaissance facelift by Giuliano da Sangallo. **Piazza Torre di Berta** is the centre of town, where on the second Sunday of September crossbow-men from Gubbio challenge the home archers in the *Palio della Balestra*, an ancient rivalry. Along Via Matteotti are many of the city's surviving 14th- and 16th-century palaces, most notably the Palazzo delle Laudi and the 14th-century palace housing the **Museo Civico** (*open daily 9.30–1 and 2.30–6; until 7.30 in summer; adm exp*). Here you can see Piero's masterpiece, the *Resurrection*, an intense, almost eerie depiction of the solemnly triumphant Christ stepping out of his tomb surrounded by sleeping soldiers and a land, more autumnal than springlike, as well as two of Piero's early works, the *Misericordia Polyptych*, a gold-background altarpiece dominated by a serene, giant goddess of a Madonna, sheltering under her cloak members of the confraternity (note the black hood on one) who commissioned the picture, and a damaged fresco of San Giuliano.

Other works are by his greatest pupil, Luca Signorelli (a *Crucifixion* with two saints on the back), Pontormo (*Martyrdom of San Quintino*), Santi di Tito, Mannerist Raffaellino del Colle, and the 16th-century Giovanni de' Vecchi, also of Sansepolcro, whose *Presentation of the Virgin* is interesting for its unusual vertical rhythms. You can see a 16th-century scene of Sansepolcro in the *Pilgrimage of the Company of the Crucifix of Loreto*, a relic of the days of the Black Death, as are the wooden panels of *Death* (one showing a fine strutting skeleton). Downstairs, a room contains sculptural fragments gathered from the town, including a rather mysterious 12th-century frieze of knights; upstairs there's a collection of detached frescoes.

Sansepolcro also has a couple of pretty churches: near the museum is the Gothic church of **San Francesco**, with a fine rose window and portal. The **Duomo** is on Via Matteotti; it was built in the 11th century but has been much restored since. Among the art inside is a fresco by Bartolomeo della Gatta and a polyptych by Matteo di Giovanni; note the huge rose window made of alabaster. Another church, **San Lorenzo**, has a *Deposizione* by Rosso Fiorentino.

## Up the Tiber: Caprese Michelangelo

Signor Buonarroti, a minor noble of Florence, was *podestà* in the tiny town of Caprese, 26km northwest of Sansepolcro, when his wife gave birth to little Michelangelo. As was the custom in those days, the baby was sent into the countryside to be nursed by a mason's wife. 'If my brains are any good at all, it's because I was born in the pure air of your Arezzo countryside,' Michelangelo later told Vasari. 'Just as with my mother's milk, I sucked in the hammer and chisels I use for my statues.' Although he only returned once to the Valtiberina, to select sturdy firs to float down the Tiber for the scaffolding in the Sistine Chapel, Caprese does not let any opportunity slip by to remind us of its most famous son, even changing its name to **Caprese Michelangelo**. The artist's purported birthplace, the 14th-century **Casa del Podestà** (*open Nov–Mar Mon–Fri 11–5, Sat and Sun 11–6; April, May and Oct Mon–Fri 10–30–5.30, Sat and Sun until 6.30; June and July Mon–Fri 9.30–6.30, Sat–Sun until 7.30; Aug daily 9.30–7.30; Sept Mon–Fri 9.30–6.30, Sat and Sun until 7.30; adm*), has been restored and now houses a museum, with photographs and reproductions of his works. Caprese's medieval castle contains questionable tributes from modern sculptors. From here it's not far into the Alpe di Catenaia and La Verna (*see* p.399).

## Caprese to Sestino

East of Caprese the countryside is the biggest attraction; between **Pieve Santo Stefano** (Roman *Sulpitia*, mostly rebuilt after the Second World War) and **Badia Tedalda** (a small resort) lie the rolling Alpe della Luna, the Mountains of the Moon.

**Sestino** (from the Roman woodland god Sextius), Tuscany's easternmost *comune* on the border of the Marches, was ruled by the Montefeltro dukes of Urbino until 1516. It has been the area's agricultural centre since antiquity and has many medieval buildings. Near its little Romanesque parish church, the **Antiquarium** (*open daily 9.30–12 and 3.30–6*) will show you the headless *Venus of Sestino* and other local finds. The 8th-century church shows the influence of Ravenna, Byzantine capital of the west; its 13th-century altar sits on a Roman boundary stone. Sestino is Tuscany's easternmost village; if you like this area, you may wish to cross the border into the Marches – specifically, into the lovely upland region called the Montefeltro above the Renaissance city of Urbino.

# South of Arezzo: the Valdichiana

The flat Valdichiana south of Arezzo is the largest, broadest valley in the Apennines, surrounded by hills and old towns. The Etruscans, headquartered at Cortona, were the first to drain its marshlands, making it their bread-basket, so rich, it is said, that even after Hannibal's troops pillaged on their way to Lake Trasimeno, there was still more than enough to feed the army and its elephants. By the Middle Ages, however, the valley had reverted to a swamp, forcing the inhabitants back into the hills. And so it stayed, until the beginning of the 19th century, when the Lorraine Grand Dukes initiated a major land reclamation scheme. Now, once again, prosperous farms are the main feature of the Valdichiana. The equally prosperous-looking cattle are a prized breed called the Chianina, descendants of the primal herds whose fossils were discovered in the vicinity.

## Monte San Savino and Lucignano

But there is more to the Valdichiana than farms and *bistecca alla fiorentina* on the hoof. On both sides of the valley are some of the most beautiful villages in this part of Tuscany. Cortona is the most famous, but there are others, like **Monte San Savino** (21km from Arezzo, on the west side of the valley), the birthplace of Andrea Contucci, better known as Andrea Sansovino (1460–1529), artistic emissary of Lorenzo de' Medici to Portugal and one of the heralds of the High Renaissance; his Florentine pupil Jacopo adopted his surname and went on to become chief sculptor and architect in Venice in its Golden Age. Monte San Savino, spread out on a low hill, is an attractive town with a *mélange* of late medieval and fine Renaissance palaces. Andrea Sansovino left several works to his home town: an attractive portal on the

# Tourist Information

**Monte San Savino**: c/o Corso San Gallo 2,
t 0575 849418.
**Castiglion Fiorentino**: Corso Italia 111,
t/f 0575 658278.

# Where to Stay and Eat

## Monte San Savino ✉ 52048
****Castello di Gargonza**, an entire walled
village 8km from Monte San Savino, just off
the SS73, t 0575 847021, f 0575 847054,
*www.gargonza.it* (*expensive*). King of the
Valdichiana for a quiet and medieval
atmosphere, with 7 rooms and 25 self-
catering apartments/houses and a pool, all
surrounded by forest; local specialities are
served at the popular restaurant (*moderate*),
boasting a choice wine list. *Closed Tues.*
***Sangallo**, Piazza Vittorio Veneto 16,
t 0575 810049, f 0575 810220, *www.hotel
sangallo.it* (*moderate*). A fine provincial hotel
in the town; no restaurant.

## Castiglion Fiorentino ✉ 52043
**Relais San Pietro in Polvano**, Località Polvano 3,
t 0575 650100 (*very expensive*). The fabulous,
panoramic terrace, where meals are served, is
one of this family-run hotel's great assets;
that and the peace and quiet of its hillside
setting. There are no TVs and small children
are discouraged; uncluttered rustic elegance
reigns throughout.
***Park**, on the main Via Umbro-Casentinese
88, t 0575 680288, f 0575 680008,
*www.parkhotelarezzo.com* (*moderate*). A big,
modern hotel with a pool; not the most
picturesque, but it's fine for a night or two.
**Antica Trattoria la Foce**, Via della Foce 30,
t 0575 658187 (*cheap*). Just outside the centre,
this doesn't look much, but it serves lovely
authentic local food. Choose from pasta with
boar, hare, duck or goose, and Valdichiana
beef as a classic *secondo*; they also do a
mean pizza. *Closed Mon and weekday lunch.*

## Lucignano ✉ 52046
**La Rocca**, Via Giacomo Matteotti 15, t 0575
836775 (*moderate*). In the delightful *centro
storico* of Lucignano, La Rocca has been
serving food since 1903. Delicious traditional
dishes such as *pici* with *sugo di nana* (duck),
tagliatelle with mushrooms or truffles, fillet
of pork with wild fennel and fantastic local
*bistecca. Closed Tues.*

church of **San Giovanni**, terracottas (along with others by the della Robbias) in the
little church of **Santa Chiara** in Piazza Jalta, and the lovely cloister of **Sant'Agostino**
(13th century, with a small rose window by Guillaume de Marcillat). Sansovino, or
Antonio da Sangallo the Elder, designed the beautiful and harmonious **Loggia dei
Mercanti**, with its grey Corinthian capitals in the early 1500s, while Antonio da
Sangallo gets credit for the simple, partly rusticated **Palazzo Comunale**, originally
the home of the Del Monte family, whose money paid for most of Monte San
Savino's Renaissance ornaments. Foremost among the medieval monuments, the
**Palazzo Pretorio** was built by the Perugians, while the city walls are the work of
the Sienese.

On a cypress-clad hill 2km east, **Santa Maria della Vertighe** was built in the 12th
century and restored in the 16th; it houses a rare 13th-century triptych by Margarito
d'Arezzo and 14th-century works by Lorenzo Monaco. Some 7km west there's the
pretty **Gargonza**, with its mighty tower dominating a tight cluster of houses on a
wart of a hill, the whole of which is now a hotel (*see* 'Where to Stay and Eat', above).

Best of all, perhaps, is cheerful little **Lucignano**, south of Monte San Savino, unique
among Italian hill towns for its street plan – it is laid out in four concentric ellipses,
like a kind of maze, with four picturesque little *piazze* in the centre. One piazza is

dominated by the Collegiata with a theatrical circular stair, another by the 14th-century **Palazzo Comunale**, now the Museo Civico, containing a good collection of 13th- to 15th-century Sienese works, a *Madonna* by Signorelli and, most famously, a 14th-century masterpiece of Aretine goldsmiths, the delicate reliquary *Albero di Lucignano*. There are more good Sienese paintings in the church of **San Francesco**. Outside the centre there's a 16th-century Medici fortress and the **Madonna delle Querce**, a Renaissance temple sometimes attributed to Vasari, with a Doric interior.

**Marciano della Chiana**, 6km northeast of Lucignano, is another old fortified village with an impressive main gate, which also does time as clock and bell tower. **Foiano della Chiana**, just to the south, is encompassed by newer buildings, but in its **Collegiata** has a good *Coronation of the Virgin* by Signorelli and a terracotta by Andrea della Robbia. Between Marciano and Foiano, keep an eye open for the curious octagonal church of **Santa Vittoria**, built by Ammannati for Cosimo I.

## Castiglion Fiorentino

To the east, on the last hill overlooking the Valdichiana plain, fortified **Castiglion Fiorentino** was Castiglion Aretino until the Florentines snatched it in 1384. Another old Etruscan settlement, with medieval streets, it nevertheless had more than a nodding acquaintance with the Renaissance. Like many a larger town (*see* Cortona, p.414), it built an ornamental geometric temple below the walls, the octagonal **Madonna della Consolazione**, untampered with since 1607. Then there's the 16th-century **Loggiato Vasariano**, overlooking the countryside from the old market square, and opposite, the **Palazzo Comunale**. The 1860 plebiscite that brought Tuscany into the kingdom of Italy made a big impression here: the Palazzo Comunale has a marble plaque recording not only the precise vote, but the exact day, hour and minute of the count. The façade also fits in a computerized tourist information screen.

Just behind and above the Palazzo Comunale, Castiglion's ancient heart is known as the Cassero (from the Roman *castrum*): here, you'll find the Palazzo Pretorio and the church of Sant'Angelo, the latter housing a small **Pinacoteca Civica** (*open Tues–Sun 10–12.30 and 4–6.30; adm*). The prizes are a French Renaissance gilded silver reliquary bust of Sant'Orsola, a pair of 13th-century crucifixes, the *Stigmata of St Francis* by Bartolomeo della Gatta, a *Portrait of St Francis* (1280) by the workshop of Margaritone di Arezzo, and the 15th-century *Probatica Piscina*, an uncommon subject (of Jerusalem's sheep pond, with curative waters) by Jacopo de Sellaio. The **Collegiata**, completely rebuilt in the 19th century, has kept its art: *Enthroned Madonnas* by Della Gatta, an *Adorazione* by Lorenzo di Credi, and in the adjacent Pieve Vecchia, Signorelli's fresco of the *Deposition*. The Gothic 13th-century church of **San Francesco** has a cloister, some frescoes and a wooden *Crucifixion* sculpted by Giambologna.

Dilapidated castles are all around Castiglion, most impressively at **Montecchio**, 4km south, with its tall honey-coloured tower and walls, a landmark visible all over the Valdichiana. For a while in the 1400s it was the stronghold of the *condottiere* Sir John Hawkwood, he of the famous 'monument' by Uccello in Florence cathedral.

## Getting Around

Cortona is just off the main Florence–Arezzo–Rome **railway** line; the nearest station is Camucia, 5km west; if you're coming up from Umbria, the station is Terontola, 10km south. Both stations have frequent LFI **buses** up to Cortona. There are also LFI train connections to Arezzo (34km/50mins), Castiglion Fiorentino, Foiano della Chiana and Castiglione del Lago on Lake Trasimeno (22km/30mins); schedules for both buses and trains, and tickets for the former, are posted in the office in Via Nazionale, near the bus terminus and car park in panoramic Piazzale Garibaldi, or call **t** 0575 398813.

## Tourist Information

**Cortona**: Via Nazionale 42, **t** 0575 630353, **f** 0575 630656, *www.apt.arezzo.it*.

## Events and Activities

**Antique furniture market**, *Aug–Sept*. Antiques are the big business in Cortona; besides the offerings in the town's shops, it hosts the national antique furniture market.
**Copperware show and market**, *April*. A showcase for another local hand-made speciality.
**Umbria Jazz Festival**, *July*. Concerts are held throughout the month in the public gardens as part of the festival.
*Sagra di Bistecca* (festival of the beefsteak), *15 August*. Featuring a huge outdoor grilling of the Valdichiana's chief product.
**Swimming**: Just off the mountain road above Torreone, set amongst the chestnut woods at Tornia is a pool called the 'Priest's Hole',

which is both prettier and more tranquil than the public pool at Il Sodo (no set fee, but they ask for a donation).
**Horse-riding**: Horses can be hired from Unione Popolare Sport Equestre, Loc. Ossaia, Montanino di Cortona, **t** 0575 67500.
**Under the Tuscan Sun Festival**: Writer Frances Mayes is the co-artistic director of this mainly music festival, which attracts an international line-up of performers. Based in Cortona, it also includes food and wine events, films, talks and seminars.

## Where to Stay

### Cortona ✉ 52044

In Cortona, available lodgings have yet to catch up with demand, especially since the town is the site of both a language school and a University of Georgia art programme operative beween June and October.
**\*\*\*\*Il Falconiere**, San Martino a Bocena, 3km away, **t** 0575 612679, **f** 0575 612927, *www.ilfalconiere.com* (*luxury*). Outside the centre; refined, frescoed and furnished with antiques and canopied beds, it also has two pools, immaculate grounds, and a first-class restaurant (*expensive*) serving creative and refined meat and fish dishes, such as duck *tortelli* in an onion and orange sauce. Also runs cookery courses. *Closed Wed in winter*.
**\*\*\*\*San Michele**, Via Guelfa 15, **t** 0575 604348, **f** 0575 630147, *www.hotelsanmichele. net* (*expensive*). In an elegant Renaissance palace with painted friezes, ancient fireplaces and old waxed floors. Private garage.
**\*\*\*\*Residence Borgo San Pietro**, Loc. San Pietro a Cegliolo, **t** 0575 604348, **f** 0575 630147, *www.borgosanpietro.com* (*moderate*).

# Cortona

High above the Valdichiana plain on terraced slopes of olives and vines, **Cortona** (pop. 27,000) is one of the crown jewels of Tuscan hill towns. Some 2,000ft above sea level, sweeping down a spur of Monte Sant'Egidio, its crooked, cobbled streets climb precipitously to the Medici fortress – even halfway up, between the houses, you can see Lake Trasimeno in Umbria and Mounts Amiata and Cetona near Siena. Three Cortonese became celebrated artists: Luca Signorelli (1441/50–1523); Baroque painter Pietro Berrettini (1596–1669), better known as Pietro da Cortona, master of the

Under the same ownership as the San Michele and 4km north. Upmarket, with pool, in a lovely 17th-century farmhouse and outbuildings, that are beautifully furnished. Well-equipped self-catering apartments sleep 2–4; minimum 3-night stay Nov–Mar and minimum one week for the rest of the year. *Closed early Jan–early Mar.*

***Oasi Neumann**, Via Contesse 1, t 0575 630354, f 0575 630477, *www.hotel oasi.org* (*moderate*). One of the nicest places to stay, with rooms in an old mansion, lovely gardens and a very warm welcome. *Open Easter–Oct.*

***San Luca**, Piazza Garibaldi 2, t 0575 630460, f 0575 630105, *www.sanluca cortona.com* (*moderate*). Simple but comfortable; many of the rooms (especially the breakfast room) enjoy wonderful views.

**Locanda del Molino**, Localita Montanare, t 0575 614192, *www.locandadelmolino.com* (*moderate*). This converted stone mill house accommodates 12 rustically romantic little rooms overlooking a brook. The excellent restaurant offers home-made local dishes.

*****Athens**, Via S. Antonio 12, t 0575 630508 f 0575 604457 (*inexpensive*). A good budget choice high up in the old town, with spacious rooms in an older building and a pretty walled garden. Only two rooms have private bath. *Open June–Nov.*

**Istituto Santa Margherita**, Via C. Battisti 15, t 0575 630336, f 0575 630549 (*inexpensive*). Rooms available with or without bath.

**Ostello San Marco**, Via Maffei 57, t 0575 601392, *www.cortonahostel.com* (*inexpensive, budget meals; IYHA card required*). One of Italy's more pleasant youth hostels, a 3km walk up from Piazza Garibaldi. *Open Mar–Oct.*

# Eating Out

Cortona's restaurants are not fancy, but make a point of using local ingredients – homemade pasta, *salumeria* and steaks from the Valdichiana, mushrooms and truffles in season, and the local white wines called *bianche vergini* (the white virgins).

**Da Tonino**, Piazza Garibaldi, t 0575 630500 (*expensive–moderate*). This is Cortona's most elegant restaurant, serving wonderful *antipasti, gnocchi di zucca* (pumpkin) with truffles and Parmesan, pasta made with chestnut flour with porcini, chicken breasts with cognac and porcini. There is a cheaper lunch menu. *Closed Mon eve and Tues.*

**La Grotta**, Piazzetta Baldelli 3, t 0575 630271 (*moderate*). A friendly but intimate restaurant that the locals would like to keep secret. Tables are laid in a pretty courtyard. *Closed Tues.*

**Miravalle**, Frazione Torreone 6, t 0575 62232 (*moderate*). On the edge of town and aptly named for its stunning views out over the valley. The food's not bad either.

**Osteria del Teatro**, Via Maffei 3, t 0575 630556 (*moderate*). In a 15th-century palazzo with old terracotta floors, beamed ceilings and a little terrace. Nice. *Closed Wed.*

**Dardano**, Via Dardano 24, t 0575 601944 (*cheap*). A simple *trattoria* with an elegant vaulted ceiling. It's popular with the locals, so can be noisy and busy, but the food is good, especially the home-made *pici* with mushroom sauce. *Closed Wed.*

**La Saletta**, Via Nazionale 26/28, t 0575 603366, *www.cortona-lasaletta.com*. Down some Tuscan wines with regional snacks at this little wine bar near the centre. They also serve the odd pasta dish and soups and excellent sandwiches.

rooms in the Pitti Palace; and Futurist-Impressionist mosaicist Gino Severini (1883–1966), all of whom left works in their home town.

According to Virgil and popular tradition, Cortona is nothing less than the 'Mother of Troy and Grandmother of Rome' – founded by Dardanus who, according to legend, was fighting against a neighbouring tribe when he lost his helmet (*corythos*) on the hill, thus giving the name *Corito* to the city that grew up on the spot. He later went to Asia to found Troy and give his name to the Dardanelles. There may be a grain of truth in this myth. The Etruscans claimed to have come from Western Anatolia (around 900 BC), and inscriptions very similar to Etruscan have been found on the Greek island of Lemnos, near Troy; artefacts from the Iron Age found in Anatolia and Tuscany suggest cultural affinities. Cortona was an important Etruscan city, one of the Dodecapolis and one of the largest in the north; ragged Etruscan stonework is still visible in the foundations of its walls. These stretch over 3km of the perimeter, but still cover only two-thirds of the area of the original Etruscan fortifications.

As a medieval *comune*, Cortona held its own against Perugia, Arezzo and Siena, while internally, its Ghibellines and Guelphs battled until the Ghibellines won out. When that fight was settled the ruling family, the Casali, spent the 14th century bumping each other off. This feast of self-destruction ended in 1409, when King Ladislas of Naples captured the city, selling it to Florence at a handsome profit.

## Palazzo Casali – Museo dell'Accademia Etrusca

*www.accademia-etrusca.org; open April–Oct Tues–Sun 10–7, Nov–Mar Tues–Sun 10–5; adm.*

The heart of Cortona, the **Piazza della Repubblica**, is a striking asymmetrical square. Dominant here is the **Palazzo Comunale** (13th century), with a tower from 1503 and monumental steps. Just behind is the impressive 13th-century **Palazzo Casali**, home of the city's murderous lordlings and now the seat of the Etruscan Academy, a cultural organization founded in the 17th century by the local nobility.

Through the palazzo's attractive courtyard awaits the **Museo dell'Accademia Etrusca**, a fascinating collection begun by the Academy in 1727, encompassing bronzes (note the two-faced god Selvans); Greek vases, attesting to the city's wealth and trading contacts of long ago; Egyptian mummies and a doll-like Egyptian funeral barque; and Cortona's most famous relic, an Etruscan bronze chandelier with 16 lamps dating back to the 5th century BC, found in a nearby field. Each lamp is a grotesque squatting figure, uncircling a ring of stylized waves and dolphins, and in the centre, an archaic gorgon.

There is a fine collection of paintings, the oldest being a Roman portrait of the Muse Polyhymnia. Others include paintings by Pietro da Cortona, *Two Saints* by Niccolò di Pietro Gerini, a 12th-century Tuscan mosaic of the Madonna, a fine polyptych by Bicci di Lorenzo, a *Madonna* by Pinturicchio, and another by Signorelli, who portrays her in the company of the saintly protectors of Cortona, with a nasty-looking devil squirming at their feet. One room is dedicated to Francesco Laperelli (1521–70) from Cortona, who built the walls of Valletta for the Knights of Malta; also ivories, globes of the earth and sky from 1714, costumes, the library founded by the Etruscan Academy in 1727, ceramics and a fine Roman alabaster Hecate, the queen of the night.

The latest permanent exhibition is a recreation of the inside of the Etruscan tumulus, the Secondo Melone di Sodo, excavated in 1991 (*see* p.419). Part of the tumulus' unique platform altar, sculpted with a man stabbing a lion while it bites off his head, is on display as well.

## Museo Diocesano

*Open Nov–Mar Tues–Sun 10–5; April–Oct Tues–Sun 10–7; adm.*

Behind the civic museum signs point the way back to the **Duomo**, an 11th-century church unimaginatively rebuilt in 1560, probably by Giuliano da Sangallo; inside there's a mosaic by Gino Severini. However, across the piazza in the deconsecrated church of Gesù there's the excellent **Museo Diocesano** with two masterpieces: Luca Signorelli's *Deposition*, with scenes of the Crucifixion and Resurrection (the latter composition inspired by his master Piero della Francesca) with an excellent predella, and a beautiful, luminous *Annunciation* by Beato Angelico, who came to Cortona to paint this solemn angel gently whispering his tremendous message; it has another exceptional predella. Note how the frame echoes the Corinthian columns of the loggia.

Other works in the collection include a 14th-century crucifix by Pietro Lorenzetti, a triptych by Il Sassetta, a fine Sienese *Madonna* by the school of Duccio di Buoninsegna, and a 2nd-century AD Roman sarcophagus with reliefs of the Battle of Lapiths and Centaurs that was closely studied by Donatello and Brunelleschi. Don't miss the fine coffered wooden ceiling of the church itself.

Below the Piazza del Duomo is one of Cortona's most picturesque lanes, the medieval Via Jannelli (or del Gesù), where some houses have *porte del morto* (doors of the dead), more common in medieval Umbria than in Tuscany. Other picturesque streets to look out for are Via Ghibellina, Via Guelfa, and Via Maffei, with its town palaces.

## Up and Down Cortona

You'll need your climbing shoes to see the other monuments of Cortona, although **San Francesco** is only a short walk up from Piazza della Repubblica. St Francis's controversial lieutenant Brother Elias was a native of Cortona and founded this little church at an interesting angle in 1245; it still retains its original façade and one side. Both Brother Elias and Luca Signorelli are buried here and on the left wall is a fine fresco of the *Annunciation*, the last work of Pietro da Cortona. On the high altar is a slice of the Holy Cross brought back from Constantinople by Brother Elias, housed in an ivory reliquary that Byzantine emperor Nicephoras Phocas carried into battle against the Saracens in the 960s, as described in the Greek inscription on the back.

From here handsome Via Berrettini continues up to Piazza Pozzo and Piazza Pescaia and the medieval neighbourhood around **San Nicolò**. This handsome little Romanesque church, built by an anachronistic architect in the 1440s, was the seat of San Bernardino da Siena's Company of St Nicholas, for whom Luca Signorelli painted a magnificent standard of the *Deposition* still hanging by the altar.

You can reach the loftiest church of them all, the **Santuario di Santa Margherita**, from San Nicolò. The views become increasingly magnificent, until you reach the pretty 19th-century neo-Romanesque sanctuary. The original church was built by Santa Margherita (1247–97), a beautiful farmer's daughter and mistress of a young nobleman; upon his sudden death, she got religion, became a Franciscan tertiary and founded a convent and hospital where she cared for the sick. Her remains are in a silver urn on the altar; her fine but empty Gothic sarcophagus on the left wall is by Angelo and Francesco di Pietro. To the right of the altar are standards and lanterns captured from the Turks in 18th-century sea battles, donated by a local commander. Just above, the overgrown **Medici Fortress** of 1556 occupies the site of the old Etruscan acropolis.

Descend from Santa Margherita to the centre by way of Via Santa Margherita and the **Via Crucis**, made up of mosaic shrines by Gino Severini, commissioned in 1947 by the people of Cortona to thank their patron saint for sparing their city from the war.

As in many Etruscan and Roman towns, Cortona's gates are orientated to the four points of the compass. The northern **Porta Colonia** has an Etrusco-Roman arch and is near some well-preserved remains of the Etruscan walls; from here, it's a 15-minute walk to the late, tall Renaissance church of **Santa Maria Nuova**, partly by Vasari and one of the more serene works to come out of the Counter-Reformation, designed in a Greek cross and crowned by a dome.

Outside the southern **Porta Berarda**, at the end of Via Nazionale, the Gothic church of **San Domenico** has an elegant interior, presided over by a grand triptych by Lorenzo di Niccolò Gerini (1402) given to the Dominicans by Lorenzo de' Medici; and in the apse there's a *Madonna with Angels* by Signorelli. Nearby is a good stretch of Etruscan wall and the beginning of the Passeggiata Pubblica through Cortona's shady public gardens, the **Parterre**, with more grandstand views over the Valdichiana.

## Around Cortona

In the Renaissance, it was fashionable in Tuscany and Umbria to decorate the outskirts of a town with a perfectly symmetrical church, exercises in geometry and divine order visible from all four sides – something, by the 16th century, impossible to do in the built-up town centres. Cortona has one of most graceful of these ornamental set pieces, **Santa Maria delle Grazie al Calcinaio**, isolated 3km down the road to Camucia. Built between 1485–1513 by Sienese architect Francesco di Giorgio Martini, this Latin cross topped with an octagonal drum has a harmonious interior, done in Brunelleschian dark and light accents, luminous and airy and pure, with accents in colour provided by fine stained glass by Guillaume de Marcillat. Unfortunately, it's rarely open but ask at the tourist office.

Ancient tombs dot the plain below. One of the most evocative, the Hellenistic **Tanella di Pitagora**, is signposted from the crossroads near Santa Maria delle Grazie (*call ahead to visit, t 0575 630415*). Named after Pythagoras – apparently the ancients confused Cortona with Croton in Calabria, where the philosopher lived – the 3rd-century BC *hypogeum* is prettily surrounded by cypress trees and has an unusual vault over its rectangular funeral chamber.

Northwest of Cortona, near the Camucia station, there's the 7th-century BC **Melone di Camucia**, an Etruscan *tumulus* containing two large chambers and corridors; and nearby, at Il Sodo (the hard-boiled egg), are two large 6th-century BC *tumuli* with massive walls, the **Meloni del Sodo** (*to visit tumulo I, call one day in advance, t 0575 630415; guided tours available; adm*), 200m in perimeter. The keeper will take you around *tumulo* I; *tumulo* II, with its five mortuary chambers, yielded the treasures and altar in Cortona's museum and is still being excavated.

Beyond Santa Maria Nuova, the road continues another 3.5km along the slopes of Monte Sant'Egidio to the **Convento delle Celle**, founded by St Francis in 1211 in a beautiful setting. Little has changed; its simple rustic buildings have preserved their Franciscan spirit better than many others – the humble founder's cell retains the saint's stone bed.

# Know Your Medici

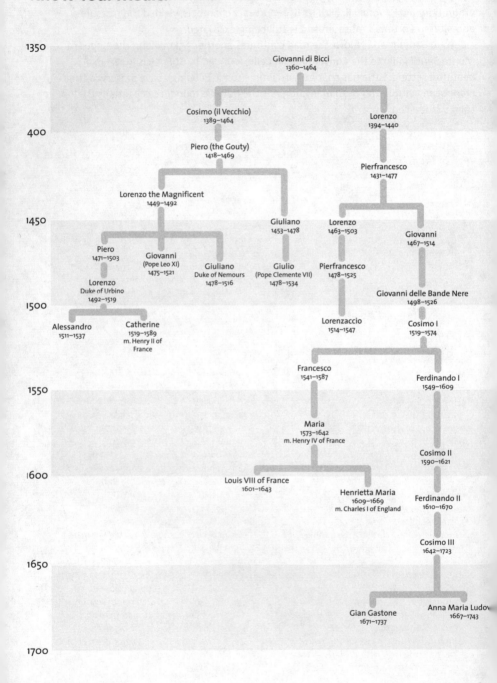

# Glossary

**acroterion**: decorative protrusion on the rooftop of an Etruscan, Greek or Roman temple. At the corners of the roof they are called *antefixes*.

**ambones**: twin pulpits (singular: *ambo*), often elaborately decorated.

**ambulatory**: aisle around the apse of a church.

**atrium**: entrance court of a Roman house or early church.

**badia**: abbey or abbey church (also *abbazia*).

*baldacchino*: baldachin, a columned stone canopy above the altar of a church.

**basilica**: a rectangular building, usually divided into three aisles by rows of columns. In Rome this was the common form for law courts and other public buildings, and Roman Christians adapted it for their early churches.

*borgo*: from the Saxon *burh* of Santo Spirito in Rome: a suburb or village.

**bucchero ware**: black, delicately thin Etruscan ceramics, usually incised or painted.

**Calvary chapels**: a series of outdoor chapels, usually on a hillside, that commemorate the stages of the Passion of Christ.

**campanile**: a bell tower.

*campanilismo*: local patriotism; the Italians' own word for their historic tendency to be more faithful to their home towns than to the abstract idea of 'Italy'.

*campo santo*: a cemetery.

**cardo**: the transverse street of a Roman *castrum*-shaped city.

**carroccio**: a wagon carrying the banners of a medieval city and an altar; it served as the rallying point in battles.

**cartoon**: the preliminary sketch for a fresco or tapestry.

**caryatid**: supporting pillar or column carved into a standing female form; male versions are called *telamones*.

*castrum*: a Roman military camp, always neatly rectangular, with straight streets and gates at the cardinal points. Later the Romans founded or refounded cities in this form, hundreds of which survive today (Lucca, Aosta, Florence, Pavia, Como, Brescia, Ascoli Piceno, Ancona are clear examples).

**cavea**: the semicircle of seats in a classical theatre.

*cenacolo*: fresco of the *Last Supper*, often on the wall of a monastery refectory.

**chiaroscuro**: the arrangement or treatment of light and dark areas in a painting.

**ciborium**: a tabernacle; the word is often used for large, free-standing tabernacles, or in the sense of a *baldacchino* (q.v.).

*comune*: commune or commonwealth, referring to the governments of the free cities of the Middle Ages. Today it denotes any local government, from the Comune di Roma down to the smallest village.

*condottiere*: the leader of a band of mercenaries in late medieval and Renaissance times.

**confraternity**: a religious lay brotherhood, often serving as a neighbourhood mutual-aid and burial society, or following some specific charitable work (Michelangelo, for example, belonged to one that cared for condemned prisoners in Rome).

*contrapposto*: the dramatic, but rather unnatural twist in a statue, especially in a Mannerist or Baroque work, derived from Hellenistic and Roman art.

*convento*: a convent or monastery.

**Cosmati work**: or *Cosmatesque*: referring to a distinctive style of inlaid marble or enamel chips used in architectural decoration (pavements, pulpits, paschal candlesticks, etc.) in medieval Italy. The Cosmati family of Rome were its greatest practitioners.

**crete**: found in the pasturelands of southern Tuscany, chalky cliffs caused by erosion. Similar phenomena are the *biancane*, small chalk outcrops, and *balze*, deep eroded ravines around Volterra.

**cupola**: a dome.

**decumanus**: street of a Roman *castrum*-shaped city parallel to the longer axis, the central, main avenue called the Decumanus Major.

**Dodecapolis**: the federation of the 12 largest and strongest Etruscan city states (*see* History and Art, p.8).

*duomo*: cathedral.

**ex voto**: an offering (a terracotta figurine, painting, medallion, silver bauble or whatever) made in thanksgiving to a god or Christian saint; the practice has always been present in Italy.

**forum**: the central square of a Roman town, with its most important temples and public buildings. The word means 'outside', as the original Roman Forum was outside the first city walls.

**fresco**: wall painting, the most important Italian medium of art since Etruscan times. It isn't easy; first the artist draws the *sinopia* (q.v.) on the wall. This is covered with plaster, but only a little at a time, as the paint must be on the plaster before it dries. Leonardo da Vinci's endless attempts to find clever short-cuts ensured that little of his work would survive.

**Ghibellines**: one of the two great medieval parties (*see* Guelphs), the supporters of the Holy Roman Emperors.

**gonfalon**: the banner of a medieval free city; the *gonfaloniere*, or flag-bearer, was often the most important public official.

**graffito**: originally, incised decoration on buildings, walls, etc.; only lately has it come to mean casually scribbled messages in public places.

**Greek cross**: in the floor plans of churches, a cross with equal arms. The more familiar plan, with one arm extended to form a nave, is called a *Latin Cross*.

**grisaille**: painting or fresco in monochrome.

**grotesques**: carved or painted faces used in Etruscan and later Roman decoration; Raphael and other artists rediscovered them in the 'grotto' of Nero's Golden House in Rome.

**Guelphs** (*see* Ghibellines): the other great political faction of medieval Italy, supporters of the Pope.

**intarsia**: decorative inlaid wood or marble.

**loggia**: an open-sided gallery or arcade.

**lozenge**: the diamond shape – this, along with stripes, is one of the trademarks of Pisan architecture.

**lunette**: semicircular space on a wall, above a door or under vaulting, either filled by a window or a mural painting.

**matroneum**: the elevated women's gallery around the nave of an early church, a custom adopted from the Byzantines in the 6th and 7th centuries.

**narthex**: the enclosed porch of a church.

**naumachia**: mock naval battles, like those staged in the Colosseum.

**opus reticulatum**: Roman masonry consisting of diamond-shaped blocks.

**palazzo**: not just a palace, but any large, important building (though the word comes from the Imperial *palatium* on Rome's Palatine Hill).

**Palio**: a banner, and the horse race in which city neighbourhoods contend for it in their annual festivals. The most famous is at Siena.

**Pantocrator**: Christ 'ruler of all', a common subject for apse paintings and mosaics in areas influenced by Byzantine art.

**pietra dura**: rich inlay decoration that uses semi-precious stones, perfected in post-Renaissance Florence.

*pieve*: a parish church.

**pluteo**: screen, usually of marble, between two columns, often highly decorated.

*podestà*: in medieval cities, an official sent by the Holy Roman Emperors to take charge; their power, or lack of it, depended on the strength of the *comune*.

**predella**: smaller paintings on panels below the main subject of a painted altarpiece.

*presepio*: a Christmas crib.

**putti**: flocks of plaster cherubs with rosy cheeks and bottoms that infested much of Italy in the Baroque era.

**quattrocento**: the 1400s – the Italian way of referring to centuries (*duecento, trecento, quattrocento, cinquecento*, etc.).

*sbandieratore*: flag-thrower in medieval costume at an Italian festival; sometimes called an *alfiere*.

**sinopia**: the layout of a fresco (q.v.), etched by the artist on the wall before the plaster is applied. Often these are works of art in their own right.

**stele**: a vertical funeral stone.

**stigmata**: a miraculous simulation of the bleeding wounds of Christ, appearing in holy men like St Francis in the 12th century, and Padre Pio of Puglia in our own time.

**telamone**: (*see caryatid*).

**thermae**: Roman baths.

**tondo**: round relief, painting or terracotta.

**transenna**: a marble screen separating the altar area from the rest of an early Christian church.

**travertine**: hard, light-coloured stone, sometimes flecked or pitted with black, sometimes perfect. The most widely used material in ancient and modern Rome.

**triptych**: a painting, especially an altarpiece, in three sections.

**trompe l'œil**: art that uses perspective effects to deceive the eye – for example, to create the illusion of depth on a flat surface, or to make columns and arches painted on a wall seem real.

**tympanum**: the semicircular space, often bearing a painting or relief, above the portal of a church.

**voussoir**: one of the stones of an arch.

# Language

The fathers of modern Italian were Dante, Manzoni and television. Each did their part in creating a national language from an infinity of regional and local dialects; the Florentine Dante, the first 'immortal' to write in the vernacular, did much to put the Tuscan dialect in the foreground of Italian literature. Manzoni's revolutionary novel, *I Promessi Sposi* (*The Betrothed*), heightened national consciousness by using an everyday language all could understand in the 19th century. Television in the last few decades is performing an even more spectacular linguistic unification; although the majority of Italians still speak a dialect at home, school and work, their TV idols insist on proper Italian.

Perhaps because they are so busy learning their own beautiful but grammatically complex language, Italians are not especially apt at learning others. English lessons, however, have been the rage for years, and at most hotels and restaurants there will be someone who speaks some English. In small towns and out-of-the-way places, finding an Anglophone may prove more difficult.

The words and phrases below should help you out in most situations, but the ideal way to come to Italy is with some Italian under your belt; your visit will be richer and you're much more likely to make some Italian friends.

## Pronunciation

Italian words are pronounced phonetically. Every vowel and consonant (except 'h') is sounded. Consonants are the same as in English, except the 'c' which, when followed by an 'e' or 'i', is pronounced like the English 'ch' (*cinque* thus becomes 'cheenquay'). Italian 'g' is also soft before 'i' or 'e' as in *gira*, pronounced 'jee-ra'. 'H' is never sounded; 'z' is pronounced like 'ts'. The consonants 'sc' before

the vowels 'i' or 'e' become like the English 'sh' as in 'sci', pronounced 'shee'; 'ch' is pronouced like a 'k' as in Chianti, 'kee-an-tee'; 'gn' as 'ny' in English (*bagno*, pronounced 'ban-yo'; while 'gli' is pronounced like the middle of the word 'million' (Castiglione, pronounced 'Ca-steely-oh-nay').

Vowel pronunciation is: 'a' as in English 'father'; 'e' when unstressed is pronounced like 'a' in 'fate' as in *mele*, when stressed can be the same or like the 'e' in 'pet' (*bello*); 'i' is like the 'i' in 'machine'; 'o' like 'e', has two sounds, 'o' as in 'hope' when unstressed (*tacchino*), and usually 'o' as in 'rock' when stressed (*morte*); 'u' is pronounced like the 'u' in 'June'.

The accent usually (but not always) falls on the penultimate syllable. Also note that, in the big northern cities, the informal way of addressing someone as you, *tu*, is widely used; the more formal *lei* or *voi* is commonly used in provincial districts.

## Useful Words and Phrases

yes/no/maybe *sì/no/forse*
I don't know *Non lo so*
I don't understand (Italian) *Non capisco (l'italiano)*
Does someone here speak English? *C'è qualcuno qui che parla inglese?*
Speak slowly *Parla lentamente*
Could you assist me? *Potrebbe aiutarmi?*
Help! *Aiuto!*
Please/Thank you (very much) *Per favore/ (Molte) grazie*
You're welcome *Prego*
It doesn't matter *Non importa*
All right *Va bene*
Excuse me *permesso*
I'm sorry *Mi scusi, mi dispiace*
Be careful! *Attenzione!*
Nothing *Niente*
It is urgent! *È urgente!*
How are you? *Come sta/stai?*

Well, and you? *Bene, e Lei/e tu?*
What is your name? *Come si chiama?/
Come ti chiami*
Hello *Salve or ciao (both informal)*
Good morning *Buongiorno (formal hello)*
Good afternoon, evening *Buonasera (also
formal hello)*
Good night *Buona notte*
Goodbye *Arrivederla (formal), Arrivederci/
Ciao (informal)*
What do you call this in Italian?
*Come si chiama questo in italiano?*
What? *Che?*
Who? *Chi?*
Where? *Dove?*
Where is/are... *Dov'è/Dove sono...*
When? *Quando?*
Why? *Perché?*
How? *Come?*
How much (does it cost)? *Quanto (costa)?*
I am lost *Mi sono smarrito*
I am hungry/thirsty *Ho fame/sete*
I am sleepy/tired *Sono stanco/a*
I am sorry *Mi dispiace*
I feel unwell *Mi sento male*
Leave me alone *Lasciami in pace*
good/bad *buono bravo/male cattivo*
well/badly *bene/male*
hot/cold *caldo/freddo*
slow/fast *lento/rapido*
up/down *su/giù*
big/small *grande/piccolo*
here/there *qui/lì*

# Transport

airport *aeroporto*
bus stop *fermata*
bus *autobus*
coach *pullman*
railway station *stazione ferroviaria*
train *treno*
platform *binario*
port *porto*
port station *stazione marittima*
ship *nave*
car *macchina*
taxi *tassì, taxi*
ticket *biglietto*
customs *dogana*
seat (reserved) *posto (prenotato)*

# Travel Directions

One (two) ticket(s) to Florence, please
*Un biglietto (due biglietti) per Firenze, per
favore*
one way *semplice/andata*
return *andata e ritorno*
first/second class *Prima/seconda classe*
I want to go to... *Desidero andare a...*
How can I get to...? *Come posso andare a...?*
How do I get to the town centre? *Come posso
raggiungere il centro città?*
Do you stop at...? *Si ferma a...?*
Where is...? *Dov'è...?*
How far is it to...? *Quanto siamo lontani da...?*
What is the name of this station? *Come si
chiama questa stazione?*
When does the next ... leave? *Quando parte
il prossimo...?*
From where does it leave? *Da dove parte?*
How long does the trip take...? *Quanto tempo
dura il viaggio?*
How much is the fare? *Quant'è il biglietto?*
Have a good trip! *Buon viaggio!*

# Driving

near/far *vicino/lontano*
left/right *sinistra/destra*
straight ahead *sempre diritto*
forwards/backwards *avanti/indietro*
north/south *nord/sud*
east *est/oriente*
west *ovest/occidente*
round the corner *dietro l'angolo*
crossroads *bivio*
street/road *strada/via*
square *piazza*
car hire *autonoleggio*
motorbike/scooter/moped *motocicletta/
Vespa/motorino*
bicycle *bicicletta*
petrol/diesel *benzina/gasolio*
garage *garage*
This doesn't work *Questo non funziona*
mechanic *meccanico*
map/town plan *carta/pianta*
Where is the road to...? *Dov'è la strada per...?*
breakdown *guasto*
driving licence *patente di guida*
driver *guidatore*
speed *velocità*

danger *pericolo*
parking *parcheggio*
no parking *sosta vietata*
narrow *stretto*
bridge *ponte*
toll *pedaggio*
slow down *rallentare*

# Numbers

one *uno/una*
two/three/four *due/tre/quattro*
five/six/seven *cinque/sei/sette*
eight/nine/ten *otto/nove/dieci*
eleven/twelve *undici/dodici*
thirteen/fourteen *tredici/quattordici*
fifteen/sixteen *quindici/sedici*
seventeen/eighteen *diciassette/diciotto*
nineteen *diciannove*
twenty *venti*
twenty-one *ventuno*
twenty-two *ventidue*
thirty *trenta*
forty *quaranta*
fifty *cinquanta*
sixty *sessanta*
seventy *settanta*
eighty *ottanta*
ninety *novanta*
hundred *cento*
one hundred and one *centouno*
two hundred *duecento*
one thousand *mille*
two thousand *duemila*
million *milione*

# Days

Monday *lunedì*
Tuesday *martedì*
Wednesday *mercoledì*
Thursday *giovedì*
Friday *venerdì*
Saturday *sabato*
Sunday *domenica*
holidays *festivi*
weekdays *feriali*

# Time

What time is it? *Che ora è?/Che ore sono?*
day *giorno*

week *settimana*
month *mese*
morning/afternoon *mattina/pomeriggio*
evening *sera*
yesterday *ieri*
today *oggi*
tomorrow *domani*
soon *fra poco*
later *dopo/più tardi*
It is too early *È troppo presto*
It is too late *È troppo tardi*

# Shopping, Services, Sightseeing

I would like... *Vorrei...*
How much is it? *Quanto costa questo?*
Where is/are...? *Dov'è/Dove sono...?*
open/closed *aperto/chiuso*
cheap/expensive *a buon prezzo/caro*
bank *banca*
beach *spiaggia*
bed *letto*
church *chiesa*
entrance/exit *entrata/uscita*
hospital *ospedale*
money *soldi*
newspaper (foreign) *giornale (straniero)*
pharmacy *farmacia*
police station *commissariato*
policeman *poliziotto*
post office *ufficio postale*
sea *mare*
shop *negozio*
telephone *telefono*
tobacco shop *tabaccaio*
WC *toilette/bagno*
men *Signori/Uomini*
women *Signore/Donne*

# Useful Hotel Vocabulary

I'd like a single/twin/double room please
*Vorrei una camera singola/doppia/
matrimoniale, per favore*
with/without bath *con/senza bagno*
for two nights *per due notti*
We are leaving tomorrow morning *Partiamo
domani mattina*
May I see the room/another room, please?
*Vorrei vedere la camera/un'altra camera*

**Is there a room with a balcony?** *C'è una camera con balcone?*

**There isn't (aren't) any hot water/soap/light/ toilet paper/towels** *Manca (Mancano) acqua calda/sapone/luce/carta igienica/ asciugamani*

**May I pay by credit card?** *Vorrei pagare con carta di credito*

**Fine, I'll take it** *Bene, la prendo*

**Is breakfast included?** *È compresa la prima colazione?*

**What time do you serve breakfast?** *A che ora è la colazione?*

**How do I get to the town centre?** *Come raggiungo il centro città?*

For a list of vocabulary relating to Italian food and drink, *see* **Food and Drink**, p.39.

# Further Reading

De Blasi, Marlena, *A Thousand Days in Tuscany: A Bittersweet Adventure* (Algonquin, 2004). An American chef married to a Venetian recounts her experiences in rural Tuscany.

Dusi, Isabella, *Bel Vino: A Year of Sundrenched Pleasure among the Vines of Tuscany* (Pocket Books, 2004). A local ex-pat follows the making of Brunello di Montalcino.

Goethe, JW, *Italian Journey* (Penguin Classics, 1982). An excellent example of a genius turned to mush by Italy; good insights, but big, big mistakes.

Hutton, Edward, *Florence; Assisi and Umbria Revisited*, in *Unknown Tuscany*, and *Siena and Southern Tuscany* (Hollis & Carter, 1995). Reprints of the travel classics.

Lasdun, James and Pia Davis, *Walking and Eating in Tuscany and Umbria* (Penguin 2005). An excellent guide to working up an appetite in the pretty countryside.

Mayes, Frances, *Under the Tuscan Sun* (Bantam, 2004). One of the better ex-pat-fixing-up-a-house-in-the-sun books that followed in the wake of Peter Mayle.

McCarthy, Mary, *The Stones of Florence* and *Venice Observed* (Penguin, 1986). Brilliant evocation of Italy's two great art cities, with an understanding that makes many other works on the subject seem sluggish and pedantic; don't visit Florence without it.

Romer, Elizabeth, *The Tuscan Year: Life and Food in an Italian Valley* (Orion, 1998). One of the best in recent years, with an emphasis on food, recipes and their cultural context.

Spender, Matthew, *Within Tuscany* (Viking, 1992). Poet Stephen Spender's son, on everything from porcupines to Pontormo's bowel movements.

## Art and Literature

Alberti, Leon Battista, *On Painting* (Penguin, 1991). Fine translation (by Cecil Grayson) of the little handbook (1435) on perspective and much much more that was a must-read for every Renaissance artist.

Ames-Lewis, Francis, *The Intellectual Life of the Early Renaissance Artist* (Yale University Press, 2002). Fascinating account of how artists struggled to get some respect.

Atalay, Bulent, *Math and the Mona Lisa: The Art and Science of Leonardo da Vinci* (Smithsonian, 2004). In search of the unity of art and science, and a paean to Leonardo.

Baxandall, Michael, *Painting and Experience in Fifteenth-Century Italy: A Primer in the Social History of Pictorial Style* (Oxford, 1988). Vividly puts Renaissance art in context with the painting trade, philosophy and social history of the period so you can 'see' paintings the way viewers did 500 years ago.

Boccaccio, Giovanni, *The Decameron* (Penguin, 2003). The ever-young classic by one of the fathers of Italian literature, full of refreshing irreverent worldliness.

Burckhardt, Jacob, *The Civilization of the Renaissance in Italy* (Penguin, 1990). The classic, published in 1860; the mark against which scholars still level their poison pens of revisionism.

Burke, Peter, *The Italian Renaissance: Culture and Society in Italy* (Polity Press, 1999). An excellent introduction to the period.

Castiglione, Baldassare, *The Book of the Courtier* (Wordsworth Editions Ltd, 2000). Essential reading for any Renaissance gent.

Cellini, B, *Autobiography of Benvenuto Cellini* (Penguin, translated by George Bull, 1999). Fun reading about the vicious competition of the Florentine art world by a swashbuckling braggart and world-class liar.

Chesterton, GK, *St Francis of Assisi* (Bantam Doubleday Dell, 1990). An enlightening biography by an author who converted to Catholicism because of St Francis.

Clark, Kenneth and Kemp, Martin, *Leonardo da Vinci* (Penguin, 1993). Classic account of the all-round genius.

**Dante,** *The Divine Comedy* (plenty of good translations). Few poems have ever had such a mythical significance for a nation. Anyone serious about understanding Tuscany or Italy and their world view will need more than a passing acquaintance with Dante.

**Ghibert and Linscott,** *Complete Poems and Selected Letters of Michelangelo* (Princeton Press, 1984).

**Hale, JR** (editor), *A Concise Encyclopaedia of the Italian Renaissance* (Thames and Hudson, 1981). An excellent reference guide, with many concise, well-written essays.

**Hall, James,** *Michelangelo: And the Reinvention of the Human Body* (Chatto and Windus, 2005). Fresh critical analysis of Michelangelo's obsession with the body, and how it influenced the way we see things, too.

**Hibbert, Christopher,** *The Rise and Fall of the House of Medici* (Penguin, 1965). One of the classics – compulsive reading. His *Florence: The Biography of a City* (1994) is also excellent.

**Hook, Judith,** *Siena* (Hamish Hamilton, 1979). A bit weak on art, but good on everything else.

**Kemp, Martin,** *Leonardo* (Oxford, 2004). Well written, with a light touch by an expert on the man of the moment.

**King, Catherine,** *Renaissance Women Patrons: Wives and Widows in Italy, c. 1300–c.1550* (University of Manchester, 2002). Readable social history of women in the Renaissance.

**King, Ross,** *Brunelleschi's Dome: The Story of the Great Cathedral of Florence* (Pimlico, 2001). Just how Brunelleschi managed it.

**Leonardo da Vinci,** *Notebooks* (Oxford, 1980).

**Levey, Michael,** *Early Renaissance* and *High Renaissance* (both Penguin, 1991). Old-fashioned accounts of the period, with a breathless reverence for the 1500s – but still full of intriguing interpretations.

**Murray, Linda,** *The High Renaissance* and *The Late Renaissance and Mannerism* (Thames and Hudson, 1977). Excellent introductions to the periods; also Peter and Linda Murray, *The Art of the Renaissance* (1963).

**Norman, Diana,** *Siena and the Virgin: Art and Politics in a Late Medieval City State* (Yale, 1999). Lavishly illustrated study of Marian art and its meaning and politics in Siena.

**Origo, Iris,** *The Merchant of Prato* (Penguin, 1992). Everyday life in 14th-century Tuscany with the father of modern accounting, Francesco di Marco Datini. Also *Images and Shadows; War in Val d'Orcia*, about a Tuscan childhood, and life during the war.

**Petrarch, Francesco,** *Selections from the Canzoniere and Other Works* (translated by Mark Musa, Oxford, 2004). The most famous poems by the 'First Modern Man'.

**Procacci, Giuliano,** *History of the Italian People* (Penguin, 2004). An in-depth view from the year 1000 up to the present – also an introduction to the wit and subtlety of the best Italian scholarship.

**Richards, Charles,** *The New Italians* (Penguin, 1995). An observant and amusing study of life in Italy during and since the political upheaval and financial scandals of the early 1990s.

**Saunders, Frances Stonor,** *Hawkwood: Diabolical Englishman* (Faber and Faber, 2004). A cracker of a read – superbly evokes the man and the world he lived in.

**Strathern, Paul,** *The Medici: Godfathers of the Renaissance* (Jonathan Cape, 2003). Popular history, written to accompany the Channel 4 series.

**Symonds, John Addington,** *A Short History of Renaissance in Italy* (University Press of the Pacific, 2002). A condensed version of the authority of a hundred years ago, still fascinating today. The same publisher has reprinted all of his works, including many others on Italy.

**Vasari, Giorgio,** *Lives of the Painters, Sculptors and Architects* (Everyman, 1996). Readable, anecdotal accounts of the Renaissance greats by the father of modern art history.

**Waley, Daniel,** *The Italian City Republics* (Longman, 1988). Fine introduction to an exciting rough and tumble time in central Italy.

**White, John,** *Art and Architecture in Italy 1250–1400* (Yale University Press, 1993). The authority on all the early masters from the dawn of the Renaissance.

# Index

Main page references are in **bold**. Page references to maps are in *italics*.

## Answers to 'A Florentine Puzzle' (*see* **Topics**, p.32)

1 Façade to **San Miniato**
2 **Baptistry**, interior apse
3 Windows at the rear of **San Iacopo sopr'Arno**, visible from Santa Trinita
4 Windows, **Orsanmichele**
5 Façade, **Santa Croce** (inspired by Orcagna's tabernacle in Orsanmichele)
6 Baptistry doors (Pisano's and Ghiberti's first set); portico of the Bigallo, interior apse, **Santa Croce**
7 **Loggia dei Lanzi**
8 Rucellai Chapel, **San Pancrazio**

# Also available from Cadogan Guides...

## France

France
Brittany
Côte d'Azur
Corsica
Dordogne & the Lot
Gascony & the Pyrenees
Loire
Normandy
Provence
Short Breaks in Northern France
South of France

## Italy

Italy
The Bay of Naples and Southern Italy
Bologna and Emilia Romagna
Central Italy
Italian Riviera and Piemonte
Lombardy and the Italian Lakes
Northeast Italy
Rome Venice Florence
Sardinia
Sicily
Tuscany
Tuscany, Umbria and the Marches
Umbria

## Spain

Spain
Andalucía
Bilbao and the Basque Lands
Granada Seville Córdoba
Northern Spain

## Greece

Greece
Athens and Southern Greece
Crete
Greek Islands

## The UK and Ireland

England
Ireland
London–Paris
London Markets
Scotland
Scotland's Highlands and Islands
Southwest Ireland

## Other Europe

Portugal
Madeira & Porto Santo
Malta, Gozo & Comino

## City Guides

Amsterdam
Barcelona
Bruges
Brussels
Dublin
Edinburgh
Florence
London
Madrid
Milan
Paris
Prague
Rome
Venice

## Flying Visits

Flying Visits Central and Eastern Europe
Flying Visits Croatia and the Adriatic
Flying Visits France
Flying Visits Germany
Flying Visits Ireland
Flying Visits Italy
Flying Visits Mediterranean
Flying Visits Scandinavia
Flying Visits Spain
Flying Visits Switzerland

Cadogan Guides are available from good bookshops, or via **Littlehampton Book Services,** Faraday Close, Durrington, Worthing, West Sussex BN13 3RB, **t** (01903) 828800, **f** (01903) 828802; and **The Globe Pequot Press,** 246 Goose Lane, PO Box 480, Guilford, Connecticut 06437–0480, **t** (800) 458 4500/**t** (203) 458 4500, **t** (203) 458 4603.

# Cadogan
# Guides
# ITALY

THE SUNDAY TIMES
**Buying a property**
ITALY

*FULLY REVISED AND UPDATED*

Monica Larner & John Howell

CADOGANguides

ROME VENICE
FLORENCE

Dana Facaros & Michael Pauls

CADOGANguides

BOLOGNA &
EMILIA-ROMAGNA

Dana Facaros & Michael Pauls

CADOGANguides

*flying visits*
ITALY
*great getaways by
budget airline*

CADOGANguides

**CADOGAN**guides

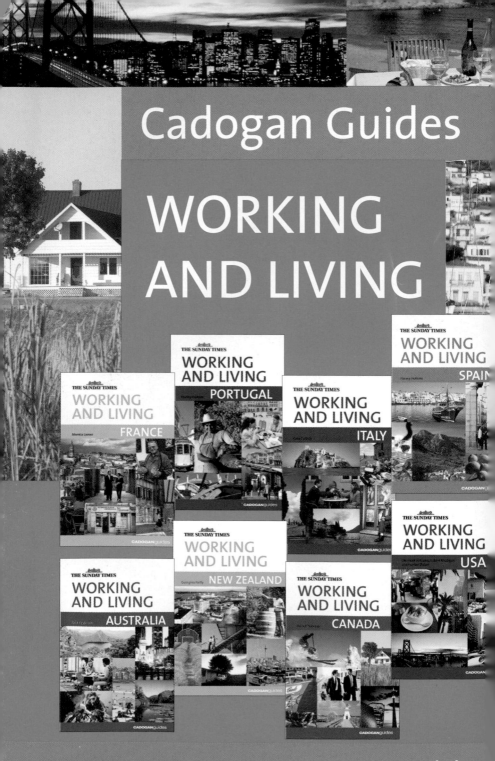

Cadogan Guides

# WORKING
# AND LIVING

THE SUNDAY TIMES
WORKING
AND LIVING
FRANCE
*Monica Larner*

THE SUNDAY TIMES
WORKING
AND LIVING
PORTUGAL

THE SUNDAY TIMES
WORKING
AND LIVING
ITALY

THE SUNDAY TIMES
WORKING
AND LIVING
SPAIN

THE SUNDAY TIMES
WORKING
AND LIVING
AUSTRALIA

THE SUNDAY TIMES
WORKING
AND LIVING
NEW ZEALAND

THE SUNDAY TIMES
WORKING
AND LIVING
CANADA

THE SUNDAY TIMES
WORKING
AND LIVING
USA

**CADOGAN**guides
*well travelled* **well read**

# Tuscany touring atlas

Ferrara

Modena

Reggio
nell'Emilia

Bologna

EMILIA-ROMAGNA

Ravenna

**1**

Pontremoli

Fivizzano

Abetone

Pietramala

Borgo S. Lorenzo

S. Benedetto
in Alpe

THE
MARCHES

Aulla

Poggio

Barga

Bagni
di Lucca

Pistoia

Pratolino

Rufina

La
Spezia

Sarzana

Carrara

Alpi

Apuane

Montecatini
Terme

Prato

Florence

Fiesole

Bibbiena

Sestino

Portovenere

Marina di Massa

Lucca

Pisa

Empoli

S. Miniato

Imprunetà

Greve in Chianti

Subbiano

Marina di Pietrasanta

Viareggio

Gombo

Pontedera

Castelfiorentino

Arezzo

Golfo

di Genova

Livorno

Casciana Terme

TUSCANY

Pietrafitta

Cortona

**2**

Gorgona

S. Gimignano

Poggibonsi

Castellina in Chianti

Lucignano

Volterra

Colle di
Val d'Elsa

Siena

Cecina

Colline Metallifere

Montepulciano

S. Vincenzo

Montalcino

Chianciano
Terme

UMBRIA

Capraia

Massa
Marittima

Populonia

Paganico

Abbadia
S. Salvatore

Piombino

Elba

Punta Ala

Grosseto

Marina di Grosseto

Saturnia

Pianosa

Talamone

Lago di
Bolsena

N

Montecristo

Giglio

Porto Sto.
Stefano

Orbetello

Capalbio

Viterbo

LAZIO

20 km

10 miles

Giannutri

Tyrrhenian Sea

Lunigiana

Garfognana

R. Magra

Capraia

Michael Montgomery

# Lear's Italy

### in the footsteps of
## Edward Lear

'Amusing and quirky, *Lear['s Italy]* would make an
excellent companion for an Italian holiday.' – *Independent*